P9-BXW-854

Sensation and Perception

Second Edition

Sensation and Perception

Second Edition

E. Bruce Goldstein
University of Pittsburgh

Wadsworth Publishing Company
Belmont, California
A Division of Wadsworth, Inc.

Psychology Editor: Kenneth King
Production Editor: Robin Lockwood
Designer: Hal Lockwood
Copy Editor: Russell Fuller
Technical Illustrators: Cyndie Clark-Huegel, Wayne Clark, Darwen and Vally Hennings, Doreen Masterson, Jere O'Boyle, Evanell Towne, Walter Yeschke

Cover: Victor Vasarely, *Vega-Nor,* 1969, oil on canvas, 78¾ × 78¾". Albright-Knox, Buffalo, New York, Gift of Seymour H. Knox, 1969

Printed in the United States of America

4 5 6 7 8 9 10—88 87 86 85

ISBN 0-534-03035-1

Library of Congress Cataloging in Publication Data
Goldstein, E. Bruce, 1941-
Sensation and perception.

Bibliography: p.
Includes index.
1. Senses and sensation. 2. Perception. I. Title.
QP431.G64 1984 152.1 83-23514
ISBN 0-534-03035-1

Credits: Photographs other than those credited here are the work of the author. Complete citations of journal articles appear in the References.

Chapter 1 *Figs. 1.8 and 1.9:* Adapted from "The Receptors of Human Color Vision" by G. Wald, *Science,* Vol. 145, pp. 1007–1017, September 4, 1964. Copyright 1964 by the American Association for the Advancement of Science. Used by permission. *Figs. 1.13, 1.14, and 1.15:* Adapted from S. S. Stevens, 1962, *American Psychologist, 17,* pp. 29–39. Copyright 1962 by the American Psychological Association. Reprinted by permission. *Box 1.2:* Figure from *Experimental Psychology,* Third Edition, edited by J. W. Kling and Lorrin A. Riggs. Copyright 1938, 1954, 1971 by Holt, Rinehart and Winston, Inc. Reprinted by permission of Holt, Rinehart and Winston. *Box 1.3:* Figure from "A Metric for Social Consensus" by S. S. Stevens, *Science,* Vol. 151, pp. 530–541, February 4, 1966. Copyright 1966 by the American Association for the Advancement of Science. Used by permission.

Chapter 2 *Fig. 2.4:* From "Biological Transducers" by W. R. Lowenstein, *Scientific American, 203.* Copyright © 1960 by Scientific American, Inc. All rights reserved. Used by permission. *Fig. 2.5:* From *Hearing: Physiology and Psychophysics* by W. Lawrence Gulick. Copyright © 1971 by Oxford University Press, Inc. Reprinted by permission. *Fig. 2.7:* From "The Stereochemical Theory of Odor" by J. E. Amoore, J. W. Johnston, Jr., and M. Rubin, *Scientific American, 210.* Copyright © 1964 by Scientific American, Inc. All rights reserved. Used by permission. *Fig. 2.16:* Adapted from J. E. Dowling and B. B. Boycott, 1966, *Proceedings of the Royal Society of London, 166, Series B,* pp. 80–111. Used by permission. *Fig. 2.18:* Adapted from *Mach Bands: Quantitative Studies of Neural Networks in the Retina* by F. Ratliff. Holden-Day, 1965. Used by permission. *Fig. 2.22:* Adapted from *Human Information Processing,* Second Edition by P. H. Norman and D. A. Lindsay. Academic Press, 1977. Used by permission. *Fig. 2.24:* Adapted from H. K. Hartline, 1938, *American Journal of Physiology, 121,* pp. 400–415. Used by permission of the author. *Fig. 2.25:* Adapted from S. W. Kuffler, 1953, *Journal of Neurophysiology, 16,* pp. 37–68. Used by permission. *Fig. 2.26:* Adapted from "Integrative Action in the Cat's Lateral Geniculate Body" by D. H. Hubel and T. N. Wiesel, 1961, *Journal of Physiology, 155,* pp. 385–398. Used by permission of Cambridge University Press. *Fig. 2.28:* Adapted from "Receptive Fields of Single Neurons in the Cat's Striate Cortex" by D. H. Hubel and T. N. Wiesel, 1959, *Journal of Physiology, 148,* pp. 574–591. Used by permission of Cambridge University Press. *Fig. 2:30:* From "Receptive Fields, Binocular Interaction and Functional Architecture in the Cat's Visual Cortex" by D. H. Hubel and T. N. Wiesel, 1962, *Journal of Physiology, 160,* pp. 106–154. Used by permission of Cambridge University Press. *Fig. 2.31:* From "Receptive Fields of Single Neurons in the Cat's Striate Cortex" by D. H. Hubel and T. N. Wiesel, 1959, *Journal of Physiology, 148,* pp. 574–591. Used by permission of Cambridge University Press. *Fig. 2.32:* From D. H. Hubel and T. N. Wiesel, 1965, *Journal of Neurophysiology, 28,* pp. 229–289. Used by permission. *Fig. 2.35:* From "The Relation Between Neural and Perceptual Intensity: A Comparative Study of Neural and Psychophysical Responses to Taste Stimuli" by G. Borg, H. Diamant, C. Strom, and Y. Zotterman, 1967, *Journal of Physiology, 192,* pp. 13–20. Used by permission of Cambridge University Press. *Fig. 2.36:* From "Stimulus-Response Functions of Primary Afferents in Psychophysical Intensity Estimation of Mechanical Skin in the Human Hand" by M. Knibestol and A. B. Vallbo in Y. Zotterman (ed.), *Sensory Functions of the Skin in Primates,* pp. 201–213. Plenum Publishing, 1976. Used by permission. *Fig. 2.38:* From "Sensory Neural Patterns and Gustation" by R. R. Erikson in Y. Zotterman (ed.), *Olfaction and Taste,* Vol. 1, pp. 205–213. Pergamon Press Ltd., 1963. Used by permission. *Box 2.2:* From "Physiological and Morphological Identification of Horizontal, Bipolar and Amacrine Cells in Goldfish Retina" by A. Kaneko, 1970, *Journal of Physiology, 207,* pp. 623–633. Used by permission of Cambridge University Press. *Box 2.3:* Figure from W. H. Dobelle, 1977, *Journal of Visual Impairment and Blindness, 71,* pp. 290–297. Used by permission.

Chapter 3 *Fig. 3.6:* From "Human Rhodopsin" by G. Wald and P. K. Brown, *Science,* Vol. 127, pp. 222–226, January 31, 1958 and "The Receptors of Human Color Vision" by G. Wald, *Science,* Vol. 145, pp. 1007–1017, September 4, 1964. Copyright 1964 by the American Association for the Advancement of Science. Used by permission. *Fig. 3.7:* From A. Chapanis, 1947, *Journal of General Physiology, 30,* pp. 423–437. Used by permission. *Fig. 3.8:* From "Human Color Vision and Color Blindness" by G. Wald and P. K. Brown, *Cold Spring Harbor Symposia on Quantitative Biology, 30,* pp. 345–359, Cold Spring Harbor Laboratory, 1965. Used by permission. *Fig. 3.11:* From "Visual Acuity" by L. A. Riggs in C. Graham (ed.), *Vision and Visual Perception.* Copyright © 1965 by John Wiley & Sons, Inc. Reprinted by permission of John Wiley & Sons, Inc. *Box 3.2:* Figure from R. W. Young and D. Bok, 1969, *Journal of Cell Biology, 42,* pp. 392–403. Used by permission. *Box 3.3:* Figure from *The Vertebrate Eye* by G. Walls. Hafner Press, 1967. Used by permission.

Chapter 4 *Fig. 4.1:* From *Living Images* by G. Shih and R. Kessell. Jones and Bartlett Publishers, Inc., 1982. Used by permission. *Fig. 4.2:* From *Fundamentals of Neurology* (6th ed.) by E. Gardner. W. B. Saunders Company, 1975. Used by permission. *Fig. 4.5:* From D. R. Kenshalo in Y. Zotterman (ed.) *Sensory Functions of the Skin in Primates,* p. 309. Plenum Publishing, 1976. Used by permission. *Fig. 4.6:* From "Nervous Outflow from the Cat's Foot

During Noxious Radiant Heat Stimulation" by P. W. Beck, *Brain Research, 67,* pp. 373–386. Used by permission. *Fig. 4.7:* Adapted from "Living Prehistory in India" by Nalini D. Kosambi, 1967, *Scientific American,* Vol. 105, pp. 110–111. Used by permission. *Fig. 4.8:* From "Sensitive Period for the Development of Human Binocular Vision" by M. S. Banks, R. N. Aslin, and R. D. Letson, 1975, *Science, 190,* pp. 675–677. Used by permission. *Fig. 4.10:* From W. R. Lowenstein, "Biological Transducers," *Scientific American, 203,* August 1960. Used by permission. *Fig. 4.11:* From "Mechanical Transmission in a Pacinian Corpuscle: An Analysis and a Theory" by W. R. Lowenstein and R. Skalak, 1966, *Journal of Physiology, 182,* pp. 346–378. Used by permission of Cambridge University Press. *Fig. 4.12:* From S. Weinstein and D. R. Kenshalo (ed.), *The Skin Senses,* 1968. Courtesy of Charles C. Thomas, Publisher, Springfield, Illinois. Used by permission. *Figs. 4.13 and 4.14:* From "The Tactile Sensory Innervation of the Glabrous Skin of the Human Hand" by A. B. Vallbo and R. S. Johanssen in G. Gordon (ed.), *Active Touch,* pp. 29–54. Pergamon Press Ltd., 1978. Used by permission. *Fig. 4.15:* Used with permission of Macmillan Publishing Company, from *The Cerebral Cortex of Man* by W. Penfield and T. Rasmussen. Copyright 1950 by Macmillan Publishing Company, renewed 1978 by T. Rasmussen. *Figs. 4.17 and 4.18:* From "Movement-Sensitive and Direction and Orientation Selective Cutaneous Receptive Fields in the Hand Area of the Postcentral Gyrus in Monkeys" by J. Hyvärinen and A. Poranen, 1978, *Journal of Physiology, 283,* pp. 523–537. Used by permission of Cambridge University Press. *Figs. 4.19 and 4.20:* From "Cortical Processing of Tactile Information in the First Somatosensory and Parietal Association Areas in the Monkey" by H. Sakata and Y. Iwamura in G. Gordon (ed.), *Active Touch,* pp. 55–72. Pergamon Press Ltd., 1978. Used by permission. *Box 4.1:* Figure from B. W. White, F. A. Saunders, L. Scadden, P. Bach-y-Rita, and C. Collins, 1970, *Perception and Psychophysics, 7,* pp. 23–27. Used by permission. *Box 4.2:* Figure from G. Békésy, 1959, *Journal of the Acoustical Society of America, 31,* pp. 1236–1249. Used by permission.

Chapter 5 *Figs. 5.4, 5.5, and 5.6:* Adapted from *Color: Its Principles and Their Applications.* Morgan and Morgan, 1972. Used by permission. *Fig. 5.9:* Adapted from "Human Color Vision and Color Blindness" by G. Wald and P. K. Brown, *Cold Spring Harbor Symposia on Quantitative Biology, 30,* pp. 345–359. Cold Spring Harbor Laboratory, 1965. Used by permission. *Figs. 5.14, 5.15, and 5.16:* From L. Hurvich and D. Jameson, 1957, *Psychological Review, 64,* pp. 384–404. Copyright 1957 by the American Psychological Association. Reprinted by permission. *Fig. 5.17:* From G. Svaetichin, 1956, *Acta Physiologica Scandinavica Supplementum, 134,* pp. 17–46. Used by permission. *Fig. 5.18:* From "Primate Color Vision" by R. L. DeValois and G. H. Jacobs, *Science,* Vol. 162, pp. 533–540, November 1, 1968. Copyright 1968 by the American Association for the Advancement of Science. Used by permission.

Chapter 6 *Fig..6.8:* From *The World Through Blunted Sight* by P. Trevor-Roper. Bobbs-Merrill, 1970. Used by permission.

Chapter 7 *Figs. 7.4 and 7.5: From Art and Visual Perception* (2nd ed.) by R. Arnheim. University of California Press, 1974. Used by permission. *Fig. 7.7: Carapace* by Diane Sloan. Collection of the Oakland Museum, gift of Mr. Joseph Chowning. Used by permission. *Fig. 7.8:* Reprinted from Jacob Beck: *Surface Color Perception.* Copyright © 1972 by Cornell University. Used by permission of the publisher, Cornell University Press. *Fig. 7.17: The Great Bridge at Rouem* by Pissarro. Museum of Art, Carnegie Institute. Pittsburgh, Pennsylvania. Used by permission. *Fig. 7.21:* From *Experimental Psychology,* Third Edition, edited by J. W. Kling and Lorrin A. Riggs. Copyright 1938, 1954, © 1971 by Holt, Rinehart and Winston, Inc. Reprinted by permission of Holt, Rinehart and Winston. *Fig. 7.22:* From *Organization and Vision* by Gaetano Kanizsa. Copyright 1979 by Gaetano Kanizsa. Used by permission of Praeger Publishers. *Fig. 7.28:* From F. Attneave, 1957, *Jorunal of Experimental Psychology, 53,* pp. 221–227. Copyright 1957 by the American Psychological Association. Reprinted by permission. *Fig. 7.29:* From "What Variables Produce Similarity Grouping" by R. R. Olson in and F. Attneave, 1970, *American Journal of Psychology, 83,* pp. 1–21. Copyright 1970 by the American Psychological Association. Used by permission. *Fig. 7.32:* From "Good Continuation Affects Visual Detection" by W. Prinzmetal and W. P. Banks, 1956, *Perception and Psychophysics, 21,* pp. 389–395. Used by permission. *Fig. 7.33:* From "Configurational Effects in Visual Information Processing" by W. Prinzmetal and W. P. Banks, 1967, *Perception and Psychophysics, 21,* pp. 389–395. Used by permission. *Fig 7.41:* From "Inferotemporal Cortex and Vision" by C. G. Gross, *Physiological Psychology, 5,* pp. 77–123. Academic Press, Inc., 1973. Used by permission. *Fig. 7.44:* From "Perceptual Organization in Information Processing" by M. Kubovy and J. Pomerantz (eds.), in *Perceptual Organization,* 1981, p. 158. Used by permission. *Fig. 7.45:* From "On the Semantics of a Glance at a Scene" by I. Biederman in *Perceptual Organization,* M. Kubovy and J. Pomerantz (eds.), 1981. Used by permission. *Fig. 7.47:* From B. R. Bugelski and D. A. Alampay, 1961, *Canadian Journal of Psychology, 15,* 205–211. Used by permission. *Fig. 7.50:* From *How People Look at Pictures* by G. T. Buswell. University of Chicago Press, 1935. Used by permission. *Fig. 7.51:* From "Cognitive Determinants of Fixation Location During Picture Viewing" by G. R. Loftus and N. H. Mackworth, *Journal of Experimental Psychology, 4,* pp. 565–572. Copyright 1978 by the American Psychological Association. Used by permission. *Box 7.1:* Figure from *Higher Cortical Functions in Man* by Aleksandr Romanovich Luria, translated from the Russian by Basil Haigh. © 1966 by Consultants Bureau Enterprises, Inc. and Basic Books, Inc., Publishers, New York. Used by permission. *Box 7.2:* Figure from A. D. Pick, 1965, *Journal of Experimental Psychology, 69,* pp. 331–339. Copyright 1965 by the American Psychological Association. Reprinted by permission.

Chapter 8 *Fig. 8.1: Vega-Nor* (1969) by Victor Vasarely. Albright-Knox Art Gallery, Buffalo, New York. Gift of Seymour H. Knox, 1969. Used by permission. *Fig. 8.3: Place des Lices, St. Topez* (1893) by Paul Signac. Museum of Art, Carnegie Institute, Pittsburgh, Pennsylvania. Used by permission. *Fig. 8.4:* Reproduced by special permission of *Playboy* Magazine; copyright © 1971 by Playboy. *Fig. 8.9: A Street with Various Buildings, Colonnades, and an Arch, c.* 1500, artist unknown, School of Donate Brumante. Museum of Art, Carnegie Institute. Pittsburgh, Pennsylvania. Used by permission. *Fig. 8.16:* D. H. Hubel and T. N. Wiesel, 1970, *Nature, 225,* pp. 41–42. Used by permission. *Fig. 8.17: Violin and Bow* (1889) by Jefferson Chalfant. Collection of the Metropolitan Museum of Art, George A. Hearn Fund, 1966. Used by permission. *Fig. 8.18:* Stereogram by Mike Chikris, 1977. Used by permission. *Fig. 8.19:* Photograph courtesy of Philip Brodatz. *Fig. 8.23:* From "Impossible Objects: A Special Type of Illusion" by L. S. Penrose and R. Penrose, 1958, *British Journal of Psychology, 49,* pp. 31–33. Used by permission of Cambridge University Press. *Box 8.2:* Figure from *Foundations of Cyclopean Perception* by B. Julesz. University of Chicago Press, 1971. Used by permission.

Chapter 9 *Figs. 9.7 and 9.8:* Adapted from A. H. Holway and E. G. Boring, 1941, *American Journal of Psychology, 54,* pp. 21–37. Used by permission of the University of Illinois Press. *Fig. 9.11:* Adapted from H. J. Wyatt and M. W. Daw, 1975, *Journal of Neurophysiology, 38,* pp. 613–626. Used by permission. *Fig. 9.23:* From "Phenomenal Regression to the Real Object. I" by R. H. Thouless, 1931, *British Journal of Psychology, 21,* pp. 339–359. Used by permission of Cambridge University Press. *Fig. 9.26:* From *Experimental Psychology,* Third Edition, edited by J. W. Kling and Lorrin A. Riggs. Copyright 1938, 1954. © 1971 by Holt, Rinehart and

Winston, Inc. Reprinted by permission of Holt, Rinehart and Winston. *Figure. 9.30: Corfu: Lights and Shadows* by John Singer Sargent, American 1856–1925, painted in 1909, Hayden Collection. Courtesy, Museum of Fine Arts, Boston. *Fig. 9.34: Sunlight in a Cafeteria* by Edward Hopper, Yale University Art Gallery, bequest of Stephen Carlton Clark. Used by permission.

Chapter 10 *Fig. 10.7:* Adapted from "Effect of Adaptation on Intensity—Response Relations in the Dorsal Lateral Geniculate Nucleus of the Cat" by D. Schweitzer-Tong. Doctoral dissertation, University of Pittsburgh, 1976. Used by permission. *Fig. 10.10:* From *Visual Perception* by T. N. Cornsweet. Academic Press, 1970. Used by permission. *Fig. 10.11:* From F. J. Verheijen, 1961, *Optica Acta, 8,* pp. 309–311. Used by permission. *Fig. 10.12:* From "Stabilized Images on the Retina" by R. M. Pritchard, *Scientific American, 204.* Copyright © 1961 by Scientific American, Inc. All rights reserved. Used by permission. *Figs. 10.14 and 10.15:* From "Perceived Lightness Depends on Perceived Spatial Arrangement" by A. L. Gilchrist, 1977, *Science, 195,* pp. 185–187. Copyright 1977 by the American Association for the Advancement of Science. *Fig. 10.16:* From "Size Adaptation: A New Aftereffect" by C. Blakemore and P. Sutton, *Science,* Vol. 166, pp. 245–247, October 10, 1969. Copyright 1969 by the American Association for the Advancement of Science. Used by permission. *Fig. 10.20:* From "Application of Fourier Analysis to the Visibility of Gratings" by F. W. Campbell and J. G. Robson, 1968, *Journal of Physiology, 197,* pp. 551–556. Used by permission. *Fig. 10.21:* From "On the Existence of Neurons in the Human Visual System Selectively Sensitive to the Orientation and Size of the Retinal Image" by C. Blakemore and F. W. Campbell, 1969, *Journal of Physiology, 203,* pp. 237–260. Used by permission. *Fig. 10.22: Requiem* (detail), pastel and acrylic, by Tom McDonald, 1982. Reproduced with permission. *Fig. 10.24:* Photograph courtesy of Jacob Beck. *Box 10.3:* Collection of the Metropolitan Museum of Art, Harris Brisbane Dick Fund, 1917. Used by permission.

Chapter 11 *Fig. 11.1: A Passing Umbrella* by Kenneth Antol, 1983. Used by permission. *Fig. 11.7:* From C. Blakemore and E. A. Tobin, 1972, *Experimental Brain Research, 15,* pp. 439–440. Used by permission. *Fig. 11.8:* Adapted from "The Velocity Tuning of Neurons in the Lateral Geniculate Nucleus and Retina of the Cat" by L. Frishman. Doctoral dissertation, University of Pittsburgh, 1979. Used by permission. *Fig. 11.12:* From "Perception" by H. L. Teuber in J. Field, H. W. Magoun, and V. E. Hall (eds.), *Handbook of Physiology,* Section 1, Neurophysiology, Vol. 3, pp. 1595–1668. American Physiological Society, 1960. Used by permission. *Fig. 11.14:* From "Paralysis of the Awake Human: Visual Perceptions" by J. K. Stevens, R. C. Emerson, G. L. Gerstein, T. Kallos, G. R. Neufeld, C. W. Nichols, and A. C. Rosenquist, 1976, *Vision Research, 16,* pp. 93–98. Copyright 1976, Pergamon Press, Ltd. Drawn by John Woolsey. Used by permission. *Fig. 11.18:* From *Aspects of Motion Perception* by P. A. Kolers, Pergamon Press, Ltd., 1971. Used by permission. *Fig. 11.21:* Courtesy of Mark Friedman. *Fig. 11.26:* From *The Intelligent Eye* by R. L. Gregory. McGraw-Hill, 1970. Used by permission. *Fig. 11.27:* From H. B. Barlow and R. M. Hill, 1963, *Nature, 200,* pp. 1345–1347. Used by permission. *Fig. 11.29:* From F. Heider and M. L. Simmel, 1944, *American Journal of Psychology, 57,* pp. 243–249. Used by permission of the University of Illinois Press. *Fig. 11.30:* From L. Burke, 1952, *Quarterly Journal of Experimental Psychology, 4,* pp. 121–138. Used by permission of the Quarterly Journal of Experimental Psychology. Copyright by Academic Press, Inc. (London) Ltd.

Chapter 12 *Fig. 12.4:* From *The Postnatal Development of the Cerebral Cortex,* Vol. 1, 1939 and Vol. 3, 1947, and *The Postnatal Development of the Human Cerebral Cortex,* Vol. 4, 1951 by J. L. Conel. Used by permission. *Fig. 12.5:* Adapted from "Visual Acuity for Vertical and Diagonal Gratings in Human Infants" by D. Teller, R. Morse, R. Borton, and D. Regal, 1974, *Vision Research, 14,* pp. 1433–1439. Copyright 1974, Pergamon Press, Ltd. Used by permission. *Fig. 12.6:* From "Infant Contrast Sensitivity Evaluated by Evoked Potentials" by M. Pirchio, D. Spinelli, A. Fiorentini, and L. Maffei, *Brain Research, 141,* pp. 179–184. Used by permission. *Fig. 12.11:* From "Assessment of Stereopsis in Human Infants" by S. L. Shea, R. Fox, R. Aslin, and S. T. Dumais, 1980. *Investigative Ophthalmology and Visual Science, 19,* pp. 1400–1404. Used by permission of the C. V. Mosby Company. *Fig. 12.12:* From "The Visual Cliff" by E. Gibson and R. Walk, *Scientific American, 202,* April 1960. Reprinted by permission of Scientific American and William Vandivert. *Fig. 12.13:* From "Pattern Perception in Early Infancy" by P. Salapatek in L. B. Cohen and P. Salapatek (eds.), *Infant Perception: From Sensation to Cognition,* Vol. 1, Academic Press, 1975. Used by permission. *Fig. 12.16:* From "Infant's Recognition of Invariant Features of Faces" by J. F. Fagan, 1976, *Child Development, 47,* pp. 627–638. Copyright 1976 by the Society for Research in Child Development. Used by permission. *Fig. 12.17:* From T. N. Wiesel and D. H. Hubel, 1963, *Journal of Neurophysiology, 26,* pp. 1003–1017. Used by permission. *Fig. 12.18:* From C. R. Olson and R. D. Freeman, 1975, *Journal of Neurophysiology, 38,* pp. 26–32. Used by permission. *Figs. 12.20 and 12.21:* From "Optically Induced Concomitant Strabismus in the Monkey" by M. L. J. Crawford, 1980, *Investigative Ophthalmology and Visual Science, 19,* pp. 1105–1109. Used by permission of the C. V. Mosby Company. *Fig. 12.22:* From C. Blakemore and G. F. Cooper, 1970, *Nature, 228,* pp. 477–478. Used by permission. *Fig. 12.23:* From H. V. B. Hirsch and D. N. Spinelli, 1971, *Experimental Brain Research, 12,* pp. 509–527. Used by permission. *Fig. 12.24:* From C. Blakemore and G. F. Cooper, 1970, *Nature, 228,* pp. 477–478. Used by permission. *Fig. 12.25:* From C. Blakemore and E. Mitchell, 1973, *Nature, 241,* pp. 467–468. Used by permission. *Fig. 12.27:* From "Sensitive Period for the Development of Human Binocular Vision" by M. S. Banks, R. N. Aslin, and R. D. Letson, 1975, *Science, 190,* pp. 675–677. Used by permission. *Fig. 12.28:* From *The World Through Blunted Sight* by P. Trevor-Roper, Bobbs-Merrill, 1970. Used by permission. *Fig. 12.29:* From "The Effect of Early Astigmatism on the Visual Resolution of Gratings" by D. E. Mitchell and F. Wilkinson, 1974, *Journal of Physiology, 243,* pp. 739–756. Used by permission of Cambridge University Press. *Box. 12.1:* Figure from R. Held and A. Hein, 1963, *Journal of Comparative and Physiological Psychology, 56,* pp. 872–876. Copyright 1963 by the American Psychological Association. Reprinted by permission.

Chapter 13 *Fig. 13.5:* From *Human Information Processing* (2nd ed.) by P. H. Lindsay and D. A. Norman. Academic Press, Inc., 1977. Used by permission. *Fig. 13.6:* From *Hearing: Physiology and Psychophysics* by W. Lawrence Gulick. Copyright © 1971 by Oxford University Press, Inc. Used by permission. *Fig. 13.8:* From "Disorders of Human Communication," Vol. 1, by E. D. Schubert, *Hearing: Its Function and Dysfunction,* p. 15, Wien, New York: Springer, 1980. Used by permission. *Fig. 13.12:* From M. M. Merzenich, P. L. Knight, and G. L. Roth, 1973, *Brain Research, 63,* pp. 343–346. Used by permission. *Fig. 13.13:* From "The Relation of Pitch to Frequency: A Revised Scale" by S. S. Stevens and J. Volkman, 1940, *American Journal of Psychology, 53,* pp. 329–353. Used by permission. *Fig. 13.18:* From "Disorders of Human Communication," Vol. 1, by E. D. Schubert, *Hearing: Its Function and Dysfunction,* p. 18, Wien, New York: Springer, 1980. Used by permission. *Fig. 13.19:* From J. Tonndorf, 1960, *Journal of the Acoustical Society of America, 32,* pp. 238–244. Used by permission. *Figs. 13.20 and 13.21:* From *Experiments in Hearing* by G. von Békésy. McGraw-Hill, 1960. Used by permission. *Fig. 13.22:* From E. A. Culler, J. D. Coakley, K. Lowy, and N. Gross, 1943, *American Journal of Psychology, 56,* pp. 475–500. Used by permission of the University of Illinois Press. *Fig. 13.25:* From "Stimulus Representation in the Discharge Patterns of Auditory Neurons" by N. Y. S. Kiang in E. L. Eagles (ed.), *The Nervous System,* Vol. 3. Raven Press, New York, 1975. Used by permission. *Fig. 13.26:* From M. M. Merzenich, P. L. Knight, and G. L. Roth, 1973, *Brain Research, 63,* pp. 343–346. Used by permission. *Fig. 13.33:* From E. I. Knudsen and M. Konishi, 1978, *Journal of Neurophysiology, 41,* pp. 870–883. Used by permission. *Box. 13.1:* Figure from "A Case of Firecracker Induced Hearing Loss" by W. D. Ward and A. Glorig, *Laryngoscope, 71,* pp. 1590–1596, 1961. Used by permission. *Box 13.2:* Figure from "Sonar System of the Blind" by W. N. Kellogg, *Science,* Vol. 137, pp. 399–404, August 10, 1962. Copyright 1962 by the American Association for the Advancement of Science. Used by permission. *Box 13.3:* Figure from "The Sensory World of the Homing Pigeon" by M. L. Kreithen in A. M. Granda and J. H. Maxwell, *Neural Mechanisms of Behavior in the Pigeon,* 1979. Used by permission of Plenum Publishing.

Chapter 14 *Fig. 14.2:* From "Stimulus Representation in the Discharge Patterns of Auditory Neurons" by N. Y. S. Kiang in E. L. Eagles (ed.), *The Nervous System,* Vol. 3. Raven Press, New York, 1975. Used by permission. *Fig. 14.5:* From *Psychology and Language: An Introduction to Psycholinguistics* by Herbert H. Clark and E. V. Clark, © 1977 by Harcourt Brace Jovanovich, Inc. Reproduced by permission of the publisher. *Fig. 14.6:* Courtesy of Ronald A. Cole, Carnegie-Mellon University, Pittsburgh. *Fig. 14.7:* From P. D. Eimas and J. D. Corbit, 1973, *Cognitive Psychology, 4,* pp. 99–109. Used by permission of Academic Press, Inc. *Figs. 14.9 and 14.10:* Courtesy of Ronald A. Cole, Carnegie-Mellon University, Pittsburgh. *Box 14.1:* Figure from "Speech Perception in Infants" by P. D. Eimas, E. R. Siqueland, P. Jusczyk, and J. Vigorito, *Science,* Vol. 171, pp. 303–306, January 22, 1971. Copyright 1971 by the American Association for the Advancement of Science. Used by permission.

Chapter 15 *Fig. 15.3:* From "The Stereochemical Theory of Odor" by J. E. Amoore, J. W. Johnston, Jr., and M. Rubin, *Scientific American, 210.* Copyright © 1964 by Scientific American, Inc. All rights reserved. Used by permission. *Figs. 15.6 and 15.7:* From *Experimental Psychology* by Robert S. Woodworth. Copyright 1938 by Henry Holt and Company, Inc., renewed © 1966 by Mrs. Greta Woodworth Herron, Svenson Woodworth, William Woodworth, and Virginia Woodworth. Reprinted by permission of Holt, Rinehart and Winston, and Mrs. Greta Woodworth Herron, Svenson Woodworth, William Woodworth, and Virginia Woodworth. *Fig. 15.8:* From "The Stereochemical Theory of Odor" by J. E. Amoore, J. W. Johnston, Jr., and M. Rubin, *Scientific American, 210.* Copyright © 1964 by Scientific American, Inc. All rights reserved. Used by permission. *Fig. 15.10:* From D. F. Matthews, 1972, *Journal of General Physiology, 60,* pp. 166–180. Used by permission of The Rockefeller University Press. *Fig. 15.12:* Figure from "Functional Organization of Rat Olfactory Bulb Analyzed by the 2-deoxyglucose Method" by W. G. Stewart, J. S. Kauer, and G. M. Sheperd, 1979, *Journal of Comparative Neurology, 185,* pp. 715–734. Used by permission. *Fig. 15.13:* From T. Tanabe, M. Iino, and S. F. Takagi, 1975, *Journal of Neurophysiology, 38,* pp. 1284–1296. Used by permission. *Fig. 15.15:* Adapted from "The Anatomy and Ultrastructure of Taste Endings" by R. G. Murray and A. Murray in G. E. W. Wolstenholme and J. Knight (eds.), *Taste and Smell in Vertebrates.* J & A Churchill, 1970. Used by permission. *Fig. 15.18:* From M. Frank, 1973, *Journal of General Physiology, 61,* pp. 588–618. Used by permission of The Rockefeller University Press. *Fig. 15.19:* From M. Sato, H. Ogawa, and S. Yamashita, 1975, *Journal of General Physiology, 66,* pp. 781–810. Used by permission of The Rockefeller University Press.

Contents in Brief

Contents

Chapter 4 Perceiving Touch, Temperature, and Pain 84

Chapter 5 Seeing Colors 111

Chapter 6 What Can Go Wrong with Your Eyes? 138

Chapter 7 Organization, Recognition, and Attention 165

Chapter 8 Perceiving Depth 203

Chapter 9 The Perceptual Constancies 231

Chapter 10 Perceiving Contrast 261

Chapter 11 Perceiving Movement 288

Chapter 12 Perceptual Development 315

Chapter 13 Basic Mechanisms of Hearing 347

Chapter 14 Perceiving Speech 382

Chapter 15 Smelling and Tasting 403

Box List

Preface

In the preface to the first edition I expressed my feeling that to understand perception fully we must attack it from both the psychophysical and physiological points of view. This idea is one of the themes of this book, and one of my goals is to identify connections between perception and physiology. Another theme of this book is that while understanding how nerve cells fire may tell us a lot about nerve cells, this knowledge, in isolation, tells us nothing about perception. Nerve cells don't perceive. Only people and animals perceive. Thus, our study of perception must be centered on the psychophysical results that describe what humans and animals perceive. If we can connect these psychophysical results to what we know about physiology, all the better. But there is much we can learn about perception by taking a purely psychophysical approach.

The generous reception given the first edition plus the feedback I've received from colleagues and students has been extremely gratifying, and has motivated me to make the second edition even better than the first. In preparing for this revision I took a critical look at the first edition and, with the aid of feedback from many people, identified things that needed to be explained more clearly, topics that could be omitted, and, most important, topics that needed to be added. The result I have tried to achieve is a book that is not simply a collection of facts, but a book that tells a connected story in which the facts about perception are presented so we can make sense of them; so we can appreciate basic principles rather than isolated results.

Although those who have used the first edition will see much that is familiar here, they will also see much that is new. Some of the more important changes and additions include:

1. A completely rewritten section on signal detection, with a typical signal detection experiment described in Chapter 1, and the theory underlying the signal detection approach described in an Appendix.

2. Chapter 2, "The Physiological Bases of Perception," has been shortened and simplified for students with no prior background in the basics of physiology. New material on the use of the 2-deoxyglucose technique to map orientation columns in the visual cortex has been added.

3. A new chapter, "Perceiving Touch, Temperature, and Pain" (Chapter 4), has been added. The rationale for placing this chapter near the beginning of the book is that the first three chapters lay the groundwork for the student's understanding of psychophysics and physiology, emphasizing examples from vision, and these approaches are then applied to the skin senses, emphasizing parallels between the skin senses and vision. This chapter also introduces the idea that perception is influenced by the perceiver's expectations and past experience. This idea, which is introduced via a discussion of the psychological aspects of pain perception, sets the stage for some of the more "psychological" topics in subsequent chapters. Also included in this chapter is new material on nociceptors, cold and warm fibers, gate control theory, endorphins, and neurons that respond to "active touch."

4. The material on color mixing in Chapter 5 has been simplified, and additions to this chapter include some well-known old work on memory color and some just published work on "blob" cells—double color-opponent cells in the cortex that may mediate our perception of color contrast.

5. A new chapter, "What Can Go Wrong with Your Eyes" (Chapter 6), has been added. The motivation behind this chapter was one of curiosity: the curiosity of my students, who often asked me questions about various eye problems, and my own curiosity about what goes on during an eye examination and during operations for conditions such as cataract, glaucoma, and detached retina.

6. The chapter on form perception from the first edition has been changed into a new chapter, "Organization, Recognition, and Attention" (Chapter 7). The section that covered Gestalt psy-

chology in the first edition has been expanded to include the information processing approach to perceptual organization, with examples from both visual and auditory perception to emphasize the generality of the Gestalt approach. New material on models of pattern recognition and attention is also included.

7. The chapter on depth perception (Chapter 8) has been reorganized and new material on J. J. Gibson's approach to the perception of space has been added.

8. A new chapter on the perceptual constancies (Chapter 9) gathers together material on size, shape, and lightness constancy that was formerly covered in different chapters and adds material on perception as hypothesis testing.

9. Chapter 10, "Perceiving Contrast", includes new material on how an object's apparent position in space affects our perception of contrast and new material on the effect of spatial frequency on contrast perception. A clear description of the Fourier approach to contrast perception is included in an Appendix.

10. The chapter on perceiving movement (Chapter 11) now includes an expanded treatment of J. J. Gibson's approach to movement perception.

11. Chapter 12, "Perceptual Development" (formerly "Experience"), includes an expanded section on infant perception that has been updated to include recent work on infant acuity, contrast sensitivity, accommodation, monocular and binocular depth perception, and form perception. As in the first edition, this chapter still includes a detailed treatment of the effect of visual deprivation on neurons in the visual cortex of both animals and humans.

12. Chapter 13, "Basic Mechanisms of Hearing," has been reorganized and new figures have been added to help the student understand the structures of the middle and inner ear. New material on tinnitus and infrasound detection by homing pigeons has been added.

13. The chapter on speech perception (Chapter 14) has been completely rewritten to include material on the motor theory of speech perception, recent work on acoustic cues for perceiving phonemes, audiovisual speech perception, and coverage of the controversy over whether the mechanisms responsible for categorical perception are linguistic or acoustic in nature. A summary of how phonemes are produced is included in an Appendix.

14. The material on olfaction and taste has been expanded so that these two senses now have a full chapter to themselves. (In the first edition they shared a chapter with touch.) New material on myths about human olfaction, cognitive factors influencing smell, the 2-deoxyglucose technique as applied to olfaction, the effect of genetic factors and past experience on taste perception, conditioned taste aversion, and specific hungers has been added.

In addition to the above changes in the text, this edition includes the following features:

1. Addition of highlighted words in the text and a glossary of over 500 definitions. Definitions are placed at the end of each chapter to make reviewing the key terms in each chapter easier for students.

2. Over 180 new drawings and photographs.

3. Over 200 new references.

One of my goals in writing this book was to transmit some of the excitement about perception I have experienced in both my physiological research on visual pigment chemistry (Goldstein, 1967, 1978) and my psychophysical research on picture perception (Goldstein, 1975, 1979) and attention (Goldstein and Fink, 1981). I hope in reading about the research described in this book you will sense this excitement and you will see that perception is more than just a list of "facts." After all, perception is something we experience all the time, and the study of perception can enhance this experience. I've found that studying perception has made me more observant of my environment, more aware of my perceptions, and more appreciative of the miraculous process that transforms energy falling on receptors into the richness of experience. I hope reading this book has the same effect on you.

E. Bruce Goldstein
Pittsburgh, November 1983

Acknowledgments

I would like to acknowledge the help of the many people who in various ways contributed to this book. First thanks go to Ken King, Wadsworth's psychology editor, who convinced me to write this book and who has provided valuable feedback and support throughout the writing of both the first edition and this revision. I would also like to thank Robin and Hal Lockwood of Bookman Productions, who made the production process (turning the manuscript into a finished book) almost painless. I thank Hal for his excellent design, Robin for overseeing the many details that went into producing the book and for many enjoyable phone conversations, and both of them for caring about my book and for making me an integral part of the whole process. I also thank Russell Fuller for his fine editing job and I thank my word processor for keeping me company throughout my writing and for making my task much easier.

During the writing of the first edition of this book I received bibliographical suggestions and feedback on various chapters from Curtis Becker of the University of Minnesota, Frank Bagrash of California State University at Fullerton, William Cain of the Pierce Foundation of Yale University, Edward Carterette of UCLA, Frank Colavita of the University of Pittsburgh, Ronald Cole of Carnegie-Mellon University, James Cutting of Wesleyan University, Dave Emmerich of SUNY at Stonybrook, Margaret Fitch of California State University at Fullerton, Donald McBurney of the University of Pittsburgh, Marvin Megibow of California State University at Chico, Virginia Parsons of Carroll College, Earl Schubert of Stanford University Medical Center, Wayne Slawson of the University of Pittsburgh, and Ronald Verillo of Syracuse University.

Suggestions and feedback for the second edition were provided by Charles Collyer of the University of Rhode Island, Lynn Cooper of the University of Pittsburgh, Nancy Dess-Beech of the University of Minnesota, Phyllis Freeman of SUNY at New Paltz, Laura Frishman of Northwestern University, Alan Gilchrist of Rutgers University, Barry Greene of Indiana University, Donald Greenfield, M.D., of the Eye Institute of New Jersey, Ronald Growney of the University of Connecticut, Steven Handel of the University of Tennessee, Leo Hurvich and Dorthea Jameson of the University of Pennsylvania, Aage Møller of the University of Pittsburgh, Charles Perfetti of the University of Pittsburgh, Edward Pollack of West Chester State College, James Pomerantz of SUNY at Buffalo, James Sawusch of SUNY at Buffalo, Robert Sorkin of Purdue University, Mark Strauss of the University of Pittsburgh, and Joshua Staller of SUNY at Oswego. I thank them all.

Finally, my heartfelt thanks go to Barbara Baker for her understanding and emotional support throughout this project.

To My Mother and Father,
To Adam and Emily,
And To Lorrin Riggs

Sensation and Perception

Second Edition

Chapter One

The Study of Perception

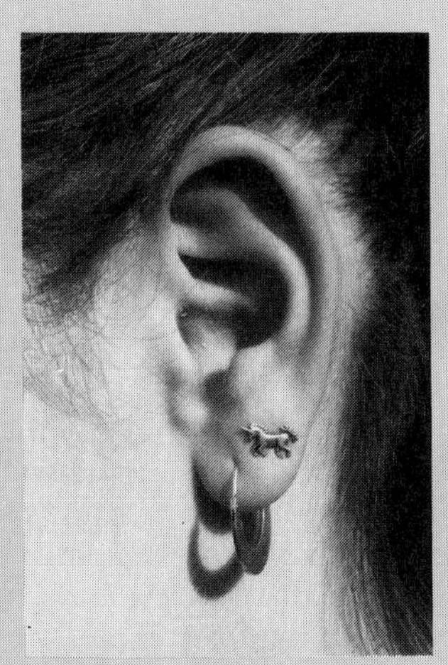
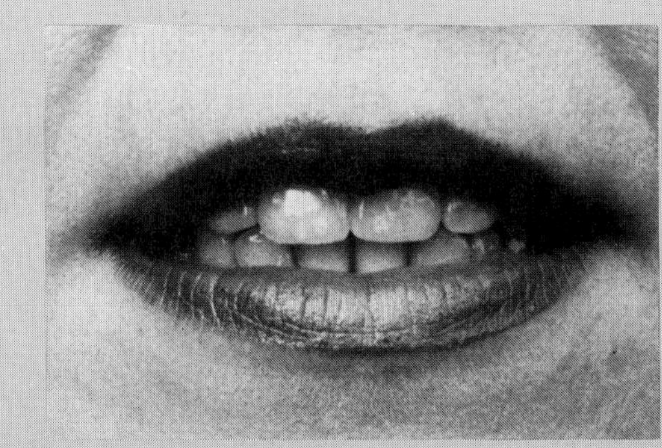
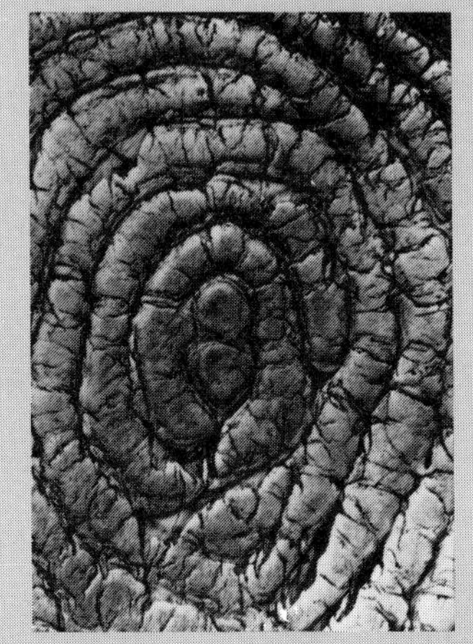
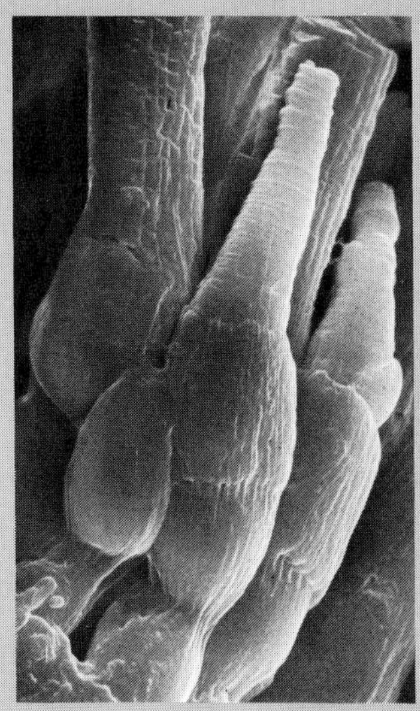

Some Questions About Perception

On the first day of class I ask my students to write down a few of their questions about perception. Most people have no trouble doing this, and I usually receive questions ranging from the far out ("Is it true that blind people have a sixth sense that enables them to detect obstacles before they hit them?" "Are there any physiological mechanisms that explain ESP?") to their own experience ("Why does the eye still see the image of a spot of light after being exposed to a flashbulb?") to other people's experience ("Does everyone perceive things in the same way, or do some people perceive things differently than I do?" "What does a person who is color-blind see?") to physiology ("What mechanisms in the ear change mechanical energy into electrical energy?").

In this book we will discuss many questions like the ones that people ask before taking a course in perception. And we will also discuss many of the questions that people hardly ever ask before taking a course in perception, such as "How do I perceive my friend Ralph?" or "Why doesn't the shape of my desk appear to change as I walk past it?" People don't ask these questions because it is usually not obvious to them that there's a problem. You probably take seeing Ralph for granted, thinking that to see Ralph you only have to look at him, because it may not have occurred to you that seeing Ralph is the end result of a long, complex process. It may also not have occurred to you that the image cast on your retina by your desk changes drastically as you look at it from different points of view and that something must be happening to keep your perception of the desk from distorting each time you look at it from a new angle. One purpose of this book is to make you aware that much of what we take for granted in perception is really very complex and, in many cases, not well understood. You will see that perception does not just "happen."

What Are Sensations and Perceptions?

Since this book (and perhaps the course you're taking) is called *Sensation* and *Perception,* it seems logical to infer that **sensation** and **perception** are two different things. And, in fact, historically, a distinction has been made between sensations and perceptions. Sensations are usually thought to be simple, basic experiences elicited by simple stimuli. Thus, we might say that we experience the sensation of "red" when presented with a small spot of red light, the sensation of "pain" in response to a pinprick, or the sensation of "light" in response to a brief flash of light. When considered from a physiological point of view, sensations are often linked to the activity of the sensory receptors. Thus, the sensation of pain might be traced to stimulation of a pain receptor in the skin, or the sensation of seeing a flash of light might be linked with activity in the receptors in the retina.

Perceptions, on the other hand, are usually thought to be more complicated experiences elicited by complex, often meaningful, stimuli. Thus, we might talk about perceiving the shapes in a painting or the melody of a song. Perceptions, being complex, are often said to be the result of a higher-order process than sensations, being the result of an integration, or putting together, of the more simple sensations. This integration process may involve other processes such as memory and may be affected by a person's past experiences. Given their nature as the result of a higher-order process, perceptions are often linked to physiological activity in the brain.

Although the above distinction between sensation and perception seems fairly clear, in practice the dividing line between the two is rather blurred. One question we might ask is: When does something that is simple (sensation) become complex (perception)? Based on the simple-complex distinction between sensation and perception, we would classify the experience caused by an isolated flash of light as a sensation. But what about the experience caused by two nearby flashes of light? Now that the stimulus is more complex, should the resulting experience be considered a perception? We could argue that perception is involved here because a higher-order process is needed to decide whether the two flashes will be experienced as separate lights or as a *group* of two lights. As we will see in Chapter 7, whether we see separate lights or a group of two depends on a number of factors, including the color of the lights and the distance between them.

Another example of the blurred distinction between sensation and perception is provided by our example of the pain caused by a pinprick. Although pain often has been classified as one of the basic sensations that can be elicited from the skin (along with coldness, warmth, and touch), we will see in Chapter 4 that the experience of pain can be influenced by higher-order factors such as the subject's culture, the subject's mental state, or the rapport between the subject and the person delivering the pinprick.

The above examples, and many others which we won't go into here, suggest that for our purposes the distinction between *sensation* and *perception* is not a fruitful one, and we will, therefore, not waste time distinguishing between the two. We will usually use the term *perception* to refer to experiences caused by stimulation of the senses, and our main goal will be to try to understand how stimulation of the senses results in these experiences.

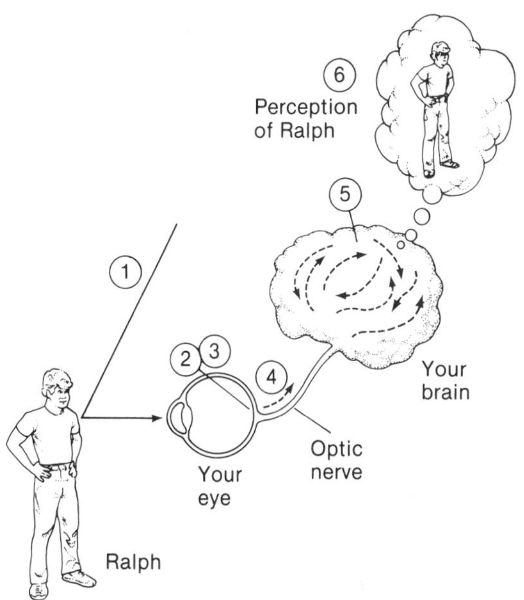

Figure 1.2 A very schematic picture of some of the steps in the perceptual process. Light bounces off Ralph (1) and into the perceiver's eye, where it forms an image on the retina (2) and generates electrical impulses in the receptors (3). Nerve impulses travel along nerve fibers (4) toward the brain, electrical signals are processed by the brain (5), and the perceiver sees Ralph (6).

Steps in the Perceptual Process

To begin our investigation of the process of perception, let's return to your friend Ralph. Figure 1.2 shows some of the steps involved in perceiving Ralph:

1. Light hits Ralph and is reflected into your eye.
2. An image of Ralph is formed on your retina.
3. Electrical signals are generated in the receptors in the retina.
4. Electrical impulses are transmitted along nerves to the brain.
5. Electrical impulses reach the brain and are processed by the brain.
6. You perceive Ralph.

From this series of steps it becomes clear that seeing Ralph is not, in fact, simple. And hearing his voice isn't simple either. When he says "hello," a pressure wave is transmitted into your ear and into the receptors of the inner ear; then electrical impulses are transmitted to and processed by the brain, and you perceive the word *hello*.

How are we to study these steps? Let's consider the two major approaches to the study of perception: the physiological approach and the psychophysical approach.

The Physiological Approach

Researchers who use the **physiological approach** study the inner workings of the perceptual systems (steps 2–5 in Figure 1.2). One of the most widely known applications of the physiological approach is David Hubel and Torsten Wiesel's study of the visual system, which we will discuss in detail in Chapter 2. They monitored the electrical activity of nerve cells in the cat's and monkey's visual cortex (Figure 1.3) and found that many cells respond only to bars of light oriented in a particular direction. For this discovery, and many others about the physiological workings of the visual system, Hubel and Wiesel were awarded the Nobel Prize for Physiol-

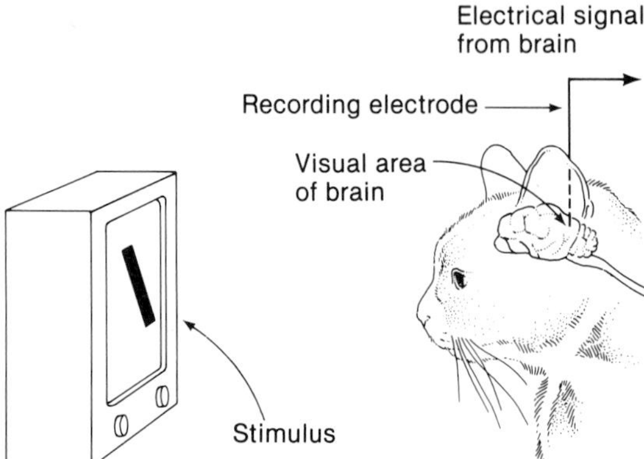

Figure 1.3 Recording electrical signals from the visual cortex of an anesthetized cat. The bar on the screen causes nerve cells in the cortex to fire, and a recording electrode picks up the signals generated by one of these nerve cells.

ogy and Medicine in 1979. However, as impressive as Hubel and Wiesel's achievements are, it is important to realize that their findings in themselves tell us little about perception. Describing how a nerve cell fires tells us a lot about the nerve cell but can't tell us about perception, because the nerve cell doesn't perceive anything.

Only people (or animals) can tell us about perception, because they are the ones who do the perceiving. Therefore, if Hubel and Wiesel's studies of nerve cells are to tell us something about perception, their findings must be combined with behavioral tests. And this has been done to some extent. For example, we will see in Chapter 11 that if we rear a cat from birth in an environment consisting of only vertical lines, cells in the cat's cortex respond not to all line orientations, as in the normal cat, but only to vertical lines. Behavioral tests show that these cats see vertical lines well but horizontal lines poorly or not at all. Pairing the physiological results with behavioral testing shows that these orientation-sensitive nerve cells in the cat are, in fact, related to perception. Again and again in this book, we will make the point that the results of physiological experiments must be combined with those of behavioral tests for the physiological results to have meaning perceptually.

Before leaving this brief introduction to the physiological approach, we should note that some researchers feel that the physiological approach is of little value in the study of perception. One such researcher, J. J. Gibson, whose work we will discuss in Chapters 4, 8, 9, and 10, believes that the physiological approach tells us little about perception. Gibson's view, however, is a minority opinion. In this book, we will take a broader view of perception, and one of our major goals will be to answer the question: What is the connection between physiology and perception?

The Psychophysical Approach

Researchers who use the **psychophysical approach** study the relationship between the stimulus (step 1 in Figure 1.2) and perception (step 6). In fact, psychophysics is more than an approach; it is a number of methods for measuring the behavioral response to perceptual stimuli (Figure 1.4). In a typical psychophysical experiment we might want to measure the relationship between the intensity of a light and a person's perception of that light's brightness. We might find, for example, that in order to double the perceived brightness of the light we have to quadruple its actual intensity. In a different experiment, we might be interested in measuring the smallest amount of pressure on the skin that results in a feeling of being touched.

We have already seen that the psychophysical approach is necessary if we are to relate the results of physiological experiments to perception, and throughout this book we will also see that the psychophysical methods are perhaps the most important tool at the disposal of the perceptual researcher. In the remainder of this chapter, we will describe in detail the various methods for measuring perception.

Describing Perceptions

Perhaps the most obvious way to measure perception is simply to ask the observer what he or she perceives. This makes sense when we consider that the first step in any area of perception research is to establish the phenomenon to be studied. For example, in his studies on the colors of the spectrum in the 1660s, Isaac Newton's first step was to accurately describe the spectrum by assigning color names

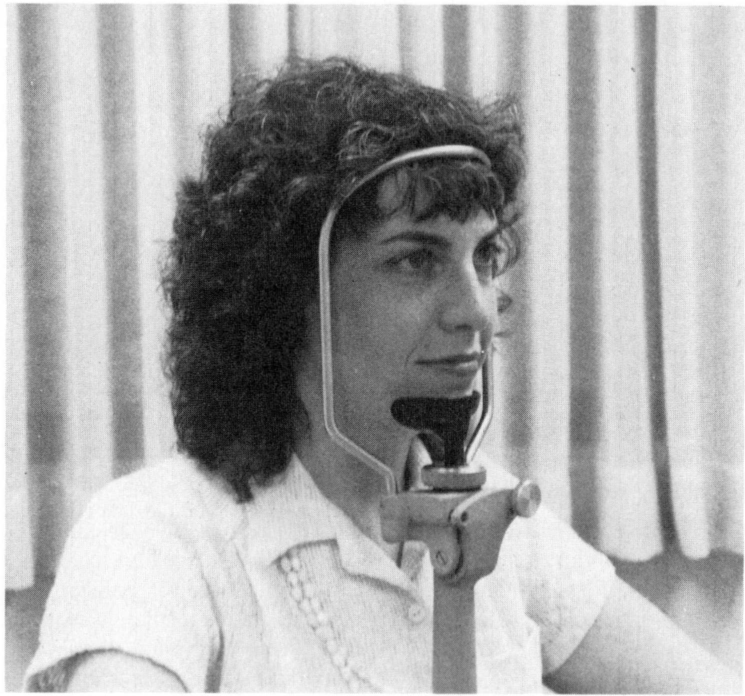

Figure 1.4 A person in a psychophysical experiment. The person's head is kept still in a chin rest as the person observes a stimulus.

to its different wavelength bands. This step then opened the way for more quantitative investigations of the mechanisms of color vision, which still continue today. Two examples below illustrate how simply asking people to describe their perceptions can lead to discoveries of new perceptions.

Effects of Brain Damage on Perception

Hans Lukas Teuber and Morris Bender (1949) studied how brain injuries affected the perceptions of soldiers who suffered schrapnel wounds in World War II. One patient with an injury in the visual cortex complained that a single motorcycle passing by looked like "a string of motorcycles standing still," as shown in Figure 1.5. This effect, discovered by means of the patient's description, was subsequently observed in a number of other patients with similar injuries. Once this effect was established, Teuber and Bender were then able in further studies to determine more precisely under what conditions it occurred. They found that patients saw multiple images when (1) an object was held stationary and the patient moved his eyes, (2) the object was moved by the examiner, or (3) the object was held steady but some other object was moved in the opposite side of the patient's visual field. One interesting aspect of these perceptions is their similarity to perceptions reported by users of hallucinogenic drugs such as mescaline, suggesting that the chemical action of these drugs may disrupt the same mechanisms of normal brain function disrupted by the removal of brain tissue.

Perceptual Effects of Marijuana

Charles Tart (1971) wanted to determine the effects, perceptual and otherwise, of marijuana. To do this he made up a questionnaire of over 200 statements, which described possible effects of marijuana. Users

Figure 1.5 What one of Teuber and Bender's (1949) brain-damaged patients saw when one motorcycle passed from left to right.

were asked to indicate how often each effect happened to them when they smoked marijuana. The results for two statements having to do with vision were as follows:

Statement: "Things seen are seen more sharply in that their edges, contours, stand out more sharply against the background."

Percent of users who experienced this effect:

Never	13
Rarely	13
Sometimes	31
Very Often	30
Usually	11

Statement: "My vision tends to be somewhat blurry; if I try to examine something visually, I can't focus as sharply as when straight."

Percent of users who experienced this effect:

Never	32
Rarely	29
Sometimes	25
Very Often	9
Usually	3

Thus, people indicate that their vision is sharper when they are high.

The descriptions of the marijuana experience provided by Tart's questionnaire have led to additional quantitative research. For example, the report of sharper vision has led a number of researchers to test the **visual acuity** of people under the influence of marijuana. A visual acuity test measures the sharpness of vision by determining how much detail a person can resolve. The most familiar kind of visual acuity test is the eye chart in your optometrist's or ophthalmologist's office.

The results of these visual acuity measurements have been surprising, however, because so far no one has been able to show that people under the influence of marijuana have better visual acuity than people not under the influence. This does not mean that results from the descriptive method are wrong but rather that the descriptive method and the standard acuity tests may be measuring different things. In this case the descriptive method appears to have detected a perceptual effect that is difficult to measure with conventional techniques.

Measuring the Absolute Threshold

Once experience is described, more precise measurements are needed to determine what mechanisms cause the experience. In the remainder of this chapter we will describe how these measurements are made. In doing this we will be concerned with measuring two things: (1) an observer's response to stimuli that are difficult to detect because they are of such low intensity and (2) the observer's response to stimuli that are of higher intensity and are therefore easy to detect. We will first consider the case in which the stimuli are of low intensity, and we will consider two different approaches to measuring these stimuli: classical threshold theory

Box 1.1 Do You See What I See?

Do you ever wonder whether you perceive things in the same way as everyone else? Most psychologists and philosophers feel it makes sense to assume that the general characteristics of most people's perceptions are the same. However, if you subscribed to a philosophical position called **radical skepticism,** you would believe that it is just as likely as not that other people perceive things very differently than you. The following statement, taken from a paper on the philosophy of perception, represents how a radical skeptic would view perception (Harman, 1974):

> You may not have the slightest reason to suppose that visual perception gives other people experiences that are anything like your visual experiences. Perhaps someone else has what would be for you auditory experiences. When he looks at the blue sky, it is like hearing middle C on the piano is for you. There seems to be no way to tell, since he would have been brought up to call that sort of experience the experience of blue. Indeed it is not clear that you have the slightest reason to suppose that others have anything you could recognize as experience. When others see things, their visual experience may be something you could not even imagine.
>
> But then is there any reason to suppose that others have experience at all? The suggestion is that, even if you could know that the people around you were made of flesh and blood, born of women, and nourished by food, they might for all you know be automatons, in the sense that behind their elaborate reactions to the environment there might be no experience. But the suggestion is not merely that you do not *know* whether other people have any experience but also that you haven't the slightest reason to suppose they do.
>
> Similarly, it might be suggested that you haven't the slightest reason to believe you are in the surroundings you suppose you are in, holding a book, reading an article on epistemology. It may look to you and feel as it would look and feel if you were in those surroundings, holding a book and reading an article. But various hypotheses could explain how things look and feel. You might be sound asleep and dreaming, or a playful brain surgeon might be giving you these experiences by stimulating your cortex in a special way. You might really be stretched out on a table in his laboratory with wires running into your head from a large computer. Perhaps you have always been on that table. Perhaps you are quite a different person from what you seem: you are a volunteer for a psychology experiment that involves having the experiences of someone of the opposite sex reading an article about epistemology in English, a language which in real life you do not understand. Or perhaps you do not even have a body. Maybe you were in an accident and all that could be saved was your brain which is kept alive in the laboratory. For your amusement you are being fed a tape from the twentieth century. Of course, that is to assume you have to have a brain in order to have experience; and that might be just part of the myth you are being given.

and signal detection theory. Each theory of measurement makes different assumptions about how an observer decides whether a stimulus is present, and each measures the observer's reactions to stimuli in different ways.

Classical Threshold Theory

Absolute threshold is defined as the smallest amount of stimulus energy necessary for an observer to detect the stimulus. The idea of an absolute threshold dates back to the early 1800s, when German philosopher J. F. Herbart suggested that for a mental event to be experienced it had to be stronger than some critical amount (Gescheider, 1976). This idea, which was developed further by Gustav Fechner in his book *Elements of Psychophysics* (1860) and by others after him, forms the basis of what has come to be called **classical threshold theory.** The basic idea underlying this theory is that at the absolute threshold there is a sharp transition between a state in which an observer cannot detect the stimulus (if the intensity is below the threshold) and in which the observer can detect the stimulus (if the intensity is above the threshold). This situation is shown in Figure 1.6. According to this idea, an observer will never be able to detect a stimulus with an intensity of 10, 11, or just under 12, and will always be able to detect a stimulus with an intensity of 12 or greater; the absolute threshold would therefore be 12 in this case.

One way to think about classical threshold theory is to relate the threshold to activity in the nervous system. In Chapter 2 we will see that there is always a level of nerve activity, called spontaneous activity, that exists even in the absence of any stimulation. It would follow from classical threshold theory that we can detect a stimulus when its presentation causes some critical increase in neural activity above the spontaneous level. Results such as those plotted in Figure 1.6 rarely occur, however. A more usual result is shown in Figure 1.7. The transition between not detecting the stimulus and detecting it is usually gradual rather than abrupt. Classical threshold theory explains this result by saying that a sharp transition between nondetection and detection occurs only if all factors remain constant during the experiment but that in reality everything is not constant. For example, the level of spontaneous activity in the nervous system, the sensitivity of receptors that pick up the stimulus, and the attention of the observer may all vary slightly with time. These variations cause slight shifts in the threshold so that the threshold is different at different points in time, and these variations cause the abrupt transition of Figure 1.6 to become the gradual transition of Figure 1.7.

In *Elements of Psychophysics,* Fechner described three methods of determining thresholds. These methods, which are known as the classical psychophysical methods, are the **method of constant stimuli,** the **method of limits,** and the **method of adjustment.**

Method of constant stimuli. To determine a threshold using the method of constant stimuli, it is first necessary to pick the stimuli to be presented to the observer. Usually five to nine stimuli are used, with the most intense being clearly above the threshold so that an observer detects it without fail and the least intense being clearly below the threshold so that an observer can never detect it. The stimuli between these two are of intermediate inten-

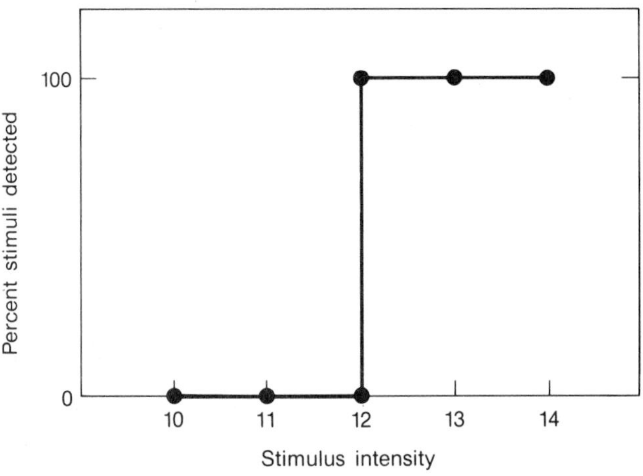

Figure 1.6 According to classical threshold theory there is a sharp step between an intensity at which an observer can't detect a stimulus (slightly below 12, in this case) and the intensity at which an observer can detect a stimulus (slightly above 12).

sity so that they are detected on some presentations and not on others. Each stimulus is presented a number of times in random order. The results for a hypothetical determination of the threshold for seeing a light are shown in Figure 1.7. Each of the six light intensities is presented ten times *in random order,* and the percentage of times that each light is detected is plotted on the vertical axis. The results indicate that the light with an intensity of 150 is never detected, the light with an intensity of 200 is always detected, and lights with intensities in between are sometimes detected and sometimes not detected. The threshold is usually taken as the intensity that results in detection on half of the trials, so in this case the threshold is an intensity of 180.

Method of limits. This method is similar to the method of constant stimuli since the experimenter presents different stimuli and asks the observer to indicate whether he or she can detect the stimulus. The major difference between the two methods is that in the method of constant stimuli the stimuli are presented in random order, whereas in the method of limits the stimuli are presented either in ascending or descending order. Table 1.1 shows the results of such an experiment. On the first series of trials, the experimenter presents a light above threshold and the observer indicates by a "yes" response that the light is seen. This response is indicated by a "Y" at an intensity of 105 on the table. The experimenter then decreases the intensity and the observer makes another judgment. This continues until, at an intensity of 98, the observer indicates by an answer of "no" that the light is not seen. This change from "yes" at 99 to "no" at 98 is the "crossover" point, and the threshold value for this run is taken as the mean between 99 and 98, or 98.5. The procedure is then repeated in reverse, starting below the threshold and increasing the intensity until the subject says "yes." Then both the descending and ascending presentations are repeated a number of times. The threshold is calculated by determining the mean of the "crossover" values for each run, so in this experiment the threshold is 98.5.

It is particularly important, when using this method, that the stimuli be presented in both ascending and descending order. One reason for this is that observers can develop response biases. For example, in descending series they may con-

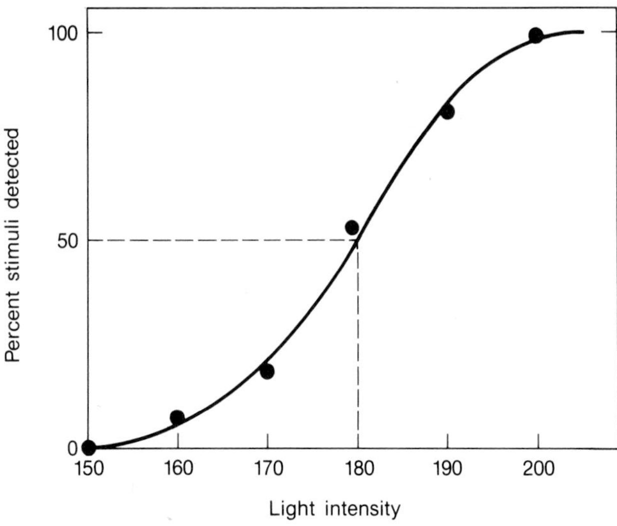

Figure 1.7 Results of a hypothetical experiment in which the threshold for seeing a light is measured by the method of constant stimuli. The threshold, the intensity at which the light is seen on half of its presentations, as indicted by the dashed line, is 180 in this experiment.

Table 1.1

Intensity	1 ↓	2 ↑	3 ↓	4 ↑	5 ↓	6 ↑	7 ↓	8 ↑
105	Y						Y	
104	Y		Y		Y		Y	
103	Y		Y		Y		Y	
102	Y		Y		Y		Y	
101	Y		Y		Y		Y	Y
100	Y	Y	Y	Y	Y		Y	Y
99	Y	N	Y	N	Y	Y	Y	Y
98	N	N	Y	N	N	N	N	Y
97		N	N	N		N		N
96		N		N		N		N
95		N		N		N		N
Crossover values →	98.5	99.5	97.5	99.5	98.5	98.5	98.5	97.5

Threshold = mean of crossovers = 98.5

tinue to say "yes" for one or two trials below the threshold because they said "yes" on the previous trials. A similar bias may occur during the ascending series, with observers continuing to say "no" for one or two trials above the threshold because they said "no" on the previous trials. But when both ascending and descending orders are used, these two biases will cancel out.

Method of adjustment. In this method, the intensity of the stimulus is slowly changed by either the observer or the experimenter until the observer says that he or she can just barely detect the stimulus. This just barely detectable intensity is then taken as the absolute threshold. When the observer adjusts the stimuli, this method has the advantage of giving the observer an active role in the proceedings, thereby maximizing the probability that he or she will stay awake during the entire experiment!

Which of these methods is usually used to measure thresholds? The answer depends on both the accuracy that is needed and the amount of time available. The method of constant stimuli is the most accurate method but takes the longest time, whereas the method of adjustment is the least accurate but is the fastest.

Why Measure Thresholds?

Now that we know how to measure the threshold, we can return to the proposition presented earlier—that once experience is described, more precise measurements are needed to determine what mechanisms cause that experience. We will illustrate how measuring thresholds has helped to determine a mechanism underlying experience by describing an experiment in the sense of vision. In order to describe this experiment, we have to introduce some facts about light. Light can be thought of as traveling in waves, much like the ripples that travel outward from a pebble dropped into a still pool of water. The distance between the peaks of these waves is the **wavelength,** and the wavelength of visible light is from about 360 nm (nm = nanometer = 10^{-7} cm) to about 760 nm. Color Plate 1.1, which shows the visible spectrum, indicates that the color of light changes with its wavelength, with short-wavelength light appearing blue, medium-wavelength light appearing green or yellow, and long-wavelength light appearing red. We will have more to say about how color changes with wavelength in Chapter 5, but for now we will be concerned with how our visual threshold changes as the wavelength of the light changes.

In our experiment, we will test an observer by having him or her look directly at a small test light that can be varied in intensity and in wavelength. We first present a 420-nm test light and determine the threshold for seeing this light by presenting different intensities according to one of the psychophysical methods described above. In an experiment such as this one, in which we will be making threshold measurements at many wavelengths, the method of constant stimuli would be too time-consuming, so we would probably choose the method of limits or the method of adjustment. After determining the threshold for seeing a 420-nm light, we then determine the threshold for seeing a 440-nm light, and so on, until we reach 660 nm. If we plot the threshold intensity necessary to see the light versus the wavelength of the light, a curve like the one in Figure 1.8 results. This curve indicates that the threshold for seeing the light is lowest in the middle of the spectrum; that is, less light is needed to see wavelengths in the middle of the spectrum than to see wavelengths at either the low or high end of the spectrum.

Figure 1.9 shows another way of plotting the same data. In this graph we have converted **threshold** to **sensitivity** by the relationship sensitivity = 1/threshold. This means that low thresholds become high sensitivities, and the curve of Figure 1.8 changes from a "U" shape to an "inverted U" shape. This curve, which is called a **spectral sensitivity curve,** tells us something very important about vision: we

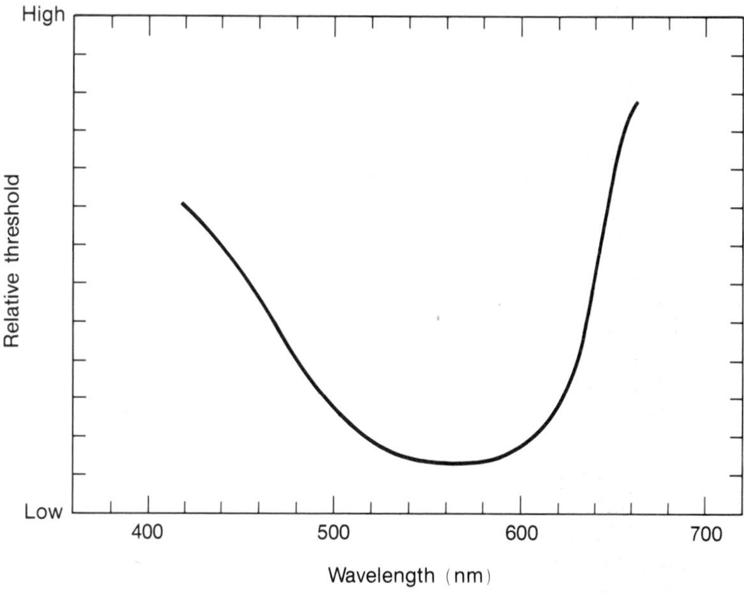

Figure 1.8 The threshold for seeing a light versus wavelength. (Adapted from Wald, 1964.)

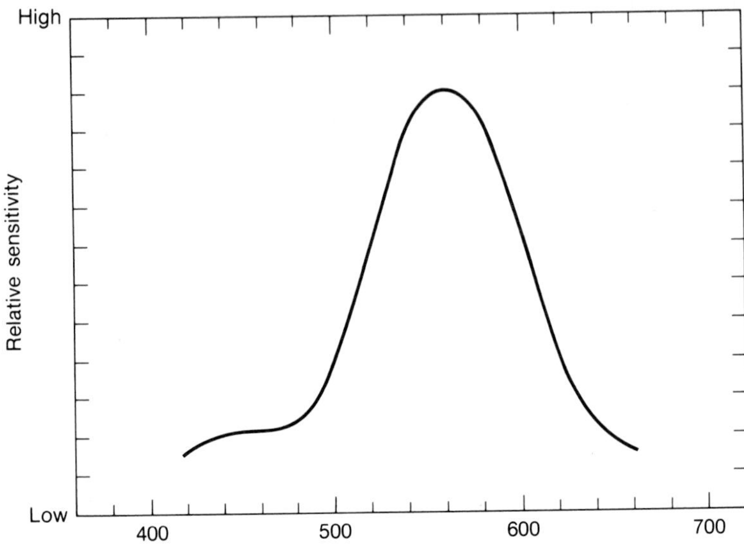

Figure 1.9 If we take the reciprocal of the thresholds in Figure 1.8 (reciprocal = 1/threshold), the curve turns over and becomes a plot of sensitivity versus wavelength, commonly known as a spectral sensitivity curve.

are not equally sensitive to all wavelengths in the visible spectrum. When we look directly at a small test light, we are most sensitive (i.e., have the lowest threshold) to light with a wavelength of about 560 nm (which looks green) and are less sensitive to lights with wavelengths higher than 560 nm (which look yellow, orange, or red) or lower than 560 nm (which look green or blue). The spectral sensitivity curve in Figure 1.9 only goes up to 660 nm, but if we were to extend our curve to 740 nm we would find that it takes over one million times more light energy to detect a 740-nm light than it does to detect a 560-nm light! This psychophysical result is important because it tells us that, in determining the physiological mechanisms responsible for vision, we should look for visual receptors that are most sensitive in the region of the spectrum to which our vision is most sensitive. And, in fact, we will see in Chapter 2 that the receptors in our eyes contain chemicals called **visual pigments,** which absorb light most effectively in exactly the region of the spectrum to which the eye is most sensitive. Thus, using psychophysics to measure the spectral sensitivity curve is an important step in identifying the physiological mechanisms responsible for vision.

Is There an Absolute Threshold?

We have seen that various psychophysical methods can be used to determine an observer's absolute threshold. By using the method of constant stimuli, for example, we can randomly present tones of different intensities to a subject and determine the tone intensity to which the subject reports "I hear it" 50 percent of the time. But can the experimenter be confident that this tone intensity truly represents the subject's sensory threshold? For a number of reasons, which we will discuss below, the answer to this question is, "Maybe not." Many researchers feel that the idea of an *absolute* measure of sensitivity, called the threshold, which can be measured by using the classical psychophysical methods, is not valid. To understand the position of these researchers, let's consider a hypothetical experiment.

In our experiment we are going to use the method of constant stimuli to measure two subjects' thresholds for hearing a tone. To do this we pick five different tone intensities, present them in random order, and ask our subjects to say "yes" if they hear the tone and "no" if they don't hear it. Our first subject, Laurie, thinks about these instructions and decides that she wants to appear supersensitive to the tones; since she knows that tones are being presented on every trial, she will answer "yes" if there is even the faintest possibility that she hears the tone. We could call Laurie a liberal responder—she is more willing to say "Yes, I hear the tone" than to report that no tone was present. Our second subject, Chris, is read the same instructions, but Chris is different from Laurie; she doesn't care about being supersensitive. In fact, Chris wants to be totally sure that she hears the tone before saying "yes." We could call Chris a conservative responder—she is not willing to report that she hears the tone unless it is very strong.

The results of this hypothetical experiment are shown in Figure 1.10. Laurie gives many more "yes" responses than Chris and, therefore, ends up with a lower threshold. But given what we know about Laurie and Chris, should we conclude that Laurie is more sensitive to the tones than Chris? It could be that their actual sensitivity to the tones is exactly the same, but Laurie's apparently lower threshold is simply due to the fact that she is more willing to report that she heard a tone than is Chris. A way to describe this difference between the two subjects is that each has a different **response criterion.** Laurie's response criterion is low (she will say "yes" to almost anything), whereas Chris's response criterion is high (she says "yes" only when she is sure that she heard the signal). That factors other than the subject's sensitivity to the signal may influence the results of a psychophysical experiment has caused many researchers to doubt the validity of the absolute threshold, as determined by these psychophysical experiments, and to create new procedures based on a theory called **signal detection theory (SDT).**

In the next section we will describe the basic procedure of a signal detection experiment and will show how such an experiment can tell us whether Chris and Laurie are, in fact, equally sensitive to the tone even though their response criteria are very different. (If you are interested in understanding the *theory* on which these signal detection procedures are based, first read the section below and then turn to Appendix A at the end of the book.)

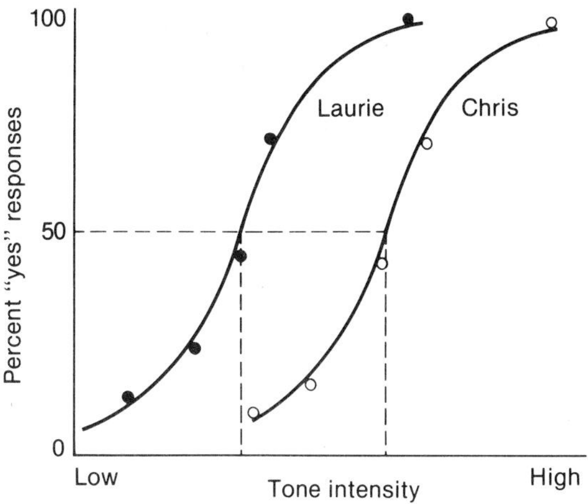

Figure 1.10 Data from experiments in which the threshold for hearing a tone is determined for Laurie and Chris by using the method of constant stimuli. These data indicate that Laurie's threshold is lower than Chris's. But is Laurie really more sensitive to the tone than Chris, or does she just appear to be more sensitive because she is a more liberal responder?

A Signal Detection Experiment

Remember that in a psychophysical procedure such as the method of constant stimuli, at least five different tone intensities are presented, with a stimulus presented on every trial. In a signal detection experiment, however, we use only a single tone intensity—a low intensity that is difficult to hear—presenting this tone on some of the trials and no tone at all on the rest. So, a signal detection experiment differs from a classical psychophysical experiment in two ways: in a signal detection experiment (1) only one stimulus intensity is presented, and (2) on some of the trials no stimulus is presented.

Let's consider the results of such an experiment, using Laurie as our subject. We present the tone for 100 trials and no tone for 100 trials, mixing the tone and no-tone trials at random. Laurie's results are as follows:

Box 1.2 How Small a Difference Can You Notice?

In 1834, E. H. Weber published the results of experiments in which he asked observers to lift a standard weight and a comparison weight and then judge which was heavier. By having observers compare a large number of different weights, Weber was able to determine the **difference threshold,** the smallest difference between two weights that could be reliably detected. He found that the size of the difference threshold, or **just noticeable difference (JND),** as it is also called, depends on the weight of the stimulus. For example, an observer can just notice the difference between a 100-gram standard weight and a 103-gram comparison weight, so the JND in this case is 3 grams. If, however, the weight of the standard is increased to 1,000 grams, the JND increases to 30 grams, so the comparison must be increased to 1,030 grams before the observer can distinguish it from the standard.

You can demonstrate to yourself that the JND gets larger as the stimulus gets larger, by doing a simple experiment with 2 boxes of wooden matches. Have a friend place 2 matches in one box (the standard) and 3 in the other (the comparison) and, comparing the weights of the 2 boxes with your eyes closed, try to decide which box is heavier. After making this judgment, repeat this procedure; if you can't correctly judge which is heavier on three out of three trials, have your friend place another match in the comparison box and try again. Continue this procedure until you can consistently judge which box is heavier. If, for example, you can consistently tell that the comparison box is heavier when it contains 6 matches, then the JND equals 4 matches. Now repeat the above procedures but start with 20 matches in the standard box and 21 in the comparison. Since the JND gets larger as the weight of the standard gets larger, you should find that the JND for the 20-match standard is larger than the JND for the 2-match standard.

Weber found that the size of the JND follows a simple rule: the size of the JND is a constant fraction of the size of the stimulus. Expressed mathematically, this idea, which is called **Weber's law,** is $JND = KS$, where K is a constant called the *Weber fraction,* and S is the value of the standard stimulus. This equation is usually expressed in the form $K = JND/S$. Applying this equation to our example of lifted weights in the first paragraph, we find that for the 100-gram standard, $K = 3/100 = 0.03$, and for the 1,000-gram standard, $K = 30/1{,}000 = 0.03$. Thus, in this example, Weber's fraction (K) is constant.

Does Weber's fraction remain constant in actual experiments? Numerous investigators have tested Weber's law and found that it is true for most senses, as long as the stimulus intensity is

When tone is presented:

- Says "yes" on 90 trials. This is a correct response and, in signal detection terminology, is called a **hit.**
- Says "no" on 10 trials. This is an incorrect response and is called a **miss.**

When no tone is presented:

- Says "yes" on 40 trials. This is an incorrect response and is called a **false alarm.**
- Says "no" on 60 trials. This is a correct response and is called a **correct rejection.**

These results are not that surprising, given that we know Laurie has a low criterion and likes to say "yes" a lot. This gives her a high hit rate of 90 percent but also causes her to say "yes" on many trials when no tone is presented at all, so her 90 percent hit rate is accompanied by a 40 percent false alarm rate. If we do a similar experiment on Chris, who has a higher criterion and therefore says "yes" much less often, we find that she has a lower hit rate (say, 60 percent) but also a lower false alarm rate (say, 10 percent). Note that although Laurie and Chris say "yes" on numerous trials on which no stimulus is presented, that result would not be predicted by classical threshold theory. Classical theory would say "no stimulus—no response," but that is clearly not the case here.

By adding a new wrinkle to our signal detection experiment, we can obtain another result that would not be predicted by classical threshold theory. Without changing the tone's intensity at all, we can not too close to the threshold. This is illustrated in the figure, which shows that the Weber fraction for lifted weights is fairly constant for two different observers, as long as the weight of the standard is greater than about 50 grams (Engen, 1972; Gescheider, 1976).

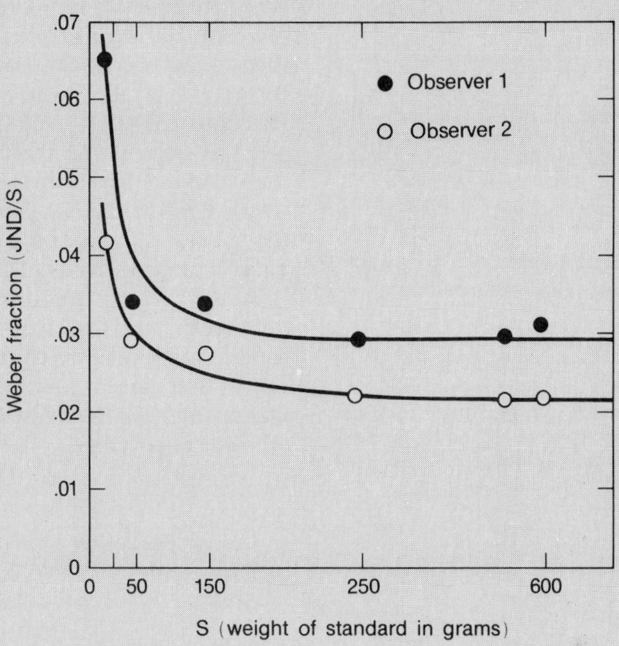

cause Laurie and Chris to change their percentages of hits and false alarms. We do this by manipulating each subject's motivation by means of **payoffs.** Let's look at how payoffs might influence Chris's responding. Remember that Chris is a conservative responder who is hesitant to say "yes." But, being clever experimenters, we can make Chris say "yes" more frequently, by adding some financial inducements to the experiment. "Chris," we say, "we are going to reward you for making correct responses and are going to penalize you for making incorrect responses. For every hit, you will receive $100 and for every correct rejection you will receive $10; but you will lose $10 for every miss or false alarm." What would you do if you were in Chris's position? Being smart, you analyze the payoffs and realize that the way to make money is to say "yes" more. You can lose $10 if a "yes" response results in a false alarm, but this small loss is more than counterbalanced by the $100 you can win for a hit. While you don't decide to say "yes" on every trial—after all, you want to be honest with the experimenter about whether or not you heard the tone—you do decide to stop being so conservative. *You decide to change your criterion for saying "yes."* The results of this experiment are interesting. Chris becomes a more liberal responder and says "yes" a lot more, responding with 98 percent hits and 90 percent false alarms.

This result is plotted as data point L (for "liberal" response) in Figure 1.11, a plot of the percentage of hits versus the percentage of false alarms. The

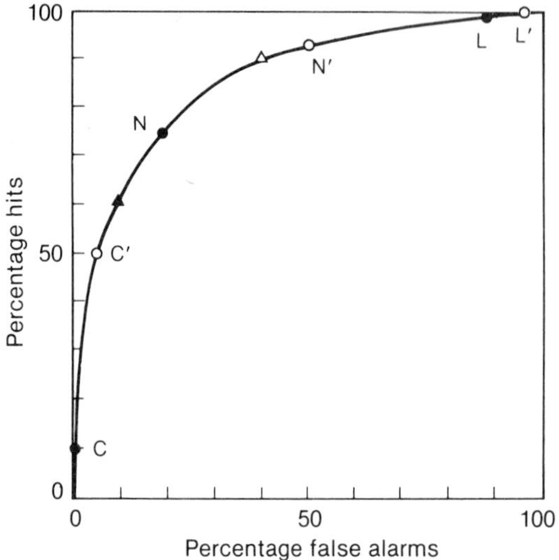

Figure 1.11 A receiver operating characteristic (ROC) curve for detection of a tone. Data points for Laurie are open and for Chris are filled. Triangles = data for first experiment (no payoffs); circles = data for second experiment (payoffs). C and C′ = payoff is for conservative response; N and N′ = payoff is neutral; L and L′ = payoff is for liberal response. That Laurie and Chris's data both fall on the same ROC curve indicates their equal sensitivity to the tone.

solid curve going through point L is called a **receiver operating characteristic (ROC) curve**. We will see why the ROC curve is important in a moment, but first let's see how we determine the other points on the curve. Determining the other points on the ROC curve is simple: all we have to do is to change the payoffs. We can make Chris raise her criterion and therefore respond more conservatively, by means of the following payoffs:

Hit	Win $10
Correct Rejection	Win $100
False Alarm	Lose $10
Miss	Lose $10

This schedule of payoffs offers a great inducement to respond conservatively since there is a big reward for saying "no" when no tone is presented. Chris's criterion is therefore shifted to a much higher level, so Chris now returns to her conservative ways and says "yes" only if she is quite certain that a tone is presented; otherwise she says "no." The result of this new-found conservatism is a hit rate of only 10 percent and a miniscule false alarm rate of 1 percent, indicated by point C (for "conservative" response) on the ROC curve. We should note that although Chris hits on only 10 percent of the trials in which a tone is presented, she scores a phenomenal 99 percent correct rejections on trials in which a tone is not presented. (This follows from the fact that, if there are 100 trials in which no tone is presented, then correct rejections + false alarms = 100. Since there was one false alarm, there must be 99 correct rejections.)

Chris, by this time, is rich and decides to go buy the Datsun she's been dreaming about. (So far she's won $8,980 in the first experiment and $9,090 in the second experiment for a total of $18,070! To be sure you understand how the payoff system works, check this calculation yourself.) However, we point out that she may need a little extra cash to have air conditioning and a stereo tape deck installed in her car, so she agrees to stick around for one more experiment. We now use the following neutral schedule of payoffs

Hit	Win $10
Correct Rejection	Win $10
False Alarm	Lose $10
Miss	Lose $10

and obtain point N on the ROC curve: 75 percent hits and 20 percent false alarms. Chris wins $1,000 more and becomes the proud owner of a Datsun with air conditioning and a tape deck, and we are the proud owners of the world's most expensive ROC curve. (Do not, at this point, go to the psychology department in search of the nearest signal detection experiment. In real life, the payoffs are quite a bit smaller than in our hypothetical example.)

Chris's ROC curve provides more evidence that factors other than sensitivity to the stimulus determine the subject's response. Remember that in all the experiments we have described so far, the intensity of the tone has remained constant. The only thing we have changed is the subject's criterion, but in doing this we have succeeded in drastically changing the subject's responses.

But what does the ROC curve tell us in addition to demonstrating that subjects will change the way they respond to an unchanging stimulus? Remember, at the beginning of this discussion, we said that a signal detection experiment can tell us whether or not Chris and Laurie are equally sensitive to the tone. The beauty of signal detection theory is that the subject's sensitivity is indicated by the *shape* of the ROC curve, so if experiments on two subjects result in identical ROC curves, their sensitivities must be equal. (This conclusion is not obvious from our discussion so far. To understand why the shape of the ROC curve is related to the subject's sensitivity, look at Appendix A after finishing this section.) If we repeat the above experiments on Laurie, we get the following results:

Liberal payoff:	Hits = 99 percent False Alarms = 95 percent
Neutral payoff:	Hits = 92 percent False Alarms = 50 percent
Conservative payoff:	Hits = 50 percent False Alarms = 6 percent

The data points for Laurie's results are shown by the open circles in Figure 1.11. Note that although these points are different than Chris's, they fall on the same ROC curve as do Chris's. We also have plotted the data points for the first experiments we did on Laurie (open triangle) and Chris (filled triangle), before we introduced payoffs. These points also fall on the ROC curve.

That Chris and Laurie's data both fall on the same ROC curve indicates their equal sensitivity to the tones, thus confirming our suspicion that the method of constant stimuli misled us into thinking that Laurie is more sensitive, when the real reason for her apparently greater sensitivity is her lower criterion for saying "yes."

Before leaving the method of signal detection, let's look at an example of how this method was used in an experiment on the perception of pain. It has been hypothesized that members of non-Western ethnocultural groups are less sensitive to pain than are Westerners (Wolff & Langley, 1968). Crawford Clark and Susanne Bennett Clark (1980) decided to test this hypothesis while on a mountain-climbing trip in the Himalayas, which gave them access to two groups of subjects: (1) five English-speaking, college-educated mountain climbers ("Occidentals"), and (2) six Nepalese porters who accompanied the Occidentals on their climb. In the first part of the experiment, Clark and Clark used the method of limits to measure the responses of both groups of subjects to an electrical shock presented to the wrist and forearm. The results of these experiments are shown in Figure 1.12. Note that the threshold intensity for just feeling the shock is the same for both groups but that the stimulus intensity for experiencing "faint pain" and "extreme pain" is much higher for the Nepalese porters. This result agrees with the hypothesis that non-Westerners are less sensitive to pain than are Westerners.

In the second part of the experiment, the method of signal detection showed, however, that there were actually no differences between the two groups of subjects. Apparently, both groups of subjects experienced the shocks in the same way, but the Nepalese porters took much higher shocks before reporting that they felt either faint pain or extreme pain. In signal detection language, we would say that the Nepalese had a higher criterion for reporting pain.

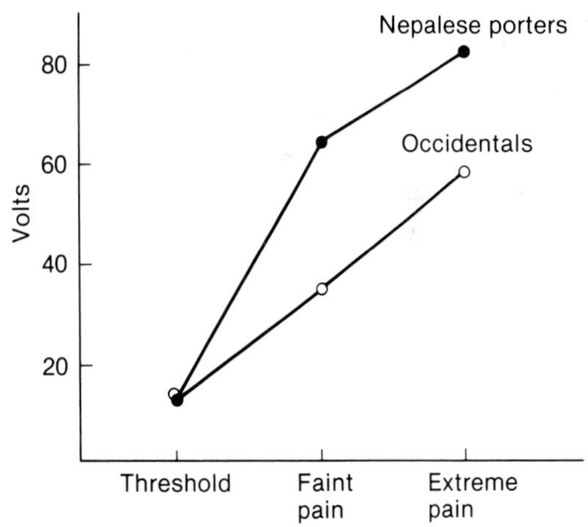

Figure 1.12 Data for the Clark and Clark (1980) experiment, which shows that the threshold for detecting a shock is the same for Western mountain climbers (Occidentals) and their native guides (Nepalese porters) but that the Nepalese porters take much higher levels of shock before reporting "faint pain" or "extreme pain." Is this result due to the fact that the Nepalese porters are less sensitive to the shocks, or does it simply mean that the porters are more conservative responders?

Although we won't go into the exact procedures used by Clark and Clark in the signal detection part of their experiment, it is important to note that signal detection procedures can be used without the elaborate payoffs that we described for Chris and Laurie. Much briefer procedures, which we won't describe here (but see Appendix A), can be used to determine whether differences in the responses of different subjects are due to differences in threshold or to differences in the subjects' response criteria.

What does signal detection theory tell us about functions such as the spectral sensitivity curve of Figure 1.9, which was determined by one of the classical psychophysical methods? When the classical methods are used to determine functions such as the spectral sensitivity curve, it is usually assumed that the subject's criterion remains constant throughout the experiment, so that the function measured is due not to changes in the subject's criterion but to changes in the wavelength or some other physical property of the stimulus. This is a good assumption, since changing the wavelength of the stimulus probably has little or no effect on factors such as motivation, which would shift the subject's criterion. Furthermore, experiments such as the one for determining the spectral sensitivity curve usually employ highly practiced subjects who are trained to give stable results. Thus, even though the idea of an "absolute threshold" may now be outmoded, many investigations using classical psychophysical methods under well-controlled conditions provide us with important information (like the spectral sensitivity curve) about the properties of sensory systems.

Measuring Magnitude Above Threshold

So far we have been focusing on stimuli of such low intensity that they are difficult to distinguish from the background noise. But the vast majority of our experience takes place above threshold, when we can easily hear someone talking to us or can easily see what's around us. Thus, it is important to ask what the relationship is between above-threshold stimuli and our perception of the stimuli. Specifically, we will ask what the relationship is between the *intensity* of a stimulus and our *perception of the magnitude* of the stimulus. If we double the intensity of a light, does it look twice as bright? If we double the intensity of a tone, does it sound twice as loud?

Before we begin discussing these questions, let's distinguish between the physical value of the stimulus (intensity in this case) and the perceived magnitude of the stimulus. Although intensity and perceived magnitude are two different things, they are often confused. Perhaps most often confused are the physical property of light intensity and the measure of perceived magnitude called "brightness." One way to compare the two is to take a small flashlight outdoors on a bright, sunny day. If we measure the intensity of the flashlight and the intensity of the sky with a light meter, we find that the sky has a much higher intensity than the flashlight. We would also say that the sky appears much brighter than the flashlight. Thus, there is a connection between intensity and brightness, and because high intensity often results in high brightness, the terms *intensity* and *brightness* are sometimes used interchangeably. To convince ourselves that they are not, in fact, the same, we only have to take our flashlight inside a dark basement. Although taking the flashlight inside does not change its intensity, it appears much brighter in the dark basement than it did in the bright backyard. (The reasons for this change in brightness are discussed in Chapter 10.) The same intensity results in different brightnesses out in the yard and inside the basement. Intensity and brightness are, therefore, not the same. To measure intensity we measure the effect of the stimulus on a measuring instrument such as a light meter; to measure brightness we measure the effect of the stimulus on a person. It is important to keep in mind that the response of the measuring instrument and the response of the person are rarely the same.

Another example of the distinction between the intensity of a stimulus and the perceived magnitude of the stimulus can be found in the spectral sensitivity curve of Figure 1.9. This curve indicates that the intensity needed to just perceive a 660-nm light is much greater than the intensity needed to just perceive a 560-nm light. In this case, vastly different stimulus intensities result in exactly the same perceived magnitude, "just barely detectable."

With this distinction between the intensity of a stimulus and the perceived magnitude of the stimulus in mind, we can discuss two approaches to measuring the relationship between the two.

Fechner's Law

Gustav Fechner derived a relationship between stimulus intensity and perceived magnitude by making the following two assumptions: (1) **Weber's law,** that the **just noticeable difference (JND)** is a constant fraction of the stimulus intensity (see Box 1.2), is valid; and (2) the JND is the basic unit of perceived magnitude, so that one JND is perceptually equal to another JND. It follows from these assumptions that the perceived magnitude of a stimulus can be determined by starting at the threshold and adding up JNDs. Thus, a light with an intensity of 20 JNDs above threshold should appear twice as bright as a light with an intensity of 10 JNDs above threshold.

Based on his two assumptions, Fechner was able to derive the following mathematical relationship between perceived magnitude and stimulus intensity: $P = K \log I$. Perceived magnitude, P, equals a constant, K, times the logarithm of the physical intensity, I, of the stimulus. (See Appendix B if you need to review logarithms.) From this equation, which is called **Fechner's law,** we can determine whether doubling the intensity of a light makes it appear twice as bright. If we set $K = 1$ and $I = 10$, then $P = 1.0$ since the log of 10 equals 1.0. If we double the intensity to 20, $P = 1.3$ since the log of 20 equals 1.3. Thus, according to Fechner's law, doubling the light's intensity does not double its brightness.

Fechner's law, however, has been questioned for three reasons: first, the law is based on the assumption that Weber's law is correct, but we saw from Box 1.2 that Weber's law is correct only at medium and high stimulus intensities. Second, Fechner's law is based on the assumption that the JND is the basic unit of measurement and that an intensity that is 20 JNDs above threshold should therefore result in a perceived magnitude twice as great as an intensity 10 JNDs above threshold. However, in 1936 S. S. Stevens showed that a sound 20 JNDs above threshold sounds much more than twice as loud as a sound 10 JNDs above threshold. Third, in 1957 Stevens proposed an alternative equation that describes the relationship between sensation and stimulus intensity for a wide range of senses more accurately than Fechner's law.

Stevens' Power Law

Stevens' equation grew from a technique, which he developed, called **magnitude estimation** (Stevens, 1957, 1961, 1962). This technique is very simple: the experimenter first presents a "standard" stimulus to the observer, let's say a light of moderate intensity, and assigns it a value of, say, 10; then lights of different intensities are presented, and the observer is asked to assign a number to each of these lights which is proportional to the brightness of the light. If the light appears twice as bright as the standard, it gets a 20, half as bright a 5, and so on. Thus, each light intensity has a brightness assigned to it by the observer.

The results of a magnitude estimation experiment on brightness are plotted in Figure 1.13. This graph plots the means of the magnitude estimates of the brightness of a light for a number of observers versus the intensity of the light. You can see from this graph that doubling the intensity does not double the perceived brightness. Doubling the intensity causes only a small change in perceived brightness, particularly at higher intensities. This result is called **response compression.** As intensity is increased, the responses increase but not as rapidly as the intensity. To double the brightness it is necessary to multiply the intensity by about nine.

Figure 1.14 shows the results of magnitude estimation experiments for brightness, for the length of a line, and for the sensation caused by an electric shock presented to the finger. You can see that there are three different kinds of curves: (1) curves that bend down, such as the one for brightness, (2) curves that bend up, such as the one for electric shock, and (3) straight lines, such as the one for estimating line length. Curves that bend down show *response compression* (doubling the light intensity causes less than a doubling of the brightness). Curves that bend up show **response expansion** (doubling the strength of a shock causes more than a doubling of the sensation of being shocked). Straight lines are *linear*

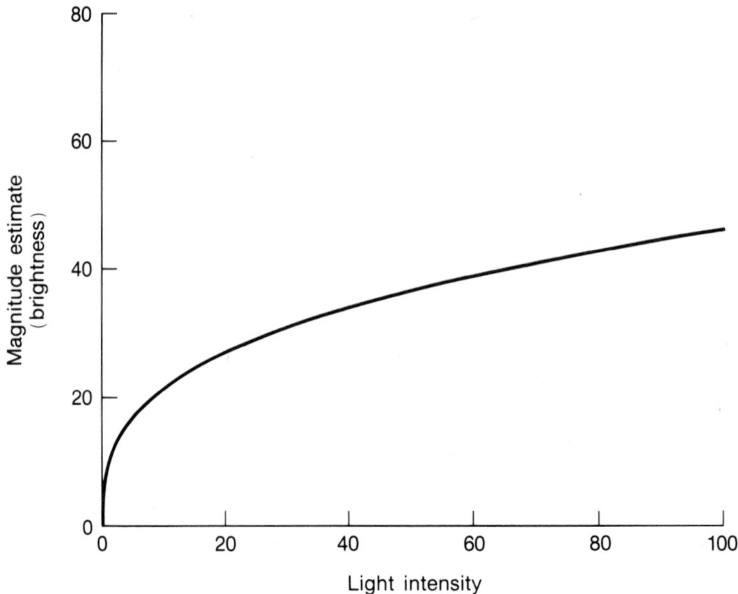

Figure 1.13 The magnitude estimates for the brightness of a light are plotted versus light intensity. (Adapted from Stevens, 1962.)

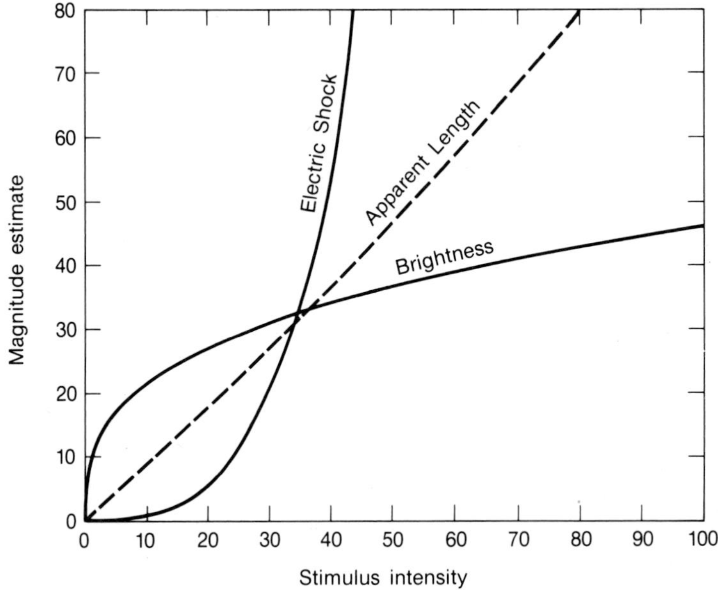

Figure 1.14 Curves showing the relationship between perceived magnitude and stimulus intensity for electric shock, line length, and brightness. (Adapted from Stevens, 1962.) The curve for brightness is the same one shown in Figure 1.13.

with a slope of close to one, so the magnitude of the response almost exactly matches increases in the stimulus (doubling the line length doubles the observer's estimate of the length of the line).

Should we conclude from the differences in the curves of Figure 1.14 that the relationship between the intensity of a stimulus and our perception of its magnitude follows different rules for each sense? The answer to this question is that even though the curves of Figure 1.14 look different, we can, in fact, find a common rule for all the senses. To find a common rule that can describe all the different curves of Figure 1.14, we have to replot the curves by plotting the *logarithm* of the magnitude estimates versus the *logarithm* of the stimulus intensity. When we do this, all three curves become straight lines, as shown in Figure 1.15; functions that are straight lines on such a log-log plot are called **power functions** and are described by the equation $P = KI^n$. Perceived magnitude, P, equals a constant, K, times the stimulus intensity, I, raised to a power, n. This relationship is called **Stevens' power law.** The power n, the exponent of the power law, indicates the slope of the lines in Figure 1.15. Remembering our discussion of the three types of curves in Figure 1.14, we can see that the slope of the curve that shows response compression is less than 1.0, the slope of the linear curve[1] is about 1.0, and the slope of the curve that shows response expansion is greater than 1.0. Thus, the relationship between response magnitude and stimulus intensity is described by a power law for all senses, and the exponent of the power law indicates whether doubling the stimulus intensity causes more or less than a doubling of the response.

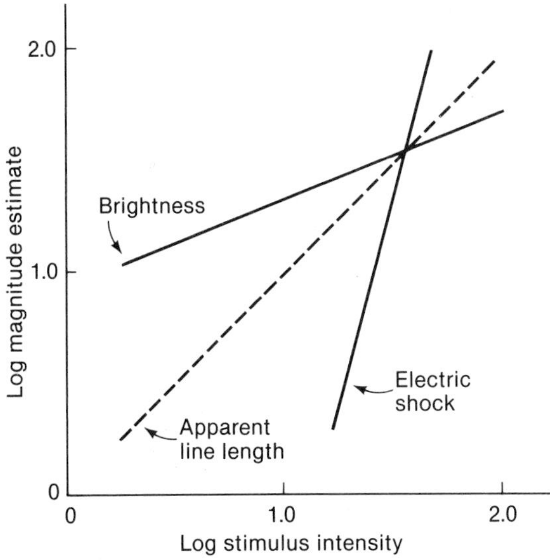

Figure 1.15 The three curves from Figure 1.14 plotted on log-log coordinates. Taking the logarithm of the magnitude estimates and the logarithm of the stimulus intensity turns the curves into straight lines. (Adapted from Stevens, 1962.)

What do these exponents mean in terms of our experience? People other than photographers, artists, lighting engineers, and perceptual psychologists aren't that conscious of the actual values of light intensities in their surroundings, so most people are surprised when you tell them that you have to multiply light intensity by nine to double the brightness. But since we can be exposed to intensity ranges of 1 to 1,000 or more on a bright, sunny day, it makes sense that our perception of brightness should not span the same large range. If it did, we should probably be faced with a scene of such high contrasts and bright glare that looking at the scene would be difficult.

Estimating line lengths is something most people have had some experience with, due to exposure to rulers and other measuring instruments, and most people are fairly good at it. Try estimating the length of line B in Figure 1.16, assuming that the length of line A is 10. (See the answer at the bottom of page 23 after making your estimate.) You probably came fairly close or overestimated slightly, as would be predicted by the exponent of 1.1 for estimating line length.

The exponent of 3.5 for shock seems compatible with our need to avoid potentially damaging stimuli. The rapid increase in pain for small increases in shock intensity serves to warn us of impending danger, and we therefore tend to withdraw even from weak shocks.

This chapter has described some of the methods used to measure psychophysical responses. As we continue our study of perception, we will see that

[1]The exponent for estimating line length is actually 1.1, but this is close enough to 1.0 so that the line in Figure 1.15 is very close to being straight.

Box 1.3 How Bright Is Your Grip?

When the method of magnitude estimation was first introduced, some people criticized the procedure of asking people to assign numbers to their sensations. The critics argued that the data collected in magnitude estimation experiments may be telling us more about how people have learned to use numbers than about the nature of the stimuli they are judging. To counter these criticisms, Stevens showed that magnitude estimation can be carried out without requiring the subject to use numbers. He accomplished this with a technique called **cross-modality matching.**

In a typical cross-modality matching experiment, a subject is presented with lights of various intensities and then asked to squeeze a hand dynamometer like the one shown in the figure with a force that matches the brightness of the lights. The result of this experiment is plotted like any other magnitude estimation experiment, with the logarithm of the force of the handgrip plotted on the vertical axis versus the logarithm of the intensity of the light plotted on the horizontal axis. Plotted in this way, the data fall on a straight line. This straight line has a slope that equals the slope of the power functions for judging the force of a handgrip divided by the slope of the power function for judging the brightness of a light. In other words, the result of the cross-modality matching experiment for matching brightness with handgrip force is accurately predicted by the results of conventional magnitude estimation experiments for handgrip and brightness alone.

Thus, Stevens succeeded in answering criticisms of the magnitude estimation procedure, by showing that a subject doesn't have to use numbers to make magnitude estimates; the subject can just as well judge the brightness of his or her grip or, more accurately, make the force of his or her handgrip equal the brightness of a light. Subjects have also been asked to make many other types of cross-modality matches, such as adjusting the loudness of a tone to match the strength of a vibration or adjusting the brightness of a light to match the length of a line. Subjects cannot only do these things but, as Stevens himself says, "Much to my surprise, and that of many observers, the matching of a sound to a vibration is satisfyingly easy." It is, in fact, apparently as easy to match a sound to a vibration as it is to match the brightness of two lights with different colors or the loudness of two tones with different pitches (Stevens, 1962).

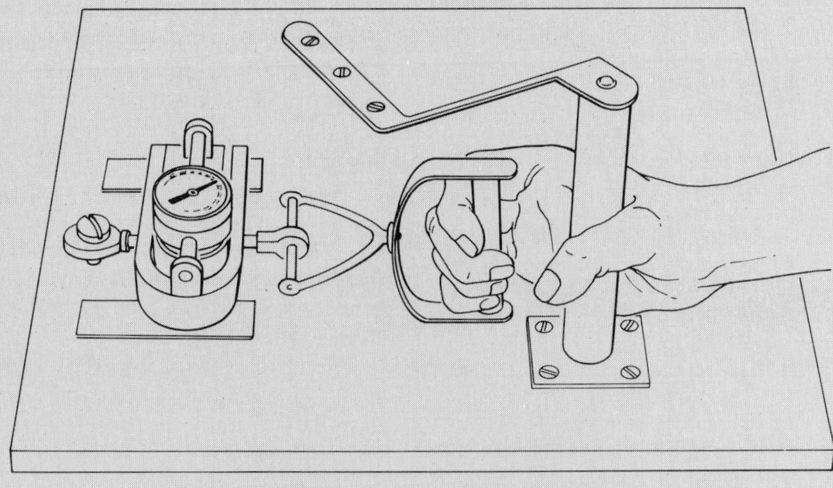

A B

Figure 1.16 If the length of line A equals 10, what is the length of line B? (No fair measuring.)

the measurement of the psychophysical response results in information that enables us to understand how the senses operate. Equally valuable information is obtained by studying the relationships between the stimulus and physiological events inside the person and the relationships between these physiological events and perception. In the next chapter, we will introduce some of the basic concepts of physiology needed to study perception and begin to describe how physiological events measured inside the person are related to the person's perceptions.

Summary

1. Although a distinction is sometimes made between *sensations* and *perceptions,* we will not distinguish between the two in this book. We will, instead, use the term *perception* to refer to experiences caused by stimulation of the senses.
2. According to a philosophical position called radical skepticism, it is just as likely as not that other people perceive things differently than you do. However, most psychologists assume that the general characteristics of most people's perceptions are the same.
3. The physiological approach to the study of perception involves the study of the inner workings of perceptual systems.
4. The psychophysical approach to the study of perception involves the determination of the relationship between the stimulus and perception.
5. The first step in perceptual research is to establish the phenomenon to be studied, and this is usually done by the process of description.
6. Classical threshold theory states that there is a sharp transition between a state in which the observer can detect a stimulus and a state in which the observer cannot. This transition takes place at the threshold.
7. The three classical psychophysical methods for determining the threshold are the method of constant stimuli, the method of limits, and the method of adjustment.
8. The measurement of thresholds helps to determine the mechanisms underlying perception. For example, the spectral sensitivity curve for vision, which is determined by measuring the thresholds for seeing across the visible spectrum, is directly related to the properties of visual pigments in the retina.
9. The difference threshold is the smallest difference that can be detected between two stimuli. According to Weber's law, the size of the difference threshold is a constant fraction of the size of the stimulus.
10. Because an observer's response to a stimulus can be influenced by the observer's response criterion, signal detection theory has been developed as an alternative to classical threshold theory.
11. In a signal detection experiment, an observer's response criterion can be manipulated by changing the observer's motivation with payoffs.
12. The receiver operating characteristic (ROC) curve is a plot of the percentage of hits versus the percentage of false alarms. The subject's sensitivity to a stimulus is indicated by the shape of the ROC curve.
13. Fechner's relationship between sensation and stimulus intensity is $P = K \log I$, where P is perceived magnitude, K is a constant, and I is the stimulus intensity.

Answer to line estimation problem: If the length of line A is 10, then the length of line B is 25.

14. The relationship between perceived magnitude and stimulus intensity can be determined directly by Stevens' technique of magnitude estimation. The relationship between light intensity and brightness determined from this technique indicates that doubling the intensity does not double the brightness. This is called response compression. In contrast, doubling the intensity of an electric shock more than doubles the response to the shock. This is called response expansion.

15. Plotting the logarithm of the magnitude estimations versus the logarithm of stimulus intensities results in a straight line that is described by the equation $P = KI^n$, where P is the perceived magnitude measured by magnitude estimation, I is the stimulus intensity, and n is an exponent that is characteristic of the sense being measured. This relationship is known as Stevens' power law.

Glossary

Absolute threshold The minimum stimulus energy necessary for an observer to detect the stimulus. (7)

Adjustment, method of A psychophysical method in which the experimenter or the observer slowly changes the stimulus until the observer detects the stimulus. (8)

Classical threshold theory The idea that for a mental event to be experienced it has to be stronger than some critical amount. (7)

Constant stimuli, method of A psychophysical method in which a number of stimuli with different intensities are presented repeatedly in random order. (8)

Correct rejection In a signal detection experiment, saying "No, I don't detect a stimulus" on a trial in which the stimulus is not presented (a correct response). (15)

Cross-modality matching A magnitude estimation procedure in which the subject matches the magnitude of a stimulus by adjusting the magnitude of another stimulus of a different modality. For example, the brightness of a light might be matched by adjusting the loudness of a tone. (22)

False alarm In a signal detection experiment, saying "Yes, I detect the stimulus" on a trial in which the stimulus is not presented (an incorrect response). (15)

Fechner's law A relationship between the physical intensity of a stimulus and perception of the subjective magnitude of the stimulus. According to Fechner, P (perception of magnitude) = K (a constant) times the logarithm of I (the stimulus intensity). (19)

Hit In a signal detection experiment, saying "Yes, I detect a stimulus" on a trial in which the stimulus is present (a correct response). (15)

Just noticeable difference (JND) The smallest difference in intensity that results in a noticeable difference between two stimuli. (12)

Limits, method of A psychophysical method in which the experimenter presents stimuli in alternating ascending and descending series. (8)

Magnitude estimation A psychophysical method in which the subject assigns numbers to a stimulus that are proportional to the subjective magnitude of the stimulus. (19)

Miss In a signal detection experiment, saying "No, I don't detect a stimulus" on a trial in which the stimulus is present (an incorrect response). (15)

Payoffs In a signal detection experiment, a system of rewards for correct responses and punishments for incorrect responses which can affect the subject's response criterion. (15)

Perception Experiences caused by stimulation of the senses. When contrasted with sensation, perception is often characterized as being more complex and involving interpretation of the stimulus. In this book, however, we will not distinguish between sensations and perceptions. (2)

Physiological approach to perception Is concerned with determining the physiological mechanisms responsible for the operation of the senses. (3)

Power function S. S. Stevens' mathematical function, which states that P (perceived magnitude) equals K (a constant) times I^n (the stimulus intensity raised to the power n). (21)

Psychophysical approach to perception Is concerned with determining the relationship between properties of the stimulus and the subject's experience. (4)

Radical skepticism A philosophical position which states that it is just as likely as not that other people perceive things very differently than you do. (7)

Receiver operating characteristic (ROC) curve A graph in which the results of a signal detection experiment are plotted as the proportion of hits versus the proportion of false alarms for a number of different response criteria. (16)

Response compression When doubling the physical intensity of a stimulus less than doubles the subjective magnitude of the stimulus. (19)

Response criterion In a signal detection experiment, the subjective magnitude of a stimulus above which the subject will indicate that the stimulus is present. (14)

Response expansion When doubling the stimulus intensity more than doubles the perceived magnitude of the stimulus. (19)

Sensation Simple sensory experiences elicited by simple stimuli. *See also* Perception. (2)

Sensitivity 1.0 divided by the stimulus intensity necessary for a subject to detect a stimulus. The lower the stimulus intensity needed to detect a stimulus, the higher is the sensitivity. (11)

Signal detection theory (SDT) States that a person's detection of a stimulus depends both on the subject's sensitivity to the stimulus and on the subject's response criterion. (15)

Spectral sensitivity curve The function relating a subject's sensitivity to light to the wavelength of the light. (11)

Stevens' power law A relationship between the physical intensity of a stimulus and the perception of the subjective magnitude of the stimulus. According to Stevens, this relationship follows a power function. *See also* Power function. (19)

Threshold *See* Absolute threshold.

Visual acuity The ability to resolve small details. (6)

Visual pigment A molecule contained in the visual receptors. The reaction of this molecule to light results in the generation of an electrical response in the receptor. (12)

Wavelength of light The distance between one peak of a light wave and the next peak. (11)

Weber's law States that the just noticeable difference *(JND)* equals a constant *(K),* called the Weber fraction, times the size of the stimulus *(S)*. This law is usually expressed in the form $K = JND/S$. (12)

Chapter Two

The Physiological Bases of Perception

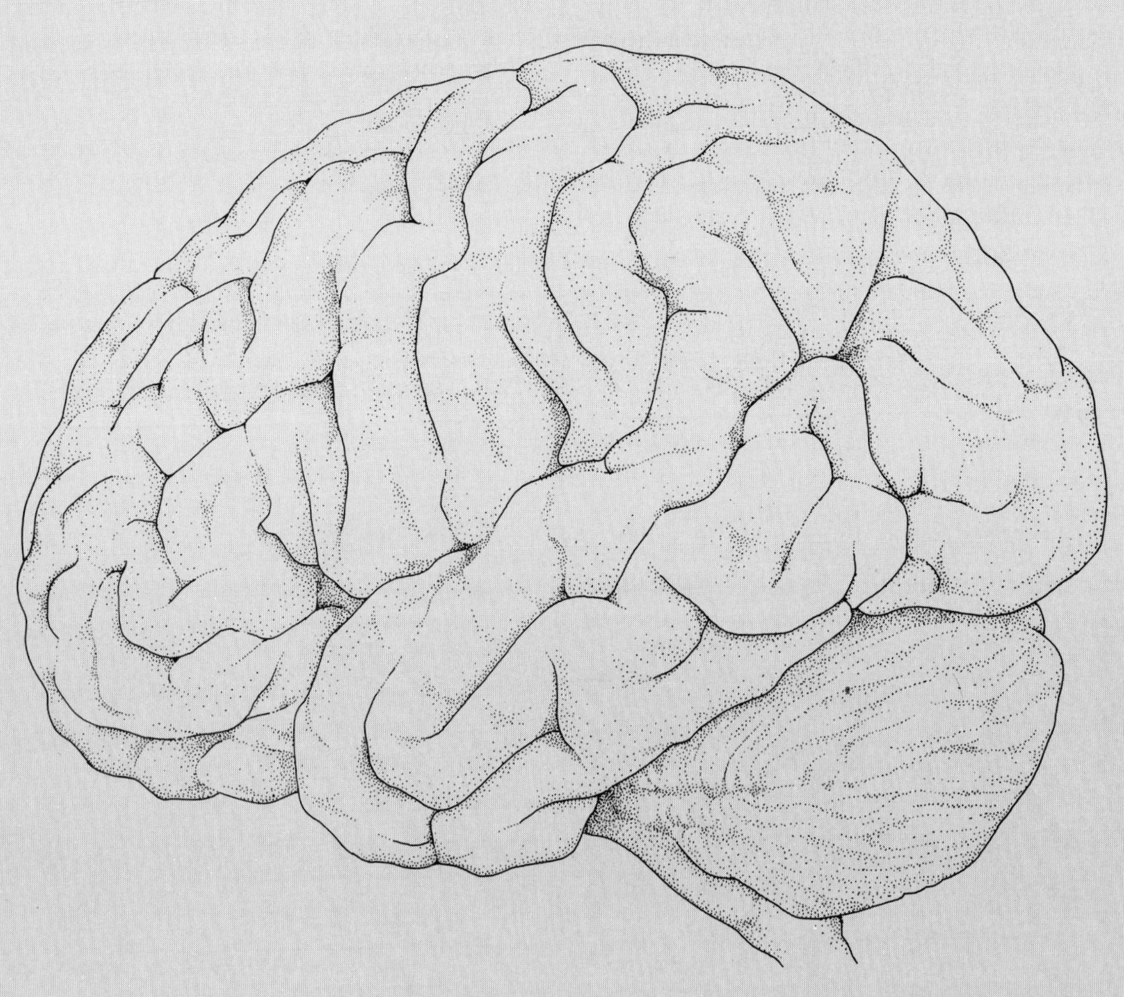

What happens to light that enters your eyes or pressure that is applied to your skin? The light and the pressure are changed into electricity by your nervous system. What happens to this electricity? It is transmitted to the brain by the nervous system. How does the electricity reaching the brain result in seeing a light or feeling someone touch your skin? In this chapter we will deal with questions such as these by looking at the physiological processes that control our perceptions. First we need to describe the structure of the nervous system and the properties of the electrical signals that travel in the nervous system.

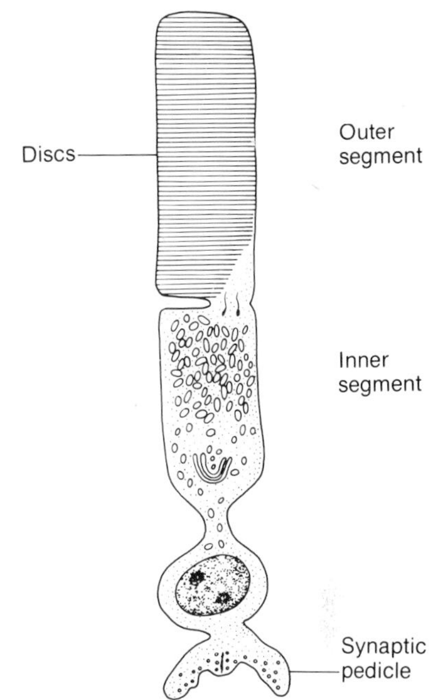

Figure 2.2 A visual receptor. The outer segment of the receptor contains a light-sensitive chemical called visual pigment.

The Nervous System

The nervous system is a communication system that transforms environmental energy into electrical energy and then transmits this electrical energy from one part of the body to another. The first job that the nervous system must perform, changing the energy in the environment into electrical energy, is carried out by the sensory receptors.

Sensory Receptors

Our ability to perceive depends on environmental information reaching the brain. Information about the environment is received by a person in the form of energy, and this energy takes a number of different forms: for seeing—light energy; for hearing and touch—mechanical energy; and for smelling and tasting—chemical energy. But the brain has a problem: electrical energy is the only thing it understands. Thus, before we can perceive any of the properties of the environment, light, mechanical, and chemical energy must be transformed into the electrical energy that the brain understands. This transformation of one kind of energy into another, which is called **transduction,** is the job of the **receptors**.

The receptors for each sense are specialized to respond to a specific kind of energy. Visual receptors, as the one in Figure 2.2, contain a chemical called **visual pigment** that changes its shape when it is hit with light. A model of this pigment, showing its shape both before and after it absorbs light, is shown in Figure 2.3. This shape change triggers a sequence of steps that leads to the generation of an electrical response in the receptor.

The receptors for touch and hearing are specialized to receive mechanical energy. Touching the skin transmits pressure through the skin, which deforms touch receptors such as the one shown in Figure 2.4. Producing sound sets up vibrations in the air, which are transmitted through various structures in the ear and bend tiny hair cells located deep inside the ear (Figure 2.5). Although we know that pushing on the touch receptor or bending the **hair cells** generates an electrical response, the exact mechanism that causes this electrical response is not known.

A similar situation exists for the senses of taste and smell. Although we know that chemicals stimulate the small cilia that are the receptors for smell (Figure 2.6) and the **taste buds** that are the receptors for taste (Figure 2.7), we don't really understand how this chemical stimulation results in electrical signals. We do know, however, that after

Box 2.1 Light, Quanta, and Vision

Light travels in waves, but, according to quantum theory, we can also think of light as being made up of small indivisible packets of energy called quanta. The figure on the top shows the path that a **quantum** follows on its way to the visual receptors. A quantum enters the eye through the cornea, passes through the lens, and then reaches the jellylike vitreous that fills the eyeball. Reaching the retina, which lines the back of the eyeball, the quantum passes through the transparent neurons of the retina, as shown in the figure on the bottom, and finally enters one of the visual receptors. (As you can see, the receptors face backward, so they can be in contact with a layer called the **pigment epithelium**, which supplies the receptors with blood and enzymes necessary for their functioning.) Inside the receptor, the quantum hits a molecule of **visual pigment**, causing the molecule to change shape and triggering a series of steps that eventually results in an electrical signal.

How many quanta must hit visual pigment molecules inside a receptor before the receptor fires? Selig Hecht, Simon Shlaer, and Maurice Pirenne (1942) answered this question by doing a psychophysical experiment in which they determined the absolute threshold for seeing a light. Using a precisely calibrated light source, Hecht determined that an observer can detect a flash of light that contains 100 quanta. Of this 100 quanta, only about half reach the retina. The other half bounce off the cornea or are reflected or absorbed by the lens or vitreous. Of the 50 quanta of light that do reach the retina, only about 7 quanta are actually absorbed by visual pigment molecules. The rest either slip between the receptors or pass through a receptor without hitting a visual pigment molecule. Thus, the activation of only 7 visual pigment molecules results in the perception of a light.

Before we leave this experiment, we still have one more fact to consider: Hecht's flash of light covered about 500 receptors. Although 7 visual pigment molecules absorb quanta, it is highly unlikely that any 2 of these 7 molecules would be in the same receptor. Look at it this way: if you released 7 ping-pong balls as you flew over an array of 500 small cylinders in a helicopter, what is the probability that 2 balls would end up in the same cylinder? The answer is *"very small,"* and it is equally unlikely that 2 visual pigment molecules in a receptor would absorb quanta in Hecht's experiment. Thus, we are led to the conclusion that when 7 visual pigment molecules in 7 *different* receptors each absorb a quantum of light, we can see the light. This means that the activity caused by the change in shape of *one* visual pigment molecule in a receptor is enough to activate that receptor, and activating 7 receptors together is enough to cause us to see the light.

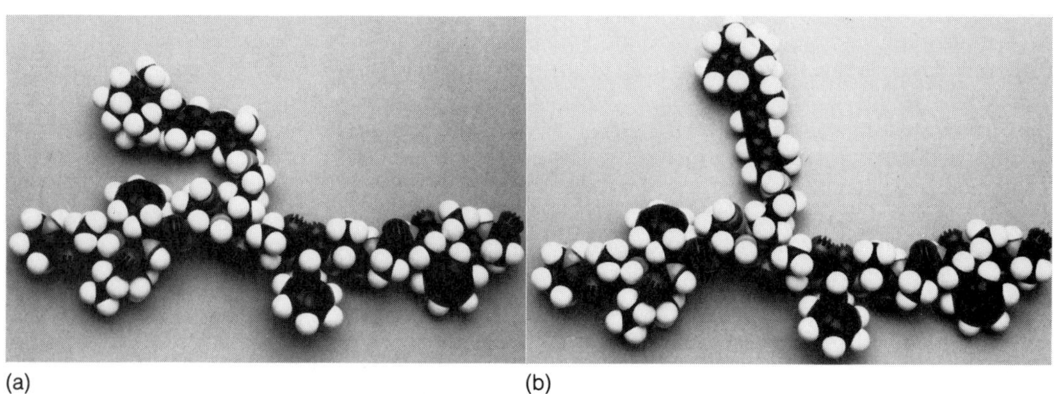

(a) (b)

Figure 2.3 Model of a visual pigment molecule, showing its shape before the molecule is hit with light (a) and after it is hit with light (b). This charge in shape results in the generation of an electrical response in the receptor.

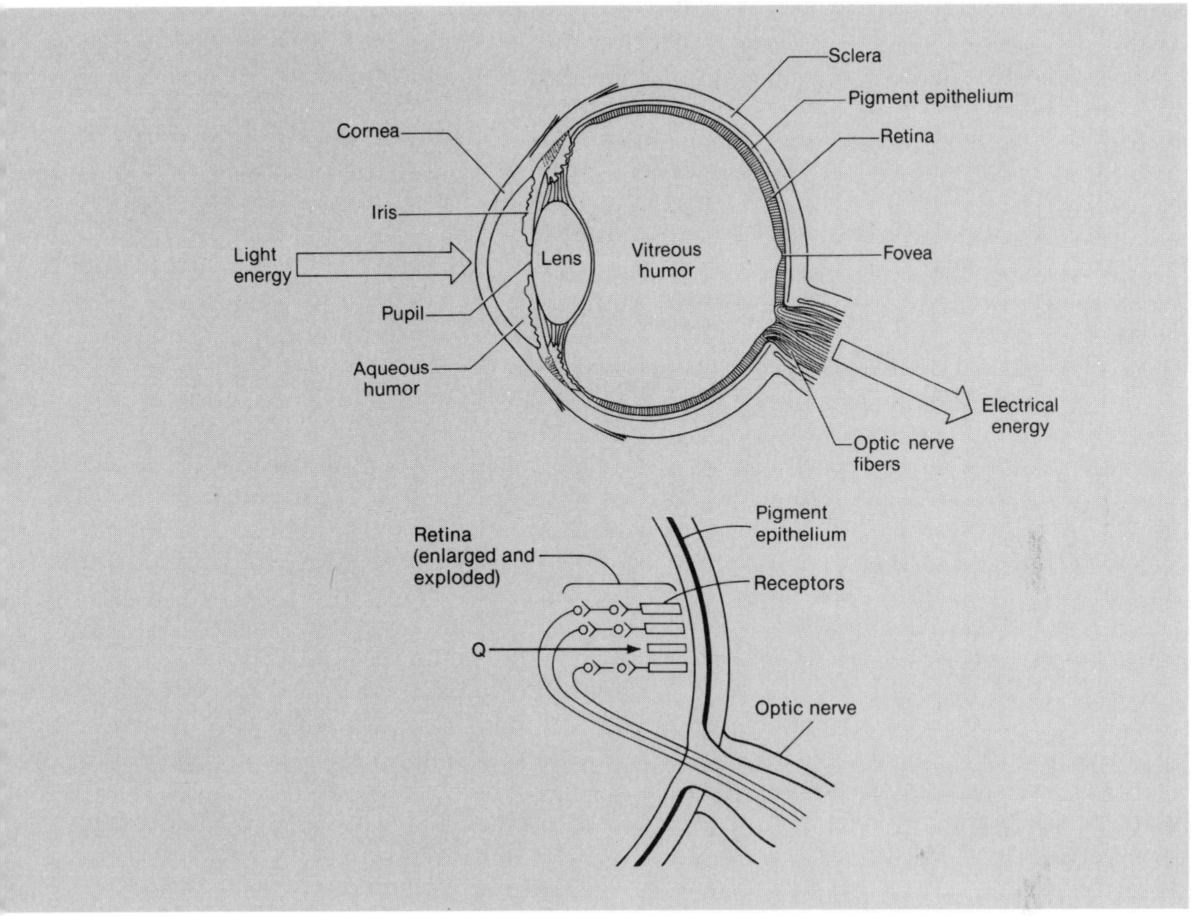

Sclera
Pigment epithelium
Retina
Cornea
Iris
Light energy
Lens
Vitreous humor
Fovea
Pupil
Aqueous humor
Electrical energy
Optic nerve fibers
Pigment epithelium
Retina (enlarged and exploded)
Receptors
Q
Optic nerve

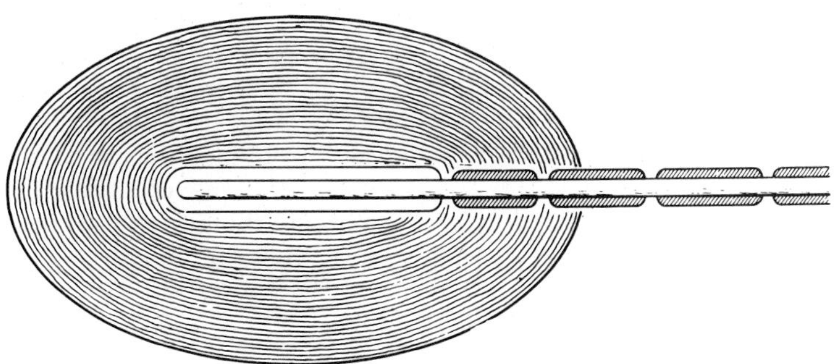

Figure 2.4 A touch receptor, which generates electrical signals in response to pressure. (From Lowenstein, 1960.)

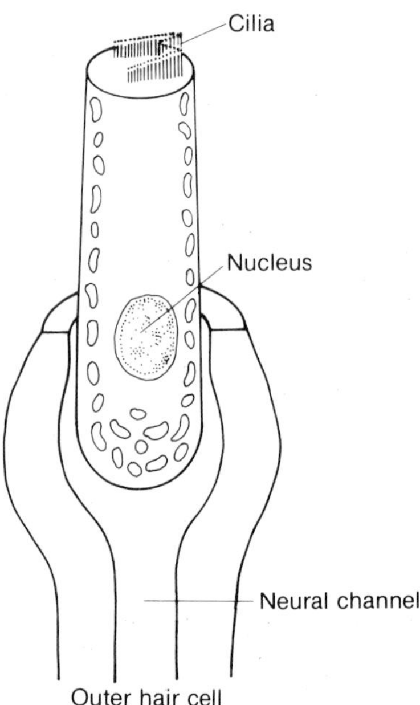

Figure 2.5 A receptor for hearing, which generates electrical signals when the cilia are bent by sound vibrations. (Adapted from Gulick, 1976.)

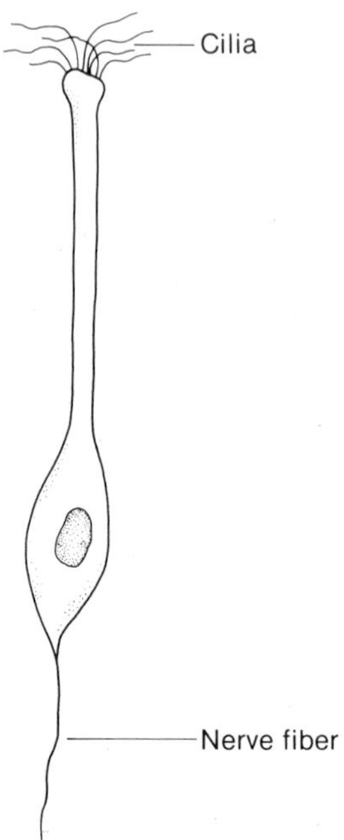

Figure 2.6 A receptor for smell, which generates electrical signals when airborne chemicals contact the cilia.

electrical signals are generated by the receptors, these signals are transmitted from the receptors toward the brain by strings of cells called neurons.

Transmission of Signals to the Brain

Strings of neurons. Signals are transmitted in the nervous system by cells called **neurons.** Receptors, as the one on the left in Figure 2.8, are specialized neurons that transform environmental energy into electrical energy. A typical neuron, shown on the right in Figure 2.8, consists of a structure called a **cell body,** which receives electrical signals, and a **nerve fiber,** which transmits these signals.

A typical sensory system, shown in Figure 2.9, is a string of neurons reaching from the receptor to the brain. In this example, a pressure-sensitive receptor in the skin transmits an electrical signal along its nerve fiber to a **synapse** at the end of the nerve fiber. The synapse, shown in more detail in Figure 2.10, is a space between the end of one neuron's nerve fiber (in this case, the receptor's nerve fiber) and the cell body of the next neuron (in this case, a neuron in the spinal cord). In order to travel up the spinal cord, the electrical signal must cross the synapse. It crosses the synapse by stimulating structures called **synaptic vesicles** that release a chemical transmitter, which in turn generates a new electrical signal in the cell body of the neuron in the spinal cord. This chemical jump across the synapse makes it possible for signals to travel long distances along many neurons.

The signal then travels up the spinal cord to synapse in a structure called the **thalamus** and then travels from the thalamus to the **cortical receiving area** for the sense of touch. Let's consider the thalamus and the different cortical receiving areas in more detail.

The thalamus. The thalamus can be thought of as a switching station for the senses, because it is here that neurons from all the senses, except the sense of smell, synapse on their way to the brain. That many

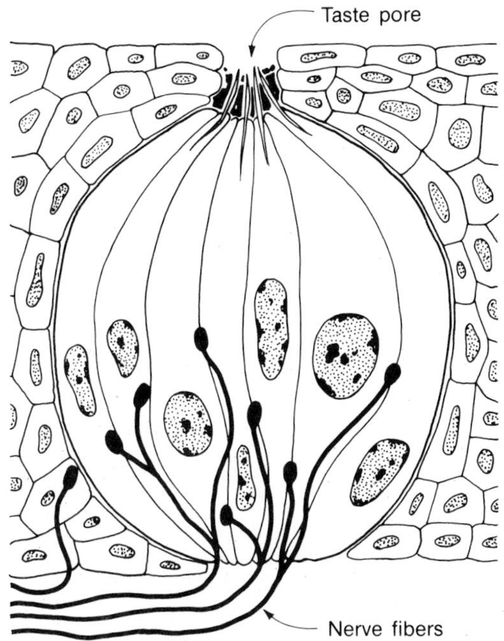

Figure 2.7 A taste bud. Chemicals entering the taste pore generate an electrical signal in the taste bud. (Adapted from Murray & Murray, 1970.)

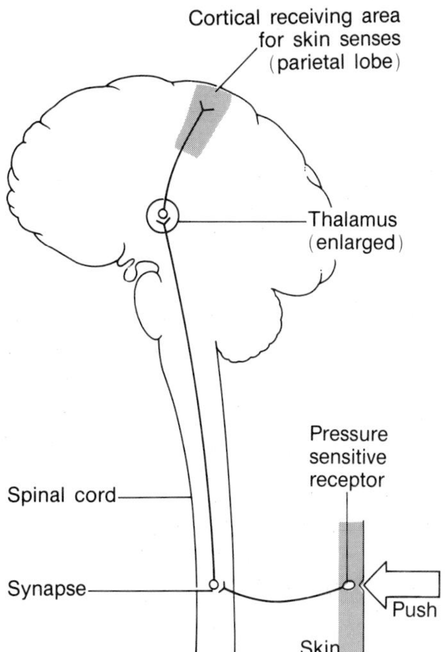

Figure 2.9 A typical sensory system. The electrical signal that originates in the receptor is transmitted along a string of neurons toward the brain.

neurons synapse together is important because this takes place throughout the nervous system, and the areas where these groups of synapses occur are called **nuclei.** The thalamus is made up of a number of nuclei, with each nucleus serving a different sense.

Cortical receiving areas. After synapsing in the appropriate nucleus in the thalamus, the nerve fibers for each sense travel to the appropriate receiving area in the cortex, shown in Figure 2.11. In this figure we see that the cortical receiving area for touch is located at the top of the cortex in the **parietal lobe**; for vision, at the back of the cortex in the **occipital lobe**; and for hearing, on the side of the cortex in the **temporal lobe.** [To help you remember which lobe goes with which sense, try remem-

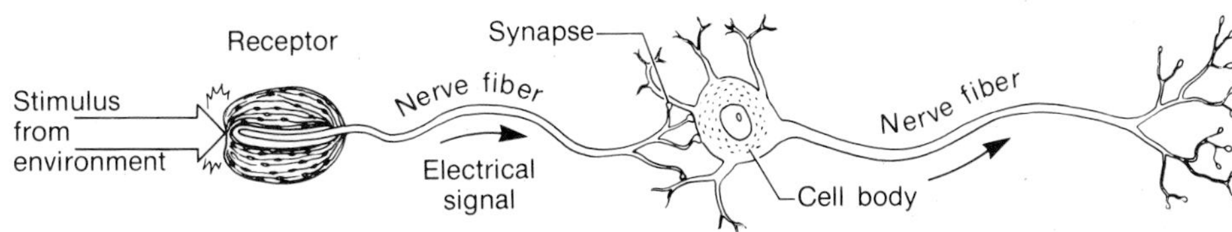

Figure 2.8 A stimulus from the environment causes a receptor to generate an electrical signal that travels to the end of the receptor's nerve fiber. The cell body of the next neuron receives the signal from the receptor's nerve fiber and generates a new electrical signal, which is transmitted down the nerve fiber of that neuron.

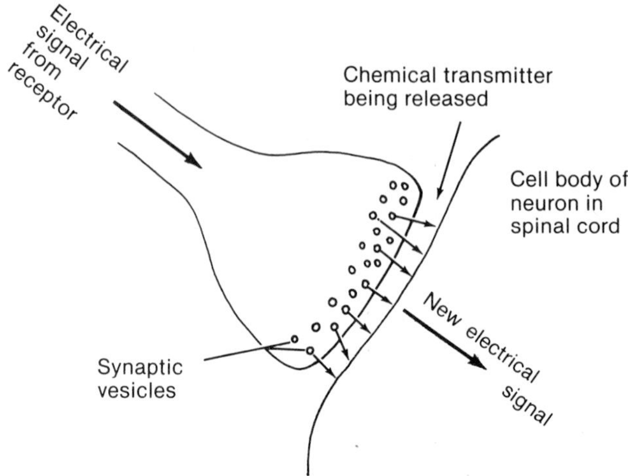

Figure 2.10 A closeup of the first synapse in Figure 2.9. The electrical signal from the receptor stimulates the synaptic vesicles, causing them to release a chemical transmitter. The chemical transmitter jumps the gap between the end of the receptor's nerve fiber and the cell body of the neuron in the spinal cord, thus generating an electrical signal in the neuron.

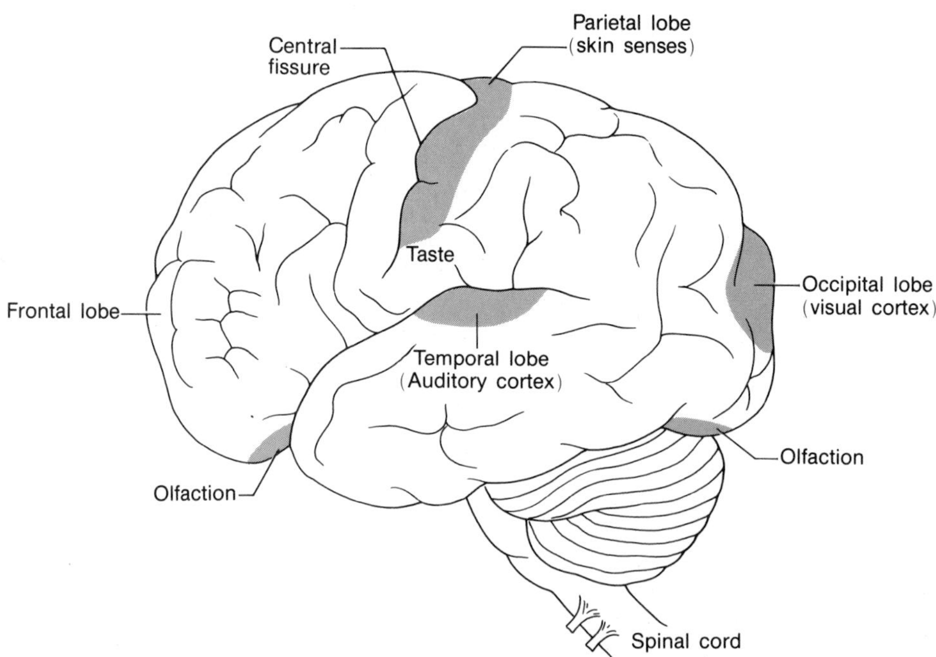

Figure 2.11 The human brain, showing the location of the primary cortical receiving areas for the senses.

bering this: Seeing *Objects* (O = Occipital); Touching *People* (P = Parietal); Hearing *Tones* (T = Temporal).] The cortical receiving areas for smell and taste are not precisely known.

Somewhere in the brain, perhaps in the cortical receiving areas, perhaps elsewhere, the electrical signals result in perception. In our example, electrical signals reaching the parietal area from the skin cause us to perceive pressure. It is important to realize that you feel pressure on your skin when the electrical signals reach the brain; it is not necessary for the electrical signals to travel back to the skin, as I've found some people mistakenly believe. When electrical signals travel from the brain back toward the skin, it is usually to stimulate muscles. Thus, if you wanted to react to someone touching your skin by touching them back, electrical signals would travel from your brain to the muscles in your arm and hand, causing your arm and hand to move. In general, perception is caused by signals that travel toward the brain, while muscle movement is caused by signals that travel away from the brain.

Before leaving our discussion of how nerve fibers transmit signals from the receptors to the brain, we should distinguish between **nerves** and **nerve fibers.** In our description of the sensory system in Figure 2.9, we followed an electrical signal as it traveled along a single nerve fiber from the skin toward the brain. It is important to remember, however, that many nerve fibers from the same area of the skin usually travel together and that nerves are bundles of thousands of such fibers. The same thing happens in vision: about one million nerve fibers leave the back of the eye together in the optic nerve.

Electrical Signals in Neurons

Now that we have a feel for how electrical signals are transmitted from the receptors to the brain, let's take a closer look at the nature of these electrical signals. When you think of electrical signals, you probably think about the electricity that travels in electrical wiring. These signals could be called "dry signals" because they are transmitted through strands of dry metal wire, and, in fact, we learn at an early age that electricity and water don't mix. However, the electrical signals that travel in nerve fibers could be called "wet signals" because they are transmitted through nerve fibers that are literally underwater. How is it possible for electricity to travel through water? We will see in the next section that it is the presence of charged molecules, particularly sodium and potassium, that makes these underwater signals possible.

How Sodium and Potassium Cause Electrical Signals

To understand how nerve fibers transmit electrical signals, let's first describe what a nerve fiber is like when it is at rest, that is, not transmitting any electrical signals.

When the nerve fiber is at rest. Nerve fibers at rest have two important properties: (1) the inside of the fiber has a negative charge compared to the outside; (2) there is a lot of sodium outside the fiber and a lot of potassium inside the fiber. Let's consider each of these properties in turn.

First, let's measure the electrical charge inside the fiber. To do this, we will use a microelectrode—a small shaft of metal or glass, with a diameter at its tip of about 1/1,000 cm—which is small enough to record electrical signals from a single nerve fiber. We position a **recording electrode** inside the nerve fiber, as shown in Figure 2.12(a), and a **null electrode** at the far end of the nerve fiber; then we record the difference in charge between them. With the electrodes positioned as shown in Figure 2.12(a), we find a 70-millivolt (1 mV = 1/1,000 volt) difference in charge between the recording and null electrodes; that is, the inside of the nerve fiber is 70 mV more negative than the outside. This 70-mV difference between the inside and outside of the fiber is called the **resting potential** of the fiber, since this is the charge inside the fiber when it is at rest.

Now, let's look at the substances inside and outside the fiber. Nerve fibers exist in a sea of liquid. They are surrounded, inside and out, with water, and this water contains numerous charged molecules called **ions.** The most abundant substance outside the nerve fiber is positively charged sodium (Na^+), and the most abundant substance inside the fiber is positively charged potassium (K^+). (There is also some sodium inside and potassium outside the fiber, along with other charged molecules, but we will focus on the sodium outside and potassium

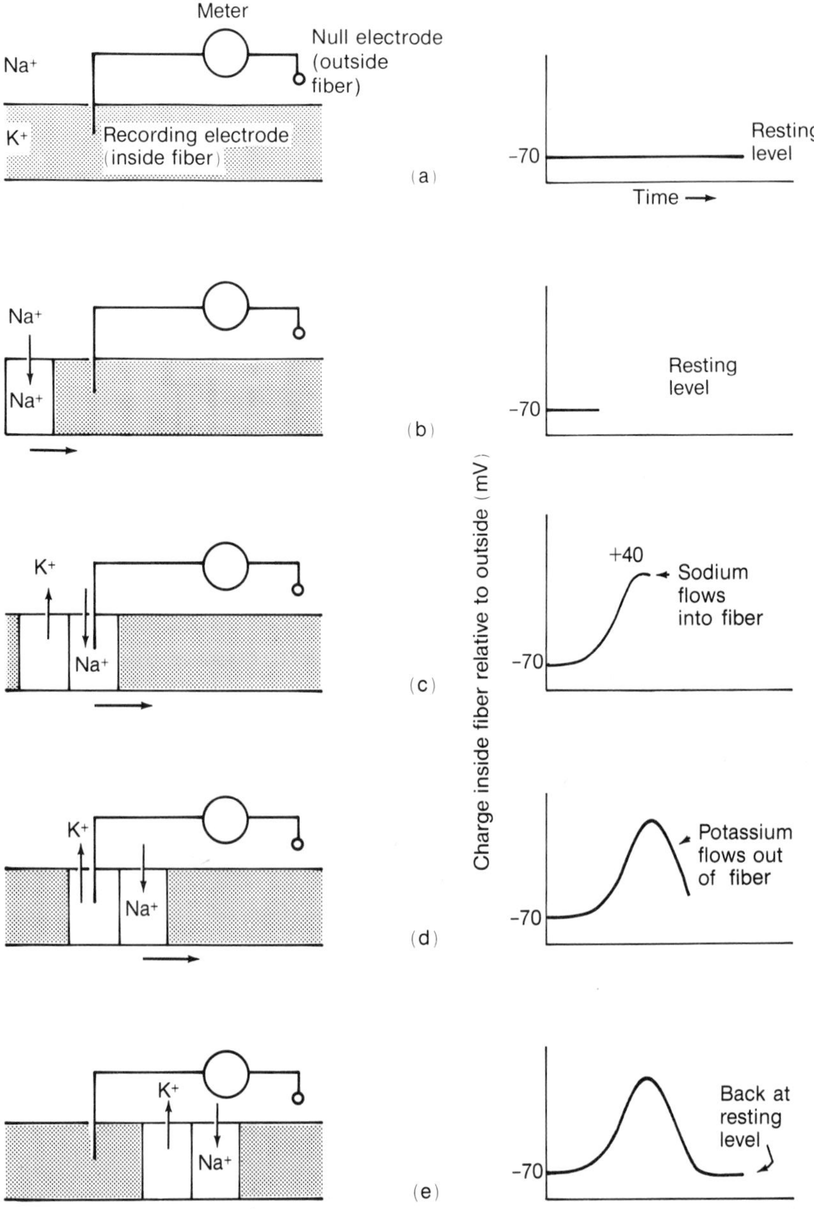

Figure 2.12 Effect of a nerve impulse as it travels down a nerve fiber. The recording setup is shown on the left, and the difference in charge between the inside and outside of the fiber is shown on the right. As long as the fiber is at rest, there is a difference in charge of −70 mV between the inside and the outside of the fiber, as shown in (a). In (b–e), we see what happens as a nerve impulse travels down the fiber. The flow of sodium into the fiber and potassium out of the fiber is shown on the left, and the resulting change in the charge measured by the electrodes is shown on the right.

inside in our discussion.) It is this sodium and potassium that cause an electrical potential to travel down the nerve fiber.

The electrical signal. Electrical signals in nerve fibers are caused by the flow of sodium and potassium across the walls of the fiber. First Na^+ flows into the fiber, and then K^+ flows out. This flow—Na^+ in, followed by K^+ out—travels down the length of the fiber. We can see how this sodium and potassium flow affects the electrical charge recorded by our electrode, by following the sequence illustrated in Figure 2.12(b–e). In (b), the sodium is flowing into the fiber in response to stimulation, but our electrode is farther down the fiber and doesn't react to the effects of this flow. The electrode, therefore, continues to record the resting potential of −70 mV, as indicated by the record on the right. Slightly later in time, at (c), the inflow of sodium reaches our electrode and causes the inside of the fiber to become more positive (because the sodium has a positive charge), increasing the charge from the resting level of −70 mV to about +40 mV. Slightly later in time, at (d), the sodium flow is past the electrode and potassium begins flowing out at the electrode. This outward flow of positively charged potassium causes the inside of the fiber to become more negative as it returns toward its resting potential of −70 mV. At (e), the flow of charged molecules has passed the electrode and the fiber has returned to −70 mV. This sequence (b–e) illustrates what happens when one **nerve impulse** passes down the fiber.

Some Basic Properties of Nerve Impulses

To illustrate some basic properties of nerve impulses, let's look at the records in Figure 2.13, which show the response of a nerve fiber to pressure on the skin. The most obvious thing about these records is that each nerve impulse appears as a sharp spike. This occurs because we have compressed the

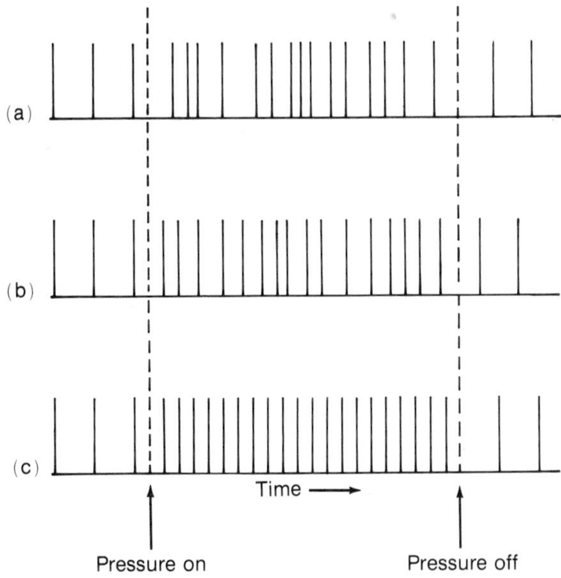

Figure 2.13 Response of a nerve fiber from the skin to (a) soft, (b) medium, and (c) strong pressure applied to the fiber's receptor. Increasing the stimulus strength increases both the rate and regularity of nerve firing in this fiber.

Box 2.2 Intracellular and Extracellular Recording

There are two ways to record the electrical signals of nerve cells. The electrode can be inserted into the cell (**intracellular recording**), or it can be positioned just outside the cell (**extracellular recording**). By far the more widely used of the two—and the one used in most of the studies described in this book—is extracellular recording, because it is much easier than intracellular recording. Intracellular recording is important, however, because it enables us to directly measure what is happening inside a cell.

The major difficulty with intracellular recording is that, because most nerve cells are very small, inserting electrodes into them is difficult. One solution to this problem is to find large cells, as A. L. Hodgkin and A. F. Huxley (1939) did in their studies of the giant squid axon. The giant squid axon measures almost 1 mm in diameter, making it possible to insert the recording electrode lengthwise into the axon, as shown in the left figure below.

In addition to making it possible to observe directly what is happening inside a cell, intracellular recording also makes possible the identification of the specific cell being studied. This is particularly important in the retina, in which many different kinds of cells exist next to each other. The cell's location in the retina can be determined at the end of an experiment, by injecting a dye into the cell through the electrode. Dyes have been developed that diffuse throughout the cell and result in pictures like the right one, below. We can tell from the shape of the dye-marker and location in the retina that this is an amacrine cell. Using this procedure, Akimichi Kaneko (1970) recorded from and identified the bipolar cells, horizontal cells, and amacrine cells in the goldfish retina (see Figure 2.16).

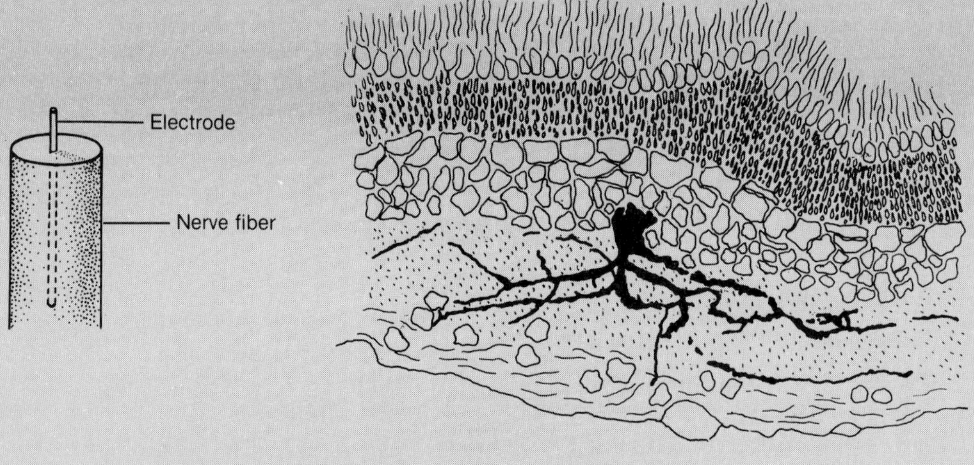

time scale, as compared to that of Figure 2.12, so that we can display a number of nerve impulses.

The three records in Figure 2.13 represent the fiber's response to three intensities of stimulation. Figure 2.13(a) shows how the fiber responds to light pressure applied to the skin, while 2.13(b) and (c) show how the response changes as the pressure is increased. Comparing these three records leads to an important conclusion: changing the stimulus intensity does not affect the size of the nerve impulses but does affect the rate of nerve firing. To put this another way, the voltage change that occurs during a nerve impulse (for most fibers, from −70 mV to +40 mV) is constant, but the rate of nerve firing can vary.

It is important to realize, however, that although increasing the stimulus intensity can increase the rate of nerve firing, there is an upper limit to the number of nerve impulses per second that can be conducted down a nerve fiber. This limit occurs because a neuron takes about one millisecond (1 msec = 1/1,000 sec) to recover from conducting a nerve impulse before it can conduct another one. This interval is called the **refractory period** of the fiber, and it sets the upper limit to the firing rate at about 500–800 impulses per second.

Another important property of nerve firing is illustrated by the beginning of each of the records in Figure 2.13. Notice that some nerve impulses occur even before the pressure stimulus is applied. In fact, many nerve fibers fire without any stimuli from the environment; this firing is called **spontaneous activity.** Although this phenomenon may seem strange, we will see later that it plays an important role in determining our perceptions.

Jumping the Synapse: Excitation and Inhibition

Once a nerve impulse is generated at one end of a fiber, it travels down the entire length of the fiber without stopping or changing its size. However, this ability to travel the fiber's entire length does not, in itself, guarantee that a signal from the pressure receptor in your skin will reach the parietal lobe of your brain, because on its journey toward the brain, the nerve impulse must traverse a number of synapses. We saw in Figure 2.10 that when a nerve impulse reaches the synapse at the end of a neuron, the transmitter in the synaptic vesicles is released onto the cell body of the next neuron, causing an electrical response in that neuron. The electrical response can be one of either **excitation** or **inhibition,** depending on the type of transmitter and the nature of the cell body's membrane. If the response is excitatory, the inside of the cell body becomes more positive and the rate of nerve firing increases (remember from Figure 2.12 that during a nerve impulse the inside of the fiber becomes more positive); if the response is inhibitory, the inside of the cell body becomes more negative and the rate of nerve firing decreases.

A neuron usually receives many excitatory and inhibitory inputs, with some neurons in the brain receiving inputs from as many as a thousand other neurons! Figure 2.14 shows how the generation of nerve impulses in a neuron depends on the interplay of the excitatory (E) and inhibitory (I) stimulation converging on the cell. When the neuron receives excitatory input, the rate of firing increases above the spontaneous level, as shown in Figure 2.14(a); but as the amount of inhibition relative to excitation increases (b–e), the firing rate decreases. In (d) and (e), the inhibition is so strong that the rate of nerve firing is decreased to below the level of spontaneous activity.

Neural Circuits

Introduction to Neural Circuits

In describing the basic structure of a sensory system, we saw that strings of neurons are connected by synapses. These strings of neurons and their synapses make it possible for nerve impulses to travel over long distances, but they also serve another purpose. Synapses are used by the nervous system to "process" electrical signals as they travel from the receptors to the brain. We will see that the electrical signals generated in the receptors are processed by the network of nerve fibers, or **neural circuits,** through which the signals travel. To illustrate how this processing works, we will look at a neural circuit that enables the nervous system to detect movement across the skin.

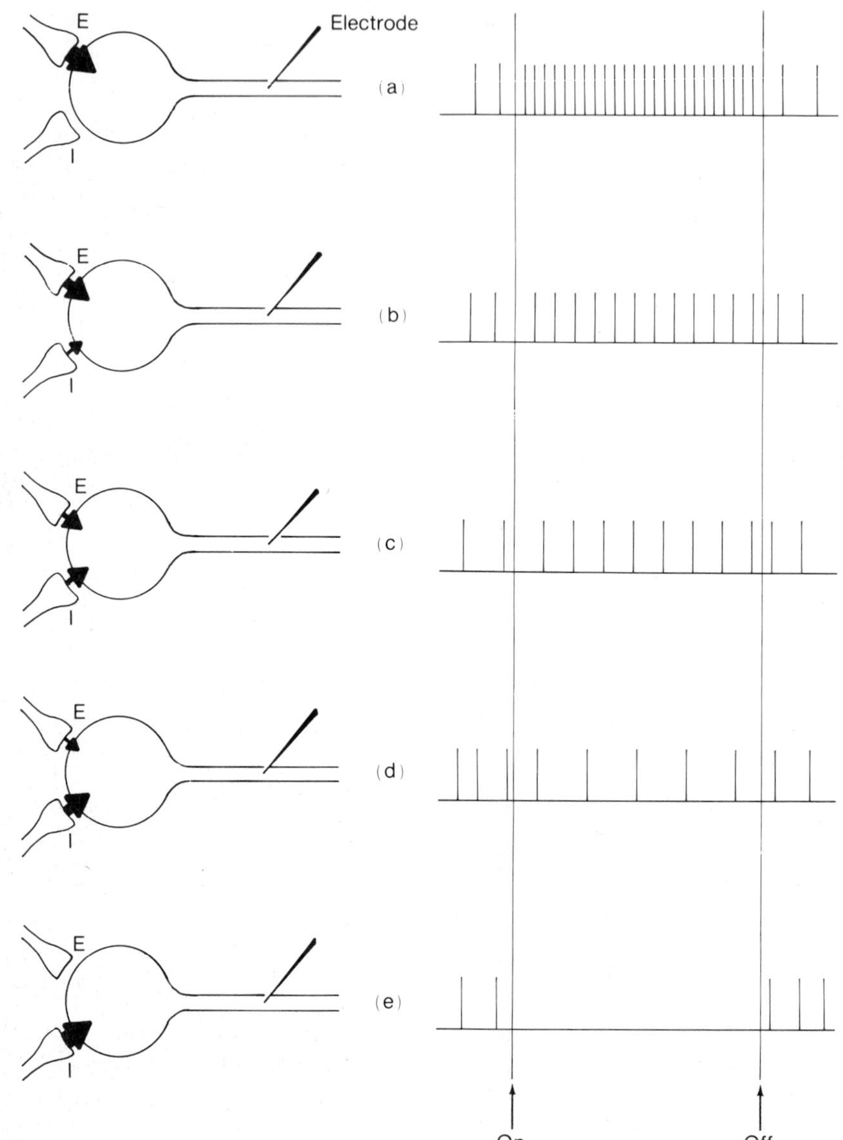

Figure 2.14 Effect of excitatory and inhibitory input on the firing rate of a neuron. The amount of excitatory and inhibitory input to the neuron is indicated by the size of the arrows at the synapse. The responses recorded by the electrode are indicated by the records on the right.

A Circuit That Detects Movement Across the Skin

We are going to look at two different circuits, circuit A in Figure 2.15, in which no processing occurs, and circuit B, in which the signals are processed. Receptors are represented by ellipses (⬭), cell bodies by circles (○), nerve fibers by straight lines (—), excitatory synapses by Y's (—<), and inhibitory synapses by T's (—|). Both circuits have receptors

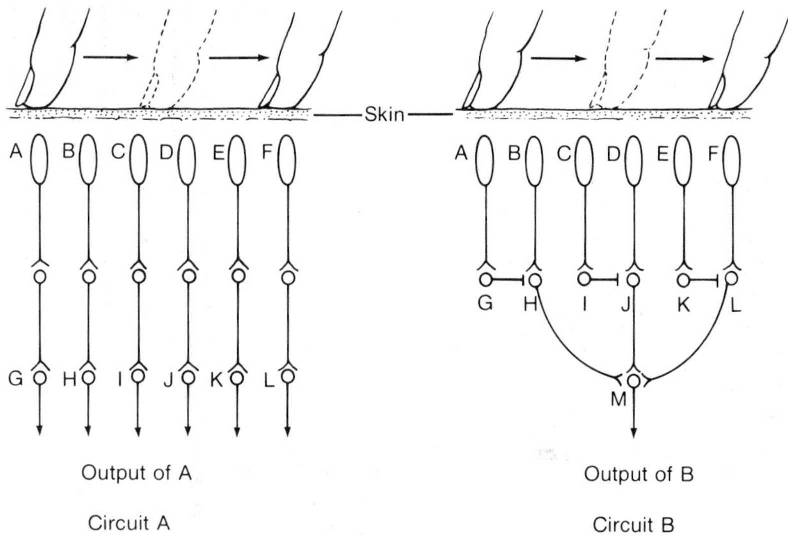

Figure 2.15 Two types of neural circuits. In circuit A the signals generated by the receptors are not processed, but in circuit B the signals are processed.

on the skin that respond to pressure. In circuit A the signals generated by receptors A, B, C, D, E, and F are each transmitted along a private line to neurons G, H, I, J, K, and L. Circuit B is more complex: signals from receptors A, C, and E stimulate cells G, I, and K, sending inhibition to neighboring neurons H, J, and L, which in turn feed into neuron M.

Let's compare the responses of these two circuits as a finger moves from left to right across the receptors. As the finger moves across the skin, the receptors in both circuits fire in sequence, starting with receptor A and ending with receptor F. The response of the *receptors* in both circuits is, therefore, the same. We can see, however, that the *output* of these two circuits is different, by measuring the response of neurons G–L in circuit A and the response of neuron M in circuit B. Moving the finger from left to right across the skin causes cells G–L to fire in sequence just as the receptors did. Thus, circuit A simply transmits unchanged the signal generated by receptors A–F to cells G–L. A similar situation occurs if the finger moves from right to left. In this case, receptors F–A fire in sequence and cells L–G fire in sequence. Again, the output of cells L–G mimics the response of the receptors.

Let's now consider circuit B. If for circuit B we begin moving the finger from left to right, receptor A is stimulated first. Receptor A then stimulates cell G, which sends an inhibitory signal to cell H. While this is occurring, the stimulus on the skin moves to receptor B and causes it to fire. Receptor B sends an excitatory signal to cell H, but cell H does not fire because it has just been inhibited by cell G. As a result, the signal that started in the receptors does not get past cell H, and the output of cell M is zero. This process is then repeated as the stimulus moves across the remaining receptors, with the net result still being no response in cell M.

Moving the finger from right to left across the skin yields a different result. Receptor F is stimulated first, and it sends a signal to cell L. The finger then moves across the skin to receptor E, which causes cell K to send inhibition to cell L. This inhibition, however, arrives at cell L too late to prevent it from firing and causing cell M to fire. This process is repeated as the finger continues to move across the remaining receptors, with the net result that cell M fires.

We can see from these examples that different things happen to signals leaving the receptors in circuits A and B. Although the response of the receptors in the two circuits is the same, the outputs are different. In circuit A, movement across the skin from left to right is indicated by sequential firing of cells G–L and movement from right to left by sequential firing of cells L–G. However, in circuit B, movement from left to right causes no response in cell M, but movement from right to left causes cell M to fire.

The lack of processing in circuit A makes it necessary to monitor the output of six neurons to determine whether a stimulus is moving from right to left. However, because of the processing in circuit B, only one neuron must be monitored to determine which way the stimulus is moving.

Why is this processing of the information generated by the receptors necessary? One reason is to transform the information falling on the receptors into a form that can be more easily understood by the brain. We can draw an analogy between information processing in the nervous system and the information processing that occurs when we analyze the data we collect in an experiment. The "raw data" from an experiment usually consist of many numbers, and it is often difficult to tell exactly what these numbers mean. However, when we plot these numbers on a graph or calculate means and standard deviations or do statistical tests, their meaning often becomes much clearer. The electrical activity of the many receptors constitutes the "raw data" of the nervous system; once this electrical activity is processed, as it is in circuit B of Figure 2.15, we can determine the nature of the stimulus by monitoring the output of only one or a few neurons.

While transforming the raw data from the receptors into a simpler form, the circuits of the nervous system also shape our perceptions. For example, what if all cells in the skin were connected together as in circuit B, so that moving a stimulus across the skin from right to left caused a large response in many neurons while moving a stimulus from left to right caused no response? If this were the case, we would be very good at perceiving right to left movement but would be unable to detect movement in the opposite direction. This hypothetical example illustrates an important principle: *the way in which neurons are wired together in the nervous system influences our perceptions.*

Having seen how information can be processed by neural circuits, we will now illustrate the principle that the way neurons are wired together influences our perceptions, by looking at some examples of information processing in the visual system. We will focus on a particularly important kind of processing called **lateral inhibition,** which occurs when cells spread inhibition laterally across nerve circuits, as did cells G, I, and K in circuit B of Figure 2.15.

Lateral Inhibition in the Retina

Structure of the Retina

To understand how lateral inhibition might operate in the retina, we need to look at the structure of the **retina.** The cross section in Figure 2.16 shows the five major types of cells in the retina. Electrical signals start in the receptors (R) and travel toward the brain via the **bipolar cells** (B) and then the **ganglion cells** (G), whose nerve fibers bundle together to form the **optic nerve.** The two remaining types of cells, **horizontal cells** (H) and **amacrine cells** (A), do not transmit signals toward the brain; instead, they transmit signals *laterally, across* the retina. Horizontal cells connect receptors to other receptors, while amacrine cells connect ganglion cells to other ganglion cells and also connect bipolar cells to each other.

Since the horizontal and amacrine cells transmit signals laterally, they can, potentially, spread inhibition across the retina. We can appreciate the possible effect of this lateral inhibition by looking at some experiments on a much simpler visual system, that of the horseshoe crab, or *Limulus.*

A Demonstration of Lateral Inhibition in the Limulus

The *Limulus,* shown in Figure 2.17, is ideally suited for vision experiments, because its eye is made up of hundreds of tiny structures called ommatidia, with each **ommatidium** having a small lens on the eye's surface that is located directly over a single receptor. Since each lens and receptor is roughly the diameter of a pencil head, it is possible to illuminate a single receptor without illuminating its neighboring receptors. This property of the Limulus eye led Kuf-

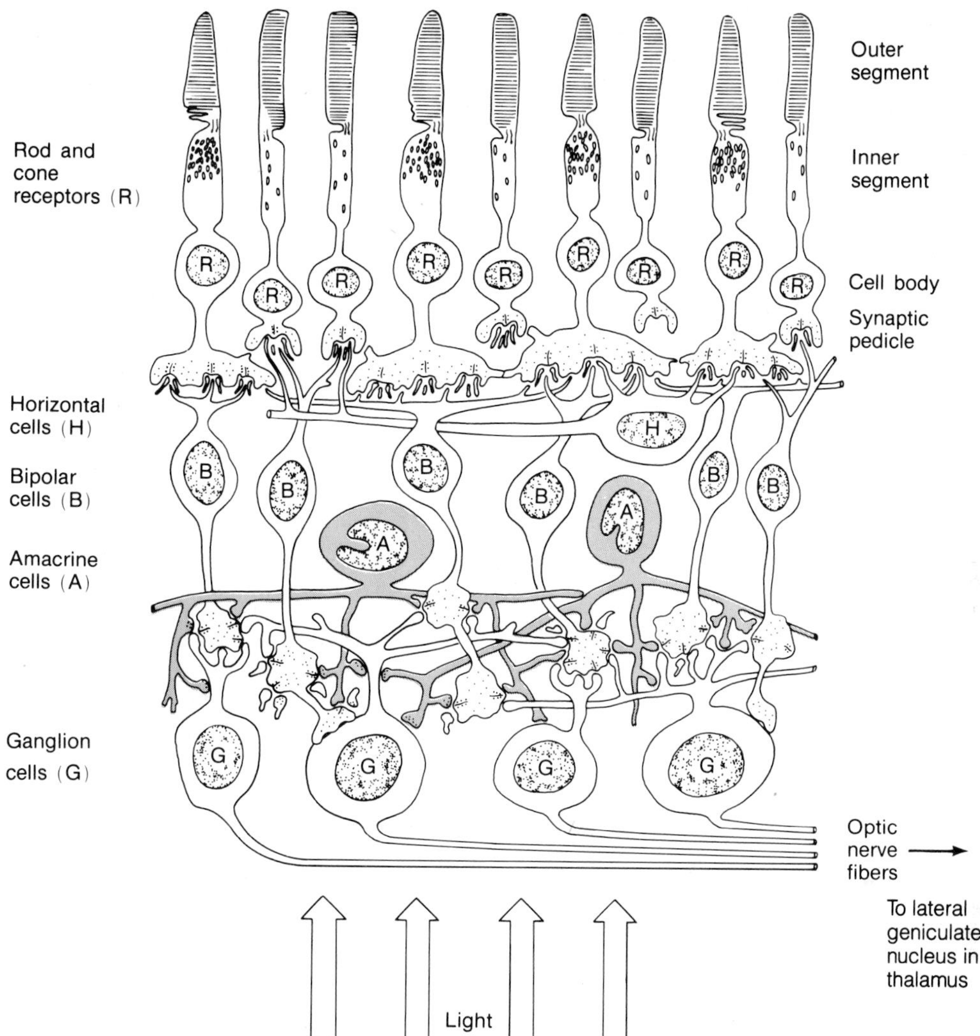

Figure 2.16 Cross section of the primate retina. Lots of processing occurs in the neural circuits of the retina, largely because of inhibition that is transmitted laterally by the horizontal and amacrine cells. (Adapted from Dowling & Boycott, 1966.)

fer Hartline, Henry Wagner, and Floyd Ratliff (1956) to do an experiment in which they demonstrated the effects of lateral inhibition.

When Hartline, Wagner, and Ratliff recorded from the nerve fiber of receptor A, as shown in Figure 2.18, they found that illumination of that receptor caused the large response shown in 2.18(a). But when they added illumination to the three nearby receptors at B, while still illuminating receptor A, they found the decreased response shown in 2.18(b). They also found that increasing the illumination of B further decreased the response, as shown in 2.18(c). Thus, illumination of the neighboring receptors *inhibited* the firing of receptor A. This lateral inhibition is transmitted along the *Limulus*'s lateral plexus, a structure that connects the *Limulus's* receptors to each other, just as horizontal cells connect receptors in the human retina.

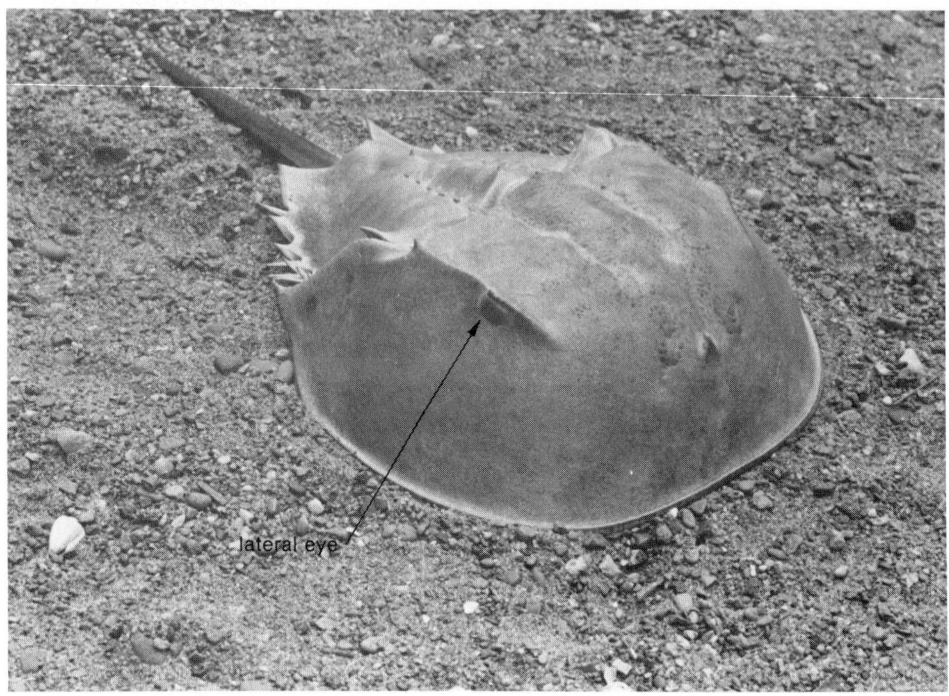

Figure 2.17 A Limulus, also known as the horseshoe crab.

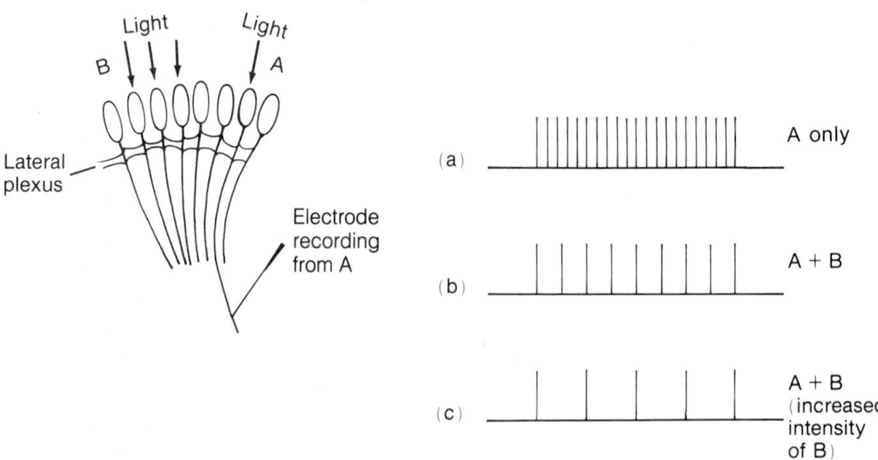

Figure 2.18 A demonstration of lateral inhibition in the Limulus. The records on the right show the response recorded by the electrode recording from the nerve fiber of receptor A when receptor A is stimulated and (a) no other receptors are stimulated, (b) the receptors at B are stimulated simultaneously, and (c) the receptors at B are stimulated at an increased intensity. (Adapted from Ratliff, 1965.)

A Perceptual Consequence of Lateral Inhibition: Mach Bands

We have shown that lateral inhibition can be demonstrated by recording from the *Limulus*, and we also know that horizontal and amacrine cells could potentially transmit this lateral inhibition across our retinas. But is there any evidence that lateral inhibition does, in fact, affect our perception? The answer to this question is "yes." A number of perceptual effects are easily explained in terms of lateral inhibition. One such effect is illustrated in Figure 2.19(a). As you look along the line from A to D, you can probably make out a faint band at B that is lighter than the rest of the light area. After you cross over to the dark side of the contour, you can see a band at C that is darker than the rest of the dark area. Figure 2.19(b) graphs the perception of lightness along the line from A to D, with the light band at B indicated by the rise in the graph at B and the dark band at C indicated by the dip in the graph at C. These light and dark bands are called **Mach bands,** after their discoverer, Ernst Mach. Mach found that light and dark bands are seen near the borders between light and dark areas, even though no bands are physically present. We can confirm that no bands are physically present by using a light meter to measure the amount of light reflected from Figure 2.19(a). When we do this, we get the result shown in 2.19(c). The intensity of the light side is the same all the way across, as is the intensity of the dark side. You can demonstrate this to yourself by covering one of the dark bands with a piece of paper. When you do this, the light Mach band should vanish, and as soon as you remove the paper, the band reappears.

A Neural Circuit That Results in Mach Bands

Although many experiments on both *Limuli* and humans support the idea that Mach bands are caused by lateral inhibition, we do not know the exact details of the circuits involved. However, a simple neural circuit that would result in Mach bands is shown in Figure 2.20. This simplified cross section of the retina shows four receptors, each of which sends lateral inhibition to its neighbors on both sides. Let's illuminate these receptors so that A and B receive intense illumination and, therefore, generate a large response of, say, 100 nerve impulses per second. Receptors C and D, on the other hand, receive dim illumination and, therefore, generate a smaller

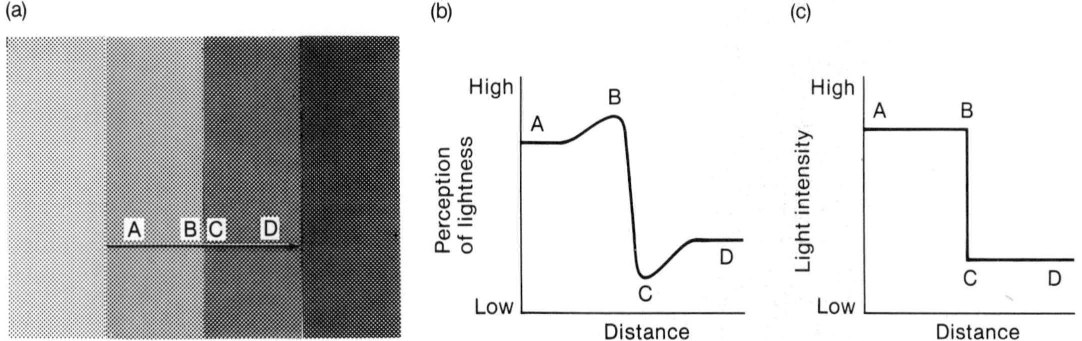

Figure 2.19 (a) Mach bands at a contour. Just to the left of the contour, near B, a faint light band can be perceived, and just to the right at C, a faint dark band can be perceived. (b) A plot showing the perceptual effect described in (a). The bump in the curve at B indicates the light Mach band, and the dip in the curve at C indicates the dark Mach band. (c) A plot showing the physical intensity distribution of the light, as measured with a light meter. Note that the bumps shown in plot (b) that correspond to the two Mach bands are not present.

response of, say, 20 impulses per second. At this point, with no inhibition involved, A and B would generate equal responses of 100, and C and D would generate equal responses of 20. However, we can show, by means of a simple calculation, how this circuit can result in an effect similar to the perceptual effect of Mach bands.

We do this calculation as follows:

1. Start with the initial response of each cell, 100 for A and B, and 20 for C and D.
2. Determine the amount of inhibition that each cell receives from its neighbor on each side. For the purposes of our calculation, we will assume that each cell sends inhibition to its neighbor equal to one-tenth of that cell's initial output. Thus, cells A and B will send 100 × 0.1 = 10 units of inhibition to their neighbors, and cells C and D will send 20 × 0.1 = 2 units of inhibition to their neighbors.
3. Determine the final output of each cell (final output = initial response − inhibition). Remember that each cell receives inhibition from its neighbor on either side. The calculation for each cell in Figure 2.20 is:

Cell A: Output = 100 − 10 − 10 = 80
Cell B: Output = 100 − 10 − 2 = 88
Cell C: Output = 20 − 10 − 2 = 8
Cell D: Output = 20 − 2 − 2 = 16

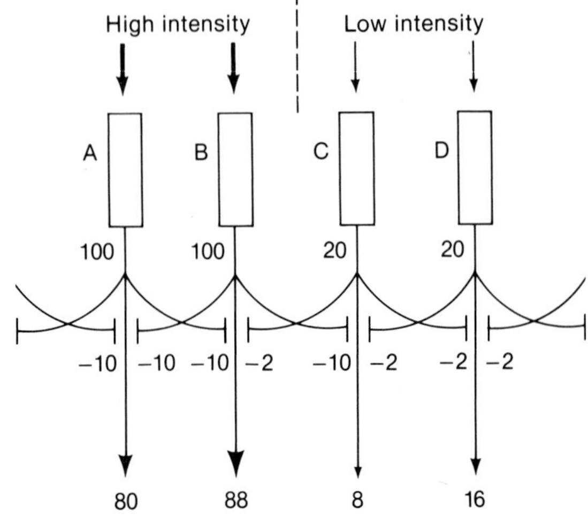

Figure 2.20 Four receptors that inhibit each other. If we know the initial output of each receptor and the amount of lateral inhibition, we can calculate the final output of the receptors. (See text for a description of this calculation.)

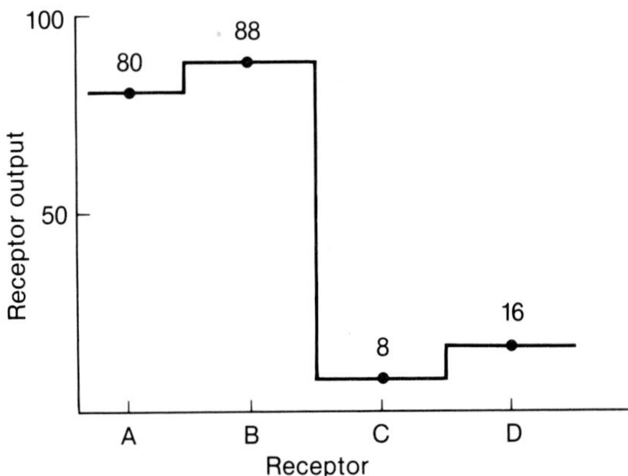

Figure 2.21 A plot showing the final receptor output calculated for the circuit of Figure 2.20. The bump at B and the dip at C correspond to the light and dark Mach bands, respectively.

The graph of these responses in Figure 2.21 looks very similar to Figure 2.19(b). There is an increase in nerve firing on the light side of the border at B and a decrease on the dark side at C. The lateral inhibition in our circuit has created Mach bands neurally, and a circuit similar to this one, but much more complex, is probably responsible for our perception of Mach bands.

This creation of Mach bands by lateral inhibition demonstrates a connection between physiology and perception, illustrating the point made in our discussion of circuits A and B, in Figure 2.15, that the way neurons are wired together influences our perceptions. Before further discussing how neural circuits can influence our perception, let's consider an implication of the nervous system's influence on our perceptions: *what we perceive is not necessarily an exact copy of the energy in the environment*. This is clearly the case with Mach bands; Mach bands are not really there, yet we see them because of lateral inhibition. We should not dismiss Mach bands, however, as simply an unusual illusion, because the same principles apply to everything we perceive. All of the energy in our environment is transformed into the electrical impulses of the nervous system and is processed by the nervous system before perception occurs. Thus, if our nervous system were different, we would perceive things differently. Eliminating lateral inhibition would eliminate Mach bands, causing us to see borders a little less sharply; it would also change the way we see colors, brightnesses, and forms, the way we hear tones, and the way we feel a touch on our skin.

Throughout this book, we will see again and again that our perceptions are not copies of what is "out there"; instead, they are the products of interactions between what is out there and our nervous system. Although this chapter focuses on how perception is influenced by a nervous system that does not exactly copy what is out there, we will see later, particularly in Chapters 8 and 14, that our perception is also strongly influenced by how we interpret what we see and hear, based on our past experiences. Such interpretation also shapes our perceptions so they are not simply copies of what is in the environment. But in talking about the effect of our past experiences on perception we are getting a little ahead of ourselves. For now, let's focus on the nervous system's influence on perception, by describing some of the neural mechanisms that may play a role in form perception.

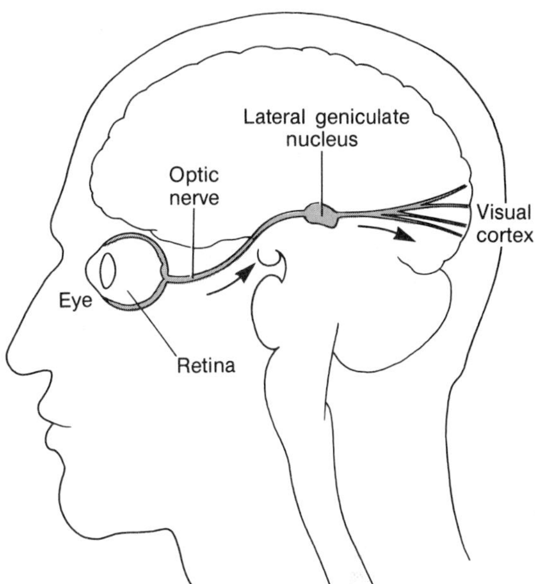

Figure 2.22 A side view of the visual system, showing the three major sites along the visual pathway where processing takes place: the retina, the lateral geniculate nucleus (LGN), and the visual receiving area of the cortex.

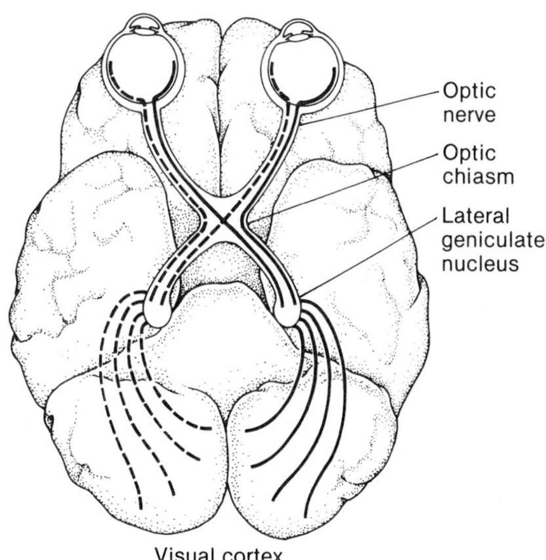

Figure 2.23 Looking at the visual system from underneath the brain. This view of the visual pathways shows how some of the nerve fibers from the retina cross over to the opposite side of the brain at the optic chiasm.

Circuits That Detect Features: Receptive Fields

The Visual Pathway

We are already familiar with the retina, the first neural network through which electrical signals generated in the visual receptors pass on their way to the brain. In this section we will follow the neural processing of these visual signals as they travel from the retina to the brain. Figures 2.22 and 2.23 show that signals leaving the retina in the optic nerve travel first to the **lateral geniculate nucleus (LGN)** in the thalamus and then to the visual receiving area in the occipital lobe of the cortex.

Receptive Fields of Optic Nerve Fibers and Cells in the LGN

As electrical signals travel from the receptors through the retina and then to the lateral geniculate nucleus on their way to the cortex, they are influenced both by lateral inhibition and by the **convergence** of signals from many receptors onto single cells closer to the brain. We can appreciate the magnitude of this convergence by considering that there are about 126 million receptors in each retina but only one million ganglion cells. Thus, on the average, signals from 126 receptors converge on each ganglion cell.

This convergence of activity, from a large number of receptors onto a smaller number of higher-order cells, means that the response of each higher-order cell can be influenced by the stimulation of those receptors that converge onto it. The receptors that influence the firing of this higher-order cell define the **receptive field** of the cell. The idea that each neuron has a receptive field made up of numerous receptors has proven to be one of the most important concepts in sensory physiology. To understand how this concept developed, we need to describe an experiment done by Hartline in 1938 and then trace the development of our knowledge about receptive fields to the present.

Hartline's 1938 paper, entitled "The Response of Single Optic Nerve Fibers of the Vertebrate Eye to Illumination of the Retina," described the response of fibers in the frog's optic nerve. (These optic nerve fibers, it should be noted, are the axons of the retinal ganglion cells shown in Figure 2.16.) Hartline found that there are three types of optic nerve fibers: **"on" fibers, "on-off" fibers,** and **"off" fibers.** The responses of these three types of fibers, shown in Figure 2.24, can be described as follows: (1) "on" fibers respond with a burst of impulses when the light is turned on, continue to fire at a lower rate throughout the illumination, and stop firing when the light is turned off; (2) "on-off" fibers respond with a burst of impulses when illumination is turned on, or when it is turned off, but do not respond during steady illumination; (3) "off" fibers do not respond when the illumination is turned on, or to steady illumination, but do respond when the illumination is turned off.

Hartline found that each type of fiber responds to an area on the retina containing many receptors.

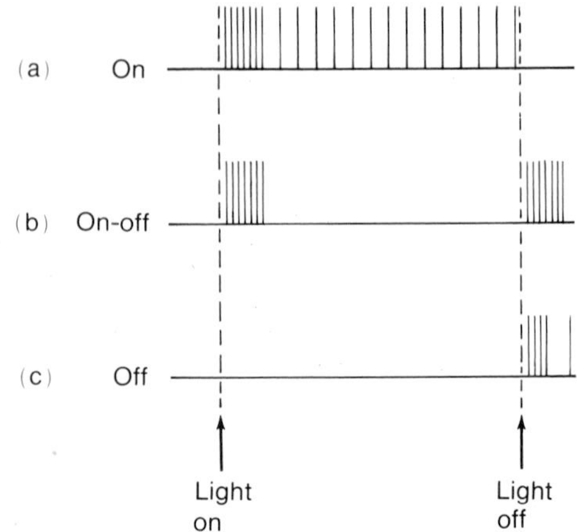

Figure 2.24 "On," "on-off," and "off" cells recorded from fibers in the frog's optic nerve. (Adapted from Hartline, 1938.)

He called this area the *receptive field* of the nerve fiber, which he defined as *"the region of the retina which must be illuminated in order to obtain a response in any given fiber."*

In 1953 Stephen Kuffler published a paper that took Hartline's findings a step further. Instead of recording from optic nerve fibers of the frog, as Hartline had, Kuffler recorded from optic nerve fibers in the cat. Whereas Hartline reported that fibers in the frog's optic nerve always respond in the same way, Kuffler found that fibers in the cat's optic nerve respond differently, depending on where the receptive field is stimulated. He found that receptive fields have a **center-surround** configuration, as shown in Figure 2.25. Stimulation of the center area of the field results in firing when the light is on (an "on" response), and stimulation of the surround area results in a burst of firing when the light is turned off (an "off" response) and inhibition when the light is turned on. Kuffler also reported an "on-off" area between the center and surround areas. Stimulation of this area results in an "on" response when the light is turned on and an "off" response when the light is turned off. (However, most descriptions of receptive fields that have appeared since Kuffler's report divide them into only "on" and "off" areas.)

The receptive field in Figure 2.25 is called an "on-center, off-surround" receptive field, or an

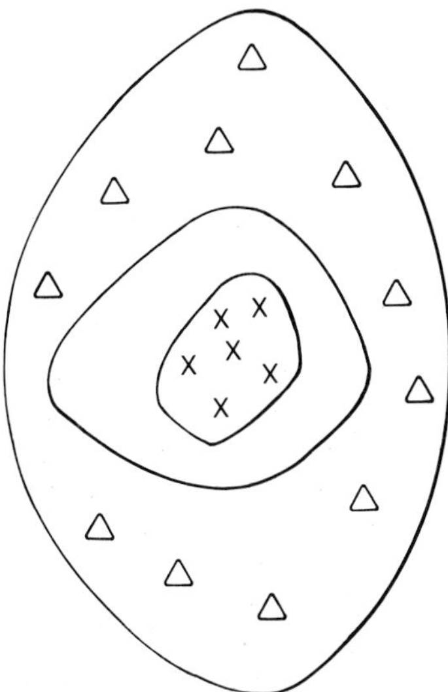

Figure 2.25 A center-surround receptive field of a cat retinal ganglion cell recorded by Kuffler (1953). Stimulation of the area marked "x" results in an "on" response, stimulation of the area marked "△" results in an "off" response, and stimulation of the area in between results in an "on-off" response.

"excitatory-center, inhibitory-surround" receptive field. There are also "off-center, on-surround" receptive fields, in which stimulation of the center causes inhibition and an "off" response, and stimulation of the surround causes an "on" response.

Both Hartline and Kuffler determined the area on the retina that, when stimulated, influenced the response of a fiber in the optic nerve. We can also determine the receptive fields of neurons closer to the visual cortex by finding the area on the retina that influences the response of these neurons. Figure 2.26 shows the receptive field of a neuron in the LGN recorded by David Hubel and Torsten Wiesel (1961). (As we continue our discussion of receptive fields, remember that wherever the neuron we record from is located, the receptive field of that neuron is always located *on the retina*. Thus, although Hubel and Wiesel were recording from a neuron in the LGN, the receptive field of this neuron is the area *on the retina* that influences the neuron's response.) Like the optic nerve receptive field in Figure 2.25, the LGN receptive field in Figure 2.26 is divided into "on" and "off" areas, which are also arranged in the center-surround configuration.

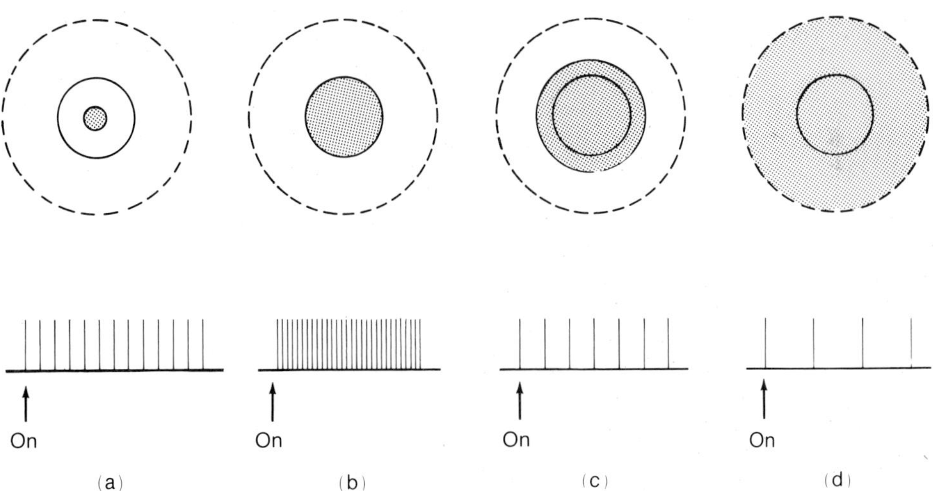

Figure 2.26 Response of an excitatory-center, inhibitory-surround receptive field. The area stimulated with light is indicated by the shading, and the response to the stimulus is indicated by the records below each receptive field. As the stimulus size increases inside the excitatory region of the receptive field in (a) and (b), the response increases. As the stimulus further increases so that it covers the inhibitory region of the receptive field, the response decreases. This cell responds best to stimulation the size of the receptive field center. (Adapted from Hubel & Wiesel, 1961.)

In this receptive field the center is excitatory ("on") and the surround is inhibitory ("off").

The fact that different areas of the receptive field can cause different types of responses becomes very important when we realize that these areas can interact with each other. Let's see how this works in our LGN cell in Figure 2.26. In (a) we see that stimulation of the center of the receptive field with a small spot of light causes an "on" response. Increasing the size of the spot, as in (b), until it completely covers the center of the receptive field, causes the "on" response to become larger. Increasing the size of the spot further, however, causes the response to become smaller, as shown in (c), because of interactions between the "on-center" and the "off-surround" of this receptive field. The "on" response due to stimulation of the center and the inhibition due to stimulation of the surround cancel each other out; consequently, further increasing the diameter of the spot, as in (d), so that it covers the entire "on" and "off" areas of the receptive field, results in a very poor response. This competition between the center and surround areas of the receptive field, called **center-surround antagonism,** makes it possible for the cell to carry out a rough analysis of the stimulus applied to the receptors. This cell responds best to a small stimulus that falls within the center of the receptive field and responds poorly to a large stimulus covering the entire receptive field.

A simple neural circuit that combines convergence and lateral inhibition to result in a center-surround receptive field is shown in Figure 2.27. This circuit operates so that stimulation of receptors in the surround excites cells A and B, which inhibit the cell we are recording from, while stimulation of receptors in the center excites this cell. There are many other circuits that would accomplish the same effect and, in fact, the actual wiring is much more complex than our example. The important point is that the excitatory and inhibitory connections of the fibers leading from the receptors to higher-order neurons are arranged so that the higher-order neurons respond to a specific feature of the stimulation presented to the retina. These higher-order cells, therefore, are often called **feature detectors,** a center-surround cell being a feature detector for small spots of light.

Receptive Fields of Cells in the Cortex

A neuron with a center-surround receptive field, such as the one in Figure 2.26, is an example of a

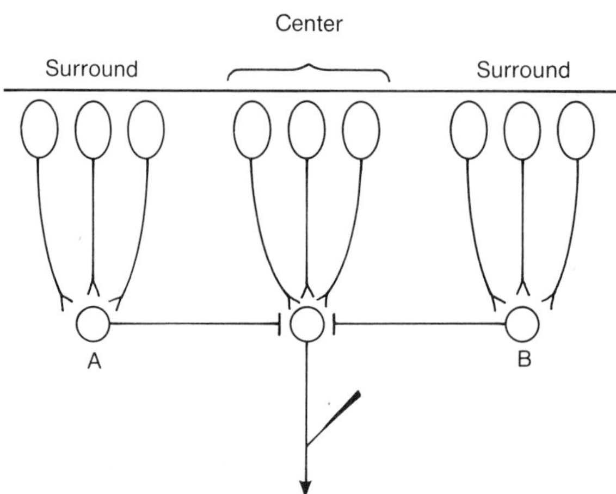

Figure 2.27 A neural circuit that would result in a center-surround receptive field. Signals from the surround receptors reach the cell from which we are recording via an inhibitory synapse, while signals from the center receptors reach this cell via a direct excitatory synapse. Thus, stimulation of the center receptors increases the firing rate recorded by our electrode, and stimulation of the surround receptors decreases the firing rate.

rather primitive feature detector. Although this neuron responds best to small spots of light, it also responds to other stimuli. For example, optic nerve and LGN neurons with center-surround receptive fields respond to spots applied to the center of the receptive field, to rectangular stimuli that fall across the receptive field, and to stimuli that move across the receptive field in any direction. If, however, we move to the cortex, we find cells that respond only to more specific stimuli. Figure 2.28 shows the receptive field of such a cell in the visual cortex. This cortical receptive field is similar to the receptive fields of optic nerve fibers and cells in the LGN because it is divided into "on" and "off" areas, but it is different because these areas are arranged side by side rather than in the center-surround configuration. A cell with this side-by-side configuration is called a **simple cortical cell,** and the receptive field is arranged so that this cell responds best to a bar of light oriented in a particular direction. A large response results when the bar is oriented along the length of the receptive field, as in (a); a smaller response results when the bar is tilted, as in (b); and no response results when the bar is perpendicular to the orientation of the receptive field, as in (c) (Hubel & Wiesel, 1959).

This preference of simple cells for bars with a particular orientation is shown graphically in Figure 2.29. This **tuning curve,** determined by measuring the responses of a simple cell to bars of light with different orientations, shows that this cell responds with 25 nerve impulses per second to a vertically oriented bar, but that the responses decrease as the bar is tilted away from the vertical, until a bar that is tilted 20 degrees from the vertical results in only a small response. While this particular simple cell responds optimally to a bar with a vertical orientation, other simple cells respond best to bars with horizontal or diagonal orientations.

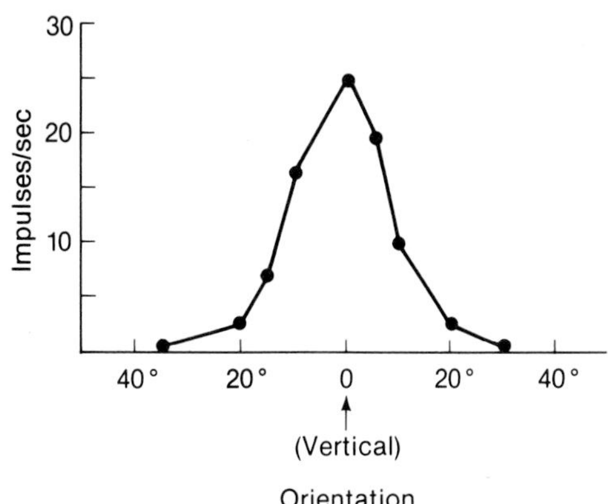

Figure 2.29 An "orientation tuning curve" of a simple cortical cell. This cell responds best to a vertical bar of light (orientation = 0) and responds less well as the bar is tilted in either direction.

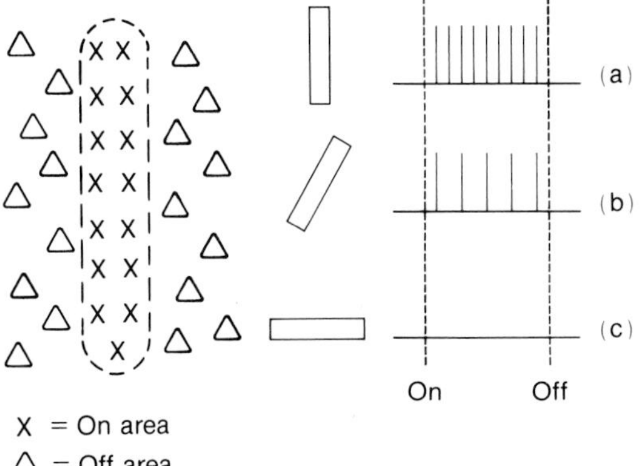

Figure 2.28 The receptive field of a simple cortical cell. This cell responds best to a vertical bar of light that covers the "on" area of the receptive field (a); it responds less well as the bar is tilted so that it covers the "off" area (b and c). (Adapted from Hubel & Wiesel, 1959.)

The difference between center-surround and simple receptive fields indicates that between the LGN and the cortex, the visual system has carried out an important step of analysis, enabling the simple cortical cells to detect lines with a specific orientation. Figure 2.30(a) shows how this analysis might be carried out by the convergence of a number of "on-center, off-surround" LGN cells onto a single cell in the cortex. We can understand how these LGN cells can be wired together to create the cortical receptive field in Figure 2.28, by considering how LGN and cortical cells respond to bars of light presented to the retina. If we present a bar that covers all the receptive field centers of the LGN cells, as shown in Figure 2.30(b), the bar increases the firing of each LGN cell, which in turn increases the firing of the cortical cell with which it synapses. If, however, we move the bar slightly to the left or right, as shown in Figure 2.30(c), so that it falls on

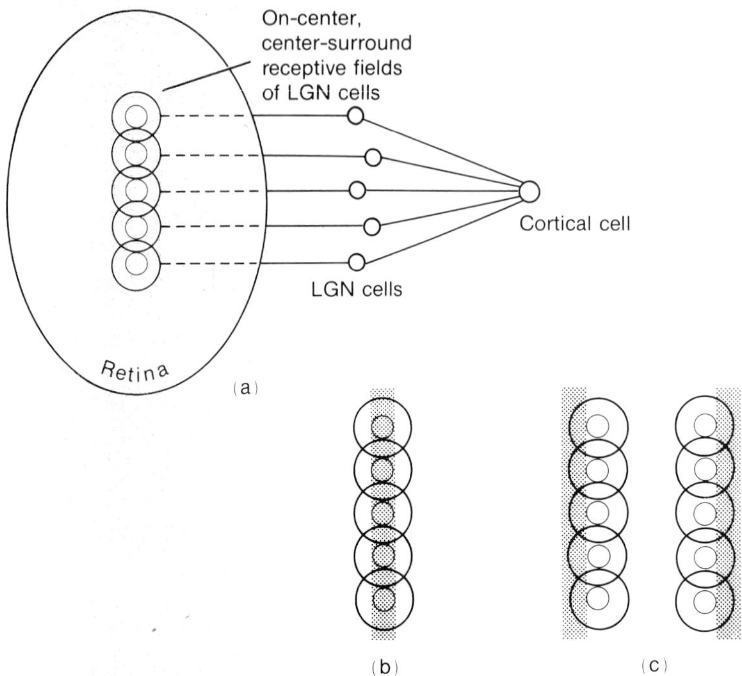

Figure 2.30 How the receptive field of a simple cortical cell can be constructed from the inputs from five LGN cells. The receptive fields of the LGN cells are positioned on the retina so that their excitatory centers line up to form the excitatory area of the cortical cell. The inhibitory surrounds of the LGN cells are positioned so that they form the inhibitory area of the cortical cell. Since the LGN cells synapse with the same cortical cell, this cortical cell will fire when the bar is positioned as in (b), but it will be inhibited when the bar is positioned as in (c). The result is a receptive field like the one in Figure 2.28. (From Hubel & Wiesel, 1962.)

the receptors in the surrounds of the LGN receptive fields, the bar decreases the firing of each LGN cell (and causes an "off" response when the bar is turned off), which in turn decreases the firing and causes an "off" response in the cortical cell. The receptive fields of a simple cortical cell, therefore, may be constructed from the receptive fields of a number of LGN cells.

The receptive fields of two other types of cells in the cortex are illustrated in Figures 2.31 and 2.32. **Complex cortical cells** respond best to bars of light oriented in a particular direction. Although both complex and simple cells respond best to bars of a particular orientation, they differ in a number of respects. Unlike simple cells, complex cells will not respond to small spots of light. For simple cells, the exact position of the stimulus on the retina is very important; for most complex cells, movement is important. A simple cell will fire only when the light is presented to the "on" area or removed from the "off" area of its receptive field, but a complex cell fires when a correctly oriented bar of light moves across the entire receptive field. Further, many complex cells respond best to a particular direction of movement.

Hypercomplex cells fire only in response to moving lines of a specific length or to moving corners or angles. The cell in Figure 2.32 responds best to a corner that is moving upward across the receptive field, as shown in record (c). While the length of the stimulus does not affect the complex cell in Figure 2.31, the hypercomplex cell will not fire if the stimulus is too long. If we try to turn the stimulus into a bar by extending its length, as in Figure 2.31(e), the cell no longer fires (Hubel & Wiesel, 1965a).

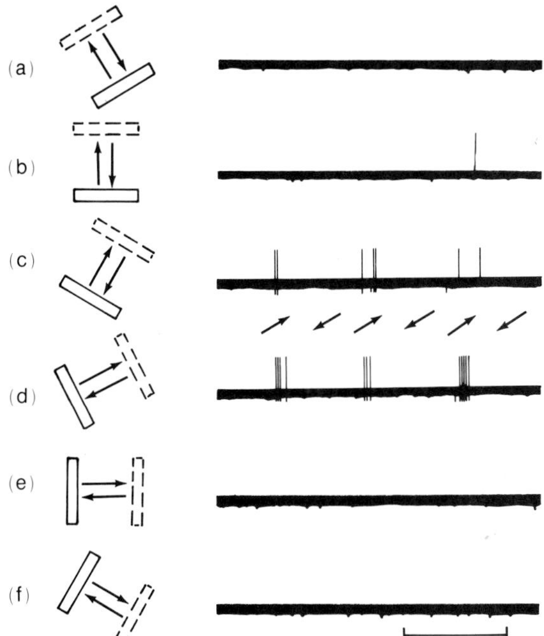

Figure 2.31 Response of a complex cell recorded from the visual cortex of the cat. The back and forth movement of the bar across the receptive field is indicated by the arrows. The records on the right show that the cell fires only when the bar is moved across the retina in a specific direction. The cell does not respond when the bar is moved back and forth, as indicated by the orientations in (a), (b), (e), and (f). A slight response occurs in (c). The best response occurs in (d), but even with the bar at this optimal orientation, a response occurs only when the bar is moved from left to right. No response occurs when the bar moves from right to left. The horizontal bar in the lower right represents 1 second. (From Hubel & Wiesel, 1959.)

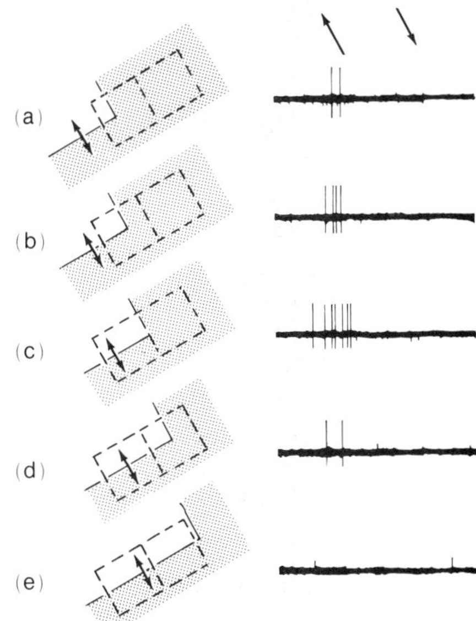

Figure 2.32 Response of a hypercomplex cell recorded from the visual cortex of the cat. This cell responds best to a light corner moving up; there is no response when the corner moves down. Note that as the corner is made longer as we progress from (a) to (b) to (c), the cell's firing rate increases, but that when the length is further increased, as in (d) and (e), the firing rate decreases. (From Hubel & Wiesel, 1965a.)

We have now come a long way from the receptors to the cortex, and we have seen that the information processing between the receptors and the cortex results in cortical neurons that fire in response to specific features of the stimulus presented to the retina. Simple cells fire to bars of light with specific orientations, complex cells to bars moving in a specific direction, and hypercomplex cells to bars, corners, or angles of a specific length that move in a specific direction. An interesting and significant property of the receptive fields we have been describing is that as we travel farther from the retina, it takes more specific stimuli to cause a cell to fire. Retinal ganglion cells will respond to just about any stimulus, whereas hypercomplex cells respond only to bars of a certain length moving in a particular direction. The characteristics of each type of cell are summarized in Table 2.1.

Columnar arrangement of cells. In the process of discovering simple, complex, and hypercomplex cells in the cortex, Hubel and Wiesel observed an interesting phenomenon. When they lowered their electrode so that its path was perpendicular to the surface of the cortex, as shown in Figure 2.33, they encountered all three types of cells—simple, complex, and hypercomplex—but the cells had something in common: their preferred orientations were the same. Thus, all cells encountered along the electrode track at A in Figure 2.33 respond best to horizontal lines, whereas all those along electrode track B respond best to lines oriented at about 45 degrees. Thus originated the idea that the cortex is organized into columns about half a millimeter in

Table 2.1

Cell	*Characteristics*
Optic nerve fiber (ganglion cell)	Center-surround receptive field. Responds best to small spots but will also respond to other stimuli.
Lateral geniculate	Center-surround receptive field. Very similar to the receptive field of an optic nerve fiber.
Simple cortical	"On" and "off" areas arranged side by side. Responds best to bars of a particular orientation.
Complex cortical	Will not respond to small spots. Responds best to movement of a correctly oriented bar across the receptive field. Many cells respond best to a particular direction of movement.
Hypercomplex cortical	Will not respond to small spots. Responds to corners, angles, or bars of a particular length moving in a particular direction.

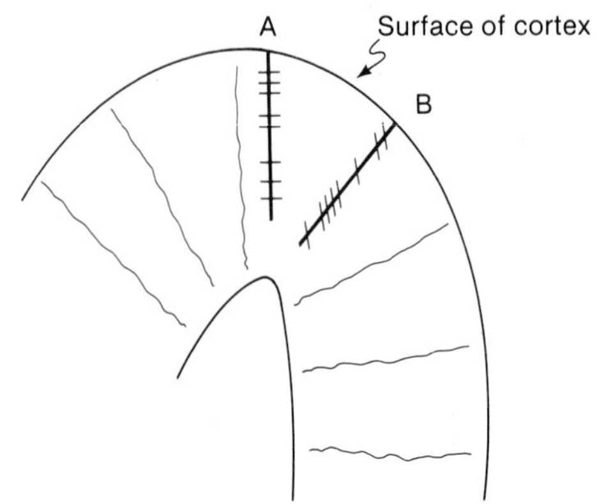

Figure 2.33 Electrophysiological evidence for orientation columns in the visual cortex. Microelectrodes oriented perpendicular to the surface of the cortex will encounter simple, complex, and hypercomplex cells along their path, but all these cells will have the same preferred stimulus orientation (indicated by the lines cutting across each electrode track).

diameter, with each column containing cells that respond best to a particular orientation. This finding supported Hubel and Wiesel's idea that just as simple cells are constructed from a number of cells with center-surround receptive fields (Figure 2.30), complex cells may be constructed from a number of simple cells with the same preferred orientation, and hypercomplex cells may be constructed from a number of complex cells with the same preferred orientation. If this idea is correct, the construction process would be made much easier if cells that respond to similar orientations are grouped together.

This columnar organization of the cortex, which Hubel and Wiesel discovered while doing electrophysiological experiments, has recently been confirmed by means of a new anatomical technique, called the **2-deoxyglucose technique.** This technique is based on the following facts: (1) brain cells depend on glucose as a source of metabolic energy; (2) cells that are more active use more glucose; (3) 2-deoxyglucose (2-DG) can masquerade as glucose (if injected into an animal, it is taken up by active cells like glucose is); and (4), after 2-DG is taken up by the cell, it begins to be metabolized, but the resultant metabolite can't cross the cell's wall and so accumulates inside the cell.

These properties of 2-DG enabled Hubel, Wiesel, and Michael Stryker (1978) to do the following experiment: after injecting radioactively labeled 2-DG into a monkey, they stimulated the monkey's visual system by moving black and white vertical stripes back and forth in front of the animal for 45 minutes. (This stripe movement increases activity in cells that prefer vertical orientations, causing them, in this case, to increase their takeup of radioactive 2-DG.) After this stimulation the monkey was sacrificed, and when its brain was examined, Hubel, Wiesel, and Stryker found that the cortex contained regularly spaced narrow bands of radioactivity. These narrow bands, which were caused by the high activity of cells that respond best to vertical stripes, showed anatomically what had previously been demonstrated electrophysiologically: the visual cortex is made up of columns that contain cells with the same preferred orientation.

Feature Detectors and Perception

I'm sure by now you're convinced that lots of information processing occurs in the nervous system. But is there any evidence that the responses of feature detectors have anything to do with human perception? We can answer this question by doing a psychophysical experiment called a **selective adaptation experiment.** To do this experiment, we use grating stimuli with different orientations, like those shown in Figure 2.34. We first determine an observer's **contrast sensitivity** for gratings of different orientations; to do this, we determine the threshold for seeing the gratings, by measuring the smallest difference in the intensities of the light and dark bars that enables the observer to just barely see the bars. We then convert threshold to sensitivity by dividing the threshold into 1.0 (see p. 11). (Since there is a big difference in the intensities of the bars in the gratings of Figure 2.34, we can see the bars easily; however, if we decrease the difference in the intensities, the bars eventually vanish, leaving only a homogeneous field.)

After determining the contrast sensitivity for these gratings, we then have the observer look at one grating (say, the vertically oriented one) for about a minute. (This is the selective adaptation part of the experiment, in which we selectively adapt the observer to one orientation, in this case vertical.) After adapting the observer to the vertical grating, we then remeasure the contrast sensitivity for all the gratings. When we do this, we find that the observer's sensitivity to the vertical grating has decreased; that is, the intensity difference between the light and dark bars must be greater after adaptation than before, in order for the observer to see the grating. The observer's sensitivity to the other gratings has also decreased, though not as much as to the vertical grating. This result is shown by the curve in Figure 2.34. Notice that adapting to the vertical grating causes a large effect on the observer's sensitivity to that grating, but that this effect diminishes as we test with orientations increasingly removed from the vertical.

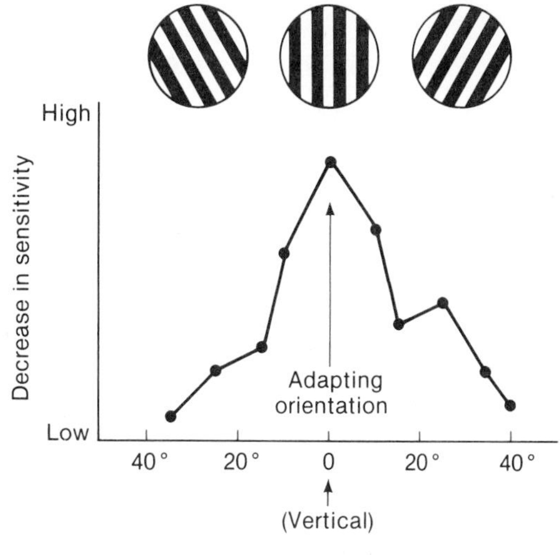

Figure 2.34 The effects of selective adaptation to a vertical grating on an observer's contrast sensitivity. This curve shows that adapting to the vertical grating causes a large decrease in the observer's ability to detect the vertical grating when it is presented again, but that this adaptation has less effect on gratings that are tilted to either side of the vertical. Gratings tilted more than about 35 degrees from the vertical are essentially unaffected by adaptation to the vertical grating.

If the curve in Figure 2.34 looks familiar, it's because it is very similar to the electrophysiological tuning curve for the simple cortical cell in Figure 2.29. This similarity in the electrophysiological tuning curves for cortical cells and the results of psychophysical selective adaptation experiments has led many researchers to explain the results of such experiments in terms of feature detectors. They suggest that adaptation to the lines of the vertical grating stimulates feature detectors that respond best to vertical lines, and that this stimulation fatigues these feature detectors, making it harder to see vertical gratings after adaptation.

Although the results of selective adaptation experiments strongly suggest that feature detectors do play a role in human perception, we cannot explain how we see the forms in our environment solely on the basis of feature detectors. Hubel and Wiesel, and many other investigators who study neurons in the visual cortex, are the first to state that these relatively simple feature detectors cannot resolve the complexities of everyday perception. Before you can perceive a chair or your friend Ralph, the simple

Box 2.3 Seeing Without a Retina: Electrical Stimulation of the Visual Cortex

In normal vision, electrical signals generated in the retina are transmitted along nerve fibers; when these signals reach the visual cortex, we see. However, more than 100,000 people in the United States and Canada are totally blind, usually due to defects in the retina or optic nerve that prevent electrical signals from being generated in the retina or from being transmitted by the optic nerve to the visual cortex. William Dobelle and a team of researchers have recently been working to develop a visual **prosthesis**: an artificial eye that can produce vision in the blind by sending electrical signals to the visual cortex. One proposed system, shown in the figure on the left, consists of a subminiature television camera mounted in a glass eye. The TV camera picks up an image from the environment and converts it into a pattern of electrical signals that is transmitted to a tiny computer mounted in a pair of dummy glasses. After being processed by the computer, these signals stimulate an array of electrodes placed on the surface of the visual cortex, causing the person to see an image corresponding to the original image received by the TV camera.

Although the system shown in the figure on the left does not yet exist, some totally blind volunteers have had an array of 64 electrodes implanted on their visual cortex. A drawing of this array, based on an X-ray, is shown on the right. Wires from the electrodes pass through a small opening in the skull, at the back of the head, and then wind beneath the scalp in an S-shaped loop, before coming through the skin and terminating in a connector attached to the skull with special bone screws. Initial testing indicates that stimulation of the cortex by a single electrode causes the observer to perceive a **phosphene**—a small glowing spot of light that appears to be located at about arm's length. Stimulation of a number of electrodes causes a number of phosphenes to be seen as a pattern. For example, Craig, a 35-year-old government employee blinded 15 years earlier in an automobile accident, was able to see letters, geometrical shapes, and simple patterns in response to various patterns of stimulation of his electrode array. When a TV camera was connected to the system, Craig could also detect white horizontal and vertical lines on a dark background.

These initial results are promising, although many problems must be solved before a visual prosthesis becomes available. For example, phos-

forms represented by feature detectors must somehow be combined into the complex forms that we see every day, and we do not yet know how this is accomplished.

Interestingly, these feature detectors are not unique to the visual system. We will see in Chapter 4 that similar kinds of feature detectors respond to movement across the skin (as in circuit B of Figure 2.15) and that they too are organized in columns. Additionally, we will see in Chapter 13 that cells which respond best to specific tone frequencies are also organized in columns. And we haven't seen the last of visual feature detectors. In Chapter 7, we will again encounter simple, complex, and hypercomplex cells, along with some others that respond to even more specific features of the stimulus, when we discuss the perception of pattern.

We have seen that the processing that occurs in the nervous system helps the brain comprehend the electrical signals generated in the receptors, by transforming the "raw data" reaching the receptors into a simpler form, such as the firing of feature detectors. This transformation of the stimuli reaching the receptors into the responses of feature detectors is relevant to the next question we will discuss: How is the information in the environment coded into electrical signals so that the brain can understand what these electrical signals mean? This is the problem of sensory coding, and we will begin our discussion of this problem by defining it in more detail.

The Sensory Code

One of my students, Bernita Rabinovitz, provided a statement of the problem of sensory coding in her response to my request for questions about perception on the first day of class:

phenes are not always seen in the position corresponding to the position of the electrode on the cortex. Adjacent electrodes may produce phosphenes that are spaced far apart in the visual field, and adjacent phosphenes are sometimes produced by widely spaced electrodes. Additionally, some phosphenes are too bright and obscure others, and phosphenes often flicker, even in response to continuous electrical stimulation. Work is now in progress to solve these problems and to develop a 512-electrode stimulation system that would transmit complicated information rapidly enough so that the prosthesis could be used by a person as he or she walks through the environment (Dobelle et al., 1974, 1976; Dobelle, 1977).

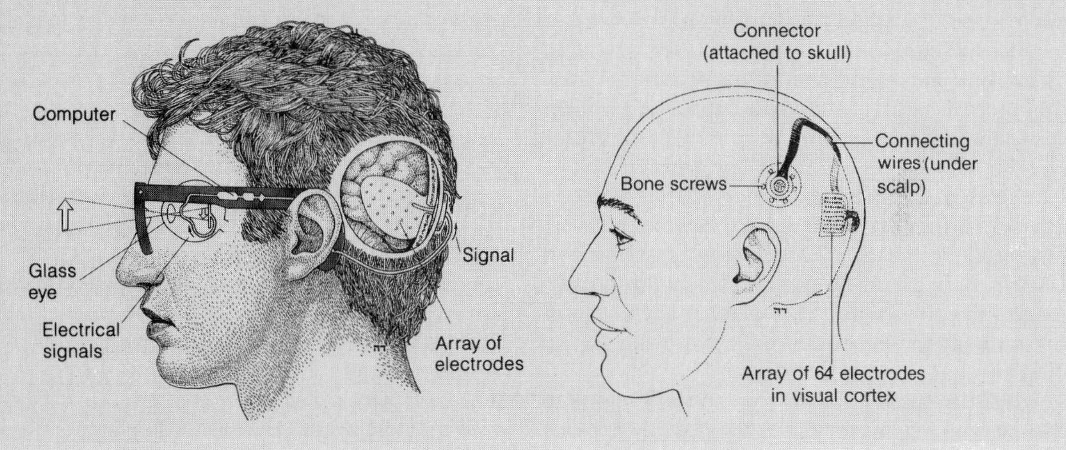

A human perceives a stimulus (a sound, a taste, etc.): This is explained by the electrical impulses sent to the brain. This is so incomprehensible, so amazing. How can one electrical impulse be perceived as the taste of a sour lemon, another impulse as a jumble of brilliant blues and greens and reds, and still another as bitter cold wind? Can our whole complex range of sensations be explained by just the electrical impulses stimulating the brain? How can all of these varied and very concrete sensations—the ranges of perceptions of heat and cold, colors, sounds, fragrances and odors, tastes—be merely and so abstractly explained by differing electrical impulses?

This is a statement of the problem of sensory coding: the electrical signals in the nervous system *represent* properties of stimuli in the environment. The electrical signals form a code that stands for various properties of the environment, the brain somehow reads this code, and we perceive the environment. Our problem is to find out what this code is.

The Code for Subjective Magnitude: How Much Stimulus Is There?

The first question we will ask is: What is the code for the subjective magnitude of the stimulus? Consider what happens to nerve impulses when we increase the intensity of a stimulus. In Figure 2.13 we saw that increasing the stimulus intensity increases the rate of nerve firing. This result, combined with the fact that increasing the stimulus intensity also increases the subjective magnitude of that stimulus (increasing the intensity of a light usually causes it to appear brighter, and increasing the intensity of a tone usually causes it to sound louder), suggests that the rate of nerve firing may be the code for magnitude. But before jumping to this conclusion, we should see whether nerve firing and subjective magnitude increase in the same way, as we increase stimulus intensity. If they do, then we would be better able to say that the rate of nerve firing may be the code for magnitude.

Gerhard Werner and Vernon Mountcastle (1965) determined the relationship between the rate of nerve firing and stimulus intensity for a pressure-sensitive neuron in the monkey's skin. They used a small plunger to push on a small touch receptor called an Iggo corpuscle, which is located close enough to the surface of the monkey's skin to be seen with a microscope. By observing the corpuscle with a microscope as it was being pushed, they were able to measure the indentation of the receptor. When they plotted the logarithm of the rate of nerve firing versus the logarithm of the indentation of the receptor, the data fell on a straight line with a slope of 0.5. Thus, in this experiment, nerve firing followed a power law like that observed in the psychophysical magnitude estimation experiments described in Chapter 1. In fact, the exponent for magnitude estimation of pressure on the skin for humans is 0.5, the same as the exponent for nerve firing in the monkey's Iggo corpuscle.

This correspondence between nerve firing in the monkey and magnitude estimates made by humans supports the idea that the rate of nerve firing may be the code for magnitude. However, rather than comparing electrophysiological data from monkeys with psychophysical data from humans, it would be more desirable to have both psychophysical and electrophysiological results for the human. These data have been provided by G. Borg and a team of investigators (1967), who recorded from the chorda tympani nerve in five patients undergoing middle ear operations. (The chorda tympani, which is made up of nerve fibers from the front of the tongue, passes through the middle ear on its way toward the thalamus.) Borg used a large electrode to record the chorda tympani response that resulted when solutions of citric acid, sucrose, and sodium chloride were flowed over the tongue. He compared these results with those of psychophysical experiments performed on the same patients two days before their operations. In these psychophysical experiments, Stevens' magnitude estimation procedure was used to determine the relationship between subjective magnitude and stimulus concentration for the same substances used in the electrophysiological experiments. One patient's psychophysical and electrophysiological responses to citric acid are shown in Figure 2.35. When response intensity is plotted versus citric acid concentration on a log-log scale, the psychophysical and electrophysiological functions are parallel, each with a slope of 0.5. These results, and similar results on some of Borg's other patients, support the idea that there is a close connection between the rate of nerve firing and subjective magnitude.

Although the two experiments described above, and a number of others (Franzen & Lindblom, 1976; Vallbo & Johansson, 1976), provide evidence that subjective magnitude is signaled by the rate of nerve firing, the correspondence between firing rate and subjective magnitude is not always so good. For example, using a technique called **percutaneous recording,** developed by Swedish investigators A. B. Vallbo and K. E. Hagbarth (1967), we can record from a single nerve fiber that responds to a touch stimulus applied to an awake person's hand, and we can compare the firing rate of this nerve fiber to the person's magnitude estimates of the touch stimulus. Figure 2.36, which shows the results of an experiment by M. Knibestol and A. B. Vallbo (1976), indicates that the relationship between nerve firing and stimulus intensity is not the same as the relationship between the person's magnitude estimates and stimulus intensity. The nerve fiber's response to the touch increases with an exponent of 0.38 (response compression, see p. 19 of Chapter 1), whereas the subjective magnitude of the touch increases with an exponent of 1.60 (response expansion). Thus, while nerve firing rate probably helps to signal the subjective magnitude of the stimulus, the brain may also look at some other properties of nerve firing to determine our perception of magnitude.

What other information about stimulus magnitude is contained in the nerve impulses? Look back at Figure 2.13. Note that increasing the stimulus intensity not only increases the firing rate but also changes the *temporal pattern* of nerve impulses. At low intensities the time between successive nerve impulses is quite variable, whereas at high intensities this time is fairly constant. Increasing the intensity often increases the regularity of nerve firing,

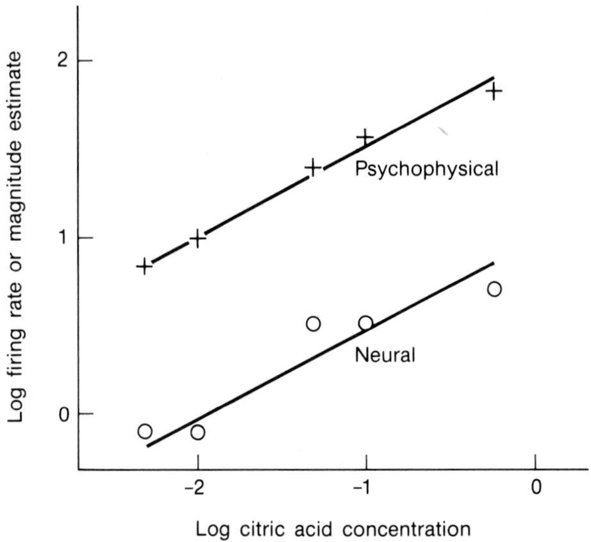

Figure 2.35 Psychophysical and neural responses to citric acid. That these two curves have the same slope argues that the increased taste intensity experienced by subjects, as the concentration of the citric acid is increased, may be caused by an increased rate of nerve firing, which also occurs as the concentration of citric acid is increased. (From Borg et al., 1967.)

and the brain may also use information such as this to determine the magnitude of the stimulus, with more regular nerve firing signaling higher stimulus intensities.

The Code for Quality

A light? A sound? A touch?: Doctrine of specific nerve energies. What is the code for quality *across* the senses? That is, how does the brain differentiate between seeing a light and hearing a sound, or between the taste of a lemon and the smell of perfume, on the basis of nerve impulses? Johannes Müller proposed an answer to this question in 1842 that has come to be known as the **doctrine of specific nerve energies.** This doctrine states that (1) the brain receives information about the environment by means of signals from the sensory nerves, and (2) the brain distinguishes between different senses by monitoring the activity in the different sensory nerves. So, activity in the optic nerve signals "light," the auditory nerve "sound," and so on. Soon after Müller's doctrine was proposed, other investigators found that each of these nerves goes to a different area of the cortex, as shown in Figure 2.11, thereby making the code for quality across the senses simple: the brain tells which sense is stimulated by the location at which the electrical signals reach the brain.

Hot or cold? Red or blue?: Specificity theory and pattern theory. But what is the code for quality *within* a sense? That is, how does the brain tell the difference between red, blue, green, and yellow, or salty, sweet, bitter, and sour, on the basis of nerve impulses reaching the appropriate areas of the cortex? Two different types of theories have been proposed. **Specificity theory** states that different qualities are signaled to the brain by activity in specific nerve fibers. **Pattern theory** states that different qualities are signaled to the brain by the pattern of activity across a large number of nerve fibers. To compare specificity theory to pattern theory, let's see how these theories might explain sensory coding in the cutaneous system.

According to specificity theory, coding in the cutaneous system might be described as follows. There are a number of types of receptors in the skin,

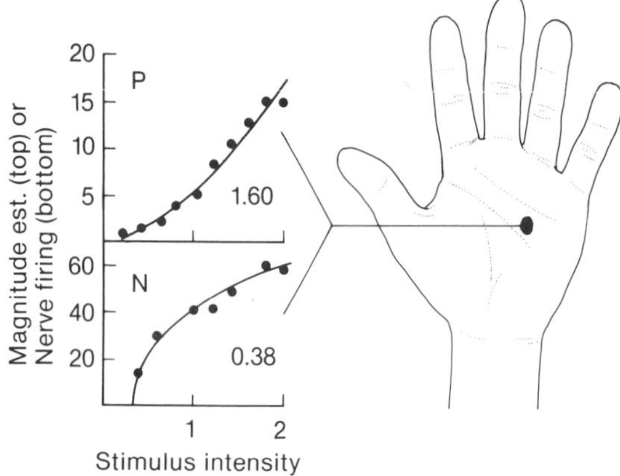

Figure 2.36 Neural and psychophysical functions for a touch stimulus presented to the hand. The neural function was determined by a technique called percutaneous recording, which makes it possible to record from single nerve fibers in awake humans. After the receptive field of a single nerve fiber, indicated by the dot, was located, the relationship between the rate of nerve firing and the pressure of a touch stimulus was determined. The resulting function, indicated by the curve marked N, has an exponent of 0.38. The psychophysical function was determined by asking the subject to estimate the magnitude of a touch stimulus presented to the center of the cell's receptive field. The resulting function, marked P, has an exponent of 1.60. (From Knibestol & Vallbo, 1976.)

and each responds only to a specific quality of stimulation. In the cutaneous system there are receptors for heat, cold, touch, and pain. Thus, a cold stimulus triggers activity only in "cold" receptors and their nerve fibers, and a warm stimulus triggers activity only in "warm" receptors and their nerve fibers. Figure 2.37(a) shows that the code for cold in this system is much activity in the cold fiber and no activity in the other fibers, and the code for warm is activity in the warm fiber and no activity in the others.

According to pattern theory, coding in the cutaneous system would be described somewhat differently. Pattern theory would say that there are a number of different receptors in the skin, but each receptor responds to a wide range of stimulation. Each receptor does not, however, respond equally to all stimuli. Thus, a given receptor might respond well to cold, less well to touch and pain, and perhaps only slightly to heat. Figure 2.37(b) shows that application of a cold stimulus results in activity not in just a single type of receptor or nerve fiber but in a large number of nerve fibers, with some fibers firing more than others. The warm stimulus causes a similar result, but the pattern of firing across nerve fibers is different than for the cold stimulus. The codes for warmth and cold in this system, therefore, are different **across-fiber patterns** of nerve firing. We will consider the evidence for specificity theory and pattern theory below.

Evidence for specificity theory. Perhaps the most convincing evidence for specificity theory comes from recent work on the skin. We will see in Chapter 4, "Perceiving Touch, Temperature, and Pain," that many nerve fibers in the skin respond only to specific stimuli. For example, **cold fibers** respond only to decreasing temperatures or steady low temperatures, **warm fibers** respond only to increasing temperatures or steady high temperatures, **pain fibers** respond only to a stimulus that damages or nearly damages the skin, and a number of types of fibers respond best to light or medium touch. We will also see in Chapter 15, "Smelling and Tasting," that some evidence favors the idea that the taste system works on the specificity principle, with activity in specific fibers signaling each of the four basic tastes—sweet, salty, sour, and bitter.

Evidence for pattern theory. We will see in Chapter 5, "Seeing Colors," that some aspects of color vision can be explained in terms of pattern theory. Each color does not have its own specific nerve fiber; rather, different colors are signaled by the firing pattern of three different receptors, each of which responds to a wide range of colors.

Some experiments by Robert Erickson (1963) provide evidence that the across-fiber pattern of nerve firing may be important in determining taste quality in the rat. To determine the across-fiber pattern of nerve activity in the rat's taste fibers, Erickson presented a number of different stimuli to the tongue and recorded the response from fibers in the rat's chorda tympani. Figure 2.38 shows the amount of nerve activity in spikes (impulses) per second for 13 nerve fibers, when stimulated with ammonium chloride (NH_4Cl), potassium chloride (KCl), and sodium chloride ($NaCl$). The solid and dashed lines

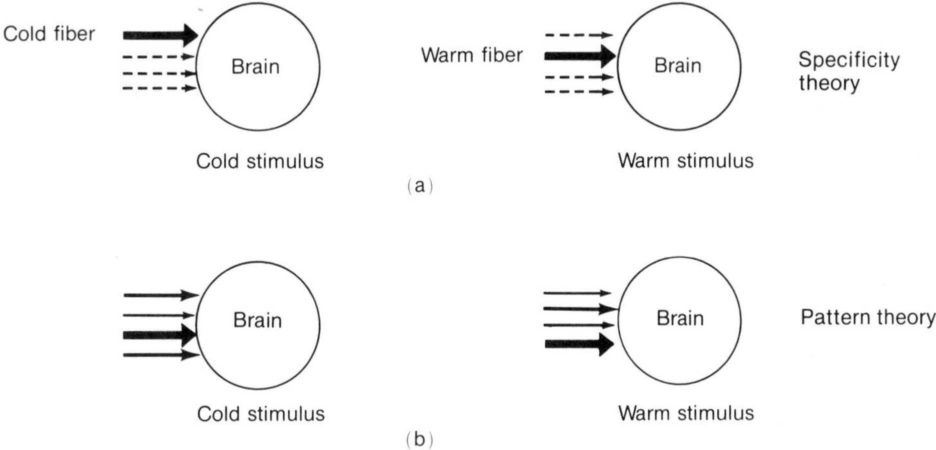

Figure 2.37 Specificity theory postulates that sensory quality is signaled to the brain by activity in specific fibers. Pattern theory postulates that quality is signaled by the pattern of activity in many fibers.

show the across-fiber pattern of these 13 neurons to NH_4Cl and KCl. These two patterns are similar to each other but not to the pattern for NaCl, indicated by the open circles.

Erickson reasoned that if the rat's perception of taste quality depends on the across-fiber pattern,

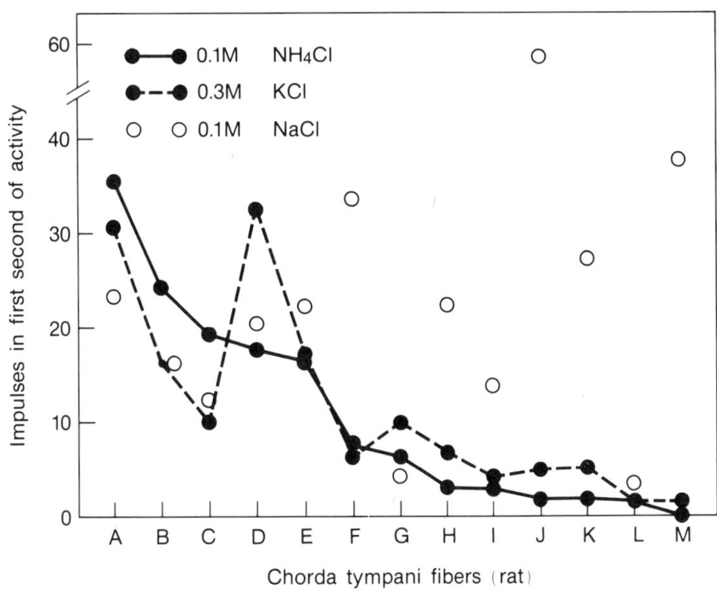

Figure 2.38 Across-fiber patterns of response in the rat to three salts. Each letter on the horizontal axis indicates a different single fiber. For each fiber the responses to three stimuli are plotted. (From Erickson, 1963.)

then two substances with similar across-fiber patterns should taste similar. Thus, the electrophysiological results would predict that NH_4Cl and KCl should taste similar and that both should taste different from NaCl. To test this idea, Erickson ran a behavioral test. He shocked rats for drinking KCl and then gave them a choice between NH_4Cl and NaCl. If KCl and NH_4Cl taste similar, then the rats should avoid the NH_4Cl when given a choice, which they did. If shocks were given for drinking NH_4Cl, the rats avoided the KCl, and if shocks were given for drinking NaCl, the rats did not preferentially avoid either the NH_4Cl or the KCl.

Erickson's results show that the rat's taste nerves are not highly specific; most nerves respond to many substances. His results also show that each substance has its own "signature," in the form of an across-fiber pattern of nerve firing, and that this signature is correlated with the taste of the substance. In Chapter 5, we will see that color vision works in a similar way: each nerve responds to a wide range of wavelengths, but each wavelength has its own across-fiber pattern signature.

Specificity, pattern, or both? Which theory of sensory coding is correct, specificity or pattern? From the evidence presented in the previous two sections, you may have guessed that the answer to this question is *both*. Since there is evidence for both theories, we needn't talk as if only one of them can be correct. In fact, the brain probably uses information from specifically tuned neurons ***and*** from the firing pattern of many neurons.

For example, the brain may be able to tell when a vertically oriented bar of light is moving from left to right across the retina, by the high firing rate of a hypercomplex cell that responds best to vertically oriented bars of a certain length. However, the response of this cell does not specify the stimulus exactly. For example, assume that hypercomplex cell A fires at 200 spikes per second to a vertically oriented 1-mm bar and at 150 spikes per second to a bar that is 0.75 mm long, 1.25 mm long, slightly tilted from the vertical, or dim. If the brain monitors only the response of cell A and finds that the firing rate is 150 spikes per second, it cannot discern whether the bar is 0.75 mm long, 1.25 mm long, slightly tilted from the vertical, or dim! One solution to this problem is to monitor the responses of other cells. For example, if there is also a good response in cell B, which responds best to 0.75-mm bars, and a poor response from cell C, which responds best to 1.25-mm bars, then we might conclude that the firing rate of cell A is lower than its maximum because the bar is shorter than cell A's 1-mm optimal length. The more cells from which we obtain information, the more precisely we can define the bar. Thus, in this example, the brain gathers information about the bar by looking both at the response of individual feature detectors ***and*** at the overall firing pattern of many of these feature detectors.

The point is that it is unlikely that our perception is ever determined by the responses of only a few fibers, even if they respond solely to very specific stimuli. For example, our perception of warmth may be determined by the responses of "warm" fibers, which respond only to increases in temperature or to steady warm temperatures. However, Kenneth Johnson and co-workers (1979) have shown that it is unlikely that the information contained in the firing of just one "warm" fiber can explain the fact that we can detect changes in temperature as small as 0.04° C. They calculated that the brain must use the information from at least 50 "warm" fibers to enable us to detect such small temperature changes.

Now that we have concluded our discussion of sensory coding, you may still wonder whether we have answered Bernita's question posed at the beginning of this section: How are experiences such as colors, sounds, and tastes explained by electrical impulses? We have seen that the nature of the environment can be signaled by neural responses in the brain, but does this really explain how these electrical signals are turned into experience? When we ask how electrical impulses become experience, we are really asking how the flow of sodium and potassium across a membrane can be turned into the perception of a blue light, a salty taste, or the feeling of pressure on the skin. The problem of how physical processes such as nerve impulses or sodium and potassium flow cause a mental experience is known as the **mind-body problem,** and the reason we have provided no answers is that we have none. Although we have accumulated much knowledge about the relationship between nerve activity and perception, we still don't know exactly ***how*** nerve activity results in perception. For example, we know that an increase in the firing rate of neurons in the visual system is often accompanied by an increase in how bright a light appears, but we don't know how the physical process of nerve impulses (or sodium and potassium flow) is changed into the mental process of the perception of brightness.

Although we can't solve the mind-body problem at this time, in the remainder of this book we will look at what we do know about the connections between physiology and perception. In doing this, we will see that physiology and perception can sometimes be matched with great precision. For example, in Chapter 3 we will see that there is a close correspondence between the properties of visual pigments and the sensitivity of the eye. But we will also see that physiology and perception cannot always be closely correlated. For example, although we can explain how feature detectors respond to spots, lines, and corners, and although we can show that similar taste stimuli result in similar across-fiber firing patterns, we are a long way from knowing the sensory code for seeing a landscape, feeling tickled, or tasting a corned beef sandwich (with mustard). At this stage of our knowledge, many of our everyday perceptions are difficult to explain physiologically; however, the eventual explanations are likely to be based on concepts such as inhibition, excitation, convergence, and receptive fields, all of which have been introduced in this chapter.

Summary

1. The nervous system is a communication system that transforms environmental energy into electrical energy and then transmits this electrical energy from one part of the body to another.
2. Receptors are neurons that are specialized to respond to a specific kind of environmental energy.
3. A sensory system consists of a series of neurons that synapse at various nuclei on the way to the brain. Fibers from all sensory systems synapse in the thalamus, from which nerve fibers travel to the cortical receiving areas for each sense. The visual receiving area is in the occipital lobe, the auditory area is in the temporal lobe, and the area for the skin senses is in the parietal lobe of the cortex.
4. The results of the Hecht, Shlaer, and Pirenne experiment indicate that it takes one quantum of light to stimulate a visual receptor and that seven receptors must be stimulated simultaneously in order for us to see a light.
5. The resting potential of the inside of a nerve fiber is −70 mV compared to the outside. The change in the charge inside the fiber during a nerve impulse is caused by the inward and outward flow of positively charged sodium and potassium. Sodium flows into the fiber until the charge inside the fiber becomes about +40 mV compared to the outside, and potassium then flows out of the fiber until the fiber returns to its original resting potential of −70 mV.
6. Increasing the intensity of a stimulus changes the rate of nerve firing but does not affect the size of the nerve impulses.
7. In intracellular recording, an electrode is inserted inside a nerve fiber. In extracellular recording, an electrode is positioned just outside the nerve fiber.
8. Many nerve fibers fire without environmental stimulation. This spontaneous firing is called spontaneous activity.
9. The transmission of nerve impulses from one neuron to another depends on the interplay of excitatory and inhibitory signals at the synapse.
10. Neural circuits "process" electrical signals as they travel from the receptors toward the brain. This processing not only transforms information falling on the receptors into a form that the brain can more easily understand, it also shapes our perceptions.
11. The retina contains five basic types of cells: receptors, bipolar cells, ganglion cells, horizontal cells, and amacrine cells. The horizontal and amacrine cells transmit electrical signals laterally across the retina.
12. Lateral inhibition has been demonstrated electrophysiologically in the *Limulus*. Mach bands, a perceptual effect that is observed by humans, is caused by lateral inhibition.

13. Hartline described "on," "on-off," and "off" fibers in the frog's retina and defined the receptive field as "the region of the retina which must be illuminated in order to obtain a response from any given fiber."

14. Kuffler demonstrated that the response of a fiber depends on which area of the receptive field is stimulated, and he showed that the receptive fields of optic nerve fibers in the cat's retina have a center-surround configuration.

15. The center-surround antagonism of cells in the optic nerve and lateral geniculate nucleus of the cat turns these cells into crude feature detectors that respond best to small spots of light.

16. Simple, complex, and hypercomplex cells in the cortex of the cat respond best to the following stimuli: simple to bars oriented in a specific direction; complex to bars that move in a specific direction; and hypercomplex to bars or corners of a specific length or size that move in a specific direction.

17. Simple cortical cells may be constructed from the inputs of a number of center-surround cells in the lateral geniculate nucleus. The idea that complex cells are constructed from simple cells with the same preferred orientation is supported by the columnar arrangement of cortical cells with the same preferred orientations.

18. The columnar arrangement of cortical cells has been demonstrated both electrophysiologically and by using an anatomical technique called the 2-deoxyglucose technique.

19. The results of selective adaptation experiments support the idea that feature detectors may play a role in human perception. However, we cannot explain the complexities of form perception solely on the basis of feature detectors.

20. Electrical stimulation of the visual cortex has been used in an attempt to develop a visual prosthesis to enable blind people to see.

21. The sensory code for subjective magnitude is probably the frequency of nerve firing, but some other property of nerve firing, such as the temporal pattern, may also be involved.

22. The sensory code for quality across the senses is the location of the electrical signals reaching the brain.

23. The specificity theory of sensory coding states that different qualities within a sense are signaled to the brain by activity in specific nerve fibers. Pattern theory states that different qualities are signaled to the brain by the pattern of activity across a large number of nerve fibers.

24. The existence of nerve fibers that respond to specific stimuli applied to the skin supports specificity theory.

25. Some evidence supports the idea that quality within a sense is signaled by the across-fiber pattern of nerve firing. The specificity and pattern principles of sensory coding probably work together to determine sensory quality within a sense.

26. The mind-body problem asks how a physical process such as the movement of charged molecules across a membrane becomes a mental process such as perceptual experience. This problem has not yet been solved.

Glossary

Across-fiber pattern The pattern of nerve activity across a large number of nerve fibers. (58)

Amacrine cell A neuron that transmits signals laterally across the retina. Amacrine cells synapse with bipolar cells and ganglion cells. (40)

Bipolar cell A neuron which is stimulated by the visual receptors and then sends electrical signals to the retinal ganglion cells. (40)

Cell body The part of a neuron that receives electrical signals from other neurons. (30)

Center-surround antagonism The competition between the center and surround regions of a center-surround receptive field. (48)

Center-surround receptive field A receptive field that consists of a roughly circular excitatory center surrounded by an inhibitory area, or a circular inhibitory center surrounded by an excitatory area. (48)

Cold fiber A neuron that fires to decreasing temperature or to steady low temperatures. (58)

Columnar arrangement of cells In the visual cortex cells are organized in columns so that all cells in a column respond best to stimuli with the same orientation. (51)

Complex cell A neuron in the visual cortex that responds best to moving bars with a particular orientation. (50)

Contrast sensitivity 1.0 divided by the smallest intensity difference between light and dark areas that can be discriminated. (53)

Convergence When many neurons synapse onto fewer neurons. (46)

Cortical receiving area The area in the cortex that receives electrical signals from one sense. For example, the cortical receiving area for vision is in the occipital lobe of the cortex. (30)

2-Deoxyglucose technique An anatomical technique that has made it possible to visualize the orientation columns in the visual cortex. (52)

Doctrine of specific nerve energies The idea that the brain receives environmental information from sensory nerves and that the brain distinguishes between the different senses by monitoring the activity in these sensory nerves. (57)

Excitation A condition that facilitates the generation of nerve impulses. (37)

Extracellular recording Recording from a cell with the tip of the electrode just outside the cell. (36)

Feature detector A neuron that responds selectively to a specific feature of the environment. (48)

Ganglion cell A neuron in the retina that receives inputs from bipolar and amacrine cells. The axons of the ganglion cells are the fibers that travel toward the brain in the optic nerve. (40)

Hair cells The receptors for hearing. (27)

Horizontal cell A neuron that transmits signals laterally across the retina. Horizontal cells synapse with receptors and bipolar cells. (40)

Hypercomplex cell A neuron in the visual cortex that responds best to angles or corners moving in a particular direction or to bars of a specific length moving in a particular direction. (50)

Inhibition A condition that decreases the likelihood that nerve impulses will be generated. (37)

Intracellular recording Recording from a cell with the tip of the electrode inside the cell. (36)

Ions Charged molecules which are found floating in the water that surrounds nerve fibers. (33)

Lateral geniculate nucleus (LGN) The nucleus in the thalamus that receives nerve fibers from the optic nerve and sends fibers to the cortical receiving area for vision. (45)

Lateral inhibition Inhibition that is spread laterally across a nerve circuit. In the retina, lateral inhibition is spread by the horizontal and amacrine cells. (40)

Limulus A primitive animal, also called the horseshoe crab, whose large visual receptors make them especially well suited for studying the electrophysiology of vision. (40)

Mach bands A perceptual effect that causes a thin dark band on the dark side of a light-dark border and a thin light band on the light side of the border. (43)

Mind-body problem The problem of how physical processes such as nerve impulses cause mental processes such as perceptual experience. (60)

Nerve A bundle of nerve fibers traveling together. (33)

Nerve fiber In most sensory neurons, the nerve fiber is the long part of the neuron that transmits electrical impulses from one point to another. (30)

Nerve impulse A rapid change in electrical potential that travels down a nerve fiber. (35)

Neural circuit A number of neurons connected by synapses. (37)

Neuron A cell in the nervous system that generates and transmits electrical impulses. (30)

Nucleus A place where many synapses occur. An example of a nucleus is the thalamus, where neurons from all the senses, except olfaction, synapse. Within the thalamus are smaller nuclei for each sense. (31)

Null electrode One of a pair of electrodes used to record nerve activity. The null electrode is positioned in a neutral area so that it is unaffected by nerve activity. (33)

Occipital lobe A lobe at the back of the cortex; it is the site of the cortical receiving area for vision. (31)

Off fiber A nerve fiber that responds with a burst of firing at the offset of stimulation. (46)

Ommatidium A structure in the eye of the *Limulus* that contains a small lens, located directly over a visual receptor. The *Limulus* eye is made up of hundreds of these ommatidia. (40)

On fiber A nerve fiber that responds with a burst of firing at the onset of stimulation and usually continues firing during stimulation. (46)

On-off fiber A nerve fiber that responds with a burst of firing at the onset of stimulation and a burst of firing at the offset of stimulation. (46)

Optic nerve About one million nerve fibers that travel from the eye toward the brain. Most of these nerve fibers synapse in the lateral geniculate nucleus of the thalamus. (40)

Pain fiber A fiber that responds to stimulation which is potentially damaging to the skin. (58)

Parietal lobe A lobe at the top of the cortex; it is the site of the cortical receiving area for touch. (31)

Pattern theory Different qualities are signaled to the brain by the pattern of activity across a large number of nerve fibers. (57)

Percutaneous recording A technique which makes it possible to record from a single nerve fiber that responds to touch stimuli in the awake human. (56)

Phosphene A small glowing spot of light. (54)

Pigment Epithelium A layer of cells, located between the retina and the back of the eyeball, that supplies the retina with blood and enzymes. (29)

Prosthesis An artificial device that substitutes for a missing part of the body. (54)

Quantum The smallest possible packet of light energy. (29)

Receptive field The receptive field of a cell in the visual system is the retinal area that, when stimulated, affects the firing of that cell. (46)

Receptor A neuron specialized to receive environmental energy and transduce it to electrical energy. (27)

Recording electrode A small shaft of metal or glass that, when connected to appropriate electronic equipment, records electrical activity from nerves or nerve fibers. (33)

Refractory period A time period of about 1/1,000 second that a nerve fiber needs to recover from conducting a nerve impulse. No new nerve impulses can be generated in the fiber until the refractory period is over. (37)

Resting potential The difference in charge between the inside and outside of a nerve fiber when the fiber is not conducting nerve impulses. (33)

Retina A complex network of neurons that covers the inside back of the eye. These neurons include the receptors, which generate an electrical signal in response to light, and the bipolar, ganglion, horizontal, and amacrine cells, which process and transmit these signals. (40)

Selective adaptation experiment Selectively adapting a person or animal to one stimulus and then assessing the effect of this adaptation by testing with a wide range of stimuli, for example, adapting with vertical bars and then testing a person's sensitivity to bars of all orientations. (53)

Sensory code The idea that electrical signals in the nervous system form a code that represents properties of stimuli in the environment. (54)

Sensory receptors Neurons that are sensitive to environmental energy and that change this environmental energy into electrical signals. (27)

Simple cell A neuron in the visual cortex that responds best to bars of a particular orientation. (49)

Specificity theory Different qualities are signaled to the brain by the activity in specific nerve fibers that fire only to that quality. (57)

Spontaneous activity Nerve firing that occurs in the absence of environmental stimulation. (37)

Synapse A small space between the end of one neuron and the cell body of another neuron. (30)

Synaptic vesicles Small packets of chemicals located on one side of the synapse. When stimulated by a nerve impulse, these chemicals are released onto the cell body on the other side of the synapse. (30)

Taste buds Receptors for taste. (27)

Temporal lobe A lobe on the side of the cortex; it is the site of the cortical receiving area for hearing. (31)

Thalamus A nucleus in the brain where neurons from all the senses, except smell, synapse on the way to their cortical receiving areas. (30)

Transduction In the senses, the transformation from environmental to electrical energy. (27)

Tuning curve For cells in the visual cortex, the function that relates the cell's firing rate to the orientation of the stimulus. (49)

Visual pigment A molecule contained in the visual receptors. The reaction of this molecule to light results in the generation of an electrical signal in the receptor. (27)

Warm fiber A neuron that fires to increasing temperature or to steady high temperatures. (58)

Chapter Three

Basic Visual Processes

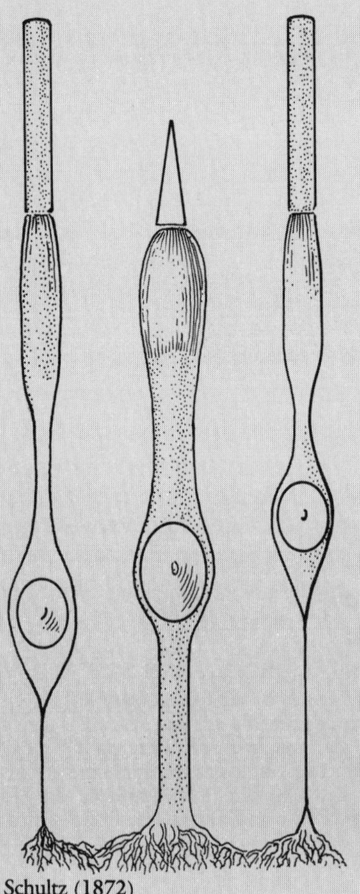

Schultz (1872)

Rods

Cones

Lewis, Zeevi, and Werblin (1969)

In the last chapter we introduced a number of facts about the visual system. We saw that the receptors transduce light into electrical energy, which is then processed by the lateral interactions and convergence of neurons in the retina, lateral geniculate nucleus (LGN), and cortex. The purpose of this chapter is to introduce additional facts about the operation of the visual system, but instead of venturing out of the retina to the LGN and visual cortex as we did in Chapter 2, we will stay closer to the receptors. Nevertheless, we are primarily interested in establishing connections between physiology and our perceptions. Keeping this purpose in mind, we will see that the properties of the receptors largely determine the nature of the information sent to higher-order neurons in the visual system and that the receptors therefore play a large role in determining our perceptions.

In studying the visual receptors, we will discuss questions that you may have asked about your own experience: "Why does it seem completely dark when I first turn out the lights in my bedroom, yet ten minutes later I see light coming in under the door and through the windows?" "Why is it hard to pick my friend's face out of a crowd?" "Why do I see in color during the day but only in shades of black and white at night?" The first step in answering these questions is to describe the visual receptors.

Duplicity Theory

In 1866 Max Schultze described two types of receptors in the retina: the **rods** and the **cones.** He differentiated these receptors on the basis of their

Box 3.1 The Blind Spot

The entire back of your eye is covered with receptors, except for the place where the optic nerve fibers leave the back of the eye on their way toward the lateral geniculate nucleus (LGN). What happens if we present a stimulus to this point? You can answer this question by closing your right eye and, with the cross below lined up with your left eye, looking at the cross while moving the book (or yourself) slowly back and forth; when the book is about a foot from your eye, the circle disappears. At this point, the image of the circle falls on the optic nerve, and for that reason, the place where the optic nerve leaves the eye is called the **blind spot.**

Why aren't we usually aware of the blind spot? There are a number of reasons. First, we usually use two eyes, so when an image falls on the blind spot of one eye, it falls on the receptors of the other. But this explanation doesn't really answer the question, because we usually aren't aware of the blind spot, even when we look with only one eye. One reason we aren't aware of it, even with one-eyed vision, is that the blind spot is located off to the side of our visual field, which means, as we will see in this chapter, that we don't see it in sharp focus. Because it isn't in sharp focus and because we don't know exactly where to look for it (as opposed to the demonstration below, in which you know that the circle will disappear), the blind spot is hard to detect.

But perhaps the most important reason that we don't see the blind spot is that some, as yet poorly understood, mechanism "fills in" the place where the image disappears. Think about what happened when the spot below disappeared. The place where the spot used to be wasn't replaced by a "hole" or by "nothingness"; it was filled in by the white page. If the spot had been surrounded by a pattern, then the pattern would have filled in the area where the spot had been.

appearance. As shown by Schultze's (1872) drawing of the rods and cones and by the modern scanning electron micrograph (Lewis et al., 1969) of these receptors (shown in the chapter-opening illustration), rods have large rod-shaped outer segments, while cones have smaller cone-shaped outer segments (see also Figure 2.16). This difference in structure formed the basis for what von Kris, in 1896, called the **duplicity theory** of vision. This theory states that the retina is made up of two types of receptors that not only look different but also have different properties and operate under different conditions. The 120 million rods in each human retina operate under dim illuminations and the 6 million cones operate under moderate and high illuminations, so that at night we see with our rods and in the daytime we see with our cones. It is as if we had two separate retinas, one that operates during the night and another that operates during the day.

Another difference between rods and cones is that they are distributed differently on the retina. There is a small area on the retina called the **fovea,** shown in Figure 3.2, that contains only cones. The fovea is located directly on the line of sight, so any time we look directly at an object, its image falls on the fovea. The fovea is small, however, so only small images fall on it completely. The rest of the retina, surrounding the fovea, is called the **peripheral retina** and contains both rods and cones.

In the remainder of this chapter, we will see that the rods and cones differ not only in shape and in distribution on the retina but also in two other ways: (1) they contain different visual pigments, and (2) they are "wired up" in different ways to other neurons in the retina. We will begin our discussion of these differences by describing how the properties of the rod and cone visual pigments determine how our eyes adjust to the dark.

Pigments and Perception

Dark Adaptation

The phenomenon of **dark adaptation** is well known: when the illumination is changed from light to darkness, you find it difficult to see anything at first, but as you spend more time in the dark, your sensitivity increases and you can eventually see things that at first seemed shrouded in darkness. Although it is apparent that your sensitivity increases as you spend more time in the dark, it is not so apparent that this increase takes place in two distinct stages,

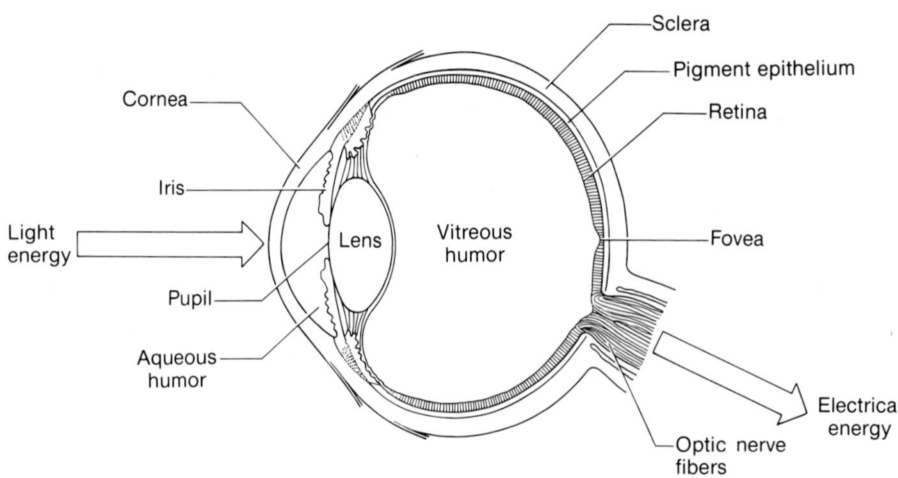

Figure 3.2 A cross section of the human eye.

an initial rapid stage and a later slower stage. In this section, we will carry out three dark adaptation experiments to show that the initial rapid stage is due to the cones and that the second slower stage is due to the rods. In our first experiment, we will describe how to measure a dark adaptation curve which shows the two-stage process of dark adaptation. In our second experiment, we will measure the dark adaptation of the cones alone; and in our third experiment, we will measure the dark adaptation of the rods alone. Finally, we will show how the different adaptation rates of the rods and cones can be explained by differences in the properties of the visual pigments contained within them.

Experiment #1: determining a two-stage dark adaptation curve. In our first dark adaptation experiment, we ask our observer to look at a display like the one in Figure 3.3. The observer looks at the small fixation point while paying attention to the flashing test light. Since the observer is looking directly at the fixation point, the point's image falls on the fovea while the image of the test light falls in the periphery. Thus, the test light stimulates both rods and cones, and any adaptation measured with this test light should reflect the activity of both the rod and cone systems.

Fixation point X   O Test light

Figure 3.3 Fixation point and test light used in an experiment to measure a dark adaptation curve.

The usual procedure in a dark adaptation experiment is to **light adapt** the observer and then determine his sensitivity in the light. As the observer views a bright adapting light, we determine his sensitivity to the test light by asking him to adjust its intensity until it can just barely be seen. The resulting sensitivity is labeled **light adapted sensitivity,** as in Figure 3.4.

After determining the light adapted sensitivity, we begin the process of dark adaptation by turning out the adapting light. Extinguishing the adapting

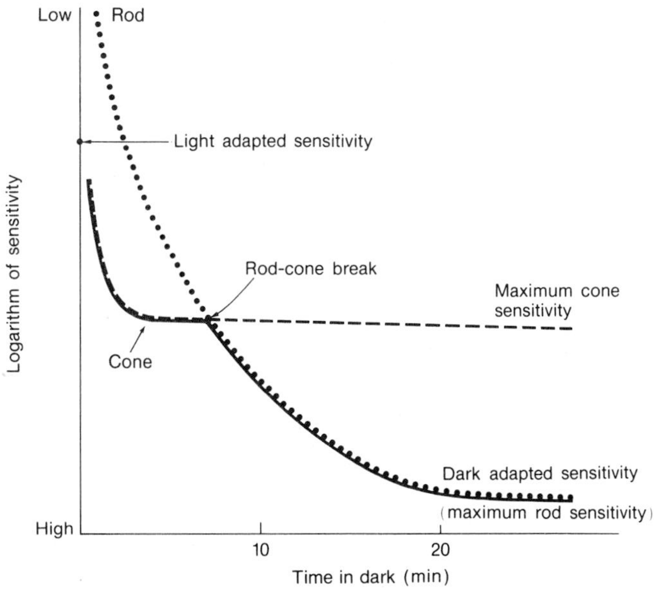

Figure 3.4 Dark adaptation curves. There are actually three curves shown in this figure. The solid line shows the two-stage dark adaptation curve measured in experiment #1, with a cone branch at the beginning and a rod branch at the end. The dashed line shows the cone adaptation curve measured in experiment #2. The dotted line shows the rod adaptation curve measured in experiment #3. Note that as these curves go down, sensitivity *increases.*

light causes the test light to appear much brighter, and the observer therefore decreases its intensity until he can again just barely see it. As dark adaptation progresses, the observer continues to adjust the intensity of the test light in this manner, and the solid line of Figure 3.4 shows the resulting dark adaptation curve. (Note that the sensitivity axis of this graph is reversed, so downward movement of the curve indicates an increase in sensitivity.) The observer's sensitivity increases in two phases. It first increases for about 3–4 minutes after the light is extinguished and then levels off; then, after about 7–10 minutes, the sensitivity increases again and continues to do so for another 20–30 minutes. In this experiment, the sensitivity at the end of dark adaptation, labeled **dark adapted sensitivity,** is about 100,000 times greater than the light adapted sensitivity measured prior to dark adaptation.

Experiment #2: measuring cone adaptation. To measure the adaptation of the cones, we repeat the first experiment but have the observer look directly at the test light, which is small enough that its entire image falls on the all-cone fovea; the resulting dark adaptation curve, indicated by the dashed curve in Figure 3.4, therefore reflects only the activity of the cones. This curve matches the initial phase of our original dark adaptation curve but does not include the second phase. Thus, the first phase of the solid dark adaptation curve must be due to the cones and the second phase to the rods. The point at which the rod phase of the adaptation curve begins is called the **rod-cone break.**

Experiment #3: measuring rod adaptation. Although the curve of Figure 3.4 shows that the cones finish adapting before the rods, we can't tell what is happening to the rods during the first 7–10 minutes of dark adaptation. Do they adapt during this time or wait until 7–10 minutes after the lights are turned out to begin adaptation? We can't answer this question by continuing our experiments on the same observer, because no area of his retina contains only rods (the fovea contains only cones and the periphery contains rods *and* cones). Thus, in our third experiment, we measure dark adaptation in a **rod monochromat**, a person whose retina contains only rods, usually due to an inherited genetic defect. The dark adaptation curve of a rod monochromat is shown by the dotted curve in Figure 3.4 (Rushton, 1961). As soon as the adaptation light is extinguished, the rods begin to gain sensitivity and continue to do so until reaching their final dark adapted level in about 30 minutes. The fact that the rods begin dark adapting immediately after the light is extinguished means that they are adapting during the cone phase of a normal person's dark adaptation curve; however, we don't see this rod adaptation because the cones are more sensitive than the rods at the beginning of dark adaptation. We see rod adaptation only after the rod sensitivity has passed the cone sensitivity, at about seven minutes after the beginning of dark adaptation.

In addition to showing that the rods begin adapting immediately after the adapting light is extinguished, the rod monochromat's dark adaptation curve also shows the much slower adaptation of the rods compared to the cones. The rods take 20–30 minutes to achieve their maximum sensitivity, compared to only 3–4 minutes for the cones. We will now show that this slower adaptation can be traced to differences in the regeneration rates of the rod and cone visual pigments.

Pigment Regeneration

To understand how the properties of visual pigments can explain the different rates of rod and cone dark adaptation, we must describe the processes of pigment bleaching and regeneration. We saw in Chapter 2 that the visual pigment molecule changes shape to start the process of transduction (see Figure 2.3). Following this change in shape, the molecule breaks in two; this process is called **pigment bleaching** because, as the molecule breaks apart, the retina changes from its original red color to orange, then to yellow, and finally becomes transparent, as shown in Color Plate 3.1. Before this bleached molecule can again change light energy into electrical energy, the pieces of molecule must reunite. This process, called **pigment regeneration,** is responsible for the increase in retinal sensitivity that occurs during dark adaptation (Wald, 1968).

Since the visual pigment changes from dark to light as it bleaches and from light back to dark as it regenerates, we can measure the concentration of pigment in the eye by determining how much light the pigment absorbs. To understand how this is done, look at Figure 3.5. A dim measuring beam with a constant intensity is projected into the eye. This beam passes through the retina, hits the back of the eye, and is reflected. On its way through the retina and back out, much of the beam's light is absorbed by visual pigment in the receptors, by other structures in the retina, and by a black layer in back of the retina called the pigment epithelium. Some light survives this absorption, however, and a beam with intensity I_{out} is reflected from the eye.

Now consider what happens when we bleach the visual pigment by exposing the eye to light. Bleaching turns the pigment molecules from dark to light. As more and more pigment molecules bleach, the pigment in the receptors gets lighter and lighter and, therefore, absorbs less and less of our measuring beam. Since less light is being absorbed by the pigment, the intensity of the light reflected from the eye, I_{out}, increases. Therefore, by measuring I_{out} we can determine how much pigment has been bleached. Conversely, if, after bleaching, we allow the visual pigment to regenerate in the dark, the pigment gets darker and the intensity of the reflected beam, I_{out}, decreases.

William Rushton (1961) used the above procedure, which is called **retinal densitometry,** to measure the concentration of cone and rod pigment during dark adaptation. He determined the rate of cone pigment regeneration by shining his measuring beam onto the fovea of a normal observer, and he determined the rate of rod pigment regeneration by shining his measuring beam onto the retina of a rod monochromat. His results show that cone pigment takes 6 minutes to completely regenerate, while rod pigment takes over 30 minutes. Rushton also measured psychophysical dark adaptation curves in both observers and found that the rate of cone dark adaptation matched the cone pigment regeneration, and the rate of rod dark adaptation matched the rate of rod pigment regeneration.

Thus, Rushton's results support the idea that visual pigment regeneration is responsible for the increased sensitivity that occurs during dark adaptation and that rods are slow to adapt because rod pigment is slow to regenerate. So the next time you turn out the lights in your bedroom, remember that both the rod and cone visual pigments begin regenerating immediately and that the resulting increases in pigment concentration cause the increased sensitivity that enables you, 10 minutes later, to detect the light coming in under the door. In the next section, we will see that in addition to determining the time course of rod and cone dark adaptation, visual pigments also determine the spectral sensitivities of rod vision and cone vision.

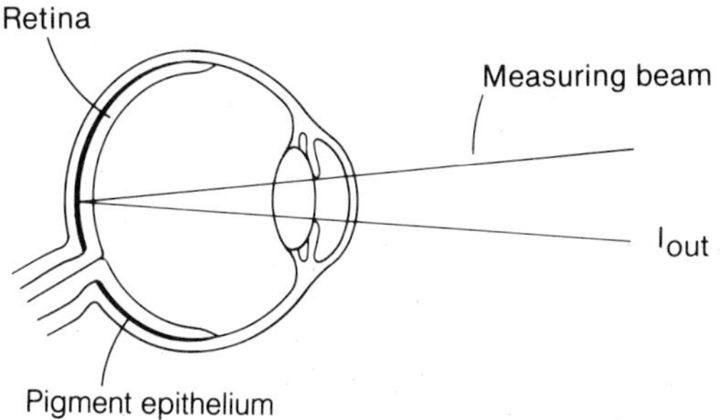

Figure 3.5 The principle underlying retinal densitometry. When the eye is exposed to light, the visual pigment molecules in the retina get lighter, causing them to absorb less of the measuring beam and increasing the amount of light reflected from the eye (I_{out}). As the molecules regenerate in the dark, they get darker, absorb more light, and decrease the amount of light reflected from the eye.

Spectral Sensitivity

We introduced the concept of spectral sensitivity in Chapter 1, when we had an observer look at a small test light to determine the threshold for seeing at wavelengths across the visual spectrum. The result of this experiment was the **cone spectral sensitivity curve** in Figure 1.9, which we have replotted as the dashed curve in Figure 3.6. This curve plots cone vision, since we positioned the test light on the all-cone fovea.

To measure the spectral sensitivity curve for rod vision, we dark adapt the eye and present our test light to the periphery. If the eye is dark adapted, presentation of threshold flashes results in a **rod spectral sensitivity curve** (solid curve, Figure 3.6). This curve shows that the rods are sensitive to shorter wavelength light than are the cones, with the rods being most sensitive to light of 500 nm and the cones most sensitive to light of 560 nm. This difference in the sensitivity of rods and cones to different wavelengths means that as our vision shifts

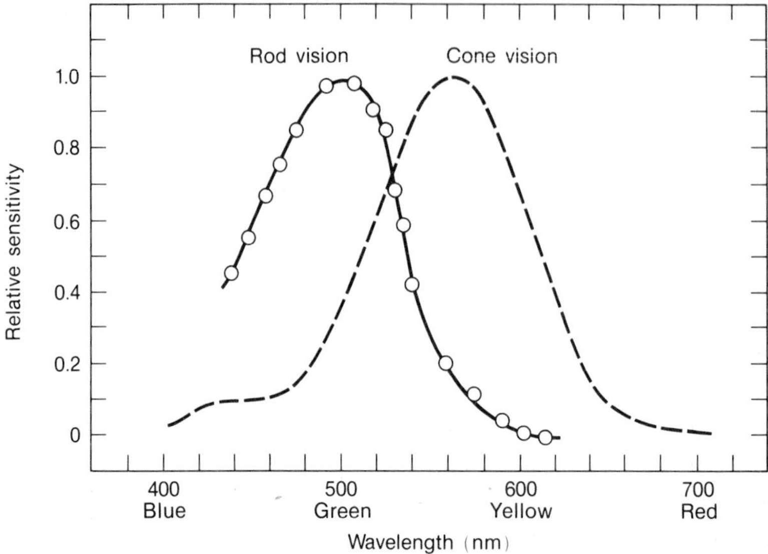

Figure 3.6 Spectral sensitivity curves for rod vision and cone vision. (From Wald & Brown, 1958, and Wald, 1964). The maximum sensitivities of these two curves have been set equal to 1.0. However, as we saw in Figure 3.4, the relative sensitivities of the rods and cones depend on the conditions of adaptation, with the cones being more sensitive in the light and the rods being more sensitive in the dark. The circles plotted on top of the rod curve represent the absorption spectrum for the red visual pigment.

from cones to rods during dark adaptation, we should become relatively more sensitive to short-wavelength light, that is, light nearer the blue end of the spectrum.

We can illustrate this sensitivity shift by doing a dark adaptation experiment using colored test flashes. Figure 3.7 shows the results of two experiments in which colored test flashes were presented to the peripheral retina. You can see that the color of the test flash makes a big difference in the dark adaptation curve. Sensitivity measured with a red test flash, which contains only wavelengths above 620 nm, shows just a small increase after the rod-cone break, while sensitivity measured with a deep blue test flash, which contains only wavelengths shorter than 485 nm, shows a large increase in sensitivity following the rod-cone break. Thus, when rod vision takes over from cone vision during dark adaptation, our sensitivity to short wavelengths increases more than our sensitivity to long wavelengths.

Let's consider this result in terms of perceiving the **brightness** of the red and blue flowers in Color Plate 3.2, by doing a simple experiment. For this experiment, first find a place where you can change the light intensity from very dark to moderately light. A good place for this is a closet where you can lower the light intensity by closing the door and raise the intensity by gradually opening the door. After selecting a closet, dark adapt one eye by closing it for about 10 minutes. This should take place in the light so that your opened eye stays light adapted while your closed eye is dark adapting. (While your eye is dark adapting, try engaging in some activity that involves depth perception, such as reaching for objects at various distances. How well can you perceive depth with one eye? We will discuss why most people see depth less well with one eye in Chapter 8.)

Once your eye is dark adapted, you are ready to do the experiment as follows:

1. With the closet door open, observe Color Plate 3.2 with your light adapted eye and compare the brightness of the blue and red flowers.

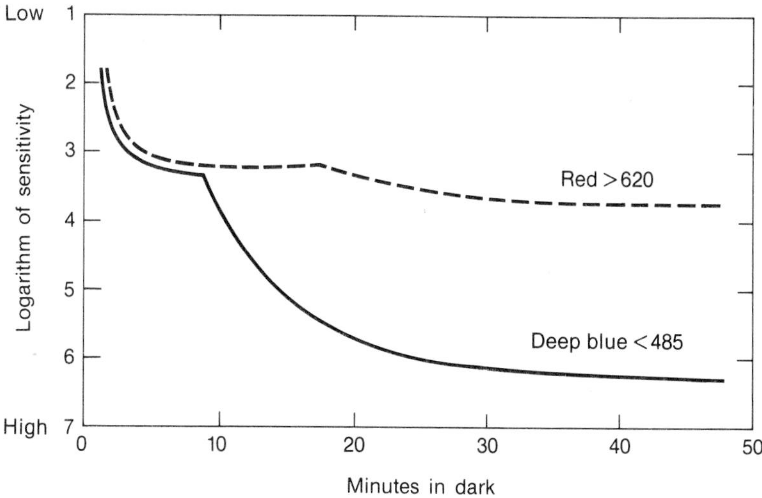

Figure 3.7 Dark adaptation curves measured with long-wavelength (red) and short-wavelength (deep blue) test flashes. The red curve has only a small rod branch because the rods are relatively insensitive to red light. (From Chapanis, 1947.)

When viewed with your light adapted eye under daylight illumination, the two flowers should have about the same brightness.

2. Close the door so that the closet is completely dark. Close your light adapted eye and open your dark adapted eye.
3. Slowly crack open the door until enough light is present for you to see the flowers with your dark adapted eye. If you have kept the light intensity low enough, you will be seeing with your rods, and the flowers should appear grey rather than red and blue (since we perceive in black and white with our rods and in color with our cones, as we will see in Chapter 5). It is important to notice that the flowers' relative brightnesses should be different than when viewed with your light adapted eye. The flower on the left should now appear slightly brighter than the flower on the right. (If you forgot how the flowers looked to your light adapted eye, close your dark adapted eye, open the door, and observe the flowers with your light adapted eye again.)

The increase in the brightness of the blue flower compared to the red one occurs because the rods are more sensitive to short-wavelength light than the cones. This shift from long-wavelength to short-wavelength sensitivity is called the **Purkinje shift,** after Johann Purkinje, who described this effect in 1825.

While your eye is dark adapted, you can carry out the following additional experiments that also illustrate differences between the rods and cones:

1. Look at Color Plate 3.2 with your light adapted eye (reclose your dark adapted eye) under bright illumination. Slowly close the door until you can no longer see the flowers and switch from your light adapted to your dark adapted eye. The flowers will become visible again because of the greater sensitivity of your dark adapted eye.
2. Look at the words in the book under bright illumination with your light adapted eye. Then slowly close the door until the illumination is very dim but still bright enough that you can read the words. Now close the door and switch to your dark adapted eye. Then slowly open the door until the page appears to be about as bright as when you read the words with your light adapted eye. Try reading the words. Since you are now using your rods,

Box 3.2 Renewable Receptors

The "business end" of a rod or cone receptor is the receptor **outer segment,** since it is here that the visual pigment resides. The outer segment consists of a series of discs stacked one on top of another, as shown in Figure 2.2 and in the left receptor in the figure on page 75. By injecting rats and frogs with radioactively labeled amino acid, Richard Young (1967) showed that the rod receptors continually add new discs to the bases of their outer segments and shed old discs from the tips. Amino acids are the building blocks of proteins. The radioactive amino acid, therefore, becomes incorporated into the protein in the animal's visual pigment, and, by means of a technique called **autoradiography,** it is possible to see the radioactive protein in the rod receptors. Young found that in animals killed within about an hour after injection, the radioactive protein is concentrated in the **inner segment,** as shown by the black dots in (a) (Young & Bok, 1969). In animals killed at longer times after injection, the protein becomes concentrated in a band that is first seen at the base of the outer segment, as in (b). Then, over a period of days, this band slowly travels the entire length of the outer segment, as shown in (c) and (d), until, after about two weeks, the band of radioactivity reaches the tip of the outer segment and disappears into the pigment epithelium, a layer of tissue located in back of the retina (see Figure 3.2).

This traveling band of radioactivity indicates that the protein, a major component of both the visual pigment and the disc membrane, forms new discs at the base of the outer segment and that these discs then move toward the tip. The disappearance of the radioactive band upon reaching the tip of the outer segment indicates that the discs are being shed into the pigment epithelium. Pictures show that small packets of half a dozen to several dozen discs are shed into the pigment epithelium, and that once there, these packets of discs are encircled by a structure called a **phagosome,** which digests the discs.

The results of the initial radioactive labeling and **disc-shedding** experiments caused researchers to conclude that disc renewal at the outer segment base and shedding at the tip occurred only in rods. The reasons for this conclusion were that no radioactive band could be seen traveling up cone outer segments, and no cone disc shedding (which is indicated by the presence of phagosomes in the pigment epithelium) was observed. Recently, however, disc shedding has been observed in the cones of a number of species, including humans. Though it is still not entirely clear why no radioactive band travels up the cone outer segments, the discovery that cones shed discs from the tips of their outer segments has led investigators to conclude that the cone outer segments are continually renewed by a process similar to the renewal process observed in rods (Steinberg et al., 1977; Anderson et al., 1978).

But if the cones shed their discs as the rods do, why wasn't this evident when rod shedding was observed? The answer is that the rods and cones shed their discs at different times of day,

you will find reading very difficult or impossible, even though you can see the page and make out the fuzzy outlines of the words. You can't read very easily with your rods because the rods see details poorly, as we will see at the end of this chapter.

Pigment Absorption Spectra

The difference we have described between the rod and cone spectral sensitivity curves can be explained by differences in the **pigment absorption spectra** of rod and cone visual pigments. An absorption spectrum is a plot of the amount of light absorbed by a visual pigment versus the wavelength of the light. George Wald, who won the Nobel Prize in 1967 for his research on visual pigments, and Paul Brown (1958) determined the absorption spectrum of human rod pigment by chemically extracting the pigment from retinas obtained from eyes donated to medical research. The resulting solution contains primarily rod visual pigment, since the rods contain about 99 percent of the visual pigment in the human retina. (This predominance of rod pigment is not surprising if we remember that the retina has 20 times more rods than cones and that the pigment-

and most of the initial disc-shedding experiments were done during times of high rod shedding but low cone shedding. This time difference in rod and cone shedding has been demonstrated by killing goldfish at different times of day and counting the number of rod and cone phagosomes in the pigment epithelium. The results of this experiment show that rod shedding occurs in early morning, while cone shedding occurs in early evening (O'Day & Young, 1978). Thus, the rods shed their discs at the end of their nighttime work hours, and the cones shed their discs at the end of their daytime work hours. Just as the participation of the rods and cones in vision is separated by one-half day, so the process of rod and cone renewal is separated by one-half day.

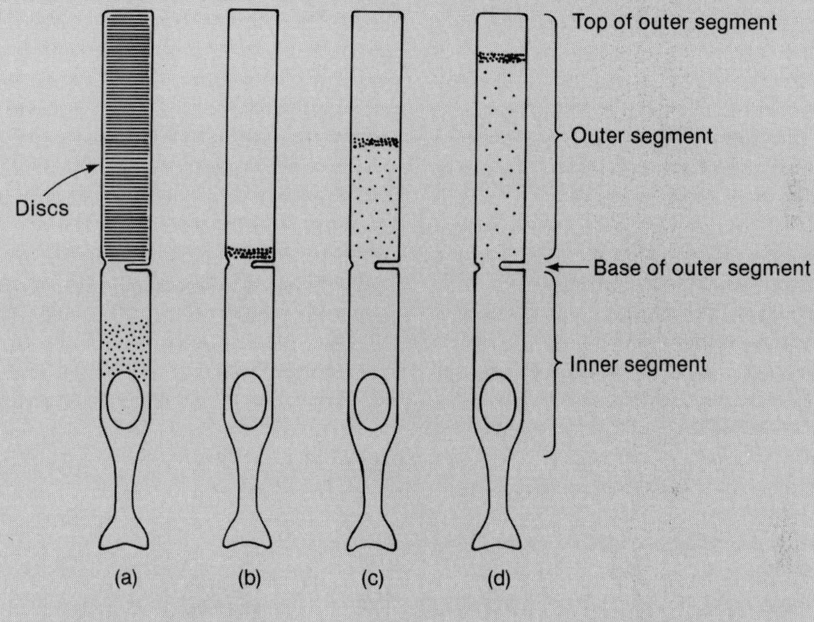

containing cone outer segments are much smaller than the rod outer segments.) When Wald and Brown measured the amount of light absorbed by the pigment solution at wavelengths across the visible spectrum, they obtained the data plotted as open circles in Figure 3.6. The match between the pigment absorption spectrum and the rod spectral sensitivity curve indicates that the spectral sensitivity of rod vision is due to the absorption of light by the rod visual pigment.

How does the spectral sensitivity curve for cone vision compare to the absorption spectrum of cone visual pigment? The answer to this question wasn't known until 1964, when the absorption spectrum of human cone pigment was first measured (the absorption spectrum of rod pigment was first measured in 1877). One reason for the delay in measuring cone pigment is that when pigment is chemically extracted, the concentration of cone pigment in the solution is so small compared to that of rod pigment that the cone pigment can't be detected. The measurement of the absorption spectrum of cone pigment had to await the development of a technique called **microspectrophotometry.**

In microspectrophotometry, rather than shining a beam of light through a solution of visual pigment extracted from the receptor, as was done to determine the absorption spectrum of rod pigment, we shine a beam of light through the pigment while it is still inside the receptor. This is difficult to do because cones are very small, but Brown and Wald (1964) successfully designed an optical system that could focus a beam of light through a single receptor. This enabled them to determine the three different curves shown in Figure 3.8. One pigment absorbs light best at about 435 nm (the short-wavelength cone pigment), one absorbs best at about 535 nm (the medium-wavelength cone pigment), and one absorbs best at about 565 nm (the long-wavelength cone pigment). Marks et al. (1964) made similar measurements.

How do we get from short-, medium-, and long-wavelength cone pigments that absorb maximally at 435, 535, and 565 nm to a psychophysical spectral sensitivity curve that peaks at 560 nm? The answer is that these three cone pigments combine to result in the spectral sensitivity curve. This was demonstrated in a psychophysical experiment by George Wald (1964). Wald reasoned that if the three cone pigments were responsible for the spectral sensitivity curve, bleaching two of the pigments should result in a spectral sensitivity curve similar to the absorption spectrum of the remaining, unbleached pigment. To see if this were so, he measured the spectral sensitivity of an observer exposed to three different adapting lights: (1) light containing long wavelengths, which bleaches the 535- and 565-nm pigments but leaves the 435-nm pigment, (2) light containing short and long wavelengths, which bleaches the 435- and 565-nm pigments but leaves the 535-nm pigment, and (3) light containing short and medium wavelengths, which bleaches the 435- and 535-nm pigments but leaves the 565-nm pigment. Wald found that when two of the three pigments are bleached, the maximum of the resulting spectral sensitivity curve falls near the peak of the absorption spectra of the remaining pigment. This experiment confirms the idea that the spectral sensitivity of the cones is due to the combined action of the three different cone pigments.

By looking at dark adaptation and spectral sensitivity, we have demonstrated that the visual pigments in the outer segments of the receptors play an important role in shaping our perceptions. We have also shown, in Chapter 2, that the way neurons are connected plays a large role in determining our perceptions. To end this chapter we will illustrate the importance of the way retinal neurons are "wired

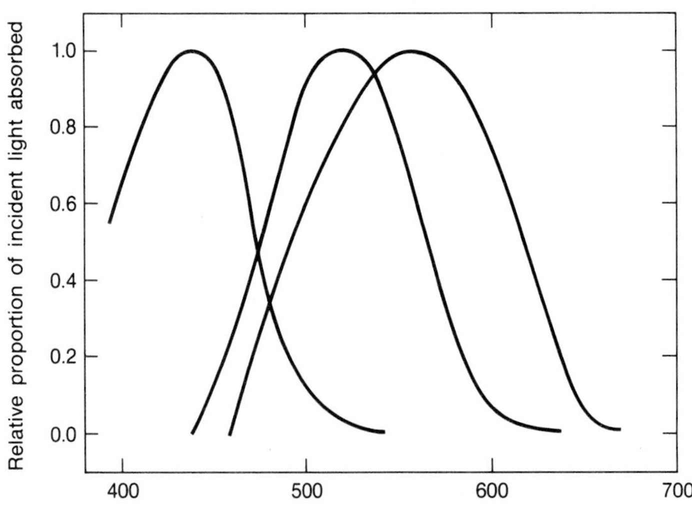

Figure 3.8 Absorption spectra of the three human cone pigments. (From Wald & Brown, 1965.)

up," by considering how rod and cone sensitivities are affected by the connections between the receptors and higher-order neurons in the retina.

Wiring and Perception

Rod and Cone Sensitivity

We already know, from the dark adaptation curve of Figure 3.4, that when the rods and cones are completely dark adapted, the rods are much more sensitive than the cones. Long before people started measuring dark adaptation curves, astronomers knew that to see a very dim star they had to look slightly to the side of the star rather than directly at it. The reason is that when you look to the side, you stimulate the rods in the peripheral retina; whereas, when you look directly at the star, you stimulate the less sensitive cones in the fovea. We will see that these differences in rod and cone sensitivity are due to differences in the way the rods and cones are connected to other cells in the retina.

When we discussed receptive fields in Chapter 2, we saw that single ganglion cells receive converging inputs from a large number of receptors. Since there are about 126 million rods and cones and only one million ganglion cells in the retina, the signals from over 120 receptors, on the average, must feed into each ganglion cell. The rods and cones both participate in this convergence, but due to their greater numbers, many more rods than cones send signals to each ganglion cell. This greater convergence of the rods is demonstrated in a very simplified diagram in Figure 3.9, which shows rods and cones synapsing with bipolar cells. In this example, five rods synapse with one bipolar cell, whereas five cones synapse with four bipolar cells. (In reality, a number of cones usually synapse with each bipolar cell, but for the purposes of this example, let's assume that we have found a few cones with private lines to their bipolars.)

To see how this wiring helps explain the rods' greater sensitivity, we present identical spots of light to the five rod receptors and the five cone receptors in Figure 3.9. Let's assume that this light causes

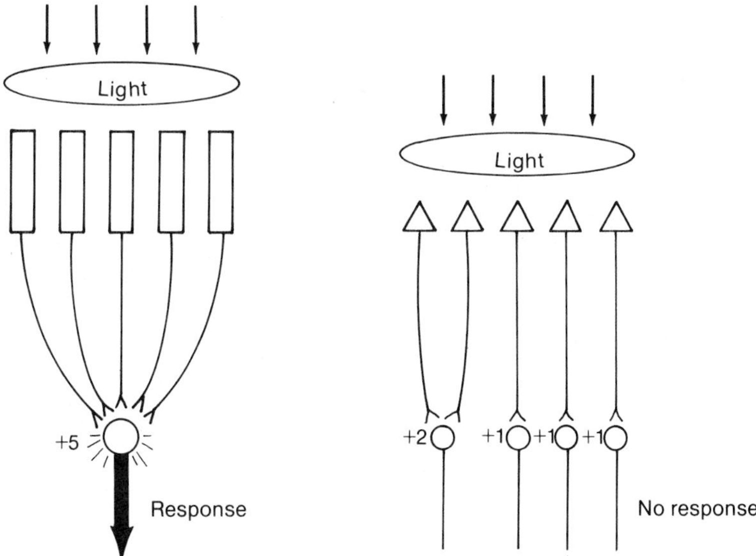

Figure 3.9 The wiring of the rods and the cones. The greater convergence of the rods results in spatial summation, which enables the rods to detect less intense light than the cones.

Box 3.3 Diurnal and Nocturnal Vision

The human eye contains both cones and rods, which enable us to see well in the brightness of the day and in the dimness of the night. However, many animals have eyes that contain only cones or predominantly rods,[1] and these animals can therefore see well only during the day or only at night. Lizards, ground squirrels, chipmunks, and prairie dogs have day, or **diurnal vision**; flying squirrels, rats, and a small mammal called the bush baby have night, or **nocturnal vision.** The all-cone retinas of the diurnal animals give them the good acuity they need to catch the small animals and insects they eat, whereas the rod-dominated retinas of the nocturnal animals give them the good sensitivity they need to see well in the dark.

Good acuity for diurnal animals and good sensitivity for nocturnal animals are also achieved by other means in addition to cones and rods. Diurnal animals achieve good acuity by having large eyes, so the image on the retina can be big and cover many cones. Thus, birds, which achieve good acuity with their cone-dominated retinas, further increase their acuity with huge eyes that take up most of the space in their head. The eyes of many birds are so large that they actually touch each other, making it possible to stimulate one eye by shining light through the wall of the other (Levine, 1955)!

Nocturnal animals achieve greater sensitivity by means of large lenses and corneas that help collect light. The eye of the opposum, a nocturnal animal, is shown on the left below. Compare the large lens and cornea of this eye to the much smaller lens and cornea of the diurnal ground squirrel eye, shown on the right (Tansley, 1965). Another means of increasing sensitivity is a reflecting surface called the **tapetum,** located behind the retinas of some nocturnal animals. The tapetum increases the amount of light hitting the receptors, by reflecting light back through the retina. The glow you see when you shine light into a cat's eye is light reflected from the cat's tapetum.

If a nocturnal animal wants to venture out into the daylight, it must have a way to protect its sensitive eyes. This protection is accomplished in some nocturnal animals by a pupil that becomes a vertical slit when it contracts in response to light. A slit pupil protects the retina against light better than a round pupil, because it can close all the way; whereas a round pupil can never close completely. Thus, an animal that is active at night can sun itself on a rock during the day, with its sensitive eyes protected by its completely closed pupil. Tansley (1965) points out, however, that truly nocturnal animals have round pupils, because they never venture into the bright daylight and therefore don't need to protect their retinas from the light.

[1]It has proven very difficult to find animals that have *only* rods. For example, although the rat has such a large proportion of rods that it's difficult to find the cones, there is a low level of cone functioning in the rat's retina.

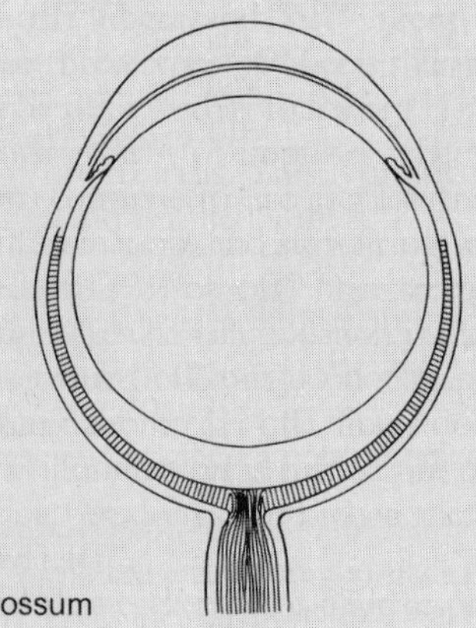

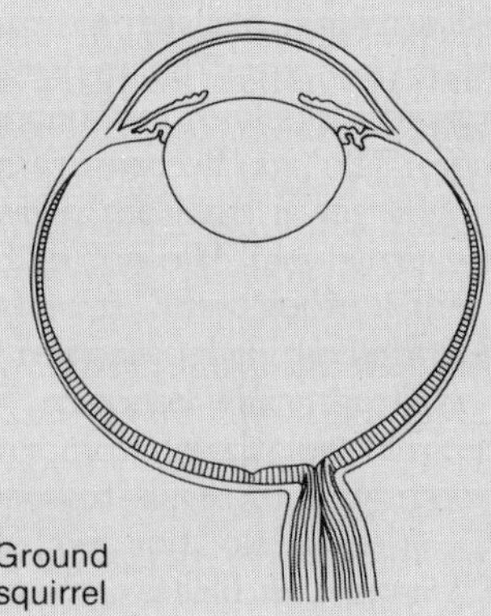

each rod and each cone to send one unit of stimulation to its bipolar cell. If we further assume that each bipolar cell must receive at least four units of stimulation to fire, then we see that the rod bipolar cell will fire (since it receives five units of stimulation, one from each rod), but the cone bipolar cells will not (since they each receive less than four units of stimulation). This hypothetical example illustrates the principle of **spatial summation.** Many rods summate, or add up, the effects of the spot of light by feeding into the same bipolar cell. The cones, on the other hand, summate less, because only a few cones feed into a single bipolar cell.

The difference in the degree of spatial summation of the rods and cones can be demonstrated psychophysically by measuring the **summation area** for rod vision and for cone vision (Bartlett, 1965). The summation area is the area within which the threshold stays the same, independent of the size or configuration of the stimulus. To illustrate what we mean by this, look at Figure 3.10. In (a) we present a spot of light 0.2 mm in diameter and find that we need to present 4 units of light to reach the observer's threshold for barely detecting the light. In (b) and (c) we increase the diameter of the spot to 0.4 mm and 0.6 mm, respectively, and find that we still need just 4 units of light to reach threshold. In (a), (b), and (c) the same amount of light is presented, but it is spread out over different areas. But, when we increase the diameter still further, to 0.7 mm, we need 6 units of light to reach threshold. Since the threshold is constant as long as the spot's diameter is 0.6 mm or less, 0.6 mm is the diameter of the summation area.

The reason the threshold remains constant as long as the spot is no larger than the summation area is that all the receptors within the summation area feed into the same ganglion cell. Thus, a small spot stimulates the ganglion cell in the same way as a larger spot, as long as the same amount of light energy is contained in both. We might expect that the greater neural convergence of the rods would cause the rods' summation area, measured psychophysically, to be larger than the cones' summation area, and, in fact, this is the case. The summation area for a spot presented to the rod-rich periphery is about 100 times greater than the summation area for a spot presented to the all-cone fovea.

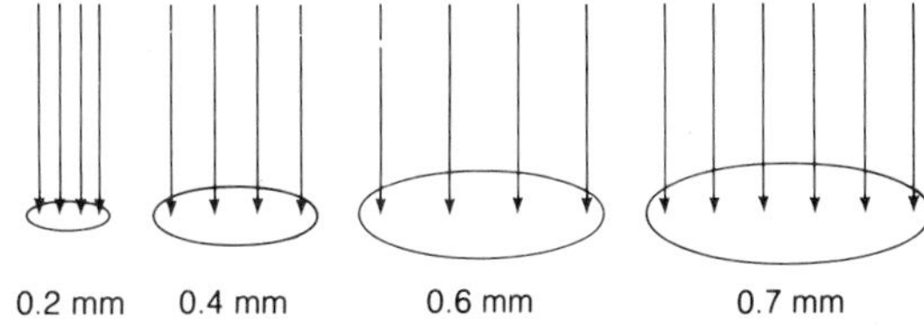

Figure 3.10 The principle of the summation area. In this example the summation area is a circle 0.6 mm in diameter. This means that the threshold for seeing a spot of light will be the same for any spot with a diameter of 0.6 mm or less. This constancy of the threshold is symbolized by the four arrows hitting each spot. When the diameter of the spot is increased to 0.7 mm, however, it takes more light (six arrows' worth) to reach threshold.

In the next section we will see that the differences in convergence of the rods and cones result not only in differences in rod and cone sensitivity but also in differences in the visual acuity, or detail vision, of the rods and cones.

Rod and Cone Acuity

The reason it is often difficult to immediately pick your friend's face out of a crowd is that to recognize a face, you must look directly at it. Only all-cone foveal vision enables us to detect small details, so only the particular face at which you are looking is seen in enough detail to be recognized, while the rest of the faces in the crowd fall on the peripheral retina and can't be recognized. You find your friend only after you move your eyes around until the image of his or her face falls on your foveas.

You can demonstrate the superiority of foveal vision over peripheral vision by looking at the title of a book on your bookshelf. Without moving your eyes from this title, see how many titles you can read to the left and right. If you do this without cheating (no fair looking to the side!), you will find that you can read only a few titles to either side. Because of the higher visual acuity of the cones compared to the rods, you can read the title of the book at which you are looking but not those which are imaged on the peripheral retina.

Visual acuity can be measured in a number of ways, one of which is to determine how far apart two dots have to be before a space can be seen between them. This is done by presenting an observer with a stimulus and asking whether there are one or two dots. Acuity can also be measured by determining how fine a checkerboard pattern (or a grating pattern of alternating light and dark lines) must be before the pattern can no longer be detected. The letters of the Snellen chart and the Landoldt rings, shown in Figure 3.11, are perhaps the most familiar ways of measuring acuity. The observer's task is to identify the Snellen letter or to indicate the location of the gap in the Landoldt rings from a fixed distance. We will discuss this method of determining acuity in Chapter 6, "What Can Go Wrong with Your Eyes."

We can demonstrate the differences between rod and cone visual acuity by measuring how acuity changes as a test pattern is moved from the fovea to the periphery or by measuring how acuity changes during dark adaptation. In each case, we find that rod acuity is much lower than cone acuity. Visual acuity drops (that is, details must be larger in order to be seen) as we move from fovea to periphery and as the retina dark adapts. Thus, although rod vision is much more sensitive to light than cone vision, rod vision is much less able to detect small details than is cone vision.

To understand how the differences in rod and cone spatial summation can explain the differences between rod and cone acuity, let's consider what happens if we stimulate rods A and E in Figure 3.12 with separate spots of light. (In reality, it is not possible to shine a spot of light onto a single receptor in the human retina, but we will assume it is possible for the purposes of our example.) Since these two rods converge onto a single bipolar cell, there is no way to tell that the activity of the bipolar cell is caused by two spots of light. A similar response in the bipolar cell could just as likely be caused by presenting a more intense light to just one of the rods. Thus, the two spots of light presented to rods A and E would be perceived as a single spot. If, however, we stimulate cones A and E, then each cone causes a separate bipolar cell to fire. That bipolar cells 1 and 4 fire but cells 2 and 3 do not indicates that the receptors feeding into 1 and 4 must be stimulated by separate spots of light. Because of this wiring of the cones, we perceive two spots of light.

Thus, the different ways the rods and cones are connected to other neurons in the retina can explain some of the differences in the sensitivity and acuity of the rods and cones. The story is not quite as simple as this, however, because factors other than wiring also influence sensitivity and acuity. For example, the spacing of retinal receptors and the fact that the eye's optical system doesn't always focus the image sharply onto the retina also help determine acuity. But the main point here is that both wiring and the properties of the visual pigments influence perception.

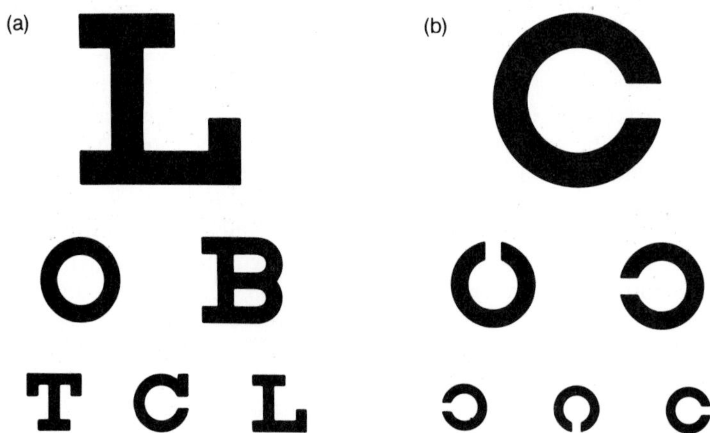

Figure 3.11 Snellen letters (a) and Landolt rings (b) used to test visual acuity. We will discuss acuity testing in more detail in Chapter 6. (From Riggs, 1965b).

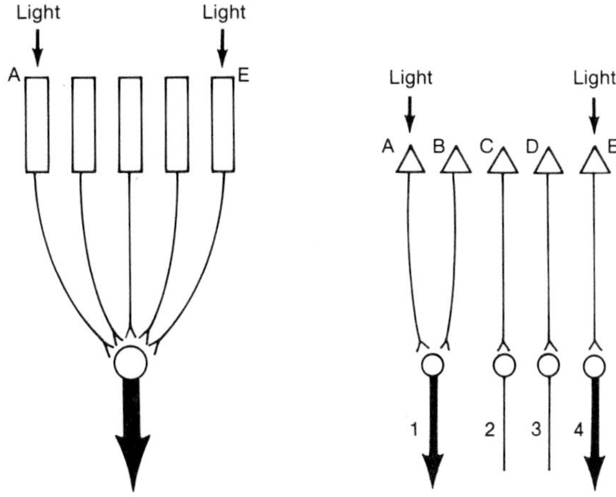

Figure 3.12 The same wiring diagrams as in Figure 3.9. In this example, the greater convergence of the rods makes it impossible for the rods to resolve the two spots of light presented to receptors A and E. The cones, however, because of their lack of convergence, can resolve these two spots.

Summary

1. Duplicity theory states that there are two different types of receptors in the retina, the rods and the cones, and that these two types of receptors serve different functions.
2. Some differences between rods and cones are listed below:

Property	*Cones*	*Rods*
shape of outer segment	conelike	rodlike
number	6 million per retina	120 million per retina
distribution	fovea and periphery	periphery only
dark adaptation	fast	slow
spectral sensitivity	most sensitive at 560 nm	most sensitive at 500 nm
dark adapted sensitivity	low	high
acuity	high	low
disc shedding	early evening	early morning

3. The place where the optic nerve leaves the back of the eye is called the blind spot. We are usually not aware of the blind spot because of a mechanism that "fills in" the place where the image disappears.
4. The cones dark adapt faster than the rods because cone visual pigment regenerates faster than rod visual pigment during dark adaptation.
5. The spectral sensitivity curve of the rods is determined by the absorption of light by the rod pigment, rhodopsin (λ_{max} = 500 nm), and the spectral sensitivity curve of the cones is determined by the absorption of light by the three cone pigments (λ_{max} = 435, 535, and 570 nm).
6. The greater dark adapted sensitivity of the rod system is due to the greater spatial summation of the rods.
7. One reason for the greater acuity of the cones is that fewer cones than rods converge onto each bipolar or ganglion cell.
8. Our retina is a duplex retina, which contains both rods and cones. Some animals, however, have retinas that contain only cones or predominantly rods, and these animals, therefore, can see well only during the day or only at night.

Glossary

Absorption spectrum A plot of the amount of light absorbed by a visual pigment versus the wavelength of light. (See Figures 3.6 and 3.8.) (74)

Autoradiography A technique that makes it possible to see radioactively labeled protein which has been taken up by a cell. (74)

Blind spot The place where the optic nerve leaves the back of the eye, causing a small area to be without visual receptors. (67)

Brightness An attribute of light that ranges from just barely visible (at low brightnesses) to dazzling (at high brightnesses). Brightness is correlated with (but is not the same as) the intensity of the light. (Brightness is discussed further in Chapter 5.) (72)

Cones Cone-shaped receptors in the retina; they are primarily responsible for vision in high levels of illumination. The cone system is responsible for color vision and detail vision. (67)

Cone spectral sensitivity curve A graph showing the cone system's sensitivity to light as a function of the light's wavelength. (71)

Dark adaptation Visual adaptation that occurs in the dark, in which the sensitivity to light increases. (68)

Dark adaptation curve The function that traces the time course of the increase in visual sensitivity that occurs during dark adaptation. (69)

Dark adapted sensitivity The sensitivity of the dark adapted eye. (70)

Disc shedding The discs at the tip of the visual receptors' outer segments are shed into the pigment epithelium. (74)

Diurnal vision Vision specialized to function during the day. (78)

Duplicity theory The idea that the rod and cone receptors in the retina operate under different conditions and have different properties. (68)

Fovea A small area in the retina that contains only cone receptors. (68)

Inner segment The part of the visual receptor, below the outer segment, that contains mechanisms important for the receptor's metabolism. (74)

Light adaptation Visual adaptation that occurs in the light, in which the sensitivity to light decreases. (69)

Light adapted sensitivity The sensitivity of the light adapted eye. (69)

Microspectrophotometry A procedure for determining pigment absorption spectra; it involves shining light through single receptors or through small numbers of receptors. (75)

Nocturnal vision Vision specialized to function at night. (78)

Outer segment The part of the visual receptor that contains the light-sensitive visual pigment. (74)

Peripheral retina All of the retina except the fovea and a small area surrounding the fovea. (68)

Phagosomes Structures in the pigment epithelium that digest discs that are shed by the receptor outer segments. (74)

Pigment absorption spectrum The function relating the amount of light absorbed by a visual pigment to the light's wavelength. (74)

Pigment bleaching When a visual pigment molecule absorbs light, a bleaching process begins in which the molecule changes shape and the color of the rod visual pigment changes from red to transparent. Sometime early in this process, visual transduction takes place. (70)

Pigment regeneration The reconstruction of the visual pigment molecule from its bleached state to its original unbleached state. (70)

Purkinje shift The shift from cone spectral sensitivity to rod spectral sensitivity that takes place during dark adaptation. (73)

Retinal densitometry A procedure for measuring the concentration of visual pigment in the living eye. It involves projecting a dim beam of light into the eye and then measuring the fraction of this beam that is reflected out of the eye. (71)

Rod-cone break The point on a dark adaptation curve at which vision shifts from cone vision to rod vision. (70)

Rod monochromat A person whose retina contains only rods. (70)

Rods Rod-shaped receptors in the retina; they are primarily responsible for vision in low levels of illumination. The rod system is extremely sensitive in the dark, but it cannot resolve fine details. (67)

Rod spectral sensitivity curve A graph showing the rod system's sensitivity to light as a function of the light's wavelength. (71)

Spatial summation When the effect of stimulation is summated (added up) over a large area. (79)

Summation area In vision, the area within which the threshold for seeing stays the same, independent of the size or configuration of the stimulus. (79)

Tapetum A reflecting surface located behind the retina in some animals (78)

Chapter Four

Perceiving Touch, Temperature, and Pain

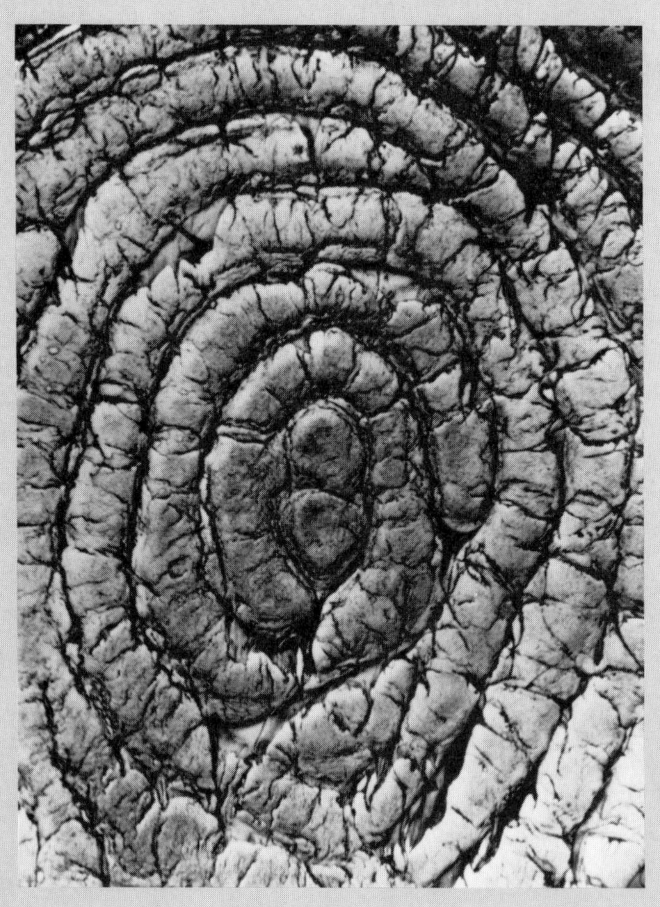

Our story so far has been dominated by the visual system. We have seen how the visual system processes electrical signals generated by the receptors to create feature detectors, single neurons that signal information about the nature of the light entering the eye. We have also raised an important question about the basic operation of the nervous system, that of sensory coding: How is environmental information coded into electrical signals so that the brain can understand what these signals mean? In this chapter we'll shift our focus to perceptions that result from stimulation of the skin—warmth, cold, touch, and pain. We wish to understand the operation of a sensory system other than vision and also to continue the discussion of sensory coding we began in Chapter 2.

In describing how a sensory system other than vision operates, we will see many similarities between what, on the surface, appear to be two very different systems. Perhaps the most striking similarity between vision and the skin senses lies in their receptive fields: the receptive fields of neurons that receive signals from the skin share many properties with those of neurons that receive signals from the retina.

We will also introduce a new idea about how the senses operate. Based on what you've read so far, you may think that perception can be explained simply by considering how nerve impulses are processed as they travel from the receptors to the brain. Unfortunately, things aren't that simple. When we discuss pain, we will see that perception is influenced not only by the nature of the electrical signals that are generated by the receptors but also by the perceiver's expectations and past experiences.

We ended Chapter 2 by introducing two theories of sensory coding: **specificity theory,** which states that sensory quality is signaled by the activities of a few nerve fibers that respond only to specific stimuli, and **pattern theory,** which states that sensory quality is signaled by the pattern of activity of many nerve fibers. In this chapter, we will elaborate on the question of sensory coding, because, historically, the skin senses have provided the battleground upon which proponents of specificity and pattern theories have presented their evidence.

Since the starting point of our perception of temperature, touch, and pain is the skin, let's start by considering the skin.

The Skin

When you look at your skin you see the skin's outer layer, the **epidermis,** which is actually several layers of tough dead skin cells. The chapter-opening illustration shows a scanning electron micrograph of the skin on the tip of a finger (magnified 27 times). Hairy skin covers most of the body, but hairless (**glabrous**) skin is found on the fingers and palms of the hands, and on the toes and soles of the feet. Both hairy and glabrous skin serve a number of functions. Skin protects us by keeping dirt and moisture from penetrating our bodies, while at the same time allowing sweat to escape, to help our bodies maintain their proper temperature.

Another function of the skin—the one we are concerned with—is to provide information about the various stimuli that contact the skin. The sun's rays heat our skin and we feel warm; a cold wind causes us to shiver; a pinprick hurts us; and, on a more pleasant note, a backrub feels great! To understand how these perceptions originate, we must look at the skin's inner layer, the **dermis,** which contains numerous nerve endings and receptors, some of which are shown in Figure 4.2. The various types of receptors in the dermis, combined with our experience of different perceptions with the skin (warmth, cold, etc.), have suggested to some researchers that perhaps each perception is signaled to the brain by a specific type of receptor. This idea, which you may recognize as a version of the specificity theory of sensory coding, was first proposed by German researcher Max von Frey. We will begin our discussion of how the skin signals the quality of experience by considering von Frey's ideas.

The Sensory Code for Quality on the Skin: Specificity or Pattern?

Von Frey's Specificity Theory

Between 1894 and 1895, Max von Frey published a series of papers in which he proposed that four primary qualities result from stimulation of the skin: warmth, cold, touch, and pain. He hypothesized that each quality is signaled by the firing of a spe-

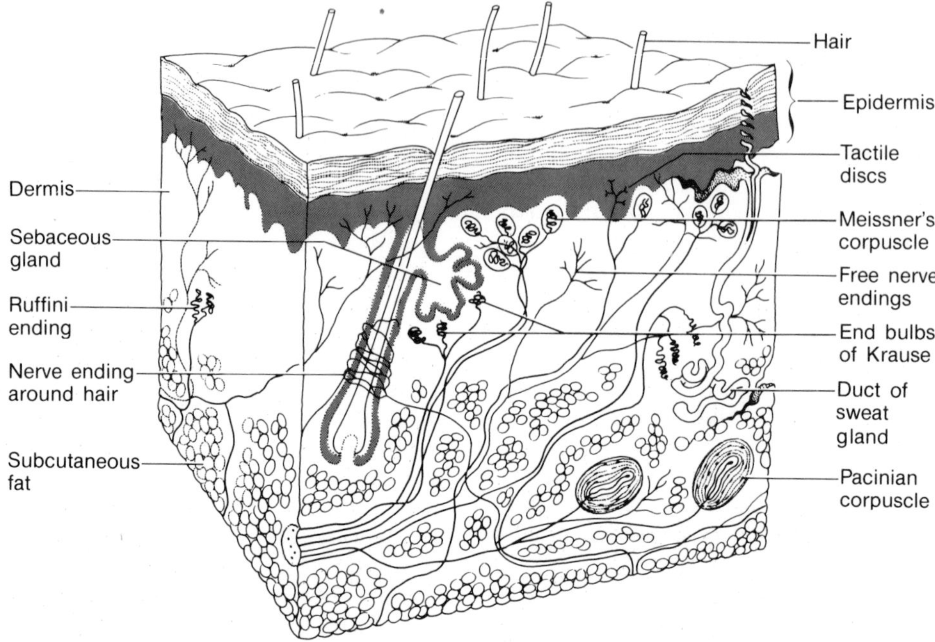

Figure 4.2 A cross section of the skin, showing the layers of the skin and some of the receptors in the dermis layer. (From Gardner, 1975.)

cialized receptor in the skin. According to von Frey, stimulation of the **Ruffini endings** (see Figure 4.2) was responsible for the sensation of warmth; the **Krause end bulbs,** for cold; the **Meissner corpuscles,** for touch; and the **free nerve endings,** for pain.

Von Frey had little evidence to support his ideas other than that receptors of many different shapes and sizes could be found in the skin. Some experiments that did seem to support von Frey's ideas involved mapping **sensory spots** on the skin, by applying stimuli to very small spots and noting the resulting sensations. The results for cold and warm stimuli are shown in Figure 4.3. Stimulation with cold results in the sensation of cold at the locations shown by the filled circles, while stimulation with heat results in the sensation of warmth at the locations shown by the open circles. Note that the cold and warm spots do not usually overlap and that many spots on the skin result in neither cold nor warm sensations. Similar results are obtained for touch and pain stimuli. Von Frey interpreted these results to mean that specialized receptors must be located under each sensory spot: Krause end bulbs should be found under cold spots, Ruffini endings under warm spots, and so on.

Von Frey's hypothesis, however, has not withstood the test of further experimentation. Many investigators have mapped sensory spots on the skin and then dissected the skin (ouch!) to see which receptors are located under each spot (Burgess & Perl, 1973). These experiments have shown little correlation between the type of sensory spot and the receptor located under it. In fact, Krause end bulbs and Ruffini endings rarely have been found under cold or warm spots.

Additional evidence that argued against von Frey's theory was provided by P. P. Lele and G. Weddell (1956), who showed that stimulation of the cornea of the eye, which contains only free nerve endings, can result in all four of von Frey's primary sensations. From such experiments, many investigators hypothesized that specificity was wrong and proposed that the skin signals quality by means of the pattern of impulses from a large number of fibers (Sinclair, 1955).

Box 4.1 Seeing with the Skin

The person sitting in the chair has her back resting against an array of 400 small vibrators. This person is blind, but by means of this **mechanical substitution system** developed by Paul Bach-y-Rita and co-workers (1969, 1970, 1972; White et al., 1970), the person can "see with her skin."

A television camera controlled by the subject takes a picture of the scene, which is translated into signals that control the vibrators in the back of the chair. Light areas of the scene cause more vibration than dark areas. After an initial period of training, subjects can learn to interpret these vibrations as representing simple objects. With further training, subjects can learn to perceive both the identities of objects and their locations relative to each other in space. Subjects are able to determine the locations of objects in space, using information provided by depth cues. For example, subjects learn that vibration higher on the back often corresponds to objects that are farther away (relative height), that the area of vibration increases as an object moves closer (relative size), and that when the vibration from one object partially obscures the vibration from another, the object with part of its vibration covered is farther away (overlap).

That subjects could tell that one object overlapped another means that they segregated the vibrations representing the foreground object from those representing the object in the background. In addition to being able to identify single objects and make depth judgments, some subjects can "see" remarkable details, as indicated by the following statements from an experienced subject: "That is Betty; she is wearing her hair down today and does not have her glasses on. Her mouth is open, and she is moving her right hand from her left side to the back of her head." This impressive demonstration of the skin's ability to "see" has led to work on more portable "mechanical substitution systems" that could be used by a blind person as he or she walks through the environment.

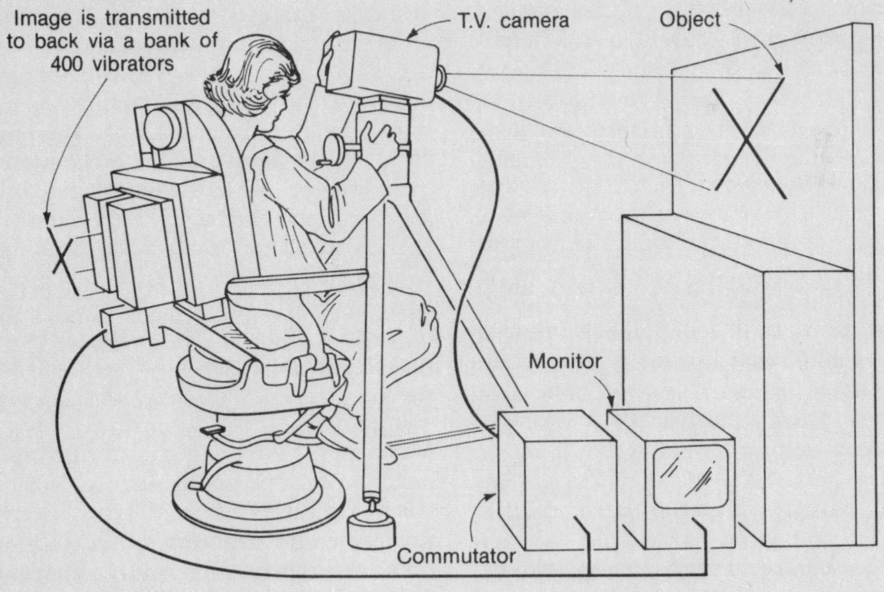

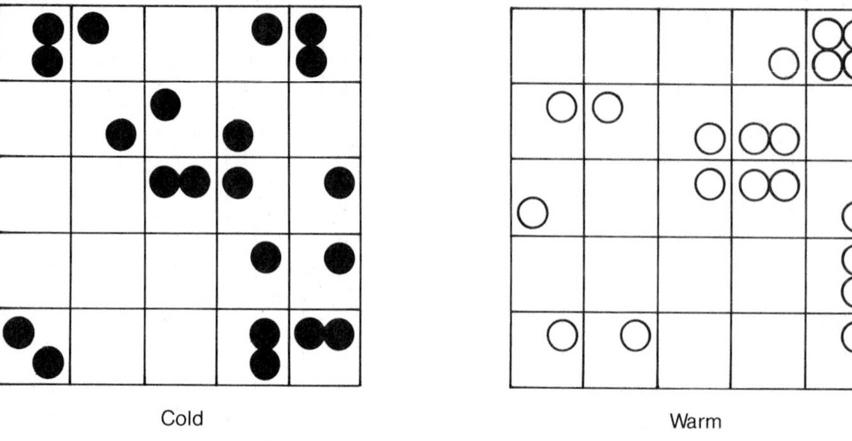

Figure 4.3 Cold and warm sensory spots on the skin. (From Dallenbach, 1927.)

Pattern Theory and the Skin

Once von Frey's theory was shown to be wrong, pattern theory was the logical alternative proposed to replace it, which D. C. Sinclair (1955) stated as follows: "What leaves the skin as a result of cutaneous stimulation is a complex spatially and temporally dispersed pattern of impulses. . . . The physical characteristics of this pattern are the determining factor in the experience of sensory quality." Pattern theory proposed that all nerve endings in the skin are alike and that different qualities are signaled by different patterns of nerve firing, as shown in Figure 2.37.

Many researchers, however, felt that pattern theory was too vague to be very useful (Melzak & Wall, 1962). It's one thing to hypothesize that warmth and pain result in two different patterns of nerve firing, but it's quite another thing to show experimentally that this is so. In addition, while pattern theory was being proposed, evidence was beginning to accumulate that not all fibers from the skin were the same—some responded only to very specific stimuli.

Fibers That Respond to Specific Stimuli

In the last 25 years, accumulated electrophysiological evidence has shown that certain fibers respond only to specific stimuli. Table 4.1 lists some of the fiber types found in the cat, along with a brief description of the stimulus that causes each type to fire (Burgess & Perl, 1973; Hensel, 1973). Let's look at the properties of a few of these fibers.

Warm and cold fibers. Figure 4.4 shows how a **warm fiber** responds to increases in temperature. This neuron (1) increases its firing rate when the temperature is increased (firing most rapidly during an increase from 40° to 45° C), (2) continues to fire as long as the higher temperature is kept on, (3) decreases its firing rate when the temperature is decreased, and (4) does not respond to mechanical stimulation (Kenshalo, 1976; Duclaux & Kenshalo, 1980). **Cold fibers,** on the other hand, increase their firing rate when the temperature is decreased and continue to fire at low temperatures. The different ways that cold and warm fibers respond to steady temperatures are shown in Figure 4.5. Cold fibers respond in the 20°–45° range, with the best response at about 30° C. Warm fibers respond in the 30°–48° range, with the best response at about 44° C.

Nociceptors. Figure 4.6 shows the response of a **nociceptor,** a fiber specialized for signaling stimuli that might damage tissue. This cat nociceptor begins firing when the temperature reaches about 45° C, the same temperature at which a human begins to feel pain (Beck et al., 1974; Zimmerman, 1979). Since most nociceptors do not respond to cold, warmth, or light mechanical stimulation but do

Table 4.1
Receptor types in the cat and their best stimuli

Receptor type	*Best stimulus*
G_1 hair receptor	Very rapid displacement of a guard hair
Intermediate hair receptor	Rapid displacement of a hair
G_2 hair receptor	Slow movement of a guard hair
D hair receptor	Slow movement of a down hair
Pacinian corpuscle	Rapid stimulation of the skin; vibration
F_1 field receptor	Rapid indentation of an area of skin
F_2 field receptor	Steady indentation of an area of skin
Type I mechanoreceptor	Indentation of skin (sensitive to the velocity of skin indentation)
Type II mechanoreceptor	Steady indentation of skin
C mechanoreceptor	Slow movement across skin, long contact
Nociceptor	Stimulus that damages or nearly damages tissue
Warm receptor	Increasing temperatures or steady high temperatures
Cold receptor	Decreasing temperatures or steady low temperatures

respond to intense heat, mechanical stimulation that deforms the skin, and chemical substances that burn the skin, it has been hypothesized that these fibers are involved in the perception of pain.

Specificity or Pattern?

Our descriptions of fibers hypothesized to play roles in the perception of warmth, coldness, and pain, as well as the descriptions of numerous fibers and their "best stimuli" in Table 4.1, may appear at first glance to be modern-day evidence for von Frey's specificity theory. In fact, these fibers do provide excellent evidence that specificity theory operates for the skin senses, but we should not confuse the idea that some nerve fibers fire only to specific stimuli with von Frey's version of specificity theory. Remember, von Frey's main hypothesis was that perceptions could be linked to *specific receptor structures.* We saw above that no evidence supports this idea, and we should

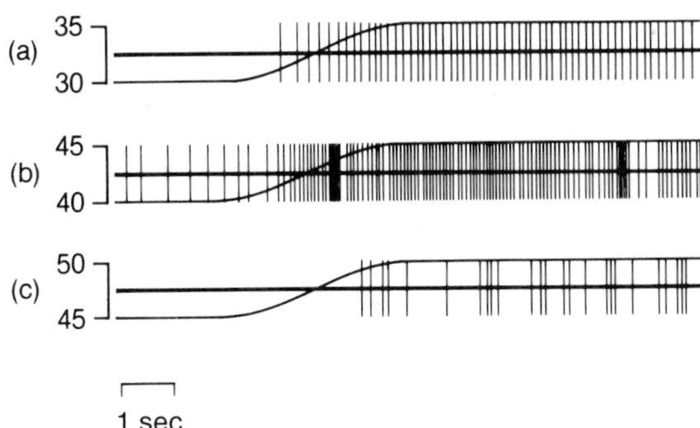

Figure 4.4 The response of a "warm" fiber in the monkey. Record A indicates that the fiber does not fire at a temperature of 30° C, but as the temperature is increased to 35° C (indicated by the sloping line), the firing rate increases, and the fiber continues to fire when the temperature is held at 35° C. Record B shows a large increase in firing when the temperature is increased from 40° to 45° C, but record C shows only a small response to an increase from 45° to 50° C. (From Duclaux & Kenshalo, 1980.)

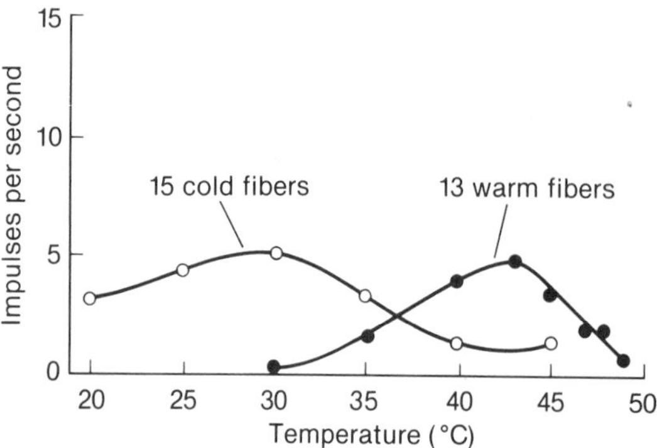

Figure 4.5 Responses of temperature-sensitive fibers in the monkey to constant temperatures. The curve on the left (open circles) shows the average response of a group of 15 "cold" fibers, which respond best at about 30° C. The curve on the right (filled circles) shows the average response of a group of 13 "warm" fibers, which respond best at about 44° C. (From Kenshalo, 1976.)

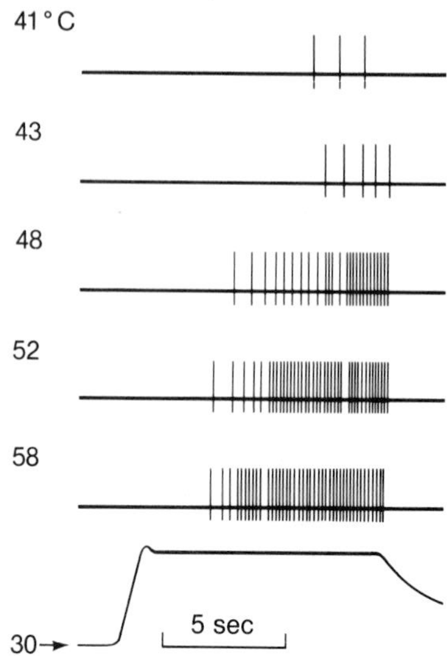

Figure 4.6 The response of a *nociceptor* in the cat to heating of the skin. This fiber begins firing at temperatures above about 45° C and reaches maximum firing rates above about 55° C. (From Beck et al., 1974.)

carefully note that, with the exception of the Pacinian corpuscle (discussed in detail later in this chapter), specific receptor structures have not been linked to the fibers in Table 4.1.[1]

Another reason that Table 4.1 cannot support von Frey's theory is that it doesn't mention *perception*. The table tells us only that certain nerve fibers respond to specific stimuli. To make the jump from nerve fiber responses to perception, we must know which perceptions result from which stimuli. This jump is sometimes easily made, sometimes not. For example, we can assume that fibers which respond only to stimuli that cause tissue damage are involved in the perception of pain, because tissue damage almost always results in pain. And we might, therefore, be justified in labeling the nociceptors in Table 4.1 "pain receptors." It has also been suggested that C mechanoreceptors are involved in the perception of "tickle," because tickling often results from slow movement across the skin (Zotterman, 1939). It is not, however, so easy to specify the perception resulting from, say, a Type I mechanoreceptor that sends information about the velocity of skin indentation.

In fact, touching the skin activates a number of the receptor types in Table 4.1. Touch involves the bending of hairs (hair receptors), indentation of the skin with some velocity (Type I mechanoreceptors), and some period of sustained pressure (F_2 field receptors, Type II mechanoreceptors, C mechanoreceptors), thereby causing a number of different fibers to fire, each one signaling a different aspect of the stimulus that causes us to perceive touch. Thus, though many fibers respond only to specific stimuli, a number of these specific fibers are probably activated by touching the skin. If this is so, then we can say that sensory quality on the skin is determined by the firing pattern of numerous fibers responding to specific stimuli. This suggested combination of specificity and pattern theories is, in fact,

[1]It is necessary to explain why Table 4.1 refers to different "receptor types." The descriptions in Table 4.1 were determined by recording from nerve fibers without looking at the structures of the receptors attached to these fibers. Thus, if one nerve fiber responded best to rapid indentation of the skin and another to slow movement across the skin, it is assumed that these fibers reflect the activity of two different receptors. Although this is a good assumption, it is important to realize that the actual receptor structures have rarely been identified—when researchers look for receptor structures, they often find only free nerve endings. In cases where two free nerve endings respond to different stimuli, there must be some difference between them, but these differences have not yet been determined.

analogous to our earlier hypothesis that the visual system pools information from many different feature detectors to more precisely specify the stimulus (see p. 60, in Chapter 2).

Though it is satisfying to suggest that our perception of different qualities by the skin is due to the firing pattern of numerous fibers that respond to specific stimuli, we shouldn't suppose that we can explain all our perceptions simply by specifying which stimuli impinge on the skin. As we stated in Chapter 2 (p. 45) and again at the beginning of this chapter, our expectations and past experience also play a role in determining our perceptions. In the next section, we will see how expectations and past experience play an important role in our perception of pain.

The Perception of Pain

Our perception of pain is not associated with one particular kind of stimulation. A sharp object, a flame, intense heat, abrasion, a sharp blow, terminal cancer, compression of nerves, and chemical burns are just a few of the things that may lead to pain. One thing that all stimuli which result in pain have in common is their potential to cause tissue damage, either to the skin or to some internal part of the body. That so many different stimuli can lead to pain makes its perception similar to that of motivational states such as hunger, thirst, and emotional feeling, which are also elicited by a wide variety of stimuli. Like these motivational states, pain is often accompanied by its own emotional reactions—reactions which lead to attempts to avoid pain or the inescapable suffering that accompanies intractable pain (Weisenberg, 1977; Mayer, 1979).

Pain also shares with motivational states a great complexity. Just as complex control systems for feeding exist at various levels of the nervous system, complicated mechanisms influence our perception of pain. There is no single center in the brain for pain; instead, pain depends on many structures in both the brain and spinal cord (Zimmerman, 1979). In this section, we will look at a few of the complexities of pain, first by describing some of the evidence which shows that psychological factors influence our perception of pain.

The Psychology of Pain

The perception of pain is determined not only by the firing of pain receptors but also by such factors as a person's culture, previous experience, and the general situation in which the pain stimulus occurs. Culture's effect on pain is most graphically demonstrated by rituals such as the hook-swinging ceremony practiced in some parts of India (Kosambi, 1967). This ritual is described as follows by Ronald Melzack (1973) in his highly readable book *The Puzzle of Pain:*

> The ceremony derives from an ancient practice in which a member of a social group is chosen to represent the power of the gods. The role of the chosen man (or "celebrant") is to bless the children and crops in a series of neighboring villages during a particular period of the year. What is remarkable about the ritual is that steel hooks, which are attached by strong ropes to the top of a special cart, are shoved under his skin and muscles on both sides of his back [Figure 4.7]. The cart is then moved from village to village. Usually the man hangs on to the ropes as the cart is moved about. But at the climax of the ceremony in each village, he swings free, hanging only from the hooks embedded in his back, to bless the children and crops. Astonishingly, there is no evidence that the man is in pain during the ritual; rather, he appears to be in a "state of exaltation." When the hooks are later removed, the wounds heal rapidly without any medical treatment other than the application of wood ash. Two weeks later the marks on his back are scarcely visible.

While it seems unbelievable that a person could feel little or no pain while hanging from steel hooks embedded in his back, this is, in fact, what happens during the hook-swinging ceremony.

In the remote Indian villages where the hook-swinging ceremony is performed, some cultural factor alters the individual's central neural activity and thereby lessens the celebrant's perception of pain. We will see how this might work when we discuss the gate control theory of pain below, but first let's consider some examples of how pain is affected by a person's mental state.

H. K. Beecher (1972) found that morphine reduces pain caused by pathological conditions accompanied by anxiety but doesn't reduce experimentally produced pain unaccompanied by anxiety. "Thus," according to Beecher, "we can state a new

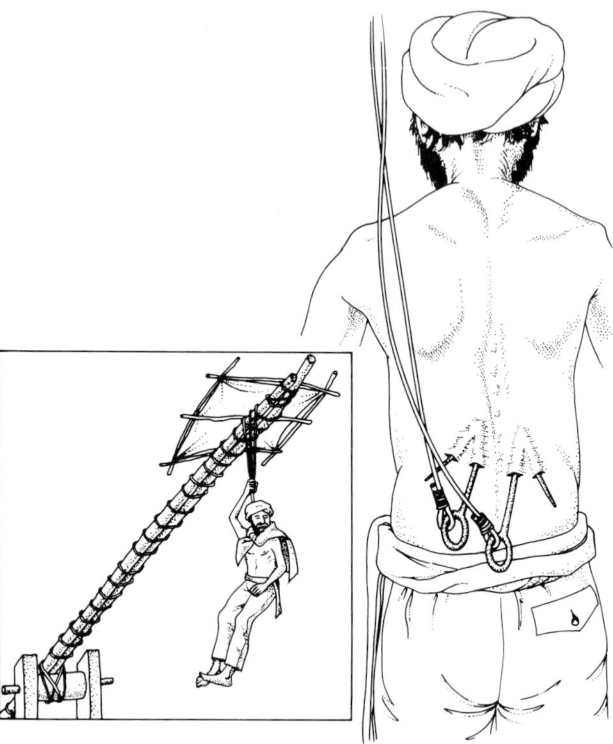

Figure 4.7 Top: two steel hooks in the back of the "celebrant" in the Indian hook-swnging ceremony. Bottom: the celebrant hangs onto the ropes as a cart takes him from village to village. As he blesses the village children and crops, he swings freely, suspended by the hooks in his back. (From Kosambi, 1967.)

principle of drug action: some agents are effective only in the presence of a required mental state."

There is ample evidence that a person's mental state affects his or her perception of pain. Beecher found that 25 percent of men seriously wounded in battle requested a narcotic for pain relief, whereas over 80 percent of civilians about to undergo major surgery requested pain relief. The difference in these percentages can be traced to the mental states of the patients. The civilians were upset about their surgical wounds because they associated these wounds with disturbing health problems. The soldiers, on the other hand, were less upset about their battle wounds, because they knew that their wounds would provide escape from a hazardous battlefield to the safety of a behind-the-lines hospital.

In a hospital study, when surgical patients were told what to expect and were instructed to relax to alleviate their pain, they requested fewer painkillers following surgery and were sent home 2.7 days earlier than patients who were not given this information. Studies have also shown that up to 35 percent of patients with pathological pain get relief from taking a **placebo,** a pill which they believe contains painkillers but which, in fact, contains no active ingredients (Weisenberg, 1977).

The above examples indicate that pain cannot be totally explained in terms of "pain receptors" that send uninterrupted signals to the brain. According to Robert Melzack and Stephen Dennis (1978), ". . . Stimulation of receptors does not mark the beginning of the pain process. Rather, stimulation produces neural signals that enter an active nervous system that (in the adult organism) is already the substrate of past experience, culture, anxiety, and so forth. . . . Pain, then, is not simply the end product of a linear sensory transmission system. Rather, it is a dynamic process which involves continuous interactions among complex . . . systems."

What is the nature of these complex systems to which Melzack and Dennis refer? In an attempt to answer this question, Melzack and Patrick Wall (1965) published a paper entitled "Pain Mechanisms: A New Theory," which proposed a gate control theory of pain perception.

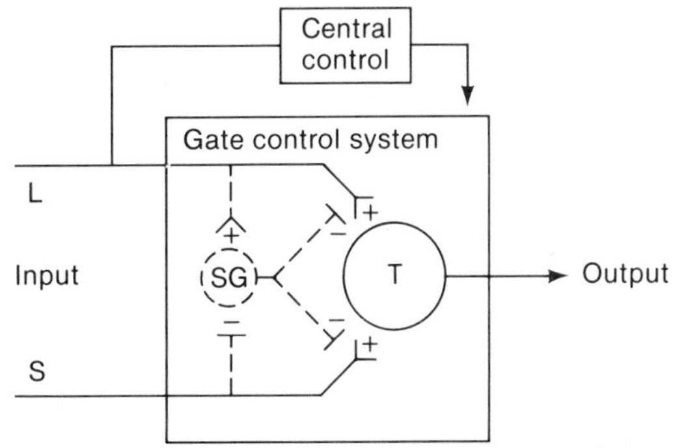

Figure 4.8 The circuit proposed by Melzak and Wall (1965) for their gate control theory of pain perception (see text for details).

Gate Control Theory

Gate control theory proposes that pain perception is controlled by a neural circuit like the one in Figure 4.8. The theory underlying this circuit is that signals which cause the perception of pain must pass through the gate control system before being transmitted to the brain. Two kinds of fibers send signals into the system: **small-diameter (S) fibers** and **large-diameter (L) fibers.** Ignoring, for a moment, the dashed structures in Figure 4.8, we can see that activation of either the S-fibers or the L-fibers causes increased activity of the **transmission (T) cell.**

The dashed structures, however, are the most important part of the circuit, because this part of the circuit controls the "gate." We saw that activity in the L-fibers excites the T-cell, but it also does something else. It closes the gate by activating a structure in the spinal cord called the **substantia gelantinosa (SG),** which, in turn, sends inhibition to the T-cell. Consequently, the net effect of activity in the L-fibers is to decrease the activity of the T-cell and thus decrease the perception of pain. Conversely, activity in the S-fibers inhibits the SG, thereby decreasing the amount of inhibition sent by the SG to the T-cell. S-fiber activity, therefore, opens the gate; with the gate open, the activity of the T-cell, and thus the perception of pain, is increased. So, according to gate control theory, we should experience more pain with a lot of S-fiber activity (because the gate is opened) and less pain with a lot of L-fiber activity (because the gate is closed).

The idea that S-fiber activity increases pain by opening the gate makes sense, because small fibers are usually associated with the nociceptors described earlier. The gate control mechanism can also be influenced by signals sent down from the brain. These signals, represented in Figure 4.8 by the box labeled "central control," are transmitted in L-fibers, so their effect is to close the gate and reduce the perception of pain.

The idea that signals sent down from the brain can reduce the perception of pain is supported by the results of an experiment done by David Reynolds (1969). Reynolds first showed that a rat responded vigorously when he pinched the rat's tail or paw. He then electrically stimulated an area in the rat's midbrain and showed that, while the stimulation was on, the animal no longer seemed to mind having his tail or paw pinched. In fact, Reynolds was even able to perform abdominal surgery on rats, with no anesthesia other than the electrical stimulation. This effect of brain stimulation, which has been confirmed in many experiments, is called **stimulation produced analgesia (SPA).**

The importance of gate control theory lies in its ability to take into account that pain is not simply determined by the activity of fibers connected to nociceptors. Gate control theory would explain some of the psychological effects we described above by saying that activity in L-fibers, or signals sent down from the brain, closes the gate. The pain reduction achieved by **acupuncture** is another effect explained by gate control theory. Acupuncture is the procedure practiced in China in which fine needles are inserted into the skin at certain "acupuncture points" in the body (Figure 4.9). Twirling these needles, or

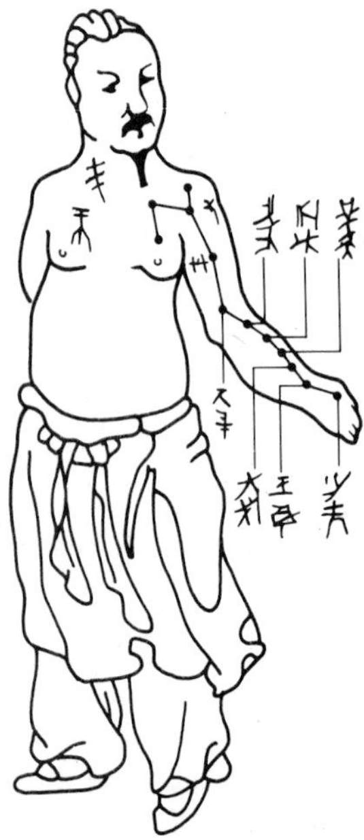

Figure 4.9 A Chinese acupuncture chart showing some sites for insertion of acupuncture needles.

passing electrical current through them, has been reported to produce a profound **analgesia** (elimination of pain without loss of consciousness), which makes it possible to perform major surgery in a totally awake patient (Melzack, 1973). Gate control theory would suggest that the stimulating needles close the gate by activating L-fibers or fibers descending from the brain.

Although certain details of gate control theory are not accepted by everyone (Nathan, 1976), most researchers feel that the way this theory accounts for input from non-pain fibers is a great advance in our understanding of pain perception. Another important development in our understanding of pain perception is the discovery that the nervous system contains **endorphins,** chemicals which are produced by the brain and have analgesic properties closely related to those of opiates such as morphine.

Endorphins

A family of substances called endorphins, ***endogenous (naturally occurring in the body) morphinelike substances,*** have recently been found in the nervous system, and a large body of evidence indicates that these substances have powerful analgesic (pain-reducing) effects (Cannon et al., 1978; Mayer, 1979; Watkins & Mayer, 1982). Some of the evidence supporting this idea follows:

1. Areas in the brain stem have been shown, using biochemical techniques, to be sites where opiates such as morphine act to produce their analgesic effects.
2. Endorphins are found at these **opiate sites.** This suggests that the naturally occurring endorphins act to reduce pain in the same way as do the opiates.
3. Stimulation produced analgesia (SPA, see above) is most effective when administered to the sites that contain endorphins. This suggests that SPA works by releasing endorphins into the nervous system.
4. Injecting **naloxone,** a substance known to inhibit the activity of opiates, into the brain decreases the effect of SPA. This suggests that naloxone inhibits the activity of the endorphins responsible for the effects of SPA.
5. Injecting naloxone into the brain also decreases the effect of acupuncture, thus supporting the idea that acupuncture works by stimulating nerve fibers to cause the release of endorphins.

This evidence strongly suggests that the brain uses endorphins to control pain.

Interestingly, it has also been shown that naloxone decreases the analgesic effect of placebos. Since placebos contain no active chemicals, their effects have always been thought to be "psychological." Apparently, however, the brain causes the placebo's pain reduction effects by releasing endorphins, which may also be responsible for the other psychological effects we described above. The discovery of endorphins also fits well with gate control theory. According to gate control theory, endorphins released by the brain stimulate L-fibers, which then close the gate and thus decrease the perception of pain.

In our discussion of pain we have established some new principles, the most important of which is that perception is not simply determined by signals, triggered in the receptors, that travel uninterrupted to the brain. Many things influence these signals during their journey, and, in the case of pain, signals travel down from the brain, perhaps caused by endorphins responding to psychological influences, that can significantly affect our perception of pain. We will see—especially in Chapter 7, when we discuss how a person's past experiences, or *perceptual set,* can influence visual perception—that similar principles hold for the sense of vision.

In the final section of this chapter, we will discuss touch. We will return to some of the themes introduced in Chapters 2 and 3, and we will note the many similarities in the principles that determine how we see and how we feel touch. We will find in touch, as in vision, that (1) the properties of the receptors influence nerve firing, (2) we can identify receptive fields, and (3) feature detectors respond to specific features of the stimulus.

Touch

How a Receptor's Structure Influences Nerve Firing

In Chapter 2 we saw that receptors play a crucial role in perception, since they transduce environmental energy into the electrical signals that travel along nerve fibers to the brain. In discussing the rod and cone receptors in Chapter 3, we showed that the importance of receptors extends beyond transduction. Properties of the rods and cones, such as the absorption spectra of their visual pigments and the way they are connected to other neurons in the retina, determine our sensitivity to light and our ability to detect details. In the sense of touch, a receptor called the Pacinian corpuscle provides an excellent example of how the properties of a receptor influence nerve firing and, therefore, presumably, perception.

The **Pacinian corpuscle,** shown in Figure 4.10, has been studied extensively because of its distinctive elliptical shape (which makes it easy to identify), its large size (about 1 mm long and 0.6 mm thick), and its accessibility (it is found in the skin, muscles, tendons, and joints, and also in the cat's mesentery, a readily accessible membrane attached to the intestine from which Pacinian corpuscles can easily be removed). Just as their visual pigments determine which wavelengths of light the rod and cone receptors can absorb, so the Pacinian corpuscle's elliptical structure determines the form of the pressure stimulus that reaches the nerve fiber inside the corpuscle.

By calculating how a push on the corpuscle at A (Figure 4.11) is translated into pressure on the nerve fiber at B, Werner Lowenstein and R. Skalak (1966) showed that the Pacinian corpuscle modifies the pressure stimulus on its way to the nerve fibers. Their results indicate that a push at A causes the pressure to change at B only at the beginning or end of the push. Continuing to push with constant pressure causes no effect at B—so as far as the nerve fiber is concerned, no stimulus is present until the pressure at A is released, at which time a brief change occurs in the pressure at B. Thus, the Pacinian corpuscle transmits pressure to the nerve fiber when the stimulus is turned on or off, but it does not transmit pressure that is continuous.

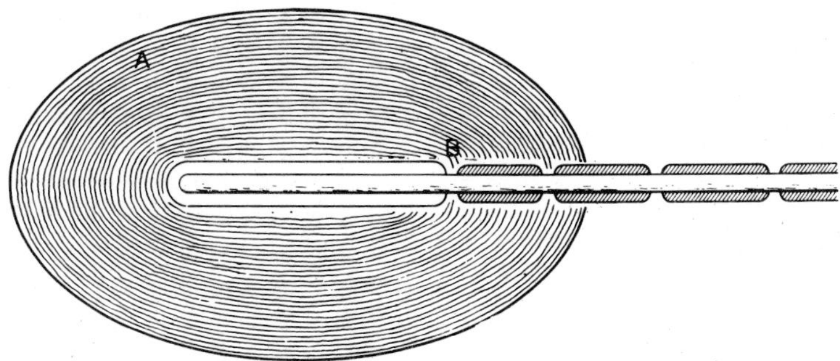

Figure 4.10 A Pacinian corpuscle. (From Lowenstein, 1960.)

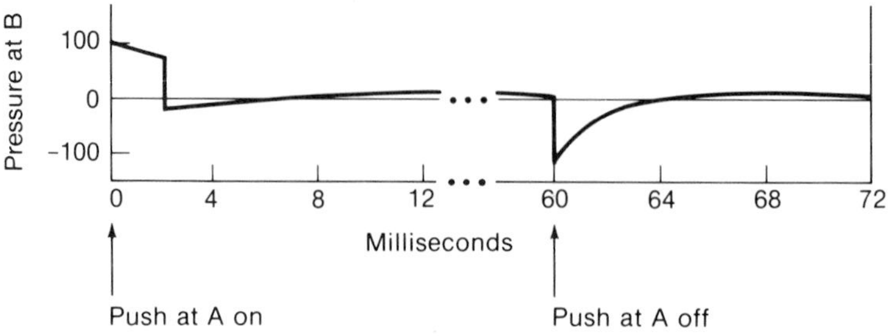

Figure 4.11 Record of the pressure at B, in the Pacinian corpuscle of Figure 4.10, caused by pushing the corpuscle at A. (From Lowenstein & Skalak, 1966).

To show that the corpuscle actually affects the response of the nerve fiber, Lowenstein and Skalak recorded electrical signals from the fiber under two conditions: (1) when the corpuscle was dissected away, so pressure could be applied directly to the nerve fiber, and (2) when the corpuscle remained, so pressure could be applied to the corpuscle. Their results were exactly as predicted in their calculations: when pressure was applied directly to the fiber, it responded when the pressure was first applied, during the time the pressure continued, and when the pressure was removed; however, when pressure was applied to the intact corpuscle, the fiber responded only when the pressure was first applied and when it was removed. Thus, the presence of the Pacinian corpuscle critically affects how the nerve fiber fires: it causes the nerve fiber to fire when the stimulus goes on or off and to not respond when the stimulus is continuous. And, in fact, the Pacinian corpuscle is thought to play a role in our perception of rapid skin vibration (Talbot et al., 1968), as we would expect of a receptor that responds only when a stimulus goes on or off.

Localization and Discrimination on the Skin

In discussing the Pacinian corpuscle, we have been concerned with how a receptor's structure influences how a nerve fiber responds to the onset and offset of stimuli applied to the skin. We are concerned here with how more central processes are responsible for our abilities to locate a stimulus applied to the skin (**localization**) and to differentiate two stimuli (**discrimination**).

Close your eyes and touch one of your fingers; that you can tell which finger you are touching demonstrates localization. Discrimination can be demonstrated by determining the **two-point threshold**—the smallest separation between two points on the skin that is perceived as two points. Hold two pencils side by side, so that their points are about 12 mm (½ inch) apart; then touch both points simultaneously to the tip of your thumb and see if you feel two points. If you feel only one, increase the distance between the pencil points until you feel two; then note the distance between them. Now move the pencil points to the underside of your forearm. With the points about 12 mm apart (or at the smallest separation you felt as two points on your thumb), touch them to your forearm and note whether you feel one point or two. If you feel only one, how much must you increase the separation before you feel two? If your results match those from the laboratory, you will find that the two-point threshold on your forearm is much larger than the two-point threshold on your thumb. Figure 4.12, which shows how the two-point threshold varies at different parts of the body, indicates that the two-point threshold is over 10 times larger on the forearm than on the thumb.

What is the physiological basis for this variation in the two-point threshold at different parts of the body? One approach to answering this question is to look at the nature of the receptive fields of neu-

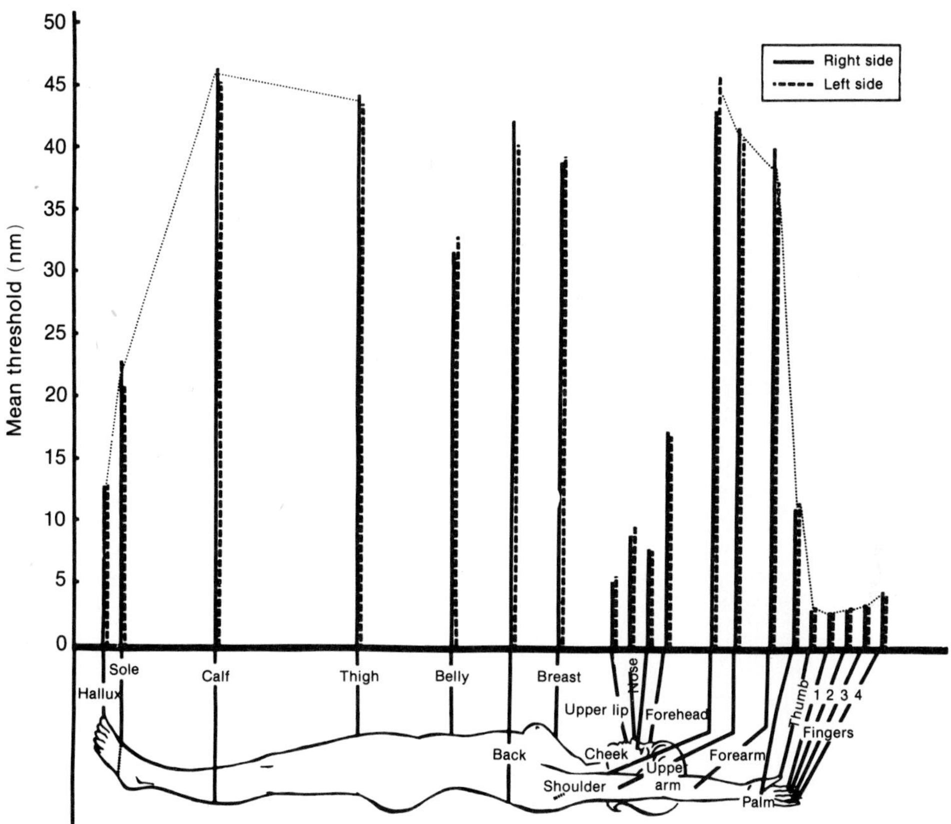

Figure 4.12 Two-point thresholds for females. Two-point thresholds for males follow the same pattern. (From Weinstein, in D. A. Kenshalo, ed., *The Skin Senses,* 1968. Courtesy of Charles C. Thomas, Publisher, Springfield, Ill.)

rons connected to receptors in the skin. Remember, from our discussion in Chapter 2, that the receptive field of a visual neuron is the area on the retina that influences the firing of that neuron. Similarly, the receptive field of a neuron connected to receptors in the skin is the area on the skin that influences the firing of that neuron. Using the technique of **percutaneous recording** (see p. 56), which allows us to record the activity of a single neuron in an awake human, we can determine the neuron's receptive field by stimulating the skin and locating the area on the skin that causes the neuron to fire. A. B. Vallbo and R. S. Johansson (1978) determined the receptive fields of neurons connected to receptors in the hand and fingers. Some were small, like those in Figure 4.13(a), and others were large, like those in Figure 4.13(b). Interestingly, Vallbo and Johansson found a higher density of small receptive fields on the fingertips than on the hand, which we would expect, since the two-point threshold is smaller on the fingertips than on the hand. In fact, Vallbo and Johansson found a direct relationship between the size of the two-point threshold and the density of neurons with small receptive fields (Figure 4.14). Thus, parts of the body responsible for fine spatial discriminations, such as the fingertips, have small two-point thresholds and small receptive fields.

Box 4.2 Two Pathways for Touch

In discussing vision, we saw that there are two systems of receptors—the rods and the cones—with the cone system being well suited to the task of resolving small details, and the rod system being poorly suited to this task. We can draw an analogy between the rod and cone systems in vision and the two major nerve pathways that carry information from the skin to the thalamus and then from the thalamus to the primary receiving area for touch, in the parietal lobe of the brain. The **lemniscal pathway** carries information from the skin to the **ventrobasal nucleus** in the thalamus, and the **spinothalamic pathway** carries information from the skin to the **posterior nucleus** in the thalamus. The difference between these two pathways becomes obvious when we look at the receptive fields of neurons in these two thalamic nuclei.

The figure on the left, below, shows the receptive fields of three neurons in the ventrobasal nucleus (lemniscal pathway), and the figure on the right shows the receptive field of a neuron in the posterior nucleus (spinothalamic pathway). The receptive fields of neurons in the lemniscal system each cover only a small area of the body, whereas the receptive fields of neurons in the spinothalamic system cover large areas of the body. This difference in receptive field size, which also occurs in the cortex, reflects differences in the function of the lemniscal and spinothalamic systems. The lemniscal system is responsible for fine tactile discriminations, such as the two-point threshold, whereas the spinothalamic system is responsible for generalized (that is, nonlocalized) tactile sensitivity. The generalized nature of the spinothalamic system is also indicated by the fact that this system contains fibers involved in the perception of temperature and pain, in addition to fibers involved in the perception of touch (Poggio & Mountcastle, 1960).

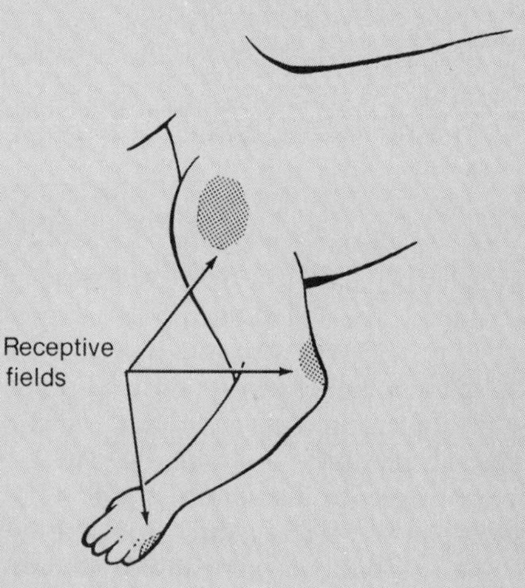

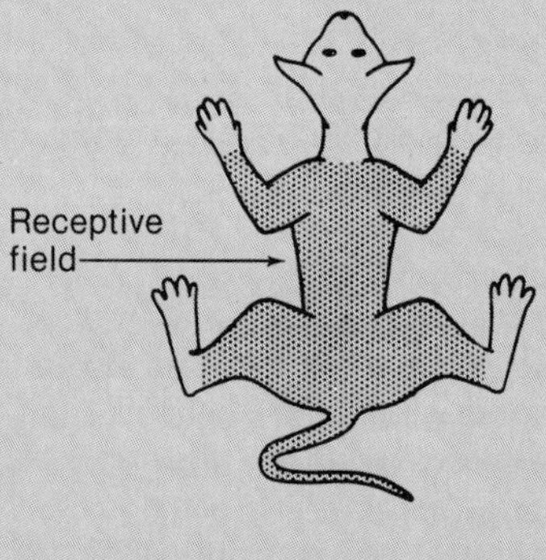

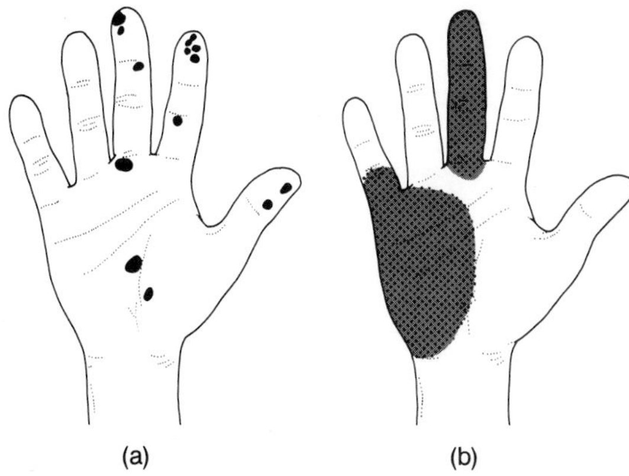

Figure 4.13 Receptive fields of single neurons in the human hand that are sensitive to touch. A number of small receptive fields are shown in (a), and two large receptive fields are shown in (b). (From Vallbo & Johansson, 1978.)

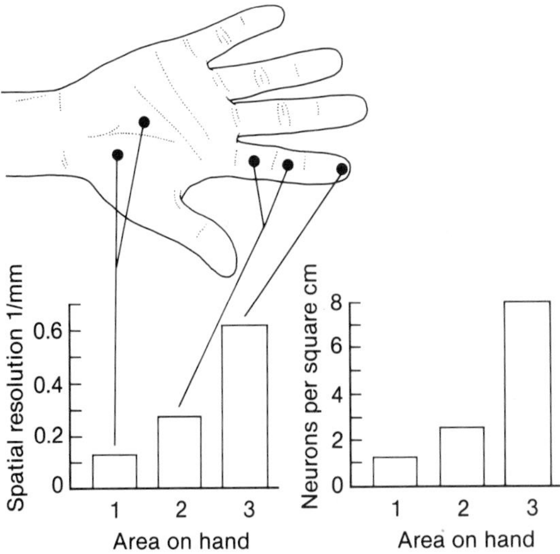

Figure 4.14 Left: the bar graph on the left shows the spatial resolution at three places on the hand and fingers. Spatial resolution, which is determined by taking the inverse of the two-point threshold (so a small two-point threshold results in high spatial resolution), increases as we move from the hand to the fingertips. Right: the density of neurons with small receptive fields at the same three locations. These data indicate that areas with high spatial resolution have high densities of neurons with small receptive fields. (From Vallbo & Johansson, 1978.)

Maps of the Body on the Brain

We can also see a relationship between the two-point threshold and physiology by moving up to the parietal cortex (see Figure 2.11), the cortical area that receives signals from the skin. For each point on the skin, there is a corresponding point or small area on the surface of the parietal cortex, as shown in Figure 4.15. The strangely shaped representation of a person on the cortex is called a **homunculus,** for "little man." Let's first describe how the homunculus is determined and then relate this strange-looking little man to the two-point threshold.

One way to chart the shape of the homunculus is by surgically placing a recording electrode on the brain and then stimulating small points on the body to locate the area which, when stimulated, causes electrical activity under the electrode. This method, called the **evoked potential** method, was used by Clinton Woolsey, Wade Marshall, and Philip Bard (1942) to determine the body map on the cortex of the rhesus monkey. By gently stroking the monkey with a camel's-hair brush and recording the evoked potentials from the cortex, they created a map similar to the one for the human in Figure 4.15. However, the evoked potential method is very time-consuming, requiring 15–40 minutes for each of the many locations on the brain, and is therefore difficult to use with humans. Thus, for humans, the relationship between points on the brain and points on the body was determined by applying a mild shock to a small area of the brain and asking the person to describe where he or she felt a sensation.

The people who allowed their brains to be electrically stimulated to produce Figure 4.15 were patients of neurosurgeons Wilder Penfield and Theodore Rasmussen (1950). Penfield and Rasmussen were operating on these patients to remove brain tumors suspected of causing epileptic seizures. A major problem in this surgery is to remove the tumor without damaging the sensory or motor areas of the brain, which are located right next to each other on either side of the central fissure (see Figure 2.11). Damage to the sensory area would cause a loss of sensation in a part of the body, and damage to the motor area would cause paralysis. Before removing the tumor, therefore, it is necessary to map the sensory and motor areas of the

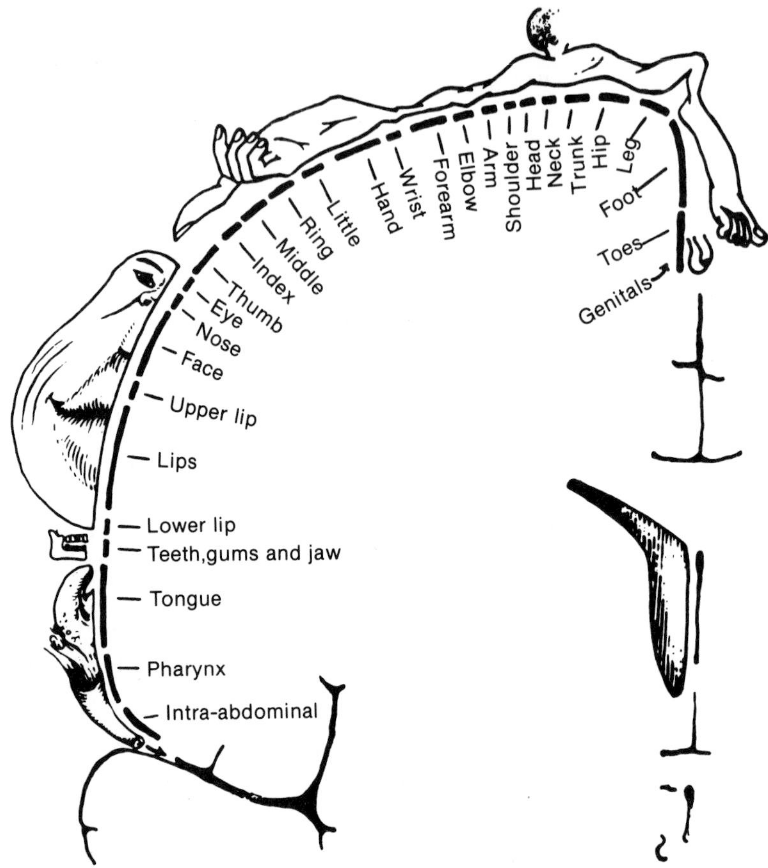

Figure 4.15 The sensory homunculus. (From Penfield & Rasmussen, 1950.)

brain in each patient. This mapping is done by opening the skull under local anesthesia and stimulating the surface of the brain with low-voltage electricity. The person experiences a sensation such as tingling, tickling, or numbness on a body part when stimulation is applied to the sensory area of the cortex, and he or she moves some body part when stimulation is applied to the motor area of the cortex. Only a local anesthetic is used because the patient must be awake to report the location and type of sensation or muscle contraction resulting from stimulation. Since the anesthesia is applied where the skull is cut and since there are no pain receptors in the brain itself, the patient feels no pain when the brain is stimulated.

Figure 4.15, the result of numerous operations performed over a twenty-year period, shows that some areas on the skin seem to be represented by a disproportionately large area on the brain. The area devoted to the thumb, for example, is as large as the area devoted to the entire forearm. (A similar situation exists in the visual system, where the area of the visual cortex devoted to the fovea, which accounts for only a small fraction of the retina's area, is as big as the cortical area devoted to a large area of peripheral vision. The reason for the fovea's distorted representation on the visual cortex is that, although small in terms of its number of receptors, the fovea is large in terms of its function; it is the area of the retina responsible for detail vision, so important in reading and in other tasks involving the perception of details.)

As with the fovea, the apparent overrepresentation of various body parts on the sensory cortex is related to the functioning of these areas. By comparing Figures 4.12 and 4.15, we can note the close relationship between the two-point threshold on the skin and the cortical representation of the skin: areas on the skin with low two-point thresholds are represented by large areas on the cortex. Thus, the map of the body on the brain may look distorted, but the distortions provide the extra neural processing that enables us to accurately sense fine details with our fingers and other parts of the body.

Before leaving our discussion, we should note that recent experiments, in which the homunculus was determined by recording from single neurons in the brains of monkeys, indicate that there is actually more than one map of the body on the brain. R. J. Nelson and co-workers (1980) found that there are at least two, and probably four, separate maps of the monkey's body in the sensory area of its brain. The apparent reason for these multiple representations is that different areas within the sensory cortex have different functions. For example, one area might be specialized for the discrimination of forms and another for the discrimination of textures. Whatever their function, these multiple maps of the body on the brain exhibit the same distortions as our simple homunculus in Figure 4.15—areas of the body that discriminate fine details are allotted large areas on the cortex.

Feature Detectors

So far, our discussion of touch has uncovered many similarities between touch and vision. Further similarities exist in the nature of the receptive fields of neurons that receive signals from the skin. If we record from neurons near the skin, in the medial nerve of the hand, we find receptive fields like the ones shown in Figure 4.13. Touching one of these simple receptive fields causes an increase in the firing rate of its neuron. Figure 4.16 shows the receptive field of a neuron in the monkey's thalamus that receives signals from receptors in the skin of the monkey's arm. This is an excitatory-center, inhibitory-surround receptive field, similar to the center-surround receptive fields of visual neurons in the retina and lateral geniculate nucleus (Mountcastle & Powell, 1959).

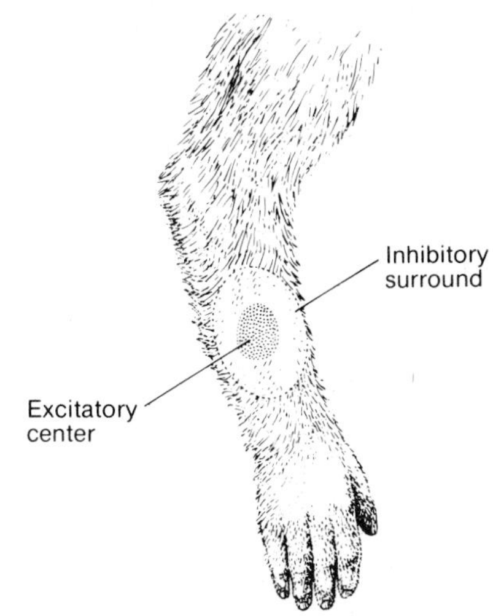

Figure 4.16 An excitatory-center, inhibitory-surround receptive field on the skin of the monkey's arm.

If we move up to the cortex, we find neurons that respond to more specialized stimulation of the skin. Figures 4.17 and 4.18 show the receptive fields

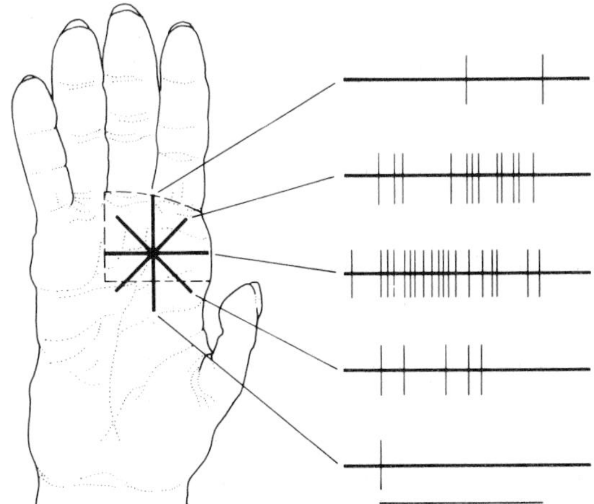

Figure 4.17 The receptive field of a neuron in the monkey's parietal cortex that responds when a metal edge is placed on the hand. This cell responds well when the edge is oriented horizontally but responds less well to other orientations. (From Hyvärinin & Poranen, 1978.)

Box 4.3 Lateral Inhibition on the Skin

Lateral inhibition, which plays such an important role in determining the nature of electrophysiologically determined receptive fields on both the retina (p. 48) and the skin (p. 101), has been demonstrated psychophysically on the skin by Georg von Békésy (1958, 1959, 1967).

The procedure for his demonstration is simple: two small pointers attached to fine hairs are touched to the skin, as shown on the hand at the top of the figure. The points stimulated on the

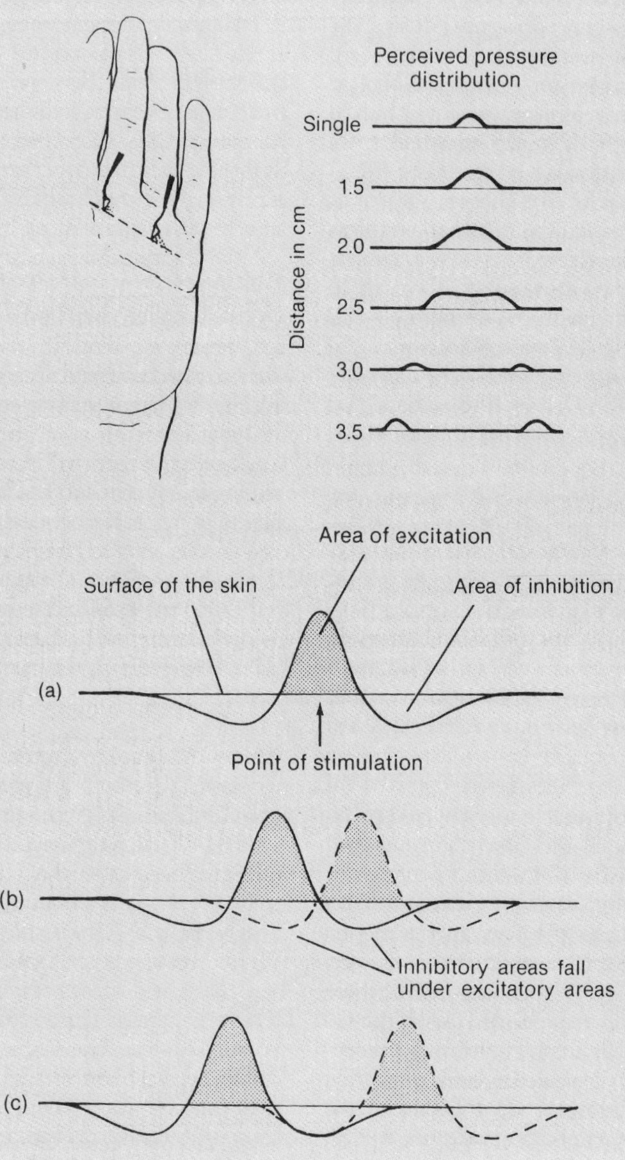

skin are separated by different distances, by varying the separation between the pointers, and the observer is asked to describe the distribution of the pressure sensation at each separation.

The results of this experiment, shown to the right of the hand, indicate that the observer feels a single pressure distribution both when a single hair is pushed into the skin and at separations of 1.5, 2.0, and 2.5 cm. When the two hairs are separated by 3.0 cm, however, the perceived pressure distribution splits in two and is greatly decreased in magnitude. When the separation between the hairs is increased further, to 3.5 cm, the perceived pressure grows so that each point is perceived to be similar to the pressure resulting from the single stimulation.

The large decrease in sensation at the 3.0-cm separation is due to lateral inhibition. We can understand how this works, by looking at diagrams (a), (b), and (c). Diagram (a) shows that pressing on the skin causes an area of excitation near the point of stimulation, and an area of inhibition surrounding the area of excitation. Diagram (b) shows what happens when two points are separated by 3.0 cm. At this separation, the inhibitory areas fall under the excitatory areas and subtract from the excitation, causing a decrease in the sensation of pressure. When the separation between the two points is increased above 3.0 cm, as shown in (c), the inhibitory areas no longer subtract from the excitatory areas, and the sensation of pressure increases. Thus, the perception of pressure on your skin depends on two things: (1) the excitation that surrounds the point of stimulation and (2) the lateral inhibition that surrounds this excitation.

of different neurons in the monkey's parietal cortex; these are quite similar to the receptive fields of simple and complex cells in the visual cortex. The cell in Figure 4.17 responds to a metal edge oriented horizontally but responds less well to other orientations. Figure 4.18 shows a cell that responds to movement across the skin in a specific direction (Hyvärinin & Poranen, 1978; see also Whitsel et al., 1972; Costanzo & Gardner, 1980). The similarity between these neurons and neurons in the visual system is striking; in both vision and touch, neurons near the receptors respond to a wide range of stimuli, whereas neurons in the cortex respond only to more specific stimuli. Similar principles of information processing apparently operate in both vision and touch.

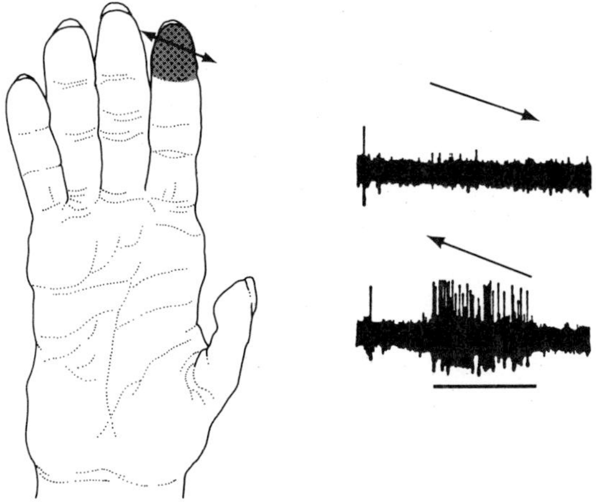

Figure 4.18 The receptive field of a neuron in the monkey's parietal cortex that responds to movement across the fingertip from right to left but does not respond to movement from left to right. (From Hyvärinin & Poranen, 1978.)

One of the more exciting developments in the physiology of touch is the recent finding that some cells in the monkey cortex respond only when the monkey grasps three-dimensional objects with specific shapes. These experiments, carried out in awake, behaving monkeys with implanted electrodes, have uncovered neurons like the one in Figure 4.19, which does not respond when the experimenter stimulates the skin but does respond when the monkey grasps certain objects. This cell responds when the monkey grasps a ruler or a block of wood but does not respond if the monkey grasps a cylinder. The cell in Figure 4.20, on the other hand, responds when the monkey grasps round objects but not when it grasps objects with straight edges. Neurons like these may

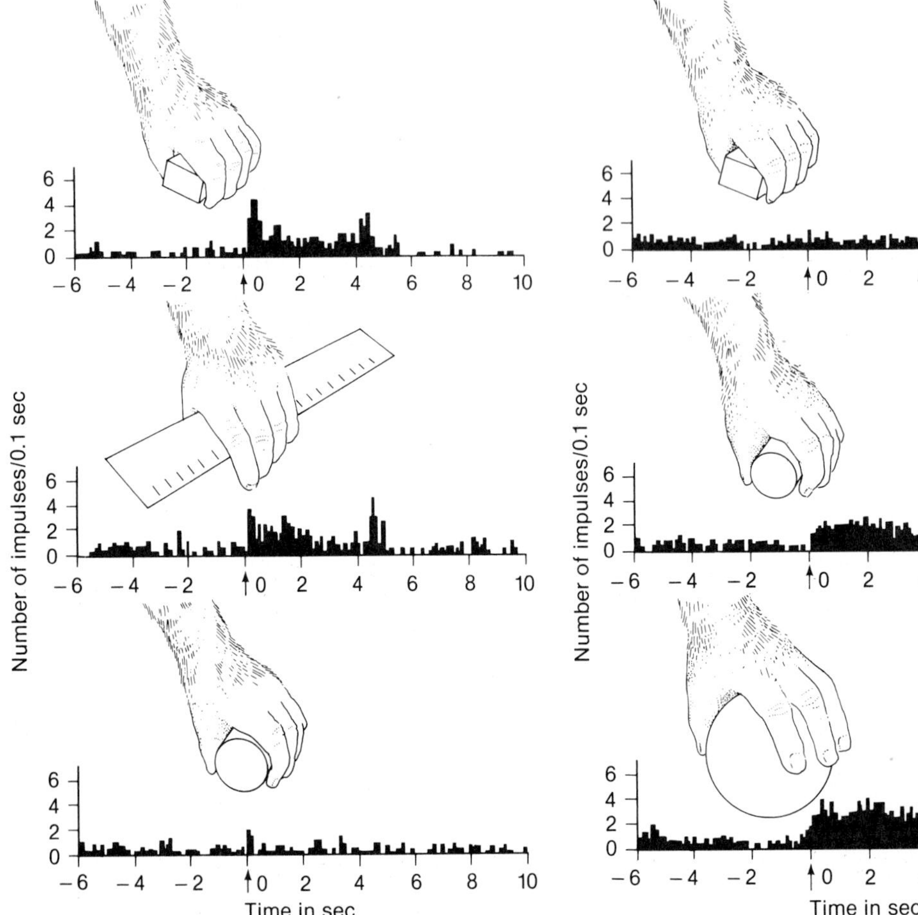

Figure 4.19 The response of a neuron in the monkey's parietal cortex that fires when the monkey grasps a rectangular block or a ruler but does not fire when the monkey grasps a cylinder. The neuron's firing rate is indicated by the height of the bars. The monkey grasps the objects at time = 0. (From Sakata & Iwamura, 1978.)

Figure 4.20 The response of a neuron in a monkey's parietal cortex that fires when the monkey grasps a cylinder or a ball but does not fire when the monkey grasps a rectangular block. (From Sakata & Iwamura, 1978.)

play a role in what has been called **active touch**—touch in which the subject plays an active role in searching out and touching stimuli.

Active Touch

With the exception of the preceding paragraph, our discussion has considered touch in a passive way. Stimulating the skin and recording evoked potentials in the brain involve experimentation on an anesthetized animal or an awake but passive human. Although these methods have yielded much information about the physiological bases of touch, they ignore the large portion of our touch experience that occurs as we interact with our environment. For example, in using our fingers to sense small details, as in reading braille (Box 4.4), or to sense the textures of different materials, we are touching in an active way. In a paper entitled "Observations on Active Touch," J. J. Gibson (1962) described the difference between *being touched*—the passive touch experienced by subjects in most physiological experiments—and *touching*—the active touch we experience in our day-to-day lives.

Perhaps the difference between active and passive touch is best described in terms of our experience. We tend to relate passive touch to the sensation experienced in the *skin,* whereas we tend to relate active touch to the *object* being touched. For example, if someone stimulates your skin with a pointed object, you might say, "I feel a prickling sensation on my skin"; however, if you feel the tip of the pointed object yourself, you might say, "I feel a pointed object" (Kruger, 1970). Another example: if you move your hand over the edges and surfaces of an object (active touch), you do not perceive the object as moving, even though it is moving relative to the skin. If, however, someone else moves an object across your skin (passive touch), you perceive the object moving across your skin.

Though we do not completely understand why these two types of touch result in such different experiences, a number of properties differentiate active from passive touch. An important property of active touch, according to Gibson, is that it is purposive; that is, when you feel something, especially an object with which you are unfamiliar, your purpose is to determine its shape. Just as you visually scan a scene by looking at its most interesting or important areas, you feel an object by touching the parts that contain information about its shape. This purposive character may be important in determining the experience of active touch.

In addition to its purposive aspect, active touch includes other properties absent from passive touch. As you feel something, you stimulate receptors not only in the skin but also in the joints and tendons that are activated as you move your fingers or hands over an object, whereas passive touch stimulates only the receptors in the skin. Moving your fingers over an object to determine its shape or texture enables you to perceive both the "touch" that occurs when a stimulus is applied to passive skin and the sounds that occur when skin moves actively over a surface. Consider the different sounds that result from touching different materials, by gently moving your fingers over a smooth surface, such as the top of your desk, and over slightly rougher surfaces, such as a page of this book or your clothes. You perceive a different sound from each material and combine this with your other perceptions to form an overall perception of the nature of the object you are touching (Taylor, Lederman, & Gibson, 1973).

The difference between passive and active touch is analogous to the difference between observing a briefly flashed stimulus while fixating on a point and freely observing a complex scene. The complexity of active touch is one reason that few experiments have been done in this area. In one experiment, Gibson (1962) found that if subjects actively feel cookie cutters of various shapes, they are able to correctly identify the shape 95 percent of the time, but if the cookie cutters are pushed onto their skin by someone else, they can correctly identify the shape only 49 percent of the time. Gibson concluded that active touch is superior to passive touch for obtaining information about the shapes of objects.

However, a dissenting view was expressed by A. S. Schwartz and co-workers (1975), who repeated Gibson's cookie cutter experiment, with one change. Schwartz used two different passive conditions. In one condition, he repeated Gibson's procedure, in which the cookie cutter was pressed onto the subject's palm, but in the other condition, he had the subject stick out his finger and feel the shape as the experimenter moved the edges of the cookie cutter across his finger. Schwartz, like Gibson, found that subjects had a hard time identifying the objects pushed into their palm by the experimenter; but Schwartz also found that when he moved the cookie cutter over the subjects' outstretched (but passive) fingers, they correctly identified the shape 93 percent of the time. Thus, Schwartz argues that although the subjective experiences of active and passive touch may be different, passive touch can provide information about a stimulus equal to that of active touch, as long as the stimulus is moved across the subject's skin. According to Schwartz, movement across the skin, not purposiveness, is what is important for discriminating shapes.

Box 4.4 Braille

What would you perceive if you ran your fingers over raised dots arranged in the pattern shown at right? You would probably perceive a bunch of raised dots! However, a person who reads **braille** would perceive the words *active touch*. The ability of the blind to read by moving their fingers over braille is an impressive example of how information can be taken in by active touch. A braille *character* consists of a *cell* made up of from one to six dots. Different arrangements of dots and blank spaces are used to represent the alphabet, as shown, and in addition to characters for each letter of the alphabet, there are also characters for numbers, punctuation marks, and common speech sounds and words.

Braille was invented by a blind Frenchman, Louis Braille, in 1824. At that time, the only reading materials available to blind people were a few books that were printed by embossing the shapes of conventional letters onto the page. These books, however, were rarely read, because each letter had to be tediously scanned in order to synthesize its complete shape. The dots of braille eliminated this problem, and braille and other raised-dot systems introduced during the 1800s gained wide popularity among the blind.

The average reading rate for experienced braille readers is about 104 words per minute, although some expert braille readers can read at rates of up to 125 words per minute. Experienced braille readers identify characters as a whole, by a kind of "tactile Gestalt" (Critchley, 1953), and Carson Nolan and Cleves Kederis (1969) have suggested that the basic unit of braille perception is the individual braille character. They base this suggestion on the results of experiments in which they determined the recognition times for individual characters and for words made up of a number of characters. They found that it takes 50–150 percent longer to identify a word than to identify all the individual characters making up the word; therefore, they concluded that the time to identify a word is made up of the time needed to individually identify each character *plus* the time needed to integrate the information derived from the recognition of each character.

This does not mean, however, that braille readers only make use of the information in the individual characters. Some of the other factors involved in braille reading are: (1) word familiarity—familiar words are recognized more rapidly than unfamiliar words; (2) content familiarity—familiar material is read faster than unfamiliar material or nonsense words; (3) knowledge of the basic properties of English spelling—knowing that the letter *q* is always followed by a *u* or that *j* is never followed by *b, c, d, f, g, j, k, l, q, r, t, v, w, x, y,* or *z* makes it possible to spend less time on some of the characters than on others; (4) experience with English syntax—a reader knows that the word following *in the event* is much more likely to be *that* than *dog*. The effect of familiarity with spelling patterns is demonstrated by the fact that braille readers read nonsense words that fol-

Summary

1. The skin serves a number of functions, of which the most important to us is to provide information about stimuli that contact the skin. This information is provided by receptors in the dermis.

2. A *mechanical substitution system* has been developed that enables blind people to detect environmental properties by sensing vibrational patterns on the skin.

3. Von Frey proposed that specific receptor structures are responsible for our perception of warmth, cold, touch, and pain. This pairing of receptor structures with perception, however, has not been supported by experiments.

4. Pattern theory states that the skin signals sensory quality by the pattern of impulses from a large number of fibers. Many researchers feel, however, that pattern theory is too vague to be useful.

5. During the last 25 years, electrophysiological

low the rules of English spelling (for example, *funts* and *lods*) more rapidly and accurately than words that violate these rules (for example, *ntsuf* and *dsol*) (Pick et al., 1966).

The above factors make it possible for experienced braille readers to identify words before they have touched all the characters (Nolan & Kederis, 1969) and to read using a continuous smooth movement of the fingers across the page, rarely pausing on any one character (Kusajima, 1974). The perception of braille depends both on the information contained in the individual characters and on the context in which these characters occur.

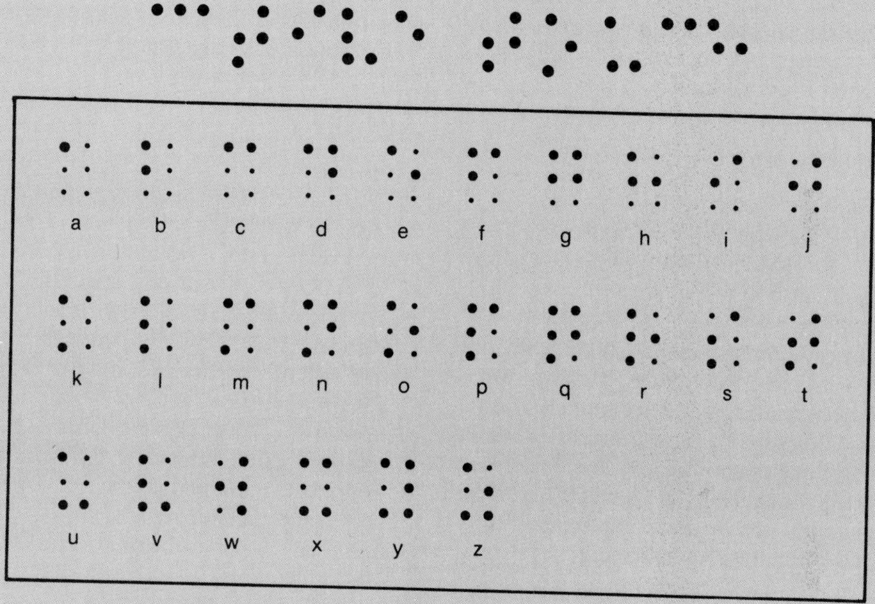

Box 4.4 The Braille Alphabet

evidence has shown that certain fibers respond only to specific stimuli, such as stimuli that cool, warm, or damage the skin.

6. Sensory quality on the skin is determined, in part, by the firing pattern of numerous fibers that respond to specific stimuli.
7. The perception of pain can be elicited by many different types of stimulation and is often accompanied by emotional reactions.
8. The perception of pain is determined not only by the firing of pain receptors but also by such factors as a person's culture, previous experience, and the general situation in which the pain stimulus occurs.
9. Gate control theory proposes that the neural signals which cause the perception of pain must pass through a neural circuit, called a gate control system, before being transmitted to the brain.
10. Electrical stimulation of specific areas in the brain can cause a reduction of pain perception called *stimulation produced analgesia*.

11. Gate control theory can explain the reduction in pain achieved by acupuncture.

12. Endorphins are chemicals which are produced in the brain and have powerful analgesic effects. Thus, the brain has an internal mechanism for controlling pain, and this mechanism may be responsible for the pain reduction effected by placebos and acupuncture. Also, endorphins may be involved in the operation of the gate control mechanism.

13. The Pacinian corpuscle acts as a *mechanical filter,* so that its nerve fiber responds only at the onset and offset of stimulation.

14. Localization is the ability to locate a stimulus applied to the skin. Discrimination is the ability to differentiate two stimuli on the skin.

15. The size of the two-point threshold differs on different parts of the body. Areas on the body with small two-point thresholds have fibers with small receptive fields.

16. The sensory homunculus, a map of the body surface on the parietal cortex, has been determined by measuring evoked potentials in monkeys and by stimulating the brains of awake humans. Both methods show that body parts important for making fine tactile discriminations, as indicated by small two-point thresholds, have large representations on the cortex.

17. The perception of pressure on the skin is affected by lateral inhibition.

18. The receptive fields of neurons that receive signals from the skin share many properties with the receptive fields of visual neurons. Some neurons near the skin have center-surround receptive fields, and some neurons in the cortex are feature detectors, which respond only to stimuli oriented in, or moving in, a particular direction. Recently, it has been found that some neurons in the monkey's cortex respond only when an awake monkey grasps stimuli with specific shapes.

19. There are two pathways that carry information from the skin to the thalamus and then to the cortex. The receptive fields of neurons in the lemniscal pathway are small, whereas the receptive fields of neurons in the spinothalamic pathway are large.

20. Most laboratory experiments involve passive touch, in which stimuli are applied to the skin of a passive observer. In contrast, active touch involves an observer who seeks out stimuli in the environment. The subjective experiences resulting from passive and active touch are different.

21. Braille is a system of raised dots that enables blind people to read. Reading braille is an example of active touch.

Glossary

Active touch Touch in which the subject plays an active role in searching out and touching stimuli, usually with his or her hands. (104)

Acupuncture A procedure in which fine needles are inserted into the skin at specific points. Twirling these needles, or passing electrical current through them, can cause analgesia. (93)

Analgesia The elimination of pain without loss of consciousness. (94)

Braille A system of raised dots in which different patterns of dots stand for different letters of the alphabet. Blind people can read by feeling these dots with their fingertips. (106)

Cold fiber A nerve fiber that responds to decreases in temperature or to steady low temperatures. (88)

Dermis The inner layer of skin; it contains numerous nerve endings and receptors. (85)

Discrimination In the skin senses, discrimination refers to the ability to discriminate one thing from another, based on touch. One example of discrimination is the ability to sense two separate points of stimulation when the skin is stimulated by two points that are close together. *See also* Two-point threshold. (96)

Endorphins Chemicals which are produced by the brain and have analgesic properties closely related to those of opiates such as morphine. (94)

Epidermis The outer layer of the skin—actually, several layers of tough dead skin cells. (85)

Evoked potential The electrical response of the brain, as recorded by relatively large electrodes that pick up activity from large numbers of neurons. (99)

Free nerve ending A nerve ending without a receptor that, according to Max von Frey, signals the sensation of pain. (86)

von Frey's theory Max von Frey proposed that the Ruffini receptors signal warmth; Krause end bulbs, cold; Meissner corpuscles, touch; and free nerve endings, pain. (86)

Gate control theory Melzak and Wall's idea that our perception of pain is controlled by a neural circuit that takes into account the relative amount of activity in large-diameter (L) fibers and small-diameter (S) fibers. (93)

Glabrous skin Hairless skin. Found on the fingers, palms of the hands, toes, and soles of the feet. (85)

Hairy skin The type of skin that covers most of the body. (85)

Homunculus "Little man." Refers to the map of the body on the parietal cortex. (99)

Krause end bulb A receptor that, according to Max von Frey, signals the sensation of cold. (86)

Large-diameter (L) fibers According to gate control theory, activity in L-fibers closes the gate control mechanism and therefore decreases the perception of pain. (93)

Lateral inhibition In the skin, stimulation at one point causes an area of excitation immediately surrounding that point and an area of inhibition surrounding the area of excitation. This inhibition is lateral because it spreads laterally from the point of stimulation. (102)

Lemniscal pathway Touch pathway to the ventrobasal nucleus. Receptive fields are small. (98)

Localization In the skin senses, the ability to tell where on the body a touch stimulus is being applied. (96)

Mechanical substitution system A system that translates the pattern of light and dark in the environment into patterns of tactile stimulation on a person's back. (87)

Meissner corpuscle A receptor that, according to Max von Frey, signals the sensation of touch. (86)

Naloxone A substance that inhibits the activity of opiates. It is hypothesized that naloxone also inhibits the activity of endorphins. (94)

Nociceptor A receptor (fiber) that responds to stimuli that damage tissue. (88)

Opiate sites Sites in the brain stem where opiates such as morphine act to produce analgesic effects. (94)

Pacinian corpuscle A receptor with a distinctive elliptical shape; it transmits pressure to the nerve fiber inside it only at the beginning or end of the pressure stimulus. (95)

Pattern theory The idea that sensations felt through the skin are signaled by the spatial and temporal pattern of nerve impulses in a large number of nerve fibers. (85)

Percutaneous recording A technique which makes it possible to record from a single nerve fiber that responds to touch stimuli in the awake human. (97)

Placebo A substance which a person believes will relieve symptoms such as pain but which, unknown to the person, contains no chemicals that actually act on these symptoms. (92)

Posterior nucleus Nucleus that receives input from the spinothalamic pathway. (98)

Ruffini ending A receptor that, according to Max von Frey, signals the sensation of warmth. (86)

Sensory spots Spots on the skin, stimulation of which results in one specific sensation. For example, stimulation of a "warm" spot results only in the sensation of warmth. (86)

Small-diameter (S) fiber According to gate control theory, activity in S-fibers opens the gate control mechanism and therefore increases the perception of pain. (93)

Specificity theory The idea that sensations felt through the skin are signaled by the activity in nerve fibers that respond only to specific stimuli. Von Frey's theory is an example of a specificity theory. (85)

Spinothalamic pathway Touch pathway to the posterior nucleus. Receptive fields are large. (98)

Stimulation produced analgesia (SPA) Brain stimulation that eliminates or strongly decreases the perception of pain. (93)

Substantia gelantinosa (SG) A nucleus in the spinal cord that, according to gate control theory, receives inputs from S-fibers and L-fibers and sends inhibition to the T-cell. (93)

Transmission (T) cell According to gate control

theory, the transmission cell receives inputs from the L- and S-fibers. Activity in the T-cell determines the perception of pain. (93)

Two-point threshold The smallest separation between two points on the skin that is perceived as two points. (96)

Ventrobasal nucleus Nucleus that receives input from the lemniscal pathway. (98)

Warm fiber A nerve fiber that responds to increases in temperature or to steady high temperatures. (88)

Chapter Five

Seeing Colors

Ewald H. Hering
(1834–1918)

Hermann Ludwig F. von Helmholtz
(1821–94)

Color is perhaps the most obvious visual quality that humans experience, and the one with which we are most actively involved. We make decisions about color whenever we decide what clothes to wear, or when we decorate a room, paint a house, or select the color for a new car. We are affected by color when a room's color scheme affects our mood or when the color of a package on the grocery store shelf influences us to buy the product in the package. We might enjoy the colors of an abstract painting or a sunset, or think that certain colors are prettier than others, but before we can make decisions about colors or be affected by them in the ways described above, we must perceive them.

It is the perception of colors that will concern us in this chapter. We will first consider the psychophysics of color, by asking questions such as: What do we mean when we say that we perceive a color? Does everyone perceive colors in the same way? How is our perception of color affected by the surroundings or by the illumination? We will then return to the physiological approach of previous chapters and ask: How does changing the wavelength of a light cause us to perceive different colors? To answer this question, we will describe two theories of color vision, and we will see that each one provides a partial answer. In combination, these theories explain many of the facts of color vision.

Defining Color

If a friend who is completely color-blind asked you to define the word *color,* what would you say? Stop for a moment and think. When you consider your response, you appreciate the difficulty of defining *color* without using examples. *Webster's* dictionary (1956) contains the following definition of *color:* "color (kul-er) n. 1. A quality of visible phenomena, distinct from form and from light and shade, such as the red of blood." Notice that the example of *red* is crucial to this definition of *color.* Or note definition 2: "A sensation evoked as a response to the stimulation of the eye and its attached nervous mechanisms by radiant energy of certain wavelengths and intensities. . . . Hue is that attribute in respect to which colors may be described as red, yellow, green, or blue." Again, *color* is defined by using the example of *red, yellow, green, or blue.* If we try looking up a specific color, such as *blue,* we find the following definition: "blue (bloo) n. 1. Any of several colors whose hue is or resembles that of the zenith of the clear sky; any color in that portion of the color spectrum lying between green and violet (reddish blue)." Again the dictionary resorts to an example, defining *blue* in terms of the color of the sky or its relationship to other colors in the spectrum.

If we can define color only by examples, we cannot help a color-blind person understand what it is like to experience color. By telling someone who is completely color-blind (and therefore sees only in shades of grey) that the sky is blue, you are saying that you experience blue when you look at the sky, but you don't convey the quality of that experience. A similar situation exists for partially color-blind people, who see some colors but not as many as a person with normal color vision. If such a person says that the sky looks blue, does he or she see the same blue as you? Probably not. The color-blind person might, in fact, be perceiving a color that you call *green* but that he or she has learned to call *blue,* since *blue* is the generally accepted name for the color of the sky. These examples illustrate that ***the perception of color is a private experience.*** We can't share the essence of experiencing "blue" with someone who has never perceived "blue" or who may perceive "blue" differently than we do.[1]

What does the privateness of the experience of color mean for people with normal color vision? It may mean that, despite our assumptions to the contrary, we actually perceive colors differently. Experiments in which people are asked to name colors suggest that we may differ in what we see, just as we differ in height, weight, reaction time, or any other measurable characteristic. This idea is supported by an experiment in which observers were shown a visible spectrum (like the one in Color Plate 1.1) and were asked to indicate which part of the spectrum appeared to be the purest orange, the purest yellow, the purest green, and so on (Chapanis, 1965). The results of this experiment indicate that individual observers make these judgments very

[1]This privacy of perception holds not only for color but for all other subjective experiences as well. Thus, just as we can't share the essence of experiencing blue with someone who has never experienced blue, we also can't share the essence of being touched or tickled, or smelling a rose, or tasting an apple, or hearing music, with someone who has never experienced these things.

reliably (that is, observers repeat their judgments very accurately) but that large differences exist between observers. One observer might say that the purest green is a 500-nm light, while another says that the purest green is a 505-nm light. A third observer might say that a 560-nm light looks yellowish green, while a fourth says that the same light looks bluish green. Do these observers perceive colors differently? Maybe or maybe not. These results indicate either that the observers perceive colors differently *or* that they perceive them in the same way but call them by different names.

Thus, although the color-naming experiment above may suggest that people with normal color vision experience colors differently, the private nature of such experience makes it impossible to know whether this is so. In the remainder of this discussion, we will, therefore, usually ignore the possibility that all people may differ somewhat in how they perceive colors. We will assume that observers with normal color vision perceive colors in approximately the same way, and we will devote our attention to describing some of the properties of color.

How Many Colors Can We See?

The above question can be answered in a number of different ways. One approach is to start at one end of the visible spectrum (see Color Plate 1.1) and slowly increase the wavelength until the observer indicates that he or she can discriminate a difference in color. When we do this, we find that observers can discriminate about 150 steps between 380 and 700 nm. We can, however, multiply these 150 discriminable colors in two ways. (1) We can vary the intensity of each step. Changing the intensity usually changes the **brightness** of the color (though we will see in Chapters 9 and 10 that brightness can be controlled by other factors, in addition to intensity). (2) We can vary the **saturation** of each step. If we start with a 640-nm light, which appears red, and then add white to it, we say that the resulting pink color is less saturated than the original red. Saturation is inversely related to the amount of whiteness in a color; that is, the more saturated a color, the less whiteness it contains. Taking into account the fact that each of the 150 discriminable colors can have many values of brightness and saturation, one investigator calculated that we can discriminate over 7 million different colors!

Another approach to determining the number of colors we can see is to ask how many color names there are. The worlds of advertising, paint manufacturing, and cosmetics expose us to such names as crushed strawberry, azure blue, Kelly green, and Chinese red. Although the ingenious names invented to describe different shades of paint, lipstick, floor tile, and fabric may not be as high as 7 million, it is still impressively high. One compilation, published by the National Bureau of Standards, lists 7,500 different color names (Judd & Kelly, 1965).

Obviously, 7 million or even 7,500 are far too many colors for us to deal with, so color scientists prefer to deal with just a few basic colors. The smallest list of basic colors has been proposed by Leo Hurvich (1981), who states that we can describe all the colors we can discriminate by using only six terms and their combinations. These terms are red, yellow, green, and blue, for the **chromatic colors,** and black and white, for the **achromatic colors.**[2] In this chapter we will focus on chromatic colors, leaving our discussion of achromatic colors for Chapters 9 and 10.

Though many schemes have been proposed to describe the relationships between different colors, perhaps the most straightforward is the color circle, shown in Figure 5.2 and Color Plate 5.1. To create a color circle, we arrange colors so that each color is perceptually similar to the color next to it. Thus, as we move around the circle, we see the colors change gradually from one to the next, and, since the colors are arranged in a circle, we eventually get back to where we started.

Hurvich describes the experience of moving around the circle in this way: if we start with red at twelve o'clock and move clockwise around the circle, the colors become increasingly yellowish, passing through various shades of orange, until we reach pure yellow at three o'clock. We call this pure yellow

[2]Another way to distinguish between colors such as red, yellow, green, and blue and colors such as black and white is to say that red, yellow, green, and blue have **hue,** whereas black and white are hueless. Thus, we should really use the term ***hue,*** rather than ***color,*** to refer to the chromatic colors. In everyday usage, however, these words have the same meaning. Since we say that "the color of the fire engine is red" rather than "the hue of the fire engine is red," we will use the word ***color*** to mean ***hue*** throughout the rest of this chapter.

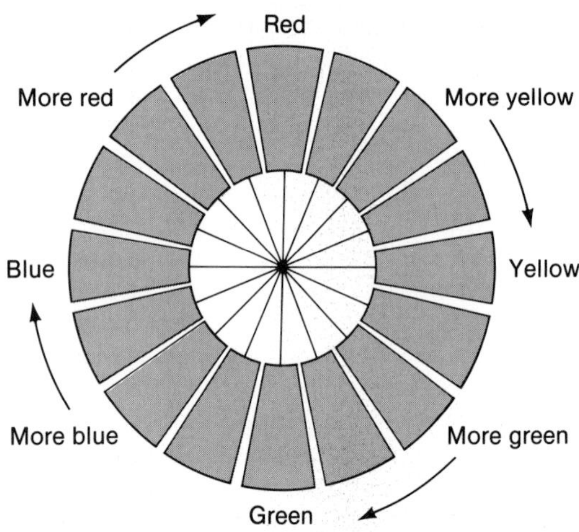

Figure 5.2 The color circle. This circle, shown in color in Color Plate 5.1, arranges colors by placing perceptually similar colors next to each other. When we do this, we find that the colors can be arranged in a circle. The four pure (or unique) colors are found at 12, 3, 6, and 9 o'clock on the circle.

because it contains no trace of the red we just left or of the green we approach as we move further around the circle. As we continue around the circle, colors become greener, until we reach pure green at six o'clock. After green, blue becomes stronger, until we reach pure blue at nine o'clock; then the blue turns to violet as red begins to reappear, until we arrive back at pure red at the top of the circle. Though we encounter many different colors as we travel around the circle, we can see from this way of organizing colors that all chromatic colors can be considered to consist of various proportions of the four basic colors: red, yellow, green, and blue.

What Determines Color Perception?

Our perception of color is determined by many different factors. In this section, we will see how the wavelength of light reflected by an object, the surroundings, the observer's state of adaptation, and the illumination influence our perception of color.

Wavelength

The logical place to begin a discussion of **wavelength** is with Sir Isaac Newton at Cambridge University in 1704. When Newton placed a prism so that sunlight shining through a hole in the shutter of his room window entered the prism, he found that the light leaving the prism formed a spectrum of colors like the one in Color Plate 1.1. When Newton recombined the colors of his spectrum with a lens, the result was the white light with which he started. On the basis of this and other experiments, Newton concluded that sunlight is made up of each of the spectral colors. Later work showed that these spectral colors differed in wavelength, with wavelengths between about 400 and 450 nm appearing violet; 450–500 nm, blue; 500–570, green; 570–590, yellow; 590–620, orange; and 620–700, red. Thus, knowing the wavelength of a light gives us a good idea of its color.

In our everyday experience, however, we are rarely exposed to single wavelengths. Light sources that illuminate the objects in our environment give off many different wavelengths, and the objects reflect many wavelengths into our eyes. Let's first describe the wavelengths given off by our three main sources of light: the sun, light bulbs, and fluorescent lights.

Figure 5.3 is a graph of the **wavelength distribution** of sunlight and of light from a tungsten light bulb. The wavelength distribution for sunlight is relatively flat, indicating that sunlight contains an approximately equal intensity of each wavelength across the spectrum. Such light is called **white light.** The wavelength distribution of light given off by fluorescent bulbs (not shown here) is approximately white, although the wavelengths emitted by a fluorescent bulb depend on the gases inside the bulb, and, since bulbs made by different companies usually contain different gases, they usually have different wavelength distributions. The wavelength distribution for light emitted by conventional light bulbs, called *tungsten* light after the bulb's tungsten filament, is much more intense at long wavelengths than at short wavelengths, as indicated by the dashed line in the figure.

Light from sources such as the sun or light bulbs can reach our eyes directly if we look at the light sources (not recommended in the case of the sun!),

Box 5.1 Rainbows

The principles underlying Newton's production of the colors of the spectrum in his room at Cambridge University and Mother Nature's production of the colors of the spectrum in rainbows are similar. Newton produced his spectrum by passing white light through a prism, and nature produces her spectrum by passing white light through tiny drops of rain that act like prisms. If the sun is behind the observer and lies low in the sky, so that it is at the correct angle relative to the raindrops, each drop of rain becomes a miniature prism and refracts light, as shown in the figure. White light entering the raindrop is separated into all the spectral colors, with the shortest wavelengths following the dashed lines and the longest wavelengths following the solid lines.

If you look at how the short and long wavelengths are refracted from a single raindrop, you might think that, since the short wavelengths are refracted to a position above the long wavelengths, you would see blue on top of the rainbow and red on the bottom. However, if we consider the relationship between the rays of light and the observer's eye, we see that the opposite is true.

Look at the upper raindrop in the figure. This raindrop, which is located at the top of the rainbow, refracts the blue and red rays so that the blue ray passes over the observer's head and the red ray enters the observer's eye. The lower raindrop does the opposite; the red ray passes below the observer and the blue ray enters the observer's eye. Thus, red is seen in the drops at the top of the rainbow and blue is seen in the drops at the bottom, with the other colors of the spectrum seen in between.

This explanation of how rainbows work also helps us understand why we can never find the pot of gold at the end of the rainbow. To see the rainbow, the angle between the rays from the sun that enter the raindrops and the rays from the raindrops that enter the observer's eye must be about 42 degrees. Unfortunately for those of us who would like that pot of gold, it is impossible to be at the end of the rainbow and at the same time still achieve an angle of 42 degrees between the rays of the sun and the rays reflected from the raindrops into our eyes.

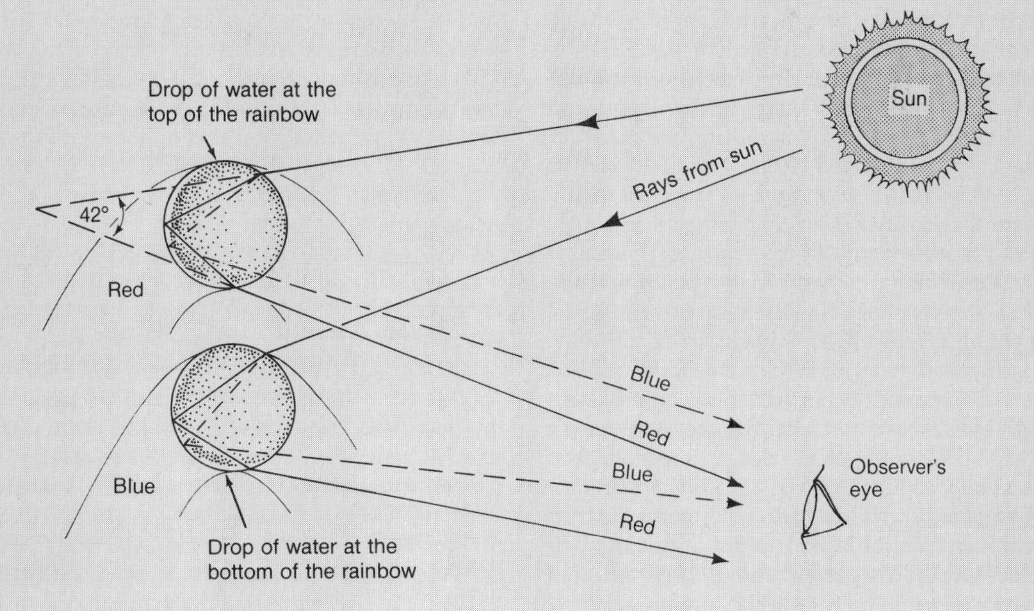

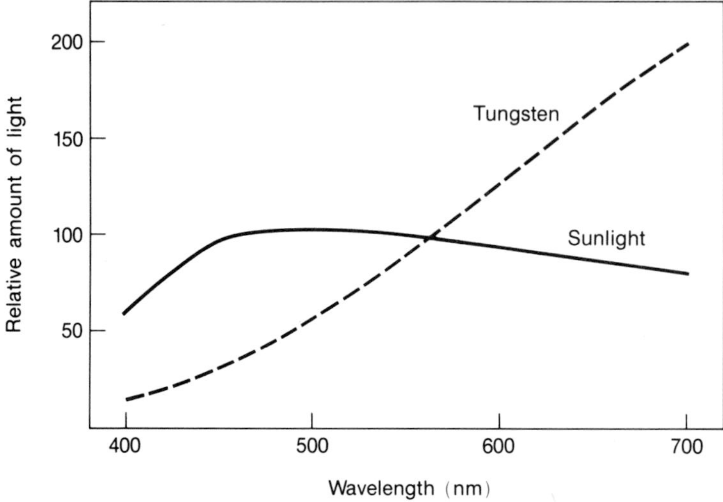

Figure 5.3 The wavelength distribution of sunlight and of light from a tungsten light bulb. (Based on data from Judd et al., 1964, and Wyszecki & Stiles, 1967.)

but most of the light we see is reflected from objects in the environment. To understand why objects have different colors, we must look at the **reflectance curves** of the objects themselves. Reflectance curves for some pigments and common objects are shown in Figures 5.4, 5.5, and 5.6. These curves show the percentage of light of each wavelength that is reflected by these pigments or objects when they are illuminated by white light. (Later in this chapter, we will consider the effect of illuminating objects with light that is not white.) Notice that each pigment or object reflects a wide band of wavelengths. As indicated in Figure 5.4, white paper reflects equally all wavelengths from 400 to 700 nm. This equal reflection of all wavelengths in the spectrum makes sense if we remember Newton's experiment, which showed that white light is made up of all visible wavelengths. A grey card and black paper also equally reflect all wavelengths but reflect less of each wavelength than the white paper: the grey card reflects about 23 percent of each wavelength; the black paper reflects only about 5 percent of each wavelength.

The objects with the reflectance curves in Figures 5.5 and 5.6, however, do not reflect all wavelengths equally. They reflect some wavelengths but absorb others. This property, called **selective reflection,** is shared by all objects that have a hue, or chromatic color, and the reflectance curves show that the region of the spectrum reflected determines the object's color. The relationship between the wavelengths reflected and the color perceived is indicated in Table 5.1, below.

The objects we have talked about so far reflect some wavelengths and absorb the rest, but what about translucent things such as liquids, plastics, and glasses? The relationship between wavelengths and color shown here also holds for translucent

Table 5.1
Relationship between color perceived and wavelengths reflected

Predominant wavelengths reflected	*Perceived color*
Short	Blue
Medium	Green
Long	Red
Long and medium	Yellow
Long and a little medium	Orange
Long and short	Purple
Long, medium, and short	White

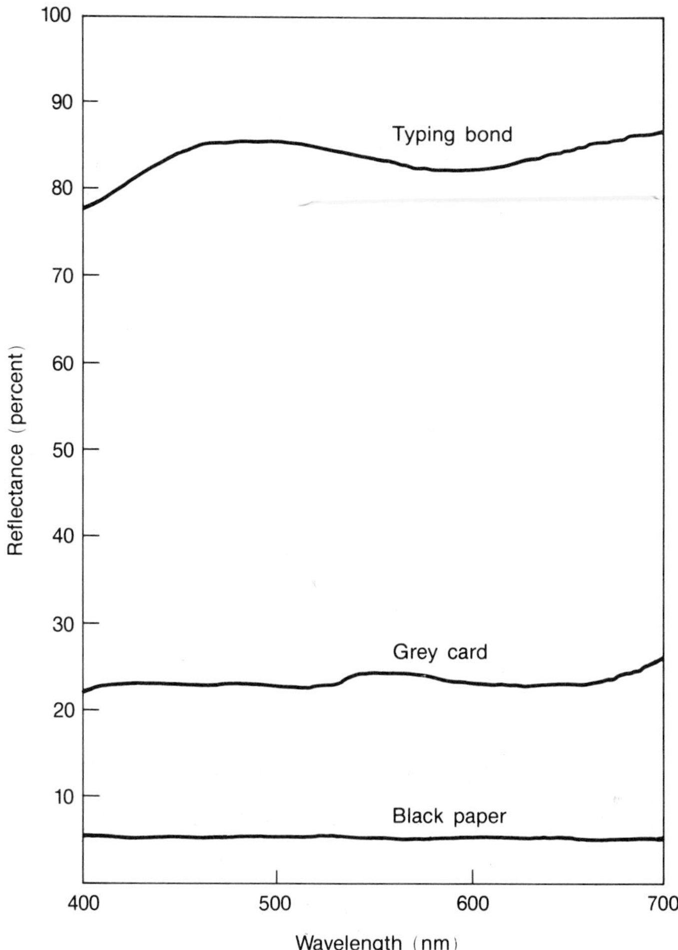

Figure 5.4 Reflectance curves for surfaces that appear white, grey, and black. (Adapted from Clulow, 1972.)

objects, except that they transmit rather than reflect light, and if they selectively transmit certain wavelengths, they appear colored. For example, cranberry juice selectively transmits long-wavelength light and appears red, while limeade selectively transmits medium-wavelength light and appears green.

Although the wavelength distribution of light reflected from or transmitted through objects plays a large role in determining the color we perceive, wavelength is not the only factor that determines color. The area surrounding an object also influences our perception of its color.

The Effect of the Surroundings: Simultaneous Contrast

A problem encountered in the famous Gobelin Tapestry Works in Paris in the early 1800s (Ratliff, 1965) illustrates the effect of the surroundings on our perception of color. The weavers complained that the color of the black-dyed wools they were using seemed washed out. To solve this problem, the tapestry works called in chemist M. E. Chevreul, who compared the black dyes used in the Gobelin Works to similar dyes used by other tapestry works. Chevreul found

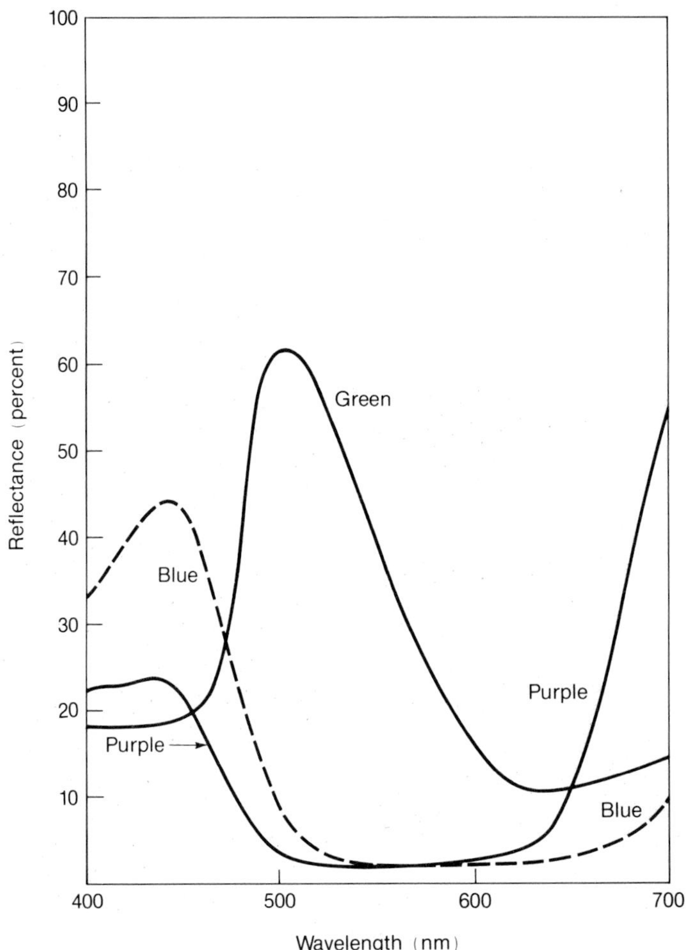

Figure 5.5 Reflectance curves for some colored pigments. Knowing which wavelengths are reflected by a pigment enables us to roughly predict the pigment's color by consulting the table on page 116. Try this for these pigments and for the foods in Figure 5.6. (Adapted from Clulow, 1972.)

that the dyes used by the Gobelin Works were as black as any of the others, but after further investigations, he concluded that the culprits were the colors woven next to the black-dyed wools in the tapestries and not the black wools themselves. The apparently washed-out blacks were caused not by poor dyes but by an effect called **simultaneous contrast**: surrounding one color with another changes the appearance of the color surrounded. Color Plate 5.2 is a demonstration of simultaneous contrast by artist Josef Albers. Although both X's are printed from the same ink and therefore reflect exactly the same wavelengths of light, the X on the top looks yellow, but the one on the bottom looks grey or violet. (Convince yourself that these two X's are, in fact, printed from the same ink, by looking at the place where they meet.)

This simultaneous contrast effect is probably caused by lateral inhibition. Cells stimulated by the light surround send a large amount of inhibition,

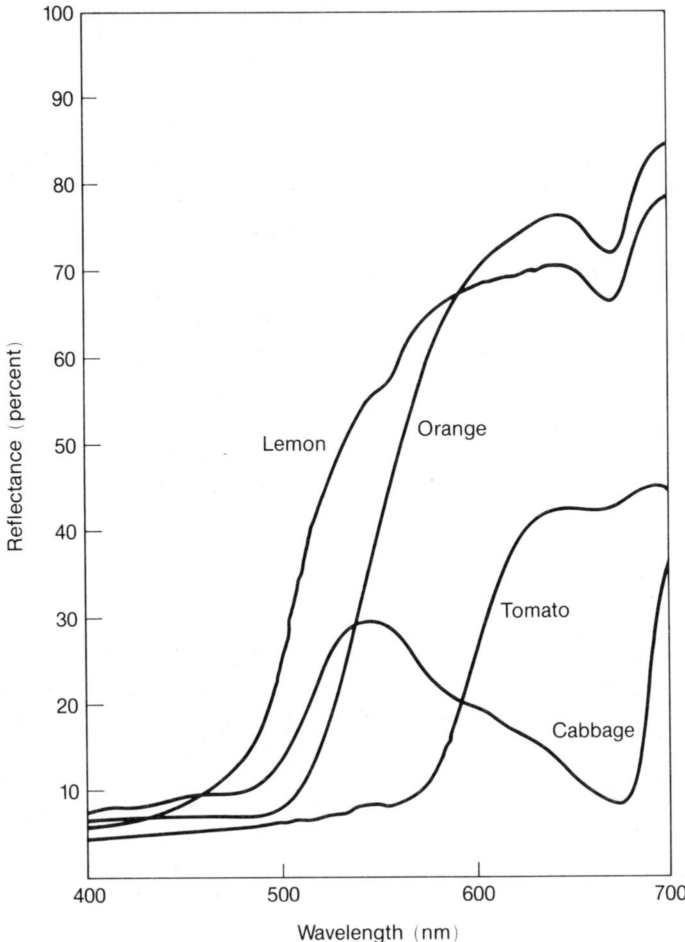

Figure 5.6 Reflectance curves of some common foods. (Adapted from Clulow, 1972.)

perhaps via horizontal and amacrine cells, to cells stimulated by the X on the left, thereby darkening this X. Cells stimulated by the dark surround send less inhibition to cells stimulated by the X on the right, and this X is therefore darkened less than the one on the left. This lateral inhibition not only affects the darkness of the X's but also influences their colors, causing the left X to look slightly violet and the right X to look yellow. Color perception, therefore, is not determined by wavelength alone; the surroundings and (as we will see next) the observer's state of adaptation affect color perception.

Adaptation of the Observer

Let's do an experiment. Illuminate the red field of Color Plate 5.3 with a bright light from your desk lamp; then, with your left eye close to the page, and keeping your right eye closed, look at the field with your left eye for about 30–45 seconds. At the end of this time, look up and around, first with your left eye and then with your right. When you do this, all the reds and oranges viewed with the left eye will look less saturated and less bright than those viewed with the right eye. You have changed your color perception by means of **selective adaptation,** similar to that used by George Wald in the experiments described on page 76. Adaptation to the red light bleaches your long-wavelength cone pigment, which decreases your sensitivity to red light.

Your perception of color can also be changed by **light adaptation** and **dark adaptation.** When you are light adapted, the cones control your vision and you see in color, but when you are dark adapted, the rods control your vision and you see in shades of grey. It is important to realize that the changes in color perception that occur as we switch from rod to cone vision (or vice versa) usually do so without any change in the wavelength distribution of light entering the eye. Thus, two lights containing the same wavelengths can result in very different perceptions of color. A dim light presented to the dark adapted eye will be perceived in shades of grey, whereas an intense light, with the same wavelength distribution, presented to the light adapted eye will be perceived in reds, blues, and greens. This dependence of color perception on the operation of the cones is another example of how our perceptions depend on the properties of the nervous system.

Memory Color

Memory color is the idea that an object's characteristic color influences our perception of that object's color. Thus, according to the idea of memory color, the knowledge that a spherical object is an orange should make the object look oranger. This idea is supported by the results of an experiment done by John Delk and Samuel Fillenbaum (1965). They showed observers figures like the ones in Figure 5.7, all of which were cut from the same sheet of orange-red cardboard. Figures such as the heart and apple were characteristically red, while others, such as the bell and mushroom, were not. The observer's task was to match the color of each object with that of a background field by adjusting the amount of redness in the background field. The result, in agreement with the idea of memory color, was that characteristically red objects, such as the heart and apple, were matched with a redder background field than were nonred objects, such as the bell and mushroom. Thus, objects that we know to be red appear redder than objects we know to be nonred.

Figure 5.7 Some of the stimuli used in Delk and Fillenbaum's (1965) experiment on memory color. Though all stimuli were cut from the same orangish red paper, the apple and heart were judged to appear slightly redder than the mushroom and bell.

Color Constancy

We saw earlier that our perception of an object's color is closely related to the wavelengths of light that an object reflects. A blue object reflects mainly short-wave light into our eyes, a green object reflects medium-wave light, and a red object reflects long-wave light. When we introduced the reflectance curves of Figures 5.4, 5.5, and 5.6, we said that they show the amount of light of each wavelength that is reflected when these pigments or objects are illuminated by white light, such as the sunlight of Figure 5.3. Now we pose two questions: (1) What happens to the *wavelengths* of light reflected from these objects when we take them indoors and illuminate them with tungsten light? (2) What happens to our *perception* of the colors of these objects when we take them indoors and view them under tungsten light?

The first question is easily answered, because we know the wavelength distribution of tungsten illumination (the dashed curve of Figure 5.3). Since tungsten illumination contains much more intensity at long than at short wavelengths, objects viewed under tungsten illumination reflect relatively more long-wavelength light than they do when viewed under white illumination. This shift to longer wavelengths is shown in Figure 5.8, in which the solid curve indicates the wavelengths reflected by a green object illuminated by sunlight, and the dashed curve indicates the wavelengths reflected by the same object under tungsten light.

How does this change in reflected wavelengths affect our perception of the object? Since the object reflects more long-wavelength light under tungsten

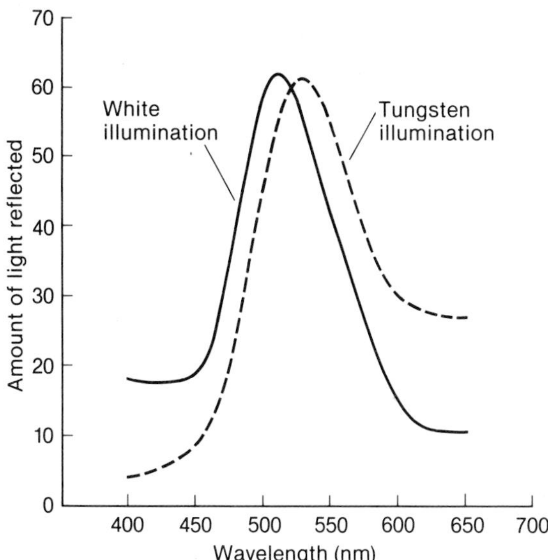

Figure 5.8 The relative amount of light reflected at each wavelength from an object that appears green when illuminated by white light. Under white illumination, the light reflected matches the object's reflectance curve, as shown in Figure 5.5. However, when illuminated by tungsten light, the object reflects more long wavelengths.

illumination, we might expect to see a different shade of green when we bring the object inside. Usually, however, we are not aware of any such shift in color. The color of your clothes and the color illustrations inside this book appear to remain approximately the same as you move from outdoor to indoor illumination. Demonstrate this to yourself by looking at one of the color illustrations first under the light of a light bulb and then under the illumination coming in through your window. This tendency to see objects as having a constant color, even under very different conditions of illumination, is called **color constancy.**

It is important to note, however, that although our perception of colors does not change as much as we might expect under different conditions of illumination, some changes do take place. When I visited the museum a few months ago, I noticed that a favorite painting had been moved from a location where it received mostly natural light to one where it received much more artificial light. Its colors had not changed so much that I could really say that the blues had become greener or the greens yellower, but the painting somehow looked different than it did before. In fact, experiments have shown that fluorescent lighting alters our perception of colors (Helson, Judd, & Wilson, 1956), and many people have found, unhappily, that their new clothes, which looked exactly right in the fluorescently lit store, have changed to a different color at home.

That our color perception does change a little when we change the illumination indicates that we usually experience not total but *approximate* color constancy. Though only approximate, color constancy is still an impressive phenomenon. An object's color is determined primarily by its reflectance curve, not by the actual wavelengths that reach the observer's eye. We will now look at a few of the explanations that have been proposed to explain color constancy.

Memory Color

Memory color partially explains why we don't see the colors of objects change: an orange stays orange under all illuminations, because we know it is an orange. While memory color may play some small role in color constancy, it cannot explain why objects without a characteristic color, such as a sweater or pieces of colored paper, stay about the same color under changing illuminations.

Selective Adaptation

Remember how adapting to the red field of Color Plate 5.3 caused other reds to become less bright? A similar thing happens when you walk into a room illuminated with tungsten light. The eye selectively adapts to the long wavelengths, which predominate in the tungsten light, and this adaptation decreases your eye's sensitivity to yellows and reds. This decreased sensitivity causes the yellows and reds to appear less bright, thus compensating for the greater amount of yellow and red light in the room. The result is a negligible change in your perception of color.

If the above explanation of color constancy is valid, then the light in our tungsten-illuminated room should appear yellower if we do not adapt to it. You can test this idea by standing outside at night and observing the window of an illuminated room from a distance. Since you are not standing in the room, you are not adapted to its light; therefore, the light you see through the window looks yellower than when seen from inside the room.

Another way to look at color constancy is to see how illumination would affect our color perception if our eyes could *not* selectively adapt. Let's consider how color film, which cannot adapt, reproduces colors under different illuminations. Color Plate 5.4 is a photograph of a desk top that is illuminated by sunlight shining through a window. The colors in this photograph correspond to those you would see if you were sitting at the desk, because the painting was photographed with "daylight" film, which is designed to give correct color reproduction in daylight illumination. If, however, we wait until dark and then turn on our desk lamp (tungsten lights), we get the photograph in Color Plate 5.5. The reddish color of this picture occurs because daylight film correctly reproduces colors in illumination that contains an equal amount of light at each wavelength, but tungsten illumination contains much more long-wavelength than short-wavelength light. Unlike the eye, daylight film can't adapt to the extra long wavelengths in the tungsten light, so the picture looks red. The different appearance of Color Plates 5.4 and 5.5 represents what we might experience under changing illuminations if our perception lacked color constancy.[3]

The Surroundings

We can illustrate the effect of the surroundings on color constancy by doing a simple experiment. Illuminate the green quadrant of Color Plate 5.6 with tungsten light; then look at it through a small hole punched in a piece of paper, so that all you see through the hole is part of the green area. Now repeat this observation while illuminating the same area with daylight from your window. With the surroundings masked off in this way, most people perceive the green area to be slightly yellower under the tungsten light than under daylight. Color constancy works less well when we mask off the surroundings, although the reason for this is complicated and not totally understood. However, it is likely, as with simultaneous contrast, that lateral inhibitory effects are involved.

We now have seen that our perception of color is determined by many factors: the illumination falling on an object, the object's reflectance, the observer's state of adaptation, and the surroundings. We will next discuss two theories that focus on how the wavelength of light results in the perception of color. These theories, first proposed in the 1800s, are the trichromatic theory and opponent-process theory of color vision.

Theories of Color Vision

Trichromatic Theory

The **trichromatic theory** of color vision was first proposed by Thomas Young in 1802 and was refined by Hermann von Helmholtz in 1852 (see the chapter-opening illustration). This theory (sometimes called the Young-Helmholtz theory) states that color vision results from the action of three cone receptor mechanisms with different spectral sensitivities. When light of a particular wavelength is presented to the eye, these mechanisms are stimulated to different degrees, and the ratio of activity in the three mechanisms results in the perception of a color. Each color, therefore, is coded in the nervous system by its own ratio of activity in the three receptor mechanisms.

We can see how this coding works, by referring to the response curves for the three mechanisms in Figure 5.9. We will label these the short-, medium-, and long-wave mechanisms in reference to the spectral regions to which they are most sensitive. With these three curves, we can determine the response of each mechanism to any wavelength. Thus, presentation of a 500-nm light results in a response of 1.3 from the short-wave mechanism, 9.0 from the medium-wave mechanism, and 6.0 from the long-wave mechanism. According to trichromatic theory, this 1.3-to-9.0-to-6.0 ratio of activity signals the

[3]To compensate for the absence of color constancy in film, we use different types of film for different illuminations. To photograph at night under tungsten illumination, we use "tungsten" film, which is designed to correctly reproduce color in tungsten light. If we photograph outdoors with tungsten film, our pictures will appear blue. This occurs because the film is designed for tungsten illumination, which contains much less short-wavelength than long-wavelength light. The blueness in our picture results from the added short wavelengths contained in daylight illumination.

Figure 5.9 Response curves for the short-, medium-, and long-wave mechanisms proposed by trichromatic theory. These curves, which are identical to the absorption spectra of the three cone pigments shown in Figure 3.8, enable us to determine the relative response of each mechanism to light of any wavelength. In the example shown here, the response of each mechanism to a 500-nm light is determined by drawing a line up from 500 nm and noting where this line intersects each curve. (Curves from Wald & Brown, 1965.)

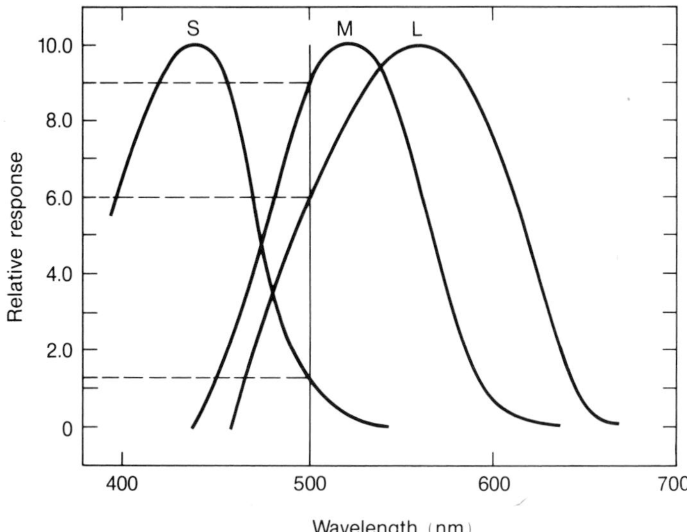

perception of a particular color, in this case the green of a 500-nm light.

You may recognize the curves of Figure 5.9 as the **absorption spectra** of the three cone pigments from Figure 3.8. These three pigments, first measured in 1964, are the receptors that correspond to the mechanisms which Young and Helmholtz proposed as the basis for trichromatic theory in the 1800s. You may wonder how Young and Helmholtz knew that there were three receptor mechanisms if the absorption spectra of the three cone pigments weren't measured until 1964.

The answer is that Young and Helmholtz used the results of psychophysical color-matching experiments to determine the existence of their three receptor mechanisms. In a color-matching experiment, observers are asked to match the color of one wavelength of light by mixing together three other wavelengths. For example, as shown in Figure 5.10, the observer might be asked to match the color of a 500-nm light presented in the test field by mixing together 420-nm, 560-nm, and 640-nm lights in the comparison field. Normal observers can do this and, in fact, can match ***any*** wavelength in the test field by mixing these three wavelengths in the appropriate proportions. (Any three wavelengths can be used in the comparison field, as long as we can't match any one of them by mixing the other two.) Observers cannot, however, match any test wavelength if they are provided with only ***two*** other wavelengths. For example, if we were given only the 420-nm and 640-nm lights to mix, we would be unable to match certain colors. Since three is the minimum number of wavelengths needed to match any wavelength in the test field, Young and Helmholtz concluded that there are three receptor mechanisms for color vision. Thus, Young and Helmholtz based a physiological theory of color vision on a psychophysical result.

The psychophysical basis for trichromatic theory tells us something very important about our perception of color: since a combination of three wavelengths can appear identical to a single different wavelength, the visual system cannot tell the difference between two physically different stimuli.

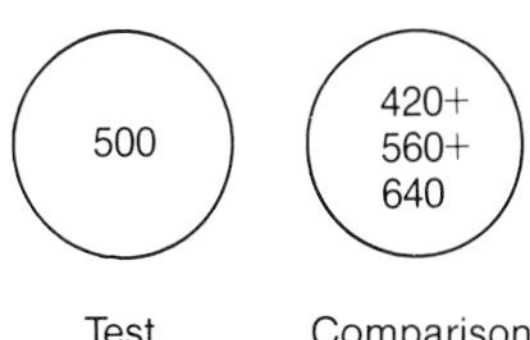

Figure 5.10 Test and comparison fields used in a color-matching experiment. In this experiment, a 500-nm light is matched by mixing lights with wavelengths of 420 nm, 560 nm, and 670 nm.

We can understand why two physically different stimuli can look identical, by considering what we would observe if we could simultaneously monitor the output of the cones responding to the test field, which contains the 500-nm light, and those responding to the comparison field, which contains our mixture of the 420-nm, 560-nm, and 640-nm lights. On the left of Figure 5.11, we see that the 500-nm light causes a 1.3-to-9.0-to-6.0 ratio of activity in the short-, medium-, and long-wave cones (remember, we determined this from Figure 5.9). On the right of Figure 5.11, we see that the mixture of three wavelengths causes the same ratio of activity in the short-, medium-, and long-wave cones. Therefore, these two physically different stimuli have identical physiological effects, and the brain has no way to tell them apart. Since the brain cannot discriminate between them, the two lights appear identical.

Two lights such as this, which have different wavelength distributions but are perceptually identical, are called **metamers,** and what we have described above is the basic principle of metamers: ***two lights with different wavelength distributions appear the same color if they stimulate the short-, medium-, and long-wave receptors in the same ratios.***

If color perception is based on the ratios of activity of the three cones and we know the response of each cone, we should be able to determine which color will be perceived. Figure 5.12 shows the relationship between the responses of the three cones and our perception of color. In this figure, responses in the short-, medium-, and long-wave cones are

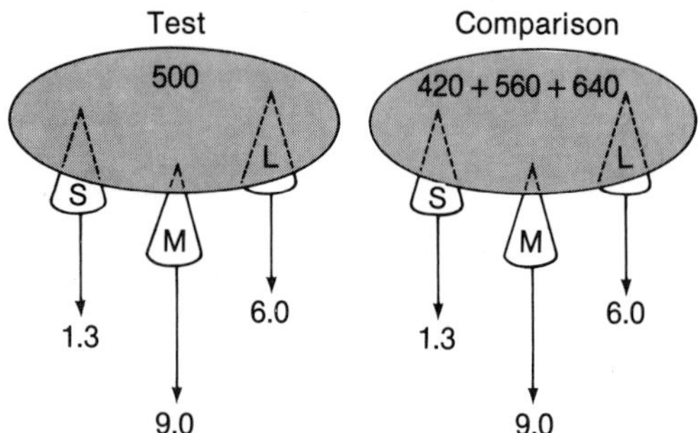

Figure 5.11 If we could simultaneously monitor the responses of the short-, medium-, and long-wave cones to the test field, which contains the 500-nm light, and to the comparison field, which contains the mixture of 420-nm, 560-nm, and 640-nm lights that perceptually match the test light, we would find no difference in the responses of the two sets of receptors. Since the responses to the two fields are identical, they will be perceptually indistinguishable.

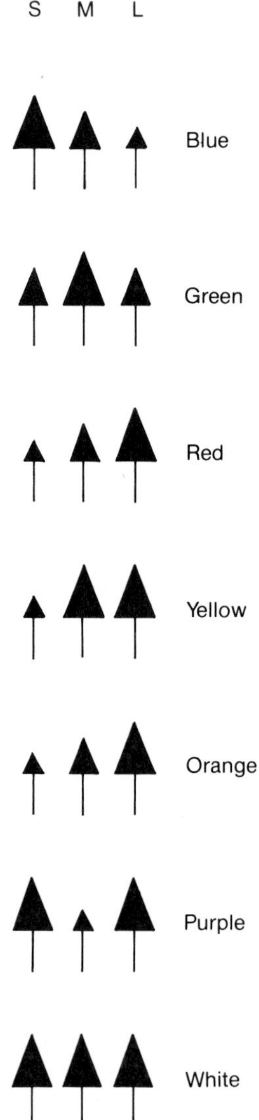

Figure 5.12 Firing patterns of the short-, medium-, and long-wave cones to different colors. The larger the receptor, the higher the rate of firing.

indicated by the size of the cone receptors. For example, blue is signaled by a large response in the short-wave cone, a small response in the medium-wave cone, and a smaller response in the long-wave cone. Yellow is signaled by a small response in the short-wave cone and large, approximately equal responses in the medium- and long-wave cones.

This theory of color vision enables us to predict which colors should result when we combine lights of different colors. For example, if we project a spot of red light onto a spot of green light, what color should result? The patterns of cone activity in Figure 5.12 show that a green light causes a large response in the medium-wave cone and a red light causes a large response in the long-wave cone. Together, therefore, they should result in a large response in the medium- and long-wave cones and a much smaller response in the short-wave cone. This is the pattern for yellow, which we do, in fact, see when red and green lights are mixed.

Let's pose another color-mixing problem: What happens when we mix blue and yellow lights? Blue light causes activity in the short-wave cones, and yellow light causes activity in the medium- and long-wave cones. Thus, combining both lights should equally stimulate all three cones, and we should perceive white. (If you are surprised by this result because you have learned that blue and yellow make green, see Box 5.2 for an explanation.)

Trichromatic theory—the idea that color perception is determined by the ratio of activity in three different receptors sensitive to different parts of the spectrum—is supported both by the results of color-matching experiments and by the measurement of the absorption spectra of single cones. Another theory of color vision, however, was proposed about 30 years after Helmholtz proposed his version of trichromatic theory. This second theory of color vision is called opponent-process theory.

Opponent-Process Theory

The **opponent-process theory** of color vision was proposed by Ewald Hering (see chapter-opening illustration) in 1878 (see Hering, 1964). The basic idea underlying Hering's theory is shown in Figure 5.13. He proposed three mechanisms, each of which responds in opposite ways to different wavelengths, or intensities, of light. The black(−)-white(+) mechanism responds positively to white light and negatively to the absence of light. Red(+)-green(−) responds positively to red and negatively to green, and blue(−)-yellow(+) responds negatively to blue and positively to yellow. According to Hering, these positive and negative responses are caused by the buildup and breakdown of a chemical in the retina: white, yellow, and red cause a chemical reaction that results in a buildup of the chemical; black, blue, and green cause a reaction that results in a breakdown of the chemical. Since the black-white mechanism is concerned with the perception of brightness rather than of the chromatic colors, we will focus our attention on the blue-yellow and red-green mechanisms.

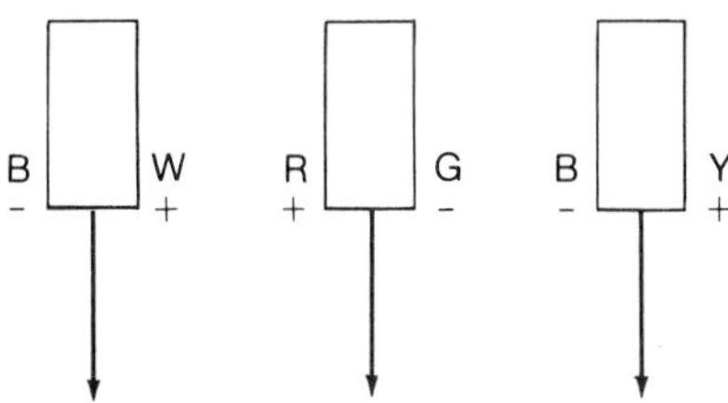

Figure 5.13 The three opponent mechanisms proposed by Hering.

Hering's idea that blue and yellow, as well as red and green, are opposites was based on the following psychophysical observations:

1. Blue and yellow cannot exist together in the same color. Nor can red and green. Can you imagine, or find an example of, a yellowish blue or a bluish yellow? How about a reddish green or a greenish red? Most people find it difficult to imagine any of these colors but can easily imagine, say, a bluish red (purple) or a greenish blue (turquoise). There is something special about the red-green and blue-yellow pairs.

2. Simultaneous contrast. If grey material is surrounded by a red background, the grey material looks slightly greenish. Similarly, a blue background makes grey material look yellow. This demonstrates simultaneous contrast, as was shown in Color Plate 5.2.

3. Afterimages. If you stare at the center of Color Plate 5.6 for 45–60 seconds and then look at the white space below, you should see

Box 5.2 When Does Blue Plus Yellow Equal Green?

It may have surprised you to read on page 125 that a blue light plus a yellow light stimulates all the cones equally and results in the perception of white. How can this be? Most people think that mixing blue with yellow results in green. In fact, these people are right, but they are talking about mixing paints rather than mixing lights. Let's consider what happens when we mix blue and yellow paints compared to what happens when we mix blue and yellow lights.

Mixing paints is called **subtractive color mixture.** To understand how subtractive color mixture causes blue and yellow to equal green, let's first consider what happens to white light that illuminates blue and yellow paint. White light is made up of all the colors of the spectrum: blue, green, yellow, orange, and red. When the white light hits the blue paint, some of these colors are absorbed (or subtracted) and some are reflected. As you can see from the figure, blue paint absorbs yellow, orange, red, and some of the green, and reflects blue and a little green. Yellow paint absorbs blue, orange, red, and some of the green, and reflects yellow and a little green.

What happens when we mix these two paints together? When they are mixed, both paints still absorb the same colors they absorbed when alone. This means that the mixture of blue and yellow paints will absorb all the blue (since yellow paint absorbs blue when alone), some of the green (blue and yellow paints both absorb some green when alone), all the yellow (absorbed by blue when alone), and all the orange and red (absorbed by both blue and yellow when alone). After all this absorbing, what's left? The only color that remains is the green reflected by both blue and yellow. (Remember that these paints don't absorb all the green.) *The only colors reflected from a mixture of paints are the colors reflected by both paints in common.* Since green is the only color reflected by *both* the blue and yellow paints, it is the only color reflected from the mixture, and we therefore perceive green.

The only reason that our blue and yellow mixture resulted in green was that there was a little green in each of the paints. What if our blue paint reflected only blue and our yellow paint reflected only yellow? These paints would have no colors reflected in common, so mixing them would result in little or no reflection across the spectrum, and, therefore, the mixture would appear black. It is rare, however, to find paints that reflect light in only one region of the spectrum. Most paints, like our original blue and yellow, reflect a broad band of wavelengths, encompassing at least two colors. If paints didn't reflect

an **afterimage** in which the green and red squares have changed places, as have the blue and yellow squares. Looking at red causes a green afterimage (and vice versa), and the afterimages for blue and yellow are similarly paired.

4. Color blindness. As we will see below, people blind to red are also blind to green, and people who can't see blue also can't see yellow.

Although Hering's opponent-process theory was supported by these psychophysical observations, only recently has it been taken as seriously as trichromatic theory. One reason for its slow acceptance was that people couldn't imagine a physiological process resulting in either the buildup or breakdown of a chemical substance. This poor acceptance of opponent-process theory is illustrated by the slight coverage given it in Yves LeGrand's 1957 book *Light, Color and Vision,* a standard reference work. Though 25 pages are devoted to trichromatic theory, opponent-process theory is dealt with in less than a page.

Despite the theory's general lack of acceptance, Leo Hurvich and Dorthea Jameson (1957) carried out an experiment that put the psychophysics of opponent-process theory on firm quantitative ground. The purpose of their experiment was to determine the strengths of the blue, yellow, red, and green components of the blue-yellow and red-green mechanisms, at wavelengths across the visible spectrum.

Let's first consider how Hurvich and Jameson

a range of wavelengths, then many of the **color-mixing** effects that painters take for granted would not occur.

Let's compare the subtractive process, which occurs when mixing paints, to the additive process, which occurs when mixing lights. Mixing lights is called **additive color mixture,** because all the wavelengths contained in each light still reach the eye when the lights are superimposed. Consider what happens when we look at blue and yellow lights that have been superimposed on a white projection screen. The short wavelengths of the blue light are reflected from the screen into our eyes, and the medium and long wavelengths of the yellow light are also reflected from the screen into our eyes. The result? Short, medium, and long wavelengths reach our eyes and we perceive white.

We can appreciate the difference between mixing paints and mixing lights, by considering that every time we add a light to some existing light, we ***add to*** the amount of light reflected from the screen into the observer's eye. However, every time we add an additional glob of paint to a mixture of paints, we ***subtract from*** the amount of light reflected from the mixture into the eye. This opposite nature of additive and subtractive color mixture is perhaps best illustrated by comparing the color that results from mixing blue, green, and red lights to the color that results from mixing blue, green, and red paints. Mixing the lights results in white, while mixing the paints results in black.

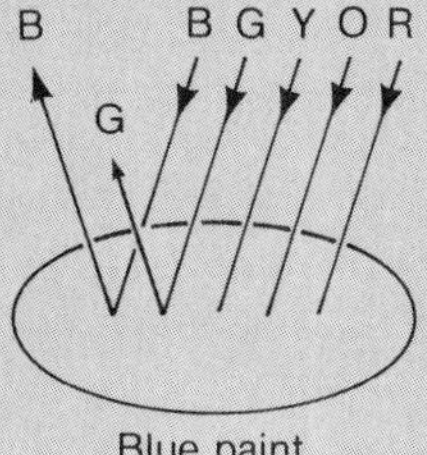

Blue paint

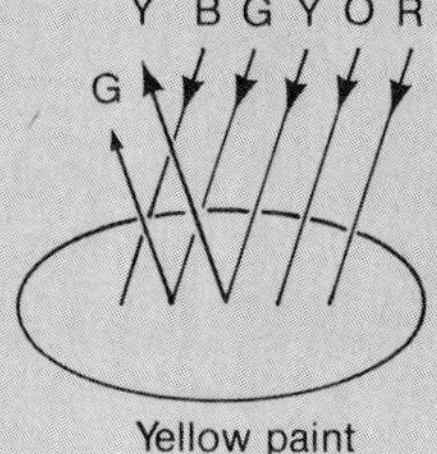

Yellow paint

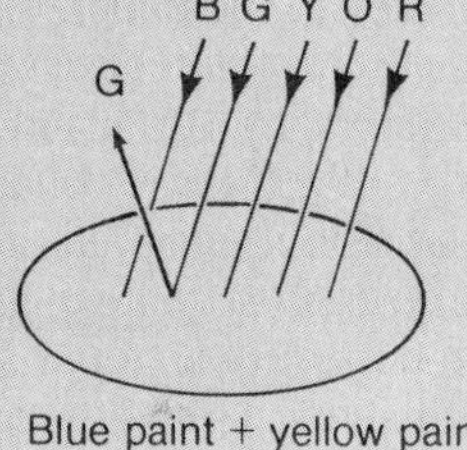

Blue paint + yellow paint

determined the strength of the blue mechanism across the spectrum, beginning at 430 nm. The blue mechanism obviously has substantial strength at 430 nm, because a 430-nm light looks violet. But how can we put a number on the amount of "blueness" in a 430-nm light? Hurvich and Jameson reasoned that since yellow is the opposite of blue and therefore cancels it, they could determine the amount of blueness in a 430-nm light by adding yellow light until it canceled all perception of blueness. As they added more and more yellow, the violet became increasingly desaturated and eventually lost all blueness. After determining how much yellow it took to eliminate all blueness at 430 nm, Hurvich and Jameson made similar measurements at longer wavelengths and obtained the dashed curve in Figure 5.14.

Figure 5.14 shows that the blue mechanism responds to lights up to 500 nm, with its maximum response occurring at about 440 nm. A 500-nm light, which looks green, appears neither blue ***nor*** yellow, but as we increase the wavelength above 500 nm, we first see a yellowish green, then a greenish yellow, a bright yellow, and finally a reddish yellow. To measure the amount of yellowness at these wavelengths, Hurvich and Jameson added blue until it eliminated all perception of yellowness. The result is the solid curve in Figure 5.14. The yellow mechanism responds to lights between 500 and 700 nm, with its maximum response at about 550 nm.

Figure 5.15 shows the results of similar experiments, in which Hurvich and Jameson measured the strengths of the red and green mechanisms. For

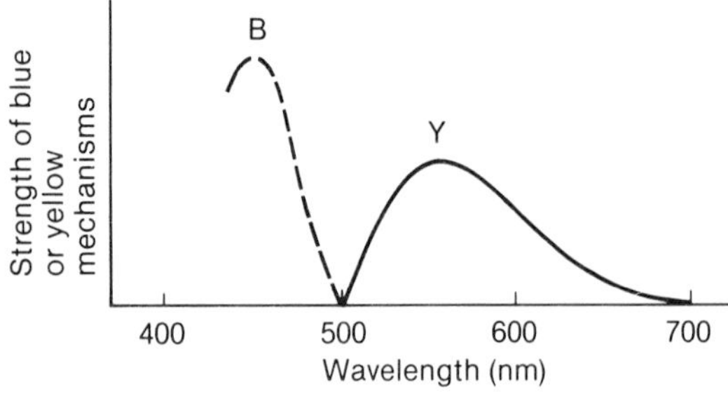

Figure 5.14 Strength of the blue and yellow mechanisms across the spectrum. Note that at no wavelength do blue and yellow occur together and that, at 500 nm, the strengths of both mechanisms are zero, indicating that a 500-nm light (which appears green) contains no traces of blue or yellow. (From Hurvich & Jameson, 1957.)

the red mechanism, they determined how much green light was needed to cancel the perception of redness at each wavelength, and for the green mechanism, they determined how much red light was needed to cancel the perception of greenness at each wavelength. The results for the red mechanism (the dotted curve), which show considerable strength not only at long wavelengths (where we would expect it) but also at short wavelengths, far from the red end of the spectrum, might seem surprising. The red mechanism's strength at short wavelengths becomes less surprising, however, if we remember that short-wavelength light looks violet (the color at about ten o'clock on the color circle of Color Plate 5.1), which contains both blue and red. The curve for the green mechanism (the solid line in Figure 5.15) indicates that this mechanism responds to wavelengths between about 490 and 580 nm, with its maximum response at about 525 nm.

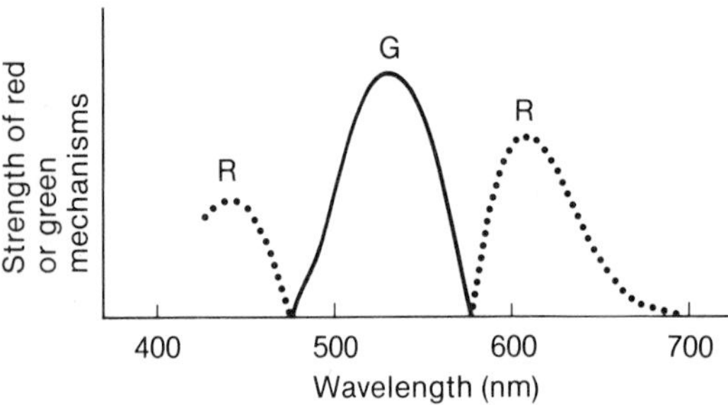

Figure 5.15 Strength of the red and green mechanisms across the spectrum. Note that at no wavelength do red and green occur together and that, at 475 nm and 580 nm, the strengths of both mechanisms are zero, indicating that neither a 475-nm light (which appears blue) nor a 580-nm light (which appears yellow) contains any traces of red or green. (From Hurvich & Jameson, 1957.)

Figure 5.16 plots the results of Figures 5.14 and 5.15 on the same graph. In this figure, the blue and green curves have been inverted to emphasize that blue (plotted as negative in the figure) opposes yellow (plotted as positive) and that green (negative) opposes red (positive). These curves could just as well be reversed, with blue and green positive and red and yellow negative.

The curves in Figure 5.16 enable us to determine the amount of each color present at any wavelength in the spectrum. For example, we can see that a 450-nm light contains a mixture of blue and red, with the blue being stronger, and that a 600-nm light contains a mixture of red and yellow, with the red being stronger. These curves also show how opponent-process theory explains color mixing. (Remember, according to trichromatic theory, mixing green and red results in yellow because this combination equally stimulates the medium- and long-wave cones, which signals yellow, as indicated in Figure 5.12.) According to opponent-process theory, a green light of, say, 560 nm causes the green

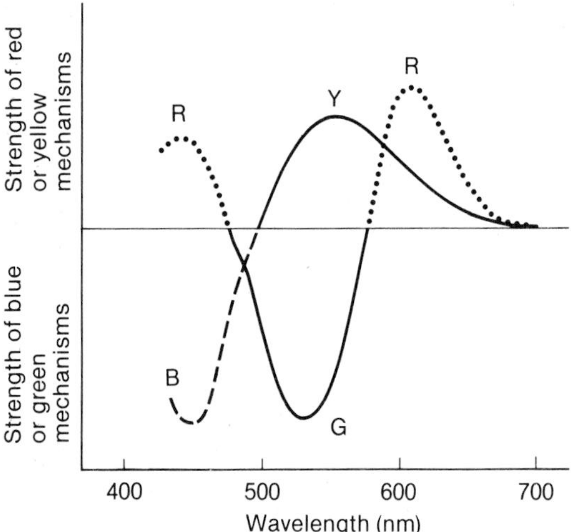

Figure 5.16 The curves of Figures 5.14 and 5.15 plotted together, with the blue and green curves inverted to indicate the opponent nature of the blue-yellow and red-green pairs. (From Hurvich & Jameson, 1957.)

and yellow mechanisms to respond, and a red light of, say, 630 nm causes the red and yellow mechanisms to respond. The mixture results in yellow because red and green oppose and cancel each other, leaving only the response of the yellow mechanism.

Though Hurvich and Jameson's measurements put the psychophysics of opponent-process theory on firm ground, it wasn't until solid physiological evidence became available that opponent-process theory began to gain equal footing with trichromatic theory. Physiological evidence was provided by Gunnar Svaetichin (1956), who recorded a slow electrical response from cells in the fish retina. This electrical response, which he called the **S-potential,** had a property that supported the opponent-process theory: the S-potentials of many cells responded positively to light at one end of the spectrum and negatively to light at the other end. This is illustrated by the S-potentials graphed in Figure 5.17. The top record is for a "red-green" cell that responds negatively at short wavelengths and positively at long wavelengths. The bottom record is for a "blue-yellow" cell that responds positively at short wavelengths and negatively at long wavelengths. Svaetichin also recorded red-green and blue-yellow cells in which the response direction was reversed from those shown here, while the opposing nature of the short- and long-wavelength responses was maintained.

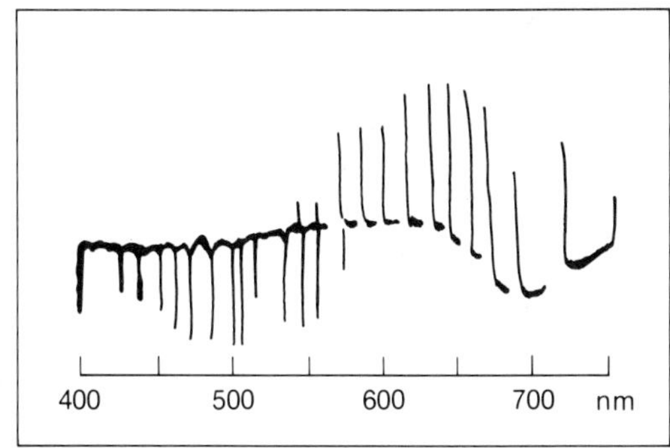

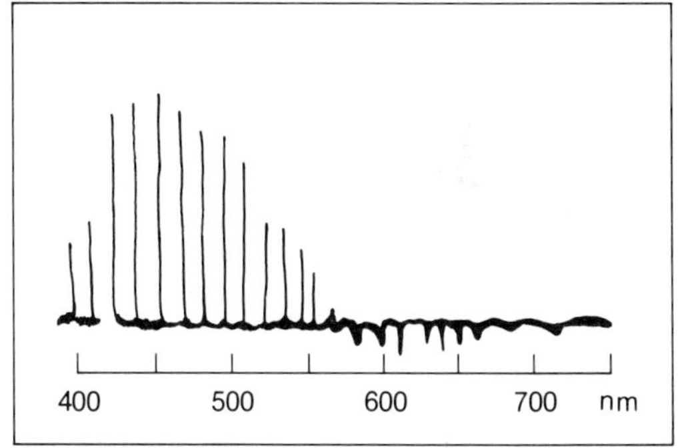

Figure 5.17 S-potentials recorded from the fish retina. The vertical lines are the responses generated by test flashes; wavelengths are indicated on the horizontal scale. (From Svaetichin, 1956.)

A few years after Svaetichin reported his results, Russell DeValois (1960) showed that cells in the monkey's lateral geniculate nucleus (LGN)—the relay nucleus for vision, which is located between the retina and the visual cortex (see Figures 2.22 and 2.23)—also have opponent properties. He found that certain cells in the LGN respond to light at one end of the spectrum with an increase in nerve firing and to light at the other end of the spectrum with an inhibition of spontaneous activity. The firing of four such cells is shown in Figure 5.18. For each cell, spontaneous activity is indicated in the top record, and the responses to 450-nm (blue), 510-nm (green), 580-nm (yellow), and 660-nm (red) lights are shown in the other records. The +B − Y cell responds to the 450-nm light with an increase in firing and to the 580-nm light with an inhibition of spontaneous activity. The +G − R cell increases its firing in response to the 510-nm light and decreases its firing in response to the 660-nm light. The +Y − B and +R − G cells also show opponent responses, but they are inhibited by short wavelengths and excited by long wavelengths. This important demonstration of opponent properties in the LGN shows that information in the slow retinal S-potentials is translated into the single-unit activity that is transmitted toward the brain.

The strong psychophysical and physiological evidence favoring both the opponent-process and trichromatic theories brings us to the question of which theory is correct.

Trichromatic or Opponent-Process?

The evidence presented so far seems to indicate that both theories of color vision are correct. But how is that possible? The answer is that two different theories can be correct if they describe what's hap-

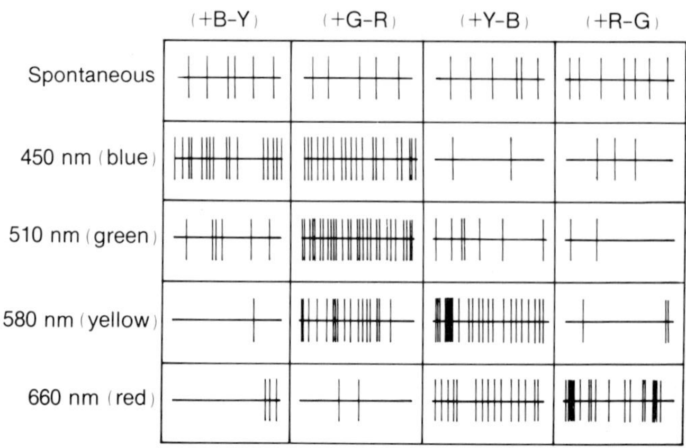

Figure 5.18 Responses of **opponent cells** in the monkey's lateral geniculate nucleus. These cells respond in opposite ways to blue and yellow (+B−Y or +Y−B) or red and green (+G−R or +R−G) light. (From DeValois & Jacobs, 1968.)

pening at different locations in the visual system. Trichromatic theory explains how the receptors function, and opponent-process theory explains how cells beyond the receptors function.

To understand how the two theories work together in the retina, look at Figure 5.19, which shows how the short-, medium-, and long-wave cone receptors of trichromatic theory might connect with bipolar cells to produce opponent responses. The blue-yellow bipolar cell receives excitatory input from the short-wave cone and inhibitory input from the long-wave cone. The red-green cell receives excitatory input from the medium-wave cone and inhibitory input from the long-wave cone.

Let's consider how the blue-yellow neuron in Figure 5.19 responds to short and long wavelengths. Short wavelengths will be absorbed best by the short-wave cone, causing an excitatory signal to reach the blue-yellow cell. We would, therefore, record a positive response from this cell. Long wavelengths will be absorbed best by the long-wave cone, causing an inhibitory signal to reach the blue-yellow cell. Therefore, we would record a negative response from this cell. We could go through a similar reasoning process for the red-green cell, with the same result: the cell would respond in an opposite manner to long- and short-wavelength light. Though the actual connections between receptors and other neurons in the retina are much more complex than is shown in Figure 5.19, our example illustrates the basic principle that appropriate inputs from cells with trichromatic properties can result in cells with opponent properties.

Our discussion so far has focused almost entirely on normal color vision. But what about color blindness? A good theory of color vision should explain the facts of normal color vision *and* of color-blind vision. After describing the major types of **color blindness,** we will see how they can be explained by the trichromatic and opponent-process theories.

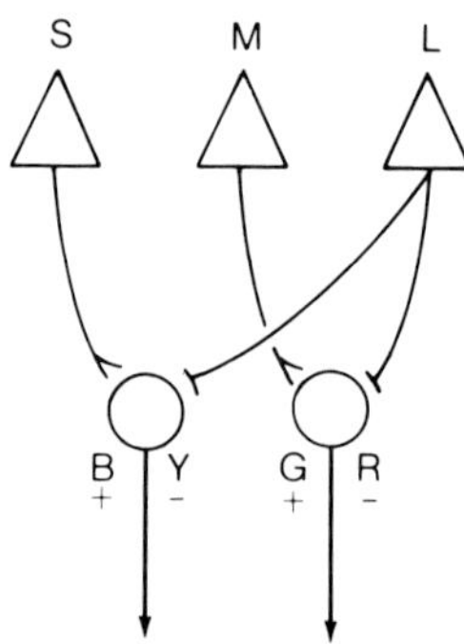

Figure 5.19 A simplified diagram showing how the short-, medium-, and long-wave cones might connect with higher-order (bipolar) cells in the retina to produce opponent responses. In the example, these connections produce one cell excited by blue and inhibited by yellow and another cell excited by green and inhibited by red.

Box 5.3 Blobs, Double Color-Opponent Cells, and Color Contrast

If the monkey's visual cortex is treated with a stain that selectively colors areas containing a substance called *cytochrome oxidase* (an enzyme involved in energy production in cells), something very interesting happens: the stain is taken up only in certain areas and, as David Hubel and Margaret Livingstone (1983) put it, these areas "form a quasi-regular polka-dot pattern of patches which we have designated by the legitimate English term 'blobs.'" These blobs, shown in the photograph below, are interesting because of the properties of the cells inside them. Hubel and Livingstone (1982, 1983) report that cells between the blobs are sharply tuned for orientation, whereas cells inside the blobs have no orientation selectivity. While these **blob cells** are insensitive to orientation, they do respond to color, with many of them having double color-opponent receptive fields, like the one shown below. The center of this particular cell's receptive field is excited by red and inhibited by green, while the surround is excited by green and inhibited by red.

These **double color-opponent cells** are particularly significant, because they may play a role in the perception of **simultaneous contrast** (see p. 117 and Color Plate 5.2). We can understand why this is so, by considering how this cell responds to different stimuli. A situation in which there is no contrast, such as a small red disc on a red background, results in little or no response, since the response of the excitatory center (+R) is canceled by the response of the inhibitory surround (−R). Similarly, little or no response occurs to a green disc on a green background. However, a situation in which there is considerable contrast, such as a red disc on a green background, will cause this cell to fire vigorously, since the excitatory response of the surround (+G) adds to the excitatory response of the center (+R). Perceptually, surrounding the red with green creates a large simultaneous contrast effect, causing the red to become much brighter and more saturated than if it were not surrounded by the green.

Blob cells are interesting because they not only may provide a physiological basis for simultaneous color contrast but also appear to operate independently of the orientation-sensitive nonblob cells. Hubel and Livingstone suggest that there are two parallel pathways: nonblob pathways, which are important for perceiving form, and blob pathways, which are important for perceiving color. Since this research is extremely recent, we must wait for the results of further research before we know the details of how cells in the blob and nonblob areas of the monkey's cortex operate.

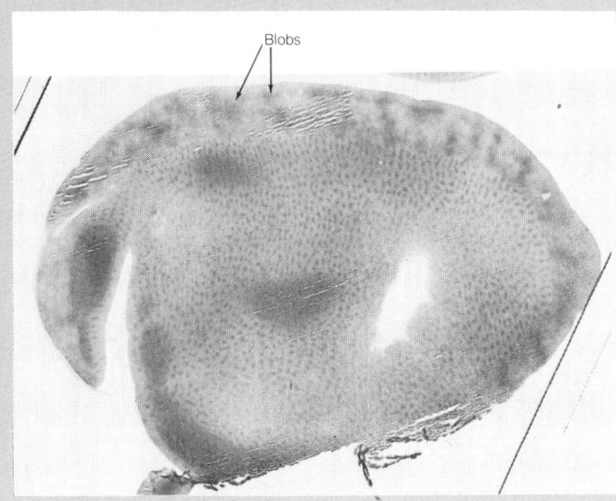

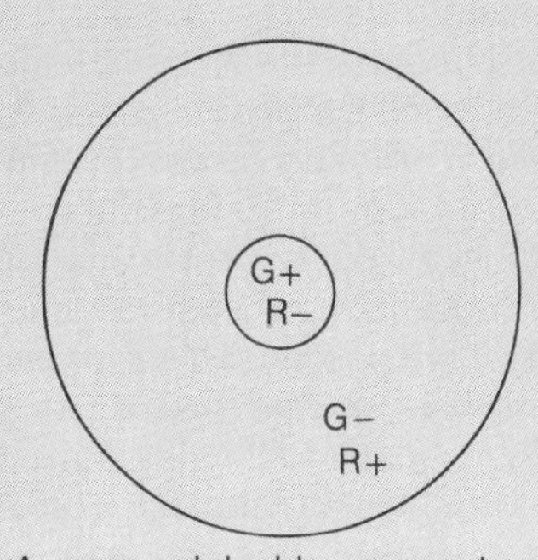

A green-red double opponent cell

Color Blindness

The color-matching experiments of trichromatic theory showed that we can match any wavelength in the spectrum by mixing three other wavelengths in the appropriate proportions. We call a person who needs three wavelengths to match any other wavelength in the spectrum a **trichromat,** and we consider trichromatic vision to be normal color vision. One difference between people with normal color vision and people who are color-blind is the number of wavelengths they need to match any other wavelength in the spectrum. A **monochromat,** a person who is totally color-blind (that is, sees everything as white, grey, or black), can match any wavelength in the spectrum by adjusting the intensity of any other wavelength. Thus, a monochromat needs only one wavelength to match any color in the spectrum.

A **dichromat,** a person who is partially color-blind (that is, sees some colors but not others), can match any wavelength in the spectrum by mixing two other wavelengths. Finally, an **anomalous trichromat** sees all colors in the spectrum and needs to mix three wavelengths to match any other, just as a normal trichromat does. An anomalous trichromat, however, mixes these wavelengths in different proportions than a trichromat and is not as good at discriminating between wavelengths that are close together.

Monochromatism

A monochromat is completely color-blind. This rare form of color blindness is usually hereditary and occurs in only about ten people out of a million (LeGrand, 1957). Monochromats usually lack a functioning cone system; therefore, their vision has the characteristics of rod vision in both dim *and* bright lights. In addition to a loss of color vision, monochromats have poor visual acuity and are so sensitive to bright lights that they often must protect their eyes with dark glasses during the day. The reason for this high sensitivity is that when rods, which are not designed to function in bright light, are the only functioning receptors, they become overloaded in strong illumination and cause a perception of glare.

Dichromatism

Since a dichromat can experience some colors (though a lesser range of color than the trichromat), this form of color blindness is less serious than monochromatism. There are three major forms of dichromatism—protanopia, deuteranopia, and tritanopia—all of which are hereditary and sex-linked. We say that they are sex-linked because women carry the gene for color blindness without being color-blind themselves, and they pass the condition to their male offspring. Thus, as we will see below, many more men than women are dichromats.

Protanopia. **Protanopia,** which affects 1 percent of males and 0.02 percent of females, results in the perception of colors across the spectrum indicated in Figure 5.20(a). A protanope perceives short-wavelength light as blue, and as wavelength is increased the blue becomes less and less saturated until, at 492 nm, the protanope perceives grey. The wavelength at which the protanope perceives grey is called his **neutral point.** At wavelengths above the neutral point, the protanope perceives yellow, which becomes increasingly saturated as the wavelength is increased until, at the long-wavelength end of the spectrum, the protanope perceives a saturated yellow.

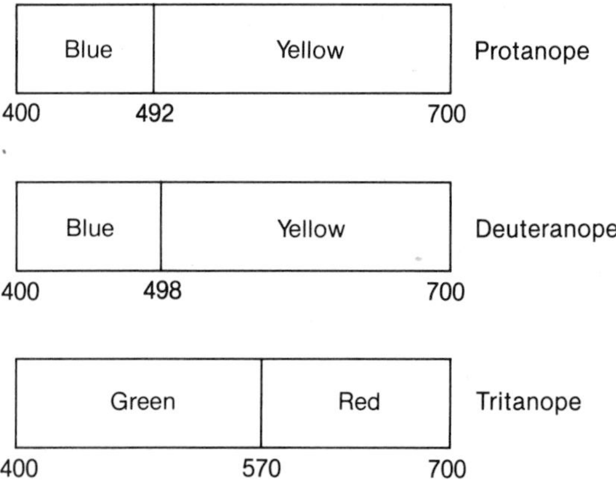

Figure 5.20 The color perceptions of the three major kinds of dichromats. The number under the dividing line indicates the neutral point, the wavelength at which grey is perceived.

Box 5.4 Color Vision in Animals

How can we tell if an animal has color vision? One way to tell is on the basis of an animal's normal behavior (Tansley, 1965). If color is a feature of one sex or is used in a species' mating or threat displays, it is likely that members of the species can perceive these colors. For example, that a territory-holding male robin attacks an intruder because of its red breast suggests that the robin has color vision. Similarly, it seems likely that peacocks would have color vision, so the female could perceive the male's colorful plumage.

We can also determine if an animal has color vision by training an animal to respond to one hue and not to another hue. However, in doing these experiments, it is important to be sure that the animal is making its judgment based on differences in hue and not on differences in brightness. Unfortunately, many experiments that claimed to provide evidence for color vision in animals are simply demonstrations that the animal can discriminate between a bright light and a dim light. To ensure that brightness plays no role in making a discrimination, it is necessary to measure an animal's spectral sensitivity curve (see Figures 1.9 and 3.6) and, based on this curve, to adjust stimuli of different wavelengths so they will appear equally bright to the animal. Using procedures such as this, it has been shown that the pigeon and chicken probably have trichromatic vision (Lashley, 1916; Hamilton & Coleman, 1933).

Another way to approach the question of whether an animal sees colors is to consider the animal's physiology. If an animal has only one visual pigment, color vision is unlikely. If an animal has more than one visual pigment, this suggests, but does not guarantee, that color vision is present. The only way to prove that an animal has color vision is by testing the animal behaviorally, as described above. The fish, for example, provides both physiological and behavioral evidence indicating the presence of color vision. Photochemical experiments show that fish have three cone pigments (Marks, 1965). Electrophysiological experiments show that fish have three types of cones (Tomita et al., 1967) and that the fish retina generates opponent S-potentials (Svaetichin, 1956; see Figure 5.17), and behavioral work indicates that goldfish have trichromatic vision (Yager & Thorpe, 1970).

Most mammals have either no color vision or minimal color vision. Though cats were originally thought to be color-blind (Tansley, 1965), recent behavioral and electrophysiological results indicate that they may be dichromats (Mello & Peterson, 1964; Sechzer & Brown, 1964; Meyer & Anderson, 1965; Pearlman & Daw, 1970). Another mammal that may be a dichromat is the squirrel (Tansley, 1965; Michael, 1969), but it appears that the dog lacks color vision.

The best color vision among nonhuman mammals is possessed by monkeys. New World monkeys such as the *Cebus* are dichromats (Grether, 1939), whereas the squirrel monkey has vision that corresponds to a human anomalous trichromat (Devalois & Jacobs, 1968). The color vision of the Old World rhesus monkey is excellent, being nearly identical to the human's. This is supported by psychophysical experiments and by microspectrophotometry, which has isolated three cone pigments similar to the human's (Marks et al., 1964; DeValois & Jacobs, 1968). Thus, the human and the rhesus monkey possess the best color vision of the mammals, and we must look to birds and fish to find comparable color vision in other species.

Deuteranopia. **Deuteranopia,** which affects about 1 percent of males and 0.01 percent of females, results in the perception of colors across the spectrum as shown in Figure 5.20(b). A deuteranope perceives blue at short wavelengths, yellow at long wavelengths, and has a neutral point at about 498 nm (Boynton, 1979).

Tritanopia. **Tritanopia** is very rare, affecting only about 0.002 percent of males and 0.001 percent of females. As indicated in Figure 5.20(c), a tritanope sees green at short wavelengths, red at long wavelengths, and has a neutral point at 570 nm (Boynton, 1972).

Before considering the physiological basis of color

blindness, let's ask how the color perceptions shown in Figure 5.20 were determined. Color-blind observers could have been asked what color they perceived at each wavelength across the spectrum, but this would be an unacceptable way to determine color perceptions. Remember, we cannot be sure that what a color-blind person calls *blue* corresponds to what a person with normal color vision calls *blue,* because the perception of color is a private experience.

The color perceptions recorded in Figure 5.20 were determined from the reports of **unilateral dichromats.** A unilateral dichromat has dichromatic vision in one eye and normal (trichromatic) color vision in the other. Such people can look at a color with the color-blind eye and then determine which color it corresponds to in the normal eye. Although unilateral dichromats are hard to find, the few who have been tested have helped us determine what colors color-blind people see (Sloan & Wollach, 1948; Graham et al., 1961).

Physiological Mechanisms

What are the physiological mechanisms for color blindness? Most monochromats are color-blind because they have just one type of cone or no cones. Dichromats are color-blind because they are missing a visual pigment. William Rushton (1964), using his retinal densitometry technique (described in Chapter 3) to measure the visual pigments in protanopes and deuteranopes, found that the protanope is missing the long-wavelength cone pigment and the deuteranope is missing the medium-wavelength cone pigment. It has been difficult to measure the visual pigments of the tritanope, both because of the tritanope's rarity and because the short-wavelength pigment is usually present only in low concentrations, even in normal retinas, but it appears that the tritanope is missing the short-wavelength pigment.

That each form of color blindness corresponds to a missing visual pigment is consistent with trichromatic theory. Trichromatic theory would predict that a person with only two pigments would need only two wavelengths to match any other wavelength, which is, in fact, the case; however, other aspects of color blindness are consistent with opponent-process theory. First, the colors perceived by color-blind observers correspond to the blue-yellow and red-green pairs of opponent-process theory (remember, this was one of the observations that led Hering to propose the theory). Second, if we compare the neutral points in Figure 5.20 to Hurvich and Jameson's psychophysical functions for normal observers in Figure 5.16, we see that the neutral points for the deuteranope and protanope fall near 500 nm, the wavelength at which the strength of the blue-yellow mechanism is zero. We would predict this location of the neutral point if deuteranopes and protanopes are missing their red-green mechanism, since seeing with only the blue-yellow mechanism would result in no perception of color at 500 nm. Similarly, the neutral point for the tritanope falls near 580 nm, the wavelength at which the strength of the red-green mechanism is zero. Thus, if tritanopes are missing their blue-yellow mechanism, we would expect them to perceive grey at 580 nm.

Perhaps our description of the physiological mechanisms of color vision makes it sound as though we can completely explain color blindness with the trichromatic and opponent-process theories. Unfortunately, things aren't that simple. We still do not understand many things about the physiology of color blindness, such as the mechanism responsible for the vision of anomalous trichromats. And other facts we have not mentioned, such as the changes in spectral sensitivity curves caused by color blindness, cannot yet be adequately explained by either theory.

Summary

1. It is difficult to define *color* without using examples, because the perception of color is a private experience.
2. People with normal color vision may perceive colors differently from one another; however, since our perception of color is a private experience, it is impossible to tell whether or not this is so.
3. There are chromatic and achromatic colors. The three main psychological attributes of chromatic colors are hue, brightness, and saturation.

4. We can discriminate about 150 different steps between 380 and 700 nm. If we vary the intensity and the saturation of each step, we can discriminate over 7 million colors. One compilation lists over 7,500 different color names.
5. The color circle is based on four pure colors: red, yellow, green, and blue.
6. Our perception of color is closely linked to the wavelength of the light. The wavelengths that reach the eye are determined by the wavelength distributions of light sources such as the sun, light bulbs, and fluorescent lights, and by the reflectance curves of objects that reflect light from these sources.
7. Objects that selectively reflect some wavelengths but not others have chromatic color.
8. Rainbows occur when white light is separated into the wavelengths of the spectrum by passing through drops of water.
9. Color perception is influenced by the surroundings through simultaneous contrast, which is probably caused by lateral inhibition.
10. Color perception is influenced by selective adaptation and by light and dark adaptation.
11. Color perception is influenced slightly by our knowledge of an object's characteristic color.
12. Changing the illumination from sunlight to tungsten light causes little change in our perception of color. This lack of color change with changing illumination is called color constancy. However, since our perception of color does change a little when we change the illumination, we usually experience not total but approximate color constancy.
13. Color constancy is due to selective adaptation and the effect of the surroundings.
14. There are two ways of mixing colors. Mixing lights together results in additive color mixing, whereas mixing paints together results in subtractive color mixing.
15. The trichromatic, or Young-Helmholtz, theory of color vision states that color vision results from the action of three cone receptor mechanisms with different spectral sensitivities. Each color is signaled by a particular ratio of activity in the three receptor mechanisms.
16. The three pigments of cone vision correspond to the three receptor mechanisms of trichromatic theory.
17. Color-matching experiments, which indicate that we can match any wavelength in the spectrum by mixing a minimum of three other wavelengths, provided the original basis for the idea that three receptor mechanisms are responsible for color vision.
18. Two lights that have different wavelength distributions but are perceptually identical are called metamers. Metamers look the same because they stimulate the short-, medium-, and long-wavelength receptors in the same ratios.
19. Opponent-process theory explains color vision by hypothesizing blue-yellow and red-green mechanisms in which blue and yellow have opposing properties and red and green have opposing properties.
20. The idea that blue and yellow are opposites and red and green are opposites is supported by the fact that we can't see a bluish yellow or a reddish green and by the nature of simultaneous contrast, afterimages, and color blindness.
21. Hurvich and Jameson's psychophysical measurements enable us to understand how opponent-process theory explains color mixing.
22. Opponent cells found in the retina and the lateral geniculate nucleus (LGN) provide physiological evidence for opponent-process theory.
23. Double color-opponent cells in the cortex provide a physiological explanation for color contrast.
24. Color vision is best explained by a combination of trichromatic and opponent-process theories, with trichromatic theory explaining the operation of the receptors and opponent-process theory explaining the operation of neurons beyond the receptors.
25. Color-matching experiments indicate that there are three major kinds of color vision defects: anomalous trichromatism, dichromatism, and monochromatism.

26. There are three kinds of dichromats: protanopes, deuteranopes, and tritanopes. These dichromats are missing long-, medium-, and short-wavelength cones, respectively, and there is evidence that protanopes and deuteranopes are missing the red-green opponent mechanism and that tritanopes are missing the blue-yellow mechanism.
27. Animals other than humans have varying degrees of color vision. Monkeys, some birds, and fish have the best color vision of nonhumans. Most mammals have either no color vision or poor color vision.

Glossary

Absorption spectrum A plot of the amount of light absorbed by a visual pigment versus the wavelength of light. (See Figures 3.6 and 3.8.) (123)

Achromatic color Color without hue. White, black, and grey are the achromatic colors. (113)

Additive color mixture Occurs when superimposing lights of different colors. (127)

Afterimage An image that results after steady fixation on a high-contrast stimulus or brief exposure to a relatively bright stimulus, such as a photographic flash. (126)

Anomalous trichromat A person who needs to mix a minimum of three wavelengths to match any other wavelength in the spectrum but mixes these wavelengths in different proportions than a trichromat. (132)

Blob cells Cells found in areas of the visual cortex that take up a stain which selectively colors tissues containing the enzyme cytochrome oxidase. Many of these cells have double color-opponent receptive fields. (131)

Brightness An attribute of light that ranges from just barely visible (at low brightnesses) to dazzling (at high brightnesses). Brightness is correlated with (but is not the same as) the intensity of the light. (113)

Chromatic color Color with hue. (113)

Color blindness A condition characterized by a deficient ability to see colors. Color-blind people see fewer colors than people with normal color vision and need to mix fewer wavelengths to match any other wavelength in the spectrum. (130)

Color constancy Our perception of an object's hue remains constant, even when the wavelength distribution of the illumination is changed. Approximate color constancy means that our perception of hue usually changes a little when the illumination changes, though not as much as we might expect from the change in the wavelengths of light reaching the eye. (121)

Color mixing Combining two or more different colors to result in a new color. *See* Additive color mixture; Subtractive color mixture. (127)

Dark adaptation Visual adaptation that occurs in the dark, in which the sensitivity to light increases. (See Chapter 3.) (120)

Deuteranopia A form of red-green dichromatism caused by a lack of the medium-wavelength cone pigment. (133)

Dichromat A person who is partially color-blind. Dichromats can match any wavelength in the spectrum by mixing two other wavelengths. Deuteranopes, protanopes, and tritanopes are all dichromats. (132)

Double color-opponent cell A cell with a center-surround receptive field; it has an opponent response to stimulation of the field's center and a reversed opponent response to stimulation of the surround. For example, if the center response is $+R-G$, the surround response will be $-R+G$. (131)

Hue The experience of a chromatic color—red, green, yellow, or blue—or a combination of these colors. (113)

Light adaptation Visual adaptation that occurs in the light, in which the sensitivity to light decreases. (See Chapter 3.) (120)

Memory color The idea that an object's characteristic color influences our perception of that object's color. (120)

Metamers Two lights that have different wavelength distributions but are perceptually identical. (123)

Monochromat A person who is completely color-blind and, therefore, sees everything as black, white, or shades of grey. A monochromat can match any color in the spectrum by adjusting the intensity of any other wavelength. (132)

Neutral point The wavelength at which a dichromat perceives grey. (132)

Opponent cell A neuron that has an excitatory response to wavelengths in one part of the spectrum and an inhibitory response to wavelengths in the other part of the spectrum. (130)

Opponent-process theory This theory states that our perception of color is determined by the activity of two opponent mechanisms—a blue-yellow mechanism and a red-green mechanism—in which the responses of the two colors in each mechanism oppose each other, one resulting in an excitatory response and the other in an inhibitory response. (This theory also includes a black-white mechanism, which is concerned with the perception of brightness.) (125)

Protanopia A form of red-green dichromatism caused by a lack of the long-wavelength cone pigment. (132)

Reflectance curve The function relating the percentage of light reflected from an object versus wavelength. (See Figures 5.4, 5.5, and 5.6 for examples of reflectance curves.) (116)

Saturation The relative amount of whiteness in a chromatic color. The less whiteness a color contains, the more saturated it is. (113)

Selective adaptation In color vision, adapting the eye to a fairly narrow range of wavelengths. (120)

Selective reflection When an object reflects some wavelengths and absorbs others. (116)

Simultaneous contrast Surrounding one color with another changes the appearance of the color surrounded. (118)

S-potential An electrical response with opponent properties, first recorded from cells in the fish retina. (129)

Subtractive color mixture Occurs when mixing together paints of different colors. (126)

Trichromat A person with normal color vision. Trichromats need to mix a minimum of three wavelengths to match any wavelength in the spectrum. (132)

Trichromatic theory This theory postulates that our perception of color is determined by the ratio of activity in three cone receptor mechanisms with different spectral sensitivities. (122)

Tritanopia A form of blue-yellow dichromatism thought to be caused by a lack of the short-wavelength cone pigment. (133)

Unilateral dichromat A person with dichromatic vision in one eye and trichromatic vision in the other. (134)

Wavelength The distance between one peak of a light wave and the next peak. (See Chapter 1.) (114)

Wavelength distribution The amount of energy in a light at each wavelength in the spectrum. (See Figure 5.3 for examples of wavelength distribution.) (114)

White light Light that contains an equal intensity of each of the visible wavelengths. (114)

Chapter Six

What Can Go Wrong with Your Eyes?

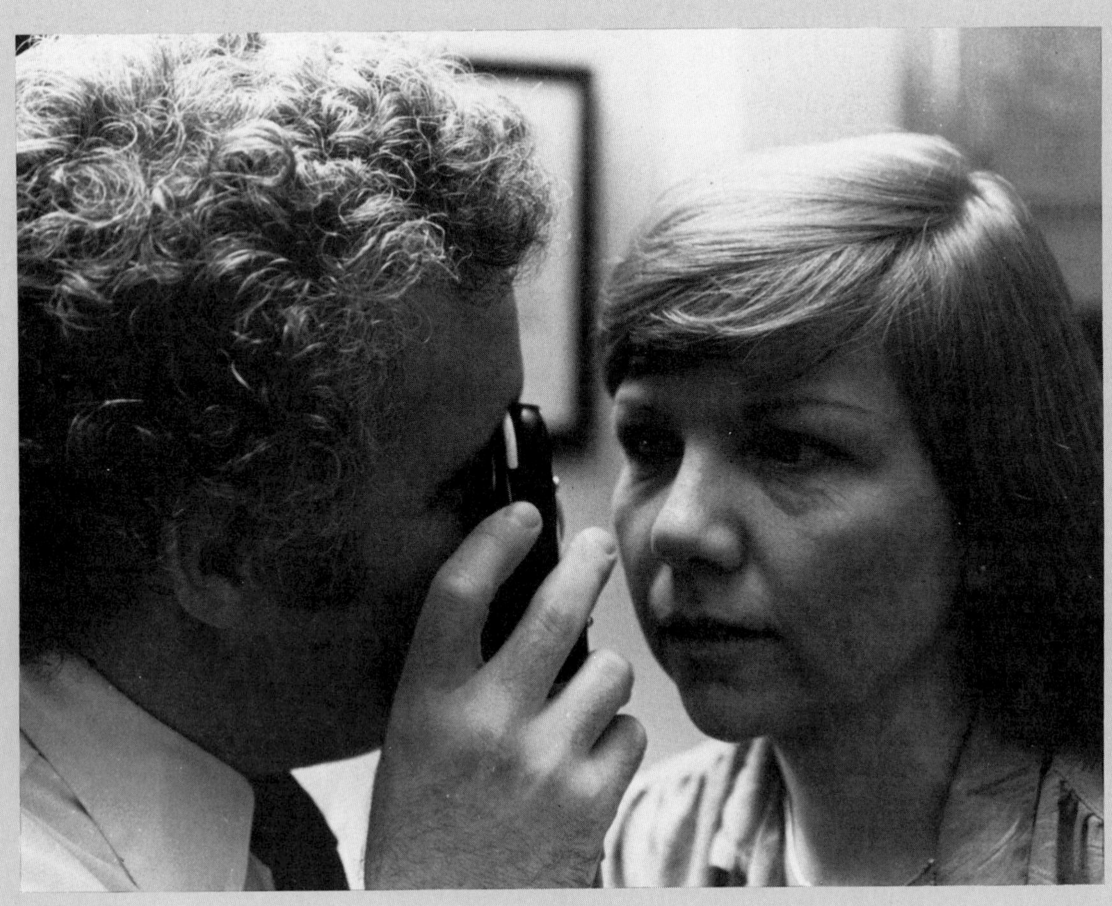

What is the man in the picture on the previous page looking at? Obviously, he's looking into the woman's eye, but what is he looking for and what is he seeing? While over 100 million Americans have had their eyes examined by an eye specialist in the process of being fitted for glasses or contact lenses, few of them could answer these or many other questions we could ask about what happens during an eye examination. As a veteran eyeglass and contact lens wearer, I have had my eyes examined many times but have never really understood, except in the most general sense, what was going on during these examinations. One purpose of this chapter is to demystify what goes on during an eye exam.

Before we can understand what the eye specialist looks for during an eye examination, we must understand the major problems that can cause poor vision. Therefore, we will start this chapter by describing these problems and how they are treated to improve or restore vision. After we understand the nature of the most common causes of visual problems, we will describe how a routine eye examination can detect these problems. (At this point, you might wish to reacquaint yourself with the basic structure of the eye, Figure 3.2, p. 68.)

What Can Go Wrong?

In our discussion, we will focus on four major types of problems that can cause poor vision:

1. Light is not focused clearly on the retina. Problems in focusing light can occur because the eyeball is too short or too long or because the lens does not function properly. We will describe the following specific problems: myopia (nearsightedness), hyperopia (farsightedness), astigmatism, and presbyopia ("old eye").
2. Light is blurred as it enters the eye. Scarring of the cornea or clouding of the lens blurs light as it enters the eye. Specific problems: corneal injury or disease, cataract.
3. Damage to the retina. The retina can be damaged by disruption of the vessels that supply it with blood, by its separation from the blood supply, and by diseases that attack its receptors. Specific problems: macular degeneration, diabetic retinopathy, detached retina, and hereditary retinal degeneration.
4. Damage to the optic nerve. The optic nerve can degenerate due to a pressure buildup inside the eyeball. Specific problem: glaucoma.

We begin by considering a problem that affects more people than all the others combined: an inability to focus incoming light onto the retina.

Focusing Problems

Accommodation

The eye has a problem—how to focus a sharp image on the retina. It solves that problem by using two focusing elements—the cornea and the lens—which, if everything is working properly, bring light entering the eye to a sharp focus on the retina.

To understand how these focusing elements work, let's first consider what happens when we look at a small spot of light located more than 20 feet away. Coming from this distance, light rays that reach the eye are essentially parallel, as shown in Figure 6.2(a), and these parallel rays are brought to a focus on the retina. If, however, we move our light closer to the eye, the rays are no longer parallel, as in Figure 6.2(b), and the point at which light comes to a focus is pushed back behind the retina. Of course, the light never comes to a focus in this situation because it is stopped by the retina, and if things remain in this state, both the image on the retina and our vision will be out of focus.

Fortunately, the eye can increase the **focusing power** of the lens to bring the image back into focus. This increase in focusing power is accomplished by a process called **accommodation,** in which tightening the ciliary muscles at the front of the eye increases the curvature of the lens so that it gets fatter, as shown in Figure 6.2(c). This increased curvature bends the light rays leaving the lens more sharply and moves the focus point forward, resulting in a sharp image on the retina and, therefore, sharp vision. The beauty of accommodation is that it happens automatically: the eye constantly adjusts the lens's focusing power to keep the image on the

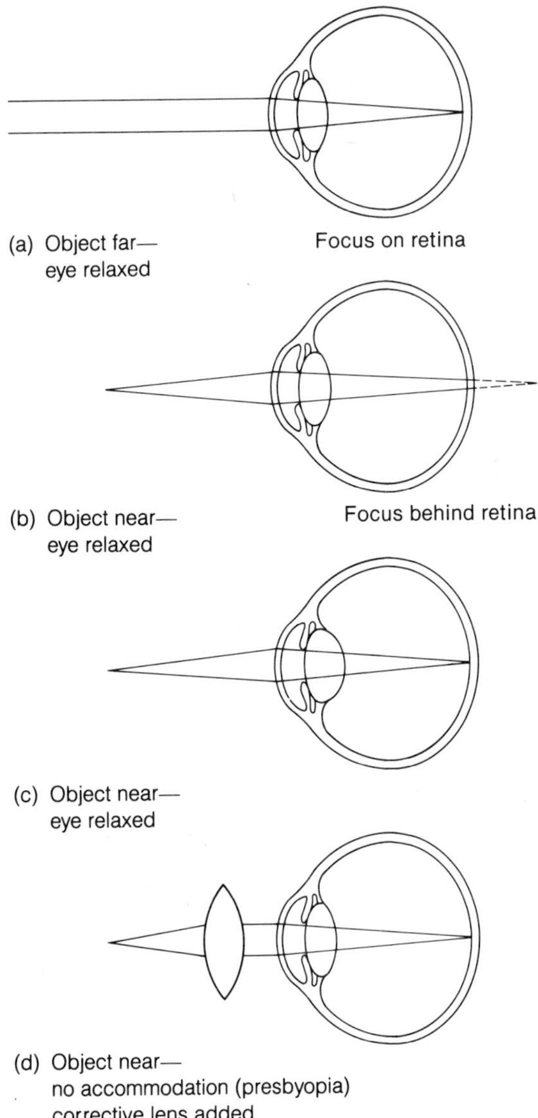

Figure 6.2 Focusing of light rays by the normal eye. (a) Parallel rays, from a spot of light greater than 20 feet away, are focused onto the retina. (b) When the spot of light is moved closer to the eye, the rays are no longer parallel and the focus point of the light is pushed back behind the retina. (c) Accommodation, indicated by the fatter lens in this picture, pushes the focus point forward onto the retina. (d) If the ability to accommodate is decreased, as in the presbyopic eye, a corrective lens is needed to bring light to a focus on the retina.

retina sharp as we look at objects located at different distances.

Because it is done unconsciously, this constant change in the focusing power of our lens, which allows us to see clearly at different distances, usually surprises most people. In fact, this unconscious focusing process works so efficiently that most people assume that everything, near and far, is always in focus. You can demonstrate to yourself that this is not so by looking at a faraway object (at least 20 feet distant) and then, while still looking at the far object, moving a pencil toward you with its point up. As the pencil point gets closer, you should notice that it looks blurred and is seen double. When the pencil point is 6–12 inches away, focus on it: the point is now seen sharply, but the faraway object is blurred.

Accommodation, therefore, enables us to bring nearby and faraway objects into focus automatically (but not simultaneously). Accommodation has its limits, however, which you can demonstrate by bringing the pencil point very close. As it approaches your nose, there will be a distance at which you can no longer see the pencil point clearly. This distance, which is called the **near point,** is the point at which your lens can no longer adjust to bring close objects into focus. As illustrated in Figure 6.3, the location of the near point depends on a person's age. The near point for most 20-year-olds is at about 10 cm, but this increases to 14 cm by age 30, 22 cm at 40, and 100 cm at 60. The reason for this loss in the ability to accommodate at close distances is that the lens hardens with age and the ciliary muscles, which control accommodation, become weaker. These changes make it more difficult for the lens to change its shape for vision at close range. Though this gradual decrease in accommodative ability poses little problem for most people before the age of 45, at around 45 years of age the ability to accommodate begins to decrease rapidly, and the near point moves beyond a comfortable reading distance. This decreased ability to accommodate (with the resulting increase in the near point) is called **presbyopia,** or "old eye."

Presbyopia affects everyone, no matter how good their eyesight is when they are young, because it is a normal consequence of aging. This means that all people eventually experience difficulty in reading,

Box 6.1 Vision Problems in the United States

Blindness and visual disability exact an enormous toll on both the people who are affected and on society. Consider these facts:

- 100 million people wear glasses or contact lenses.
- 10 million people over 25 have some non-correctable loss of sight.
- 1.4 million people can't see ordinary newsprint, even with glasses.
- 500,000 people are legally blind.
- 47,000 new cases of blindness are reported every year.
- 34 million office visits are made each year for eye care.
- 770,000 eye operations are performed each year.
- Over $5 billion are spent each year on doctors' bills and benefits related to eye care.

Source: *Vision Problems in the United States,* National Society to Prevent Blindness, New York, 1978.

when their inability to accommodate makes it impossible for them to focus at a comfortable reading distance—about 18 inches. The solution to this problem is a corrective lens that adds the necessary focusing power to bring light to a focus on the retina, as shown in Figure 6.2(d).

Myopia

Myopia, or nearsightedness, is an inability to see distant objects clearly. The reason for this difficulty, which affects over 70 million Americans, can be understood by looking at Figure 6.4(a): in the myopic eye, parallel rays of light are brought to a focus in front of the retina, so the image reaching the retina is blurred. This problem can be caused by either of two factors: (1) **refractive myopia:** the cornea and lens bend the light too much, or (2) **axial myopia:** the eyeball is too long. Either way, light comes to a focus in front of the retina, so the image on the retina is out of focus, and faraway objects looked blurred.

How can we deal with this problem? Accommodation can't help us, because increasing the power of the lens moves the focus point forward, as we saw in Figure 6.2(c), which only makes matters worse. However, by observing what happens when we move our spot of light closer to a normal eye,

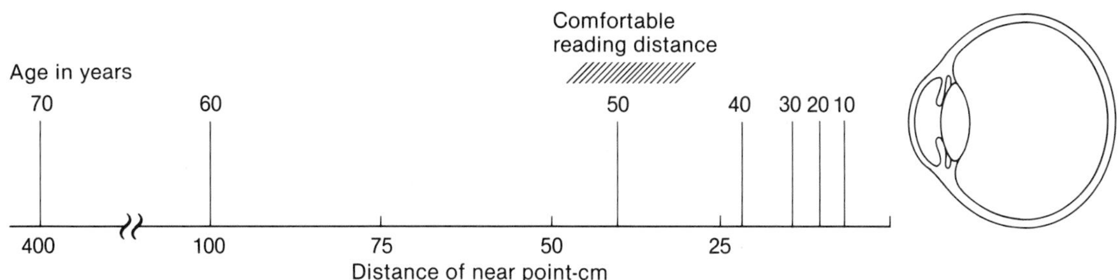

Figure 6.3 Near point as a function of age. The distance of the near point in centimeters is indicated on the scale at the bottom, and various ages are indicated by the vertical lines. Objects between the eye and the near point cannot be brought into focus by accommodation. Thus, as age increases, the ability to focus on nearby objects becomes poorer and poorer; eventually, past the age of about 50, reading becomes impossible without corrective lenses.

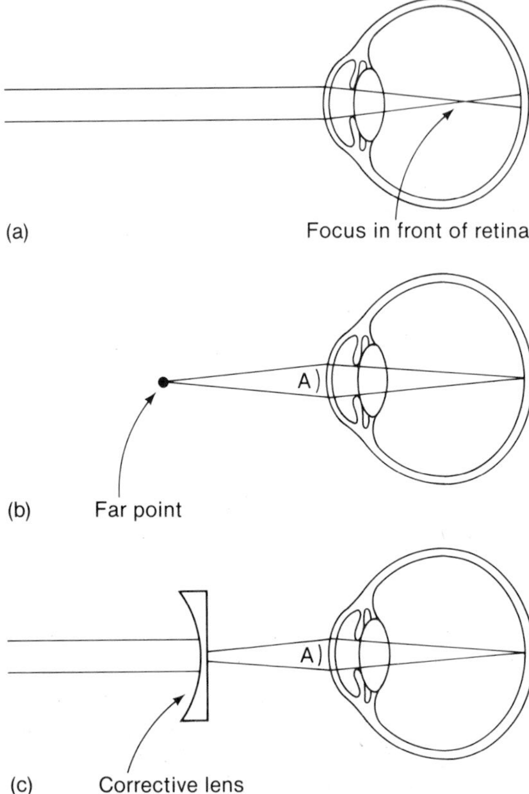

Figure 6.4 Focusing of light by the myopic (nearsighted) eye. (a) Parallel rays from a distant spot of light are brought to a focus in front of the retina, so distant objects appear blurred. (b) As the spot of light is moved closer to the eye, the focus point is pushed back until, at the far point, rays are focused on the retina and vision becomes clear. Vision is blurred beyond the far point. (c) A corrective lens, which bends light so it enters the eye at the same angle as light coming from the far point, brings light to a focus on the retina. Angle A is the same in (b) and (c).

we can see another solution: when the spot of light is far from the eye, rays are focused on the retina (Figure 6.2a), but when we move the spot closer, the focus point moves back (Figure 6.2b). The same thing happens in a myopic eye: when the spot of light is far from the eye, rays are focused in front of the retina (Figure 6.4a), but when we move the spot closer, the focus point moves back, and if we move the spot close enough, we can push the point of focus onto the retina (Figure 6.4b). The farthest distance at which the spot of light is focused on the retina is called the **far point,** and when our spot of light is at the far point, a myope can see it clearly.

What happens if we move our spot of light closer than the far point? By moving the spot closer, we push the focus point back behind the retina (see Figure 6.2b); fortunately, however, we can now use accommodation to push the focus point forward, back onto the retina. A myope, therefore, can see objects clearly if they are at the far point or closer.

Our proposed solution—moving objects closer to the eye—enables the myope to see nearby objects clearly (which is why a myopic person is called "nearsighted"), but it still leaves the myope with fuzzy vision for objects beyond the far point. The solution to this problem is well known to anyone with myopia: corrective glasses or contact lenses that bend incoming light so that it appears to be at the far point. This is illustrated in Figure 6.4(c). Notice that the lens placed in front of the eye bends rays so that light enters the eye at exactly the same angle as light coming from the far point in Figure 6.4(b).

Before leaving our discussion of myopia, let's consider one more problem: How strong must a corrective lens be to give the myope clear far vision? To answer this question, we have to keep in mind what is required of a corrective lens: it must bend parallel rays so that light enters the eye at the same angle as would a spot of light positioned at the far point. Figure 6.5 shows what this means for two different locations of the far point. When the far point is close, as in Figure 6.5(a), we need a powerful corrective lens to bend the light in the large angle shown in Figure 6.5(b). However, when the far point is distant, as in Figure 6.5(c), we need only a weak corrective lens to bend the light in the small angle shown in Figure 6.5(d). Thus, the strength of the corrective lens depends on the location of the far point: a powerful lens is needed to correct vision when the far point is close, and a weak lens is needed to correct vision when the far point is distant.

When ophthalmologists or optometrists write a prescription for corrective lenses, they specify the strength of the lens in **diopters,** using the following relationship: number of diopters = 1/far point in meters. Thus, a slightly myopic person, with a far point at 1 meter (100 cm), requires a 1-diopter correction (diopters = 1/1 = 1.0). However, a very

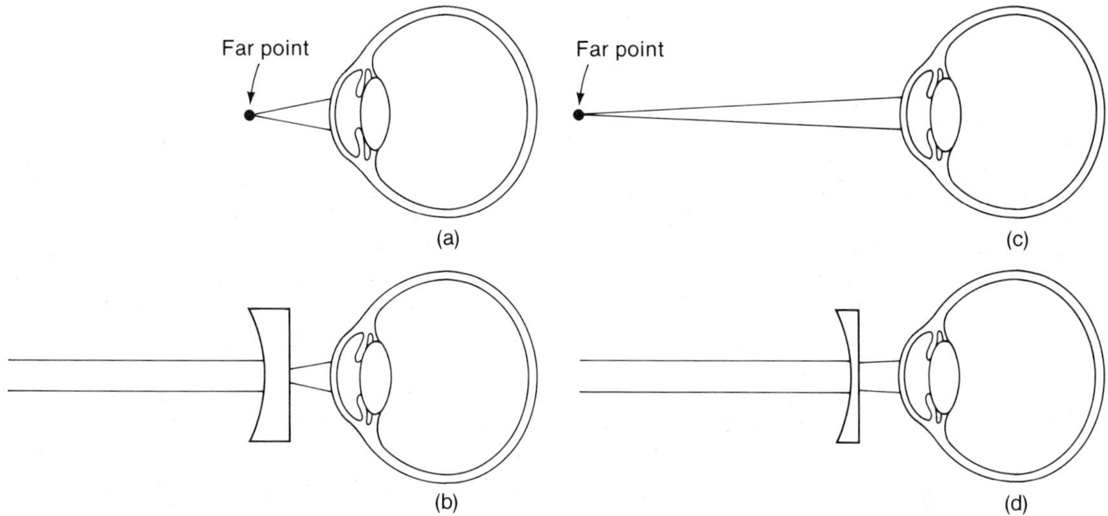

Figure 6.5 The strength of a lens required to correct myopic vision depends on the location of the far point. (a) Close far point requiring (b) strong corrective lens. (c) Distant far point requiring (d) weak corrective lens.

myopic person, with a far point at two-tenths of a meter (20 cm), requires a 5-diopter correction (diopters = 1/0.2 = 5.0). This relationship between the distance of the far point and the required number of diopters of correction is shown in Figure 6.6.

Hyperopia

A person with **hyperopia,** or farsightedness, can see distant objects clearly but has trouble seeing nearby objects. We can understand hyperopia by looking at Figure 6.7. In the hyperopic eye, the focus point for parallel rays of light is located behind the retina, usually because the eyeball is too short. By accommodating to bring the focus point back to the retina, hyperopes are able to see distant objects clearly.

Nearby objects, however, are difficult for the hyperope to deal with, because, as we saw in Figures 6.2 and 6.4, moving an object closer pushes the focus point farther back. The hyperope's focus point,

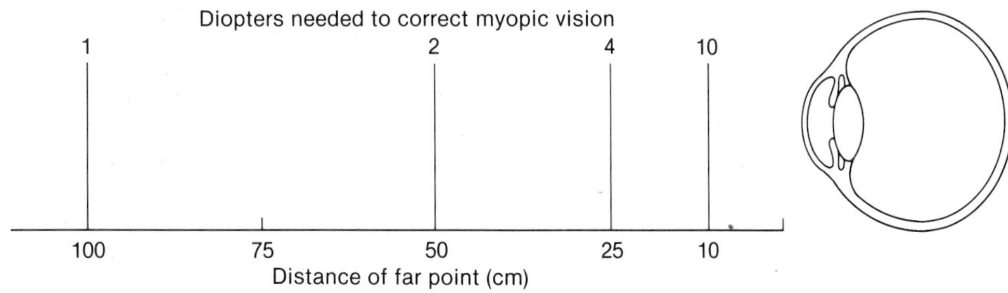

Figure 6.6 The number of diopters of lens power needed to correct myopic vision for different far points. Without a corrective lens, vision is blurred at distances greater than the far point. A far point of 10 cm represents severe myopia, and a far point of 100 cm represents mild myopia.

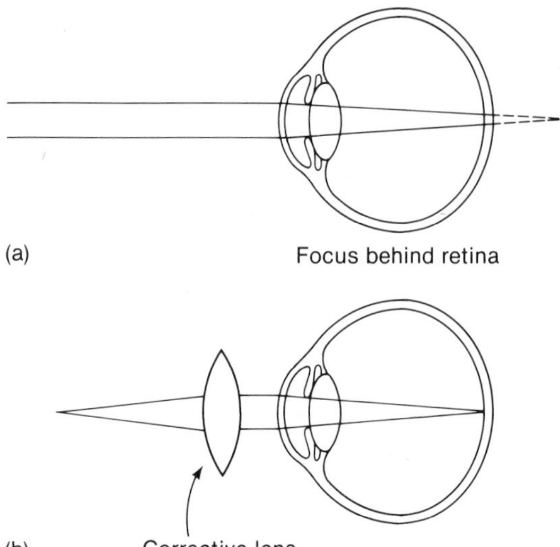

Figure 6.7 Focusing of light by the hyperopic (farsighted) eye. (a) Parallel rays from a distant spot of light are brought to a focus behind the retina, so, without accommodation, far objects are blurred. Hyperopes can, however, achieve clear vision for distant objects by accommodating. (b) If hyperopia is severe, the constant accommodation needed for clear vision may cause eyestrain, and a corrective lens is required.

behind the retina for far objects, is pushed even farther back for nearby objects, so the hyperope must exert a great deal of accommodation to return the focus point to the retina. The hyperope's constant accommodation when looking at nearby objects (as in reading or doing close-up work) results in eyestrain and, sometimes, headaches. These symptoms of hyperopia are easily prevented by a corrective lens that brings the focus point forward onto the retina, as shown in Figure 6.7(b).

Astigmatism

Imagine what it would be like to see everything through a pane of old-fashioned wavy glass, which causes some things to be in focus and others to be blurred. This describes the experience of a person with a severe **astigmatism,** because an astigmatic person sees through a misshapen cornea, which correctly focuses some of the light reaching the retina but distorts other light. The normal cornea is spherical, curved like a round kitchen bowl, but an astigmatic cornea is somewhat elliptical, curved like the inside of a spoon. Because of this elliptical curvature, a person with astigmatism will see the "astigmatic fan" in Figure 6.8(a) partially in focus and partially out of focus, as shown in Figure 6.8(b). As in hyperopia, eyestrain is a symptom of astigmatism because, no matter how much the person accommodates to try to achieve clear vision, something is always out of focus. Fortunately, astigmatism can be corrected by glasses or contact lenses.

Decreased Transmission of Light

The focusing problems described above are the most prevalent visual problems, as evidenced by the large number of people who wear glasses. Because these problems usually can be corrected with glasses or contact lenses, most people with focusing problems see normally or suffer only mild losses of vision. We will now consider situations in which disease or physical damage can cause severe visual losses or, in some cases, blindness. But before we begin to discuss these problems, we should define what we mean by **blindness.**

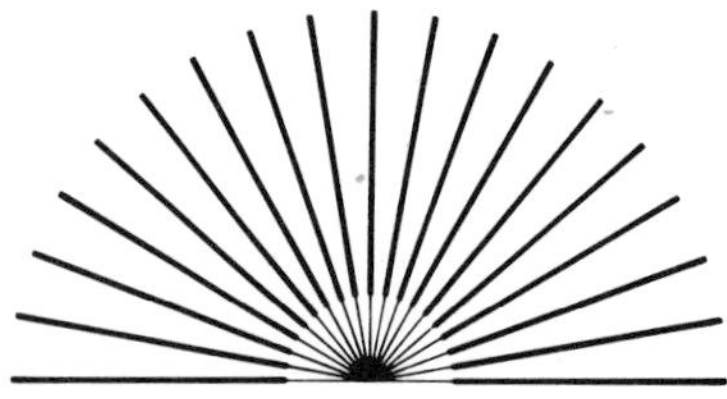

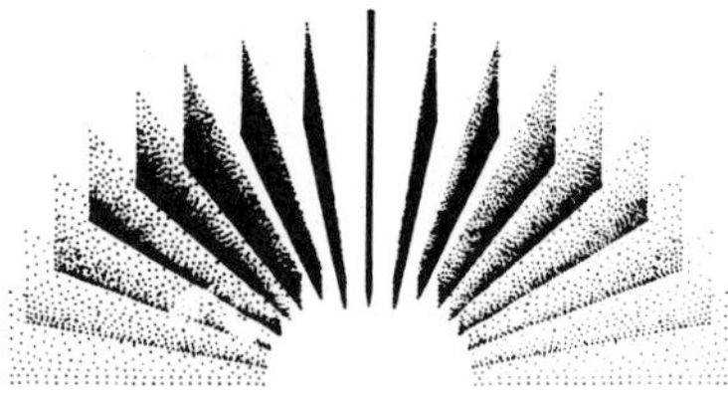

Figure 6.8 An "astigmatic fan" (a) as it appears to someone with normal vision, and (b) as it appears to someone with an astigmatism.

What Is Blindness?

It is a common conception that a person who is blind lives in a world of total darkness or formless, diffuse light. While this description is true for some blind people, many people who are classified as legally blind do have some vision. According to the definition accepted in most states, a person is considered legally blind if, after correction with glasses or contact lenses, he or she has visual acuity of 20/200 or less in the better eye. To understand this definition, consider that 20/20 acuity means that a person can see at 20 feet what a person with normal vision can see at 20 feet. However, a person with an acuity of 20/200 needs to be at a distance of 20 feet to see what a person with normal vision can see from a distance of 200 feet.

When we define blindness in terms of visual acuity, we are evaluating a person's ability to see with his or her fovea (which, as we saw in Chapter 3, is the cone-rich area of the retina that is responsible for detail vision). While poor foveal vision is the most common definition of blindness, a person with good foveal vision but little peripheral vision can also be considered legally blind. Thus, a person with normal (20/20) foveal vision but little or no vision in the periphery can be legally blind. This situation, which is called **tunnel vision,** results from diseases we will discuss below, such as advanced glaucoma or retinitis pigmentosa (a form of retinal degeneration), which affect peripheral vision but leave the foveal cones unharmed.

Corneal Disease and Injury

The **cornea,** which is responsible for about 70 percent of the eye's focusing power (Lerman, 1966), is the window to vision, because light first passes through this structure on its way to the retina. In order for a sharp image to be formed on the retina, the cornea must be transparent, but this transparency is occasionally lost when injury, infection, or allergic reactions cause the formation of scar tissue on the cornea. This scar tissue causes decreased visual acuity and sometimes makes lights appear to be surrounded by a halo, which looks like a shimmering rainbow. In addition, **corneal disease and injury** can also cause pain.

- 2 million cases of corneal disease are diagnosed each year.*
- 1.3 million injuries occur each year.
- The most common causes of eye injuries are (in order of incidence) metal pieces, contact lenses, motor vehicles, chemicals, baseballs, and glass.
- More than 35,000 Americans suffer eye injuries from sports each year. Baseball, racquet sports, and basketball account for the largest number of sports-related injuries.
- Corneal problems are the leading cause of monocular (one-eyed) blindness.
- 10,000 corneal transplant operations are performed each year.

Drugs, which can often bring the cornea back to its transparent state, are the first treatment for corneal problems. If drugs fail, however, clear vision can often be restored by a **corneal transplant** operation. The basic principle underlying this operation is shown in Figure 6.9. The scarred area of the cornea, usually a disc about 6–8 mm in diameter, is removed and then replaced by a piece of cornea

*All data in this chapter regarding the incidence of vision problems are from *Vision Problems in the United States,* National Society to Prevent Blindness, New York, 1978. Note that these numbers refer only to vision problems in the United States.

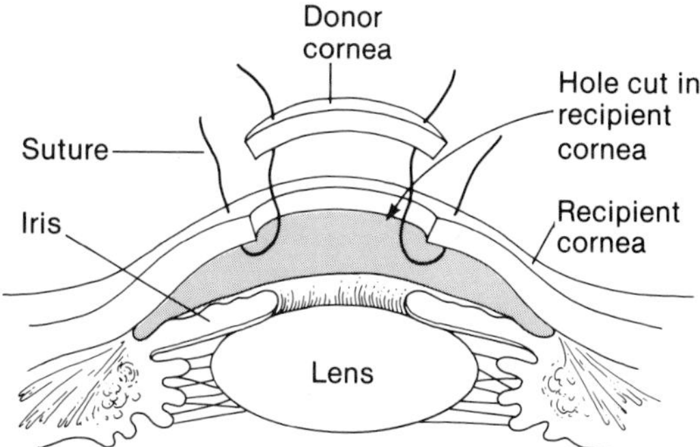

Figure 6.9 Corneal transplant operation. The scarred part of the cornea has been removed, and the donor cornea is about to be sutured in place.

taken from a donor. For best results, this donor should be a young adult who died from an acute disease or from an injury that left the corneal tissue in good condition. In the past, a major problem with this operation was the necessity of transplanting the donor cornea within a few hours of the donor's death. Recently, however, two procedures have been developed that make it possible to store corneal material for long periods of time. A donor cornea stored at 4° C, in a special solution called M-K, will keep for up to a week, and a cornea that is slowly brought down to a temperature of – 120° C (a technique called **cryopreservation**) will keep indefinitely.

We tend to think of operations such as heart and liver transplants as risky and sometimes unsuccessful, because of the frequent rejection problems that occur. But these rejections occur because of antibodies carried in the blood, which is not a problem for corneal transplants, because the cornea is not in contact with the blood supply. Thus, of the approximately 10,000 corneal transplants performed every year, 85 percent are successful. Remember, however, that a corneal transplant operation involves only a small piece of the eye—there is no such thing as an eye transplant. Indeed, the problems involved in transplanting a whole eye are overwhelming. Besides the difficulties involved in keeping the donor eye's retina alive (once its circulation is cut off, the life expectancy of a retina is very short), there is the problem of connecting the one million optic nerve fibers of the donor's eye to the corresponding fibers of the patient's optic nerve. At this point, whole eye transplants are purely science fiction.

Clouding of the Lens (Cataract)

Like the cornea, the **lens** is transparent and is important for focusing a sharp image of the incoming light on the retina. Clouding of the lens, which is called a **cataract,** is sometimes present at birth (**congenital cataract**), can be caused by another eye disease (**secondary cataract**), or can be caused by injury (**traumatic cataract**), but the most common cause of cataract is old age (**senile cataract**). Cataracts develop, for reasons as yet unknown, in 75 percent of people over 65 and in 95 percent of people over 85.

- Cataracts are the third leading cause of blindness, accounting for 42,000 cases.
- 41.2 million people over 40 have cataracts.
- Three out of four people over 65 (25 million people) have cataracts.
- 5–10 million people become visually disabled every year due to cataracts.

Although millions of people have cataracts, in only about 15 percent of the cases does the cataract interfere with a person's normal activities, and only 5 percent are serious enough to require surgery—the only treatment for cataract.

The basic principle underlying a cataract operation is illustrated in Figure 6.10. A small opening is made in the eye, through which the lens is removed by **cryoextraction,** a technique in which a very cold probe is inserted into the eye so its tip touches the lens. The extreme cold causes the lens to stick to the probe, which then pulls the lens out of the eye. Another technique, **phacoemulsification,** uses ultrasound to remove the lens: a hollow needlelike instrument, vibrating 40,000 times per second, is inserted into the lens; the high-frequency vibrations break up the lens, and the resulting pieces are sucked out of the eye through the hollow needle.

Removal of the clouded lens clears a path so that light can reach the retina unobstructed, but in

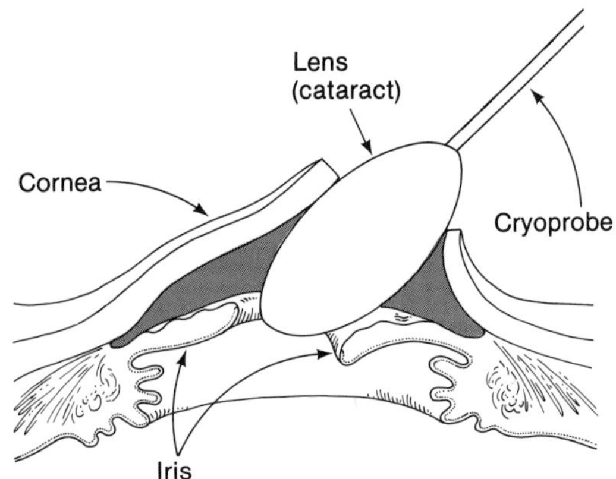

Figure 6.10 Last stage of a cataract operation. The figure shows the lens being removed from the eye with a cryoprobe.

removing the lens we have also removed some of the eye's focusing power. (Remember that the cornea accounts for 70 percent of the eye's focusing power; the lens is responsible for the remaining 30 percent.) Although we can fit the patient with glasses, this creates problems of its own, because glasses can enlarge the image falling on the retina by as much as 20–35 percent. If one eye receives this enlarged image and the other receives a normal image, the brain cannot combine these images to form a single, clear perception. A better solution is to fit the patient with contact lenses, which only enlarge the image by about 6 percent, but many older people have difficulty inserting and removing these lenses every day. They need a lens that neither changes image size nor requires daily insertion and removal. This need appears to be met by a relatively new development in the treatment of cataract—the **intraocular lens.**

The idea of implanting a lens inside the eye where the old lens used to be goes back 200 years, but the first workable design for an intraocular lens was not proposed until 1949. These early lenses were not very successful because they were too heavy, but recent developments in lightweight plastics have resulted in ultralightweight lenses, like the one shown in Figure 6.11. Although the intraocular lens was still considered experimental in the early 1970s, today the intraocular lens appears to be on its way to becoming a routine part of the cataract operation.

Damage to the Retina

The retina's source of life is the nourishment it receives from the retinal circulation and from the **pigment epithelium** upon which it rests. All four conditions described below affect the retinal circulation or the relationship between the retina and the pigment epithelium in some way, resulting in a loss of vision.

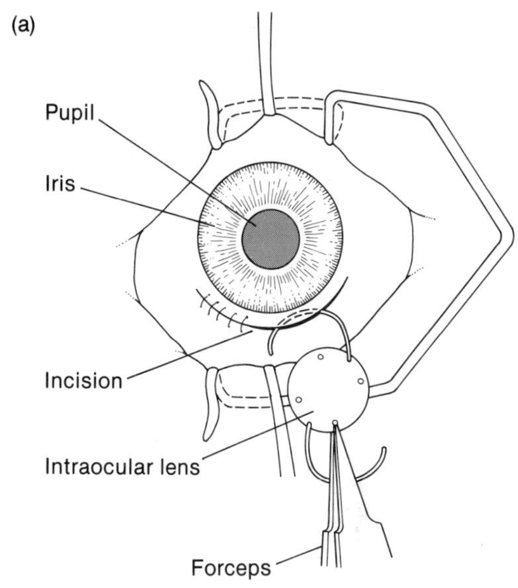

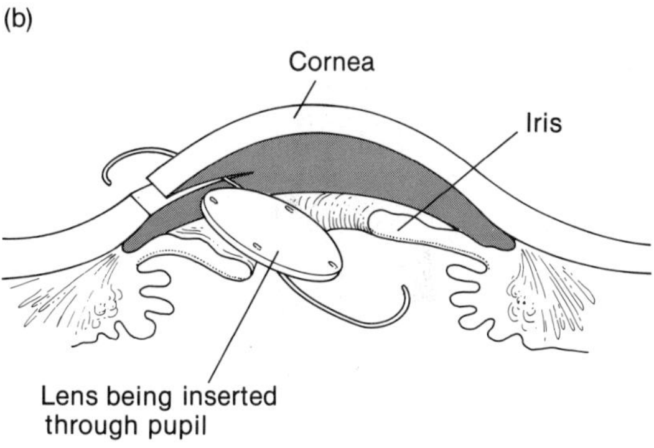

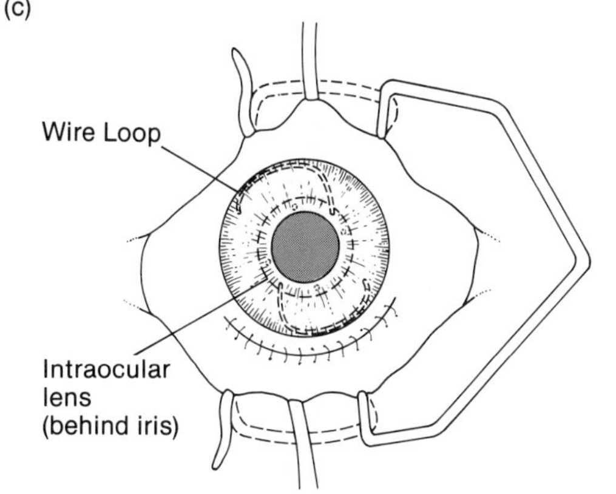

Figure 6.11 Installing an intraocular lens in the eye after the cataract (the person's clouded lens) has been removed. (a) Top view of the eye, showing the lens being inserted into the eye through an incision. (b) Side view, showing the lens partially inserted. (c) Top view, showing the lens in place behind the iris. The small wire loops hold the lens in place.

Diabetic Retinopathy

Before the isolation of insulin in 1922, most people with severe **diabetes,** a condition in which the body doesn't produce enough insulin, had a life expectancy of less than 20 years. The synthesis of insulin (which won for its discoverers the 1923 Nobel Prize) greatly increased the life expectancy of diabetics, but one result of this greater life expectancy has been a great increase in an eye problem called **diabetic retinopathy.** Of the 10 million diabetics in the United States, about 4 million show some signs of this problem.

Figure 6.12 shows what happens as the disease progresses. At first the capillaries swell, as shown in Figure 6.12(a), and may leak slightly. At this point vision is usually not seriously affected, and most cases of diabetic retinopathy stop here. However, if the disease progresses further, a process called **neovascularization** occurs. Abnormal new blood vessels are formed, as shown in Figure 6.12(b), which do not supply the retina with adequate oxygen and which may rupture and bleed into the **vitreous humor** (the jellylike substance that fills the eyeball), interfering with the passage of light to the retina and causing, in some cases, scarring and retinal detachment (see below).

One technique for stopping neovascularization is called **laser photocoagulation,** in which a laser beam of high-energy light is aimed at leaking blood vessels. The laser "photocoagulates," or seals off, these vessels, thereby stopping the bleeding. Recently, a new procedure, called **panretinal photocoagulation,** has been used with some success. In this technique, the laser scatters 2,000 or more tiny burns on the retina, as shown in Figure 6.13. For some reason, though the burns do not directly hit many of the leaking blood vessels, they cause them to dry up and go away.

- 4 million people suffer from diabetic retinopathy.
- Diabetic retinopathy accounts for 37,000 cases of blindness.
- 300,000 diabetics suffer severe decreases in vision due to diabetic retinopathy.

If laser photocoagulation is not successful in stopping neovascularization, an attempt to eliminate the blood inside the eye is made by means of an operation called a **vitrectomy,** shown in Figure 6.14. A hollow needle placed inside the eye sucks out the vitreous humor and the blood which is blocking vision, then replaces the vitreous humor with a salt solution. While this procedure removes the blood inside the eye, it does not stop neovascularization, which caused the bleeding in the first place.

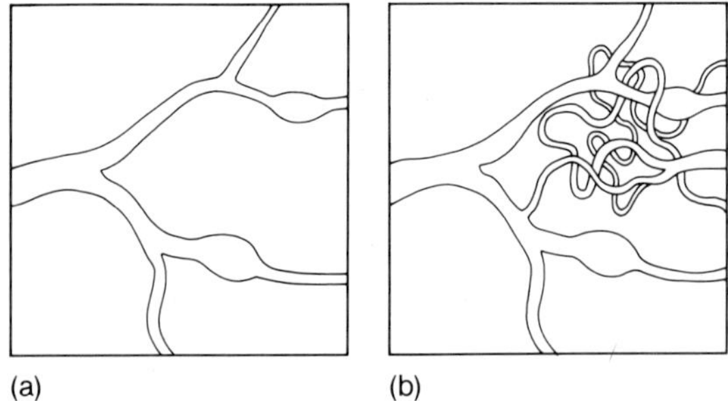

Figure 6.12 Blood vessels in diabetic retinopathy. (a) In early stages of the disease, blood vessels swell and leak slightly. (b) In later stages, abnormal new blood vessels (neovascularization) grow on the surface of the retina.

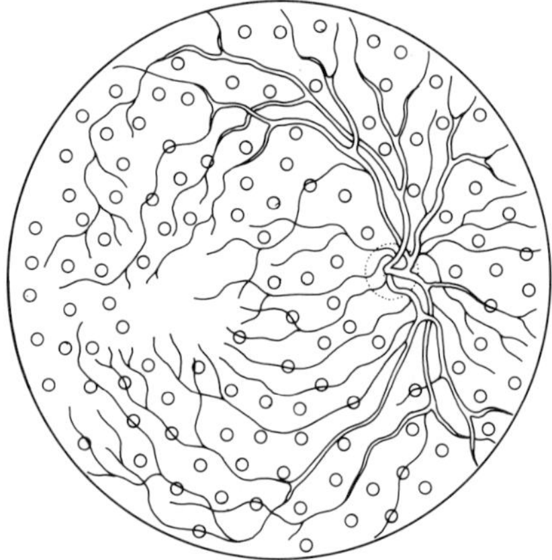

Figure 6.13 Laser photocoagulation for the treatment of diabetic retinopathy. The picture shown here illustrates the technique of panretinal photocoagulation. Each dot represents a small laser burn.

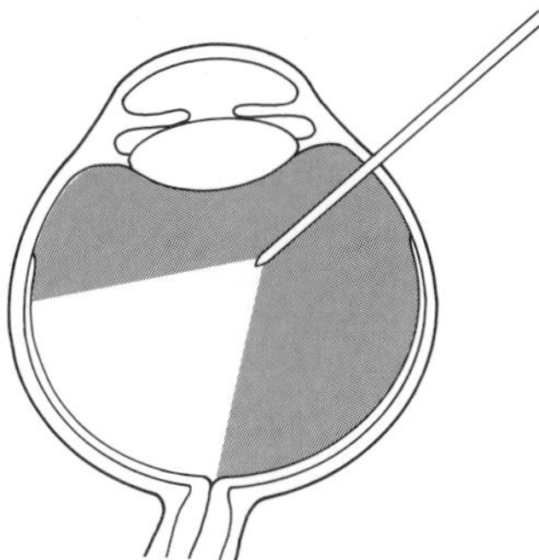

Figure 6.14 Vitrectomy. The hollow needle inserted into the eyeball first sucks out the liquid inside the eye and then fills the eyeball with a salt solution.

Although a complete cure for diabetic retinopathy has not yet been discovered, a recent series of tests, carried out by the National Eye Institute, indicates that laser photocoagulation reduces by 60 percent the chance that someone with diabetic retinopathy will suffer severe visual loss.

Macular Degeneration

Imagine your frustration if you could see everywhere *except* where you were looking—if every time you looked at something, you lost sight of it. That is exactly what happens if a region of the retina called the **macula** is damaged. The macula is an area about 5 mm in diameter that surrounds and includes the cone-rich fovea. If the macula degenerates, blindness results in the center of vision, as in Figure 6.15. This condition is extremely debilitating because, although peripheral vision remains intact, the elimination of central vision makes reading impossible.

- Macular degeneration is the second leading cause of blindness, accounting for 60,000 cases.
- Macular degeneration is the leading cause of blindness in people over 75 years old.

There are a number of forms of **macular degeneration,** but the most common is called **senile mac-**

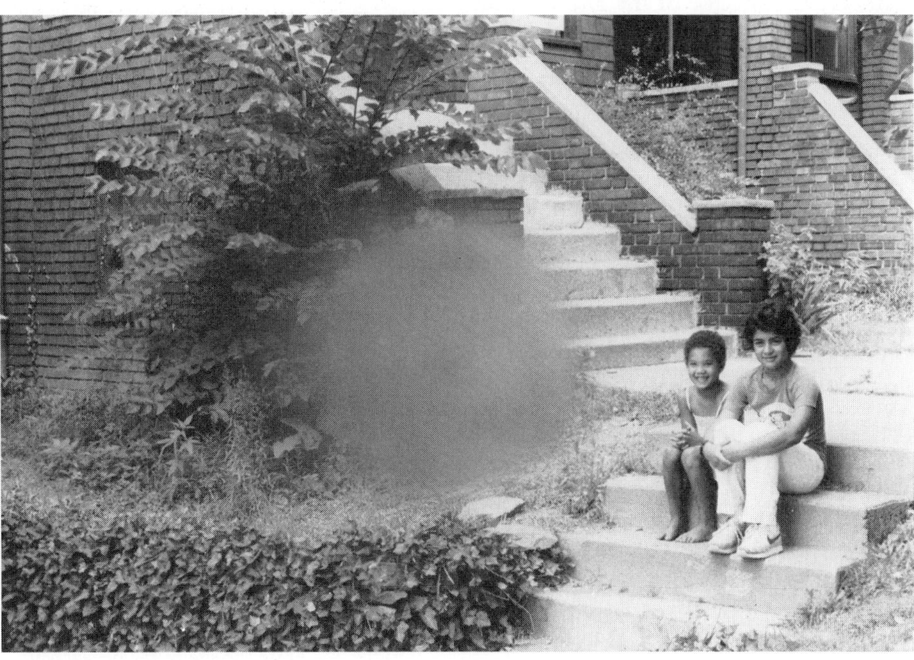

Figure 6.15 Macular degeneration causes a loss of central vision, as shown above.

ular degeneration, because it occurs, without obvious reason, in older people. In its mild form, there is a slight thinning of the cone receptors and the formation of small white or yellow lumps on the retina. This form of macular degeneration usually progresses slowly and may not cause serious visual problems. In 5–20 percent of the cases, however, small new blood vessels, similar to those formed in diabetic retinopathy, grow underneath the macula area of the retina. These new blood vessels form very rapidly—over a period of only 1–2 months—and leak fluid into the macula, killing the cone receptors.

Until recently, there was no treatment for senile macular degeneration. However, a recent study by the National Eye Institute indicates that in many patients with severe degeneration, laser photocoagulation can stop or greatly reduce leakage from the newly formed vessels. This study, originally intended to last five years, was termed a success after only three, and in 1982 the Eye Institute held a press conference to alert ophthalmologists to this new way of treating this form of senile macular degeneration.

Dr. Carl Kupfer, director of the Eye Institute, stated at the press conference, "We believe that these findings may save as many as 13,000 Americans from going blind in the next year. That would mean that the expected nationwide incidence of blindness can be reduced by almost 14 percent over the next year." To achieve such dramatic results, however, laser treatment should be started as soon as the abnormal blood vessels begin forming and must be started before the disease progresses to where the fovea, at the macula's center, becomes damaged by the leaking vessels. Since this disease progresses so rapidly once it begins, speedy treatment is essential if blindness is to be prevented.

Detached Retina

Before I came to Pittsburgh, I lived in Boston for two years. I was lucky enough to be there in 1967, when the Boston Red Sox won the American League pennant for the first time since 1946. One of the star players on that team, Tony Conigliaro, was hit by a pitch six weeks before the World Series and began complaining that he could not see well—he had fuzzy vision and found it difficult to catch what would have been routine fly balls. Tests at the Massachusetts Eye and Ear Infirmary showed that the reason for Conigliaro's fuzzy vision was that his retina had become detached from the underlying pigment epithelium, as shown in Figure 6.16. Although attempts were made to reattach his retina, Conigliaro's vision never returned to normal, and his baseball career was ended. More recently, it was discovered that Sugar Ray Leonard, the welterweight boxing champion, had suffered a detached retina, and his doctors told him that he would risk losing all vision in the affected eye if he continued boxing.

A **detached retina** affects vision for two reasons. (1) For good image formation, the retina must lie smoothly on top of the pigment epithelium. (2) More importantly, when the retina loses contact with the pigment epithelium, the visual pigments in the detached area are separated from enzymes in the epithelium necessary for pigment regeneration. When the visual pigment can no longer regenerate, that area of the retina becomes blind.

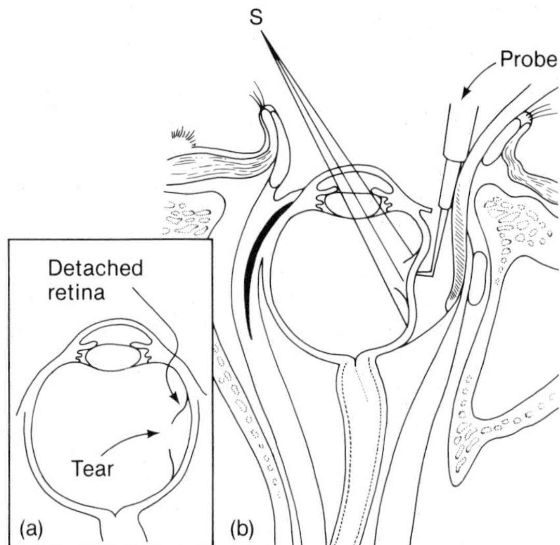

Figure 6.16 (a) A detached retina. (b) Procedure for reattaching the retina. To locate the site of detachment, a probe pushes the eyeball from outside while the surgeon, at S, looks into the eye. Once the site of the detachment is located, the outside of the eye is marked and a cooling or heating probe is applied at the marked point.

- 25,000 cases of detached retina are reported each year.
- 6,000 people lose vision in one eye, due to detached retina, each year.

The treatment for a detached retina is an operation that attempts to reattach it. The basic idea of this operation is to cause the formation of scar tissue inside the eye that will attach itself to the retina and anchor it in place. This is accomplished by applying either a cooling or a heating probe to exactly the right place on the outside of the eyeball. Figure 6.16(b) shows the procedure used to determine where to apply the probe. While looking into the eye with a special viewing device, the surgeon presses on the outside of the eyeball, which causes an indentation that can be seen inside the eye. The surgeon presses at a number of points, until the indentation inside the eyeball matches the location of the tear or hole in the retina, where the detachment originated. Once the correct point is located, it is marked on the outside of the eyeball, and that point is cooled or heated to create an inflammatory response. This inflammation causes scarring that "welds" the retina back onto the pigment epithelium. If the area of detached retina is not too big, there is a 70–80 percent chance that this procedure will work. In most cases this procedure restores vision, although vision is sometimes not restored even though the retina is successfully reattached. The larger the detached area, the less likely it is that this operation will work.

Hereditary Retinal Degeneration

The most common form of retinal degeneration is a disease called **retinitis pigmentosa,** a disease that has blinded 26,000 people. We know that retinitis pigmentosa is a **hereditary retinal degeneration**—it is passed on from one generation to the next—but we know little about what actually causes the disease. One hypothesis is that it is caused by a problem in the pigment epithelium.

The first symptom of retinitis pigmentosa, which usually appears around adolescence, is difficulty in seeing at night, since the disease first attacks the rod receptors. As the person gets older, the disease slowly progresses, causing further losses of vision in the peripheral retina. Then, in its final stages, which may not occur until late in the person's life, retinitis pigmentosa also attacks the cones, resulting in complete blindness.

Optic Nerve Damage

Glaucoma

Glaucoma, the leading cause of blindness in the United States, causes nerve fibers in the optic nerve to degenerate, thereby preventing the nerve impulses generated by the retina from being transmitted to the brain. Although the end result of glaucoma is damage to the optic nerve, the source of the problem is at the front of the eye.

- Glaucoma is the leading cause of blindness, accounting for 62,000 cases.
- 2 million people over 35 have glaucoma.
- 178,000 new cases of glaucoma are reported each year.
- Over $30 million per year is spent for just one type of eyedrop used to treat glaucoma.

Figure 6.17(a) is a cross section of the front of the eye. Under normal conditions, **aqueous humor**—the liquid found in the space between the cornea and lens—which is continuously produced at A, passes between the iris and lens (following the path indicated by the arrows), then drains from the eye at B. In glaucoma the drainage of aqueous humor is partially blocked. In **closed-angle glaucoma** the iris is pushed up, as shown in Figure 6.17(b), thereby closing the angle between the cornea and iris. This pushing up of the iris hinders the flow of aqueous humor in two ways: (1) a **pupillary block** constricts the opening between the iris and lens, making it more difficult for the aqueous to get through the opening; and (2) the pushed up iris blocks the area at B, where the aqueous leaves the eye. In **open-angle glaucoma** the eye looks normal, as in Figure 6.17(a), but the drainage area at B is partially blocked, making it difficult for the aqueous to leave the eye.

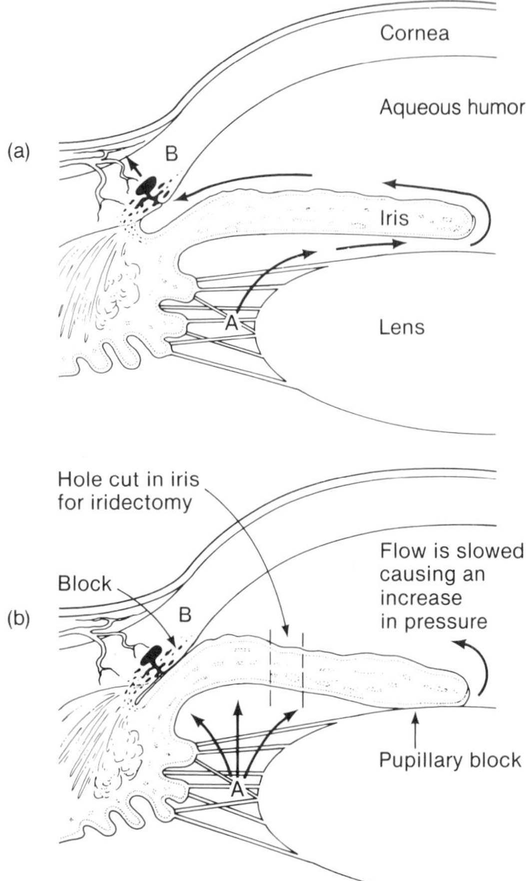

Figure 6.17 (a) Arrows indicate the flow of aqueous humor in the normal eye. The aqueous is produced at A and leaves the eye at B. In open-angle glaucoma, the aqueous cannot leave the eye, due to a blockage at B. (b) In closed-angle glaucoma, the raised iris causes a pupillary block that hinders the flow of aqueous from the eye. An iridectomy—cutting a hole in the iris—can be performed to provide a way for the aqueous to reach B.

The blocks that occur in both closed- and open-angle glaucoma result in a large resistance to the outflow of aqueous humor, and, since the aqueous continues to be produced inside the eye, the **intraocular pressure**—the pressure inside the eyeball—rises. This increase in intraocular pressure has two effects: (1) it compresses the blood vessels that provide nourishment to the retina, and (2) it presses on the head of the optic nerve at the back of the eye. These effects result in degeneration of the optic nerve fibers, and this degeneration results in blindness.

The increase in pressure that occurs in closed-angle glaucoma usually happens very rapidly and is accompanied by pain. The treatment for this type of glaucoma is an operation called an **iridectomy,** in which a small hole is cut in the iris, as shown in Figure 6.17(b). This hole opens a channel through which the aqueous can flow and also causes the iris to flatten out, thereby uncovering the area at B so the aqueous can flow out of the eye.

Intraocular pressure increases more slowly in open-angle glaucoma, which can often be treated by medication that brings down the pressure, either by slowing the production of aqueous or by opening the blockage at B. Fortunately, open-angle glaucoma (by far the most common type, accounting for about 85 percent of all glaucoma) progresses slowly enough that, if it is diagnosed in time, medication will probably decrease the pressure. In 5–10 percent of the cases of open-angle glaucoma, medications do not decrease the pressure, and an operation becomes necessary. The goal of this operation is to cut an opening at B that enables the aqueous to flow out. Recently, some success has been achieved by using lasers to open this area.

The Eye Examination

So far, we have described some of the things that can go wrong with the eye and how these problems are treated. In this part of the chapter, we will describe the procedures used to uncover some of these problems. Before describing the eye examination, however, we should consider who examines the eye.

Who Examines Eyes?

There are three types of professionals involved in eye care: ophthalmologists, optometrists, and opticians. We will consider each in turn.

1. Ophthalmologists. An **ophthalmologist** is an M.D. who has completed undergraduate school and four years of medical school, which provide general medical training. In order to

become an ophthalmologist, a person needs four or more years of training after graduation from medical school to learn how to medically and surgically treat eye problems. Some ophthalmologists receive even further training to specialize in specific areas such as pediatric ophthalmology (practice limited to children), diseases of the cornea, retinal diseases, or glaucoma. Most ophthalmologists, however, treat all eye problems, as well as prescribing glasses and fitting contact lenses.

2. Optometrists. An **optometrist** has completed undergraduate school and, after four years of additional study, has received a doctor of optometry (O.D.) degree. Optometrists can examine eyes and fit and prescribe glasses or contact lenses, but if they find eye diseases, they refer patients with these problems to an ophthalmologist. In general, optometrists cannot prescribe drugs, although this is a controversial issue, and bills have been introduced in some state legislatures that would allow optometrists to make limited use of some drugs.
3. Opticians. **Opticians** are trained to fit glasses and, in some states, contact lenses, on the prescription of an ophthalmologist or an optometrist.

What Happens During an Eye Exam?

The basic aims of an eye exam are: (1) to determine how well the patient can see, (2) to correct vision if it is defective, (3) to determine the causes of defective vision by examining the optics of the eye and checking for eye diseases, and (4) to diagnose diseases that the patient may not even be aware of. To accomplish these aims, an ophthalmologist usually performs the following procedures:

Taking a medical history. The first step in an eye exam is to take a medical history. This history focuses on any eye problems that the patient may have had in the past and on any current eye problems.

Measuring visual acuity. This is the familiar part of the eye exam, in which you are asked to read letters on an eye chart like the one in Figure 6.18.

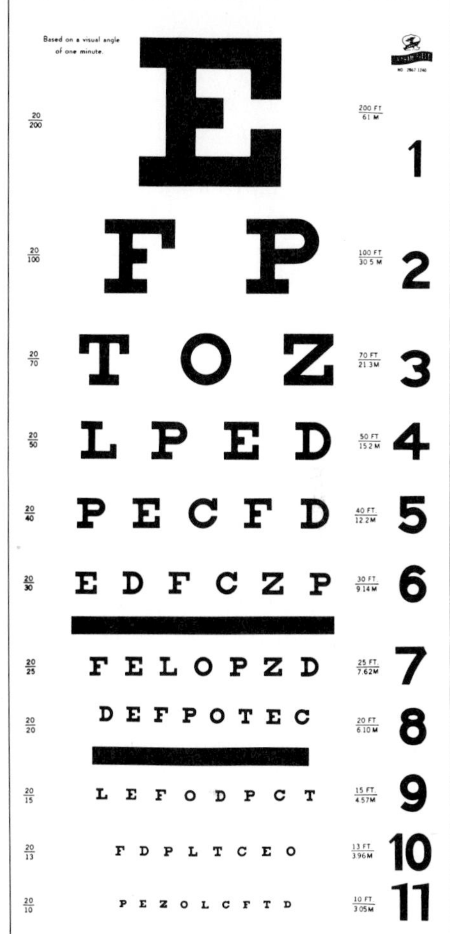

Figure 6.18 Snellen eye chart used to test visual acuity.

The *E* at the top of the chart is usually the 20/200 line, which means that a person with normal vision should be able to see the *E* from a distance of 200 feet. Since the eye chart is usually viewed from about 20 feet, people with normal vision see the *E* easily. When asked to read the smallest line he or she can see, the patient usually picks a line that is easily read. With a little encouragement, however, the patient finds that he or she can see lines smaller than the one originally picked, and the examiner has the patient read smaller and smaller lines until letters are missed. The smallest line a person can read indicates his or her visual **acuity,** with normal vision defined as an acuity of 20/20. A person with worse than normal acuity, say, 20/40, must view a display from a distance of 20 feet to see what a person with normal acuity can see at 40 feet. A person with better than normal acuity, say, 10/20, can see from a distance of 20 feet what a person with normal vision must view from 10 feet.

It is important to realize that the visual acuity test described above tests only foveal vision. When you read an eye chart, you look directly at each letter, so the image of that letter falls on your fovea. Thus, as mentioned earlier, a person who scores 20/20 on a visual acuity test can still be classified as being legally blind, if he or she has little or no vision in the periphery. Testing peripheral vision is usually not part of a routine eye exam, so we will describe how this is done at the end of the chapter.

In addition to testing far vision, it is also customary to test near vision, especially in older patients who may be experiencing the effects of presbyopia (see p. 140). This is done by having them read the smallest line of a card, like the one in Figure 6.19, from a comfortable reading distance.

No. 1

In short-sighted persons the eye-ball is too long, and the light rays come to a focus in front of the retina,

No. 2

while in far-sighted persons the eye-ball is too short, and the focal point, therefore, falls be-

No. 3

hind the retina. In either case a blurred image is received upon the retina. In order

No. 4

to overcome this blurring, and thus correct the optical defect, the eye un-

No. 6

consciously makes an effort by which the ciliary muscle acts on

No. 8

the lens. This effort explains why eye-strain may cause

No. 10

pain and discomfort. An optical correction for

No. 12

the refractive error is found in specta-

Figure 6.19 Card for testing close vision. The patient's close vision is measured by determining the smallest line that he or she can read from a comfortable reading distance.

Refraction. A score of 20/60 on a visual acuity test indicates worse than normal acuity but does not indicate what is causing this loss of acuity. Acuity could be decreased by one of the diseases described earlier or by a problem in focusing—myopia, hyperopia, or astigmatism. If the problem lies in the focusing mechanism of the eye, it is usually easily corrected by glasses or contact lenses. **Refraction** is the procedure used to determine the power of corrective lenses needed to achieve clear vision.

The first step in refraction is a **retinoscopy exam**—an examination of the eye with a device called a retinoscope. This device projects a streak of light into the eye that is reflected into the eye of the examiner. The examiner moves the retinoscope back and forth and up and down across the eye, noticing what the reflected light looks like. If the patient's eye is focusing the light correctly, the examiner sees the whole pupil filled with light, and no correction is necessary (in this case, the patient usually will have tested at 20/20 or better in the visual acuity test). If, however, the patient's eye is not focusing the light correctly, the examiner sees a streak of light move back and forth across the pupil as the streak of light from the retinoscope is moved across the eye.

To determine the correction needed to bring the patient's eye to 20/20 vision, the examiner places corrective lenses in front of the eye while still moving the streak of light from the retinoscope back and forth. One way of placing these lenses in front of the eye is to use a device like the one shown in Figure 6.20. This device contains a variety of lenses that can be changed by turning a dial. The examiner's goal is to find the lens that causes the whole pupil to fill up with light when the retinoscope is moved back and forth. This lens brings light to a focus on the retina and is usually close to the one that will be prescribed to achieve 20/20 vision.

The retinoscopy exam results in a good first approximation of the correct lens to prescribe for a patient, but the ultimate test is what the patient sees. To determine this, the patient looks at the eye chart while the examiner places first one lens and then another in front of the patient's eyes and asks which one results in the clearest vision. When the examiner determines which lens results in 20/20 vision, he writes a prescription for glasses or contact lenses. To fit contact lenses after determining the prescription, the examiner must match the shape of the contact lens to the shape of the patient's cornea.

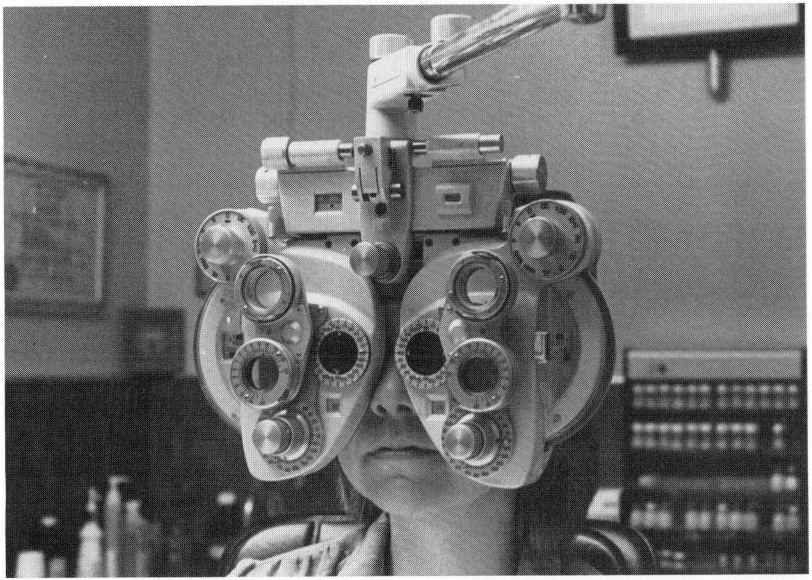

Figure 6.20 A device for placing different corrective lenses in front of the patient's eyes. Different lenses are placed in front of the eye during the retinoscopy exam and again as the patient looks at the eye chart.

The procedure described above is used to determine the correction needed to achieve clear far vision. Using a procedure we will not describe here, the examiner also determines whether a correction is needed to achieve clear near vision. This is particularly important for patients over 45 years old, who may experience reading difficulties due to presbyopia.

External eye exam. In an **external eye exam,** the examiner uses a variety of tests to check the condition of the external eye. He checks pupillary reaction by shining light into the eye, to see if the pupil responds by closing when the light is presented and opening when the light is removed. He also checks the color of the eye and surrounding tissues. "Red eye" may indicate that an inflammation is present. The examiner checks eye movement by having the patient follow a moving finger, and he checks the alignment of the eyes by having the patient look at a target. If they are aligned correctly, both eyes will look directly at the target; but if the eyes are misaligned, one eye will look at the target, and the other will veer off to one side.

Slit lamp examination. The **slit lamp examination** checks the condition of the cornea and lens. The slit lamp, shown in Figure 6.21, projects a narrow slit of light into the patient's eye. This light can be precisely focused at different places inside the eye, and the examiner views this sharply focused slit of light through a binocular magnifier. This slit of light is like the sharp edge of a knife that cuts through the eye.

What does the examiner see as he looks at the "cutting edge" of light from the slit lamp? By focusing the light at different levels inside the cornea and lens, the examiner can detect small imperfections—places where the cornea or lens is not completely transparent—which cannot be seen by any other method. These imperfections may indicate corneal disease or injury or the formation of a cataract.

Tonometry. **Tonometry** measures the intraocular pressure—the pressure inside the eye—and is, therefore, the test for glaucoma. Nowadays, an instrument called a **tonometer** is used to measure intraocular pressure, but before the development of

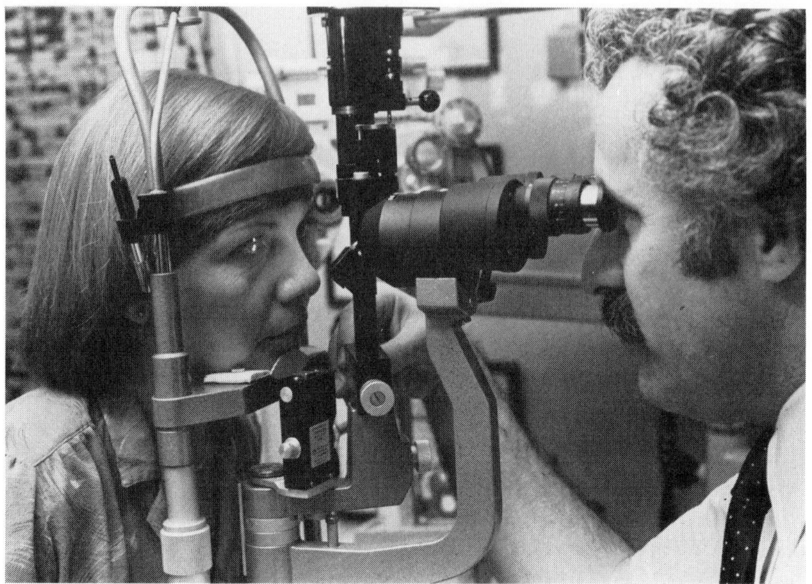

Figure 6.21 A patient being examined with a slit lamp. The examiner is checking the condition of the lens and cornea by viewing the slit of light through a binocular magnifier.

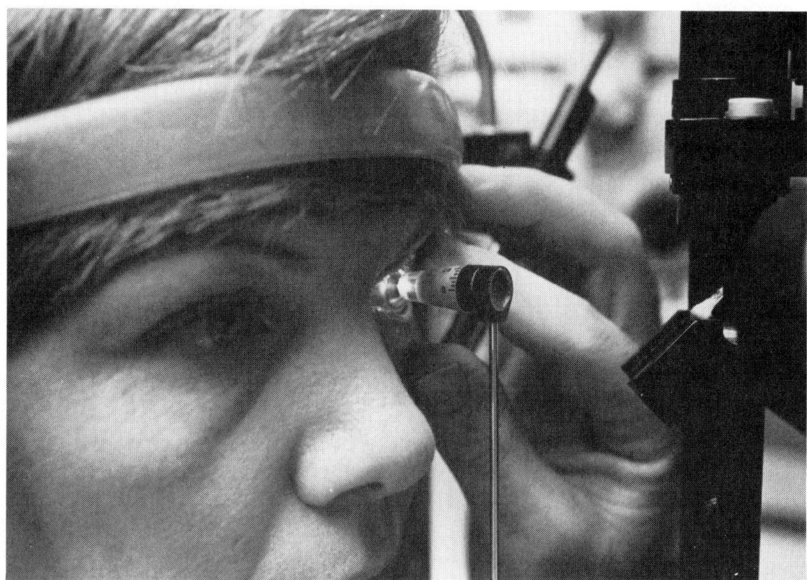

Figure 6.22 An applination tonometer being applied to a patient's cornea.

this device, it was known that large increases of intraocular pressure, which accompany severe cases of glaucoma, cause the eye to become so hard that this hardness could be detected by pushing on the eyeball with a finger.

There are several types of tonometers, which measure the intraocular pressure by pushing on the cornea. The Schiotz tonometer is a hand-held device that consists of a small plunger attached to a calibrated weight. The weight pushes the plunger and indents the cornea. If the intraocular pressure is high, the plunger causes a smaller indentation than if the intraocular pressure is normal. Thus, intraocular pressure is determined by measuring the indentation of the cornea. (Though this procedure may sound rather painful, it is not, because the examiner applies a few drops of anesthetic to the cornea before applying the tonometer.)

The applination tonometer, shown being applied to a patient's cornea in Figure 6.22, is a more sophisticated and accurate instrument than the Schiotz tonometer. After a few drops of anesthetic are applied to the cornea, the flat end of a cylindrical rod, called an **applinator,** is slowly moved against the cornea by the examiner, who watches the applinator's progress through the same magnifiers used for the slit lamp exam (Figure 6.21). The examiner pushes the end of the applinator against the cornea until enough pressure is exerted to flatten a small area on the cornea's curved surface. The greater the force that must be exerted to flatten the cornea, the greater the intraocular pressure.

Ophthalmoscopy. So far, we have looked at the outside of the eye (external eye exam), examined the lens and cornea (slit lamp exam), and measured the intraocular pressure (tonometry), but we have yet to look at perhaps the most important structure of all—the retina. Since there is a hole in the front of the eye, it should be simple to see the retina; we only have to look into the hole. Unfortunately, it's not that simple; if you've ever looked into a person's pupil, you realize that it's dark in there. In order to see the retina, we must find some way to light up the inside of the eye.

We might try placing a light at L, as shown in Figure 6.23. This seems like a good idea until we try to look into the patient's eye. If I place my eye

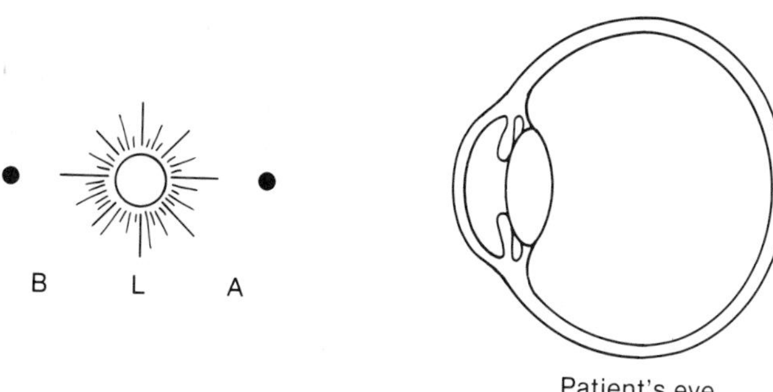

Figure 6.23 Ways to light up the inside of the eye that won't work. The light at L is blocked if the examiner's eye is positioned at A, and it blinds the examiner's eye positioned at B.

at A, my head blocks the light from L, and if I place my eye at B, I am blinded by the light at L. Clearly, neither of these methods will work.

It was not until 1850 that Hermann von Helmholtz, of the Young-Helmholtz theory of color vision (Figure 5.1), invented a device called the **ophthalmoscope.** The principle underlying Helmholtz's ophthalmoscope is shown in Figure 6.24. Helmholtz solved the problem of the blocked or blinding light of Figure 6.23 by placing the light off to the side and directing it into the patient's eye with a half-silvered mirror. The important property of a half-silvered mirror is that it simultaneously reflects and transmits light, so an examiner positioned as shown in Figure 6.24 can see through the mirror and into the patient's eye. Actual ophthalmoscopes are much more complicated than the one diagramed in Figure 6.24, consisting of numerous lenses, mirrors, and filters, but the basic principle remains the same as in the original ophthalmoscope designed by Helmholtz in 1850.

Figure 6.25 is a patient's-eye view of an examination with an ophthalmoscope. (See also chapter-opening illustration, which shows a patient being examined with an ophthalmoscope.) Color Plate 6.1 shows what the ophthalmologist sees if the patient has a normal retina. The most prominent features of this view of the retina are the place where the optic nerve leaves the eye (called the **optic disc**, or blind spot), and the arteries and veins of the retina. In his examination, the ophthalmologist focuses on these features, noting any abnormalities in the appearance of the optic disc and retinal circulation. For example, the ophthalmologist could detect the

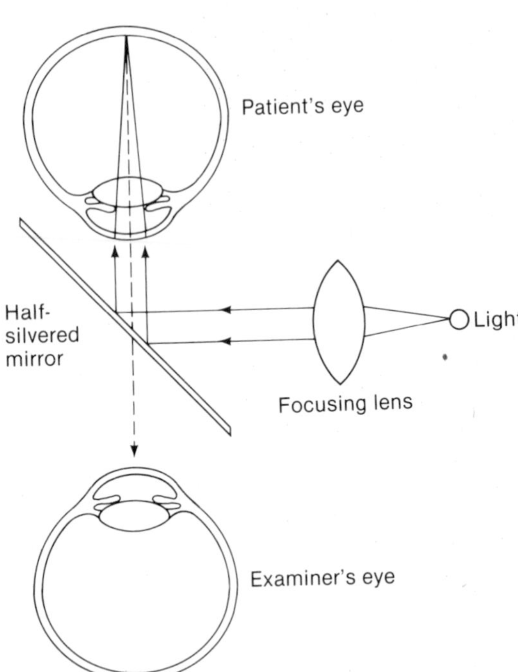

Figure 6.24 Principle behind the opthalmoscope. Light is reflected into the patient's eye by the half-silvered mirror. Some of this light is then reflected into the examiner's eye (along the dashed line), allowing the examiner to see the inside of the patient's eye.

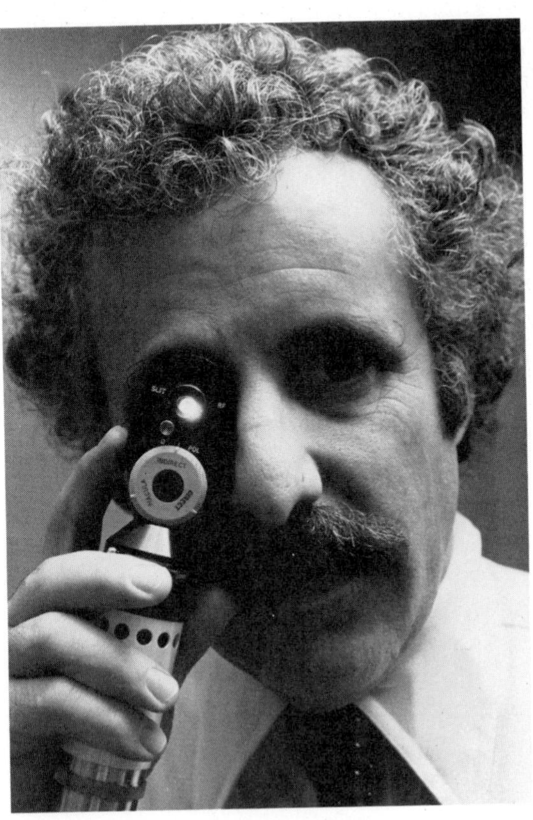

Figure 6.25 An ophthalmologist looking into your eye.

presence of diabetic retinopathy by noticing a number of very small blood vessels (neovascularization). In fact, all the retinal injuries and diseases described above cause some change in the appearance of the retina, which can be detected by looking at the retina with an ophthalmoscope.

Color Plate 6.2 shows the effect of glaucoma on the appearance of the retina. Compare the blood vessels near the optic discs in Color Plates 6.1 and 6.2. Notice that the blood vessels in the normal retina remain visible until they leave the eye in the middle of the optic disc, whereas the vessels in the eye with glaucoma vanish as they enter a depression in the optic disc. This effect results from the optic disc having been pushed in, or "cupped," by the high pressure inside the eye, as shown in Figure 6.26.

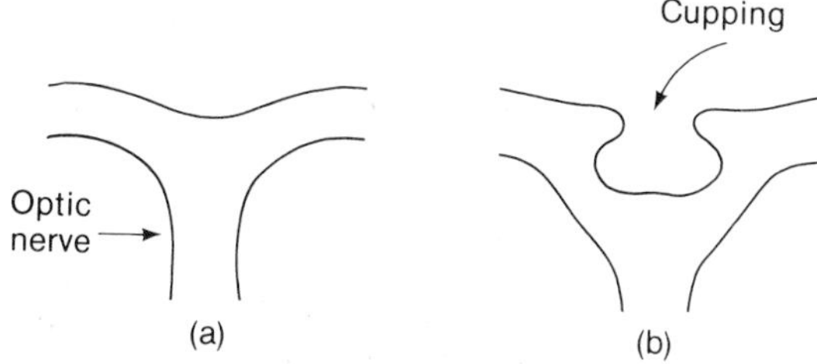

Figure 6.26 Side view of the optic nerve where it leaves the eye. (a) Normal optic nerve. (b) Optic nerve in eye with glaucoma, which shows "cupping" of optic disc.

Our description of an eye examination has covered most of the tests included in a routine exam. The ophthalmologist might decide to carry out a number of other tests if some problem were suggested by the routine tests. For example, a technique called **fluorescein angiography** is used to more closely examine the retinal circulation in patients with diabetic retinopathy. A fluorescent dye is injected intravenously into the arm, and when this dye reaches the retina, it outlines the retinal circulation. If the circulation is normal, the retinal arteries and veins are outlined sharply, as shown in Figure 6.27. If, however, the circulation is damaged by diabetic retinopathy, a splotchy angiogram results as shown in Figure 6.28.

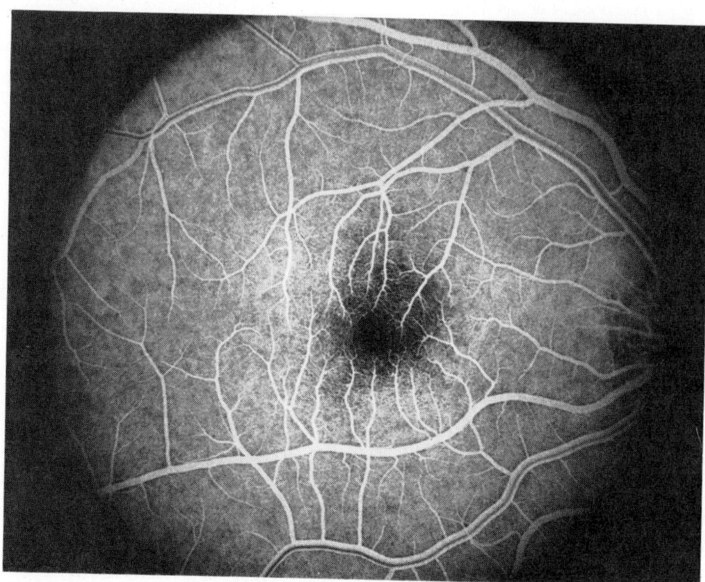

Figure 6.27 Fluorescent angiogram of a normal eye. In the normal eye, the blood vessels stand out in sharp contrast to the background. (Photograph courtesy of Eye and Ear Hospital of Pittsburgh.)

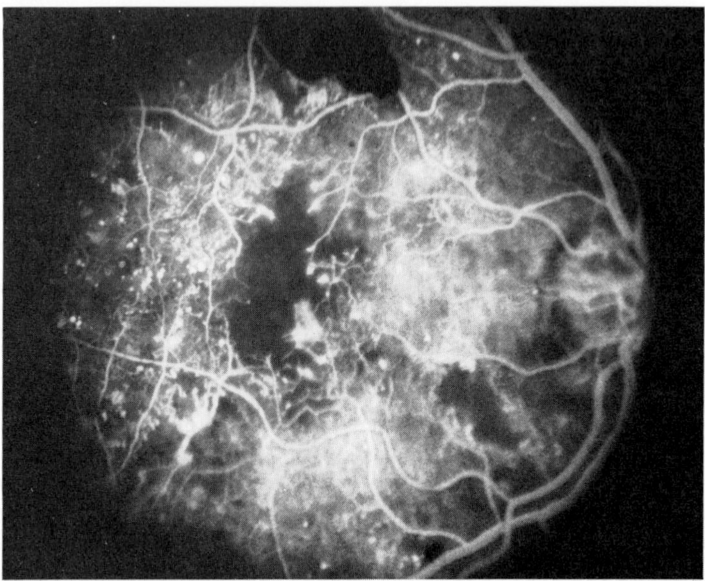

Figure 6.28 Fluorescein angiogram of an eye with diabetic retinopathy. The white areas and splotches indicate leakage of fluid. The dark form at the top is a blood clot inside the eye. (Photograph courtesy of Eye and Ear Hospital of Pittsburgh.)

Other tests, which we will not describe in detail here, include the **electroretinogram,** which measures the electrical response of the rod and cone receptors (useful in diagnosing retinal degenerations such as retinitis pigmentosa), and the **visual field test,** which measures a person's ability to see in both the fovea and the periphery. This test locates blind spots (called *scotomas*) that might be caused by retinal degeneration, detachment of the retina, or diseases such as glaucoma.

Summary

1. There are four major types of problems that can cause poor vision: (1) light is not focused clearly on the retina; (2) light is blurred as it enters the eye; (3) the retina is damaged; and (4) the optic nerve is damaged.
2. The cornea and the lens are the major focusing elements of the eye.
3. Accommodation is a process in which the focusing power of the eye is increased by tightening the ciliary muscles. This tightening of the ciliary muscles increases the curvature of the lens. Accommodation enables us to adjust the lens's focusing power to keep the image on the retina sharp as we look at objects located at different distances.
4. The near point is the distance at which a person's eye can no longer use accommodation to bring nearby objects into focus. The near point increases as a person ages until, at about 45 years of age, it moves past a comfortable reading distance. This decrease in the ability to accommodate to nearby objects, as age increases, is called presbyopia.
5. Myopia is the inability to see distant objects clearly. In the myopic eye, parallel light rays come to a focus in front of the retina. The blurred vision of myopia can be corrected by glasses or contact lenses.

6. Hyperopia is the inability to see nearby objects clearly. In the hyperopic eye, the focus point for parallel light rays is behind the retina. Hyperopia can be corrected with glasses or contact lenses.
7. Astigmatism, which is caused by a misshapen cornea, results in blurring of some objects but not others. This condition can be corrected by glasses.
8. A person is considered legally blind if, after correction with glasses or contact lenses, he or she has visual acuity of 20/200 or less in the better eye. A person with good central (foveal) but little peripheral vision can also be considered legally blind.
9. Disease or injury can decrease the transparency of the cornea and cause a blurred image on the retina. Corneal problems can be treated with drugs or corrected by a corneal transplant operation.
10. The most common cause of clouding of the lens, or cataract, is old age. In severe cases of cataract, the lens is removed and often replaced with an intraocular lens, which is implanted inside the eye.
11. Diabetic retinopathy is a condition that causes damage to the retina of some people with diabetes. Loss of vision can often be prevented by an operation called laser photocoagulation.
12. Macular degeneration is a degeneration of the macula, the area surrounding the fovea. Laser photocoagulation can often decrease the loss of sight caused by a severe form of macular degeneration.
13. Detached retina, the detachment of the retina from the underlying pigment epithelium, causes a loss of vision in the area of detachment. The retina can often be reattached by heating or cooling the area on the outside of the eyeball adjacent to the detachment.
14. Retinitis pigmentosa is a hereditary disease that causes degeneration of the retina. There is no known treatment for this disease.
15. Glaucoma, the leading cause of blindness in the United States, causes nerve fibers in the optic nerve to degenerate, due to a buildup of pressure inside the eye. This buildup of pressure can usually be decreased by means of drugs or surgery.
16. The three types of professionals involved in eye care are ophthalmologists, optometrists, and opticians.
17. A basic eye exam consists of the following procedures: taking a medical history, measuring visual acuity, refraction, external eye exam, slit lamp examination, tonometry, and ophthalmoscopy.
18. Visual acuity, a test of foveal vision, is measured by having a person read an eye chart.
19. The eye is refracted by using a device called a retinoscope. The result of this procedure is an estimate of the correction needed to bring a person's eye to 20/20 visual acuity.
20. The slit lamp examination checks the condition of the cornea and the lens.
21. Tonometry, which measures the intraocular pressure, is used to detect glaucoma.
22. A device called an ophthalmoscope enables an examiner to see the optic disc, as well as the arteries, veins, and other features of the retina.
23. Fluorescein angiography is used to examine the retinal circulation in patients with diabetic retinopathy and other conditions that affect the retinal circulation.

Glossary

Accommodation The eye's ability to bring objects located at different distances into focus by changing the shape of the lens. (139)

Acuity The ability to resolve small details. During an eye examination, acuity is measured by determining the smallest letters that a person can read on an eye chart. (153)

Applinator The part of an applination tonometer that is pushed against the patient's cornea to determine the intraocular pressure. (156)

Aqueous humor The liquid found in the space between the cornea and lens of the eye. (151)

Astigmatism A condition in which objects in some orientations are seen as blurred because the cornea is misshapen. (144)

Blindness A person is considered legally blind if he or she has visual acuity of 20/200 or less after correction, or if he or she has little peripheral vision. (144)

Cataract A lens that is clouded. (148)

Cataract, congenital A cataract present at birth. (146)

Cataract, secondary A cataract caused by another eye disease. (146)

Cataract, senile A cataract due to old age. This is the most common form of cataract. (146)

Cataract, traumatic A cataract caused by injury. (146)

Cornea The transparent structure at the front of the eye that is the eye's major focusing element. (145)

Corneal disease and injury Any disease or injury that damages the cornea, causing a loss of transparency. (145)

Corneal transplant The replacement of a damaged piece of cornea with a piece of healthy cornea taken from a donor. (145)

Cryoextraction Extraction of a cataract by placing a very cold probe on the lens. The lens sticks to this probe and is then lifted out of the eye. (146)

Cryopreservation A technique that preserves a donor cornea by slowly bringing it down to a temperature of $-120°$ C. (146)

Detached retina A condition in which the retina is detached from the back of the eye. (150)

Diabetes A condition in which the body doesn't produce enough insulin. One side effect of diabetes is a loss of vision due to diabetic retinopathy. (148)

Diabetic retinopathy Retinal damage that is a side effect of diabetes. This condition sometimes causes neovascularization—the formation of abnormal small blood vessels, which do not supply the retina with adequate oxygen and which bleed into the vitreous humor. (148)

Diopter The focusing power of a lens needed to achieve clear vision. The number of diopters needed to achieve clear vision = 1/far point in meters. Therefore, the closer the far point, the greater the required number of diopters. (See Figure 6.6.) (142)

Electroretinogram An electrical response of the rod and cone receptors to light, which is useful in diagnosing retinal degenerations such as retinitis pigmentosa. (160)

External eye exam Examination of the condition of the external eye. This exam includes, among other things, examination of the reaction of the pupil to light, the color of the eye, and alignment of the eyes. (155)

Far point The farthest distance at which a stimulus results in a focused image on the retina. The far point is at infinity for people with normal vision but is closer for people with myopic vision. Therefore, without a corrective lens, myopes cannot bring stimuli beyond the far point into focus on the retina. (142)

Fluorescein angiography A technique in which a fluorescent dye is injected into a person's circulation. The way this dye outlines the retinal arteries and veins indicates the condition of the retinal circulation. (159)

Focusing power The degree to which a structure such as the lens or cornea bends light. The greater the focusing power, the more the light passing through that structure is bent. (139)

Glaucoma A disease of the eye that results in an increase in intraocular pressure. (151)

Glaucoma, closed-angle A form of glaucoma in which the iris is pushed up so that it closes the angle between the iris and cornea, thereby blocking the area through which the aqueous humor normally drains out of the eye. (151)

Glaucoma, open-angle A form of glaucoma in which the area through which the aqueous normally drains out of the eye is partially blocked. In this form of glaucoma, the iris remains in its normal position, so the angle between the iris and cornea remains open. (151)

Hyperopia (farsightedness) Inability to see near objects clearly because the focus point for parallel rays of light is behind the retina. (143)

Intraocular lens A corrective lens that is permanently implanted in the eye to replace the lens removed in a cataract operation. (147)

Intraocular pressure Pressure inside the eyeball. (152)

Iridectomy A procedure used to treat closed-angle glaucoma, in which a small hole is cut in the iris. This hole opens a channel through which aqueous humor can flow out of the eye. (152)

Laser photocoagulation A procedure in which a laser beam "photocoagulates" blood vessels that are leaking due to neovascularization. This photocoagulation seals off the blood vessels and stops the leaking. (148)

Lens The transparent focusing element of the eye through which light passes after passing through the cornea and aqueous humor. (146)

Macula An area about 5 mm in diameter that surrounds and includes the cone-rich fovea. (149)

Macular degeneration A degeneration of the macula. (149)

Macular degeneration, senile Degeneration of the macula that occurs in older people. This is the most common form of macular degeneration. (149)

Myopia (nearsightedness) Inability to see distant objects clearly because parallel rays of light are brought to a focus in front of the retina. (141)

Myopia, axial Myopia that occurs when the eyeball is too long. (141)

Myopia, refractive Myopia that occurs when the cornea and lens bend light too much (they have too much focusing power). (141)

Near point The distance at which the lens can no longer accommodate to bring close objects into focus. Objects nearer than the near point can only be brought into focus by using corrective lenses. (140)

Neovascularization The formation of abnormal small blood vessels that occurs in some patients with diabetic retinopathy. (148)

Ophthalmologist A person who has specialized in the medical treatment of the eye by completing four or more years of training after receiving the M.D. degree. (153)

Ophthalmoscope A device that enables an examiner to see the retina and retinal circulation inside the eye. (158)

Ophthalmoscopy The use of an ophthalmoscope to visualize the retina and retinal circulation. (156)

Optic disc The disc-shaped area at the back of the eye where the optic nerve leaves the eye. (158)

Optician A person who is trained to fit glasses and, in some cases, contact lenses. (153)

Optometrist A person who has received the doctor of optometry (O.D.) degree, by completing four years of postgraduate study in optometry school. (153)

Panretinal coagulation A procedure used to stop the bleeding caused by neovascularization, in which a laser scatters 2,000 or more tiny burns on the retina. (148)

Phacoemulsification A technique for removing a cataract by breaking up the lens with ultrasonic vibrations and then sucking the pieces of lens out of the eye through a hollow needle. (146)

Pigment epithelium A layer of cells that lines the inside of the eyeball. The retina rests on the pigment epithelium. (147)

Presbyopia ("old eye") Inability of the eye to accommodate due to the hardening of the lens and weakening of the ciliary muscles, which occur as people get older. (140)

Pupillary block A blockage that constricts the opening between the iris and lens of the eye, making it difficult for aqueous humor to leave the eye. It is caused by the pushed up iris that is characteristic of closed-angle glaucoma. (151)

Refraction A procedure used to determine the power of corrective lenses needed to achieve clear vision. (154)

Retinal degeneration, hereditary Degeneration of the retina that is inherited. There are many different forms of retinal degeneration, the most common being retinitis pigmentosa. (151)

Retinitis pigmentosa A hereditary retinal disease that causes a gradual loss of vision and can ultimately result in blindness. (151)

Retinoscopy exam Examination with a device called a retinoscope, which indicates the power of the corrective lens needed to achieve normal vision. (154)

Slit lamp exam An examination that checks the condition of the cornea and lens. (155)

Tonometer A device that measures the pressure inside the eye by pressing on the surface of the cornea. (155)

Tonometry An examination that measures the pressure inside the eye. (155)

Tunnel vision A condition in which peripheral

vision is absent, but some central vision remains. Perceptually, the effect of this loss of peripheral vision is like looking down a tunnel. (145)

Visual field test A test that measures a person's ability to see in both the fovea and the periphery. (160)

Vitrectomy A procedure in which a hollow needle placed inside the eye sucks out the vitreous humor and replaces it with a salt solution. This procedure is used when the vitreous humor is filled with blood from leakage of the retinal circulation. (148)

Vitreous humor The jellylike substance that fills the eyeball. (148)

Chapter Seven

Organization, Recognition, and Attention

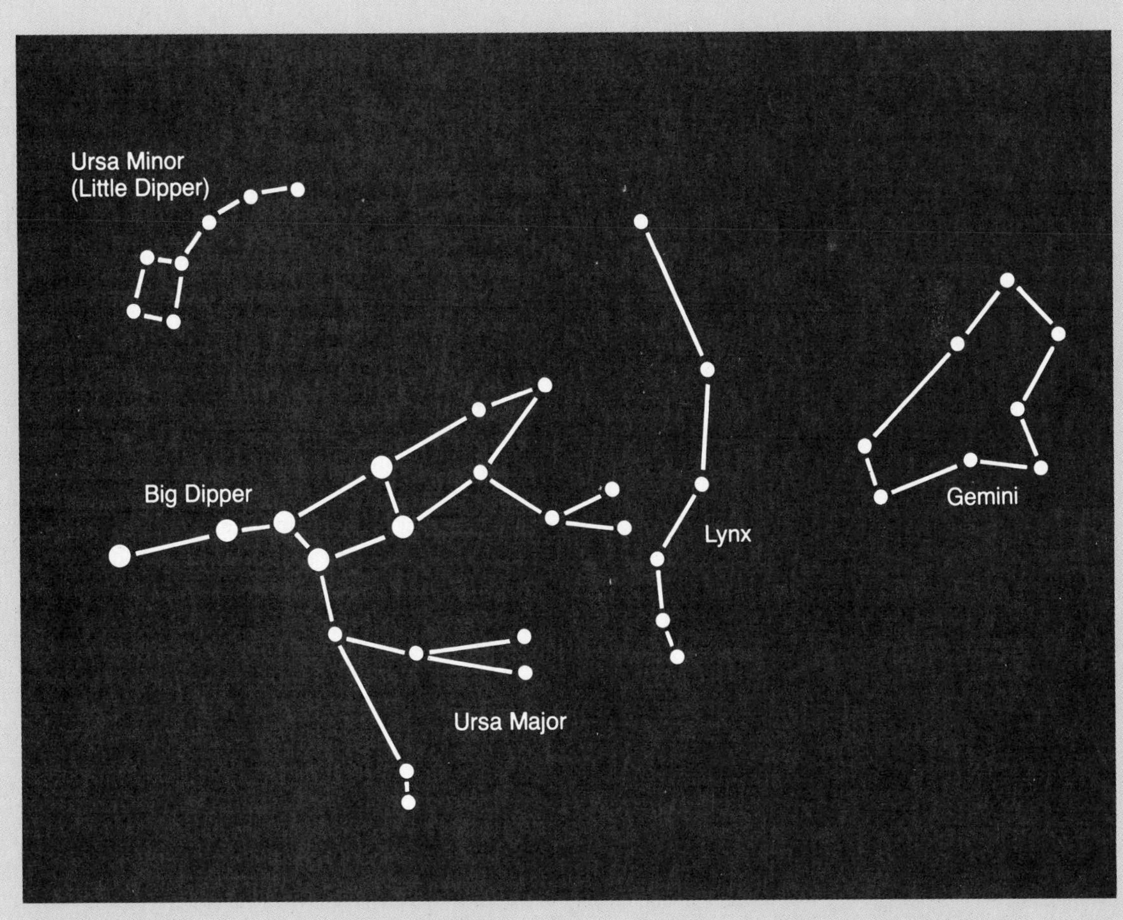

> Many mornings at breakfast I come face-to-face with form perception when my six-year-old son Adam tells me that he is about to eat the elephant (or some other animal) which has appeared in his scrambled eggs. Adam's perception of an elephant in his scrambled eggs means that the pieces of egg on his plate have become perceptually organized so that they look like an elephant.
>
> —From the First Edition

Adam is now eleven and he still sees animals in his eggs. There is, however, nothing strange about his behavior. People have been organizing small elements into larger objects since before written history, as evidenced by the constellations shown in the chapter-opening illustration.

We should not, however, suppose that perceptual organization is simply a curiosity that creates animals from food and big and little dippers from the stars. Perceptual organization is essential for making sense of the world. When you look at a country scene and see a barnyard surrounded by trees, the process of organization enables you to separate the barnyard from the trees and to see each tree as a separate entity. Similarly, when you talk with a friend in a noisy room, the process of organization enables you to differentiate your friend's voice from all the other sounds that simultaneously reach your ears.

One way to consider the processes that enable you to make sense of the stimuli reaching your eyes and ears is to think in terms of: (1) **organization**—small units are grouped into a larger form; and (2) **recognition**—the form is perceived as a meaningful object. These two processes, organization and recognition, are closely linked. Before Adam can recognize the elephant in his eggs, he must perceptually organize the pieces so that they look like an elephant. Therefore, Adam's recognition of the elephant depends on his organization of the pieces of eggs, but his organization of the pieces depends to some extent on his previous experience in recognizing elephants.

Though it may seem strange to say that recognition depends on organization and organization depends on recognition, the nature of this close interplay between these two processes will become clearer when we discuss them in more detail. We will begin by focusing on research that has addressed the problem of perceptual organization: How do small units become perceptually organized into parts of a larger form?

Perceptual Organization: The Gestalt Approach

Real progress in the study of perceptual organization began with a group called the Gestalt psychologists, which was formed about 1912 by Max Wertheimer. According to Edwin Boring (1950), the birth of **Gestalt psychology** can be traced to a train ride taken by Wertheimer in the summer of 1910. As the story goes, Wertheimer was on his way to a vacation in Rhineland, in the west of Germany, when he suddenly experienced a flash of insight about movement perception. He got off the train at Frankfurt, checked into a hotel, and purchased a toy stroboscope (a device like a "flip book," in which still pictures appear to move when the pages are rapidly flipped). Wertheimer first began work in his hotel room but soon moved his makeshift setup to the psychology laboratory at the University of Frankfurt.

Wertheimer's experiments in movement perception at the Frankfurt lab, the results of which he published in 1912, marked the founding of Gestalt psychology. In one experiment reported in this paper, Wertheimer flashed two vertical lines, which were 1 cm apart, one after the other. He found that when the time interval between the flashed lines was from about 30 to 200 msec, observers reported that a single line appeared to move from one position to the other. Wertheimer interpreted this result, which he called **phi movement** (see Chapter 11), as an illustration of the principle that "the whole is different from the sum of its parts."

Wertheimer's conclusion that the whole is different from the sum of its parts was a logical inference from his demonstration of phi movement. Consider his experiment, diagramed in Figure 7.2: (a) one line flashes on and off; (b) there are 50 msec of darkness; and (c) another line, 1 cm from the first, flashes on and off. Though nothing actually happened in the space between the two lines, the observer's perception, shown at (d), was that the first line moved *through the empty space* to the posi-

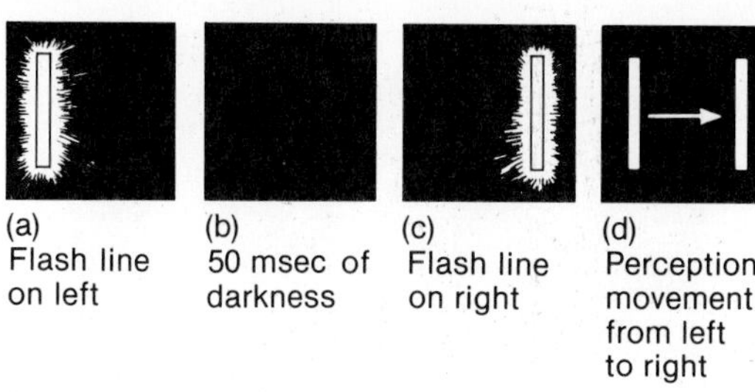

Figure 7.2 Wertheimer's experiment in movement perception.

tion of the second line. Movement of a line from one position to another is certainly different from two singly flashed lines.

While Wertheimer's conclusion may seem almost obvious now, it was a revolutionary idea at the time it was proposed. When Wertheimer's paper was published, most psychologists believed that perceptions were constructed from elementary "sensations" and that perceptions, therefore, could be explained by adding up the many sensations caused by an object. According to this reasoning, each of the dots that make up the face in Figure 7.3 results in a sensation, and the sum of these sensations creates our perception of the face.

The Gestalt school of psychology rejected the idea that perceptions are constructed from sensations in favor of the idea that the stimulus must be considered as a whole. Much of the evidence for

Figure 7.3 A face made up of "sensations." Each dot on this face represents an elementary sensation. According to psychology *circa* 1900, the sum of these sensations creates our perception of the face.

Figure 7.4 A rearing horse. (From Arnheim, 1974.)

Figure 7.5 One horse following another horse. (From Arnheim, 1974.)

this view comes from examples such as Wertheimer's, which show that our perception of one part of a stimulus depends on the presence of other parts of the stimulus. Look, for example, at Figures 7.4 and 7.5. The horse in Figure 7.4 looks as if it is rearing back, but the identical horse in Figure 7.5 appears to be moving forward. The presence of the rider in Figure 7.4 and the lead horse in Figure 7.5 make the same horse look different in the two pictures.

Figures 7.6, 7.7, and 7.8 show other examples supporting the idea that our perception of parts of a stimulus depends on the overall stimulus configuration. Figure 7.6 is an example of **subjective contour.** The contours of the triangle are not physically present; they are caused by the rest of the configuration. You can prove this to yourself by covering the three circular objects with small pieces of paper. When you do this, the subjective contours vanish. No theory which holds that perceptions are constructed from individual sensations can explain this result.

Figure 7.7 is a picture of a woman holding some flowers and a transparent veil. Though we can see some reflections on the right of the veil near the flowers, there are no reflections further to the left; and since the veil is transparent, it becomes almost invisible. How then do we know that the veil is there? The answer lies in the embroidery. The embroidery defines the veil and causes us to assume its presence, even though we can't see it.

Look at the two vases in Figure 7.8. The one on the left has a glossy finish and the one on the right a dull finish. Or do they? Cover up the highlights on the left vase and observe what happens. It becomes the same as the right vase, because both vases are identical except that the highlights have been removed from the right vase. In this example, as in the previous ones, our perception of parts of an object is determined by the other parts of the object.

Figure 7.7 Diane Sloan, *Carapace No. 3.* (Collection of the Oakland Museum, gift of Mr. Joseph H. Chowning).

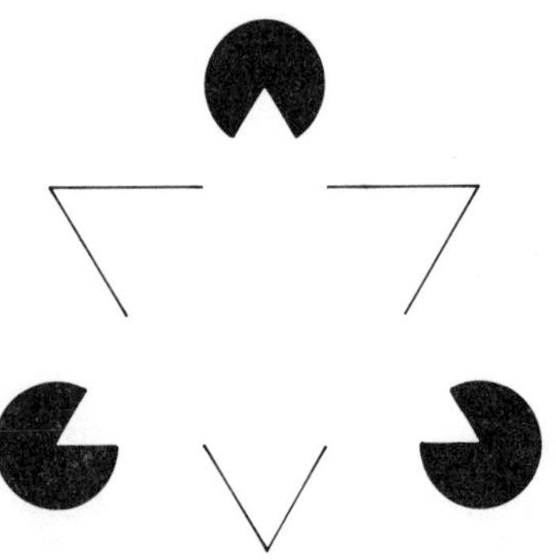

Figure 7.6 The white triangle with its base down in the above figure is constructed from subjective contours. When the black circles are covered the triangle vanishes, and when they are uncovered it reappears. (From Kanizsa, 1955.)

The Laws of Organization

The Gestalt psychologists were interested not only in demonstrating that the whole is more important than the sum of its parts but also in determining rules to tell us why we perceive a given stimulus in the way we do. Look at Figure 7.9. What do you see? If you see a dog, then you have succeeded in transforming a mass of black and white shapes into a dalmation! How does this particular arrangement of black and white shapes enable us to differentiate the spotted dog from the spotted background? A Gestalt psychologist would answer this question by referring to the **laws of organization.** These laws are a series of rules that describe what your perception will be, given certain stimulus conditions. Let's look at the four most important Gestalt laws.

Figure 7.8 Two vases, showing how highlights on the surface on the left make the whole surface appear glossy. (From Beck, 1972.)

Figure 7.9 Some black and white shapes that become perceptually organized into a dalmation. (Photograph by R. C. James.)

Pragnanz. Pragnanz, roughly translated from the German, means "good figure." The **law of Pragnanz**—the central law of Gestalt psychology—which is also called the law of good figure or the law of simplicity, states: *every stimulus pattern is seen in such a way that the resulting structure is as simple as possible.* According to the law of simplicity, you should perceive Figure 7.10(a) as a square and an elliptical object, as in (b), because these two objects are simpler than some other possibilities, such as those shown in (c) and (d). Similarly, Figure 7.11 is perceived as a triangle overlapping a rectangle, not as a complicated, eleven-sided figure.

Similarity. Most people perceive Figure 7.12(a) as either horizontal rows or vertical columns of circles, or as both. But when we change some of the circles to squares, as in Figure 7.12(b), most people perceive vertical columns of squares. This perception illustrates the **law of similarity** at work: *similar things appear to be grouped together.* This law causes the circles to be grouped with other circles and the squares to be grouped with other squares. Grouping can also occur due to similarity of lightness (Figure 7.13), color, orientation, or size.

Similar auditory stimuli also group perceptually. This was common knowledge to composers in the Baroque period (1600–1750), who, by playing a series of rapidly alternating high and low tones on one instrument, created the illusion of two instruments, one playing the high tones and one playing the low tones. An excerpt from a composition by J. S. Bach that used this device is shown in Figure 7.14. When this passage is played rapidly, the low notes sound as if they are a melody played by one instrument, while the high notes sound like a different melody played by another instrument. This grouping due to similarity of pitch has been called *implied polyphony* or *compound melodic line* by musicians, and it has been called **auditory stream segregation** by psychologists Albert Bregman and Jeffry Campbell (1971).

Auditory stream segregation has been demonstrated experimentally by alternating high and low tones, as shown in the sequence in Figure 7.15. When the high-pitched tones are slowly alternated with the low-pitched tones, as in Figure 7.15(a), the tones are heard in one stream—one after another—hi-lo-hi-lo-hi-lo, as indicated by the dashed line. If, however, the tones are alternated very rap-

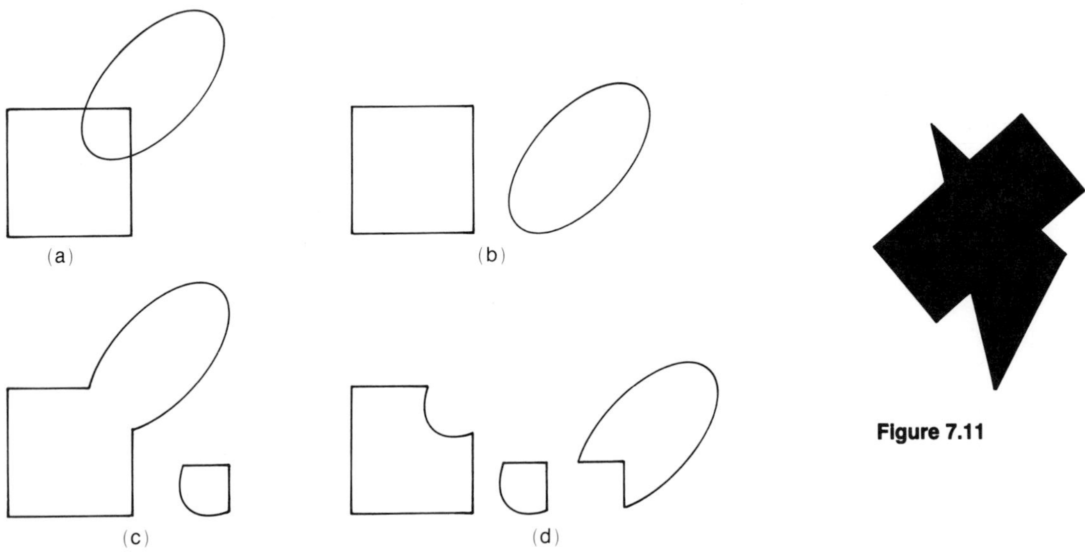

Figure 7.10

Figure 7.11

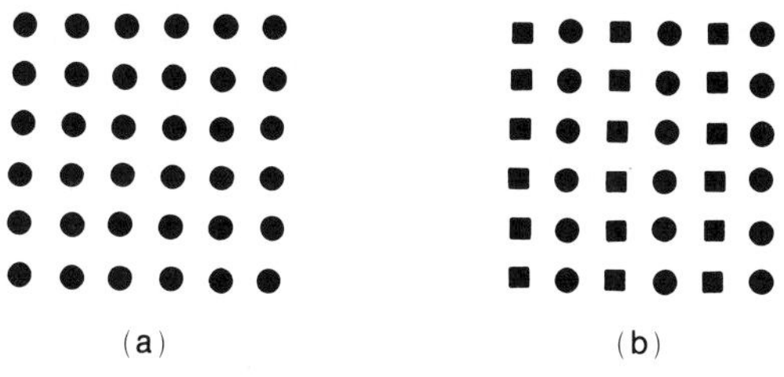

Figure 7.12 (a) Perceived as horizontal rows or vertical columns, or both. (b) Perceived as vertical columns.

idly, as in Figure 7.15(b), the high and low tones become perceptually grouped into two auditory streams so that the listener perceives two separate streams of sound, one high pitched and one low pitched, occurring simultaneously.

Good continuation. The series of points starting at A in Figure 7.16 flows smoothly to B. It does not go to C or D, because that path would involve making sharp turns and would violate the **law of good continuation,** which states: *points that, when connected, result in straight or smoothly curving lines are seen as belonging together, and lines tend to be seen in such a way as to follow the smoothest path.*

Good continuation is illustrated by the bridge and smokestack in Pissaro's painting *The Great Bridge at Rouen,* shown in Figure 7.17. Although the smoke cuts the bridge in two and cuts the smokestack into three pieces, we assume, due to good continuation, that the various parts belong together, and the bridge and smokestack, therefore, do not fall apart.

Good continuation also works for tones. Auditory good continuation, as demonstrated by Richard Warren, C. J. Obuseck, and J. M. Acroff (1972), is shown in Figure 7.18. When bursts of tone are interrupted by gaps of silence, as in 7.18(a), listeners perceive both the tones and the silence between the tones. If, however, the silent gaps are filled in with a hissing sound, called "noise," as in Figure

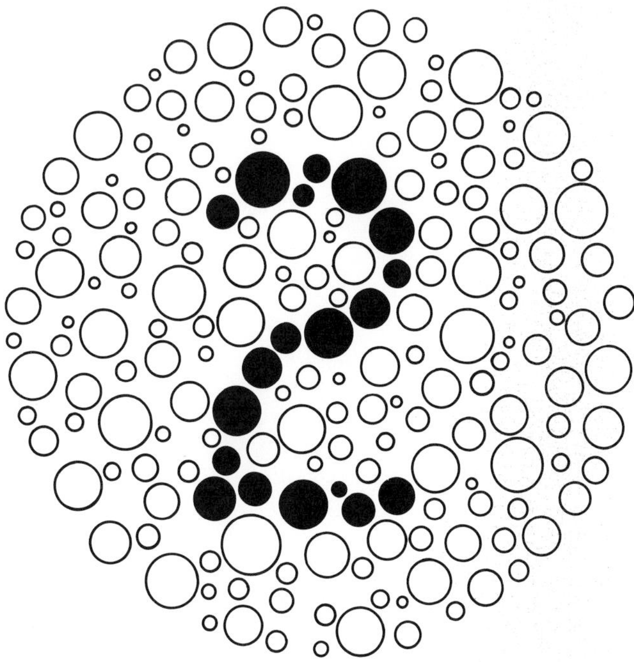

Figure 7.13 Grouping determined by similarity of lightness. The light objects form one group and the dark objects form another group.

Figure 7.14 Four measures of a composition by J. S.Bach (*Chorale Prelude on Jesus Christus unser Heiland,* 1739) that result in auditory stream segregation.

7.18(b), the listeners perceive the tone as continuing under the noise, as shown in 7.18(c). Just as Pissaro's smokestack is perceived as continuous even though it is twice interrupted by smoke, an interrupted tone can also be perceived as continuous if the interruptions are filled in with bursts of noise.

Proximity or nearness. Figure 7.19(a) is perceived as horizontal rows of circles. This is the **law of proximity** at work: *things that are near to each other appear to be grouped together.* And, although every other circle is changed to a square in Figure 7.19(b), we still perceive horizontal rows; in this case, the law of proximity overpowers the law of similarity.

Auditory stream segregation provides an example of how proximity affects our perception of tones. Stream segregation requires that one series of tones be high pitched and the other low pitched. But, in addition to being different in pitch, these tones must also obey the law of proximity: tones that are similar in pitch *and* follow each other rapidly will form streams. If the tones are too far apart in time, as in Figure 7.15(a), streaming will not occur, even if the tones are similar in pitch.

Let's now apply some of these Gestalt laws to the spotted dog in Figure 7.9. What is it about the dog's spots that differentiate them from the other spots in the scene? If you look at the spots on the dog's body, you will notice that they are similar, more rounded, and in sharper focus than most of the spots in the background. The law of similarity helps us differentiate the dog's spots from those in the background. Similarity of orientation is also at work on the five spots that run along the top of the dog's back. Notice how they group themselves together and, perhaps aided by the law of good continuation, help to form the contour of the dog's back. These factors, plus others we will discuss later, all work together to turn the spots into a dog.

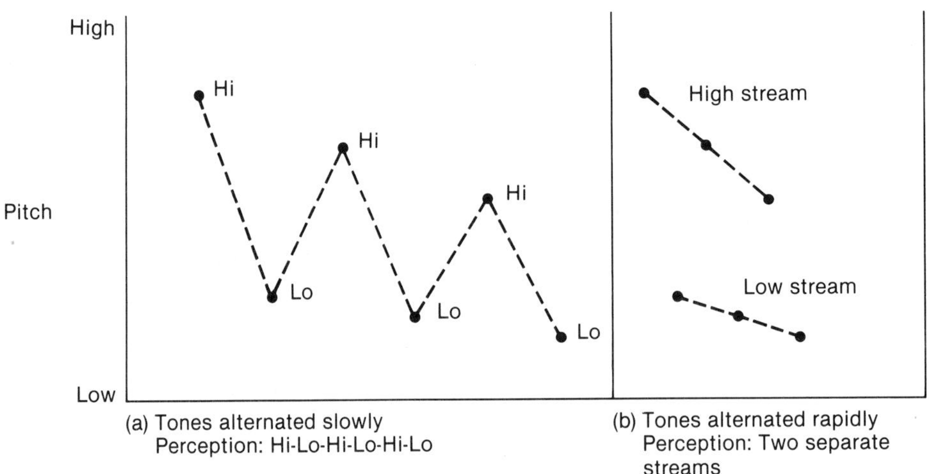

Figure 7.15 (a) Slow alternation of high and low tones does not result in auditory stream segregation. (b) Faster alternation results in segregation into high and low streams.

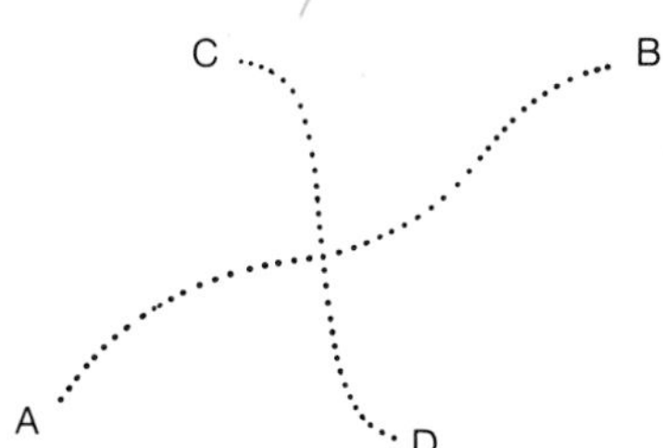

Figure 7.16 Good continuation.

Figure-Ground

Our spotted dog forms a figure against a background. This separation of figure and background has been of great interest to the Gestalt psychologists, because we must segregate an object from its background in order to perceive it. Figure 7.20 illustrates a **figure-ground** pattern similar to those introduced by Danish psychologist Edgar Rubin in 1915. This is called a **reversible figure-ground** pattern, because it can be perceived either as two black faces looking at each other, in front of a white background, or as a white vase on a black background. Some of the properties of the figure and ground are:

1. The figure is more "thinglike" and more memorable than the ground.
2. The figure is seen as being in front of the ground.
3. The ground is seen as unformed material and seems to extend behind the figure.

You can demonstrate these properties to yourself by looking at Rubin's face-vase reversible figure-ground in Figure 7.20. Note that when the vase

Figure 7.17 Camille Pissaro, *The Great Bridge at Rouen* (1896). (Museum of Art, Carnegie Institute, Pittsburgh, Pa.)

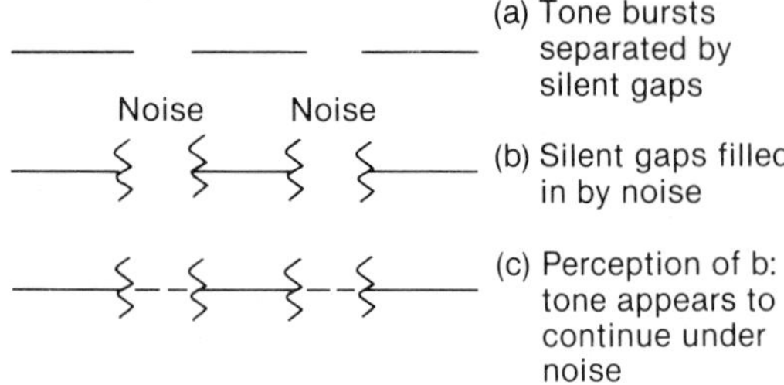

Figure 7.18 A demonstration of good continuation, using tones.

Figure 7.20 A version of Rubin's reversible face-vase figure.

is seen as figure, it appears to be in front of the black background, and when the faces are figure, they are sitting on top of the white background. Also notice that when you are perceiving the vase as figure, it is difficult, if not impossible, to simultaneously perceive the faces. Remember that the ground is seen as "unformed material"; as soon as you perceive the white area as figure, the vase is seen in front, and the black area becomes "unformed material" that extends behind the vase.

What determines which part of a stimulus will be the figure and which will be the ground? Rubin and others have identified a number of factors:

1. *Symmetry.* Symmetrical areas tend to be seen as figure. In Figure 7.21, the symmetrical black areas on the left and the symmetrical white areas on the right are seen as figure.
2. *Convexity.* Convex (i.e., outwardly bulging) shapes tend to be seen as figure, and the convexity can sometimes overpower symmetry, as shown in Figure 7.22.
3. *Area.* Stimuli with comparatively smaller areas are more likely to be seen as figure. This effect was demonstrated by an experiment in which subjects were shown a stimulus such as the one in Figure 7.23. The subjects were asked to report whether they saw the "plus-figure" or the "cross-figure" when the stimulus was first presented, and on each trial the angle of the cross-figure was changed. The results of this experiment show that the smaller the angle of the cross-figure, the more often it was seen

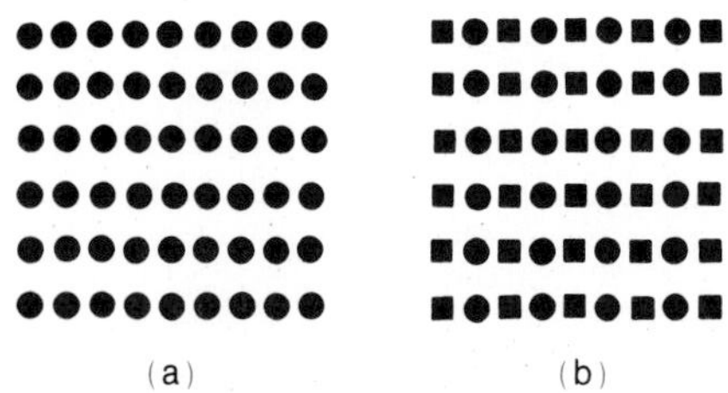

Figure 7.19 Two examples of the law of nearness: (1) perceived as horizontal rows of circles; (b) still perceived as horizontal rows, even though half of the circles have been changed to squares.

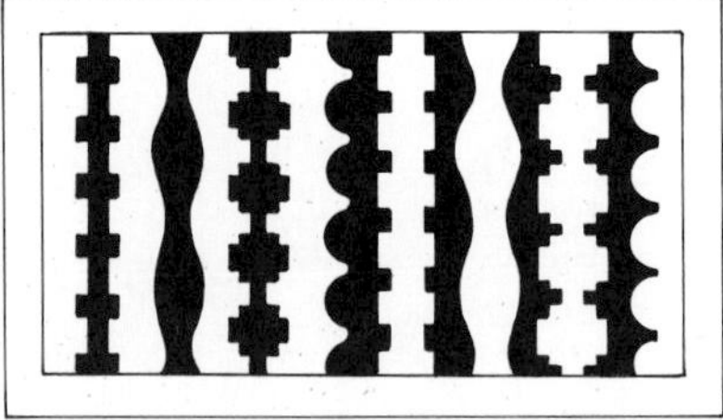

Figure 7.21 Symmetry and figure-ground. Look to the left and to the right and observe which colors become figure and which become ground. (Adapted from Hochberg, 1971.)

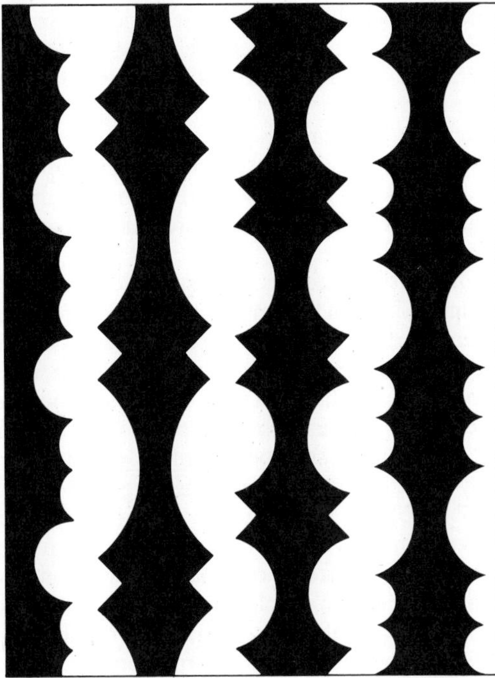

Figure 7.22 Although the black columns are symmetrical, they are not perceived as figure. The white columns are perceived as figure because they are convex. (Kanizsa, 1979.)

as figure. A cross-angle of 5 degrees was seen as figure 80 percent of the time, while a cross-angle of 70 degrees was seen as figure less than 10 percent of the time (Künnapas, 1957; see also Oyama, 1960).

4. *Orientation.* Vertical or horizontal orientations are more likely to be seen as figure than are other orientations. This tendency of verticals and horizontals to be seen as figure is shown in Figure 7.24.

What Does Gestalt Psychology Tell Us?

Gestalt psychology tells us that we should pay attention to the overall stimulus pattern. It also offers a number of laws of organization that supposedly govern the way we group parts of a stimulus together and the way we separate figure from ground; however, while the laws of organization seem to work well when applied to the examples picked to illustrate them, the operation of some of the laws is not always as straightforward as in the examples.

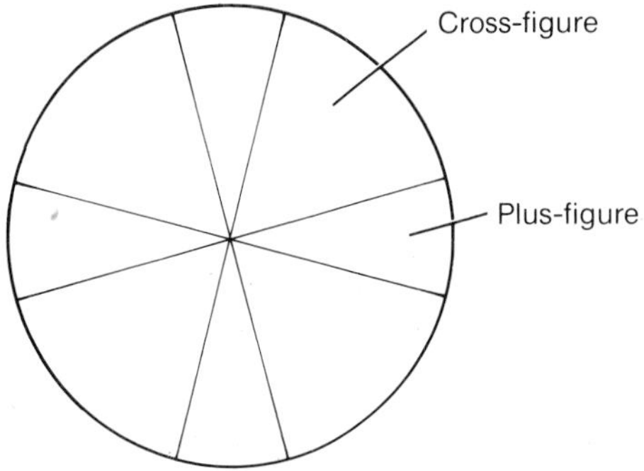

Figure 7.23 Effect of area on figure-ground perception. The smaller plus-figure is more likely than the cross-figure to be seen as figure.

One problem lies in the application of the law of simplicity. How do we tell if one figure is simpler than another? This is not an easy question to answer; although we can easily measure properties such as lightness or nearness, there is no easy way to measure simplicity.

Particularly troublesome for the law of simplicity are pictures that can be seen in either two or three dimensions. Look, for example, at Figure 7.25.

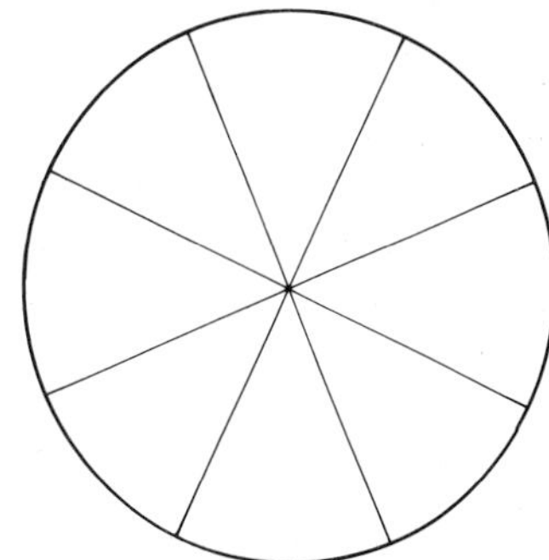

Figure 7.24 Effect of orientation on figure-ground perception. When the area and colors of the sectors are equal, there is a tendency to see the vertical and horizontal areas of the cross as figure. What is your initial perception? Allow your perception to flip back and forth between the two alternatives. Which perception is present the longest?

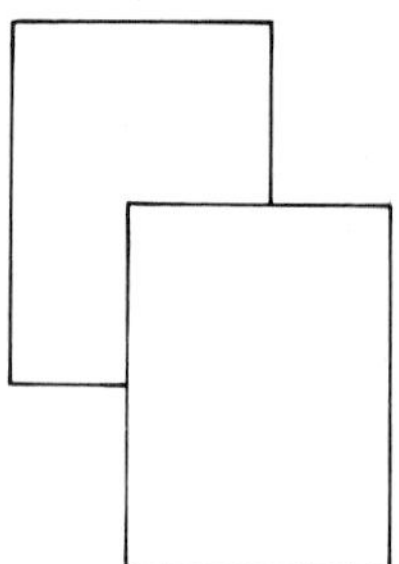

Figure 7.25 Which is simpler, two overlapping rectangles or a rectangle and an upside-down, L-shaped object in the same plane?

Which is simpler, two overlapping rectangles or a rectangle and an upside-down L-shaped object in the same plane? Does the fact that the perception of two rectangles involves three rather than two dimensions make this perception more simple or more complex than the perception of a rectangle and L-shaped object? Since the law of simplicity provides us with no rules for determining which is simpler, it is hard to answer these questions except to say that most people tend to see this figure in three dimensions, with one rectangle positioned in front of the other.

Consider Figure 7.26(a). This figure is often initially perceived as a flat, six-pointed star; however, after it is viewed for a while, a number of alternative perceptions appear. For example, it can be perceived as two intersecting *V*s, one right side up and one upside down, as in Figure 7.26(b) (the upside-down *V* is shaded). It can also be perceived as a three-finned propeller on top of a triangle. To see the figure in this way, try to perceive the shaded area of 7.26(b) as the triangle and the light area as the three-finned propeller. (You can also reverse this perception by seeing the light area as the triangle and the shaded area as the fins of the propeller.) Finally, look at 7.26(c) and imagine that the shaded areas on the left and right represent the pages of opened books.

Obviously, there are many possible perceptions of Figure 7.26 (in fact, my students have discovered others in addition to those described here: Can you find two chairs, each missing their legs on one side?). Though we might expect the law of simplicity to predict that the simplest perception would be the flat, symmetrical star, people often see the seemingly more complex perceptions suggested by Figure 7.26(b) and (c). In fact, many people find that their perceptions change between two or even three different objects as they continue to view this figure. Can something be simple one minute and not simple the next? Unfortunately, the law of simplicity does not provide enough information about what simplicity is for us to know what it predicts about perception in situations such as this.

Another question we can ask about the Gestalt laws is: How applicable are they to real-life situations? Most examples of the Gestalt laws are illustrated by simple line drawings that consist of dots or lines. But what happens when we move from the flat pages of a book to the three-dimensional world, where objects are separated in depth? In Chapter 8, we will see that various kinds of depth information help us see that one object is in front of another,

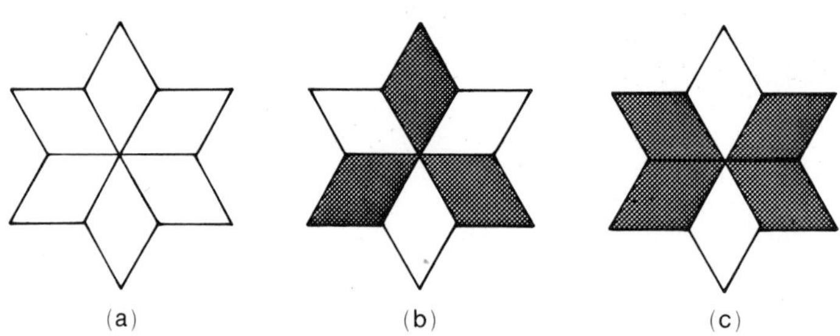

Figure 7.26

thereby making it unnecessary to use the laws of organization to explain why we see one thing as figure and another as ground.

Another important aspect of our perception of objects, usually ignored by the Gestalt laws, is our familiarity with the objects in our environment. Edgar Rubin (of the face-vase, figure-ground demonstration in Figure 7.20) lists familiarity as a factor in helping to separate figure from ground, and Harry Helson (1933), who compiled a list of over 100 Gestalt principles, states that if a pattern has two possible organizations, the more meaningful organization tends to prevail. However, most lists of the Gestalt laws of organization ignore familiarity and meaning. One reason for this is that becoming familiar with an object or apprehending an object's meaning requires learning, which doesn't fit with the Gestalt psychologists' idea that the laws of organization are "built in" at birth and, therefore, require no learning. But what we have learned about dogs in the past must help us to see the dog in Figure 7.9. One reason why the spots group into a perception of a dog is that this particular pattern of spots fits our ideas of what dogs are supposed to look like. If we had never seen a dog or a doglike animal, we might not group the spots in the same way. Perhaps another Gestalt law is needed: *stimuli that, when seen together, have meaning or look familiar will tend to be grouped together.*

In addition to the above difficulties, there are other problems with the Gestalt laws. We saw in Figure 7.12 that circles were grouped with circles and squares with squares to form vertical columns (the law of similarity), but in Figure 7.19 the same circles were grouped with squares to form horizontal rows (the law of nearness). Clearly, at some point between these two extremes, the two laws will balance each other, as in Figure 7.27, and we will be uncertain as to whether we see columns or rows. The law of similarity causes us to see Figure 7.27(a) as vertical columns, but if we move the squares and circles closer together, as in Figure 7.27(b), the law of nearness begins to influence our perception—sometimes we perceive horizontal rows and sometimes vertical columns. When the spacing between the squares and circles is decreased even farther, as in Figure 7.27(c), the law of nearness dominates our perception—we see only horizontal rows.

The problem of conflicts between laws brings us back to the problem of measurement. Though we can measure nearness with a ruler, we don't know how to translate that measurement of nearness into psychological units. That is, knowing that two objects are 10 mm apart does not tell us whether they will be perceived as belonging together. Thus, while we can predict a conflict between the laws of nearness and similarity in Figures 7.12, 7.19, and 7.27, we cannot predict which law will win out in a given

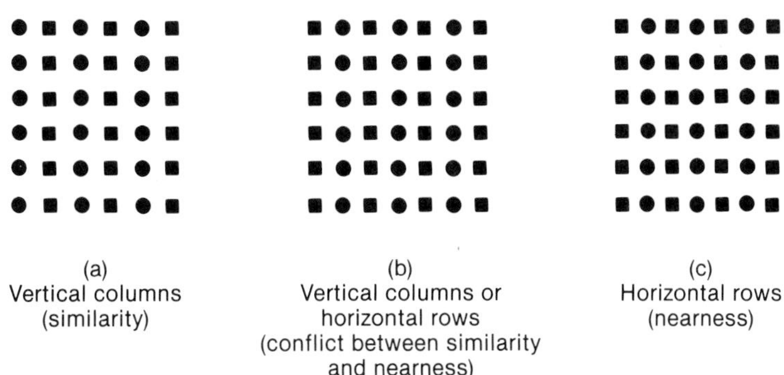

Figure 7.27 (a) Perceived as vertical columns (law of similarity); (b) perceived as either vertical columns or horizontal rows (conflict between the laws of similarity and nearness); and (c) perceived as horizontal rows (law of nearness).

situation. The usual procedure with the Gestalt laws is to start with perception (Perception: in Figure 7.12 I see the circles in vertical columns) and then explain why the stimulus patterns resulted in that perception (Explanation: the circles were grouped together by the law of similarity, which was stronger than the law of nearness in this case).

But does this "explanation" really explain anything? It's really more a description of what's happening in this situation than an explanation that can help us predict what's going to happen in other situations. This tendency of the Gestalt approach to *describe* rather than to *explain* has led many present-day researchers to question the Gestalt approach. Recently, James Pomerantz (1981) has aptly described the Gestalt approach as the "look-at-the-figure-and-see-for-yourself" method: an observer looks at a figure and reports what he or she sees. Pomerantz and others have argued that we need a more quantitative approach to the Gestalt principles, and, in an attempt to do this, a number of researchers have begun to apply a more experimental approach to the study of the Gestalt laws. In the next section, we will describe some recent experiments resulting from this new approach to Gestalt psychology.

Gestalt Psychology: Experimental Studies

Beginning in the 1950s, researchers began to apply the experimental method to the Gestalt laws in an attempt to understand, in a more quantitative way, how these laws work.

Simplicity

A number of experimenters have tried to determine what it is about a figure that makes it simple. Fred Attneave (1957) presented 72 different figures like the ones in Figure 7.28 and asked subjects to rate them on a scale from 0 (extremely simple) to 6 (extremely complex). The mean rating for the 72 figures ranged between 0.82 and 5.24. Attneave found that figures with fewer turns, greater symmetry, and larger angles than others were more likely to be called simple. Unfortunately, even with these data, it is still difficult to measure simplicity, especially for objects different from those in Attneave's experiment.

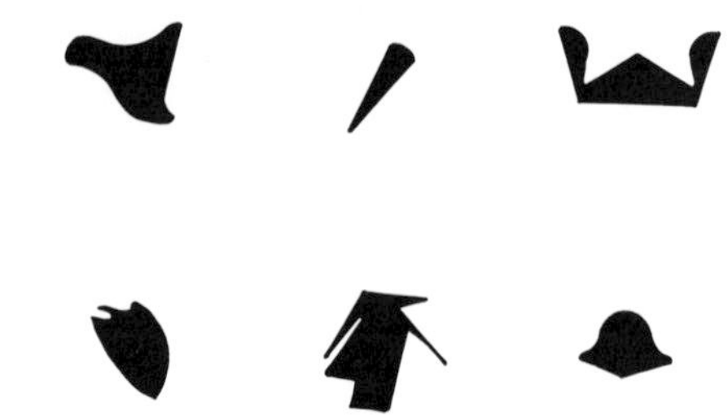

Figure 7.28 Some of the stimuli used in Attneave's (1957) experiment.

Similarity

Visual similarity. An experiment by Richard Olson and Fred Attneave (1970) illustrates the use of the experimental method to study similarity grouping. To determine which variables produce similarity grouping, Olson and Attneave made up 14 displays like the ones in Figure 7.29. The observer's task was to determine as quickly as possible the position of the "odd" stimuli. Thus, for the display in Figure 7.29(a), the odd stimuli (vertical lines) are in the lower right position, whereas in Figure 7.29(b), the odd stimuli (corners facing to the right) are in the middle right position.

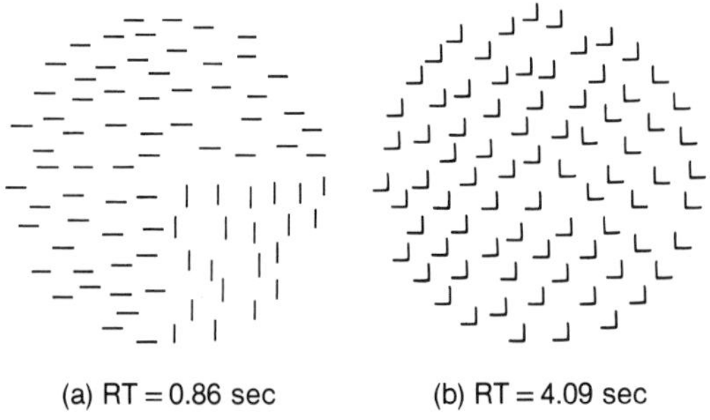

Figure 7.29 Two of the stimuli used in Olson and Attneave's (1970) experiment.

The key measure in this experiment was the observer's reaction time—how long it took to locate the odd stimuli. A fast reaction time indicates that perceptual grouping causes the odd stimuli to be easily identified, whereas a long reaction time indicates that grouping is less effective in differentiating the odd stimuli from the rest of the display. Excellent grouping occurs when the slopes of the two elements are different, as in Figure 7.29(a), which produced an average reaction time of 0.86 seconds. However, grouping is poor when different arrangements of the same slopes are used, as in Figure 7.29(b), which produced an average reaction time of 4.09 seconds. This is a striking difference in performance: when the slopes differ, observers can almost immediately identify the odd elements; however, when the slopes are similar (but are arranged differently), the observer takes a number of seconds to search for the odd elements. Olson and Attneave concluded, therefore, that differences in slope produce excellent grouping.

The advantage of such an experiment over the "look-at-the-figure-and-see-for-yourself" method used by the original Gestalt psychologists is that Olson and Attneave could assign a number to each display that was related to the goodness of perceptual grouping. This enabled them to draw precise conclusions about what type of displays cause good and poor similarity grouping.

Though Olson and Attneave's result shows that line slopes play an important role in similarity grouping, the question of how grouping by similarity operates is still far from solved. For example, though Olson and Attneave showed that good grouping occurs when the slopes of large groups of lines are different, as in Figure 7.29(a), James Pomerantz (1981) has shown that differences in slope do not always result in good grouping. For example, since three of the four diagonal lines in Figure 7.30 have similar slopes, we would expect, based on similarity grouping, that they would group together, leaving the line in the upper right, with its different slope, as the "odd-line-out." However, when Pomerantz asked observers to identify the odd line in this display, he found that "they see the lower left element as odd, although a little scrutiny shows that in reality, the odd one is hiding in the upper right." Apparently, many observers see this display as an open box facing downward, with a stick (the lower left diagonal) popping out. Thus, line slope may cause good grouping in some displays but not in others.

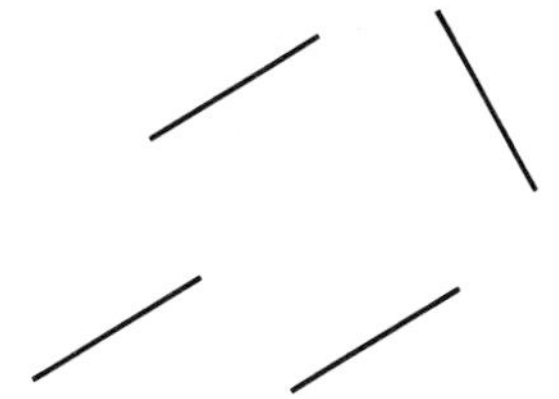

Figure 7.30 Which is the odd-line-out? (From Pomerantz, 1981.)

Though Pomerantz's result does not support Olson and Attneave's conclusion that lines with similar slopes tend to be grouped together, both experiments do show that perceptual grouping influences our ability to extract information from a display. Clearly, the way similarity grouping organizes a stimulus array affects our ability to distribute attention to various parts of that array. For example, in Figure 7.30, the grouping of the upper right line with the two lines near it makes it difficult for us to single out that line and correctly identify it as the odd one.

The idea that grouping can affect our ability to attend to elements in a display has been applied not only to visual stimuli but also to auditory stimuli. Albert Bregman and his colleagues have shown that the grouping caused by auditory stream segregation has significant effects on a listener's ability to make judgments about the relationships between individual tones.

Auditory similarity. Auditory stream segregation, the organization of a rapid sequence of alternating high- and low-pitched tones into two separate streams—the high-pitched tones belonging to one stream and the low-pitched tones belonging to the other—is a good example of auditory grouping based on similarity of pitch.

A demonstration of how auditory stream segregation affects a listener's judgment is provided by Albert Bregman and Alexander Rudnicky's (1975) experiment, diagramed in Figure 7.31. The listener is first presented with two standard tones, A and B

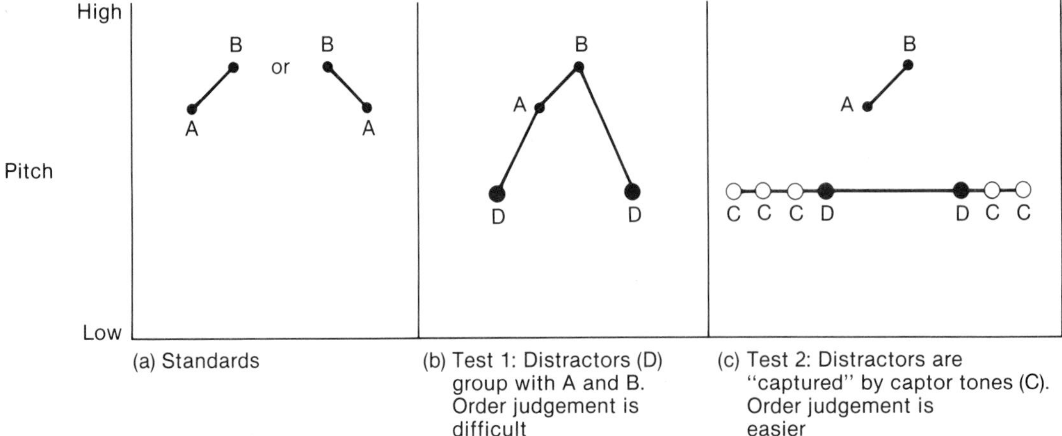

Figure 7.31 Bregman and Rucnicky's (1975) experiment. (a) The standard tones. (b) Test 1: the distractor (D) tones group with A and B, making it difficult to judge the order of A and B. (c) Test 2: the addition of captor (C) tones with the same pitch as the distractor tones causes the distractor tones to form a separate stream (law of similarity) and makes it easier to judge the order of tones A and B.

(7.31a). When these tones are presented alone, it is easy to perceive their order (AB or BA). However, when these tones are sandwiched between two distractor (D) tones (7.31b), it becomes very hard to judge their order. The name "distractor tones" is well taken—they distract the listener, making it difficult to judge the order of the tones A and B. Thus, if the listener is first presented with one of the standards (7.31a) and is then presented with the standards plus the distractors (7.31b), she can determine whether tones A and B are in the same or different order as when they were first presented alone (7.31a) only 65 percent of the time.

Bregman and Rudnicky decided to use the law of similarity to eliminate the distracting effect of the D tones. Their strategy was to make the D tones part of a stream that did not include tones A and B. To do this, they added a series of "captor" (C) tones with the same pitch as the distractors (7.31b). Since these captor tones have the same pitch as the distractors, they "capture" the distractors and form a stream that separates the distractors from tones A and B. In this situation, A and B are perceived as belonging to a separate stream, and listeners correctly detect their order 82 percent of the time.

Good Continuation

Decide, as quickly as possible, whether there is a *T* or an *F* present in each of the displays in Figure 7.32. You probably noticed that it was easier to pick out the *F* in display A than in display B. William Prinzmetal and William Banks (1977) did a reaction time experiment (like Olson and Attneave's similarity experiment) and found that observers identified the target letter faster in display A than in display B. From the slower detection in B, they concluded that the Gestalt principle of good continuation had caused the *F* in B to be grouped with the line of irrelevant stimuli, thereby making it harder to detect. In A, however, the *F* is not grouped and, therefore, stands out more and is detected faster.

Proximity

In addition to showing that grouping due to good continuation can affect an observer's ability to detect a target letter, Banks and Prinzmetal (1976) have shown that grouping due to proximity has a similar effect. Observers detected the target letter in Figure 7.33(a) faster than they detected the target in Fig-

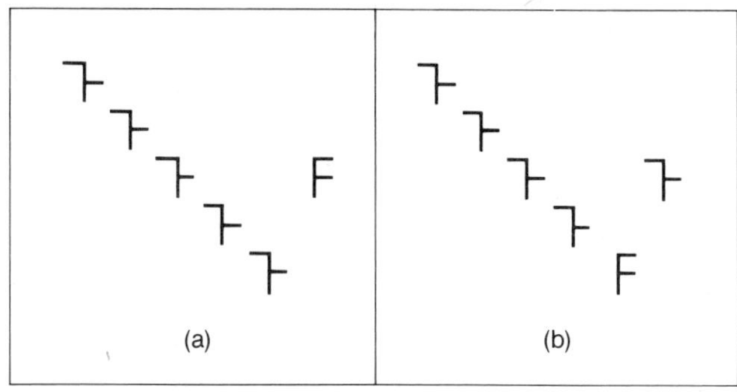

Figure 7.32 Two of the stimuli used in Prinzmetal and Banks' (1977) experiment, illustrating how grouping due to good continuation affects an observer's performance.

ure 7.33(b). The reason for this difference in performance, according to Banks and Prinzmetal, is that in B the target is grouped with the irrelevant stimuli, which causes the irrelevant stimuli to interfere with the target. In A this grouping does not occur, so the target is more easily detected.

Organization and Recognition

From about the 1920s on, the study of perceptual organization has focused on the basic organizational principles set forth by the Gestalt psychologists. But we have gone beyond the original Gestalt procedures to experiments such as those described above, which show that perceptual organization influences an observer's ability to attend to different parts of a display. Some of these experiments have also shown that Gestalt principles govern not only how we see visual displays but also how we hear sequences of tones.

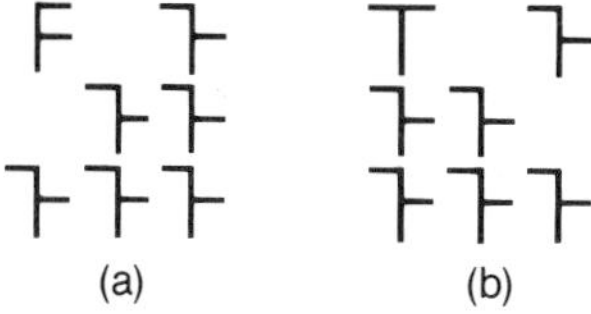

Figure 7.33 Two of the stimuli used in Banks and Prinzmetal's experiment, illustrating how grouping due to proximity affects an observer's performance.

However, despite recent advances made by applying the experimental method to the study of organization, many questions remain unanswered. We can still ask, for example, how to measure *simplicity* and *similarity* and how to predict, given a specific stimulus configuration, which areas will be figure and which will be ground.

We can also ask how we can recognize a particular stimulus as something familiar. Questions like this one bring us to the topic of **pattern recognition.** At the beginning of this chapter, we said that perceptual organization and pattern recognition are closely related. In fact, many of the experimental studies of the Gestalt laws involve an ability to recognize patterns. When we ask observers to tell us whether or not a stimulus contains a *T* or an *F*, or which of two tones comes first, we are asking them to recognize a specific pattern.

Many researchers interested in how we recognize patterns have not focused on the Gestalt laws but have, instead, proposed *models* of pattern recognition. In an attempt to explain how we recognize patterns, these models consider the sequences of mental processes that occur between the presentation of a stimulus and our recognition of this stimulus. Their concern for mental processes has led researchers to consider what's going on inside people's heads and has often led to hypothetical links between these mental processes and some of the physiological processes, such as feature detectors, that we discussed in earlier chapters.

Box 7.1 Visual Agnosia

One of the central acts of perception is the synthesis of the parts that make up an object into an integrated whole. By studying individuals who have suffered brain damage from war wounds or accidents, we have been able to show that this integration process breaks down when certain areas of the cortex are damaged. Damage to the primary visual receiving area in the occipital cortex causes blindness, with the degree of blindness depending on the size of the area that is damaged. This area is, however, apparently not crucial for the integration process since what *is* seen is perceived as a meaningful whole. If, however, a person's primary visual cortex remains intact but nearby areas in the occipital and parietal lobes are damaged, the person can see clearly, but has a condition called **visual agnosia** that interferes with his ability to recognize what he sees. For example, a patient with visual agnosia might respond as follows to a picture of a monkey: "eyes . . . mouth . . . of course, it's an animal!" Or a picture of a telephone might elicit the following response: "a dial . . . numbers . . . of course, it's a watch or some sort of machine!" Apparently, these patients are basing their identifications on only one or two parts of each picture and are not combining these parts with the other components of the picture to form a whole.

Support for this idea comes from experiments which show that covering part of a picture has little effect on a patient's ability to identify the picture. Whether they see the whole picture or only part of it, they just identify isolated parts of the picture. This inability to synthesize an object into an integrated whole is also illustrated by the attempts, shown below, of a patient with a bilateral wound of the occipital region to copy a picture of an elephant to complete a picture of a camel which had been started, and to draw a picture of a man from spoken instructions (Luria, 1966).

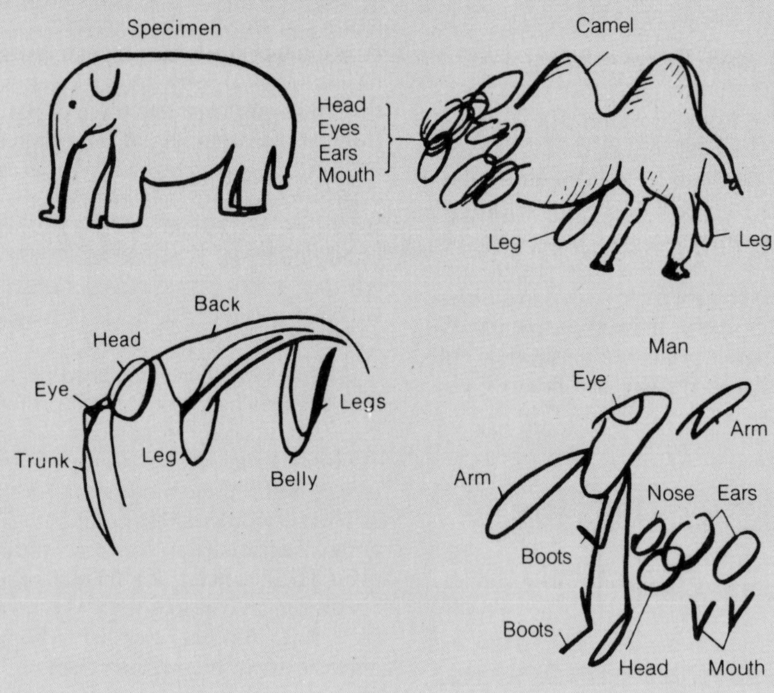

Pattern Recognition

How do you recognize things in your environment? You easily recognize the words on this page, the objects scattered on your desk, and your friend's face when he or she interrupts your studying. The great ease with which you do these things makes the question "How do you recognize things?" seem to be an easy one to answer. However, the complexity of recognition becomes apparent when we try to design a device that can recognize even simple forms.

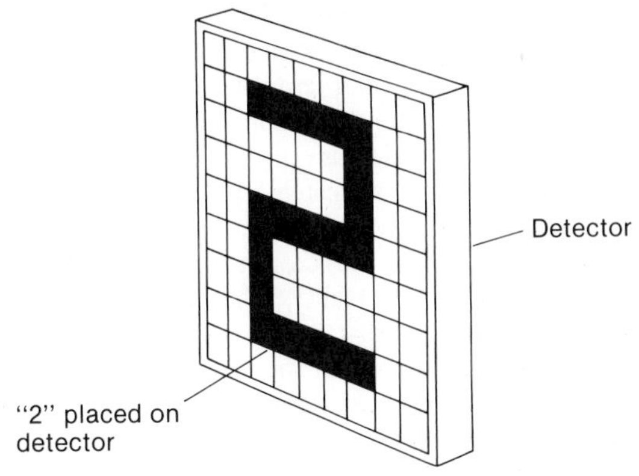

Figure 7.35 When the number two is placed on top of the detector unit, it blocks the light from some of the light-sensitive cells and modifies the signal reaching the comparator unit.

A Template-Matching Device

A hypothetical device that can recognize numbers is shown in Figure 7.34. For the first stage of our device, we construct a *detector unit,* a grid of light-sensitive cells, each of which generates an electrical signal when illuminated. When we place a black image of the number two on top of the detector unit, as shown in Figure 7.35, the image blocks the light from some of the light-sensitive cells and, therefore, turns them off. Thus, by placing our black two on the detector unit, we cause the pattern of electrical signals sent out by the detector to match the shape of the number placed on top of it, and these electrical signals are sent to the second stage of our number-recognition device, the *comparator unit.*

The key feature of the comparator unit is that it contains **templates,** each one matching the shape of a number, as shown in Figure 7.36. The comparator determines which number was presented to the detector by comparing the pattern of electrical signals received from the detector to each of these templates. If the pattern of signals and the template

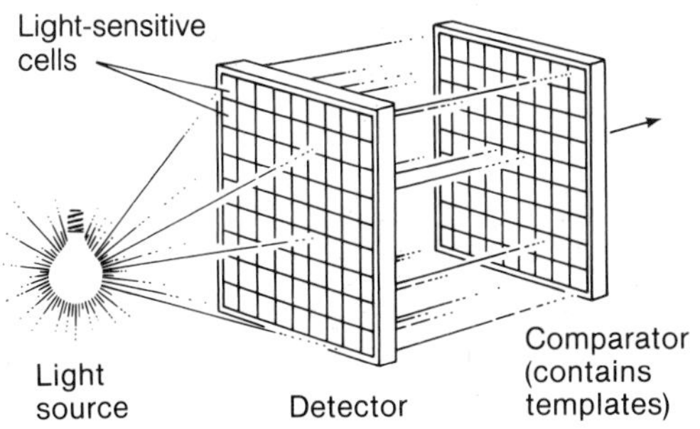

Figure 7.34 A hypothetical device to recognize numbers. The light-sensitive cells of the detector unit feed their signals back to the comparator unit, which contains templates (see text).

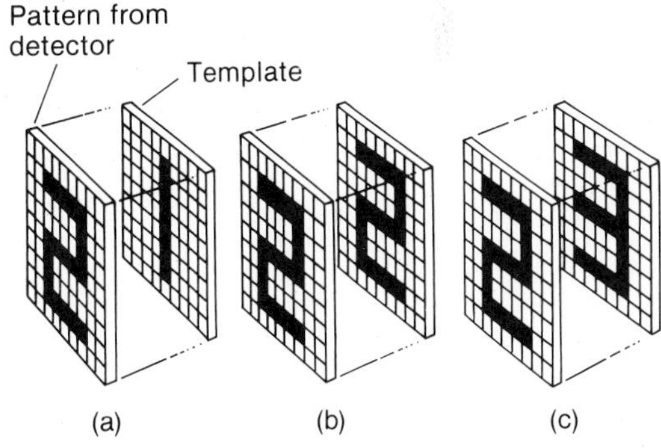

Figure 7.36 The pattern of signals from the detector is compared to each template in the comparator. The pattern generated by placing the 2 on the detector does not match the template for 1 or 3 (a and c) but does match the template for 2 (b).

match exactly, as in Figure 7.36(b), the comparator recognizes the number. If there is no exact match between the signals and templates, the comparator must decide which template comes closest to matching the pattern of signals.

Although template-matching systems similar to that described above have been used successfully for tasks such as reading the account numbers on checks (see Figure 7.37), in reality, it has been impossible to build a machine that can recognize numbers or letters with anywhere near the ease that humans do.

To understand the limitations of template matching, consider what would happen if the numbers in Figure 7.36 were misaligned. Tilting the two destroys the overlap between the signal from the detector and the template, which makes it unlikely that the "2" will be recognized. Thus, the template-matching system works only if the numbers are presented exactly upright and are perfectly aligned with the templates. The template system also requires that the numbers to be recognized be exactly the same size as the template numbers, since differences in size would prevent a match.

Perhaps the most serious drawback of the template system is that the number to be recognized must look exactly like the template. Thus, while the template system can recognize a 2, it might fail to recognize twos such as 2, 2, *2*, 2, *2* or **2**, even though all these symbols are easily recognized as "twos" by a human observer. The only way a template system can handle all these different-looking twos is to store a template for each one. Since humans have devised hundreds of different ways to make each number and letter (just consider the wide variations in people's handwriting), this adds up to a lot of templates!

These drawbacks of the template system have led psychologists to reject it as a possible mechanism for human pattern recognition. A better system is called **feature analysis.**

Feature Analysis

The feature analysis model of pattern recognition was described by O. G. Selfridge in 1959, and Selfridge's model (or variations of it) remains the most promising explanation of the way human pattern recognition works. As we will see, this system avoids many of the problems of the template-matching system. In addition, it has the advantage that many of its properties can be related to what we know about the physiology of the visual system.

The feature analysis model involves a number of stages. Whereas the template model has only two stages—a detector that picks up the signal and a comparator that compares this signal to stored templates—the feature analysis model has four stages. An amusing description of each stage is provided by Peter Lindsay and Donald Norman (1977), who

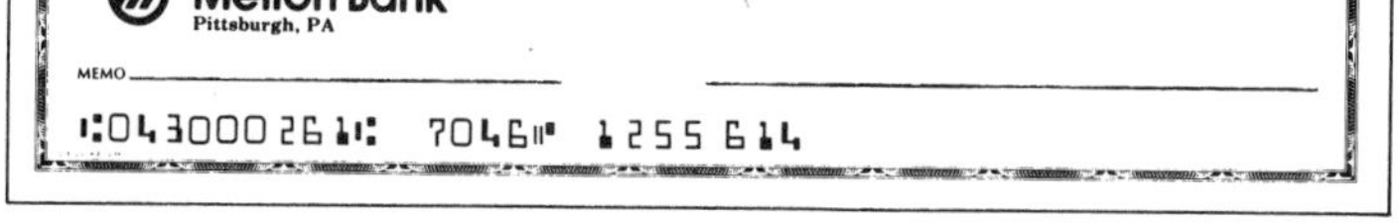

Figure 7.37 The numbers at the bottom of this check have been specially designed so that they can be recognized by an electronic reader, which operates according to the principles of a template-matching system.

state that each of the stages is inhabited by "demons" with specific jobs. In stage one, the **image demon** records the image of whatever stimulus is presented; in stage two, **feature demons** break the image into parts called features; in stage three, **cognitive demons** look for specific patterns of these features; and in stage four, a **decision demon** uses the information provided by the cognitive demons to decide which stimulus was presented.

Though this description of the model makes it sound as if your head is populated by little people, we will see that these "little people" may actually be neurons that perform specialized tasks. We will now describe in more detail which tasks each of these "demons" perform.

Image demons. The image demon's job is simply to record the image. This function, which is the same as that of the detector unit in the template-matching scheme, is carried out physiologically by the receptors. In the case of vision, the image forms on the rod and cone receptors of the retina, which results in the electrical signals that are sent along the optic nerve toward the brain.

Feature demons. The feature demons take the electrical signals generated by the image demon and analyze them in terms of features. We can understand how this works by looking at Figure 7.38. The letter *R* on the left is the stimulus to be recognized. The *R* is recorded by the image demon, and the generated signals are sent to the feature demons. There are a number of these demons, each responsible for a particular feature, or part, of the stimulus. The figure shows demons that are responsible for seven different features (there are many other feature demons, which, for purposes of simplicity, aren't shown here). Feature demons that respond to a curve open on the left, a downward facing angle, a vertical line, a right angle, and a slanted line are activated by the *R*, as indicated by the arrows. Compare this result to what happens if we present the letter *T* (Figure 7.39). Presenting a *T* activates the feature demons responsible for the vertical line, the horizontal line, and two right angles.

Cognitive demons. The cognitive demons determine which groups of features are present. According to the feature analysis model, each cognitive demon is activated by particular features. One cognitive demon might be activated by the features that make up a chair, another by the features that make up your friend's face, another by the features that make up an airplane, and so on. Since we are concerned here with recognizing letters of the alphabet, we will assume that a cognitive demon is activated

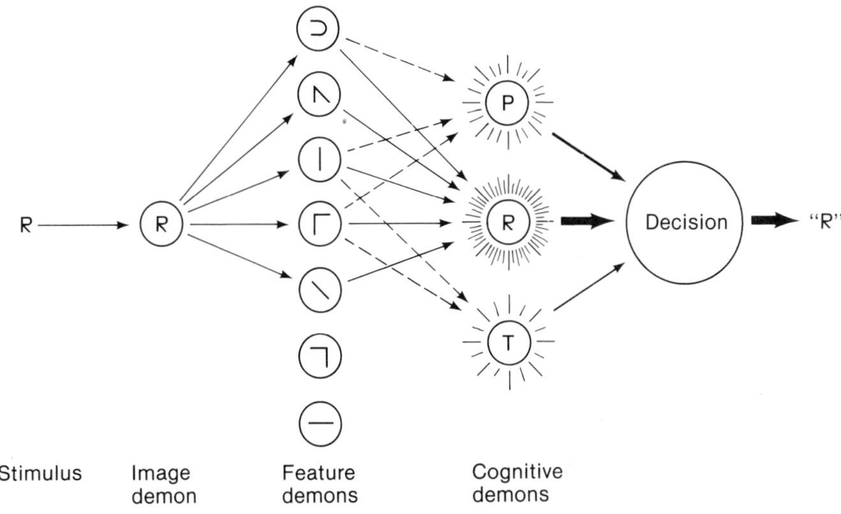

Figure 7.38 A feature analysis system at work recognizing the letter *R*.

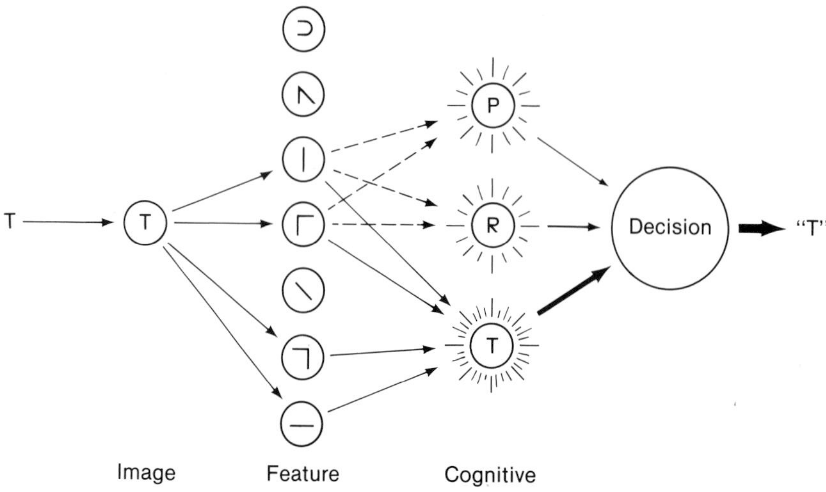

Figure 7.39 A feature analysis system at work recognizing the letter *T*.

by the features that make up each letter, and in Figures 7.38–7.40, we show the cognitive demons for the letters *R*, *T*, and *P*.

Look at the cognitive demons in Figure 7.38. The response of each cognitive demon is determined by how many of its features have been activated. The *T*'s cognitive demon is activated slightly, because two of its features have been activated (the vertical line and a right angle); the *P*'s demon is activated more than the *T*'s, because three of its features have been activated; and the *R*'s cognitive demon is activated most of all, with five of its features being activated.

To see what happens when we present the letter *T*, look at the cognitive demons in Figure 7.39. The letter *T* activates one of the feature demons for *P*, two for *R*, and four for *T*. Thus, in this case, the cognitive demons for *R* and *P* are excited slightly, and the demon for *T* is excited more strongly.

Decision demons. The final stage in this process brings us to the decision demon. It is the decision demon's job to recognize the letter that was presented at the beginning of this process, which it accomplishes by identifying the most active cognitive demon. In Figure 7.38 the decision demon would pick *R*, and in Figure 7.39 the choice would be *T*, because these letters have the most active cognitive demons.

Before leaving the decision demon, let's consider what happens if we present a *P*. The result of presenting a *P*, shown in Figure 7.40, poses a problem for the decision demon, because the cognitive demons for *R* and *P* are equally active. This occurs because the *P* and the *R* have very similar features; their only difference is the *R*'s slanted line, a feature that the *P* lacks. For the decision demon to recognize that a *P* was presented in Figure 7.40, we need to modify the feature analysis model slightly. One possibility would be to specify that a cognitive demon can be maximally excited only if all the possible feature demons for that letter are excited. If the cognitive demons follow this rule, then the cognitive demon for *P* would be maximally excited (since all three of its possible feature demons are excited), whereas the cognitive demon for *R* would not be maximally excited (since one of its feature demons, the one for the slanted line, is not excited). With this modification, the feature analysis model does a good job of recognizing the letters of the alphabet.

Advantages of Feature Analysis

A clear advantage of feature analysis over template matching is that feature analysis can recognize a much wider range of stimuli. Whereas template matching looks for a stimulus that exactly matches the size, orientation, and shape of a specific template, feature

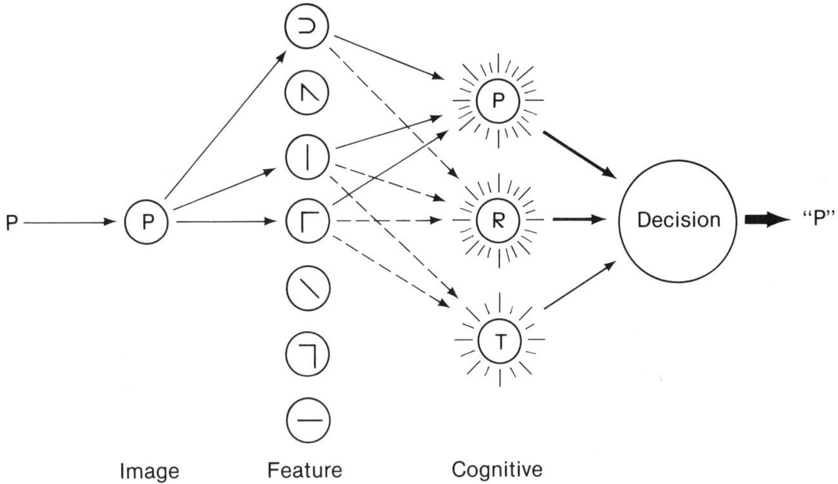

Figure 7.40 A feature analysis system at work recognizing the letter *P*. Note that the cognitive demons for the *R* and *P* both receive input from three feature demons, but the decision demon still correctly identifies the letter as a *P* (see text).

analysis looks for a stimulus with a particular set of features. Thus, feature analysis can recognize *R*s of many sizes and shapes, as long as a particular set of features is present.

Another advantage of feature analysis is that we can relate some components of the model to physiological events inside the person. The function of the image demon may be carried out by the receptors in the retina, and the feature demons may correspond to feature detectors in the visual cortex—the simple, complex, and hypercomplex cells we described in Chapter 2.

Though it is easy to find cortical neurons that correspond to many of our feature demons, finding physiological processes that correspond to cognitive demons is more difficult. A neuron that functions as a cognitive demon would have to be activated only by stimuli that contain a specific set of features. So far, there is little evidence for the existence of such neurons, although Charles Gross, Carlos Rocha-Miranda, and David Bender (1969) have found neurons in the monkey's inferotemporal cortex (an area outside the visual receiving area near the temporal lobe) that respond best to complex shapes like the ones in Figure 7.41 that look very much like a monkey's hand. Perhaps further research will uncover more neurons that respond best to specific sets of features, but, with the exception of Gross's monkey-hand detector, these cells have been difficult to find. Similarly, at this time there is no known neuron that corresponds to the decision demon. Such a neuron (or network of neurons) would have to

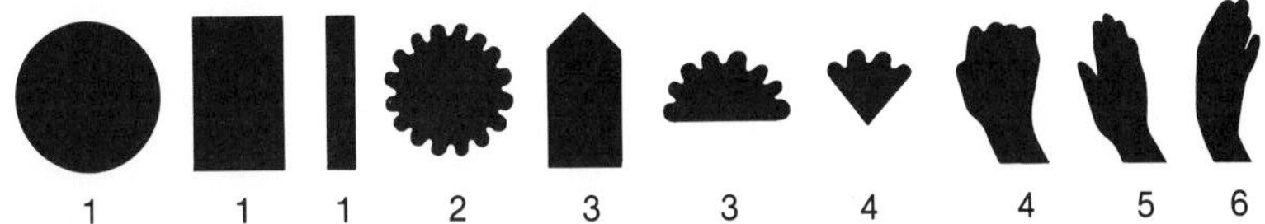

Figure 7.41 Some of the shapes used in Gross et al.'s (1969) experiment. The stimuli are arranged from left to right in order of increasing ability to cause a response in a neuron in the monkey's inferotemporal cortex. One = no response, 2 or 3 = small response, and 6 = maximum response. This neuron responds best to a shape that resembles a monkey's hand.

Box 7.2 Perceptual Learning

In her book *Principles of Perceptual Learning and Development* (1969), Elinor Gibson points out that while she perceives the sound of many birds singing together as a conglomeration of many unidentifiable birdsongs, an ornithologist could easily separate and identify each of the birdsongs. There are many other examples of situations in which some people can make fine discriminations that are exceedingly difficult for most other people. The following is a particularly striking example from an account of a wine-tasting competition (Root, 1974; cited in Walk, 1978):

> The competing sommeliers were called upon to identify 14 different vintages. It turned out that all 14 were the same wine of the same year; the contest boiled down, therefore, to naming the *clos,* the individual plot of land on which each wine had been grown, some of them only a few acres apart. *All* of the contestants realized that they were faced with 14 wines of the same category, and named correctly the wine and the year. The winner identified the 14 *clos* correctly; two others were right on 13.

The highly developed skills of the ornithologist and the expert wine taster are examples of the results of **perceptual learning.** Perceptual learning, then, is primarily a problem in **discrimination.** The basic question perceptual learning asks is: How do we learn to discriminate between two or more stimuli that initially appear to be the same?

Many researchers feel that an important part of learning to discriminate between two stimuli is learning to attend to the distinctive features of the stimuli. An experiment by Anne Pick (1965) demonstrates how practice with distinctive features can improve discrimination performance. In the training phase of her experiment, Pick showed kindergarteners pictures of three standard stimuli, two of which are shown on the upper left of the figure below. She then presented pictures of the standards along with three transformations of the standards. These transformations, two of

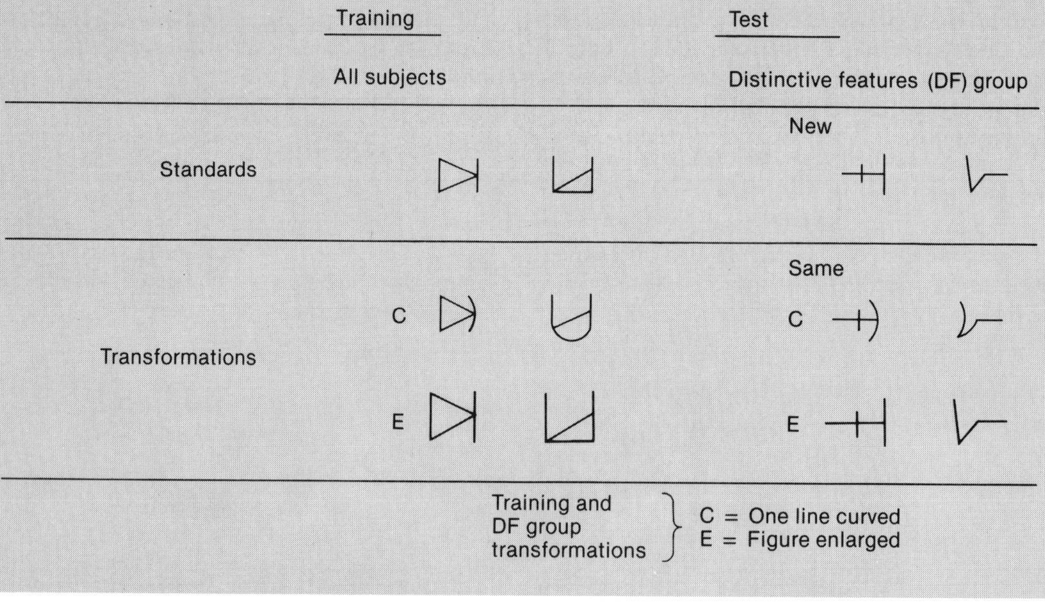

Training

All subjects

Test

Distinctive features (DF) group

New

Standards

Same

Transformations

C

E

C

E

Training and DF group transformations } C = One line curved
E = Figure enlarged

which are shown on the lower left of the figure, differed from the standard in some basic feature; for example, a straight line is changed to a curved line in transformation C, and the stimulus is enlarged in transformation E. The subject's task was to pick the pictures that were identical to the standards. Training continued until subjects were able to pick the standard pictures, without picking any of the transformations.

In the text phase of the experiment, which followed the training, Pick divided her subjects into three groups. For subjects in the *distinctive features group,* the above procedure was repeated, with new standards but with the same transformations they had seen in training. For example, if they saw the curved transformation and the size transformation in training, they saw the same transformations of the new standards. Subjects in the *prototype group* saw the same standards they saw in training but with new transformations, and subjects in the *control group* saw new standards *and* new transformations. The subjects in all groups had the same task as in training: to pick the stimuli that matched the standards.

The results of this experiment showed that subjects in the distinctive features group made fewer errors than those in the other two groups. One explanation of the superior performance of the distinctive features group is that, during training, these subjects learned to pay attention to the distinctive features they experienced. For example, they may have learned to pay attention to straightness and curviness during training, so attending to the straightness and curviness of the transformed stimuli in the second part of the experiment made it easier for them to discriminate between the different stimuli.

Distinctive feature learning undoubtedly plays an important role in developing skills such as those possessed by ornithologists and expert wine tasters. Wine tasters learn to tell the difference between two seemingly identical wines, by learning to focus their attention on a particular property of the wine, such as sweetness or dryness, or on some other, more subtle, individual property, which for us is lost in the overall taste of the wine.

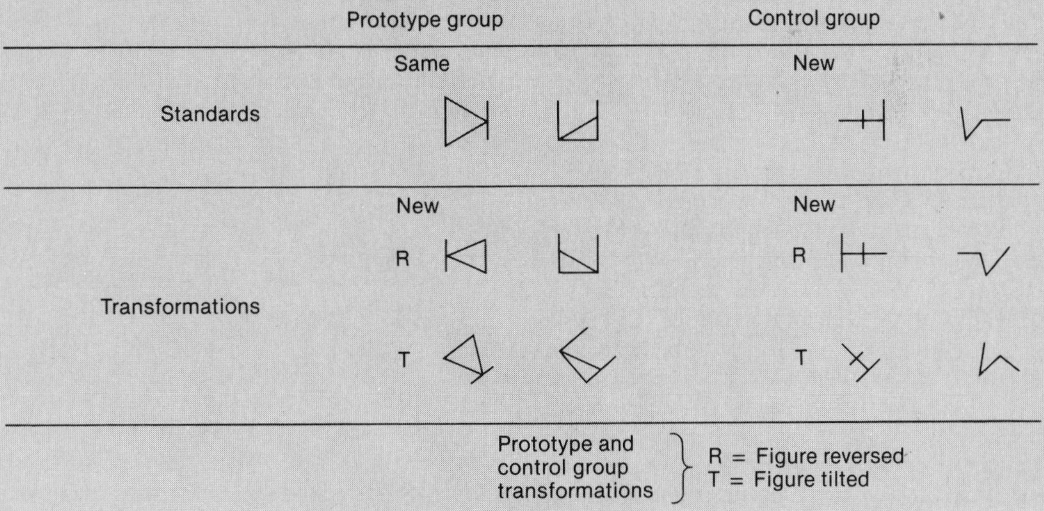

be capable of deciphering the meaning of all these inputs. So far, this "master neuron" exists only in the wildest fantasies of neurophysiologists.

The idea of pattern recognition based on features is appealing, not only because of the physiological evidence for feature detectors but also because the results of some psychophysical experiments show that features may play a role in recognition. Kinney, Marsetta, and Showman (1966) asked observers to identify letters that were flashed so briefly they were difficult to see. They found that, under these difficult conditions, observers made some errors in their identification of letters and that these errors followed a pattern: letters with common features tended to be more easily confused than those without. For example, the letter *C* was most likely to be confused with *G, O,* or *B,* all of which share features with *C,* but was never confused with letters such as *A, E,* or *F,* which have completely different features.

Problems with Feature Analysis

Though feature analysis is a good starting point for explaining human pattern recognition, a number of problems remain to be solved. In the sections below we will consider some of these problems.

What is a feature? Up till now we have defined features as parts of objects. With this definition in hand, we dissected the letter *R* into a number of smaller parts—lines, angles, and curves. It is convenient to define features in this way, because it is easy to relate straight lines or angles to feature detectors known to exist in the cortex. However, in some situations, our perception is determined not by these small parts of figures but, rather, by larger, more "global" aspects of the figure.

A good example of the use of global features is provided by an experiment done by L. Kozlowski and Jim Cutting (1977). They put small lights on people and then had them walk in a darkened room. Kozlowski and Cutting found that observers could easily tell whether the person walking was a male or a female, based solely on the pattern of moving lights. It is difficult to explain this result based on the firing of feature detectors that respond to small portions of the stimulus, because the crucial information for this task appears to be the complicated relations among the moving dots of light. In other words, the stimulus as a whole is what is important, rather than individual parts of the stimulus.

Another illustration that the recognition of an object may not depend on the recognition of its individual parts is provided by an experiment done by Jim Pomerantz, Lawrence Sager, and Robert Stoever (1977). The observer's task was to look at a stimulus like the one in Figure 7.42 and identify, as quickly as possible, the quadrant containing the odd stimulus. According to the theory of feature detectors, the observer accomplishes this task by using information provided by feature detectors that fire to each slanted line segment. If this is so, Pomerantz asked, what should happen if identical right angles are added to each line segment, as shown in Figure 7.42(b)? If, in fact, the crucial information for detecting the odd quadrant is provided by feature detectors that fire to individual line segments, then adding identical patterns to each quadrant should have no effect on the observer's ability to pick the odd quadrant. Pomerantz, however, found otherwise. Observers took an average of 1,884 msec to identify the odd quadrant in (a) but took only 749 msec to identify the odd quadrant in (b). Thus, adding identical stimuli to each quadrant improved the observer's performance.

According to Pomerantz, adding the right angles creates new, larger, **emergent features**—in this case, the triangle. While feature detectors for slanted lines may help the observer looking at (a), the new feature (the triangle), which emerges from the addition of the right angle, determines the observer's faster reaction time in (b).

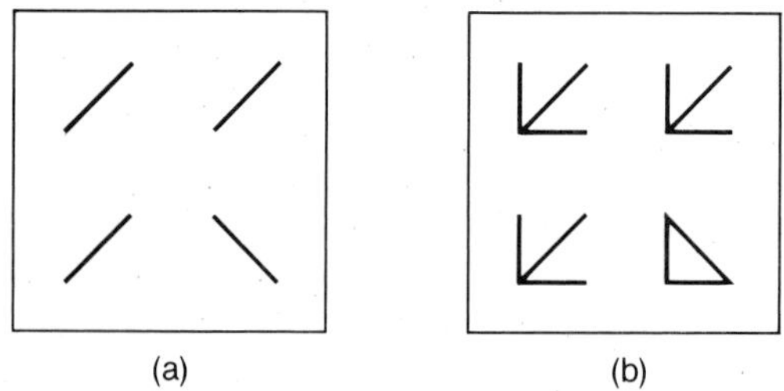

Figure 7.42 Stimuli used in Pomerantz, Sager, and Stoever's (1977) experiment.

Finally, an experiment by Navon (1977), using stimuli in which a large letter is made up of a number of smaller letters (Figure 7.43), also shows that larger, more "global," parts of a stimulus can take precedence over smaller parts of the stimulus. He showed this by asking observers to identify either the large letter (global-directed condition) or the small letters that make up the large letter (local-directed condition).

Navon found that in the global-directed condition, observers could ignore the small letters; that is, they identified the *H* just as rapidly when the small letters were *E*s as when they were *H*s. In the local-directed condition, however, the observers' ability to identify the small letters was affected by the large letter. They responded rapidly when the large letter matched the small one, as in Figure 7.43(a), but their performance declined when the large letter did not match, as in Figure 7.43(b). Navon interpreted this interfering effect of the large letter as an indication that we identify large letters before smaller ones. In terms of features, Navon's observers paid attention to the features defined by the large letter before paying attention to those of the smaller letters.

With the results of these three experiments in mind, we need to rethink our conception of what a feature is. It appears that features are sometimes individual line segments, which can easily be dealt with by cortical feature detectors. In other instances, however, features are larger, such as the overall movement pattern of numerous lights or a triangle or other geometrical figure, and cannot easily be dealt with by traditional feature detectors.

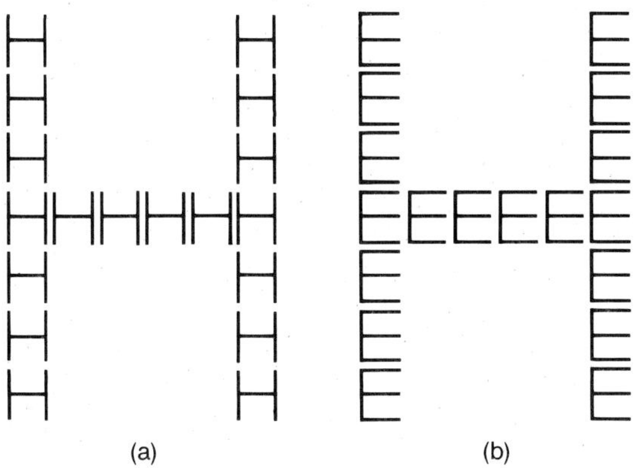

Figure 7.43 Stimuli used in Navon's (1977) experiment.

Organizational effects. Many of the organizational effects used to illustrate Gestalt principles are extremely difficult to explain in terms of features or feature detectors. For example, consider the Prinzmetal and Banks experiments that used the stimuli shown in Figures 7.32 and 7.33. According to the feature analysis model of pattern recognition, the first step in recognizing the target would be to analyze it in terms of its features. But if individual features are what is important, how can we explain why the larger patterns near the target influenced the observer's performance? Something besides features must be influencing our perception in these examples.

The effect of context. The examples from Figures 7.32 and 7.33, which show that the pattern surrounding a target can influence our ability to detect the target, indicate that the **context** in which the target appeared influences the target's detectability. In this section, we will look at some examples of how context created by an observer's past experience can influence object recognition. We will first consider two experiments, one by Stephen Palmer (1975) and one by Irving Biederman (1981).

In Palmer's experiment, the observer is shown two slides: first a *context* scene, like the one on the left of Figure 7.44, followed by one of the target objects on the right. Palmer found that an observer's ability to name the target object was affected by his viewing the scene that preceded it. A target object appropriate to the scene, such as a loaf of bread for the kitchen scene, was detected correctly about 80 percent of the time, but a target object inappropriate to the scene, like the drum or the mailbox, was detected correctly only about 40 percent of the time. Palmer's result occurs because the observers knew from past experience which objects belong in kitchens (bread) and which objects do not (mailboxes and drums).

Biederman demonstrated that an observer's past experience influences perception by flashing scenes on a screen, such as the one in Figure 7.45, then

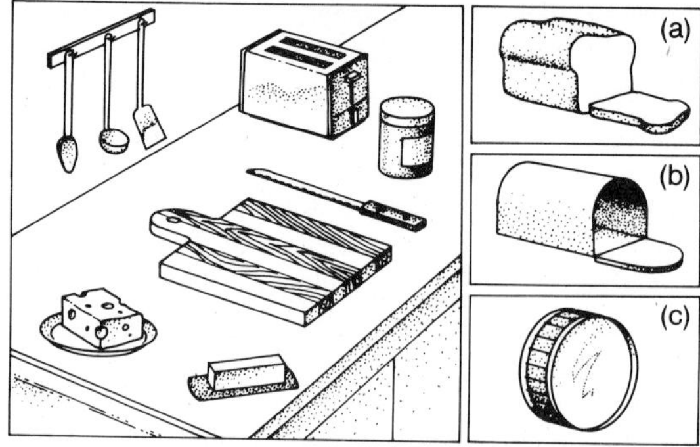

Figure 7.44 Stimuli used in Palmer's (1975) experiment. The scene at the left is presented first, and the observer is then asked to identify one of the objects on the right.

asking observers to identify an object located at a particular place in the scene (they were told where to look immediately before seeing the picture). For the picture in Figure 7.45, observers were asked to identify the fire hydrant. Biederman found that observers made more errors when the hydrant was in a strange location, such as on top of the mailbox, than when it was located where it belonged, on the sidewalk. The observers' knowledge of where fire hydrants belong influenced their ability to recognize the hydrant.

Top-Down and Bottom-Up Processing

When a person's knowledge of the world influences perception, we are dealing with a much different level of analysis than that hypothesized by the feature analysis model. Feature analysis is often referred to as **bottom-up processing,** because processing starts with small units (features), and our perception is then built on the foundation laid by these small units. In contrast, analysis that involves a person's knowledge of the world is referred to as **top-down processing,** because processing starts with higher-level information, such as the context in which a stimulus is seen or other information that causes us to expect that a particular stimulus will be presented. The Palmer and Biederman results support the idea of top-down processing, because our perceptions in both situations are clearly influenced by higher-level information.

Figure 7.45 Stimulus used in Biederman's (1981) experiment. In this picture observers were asked to identify the fire hydrant.

Other examples of top-down processing are provided by Figures 7.46–7.48. When we read the top line of Figure 7.46, we interpret the stimulus under the arrow as the letter *B,* because it is seen with letters of the alphabet. However, when we read the bottom line, we see the identical stimulus as the number 13, because it is seen with numbers (Bruner & Minturn, 1955).

The rat-man demonstration, shown in Figure 7.47, is one that I have used to demonstrate to my class the effect of **perceptual set** —the fact that a person's expectations can influence what the person perceives. I present the picture of a rat in (a) to half the class and the picture of the man's head in (b) to the other half. When the picture in (c), which can be interpreted as either a rat or a man, is flashed on the screen for the whole class, the half who originally saw the rat say that 7.47(c) is a rat, and the half who originally saw a man say that the same picture is a man. The expectation, or perceptual set, established by the first presentation clearly influences their perception.

Figure 7.48 is a picture similar to the rat-man demonstration in that it can be seen in two ways, as a pretty young wife or as an old haggard mother-in-law. Just as our perception of the rat-man figure is influenced by previous exposure to a picture that is clearly a rat or clearly a man, our perception of the wife–mother-in-law picture can also be influenced by first seeing a picture that is clearly the wife or clearly the mother-in-law (Leeper, 1935). (Hint: the wife's neckband is the mother-in-law's mouth; the wife's chin is the tip of the mother-in-law's nose.)

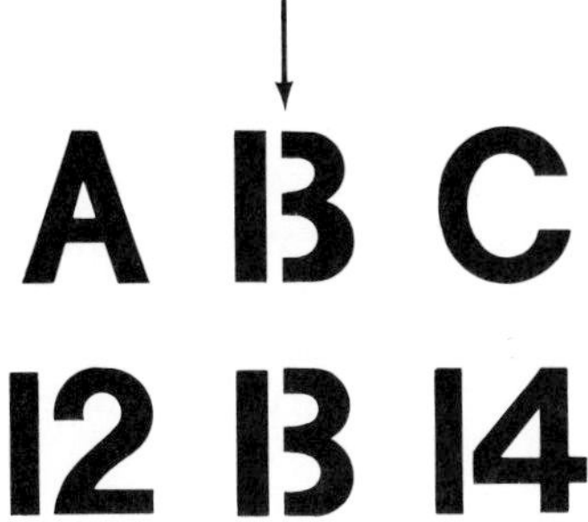

Figure 7.46 Our perception of the object under the arrow is affected by perceptual set (see text).

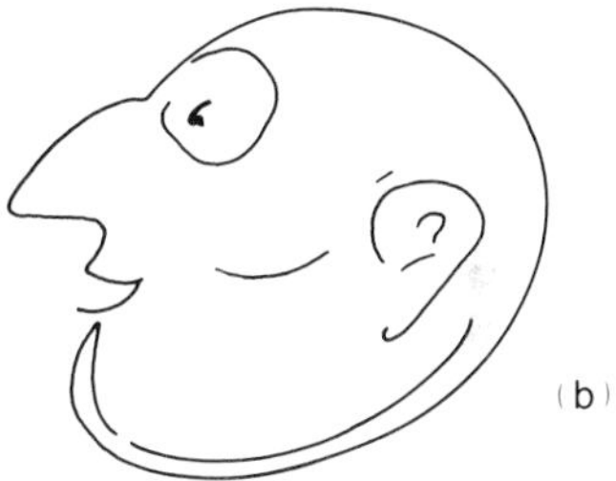

Figure 7.47 The rat-man demonstration. Figure 7.47 (c) is from Bugelski and Alampay (1961), and the others are adapted from this figure.

In all these examples (*B*/13, rat/man, and wife/mother-in-law), top-down processing influences our perception such that, even though the features that make up these pictures remain constant, our interpretation of the pictures changes with the context in which we view them.

Figure 7.48 The wife–mother-in-law figure. (From Boring, 1930.)

The importance of top-down processing is further illustrated by considering how people read. If we used only bottom-up processing for reading, we would have to detect each letter in a word by first identifying each of the letter's features. If each letter contains 4–5 features, a person who reads one page per minute will need to detect 30–50 letters, containing 120–250 features, every second! Dealing with this much information would be a great strain, and, fortunately, we needn't pay attention to every feature, every letter, or even every word in order to read. The contribution of top-down processing, which takes context into account, enables us to skip many features, letters, and words without sacrificing understanding. For example, in reading the sentence "Carl Yastrzemski hit a home _____ over the left field wall," our knowledge of baseball enables us to fill in the missing word *run,* even though it isn't there. And if the word *run* were there, we would not need to pay very much attention to it to understand the sentence. Thus, the use of context enables us to read without paying attention to every feature, letter, and word in a sentence (cf. Tulving & Gold, 1963; Tulving, Mandler, & Baumal, 1964; Smith & Spoehr, 1974).

The examples of top-down processing for visual perception and reading presented here, plus numerous examples in the area of speech perception (see pp. 383–400, in Chapter 14), have convinced most researchers that a full description of how we recognize patterns must involve a combination of top-down and bottom-up processing, with these two levels of analysis working together. Thus, for our description of pattern recognition to be complete, we must add the contributions of context and meaning to the feature analysis model. In fact, some versions of feature analysis models incorporate both bottom-up and top-down processing, by giving the decision demon the added responsibility of taking context and meaning into account before deciding which pattern is present (Lindsay & Norman, 1977).

Attention

As you read the text of this book, your **attention** is captured by the words on the page and by the figures that accompany them. You must pay attention to the words in order to understand them and to know when to attend each of the figures. But the directed attention that you experience when reading this book is not the same as your experience with the real world. Many stimuli compete for your attention in the real world, and you must somehow decide which ones will win your attention.

The topic of attention is important because attention and perception usually go hand in hand: you attend to the things you are interested in perceiving, and you usually perceive the things you attend to. Attention is a vast topic, which has interested not only perceptual psychologists but also cognitive psychologists interested in topics such as memory, thinking, and problem solving (Norman, 1976; Spoehr & Lehmkuhle, 1982). We will, however, limit ourselves to a few questions relevant to perception: (1) What determines where you direct your attention? (2) Is it possible to selectively attend to a small portion of the environment? (3) Is it possible to attend to two or more things at once?

Determinants of Attention

The first question we should ask is: Why is attention necessary? In the case of vision, attention is necessary because we can see clearly only that part of the scene which falls on our foveas (see p. 68, in Chapter 3), and our foveas can be directed to only a small part of the scene at a time. In vision, therefore, we direct our foveas to that part of the scene we want to attend. The rest of the scene falls in our peripheral vision, and though we can still see and perhaps even pay attention to this part of the scene (an important skill for athletes), the major portion of our attention is usually directed at the thing we are looking directly at.

That we can easily pay attention to only one thing at a time is illustrated by looking at Figure 7.49(a). At first this object looks entirely reasonable, but after you have looked at it for a while, you realize that there is something funny going on. In fact, this object is called an **impossible object,** because it can't really exist in three-dimensional space. Only after you have had time to successively attend to different parts of the object you notice that when you combine the left half with the right half, the object simply doesn't make sense. A similar process occurs for the object in Figure 7.49(b), but it takes less time to realize that this shortened object is impossible, because its features are closer together and the halves, therefore, are easier to compare.

Even if we could see or hear everything clearly, attention would still be necessary because our brain can't handle all the information that is out there. To realize this, you need only consider the scene at a noisy bar or at a party. The conversations, people, music, and everything else that is happening is simply too much to deal with all at once, so you resolve this *information overload* by focusing your attention on only a small fraction of the information in your environment.

How can we determine what attracts people's attention? One way is to observe their looking behavior, preferably in as natural a setting as possible. In fact, devices have been developed that can measure where a person is looking; however, since these devices are most easily used in the laboratory, most of our information about where people look has been determined by measuring people's **eye movements** as they look at pictures. The results of one of these experiments is shown in Figure 7.50. These eye movement records consist of two components: fixations, indicated by the dots, and eye movements, indicated by the lines connecting the dots. As the observer looks at the picture, he or she makes a series of fixations and eye movements. Each fixation lasts 300–900 msec, and each eye movement lasts 10–80 msec. The observer makes 1–3 fixations per second, separated by very rapid eye movements (Yarbus, 1967).

One interesting thing about the eye movement record in Figure 7.50 is that there are many areas of the picture at which the observer never looks! Apparently, the observer picks only certain areas of the picture on which to fixate, and, according to an experiment by Norman Mackworth and Anthony Morandi (1967), these areas seem to have a high information content. Mackworth and Morandi first measured observers' eye movements while they looked at a picture. The picture was then divided into 64 squares, and an independent group of observers was asked to rate the "informativeness" of each square. Informativeness was defined in terms of *recognizability.* A square was rated high in informativeness if the subject judged that it would be easy to recognize on another occasion. The results showed that observers fixated on the areas of the picture

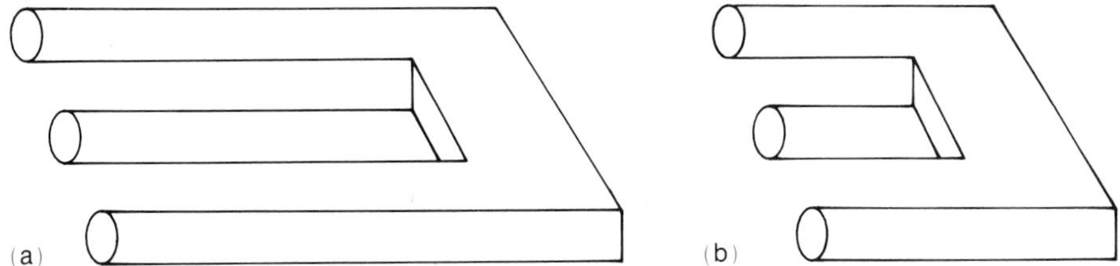

Figure 7.49 (a) An impossible object. Since we cannot attend to the entire object at once, we must compare the parts of the object before we realize that it is impossible. (b) It is easier to see that this smaller object is impossible, because we don't have to distribute our attention over such a large area.

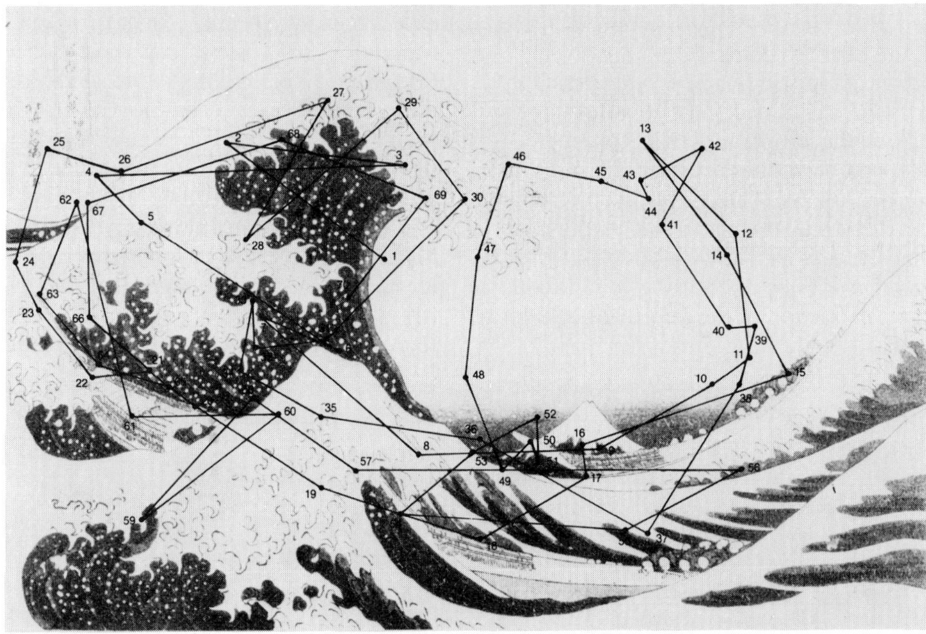

Figure 7.50 A picture of *The Wave* by Hokusai Katsushika (1760–1850) that was presented to observers by Buswell (1935) in his study of the eye movements. The record below indicates the pattern of fixations and eye movements made by an observer viewing this picture.

Box 7.3 Orientation and Form Perception

What happens when we tilt a square at a 45-degree angle? As you can see from the figure below, a tilted square is perceived as a diamond and *not* as a tilted square! Why does this occur? Is it because rotating the square 45 degrees results in a tilted image of the square on your retina? You can easily answer this question by cutting out a paper square and taping it to your wall so that the bottom of the square is parallel to the floor. First, view the square with your head upright, then with your head tilted at a 45-degree angle. What do you see? You will probably continue to perceive the square as a square, even though, when you view it at a 45-degree angle, the square's image on your retina is oriented like a diamond. You can also tilt the square on the wall so that it looks like a diamond when viewed upright, and then tilt your head so that the diamond's image on your retina is oriented like an upright square. The result? The diamond will continue to look like a diamond, no matter how you look at it.

These demonstrations show that the orientation of the retinal image does not determine whether we see a square or a diamond. Something else must determine which form we see. Irvin Rock (1974) suggests that whether we see a square or a diamond is determined by a cognitive process in which we assign the locations of the top, bottom, and sides to different parts of the figure. This cognitive process assigns the role of "top" to side "a" for the square and to angle "A" for the diamond: once this is established, we perceive the figure as a square or a diamond as long as the top is "up" in relation to the rest of the environment. We perceive the top of the square or the top of the diamond as being upright with respect to the environment, even when we tilt oul head, because of another cognitive process that compensates for the tilt of these figures on our retina.

This compensation process, however, does not work for all figures. Look at the inverted face below. When the face is upside down, it looks strange, even if you know whose face it is. This result contradicts our experience with the square or diamond, which continues to look like a square or diamond, no matter how we view it. If we correct for the change in the retinal orientation of a square or a diamond, why can't we correct for the change in the retinal orientation of a face? Since we can easily locate the top, bottom, and sides of the face, it would seem that compensation for the upside-down retinal image should be easy. Rock suggests that the reason the appearance of the inverted face changes is that the mechanism which compensates for the tilt of the square and the diamond can't compensate for all the features of the more complex face. While our attention is focused on correcting the mouth, we can't correct the rest of the features at the same time; therefore, we find it difficult to recognize the inverted face. Thus, our perception of disoriented figures depends on their orientation on the retina for complex figures, such as faces, but does not depend on their orientation on the retina for simple figures, such as squares or diamonds.

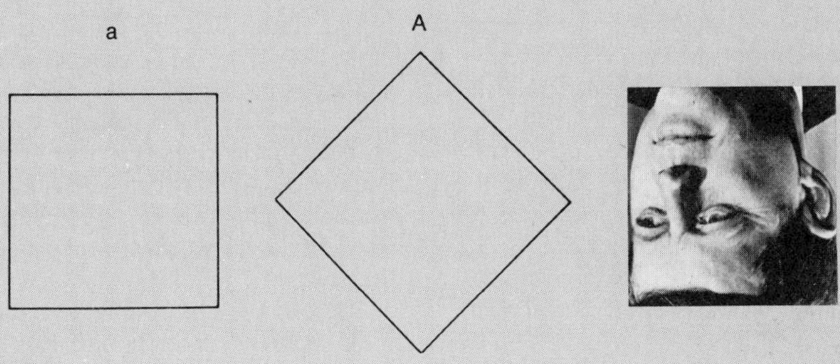

that were rated highest in informativeness.

In a later experiment, Mackworth collaborated with Geoffrey Loftus (Loftus & Mackworth, 1978) to show that people direct their attention to objects they would ordinarily not expect to find in a particular context. For example, most observers who look at Figure 7.51 rapidly focus on the octopus in the middle of the farm scene and continue to look at it for much longer than they look at a picture of a tractor presented in the same position in that scene. This is top-down processing in action. People focus their attention on the octopus because they know that a farm is an absurd place to find one.

Figure 7.51 One of the stimuli used by Loftus and Mackworth (1978). Observers attend to the incongruous octopus more than to a tractor located in the same position.

Selective Attention

We have seen that we tend to pick certain objects to look at, and, because we can see clearly only a small area, we usually focus our attention on that particular area. But consider the problem we face for the sense of hearing. If you are at a party where perhaps five to ten conversations are taking place at once, the sounds from each conversation enter your ears, stimulate the receptors in your ears, and send nerve impulses down the auditory nerve toward the brain. When considered from this point of view, we might think that all this talk would end up as a meaningless garble. However, in spite of this apparent overstimulation, we somehow solve what psychologists call the **cocktail party problem** by **selective attention,** that is, by selecting one conversation to listen to while ignoring the others.

Colin Cherry (1953) demonstrated this ability to selectively attend to one conversation, by presenting two messages dichotically, that is, one message to the left ear and a different message to the right ear. In **dichotic listening** experiments, a person is told to pay attention to a spoken message presented to the left ear and ignore the message presented simultaneously to the right ear. To assure that a subject is paying attention to the message in the left ear, the person is asked to repeat the message as he or she hears it, a technique Cherry called **shadowing.** Cherry found that people could easily shadow the attended message, ignore the other one, and even be unaware of such drastic changes as backward speech or a switch to a different language in the unattended message.

Recently, Ulric Neisser and R. Becklen (1974) did an analogous experiment for the sense of vision. Rather than present one image to the left eye and another to the right eye (which would cause a condition called **binocular rivalry,** in which the left and right images alternate with each other every few seconds), Neisser and Becklen superimposed two images, as shown in Figure 7.52. They presented two superimposed films, one of a "hand-slapping" game and the other of three people throwing a ball back and forth, then asked observers to pay attention to one film and ignore the other. To be sure the observers were, in fact, paying attention to the film they were supposed to be paying attention to, the observers had to press a key every time the ball was thrown (if they were attending to the ball-throwing film) or every time the hands moved (if they were attending to the hand-slapping film). The results of Neisser and Becklen's vision experiment paralleled the results of Cherry's hearing experiment: observers could selectively attend to one of the films, and, while they were attending to this film, they took in little information from the other, unattended film. (See also Goldstein & Fink, 1981, for a similar experiment with superimposed still pictures.)

Thus, in both hearing and vision, we can selectively attend to one stimulus and ignore another

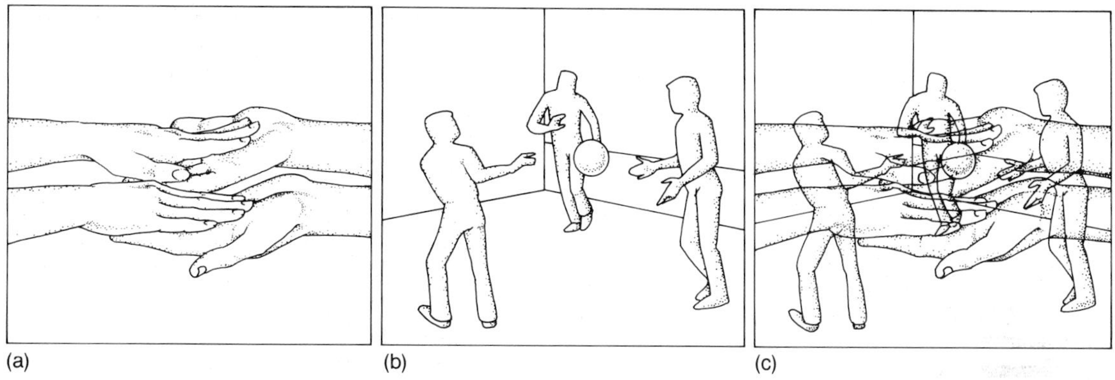

Figure 7.52 Stimulus for Neisser and Becklen's (1974) experiment. A videotape of a hand-slapping game (a) was superimposed on a videotape of three people throwing a ball (b) to produce the stimulus in (c).

one, and, in doing so, we perceive little information from the unattended stimulus.

Divided Attention

While our ability to selectively attend to one message makes it easy to solve the cocktail party problem—talking to one person while ignoring everyone else—another, more difficult problem often occurs at parties—the problem of **divided attention.** This happens when you are having a conversation with one person but actually want to hear what is being said by another person. If you have ever tried to listen to two conversations at once, you know that it is difficult if not impossible, and this has been confirmed by dichotic listening experiments in which people try to simultaneously listen to different messages presented to the left and right ears. Unless very simple or familiar messages such as nursery rhymes or Christmas carols are presented, it is extremely difficult to follow both messages at once.

Our inability to attend to two messages at once led Donald Broadbent (1958) to propose his **filter model of attention.** Broadbent's model says the stimuli that enter a person's ears must pass through a filter before entering memory and that this filter can only admit one message at a time. While a number of messages may get into the ear, all but the one being attended to are filtered out before they can be perceived or stored in memory. Later experiments have shown, however, that when a person is attending to one message, some information from the unattended message may be recognized. For example, you may have heard someone to whom you were not even listening mention your name, halfway across the room. Results such as this show that Broadbent's filter model is too simple to account for all the facts of attention, and a number of other models have been proposed (Norman, 1968; Triesman, 1969).

The fact remains, however, that in high-information situations such as parties, you can deal only with a small fraction of the information entering your ears. So the next time you find yourself listening to one person but really wanting to listen to someone else, remember that it is impossible to listen to both people at once; your only solution is to excuse yourself from one conversation and switch to the other.

Summary

1. This chapter considers organization as the process by which small units are grouped into a larger form and recognition as the process by which a form is recognized as a meaningful object.

2. Gestalt psychology was founded in 1912 by Max Wertheimer. His experiments with *phi movement* led him to state the principle that "the whole is different from the sum of its parts."

3. The Gestalt school of psychology rejected the idea that perceptions are constructed from sensations in favor of the idea that the stimulus must be considered as a whole.

4. The Gestalt laws of organization—Pragnanz, similarity, good continuation, and nearness—provide us with rules for how parts of stimuli are grouped together.

5. A form is usually perceived as a figure in front of a background, and a number of rules help us determine which part of a pattern will be the figure and which part will be the ground.

6. The Gestalt laws of organization are sometimes difficult to apply. Some of the problems with them include difficulty in telling when one object is simpler than another, conflicts between the laws, and the lack of applicability to the three-dimensional world.

7. The tendency of the Gestalt approach to describe rather than to explain has led many present-day researchers to question the Gestalt approach.

8. Recent research based on the Gestalt approach has concentrated on applying the experimental method to Gestalt psychology in an attempt to understand, in a more quantitative way, how these laws work. Researchers have used both visual and auditory stimuli in these experiments.

9. One example of how the Gestalt laws of organization can be applied to auditory stimuli is the phenomenon of auditory stream segregation, which demonstrates auditory grouping based on similarity of pitch.

10. A person suffering from visual agnosia can see clearly but has difficulty recognizing what he has seen.

11. The template system of pattern recognition only works in very restricted situations. Its drawbacks have led psychologists to reject it as a possible mechanism for human pattern recognition.

12. The feature analysis model of pattern recognition, which involves an analysis of an image by image demons, feature demons, cognitive demons, and decision demons, is the most promising explanation of the way human pattern recognition may work.

13. An important part of learning to discriminate between two stimuli is learning to attend to the distinctive features of the stimuli.

14. Though the feature analysis model is a good start toward explaining human pattern recognition, a number of problems remain to be solved. One such problem is that it is sometimes difficult to define exactly what we mean by a feature, and another is that the context in which a pattern occurs influences our recognition of that pattern.

15. Bottom-up processing starts with small units such as features, whereas top-down processing starts with higher-level information, such as the context in which a stimulus is seen or other information that causes us to expect that a particular stimulus will be presented.

16. Our ability to recognize objects that are tilted or inverted depends, at least partially, on a cognitive process that assigns the locations of the top, bottom, and sides to different parts of the object.

17. Attention is necessary in vision because we can see clearly only that part of a scene which falls on our foveas, and our foveas can be directed to only a small part of the scene at a time.

18. We can easily pay attention to only one thing at a time.

19. When looking at pictures, we tend to look at areas that are high in informativeness and novelty.

20. The results of dichotic listening experiments indicate that we can selectively attend to one of two auditory messages presented simultaneously. Experiments in which subjects view two superimposed films indicate that we can selectively attend to one of two visual images presented simultaneously.

Glossary

Agnosia Visual agnosia is a condition in which a person can see clearly but has difficulty recognizing what he has seen. This condition, often caused by brain injury, makes it difficult for people to synthesize parts of an object into an integrated whole. (182)

Attention The process by which we focus consciousness onto a specific stimulus. (194)

Auditory stream segregation When a series of tones that differ in pitch are played so that the high- and low-pitched tones alternate rapidly, the high and low pitches become perceptually separated into simultaneously occurring, independent streams of sound. (170)

Binocular rivalry When one image is presented to the left eye and another is presented to the right eye, we do not see both images simultaneously; instead, binocular rivalry causes our perception to alternate between the left and right images. (198)

Bottom-up processing Processing that starts with the analysis of small units such as features. The feature analysis model of pattern recognition described in this chapter is an example of bottom-up processing. (193)

Cocktail party problem The problem we face at a party in which we must select one of many conversations to listen to. (198)

Cognitive demons Devices hypothesized by the feature analysis model of pattern recognition that are activated by particular features. Whereas each feature demon is activated by only one feature, each cognitive demon is activated by all the features that make up a particular pattern. For example, one cognitive demon might be activated by all the features that make up the letter *R*. (185)

Context Stimuli that potentially affect the perception of other stimuli. (191)

Decision demons Devices hypothesized by the feature analysis model of pattern recognition that recognize a pattern by identifying the most active cognitive demon. (185)

Dichotic listening When one message is presented to the left ear and another message is presented to the right ear. (198)

Discrimination In perceptual learning, the ability to discriminate between two stimuli that initially appear the same. (188)

Distinctive feature learning Learning to discriminate between two objects by learning to pay attention to specific features of the object. (189)

Divided attention Paying attention to two or more stimuli that are presented simultaneously. (199)

Emergent features Large features that "emerge" when additional stimuli are added to small features. (190)

Eye movements The voluntary eye movements, which occur as an observer looks at a scene, are rapid movements of the eyes that last 10–80 msec and are separated by fixations that last 300–900 msec. (195)

Feature analysis A model of pattern recognition that involves a number of stages in which a pattern is broken down into its component features and the information provided by these features is used to recognize the pattern. (184)

Feature demons Devices hypothesized by the feature analysis model of pattern recognition, each of which is activated by a specific feature of the stimulus. (185)

Figure-ground The separation of a pattern into a figure and a background. The figure is seen as being in front of the ground, which extends behind the figure. (173)

Filter model of attention Donald Broadbent's idea that incoming stimuli must pass through a filter before being perceived and that this filter can only admit one message at a time. (199)

Gestalt psychology A school of psychologists that has focused on developing principles of perceptual organization. (166)

Good continuation, law of Points that, when connected, result in straight or smoothly curving lines are seen as belonging together, and lines tend to be seen in such a way as to follow the smoothest path. (171)

Image demons Devices hypothesized by the feature analysis model of pattern recognition that record the image of the stimulus. (185)

Impossible object An object that can be represented by a two-dimensional picture but cannot exist in three-dimensional space. (195)

Laws of organization A number of rules developed by the Gestalt psychologists that describe how small elements are grouped into larger configurations. (168)

Organization The perceptual process by which small units are grouped into larger forms. (166)

Pattern recognition The process by which we recognize patterns. This process is often accompanied by the assignment of meaning to the pattern. (181)

Perceptual learning The process of learning to discriminate between two or more stimuli that initially appear to be the same. (188)

Perceptual set A person's expectations can influence what they perceive. (193)

Phi movement The illusion of movement between two stimuli that is observed when the two stimuli are rapidly presented one after another. (166)

Pragnanz, law of Also called the law of good figure or the law of simplicity. States that every stimulus pattern is seen in such a way that the resulting structure is as simple as possible. (170)

Proximity, law of Things that are near to each other appear to be grouped together. Also called the law of nearness. (172)

Recognition The perceptual process by which a form is recognized as a meaningful object. (166)

Reversible figure-ground A figure-ground pattern that reverses as it is viewed, so the figure becomes the ground and the ground becomes the figure. (173)

Selective attention Paying attention to one stimulus while ignoring other, simultaneously presented stimuli. (198)

Shadowing When a person repeats a message aloud as he or she hears it. (198)

Similarity, law of Similar things appear to be grouped together. (170)

Subjective contour The perception of a contour when no contour is physically present. (167)

Template A standard pattern, hypothesized to be stored inside an organism, against which incoming patterns are compared. (183)

Template matching A process in which a pattern is matched against a series of templates to determine which template most closely matches the pattern. (183)

Top-down processing Processing that starts with the analysis of high-level information, such as the context in which a stimulus is seen. (193)

Chapter Eight

Perceiving Depth

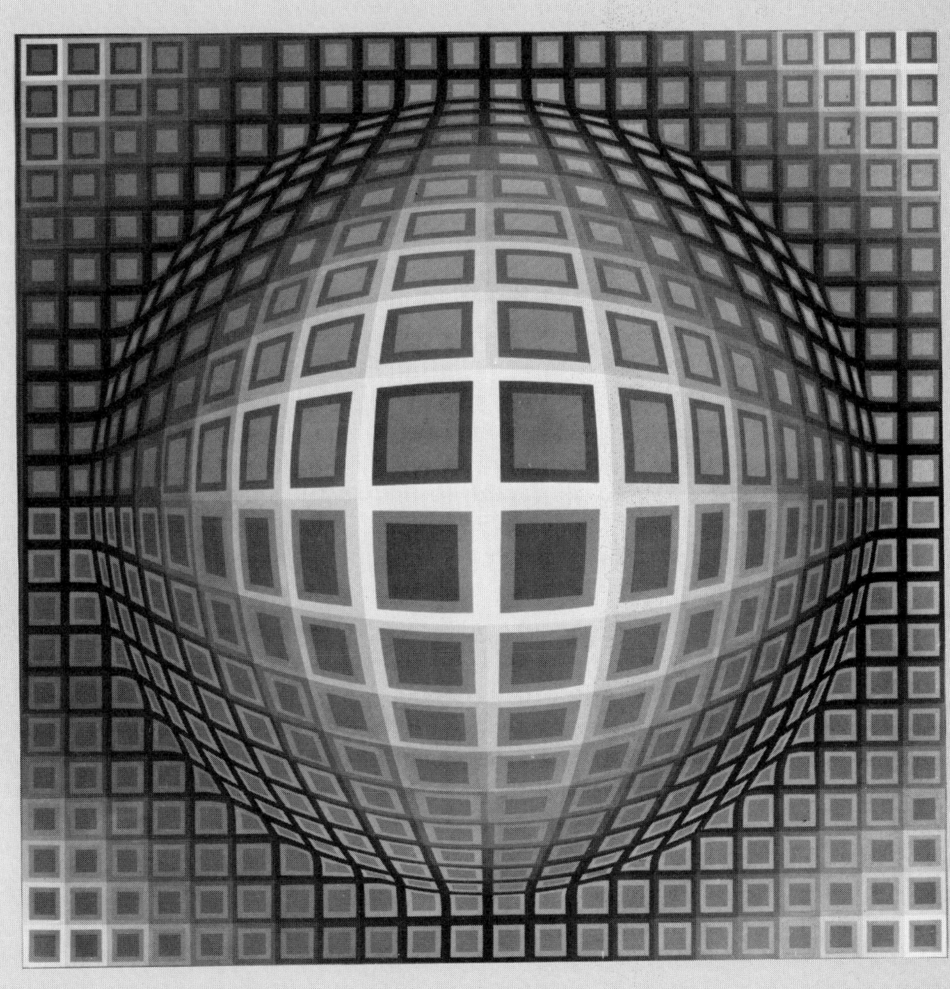

Imagine that you are standing on a hill looking out over the neighborhood of Figure 8.2. Imagine that you are actually *there, observing the three-dimensional scene.* You can see from the car in the foreground down to the cross-street at the bottom of the hill, and then up the next hill to the houses that line the ridge in the distance. And it takes no particular skill on your part to know that the car is nearby and the ridge is far away.

The amazing thing about this effortless process is that you can perceive the scene in three dimensions—height, width, and depth—based on information reflected from the scene onto the two-dimensional surface of your retina. That we can perceive three dimensions, even though the surface of our retina is flat, has led many investigators to propose that our perception of depth is caused by various **depth cues**—two-dimensional information on the retina that signifies the three dimensionality of the scene. This approach to depth perception largely treats the observer as observing a scene from a stationary viewpoint, since all the depth cues but one involve a stationary picture on the retina. Some investigators, however, feel that the best way to understand depth perception is not to focus on the two-dimensional picture formed on the retina of a stationary observer; instead, they look at the information available to an observer as he or she moves through the environment. In this chapter, we will consider each of these approaches to depth perception, starting with the idea of depth cues.

Depth Cues

To get from the two-dimensional image on the retina to our perception of the three-dimensional scene, there must be two-dimensional information on the retina that signifies the three dimensionality of the scene. Since a number of these depth cues can be depicted in pictures (and are therefore called **pictorial depth cues**), we will, when appropriate, use works of art to illustrate these cues.

Overlap

The depth cue of **overlap** (also called interposition) is illustrated by the way the houses in Figure 8.2 overlap and, therefore, cover each other. Houses in the front cover houses that are farther back. If object A covers object B, then object A is seen as being in front of object B.

Figure 8.2 A neighborhood in Pittsburgh that contains many depth cues.

Paul Signac's painting *Place des Lices, St. Tropez* (1893), shown in Figure 8.3, makes extensive use of overlap. Place a piece of paper so that it covers everything below mark A and notice how overlap helps you determine the relative positions in depth of the branches in the top half of the picture. Then move your paper up so that it covers everything below mark B. Since there is little overlap in the upper left of the picture, it is difficult to tell which branches are in front and which are in back.

Relative Size

In addition to noticing that the houses in the background in Figure 8.2 are overlapped by those in the foreground, you can also see that the houses in the background take up less of your field of view than those in the foreground. This cue of **relative size,** which apparently has fooled the large person in Figure 8.4 into thinking that a small person was far away, was demonstrated by Adelbert Ames, who had observers view illuminated balloons in a darkened room. When he increased the size of one balloon by pumping more air into it, the observers reported that the expanding balloon appeared to be moving closer. Large relative size causes an object to appear close.

Relative Height

As you notice that houses farther in the background take up less of your field of view, you may also realize that they are higher in your field of view. This is the cue of **relative height.** Objects that are higher

Figure 8.3 Paul Signac, *Place des Lices, St. Tropez* (1893). (Museum of Art, Carnegie Institute, Pittsburgh, Pa.)

"Excuse me for shouting—I thought you were farther away."

Figure 8.4 Reproduced by special permission of *Playboy* magazine. (Copyright 1971 by Playboy.)

in your field of view, like the men in Figure 8.5, are usually seen as being more distant. This rule holds for objects below the horizon line (the men) but not for objects above the horizon line (the clouds). If an object is *above* the horizon line, being higher in your field of view makes it appear to be *closer*. Returning to Figure 8.2, notice that the houses on the ridge are the highest and most distant objects in the scene. You may also notice that the houses on the ridge are seen slightly less sharply than those in the foreground, which brings us to our next depth cue—atmospheric perspective.

Atmospheric Perspective

When we look at a distant object, **atmospheric (or aerial) perspective** results, because we are also looking at the air and the particles suspended in the air between us and the object. The farther away an object is, the more air and particles we have to look through, which makes far objects look less sharp than close objects. Figure 8.6, which shows a group of musicians on a hill overlooking Pittsburgh, is a good illustration of atmospheric perspective. Compare the sharpness of the musicians and other objects in the foreground to the fuzziness of downtown Pittsburgh in the background. Returning to our photograph in Figure 8.2, we can see a similar but less striking effect of atmospheric perspective, by comparing the sharp houses in the foreground to the slightly washed-out houses on the far hill in the background. If, instead of viewing hills in Pittsburgh, you were to view hills on the moon, where there is no atmosphere and hence no atmospheric perspective, the far hills would look just as sharp as near hills. But back here on earth there is atmospheric perspective, the exact amount being dependent on the nature of the atmosphere.

A few years ago, my friend Walt took a trip from Pittsburgh to Montana and learned firsthand about atmospheric perspective. He wanted to climb a mountain that appeared to be perhaps a three-hour hike away, only to find after three hours of hiking that he was not even halfway there. Walt's perceptions were calibrated for Pittsburgh, so he found it difficult to accurately estimate distances in the clearer

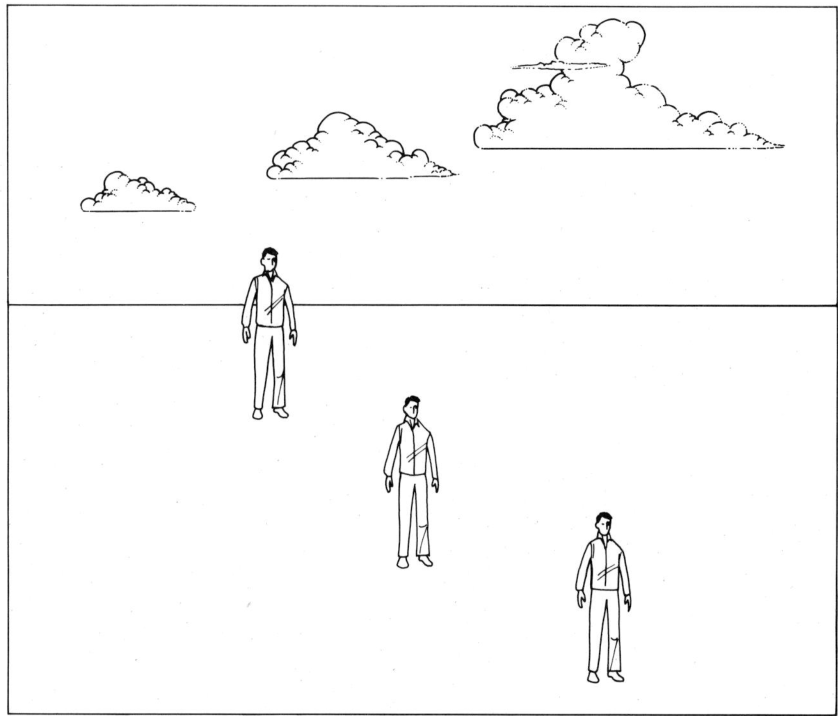

Figure 8.5 Relative height. Other things being equal, objects below the horizon that appear higher in the field of view are seen as being farther away. Objects above the horizon that appear lower in the field of view are seen as being farther away.

air of Montana. Because of the difference in atmospheric perspective, the mountain that would have looked three hours away in Pittsburgh was over six hours away in Montana!

In addition to making far objects look fuzzy, the atmosphere also makes them look blue. In Color Plate 8.1, you can see that the hills in the background look much bluer than the trees and grass in the foreground. (The reason for this blueness is explained in Box 8.1.)

Examples of the use of atmospheric perspective, as well as relative height and relative size, are illustrated by Gerard David's painting *Rest on the Flight to Egypt,* shown in Color Plate 8.2. That Joseph in the background is much smaller and higher than Mary in the foreground illustrates relative size and height. And atmospheric perspective is depicted in the painting by objects that become bluer and bluer as they recede into the background.

Atmospheric perspective was widely used by painters in the fifteenth and sixteenth centuries, and many art academies of the day hung a series of blue-tinted curtains between the art students and the objects they were painting, in order to make these students paint faraway objects blue. This training often resulted in an exaggeration of atmospheric perspective, so that many mountains were painted much bluer than they may have looked in the original scene.

Familiar Size

Look at the coins in Figure 8.7. If they were real coins, which would you say is closer? If you are

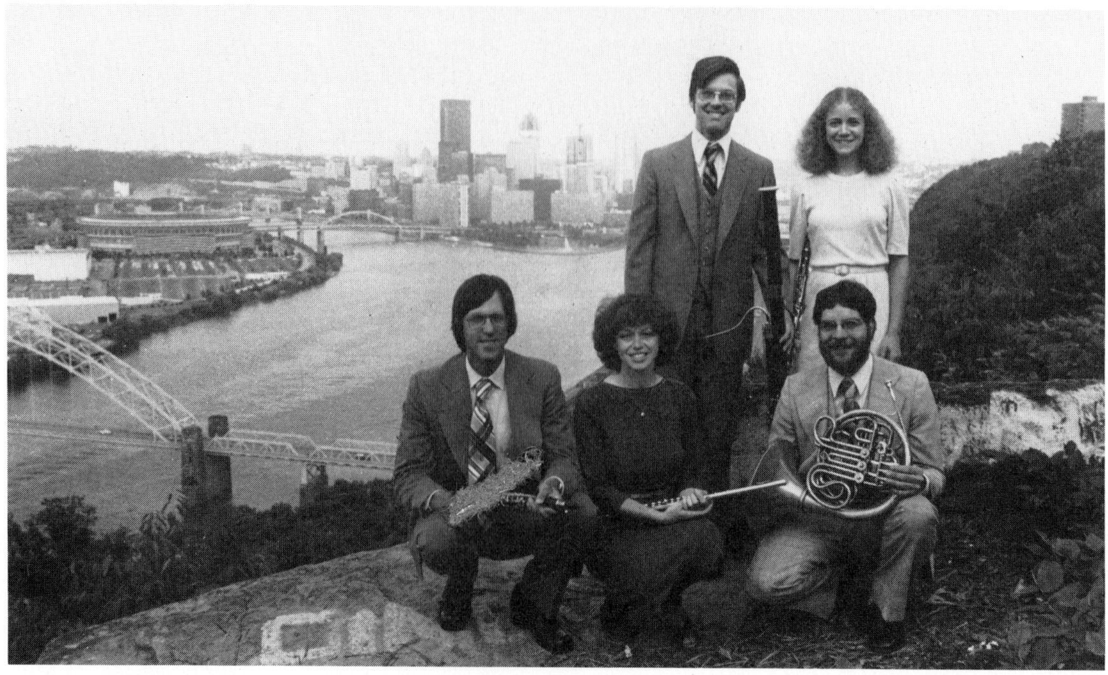

Figure 8.6 The Renaissance City Woodwind Quintet on a hill overlooking downtown Pittsburgh. (Photograph courtesy of Jim Whipple, 1983.)

influenced by your knowledge of the actual sizes of pennies, quarters, and half dollars, you would probably say that the penny is closer. If you did, the cue of **familiar size** is influencing your judgment of depth. In fact, an experiment by William Epstein (1963) shows that under certain conditions, our knowledge of an object's size can influence our perception of that object's depth. The stimuli in Epstein's experiment were photographs of a dime (enlarged to the size of a quarter), a quarter (actual size), and a half dollar (reduced to the size of a quarter). The photographs were realistic enough so that when viewed at a distance with one eye they appeared to be real coins.

In this experiment, the observer's task was to adjust the distance of each coin so it appeared to be at the same distance as a pack of cigarettes located 135 cm away. When the observers did this, they positioned the oversized dime about 23 cm closer than the cigarettes, the quarter only about 2 cm closer than the cigarettes, and the undersized half dollar 29 cm farther away than the cigarettes. This result is exactly what we would expect if familiar size is influencing the observers' judgment of distance. Consider the oversized dime. For a dime to appear as large as it did to the observers (who did not know that they were actually viewing an over-

Figure 8.7 Stimuli for a familiar size experiment.

Box 8.1 Why Blue?

Atmospheric perspective causes faraway objects to look fuzzy and blue. But why blue? A faraway object looks blue because, to see it, you must look through the short-wavelength light between you and the object. But if the sun's light is white, why is there short-wavelength light between you and the object? We can answer this question by considering what happens to the sun's light on its way into the earth's atmosphere. Sunlight entering the atmosphere encounters many small particles, which scatter the light. When these particles are small in relation to the wavelength of the light, a condition known as **Rayleigh scattering** occurs (named after Lord Rayleigh, who first described the effect and who also won the Nobel Prize for discovering argon), and the scattering is *inversely* proportional to the fourth power of the wavelength of the light. This inverse proportionality means that short wavelengths are scattered *more* than long wavelengths, with the result shown in the figure to the left below. The scattering of most of the short-wavelength light makes the sky appear blue and simultaneously results in the atmospheric perspective effect, since the short wavelengths that give the sky its blue color are also scattered down to the level of an observer positioned on the ground. The long-wavelength light is not scattered as much, and most of it is transmitted directly through the atmosphere to the observer, making direct sunlight appear yellow.

Rayleigh scattering also explains why the setting (and rising) sun looks red. In this case, illustrated in the right figure, the light from the setting sun travels a greater distance through the atmosphere than it does at noon, and this increases the amount of short and medium wavelengths that are scattered. By the time the light reaches the observer, only the longest wavelengths remain, and the sun therefore appears red.

The physics of light scattering also helps us understand why objects observed through a mist appear white. This occurs because the particles in mist are large compared to the wavelength of light and do not scatter short wavelengths preferentially, as in Rayleigh scattering. With all wavelengths scattered equally, we perceive a misty white (Riggs, 1965a; Ross, 1974).

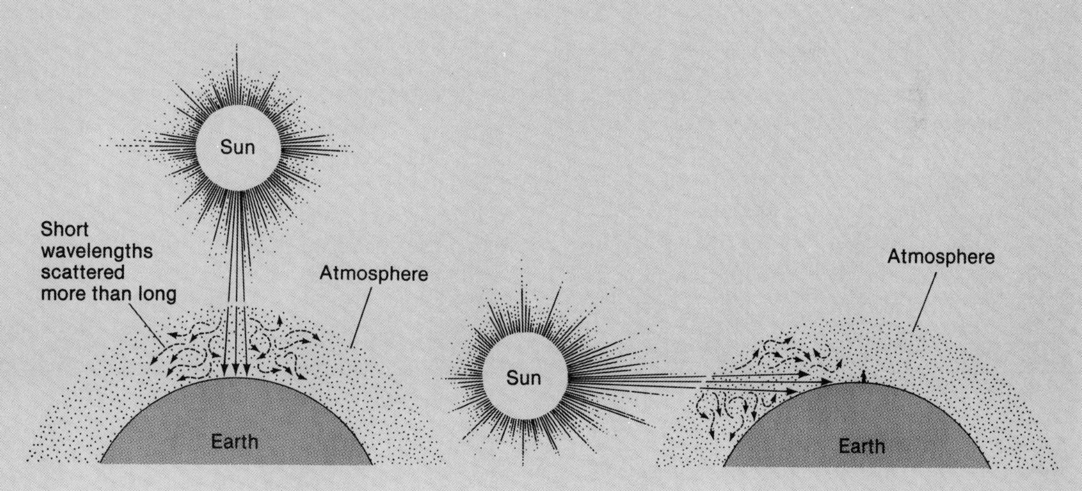

sized dime), it would have to be close. Similarly, for a half dollar to appear as small as it did, it would have to be far away. But the quarter, which was its actual size, was positioned at just about the right distance. Clearly, the observers' judgments were influenced by their knowledge of the sizes of real dimes, quarters, and half dollars. It is important to note, however, that this result occurred only when the observers viewed the stimuli with one eye. When they viewed the stimuli with both eyes, familiar size had little or no effect on their judgments. As we will see below, the use of two eyes provides important information for the perception of depth; so, when the observers in Epstein's experiment used two eyes, this extra information enabled them to disregard the effect of familiar size and correctly judge the distances of the oversized dime and undersized half dollar. Familiar size, therefore, appears to play an important role in depth perception only when other information about depth is absent (see also Schiffman, 1967). (In the next chapter, we will discuss in more detail the relationship between our perception of depth and our perception of size.)

Linear Perspective

How can we create a three-dimensional impression of depth on the two-dimensional surface of a picture? This question has concerned artists since before the ancient Greeks, but it wasn't until 1435 that Leon Battista Alberti wrote *De Pictura,* the first book describing the principles of a drawing system called **linear perspective,** which made it possible to convincingly depict depth on a two-dimensional surface (see White, 1968). Alberti's book describes how to draw a picture in linear perspective by using a fairly complex geometrical procedure. A more straightforward way of describing perspective has been provided by Leonardo da Vinci: "Perspective is nothing else than seeing a place behind a plane of glass, quite transparent, on the surface of which the objects behind the glass are to be drawn" (Gombrich, 1960). This technique, which has been called **Alberti's window,** enables anyone to draw in perspective. You need only obtain a transparent surface, such as a piece of glass or a rigid piece of transparent plastic; then, keeping your eye fixed in one place, look at a scene through the transparent surface and trace the scene onto the surface. This procedure is being used by the artist in Figure 8.8; instead of drawing the picture on the window, however, he is transferring it to a canvas. This procedure results in a picture drawn in linear perspective that creates an impression of depth on the canvas. Another way to create a perspective picture is to take a photograph. The optical system of a camera accomplishes essentially the same thing as Alberti's window and records the result on film.

When a picture is drawn in linear perspective, an interesting result occurs: lines that are parallel in the scene (such as the sides of the street in Figure 8.2) converge as they get farther away. The greater the distance, the greater the convergence, until, at a distance of infinity (far away!), these lines meet at a vanishing point. What is important for our purposes is that this convergence occurs not only in perspective pictures, such as Figure 8.9, but also in the world. This convergence of parallel lines, to which most people have been introduced by viewing railroad tracks that vanish into the distance, is usually referred to as the depth cue of *linear perspective.*

Movement Parallax

So far, you have been patiently standing on the hill, observing the scene of Figure 8.2. Let's consider what happens if you get restless and decide to take a walk. As you walk along the top of the hill and look out over the houses, the nearby houses will pass rapidly across your field of vision, and the houses on the far ridge will hardly appear to move at all. This speed of movement is directly related to distance: the farther away a house is, the more slowly it appears to move. This effect is particularly apparent when you look out the side window of a moving car or train. Nearby objects appear to speed by in a blur, while objects on the horizon move very slowly. This difference in the speed of movement for near and far objects is called **movement parallax,** and we can use this cue to perceive the depths of objects based on how fast they move as we move: far objects move slowly; near objects move rapidly.

We can understand why this movement parallax effect occurs, by looking at Figure 8.10. This figure shows a single eye that moves from position 1 to position 2, and two objects, a near object at A and a far object at B. First consider how the image of the near object moves across the retina as the eye moves from 1 to 2. When the eye is at 1, the image of object A is at A_1 on the retina; and when the eye has moved to 2, the image of object A has moved all the way across the retina to A_2. This means that when the eye moves from position 1 to position 2,

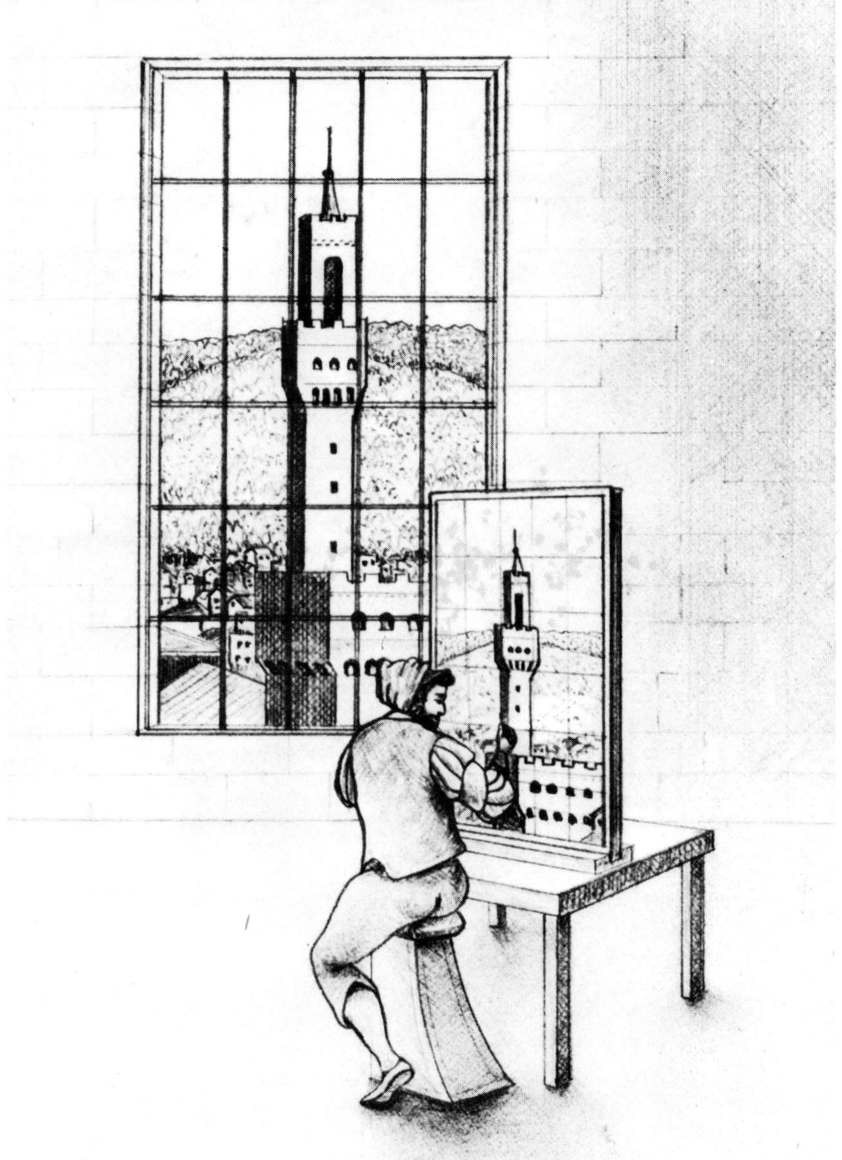

Figure 8.8 An artist drawing a picture in perspective by using the method of Alberti's window (see text).

the image of object A moves from one side of the observer's field of view to the other. The image of object B, on the other hand, moves only from B_1 to B_2 on the retina and, therefore, moves only a short distance across the observer's field of view. Thus, as the observer moves from left to right, the

Figure 8.9 *A Street with Various Buildings, Colonnades, and an Arch,* circa 1500, artist unknown (School of Donate Brumante). This is an example of a picture drawn in perspective, so that parallel lines in the scene would converge to a vanishing point if infinitely extended. Something interesting happens in this picture near the last building on the left. The squares in this part of the street are not lined up exactly parallel with those in the foreground, which creates the impression of a slight rise in the street. We can't tell, however, whether the artist meant to show a slight rise in the street, or whether this rise is the result of faulty perspective. (Museum of Art, Carnegie Institute, Pittsburgh, Pa.)

near object travels a large distance across the retina and therefore travels rapidly across the observer's field of view, but the far object travels a much smaller distance across the retina and therefore travels much more slowly across the observer's field of view.

At the beginning of this discussion, we asked how it is possible that a two-dimensional image on the retina could result in a three-dimensional perception of our view from the hill. Now we can see that although the image on the retina may contain only two dimensions, it also contains a large amount of information that is correlated with the depth in the scene. The pictorial depth cues of smaller size, greater fuzziness or height, blueness, linear perspective, and overlapping are all correlated with increased depth, and if the observer is moving, movement parallax also provides depth information. This environmental information is transformed into retinal information, which is then transduced into nervous system information in the form of nerve impulses transmitted to the brain. That the retinal information exists in two dimensions is not important to the brain, because it doesn't see the image on the retina; it "sees" only the nerve impulses. The important thing is that *information* about depth reaches the brain, but this information itself need not have depth.

Before considering further sources of depth information, we should consider some important points about the depth cues we have already discussed. Few of them are foolproof. Any single cue can provide erroneous information. For example, the porch on the left in Figure 8.2 is higher than the house just below it, even though it is actually closer to us, not farther away, as would be predicted by the cue of relative height. Fortunately, we usually don't have to rely on any single depth cue. Many cues provide overlapping information in any scene, and this overlapping of the cues gives us the most accurate information about depth. This shouldn't be taken to mean, however, that every cue is necessary for us to perceive depth. Experiments have shown that, when a number of sources of depth information are present, elimination of one of them seldom greatly impairs our perception of depth. That's why we still perceive depth on the moon, even without atmospheric perspective. The available depth cues contain enough information to enable us to judge the distances of nearby and faraway craters.

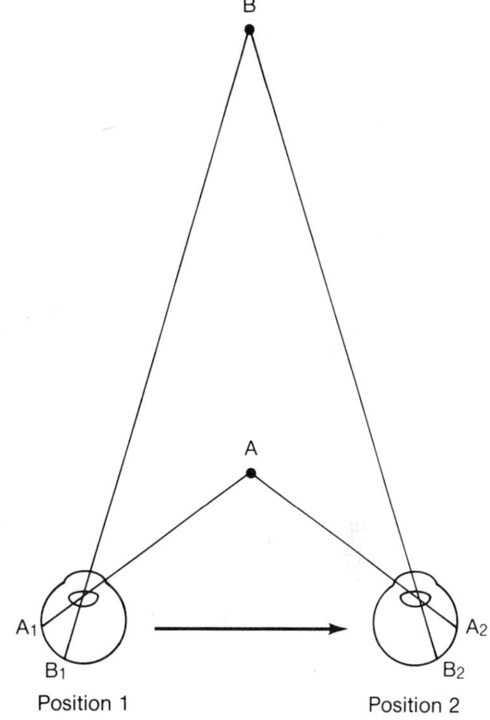

Figure 8.10 One eye, moving from left to right, showing how the images of two objects (A and B) change their position on the retina due to this movement.

Accommodation and Convergence

All the depth cues we have considered until now have depended on information imaged on the retina, but **accommodation** and **convergence,** two other cues, provide information not from the image on the retina but from the muscles of the eye. Hold your finger about two inches from your nose and look at it. When you do this, two things happen: (1) the lens of the eye (see Figure 3.2) bulges from the action of the ligaments that hold it in place, and (2) the eyes converge, as shown in Figure 8.11(a), due to the action of the eye muscles. If you move your finger farther away, the lens flattens and the eyes diverge, as shown in Figure 8.11(b). Accommodation is the change in the shape of the lens that varies with distance (see pp. 139–140, in Chapter 6), and convergence is the way your eyes move inward and outward with changes in distance.

It is thought that accommodation and convergence can serve as cues to depth because the shape of the lens and the position of the eyes are correlated with the distance of the object we are observing. There is, however, some doubt as to the effectiveness of these cues, and, at best, they may provide depth information for objects not farther than about ten feet from the observer.

Binocular Disparity

This cue has been saved for last because it is the most important cue for depth. All the other cues we have discussed, with the exception of convergence, are **monocular depth cues,** because they still work if we look through only one eye, but **binocular disparity** depends on both eyes. This cue is based on the fact that our eyes see the world from the slightly different positions determined by the distance between them. Because of this, we see two different views of the world. You can demonstrate this double view to yourself by closing your left eye and holding one finger upright about 6 inches in front of you. Then position a finger from your other hand about 6 inches farther back, so that it is completely hidden by the front finger. You should now be able to see just the front finger. But if you now close your right eye and open your left eye, which sees from a different point of view, you can see the rear finger. Your left eye has looked around your front finger!

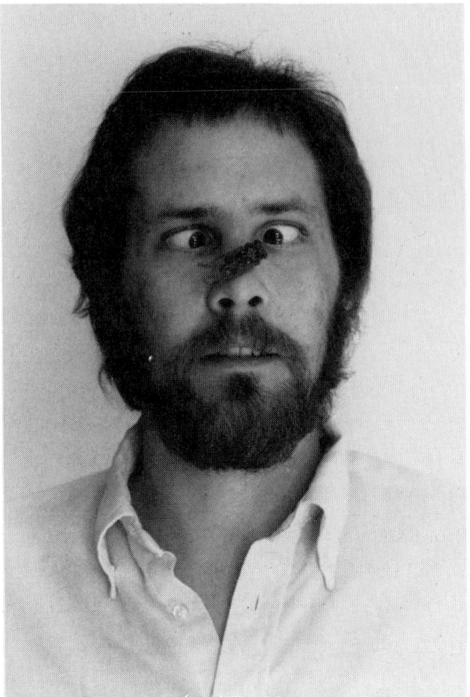

Figure 8.11 The eyes converge (left) when they look at something very close and diverge (right) when they look at something far away.

But how do the different views of our two eyes result in an impression of depth? To understand this, we must describe binocular disparity in more detail, and to understand binocular disparity, we must first understand the concept of **corresponding retinal points.** For every point on one retina, there is a corresponding point on the other retina. Corresponding points are the places on each retina that would overlap if one retina could be slid on top of the other retina. So, the two foveas, F and F′, fall on corresponding points, as shown in Figure 8.12, and A and A′ and B and B′ also fall on corresponding points.

To apply our knowledge of corresponding points to depth perception, let's assume that you are sitting in the lifeguard chair of Figure 8.13. If you look directly at your friend Ralph, Ralph's image will fall on your foveas (F and F′), which are corresponding points. However, Ralph is not the only person whose image falls on corresponding points. The images of everyone who is located on the dashed line also fall on corresponding points. This dashed line, which is called the **horoptor,** is part of an imaginary surface that passes through the point of fixation (Ralph's head) and, in our example, also through the heads of Harry and Susan. This means that Harry's and Susan's images fall on corresponding points on the

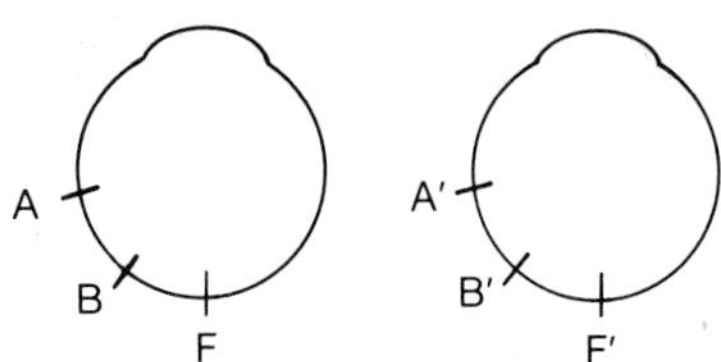

Figure 8.12 Corresponding points on the two retinas. To determine corresponding points, slide one eye on top of the other one.

retina, as shown in Figure 8.14. (It is important to remember that the situation we are describing here holds only as long as you are looking at Ralph. If you change your point of fixation, then a new horoptor passes through the new point of fixation.)

What does this have to do with depth perception? While still looking at Ralph, let's consider where Carol's and Charlie's images fall on the retina. Since their heads are not located on the horoptor, their images fall on **noncorresponding** (or **disparate**) **points,** as indicated in Figure 8.15. For example, Carol's image falls on noncorresponding points B and G′. (Note that if you slid the retinas on top of each other, points B and G′ would not overlap and are therefore noncorresponding.) The corresponding point to B is, in fact, located at B′, far from G′. The distance between G′ and B′ is called the **degree of disparity,** and the key to binocular depth perception is that *the farther the object is from the horoptor, the greater is the degree of disparity.* You can see this by comparing the disparity of Carol's and Charlie's images in Figure 8.15. Carol's disparity, as we saw above, is the distance between G′ and B′, whereas Charlie's is the distance between H′ and A′. Charlie's images are more disparate because he is located farther from the horoptor. Thus, knowing the amount of disparity tells us how far Charlie and Carol are from where we are looking. Since Charlie's disparity is greater than Carol's, he must be located farther from the horoptor and, therefore, closer to us.

Though we can now see that disparity provides information about the relative distances of objects in a scene (or swimmers in a pool), one problem remains. How is this information used by the brain? This question was answered by Horace Barlow, Colin Blakemore, and John Pettigrew (1967), who found cells in the cortex of the cat that respond best to stimuli that fall on points separated by a specific degree of disparity on the two retinas. Records from such a cell in the visual cortex of the monkey, which David Hubel and Torsten Wiesel (1970b) call a **binocular depth cell,** are shown in Figure 8.16. Record (a) shows that this cell does not respond when corresponding points (indicated by the overlap of the cross hairs) on the two eyes are simultaneously stimulated by a bar moving either from left to right or from right to left. Records (b), (c), (d),

Figure 8.13 When the lifeguard looks at Ralph, this causes the images of Ralph, Susan, and Harry to fall on the horoptor, indicated by the dashed line. This means that Ralph's, Susan's, and Harry's images fall on corresponding points on the lifeguard's retina, and the images of all the other swimmers fall on noncorresponding points.

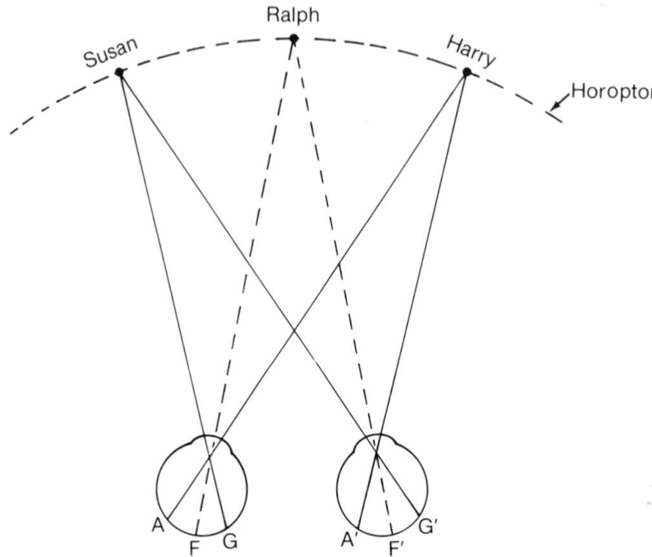

Figure 8.14 What's happening to the images of Susan, Ralph, and Harry inside the lifeguard's eye? Susan's image falls on corresponding points G and G′, Ralph's falls on the foveas F and F′ (which are corresponding points), and Harry's falls on corresponding points A and A′.

and (e) show that this cell does respond, however, when the disparity of the moving bar is increased, with the maximum response occurring in record (c), at 30 minutes (half a degree) of disparity. Records (f) and (g) indicate that, if each eye is *individually* stimulated by bars separated by 30 minutes of arc, no response occurs, even though a large response results when these same bars are presented simultaneously, as in (c).

The existence of binocular depth cells in the cat and monkey means that, if the animal's convergence is fixed (that is, if its eyes are positioned to look at a particular point in space and don't move), cells that fire best to different disparities will be excited by stimuli lying at different distances from the animal. Thus, in Figure 8.13, each swimmer causes a different group of the lifeguard's binocular depth cells to fire, which signal information about the distance between the lifeguard and each swimmer.

This description of binocular disparity completes our list of depth cues. Remember that no single cue is crucial for our perception of depth; we can eliminate any monocular depth cue or close one eye to eliminate binocular disparity and still see in depth. However, the more cues we have, the better our chances to accurately deduce the three dimensions of the world from the two-dimensional information on our retinas.

The Special Problem of Pictures: Flatness Cues

We discussed earlier that artists had searched for centuries for ways to create an impression of depth in a picture before the Renaissance artists finally discovered linear perspective. One reason that a picture drawn in linear perspective creates a good impression of depth is that such a picture contains many of the depth cues present in the three-dimensional scene. If the depth cues of overlap, relative size, relative height, and linear perspective are present in the original scene, they will automatically be transferred to the canvas by using the method of linear perspective. If we then add atmospheric perspective to our picture, we can further increase the impression of depth. Even if we take these measures, however, we can still only create the *impression* of depth in a picture. It is difficult for a picture to create so convincing an *illusion of depth* that it will be mistaken for the actual scene. One reason for this

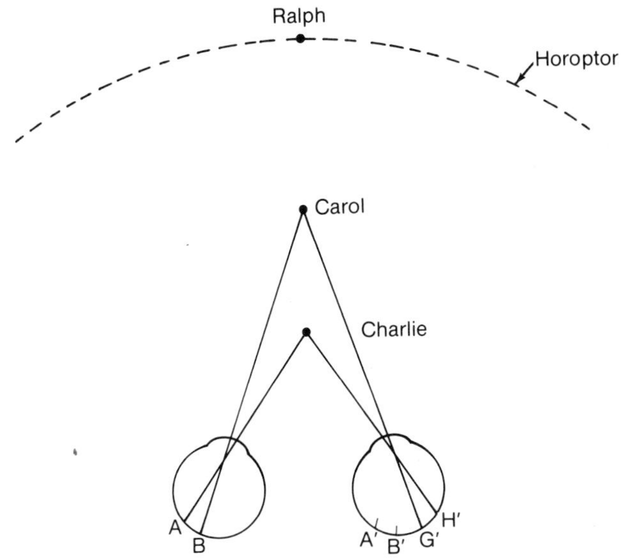

Figure 8.15 What's happening to the images of Carol and Charlie in the lifeguard's eye? Since Carol and Charlie are not located on the horoptor, their images fall on noncorresponding points.

difficulty is that some depth cues cannot be used in pictures. Accommodation, convergence, movement parallax, and binocular disparity can't be used in ordinary still pictures because they all depend on the presence of actual depth. (As we will see below, however, binocular disparity is used in stereoscopic still or moving pictures.)

But the problem of creating pictorial depth is not simply that some depth information in the world is absent from the picture. Pictures not only contain fewer depth cues than the world, they also contain **flatness cues,** which decrease our impression of depth. Let's explain what we mean by this.

When we walk past a real scene, we experience movement parallax, which causes objects to change their positions in relation to one another. Demonstrate this to yourself by holding up one finger on each hand, about 6 inches apart and one in front of the other. While observing the fingers with one eye, move your head back and forth. What happens? The front finger moves back and forth, so it is sometimes seen to the left of the rear finger and sometimes to the right. But if we try this procedure on the trees in Figure 8.3, the trees do not move relative to one another. The tree on the far right stays on the far right, no matter where we move our head. This lack of movement parallax in the picture is a cue that the picture is flat.

We can also compare binocular vision's effects on our perception of a three-dimensional scene to its effects on our perception of a picture. Remember the demonstration on page 213, in which you looked at your two fingers first with one eye and then with the other? By blinking back and forth, you saw two different views of your fingers. But what happens if you try this on the trees in Figure 8.3? Blinking back and forth has no effect on your perception of the trees' position. This means that we do not experience binocular disparity when looking at a picture, and this lack of binocular disparity serves as a cue that we are looking at a flat picture. Such flatness cues as our perception of brush strokes, glare, and the frame of the painting also make us aware that we are looking at a picture.

The presence of flatness cues limits our ability to create a convincing illusion of depth in a picture that hangs on a wall. Most people move around as they look at pictures and are usually aware of brush strokes, glare, and the picture frame. However, with special viewing conditions, it is possible to overcome these flatness cues.

Viewing a picture with one eye eliminates the

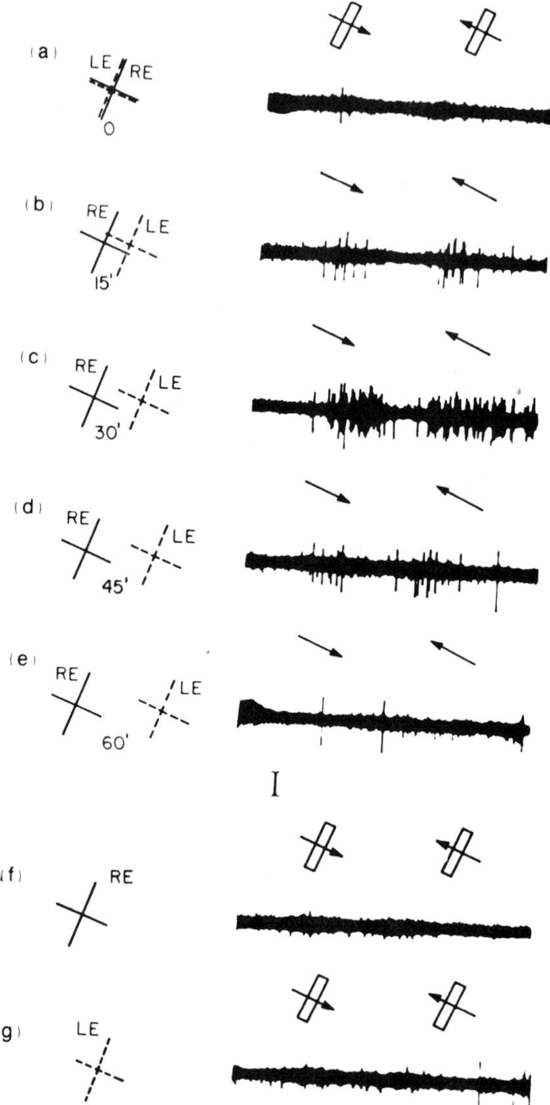

Figure 8.16 The response of a binocular depth cell in the visual cortex of the monkey. The positions of the cross hairs indicate the position of the bar for the right eye (RE) and the left eye (LE). This cell responds to movement of the bar in either direction (indicated by the arrows), but it responds best when the two bars are presented simultaneously and are displaced 30 minutes in position, as shown in record (c). In records (f) and (g), bars are presented to the same positions as in record (c), but each bar is presented to the left and right eye separately. The cell does not respond because both eyes must be stimulated to cause a binocular depth cell to fire. (From Hubel and Wiesel, 1970b.)

flatness cue of lack of binocular disparity, because the brain can only tell that there is no disparity by comparing the input from two eyes. By adding a peephole through which to view the picture, we can ensure one-eyed viewing, eliminate the lack of movement parallax by eliminating movement, and restrict the field of view to eliminate the perception of the picture frame. Though looking through a peephole may be a strange way to view a picture, this viewing method can so increase the illusion of depth that an unsuspecting viewer will be fooled into thinking he is looking at an actual scene instead of a picture. Patricia and Olin Smith (1961) achieved this illusion by having observers view a large photograph of a room through a peephole and found that the observers, unaware that they were looking at a photograph, thought they were viewing a real room.

In addition to viewing through peepholes, there are other ways of creating convincing illusions with pictures. One way, which was used by the **trompe l'oeil** (*fool the eye;* pronounced "trump l'oy") painters who were active in America in the nineteenth century, was to paint pictures that contained little depth. For example, Jefferson Chalfant's painting *Violin and Bow,* shown in Figure 8.17, has little depth; and, since the violin is painted life-sized and in color, this painting is easy to mistake for a real violin. We should note, however, that although the trompe l'oeil painters created convincing illusions, they succeeded in doing this only by picking scenes with very little depth, such as a violin hanging on a wall.

Figure 8.17 Jefferson Chalfant, *Violin and Bow* (1899). (Collection of the Metropolitan Museum of Art, N.Y. George A. Hearn Fund, 1966.)

Perhaps the most familiar technique for producing an illusion of depth is the **stereoscope,** an extremely popular device among adults in the 1800s and now familiar to most children as the View Master. The basic principle underlying the stereoscope is the duplication of binocular disparity that a person would experience in each eye if he or she were viewing the actual scene. To accomplish this, two photographs are made with a special camera that has two lenses with the same separation as the eyes. This results in two slightly different views, like those shown in Figure 8.18. The stereoscope presents the left picture to the left eye and the right picture to the right eye so that they combine to result in a convincing three-dimensional perception of the scene.

The principle behind the stereoscope—presenting one image to the left eye and the other to the right eye—has also been used in 3-D movies. These movies, particularly the horror movies, became quite popular when introduced commercially in the 1950s. (I still remember the terror I experienced when a huge froglike creature jumped out of a spooky castle and plummeted toward the audience.) After the novelty wore off, however, and people got tired of wearing the special glasses needed to present different images to the left and right eyes, these movies disappeared from the theaters. Recently, however,

Figure 8.18 Stereoscopic photograph of Terry Bradshaw (right) of the Pittsburgh Steelers talking to Joe Ferguson of the Buffalo Bills after a game at Three Rivers Stadium in Pittsburgh. The picture on the left is the view seen by the left eye, and the picture on the right is the view seen by the right eye. Though the two pictures may at first glance look the same, a closer look shows that the relationship between the foreground and background is different in the two views. For example, compare the distance between Bradshaw's head and the lighted upper stands in the background, or compare the people in the stands in the space between Bradshaw and Ferguson. When the two views are presented to each eye separately in a stereoscope, this slight displacement results in binocular disparity and we see the scene in depth. (Stereogram by Mike Chikiris, Pittsburgh Stereogram Company, Pittsburgh, Pa., 1977.)

3-D movies have reappeared and been introduced to a new generation of moviegoers.

Depth Information in the Scene: The Approach of J. J. Gibson

The Moving Observer

Let's consider the approach we have taken to perception so far in this book, by remembering a few of the experiments we have discussed in past chapters. In Chapter 3, we measured a dark adaptation curve by having an observer in a dark room look at a fixation light while adjusting the intensity of a flashing test light so that it stayed at threshold. We then saw that the rate of the observer's dark adaptation was paralleled by the rate of visual pigment regeneration in the receptors. In Chapter 4, we applied stimuli to a subject's skin and asked the subject to estimate the magnitude of the resulting touch sensation. We then compared the subject's magnitude estimates with recordings made from nerve fibers serving the skin.

The two experiments described above, and many others we have described earlier, have two things in common. First, the psychophysical experiments usually involve a passive observer; stimuli are presented to a stationary observer by an experimenter. Second, we try to correlate the results of these psychophysical experiments with those of physiological experiments done on either humans or animals. This approach has greatly increased our understanding of both the psychophysics of perception and the relationship between perception and physiology. However, J. J. Gibson (1950, 1966, 1979) feels that this approach is not the most fruitful way to study perception.

Gibson feels that we can best learn about perception by ignoring physiology and concentrating on the psychophysical approach. He also feels that when we do psychophysics, we should concentrate

Box 8.2 Depth in Random Dot Patterns

The depth cue of *retinal disparity* is used to create an illusion of depth from two-dimensional pictures in stereoscopes, which present the left eye's view to the left eye and the right eye's view to the right eye. Although the disparity created by presenting a different view to each eye creates depth in these stereoscopic pictures, most stereoscopic pictures contain depth information in addition to disparity. *Relative size, overlap, relative height,* and other *monocular depth cues* may contribute to the depth seen in stereoscopic pictures. Bela Julesz (1971), however, has created the illusion of depth by using a stereoscope with random dot patterns, which contain no depth information other than disparity. Two such random dot patterns, which constitute a **random dot stereogram,** are shown above.

The patterns below were constructed by first generating two identical random dot patterns with a computer and then shifting a square-shaped section of the dots to the right, in the pattern on the right. This shift is too subtle to see in these dot patterns, but we can understand how it is accomplished, by looking at the diagrams below the dot patterns. In these diagrams, the black dots and white dots in the patterns are indicated by 0's and 1's and by A's and B's. The A's and B's indicate the square-shaped section where the shift takes place. Notice that the A's and B's are shifted one unit to the right in the right pattern. The X's and Y's indicate areas uncovered by the shift that must be filled in with new black dots and white dots to complete the pattern.

The effect of shifting one section of the pattern in this way is to create disparity, which causes the perception of depth when the patterns are viewed in a stereoscope. When viewed stereoscopically, the dot patterns are perceived as a small square floating above the background. This demonstration shows that even when no other depth information is present, retinal disparity can cause the perception of depth.

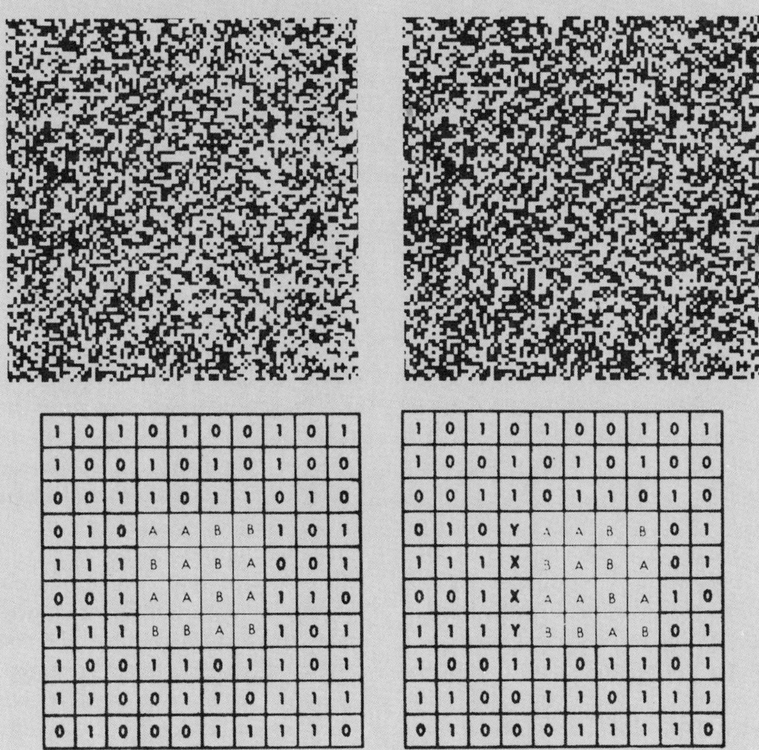

on the perceptions of active observers. Psychophysics as studied for the past 80 years, Gibson argues, has been done in artificial situations. In real life, people do not sit in dark rooms and look at fixation lights. Instead, people actively move through their environment, looking this way and that as they walk from one place to another. Gibson's philosophy has led him to a new approach to perception, one that takes the movement of an active observer into account. We have already seen how this approach has been applied to the study of touch, in our discussion of *active touch* in Chapter 4. In the remainder of this chapter, we will consider how Gibson's approach has been applied to the study of depth perception. To do this, we will describe the three main ideas that form the basis for Gibson's approach to perception: (1) the ground theory of space perception, (2) invariants, and (3) direct perception.

The Ground Theory of Space Perception

Gibson's approach grew out of some perception experiments he did during World War II, in which he tried to determine how to improve a pilot's ability to land an airplane. From these experiments, Gibson concluded that the traditional depth cues could not sufficiently explain how an airplane pilot judges the distance to a runway as he comes in for a landing. Depth cues, according to Gibson, belong to **air theories of space perception,** because such cues as overlap, relative size, and relative height depend on objects or groups of objects in the air. Based on his aviation experiments, Gibson proposed that air theories be replaced by his **ground theory of space perception.** According to the ground theory, visual space is determined not by objects that protrude into the air but by information contained on the ground, upon which these objects rest.

The best example of information contained on the ground is a **texture gradient,** such as the one created by the ridges in the sand of Figure 8.19. This figure shows how the elements that make up a textured surface appear to be packed closer and closer together as the surface stretches into the distance. This gradient results in an impression of depth, and the spacing of the gradient's elements provides information about the distance at any point on the gradient. Other examples of texture gradients are shown in the checkerboard of Figure 8.20, the Renaissance street of Figure 8.9 and the modern painting of Figure 8.1 (the chapter-opening illustration).

These texture gradients may seem to share with depth cues such features as linear perspective (the way parallel lines in the gradients of Figures 8.9 and 8.20b and c converge toward a vanishing point) and relative size (the way the more distant elements of the gradients get smaller), and, in fact, they do. Texture gradients contain the traditional depth cues of linear perspective, relative size, and relative height. However, a texture gradient has an important property that the traditional depth cues lack: a texture gradient extends over a large area, and no matter where you move on the gradient, the elements of the gradient provide information that enables you to determine the distance between where you are and another point on the gradient. For example, consider the checkerboard of Figure 8.20. The elements of the gradient provide information that make it possible to determine the distance to 3 when you are at 1 (8.20b), when you are at 2 (8.20c), or when you are anywhere else on the gradient. That gradients allow an observer to move without losing depth information is an important feature of Gibson's approach to perception, which brings us to the idea of **invariants.**

Invariants

Given that texture gradients on the ground provide information about the depth of a scene, the next step is to ask what happens when an observer moves on the gradient. Movement of the observer creates a problem, because it results in a constantly changing image on the retina. Gibson deals with this problem by noting that, although an observer's movement may cause the image on the retina to be in constant flux, some *information* on the retina remains constant, or, in Gibson's terminology, *invariant*. For example, as an observer moves relative to a texture gradient, the contours that define the textures of the gradient sweep across the retina, but the texture of the gradient remains invariant—that is, the elements of the gradient always appear

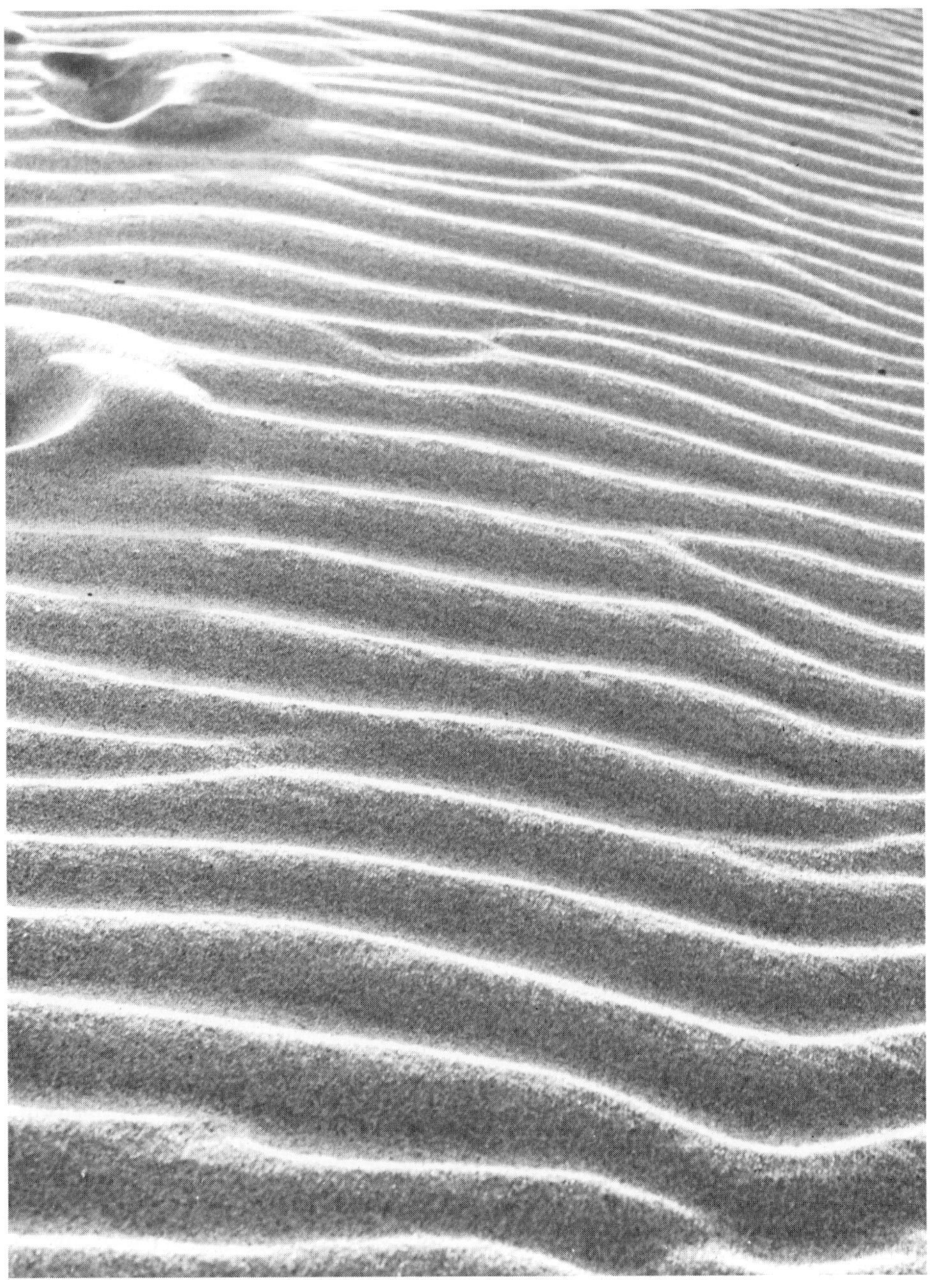

Figure 8.19 A texture gradient made up of ridges in the sand. If viewed from above, the distance between each sand ridge appears approximately equal; however, when viewed from the ground, the ridges appear to be spaced closer and closer together as distance increases. (Photograph courtesy of Philip Brodatz, 1976.)

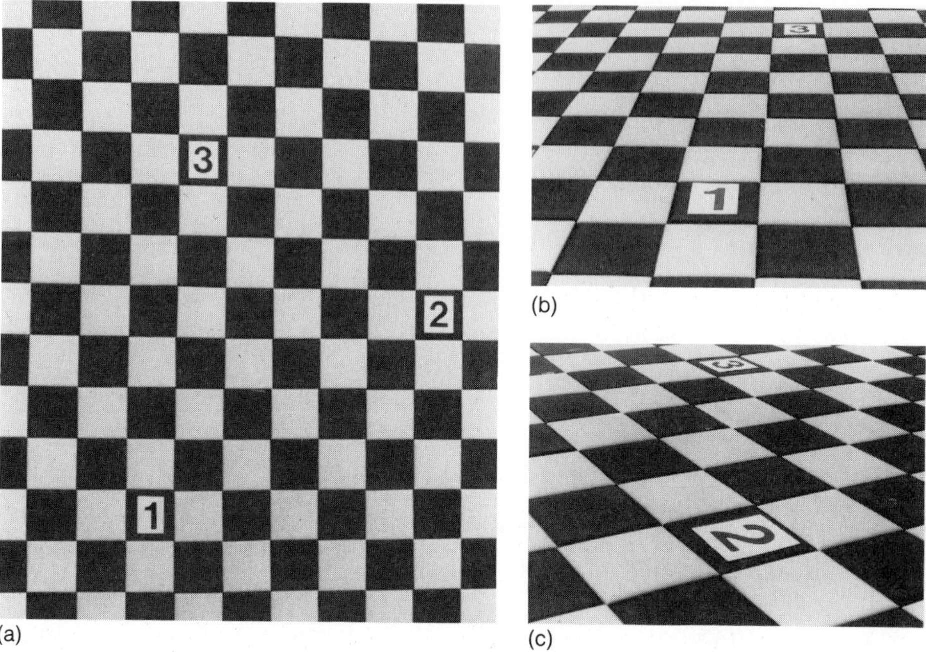

Figure 8.20 (a) Top view of a checkerboard pattern showing the location of 1, 2, and 3. (b) Looking at 3 from 1. (c) Looking at 3 from 2. No matter where you are on a texture gradient, information is present that indicates distance. When standing at 1 the number of gradient units indicates the distance of 3. If we move to 2, we can still use the information provided by the number of texture units to determine the distance to 3.

more closely spaced as distance increases—and the scale of depth in the scene, therefore, remains constant. According to Gibson, it is this invariant information that we use in everyday perception as we move through the environment.

Another example of invariance is provided by the way movement of an observer causes textures in the environment to flow. This flow of the environment, illustrated in Figure 8.21, shows how the environment speeds past an observer who is traveling toward point A. In this situation, there is flow everywhere except at the point toward which the observer is moving. Since this point is at the center of the optical **flow pattern,** it does not change—it stays invariant. Thus, to stay on course while moving toward an object, a person only needs to keep the invariant center of the flow pattern centered on the object.

Direct Perception

The next question Gibson asks is: How does the observer use this invariant information? His answer is that we pick up invariants by **direct perception** and just use them. To understand what this means, let's anticipate some material we will be covering in the next chapter on how we perceive the sizes of objects.

One thing we will discuss is that we are pretty good at perceiving the correct sizes of objects, even if these objects are located at different distances from us. If we are presented with a 5-foot-tall pole at a distance of 3 feet, we can accurately estimate its height as being about 5 feet. If we then move this pole to a distance of 30 feet, we can still accurately estimate its height. And we make these accurate height judgments despite the fact that, when we move the pole

Figure 8.21 The flow of the environment as seen from a car speeding across a bridge toward point A. The flow, shown by the arrows is more rapid closer to the car (as indicated by the increased blur) but occurs everywhere except point A, the point toward which the car is moving.

from 3 feet to 30 feet, the pole's image on our retina gets smaller. Though we don't see the image on our retina, we do notice that when we move the pole to a distance of 30 feet, it takes up much less of our field of view than it did previously. Since the pole now takes up much less of our field of view, why don't we perceive it as being smaller? We can postulate that we take the pole's distance from us into account. Our perception of the pole's size, according to this explanation (which we will consider in more detail in the next chapter), results from an unconscious mental process in which we account for both the object's size in our field of view *and* its distance from us.

Gibson, however, feels that the information provided by invariants is present in a form that can be used immediately, without being processed in any way. Thus, Gibson's explanation for our ability to accurately estimate the height of a pole at any distance is that we note how many units of a texture gradient are covered by the base of the object. For example, in Figure 8.22, the bases of the two poles each cover about half a unit on the texture gradient, which indicates *directly,* without further mental processing, that the bases of the two poles are the same size. Similarly, to perceive the depth in a scene, rather than take into account the scattered information provided by a number of different depth cues, we only have to perceive directly the information provided by a texture gradient.

Evaluation of Gibson's Theory

Most perception researchers feel that Gibson is on the right track in studying the perception of active explorers of the environment. (These same researchers, however, would also maintain that we have learned much about perception by testing passive observers in the laboratory.) It also seems reasonable to these researchers that texture gradients and the optical flow past a moving observer do provide information that an observer could use to perceive depth. However, it is still not clear whether the information provided by texture gradients, flow

Figure 8.22 A texture gradient with two poles. According to Gibson, the fact that the bases of both poles cover the same number of units on the gradient provides direct information that the bases of the two poles are the same size.

patterns, and other invariants is actually *used* by an observer to perceive depth. (See Goldstein, 1981, for a description of some of the other invariants Gibson has proposed.) That is, it is one thing to say that certain information is *available* for the perception of depth, but it is another thing to *show* that this information is actually used by observers to perceive the environment. As David Marr (1982) says, regarding Gibson's idea that we can detect the invariants in the environment, Gibson "vastly underrated the sheer difficulty of such detection." Therefore, the question of whether we actually use these invariants in perceiving is one that must await further experimentation.

There are a few additional problems with Gibson's ideas. Although Gibson implies that our world is full of texture gradients, they are sometimes difficult to find. Also, Gibson's theory deals almost exclusively with the moving observer, ignoring our ability to see depth even when we are completely stationary.

The most controversial feature of Gibson's theory is his idea of direct perception. Most researchers feel that some mental processing is necessary, as should be clear from the first eight chapters of this book. Though we have already given many examples of how perception is affected by information processing, let's look at another example, which Julian Hochberg (1970) feels argues against Gibson's idea that no processing is necessary.

Hochberg bases his argument on the fact that we are continually making eye movements so that we can perceive various parts of a scene in detail (see Figure 7.50). According to Hochberg, eye movements are necessary not only to help us see the various parts of a scene in detail but also to help us piece together, or ***integrate,*** the scene. Hochberg feels that our perception of a scene as being coherent and meaningful depends on our creating a ***mental map*** of the scene by means of a series of eye movements.

Hochberg supports this idea by referring to objects such as those in Figure 7.49 and the one in Figure 8.23, below. When we first look at these objects they appear to be reasonable, but on closer

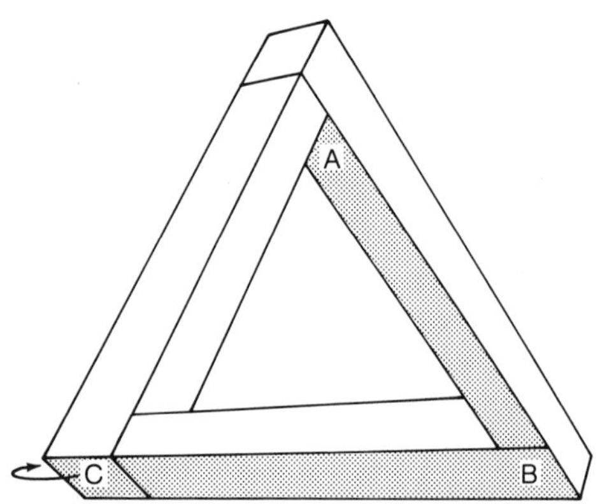

Figure 8.23 Penrose and Penrose's (1958) impossible figure. Imagine that this is a three-dimensional object and try to trace the path your finger would follow along its faces if you went from A to B to C and then around the corner, as indicated by the arrow. Can you ever get back to A without turning around?

inspection we begin to see that something's wrong. For example, face A-B in Figure 8.23 is on the inside and the outside of the object simultaneously. The object, therefore, is called an *impossible object,* since it can exist in two-dimensional drawings but not in the three-dimensional world. Hochberg says that we become aware that this is an impossible object by successively fixating on its different parts and that we see the object as impossible only after we have been able to compare the results of these fixations.

The point of Hochberg's impossible objects, relative to Gibson, is that there is nothing direct about how we perceive these objects. We make a series of eye movements and fixations and must compare what we see at each fixation before we can decide that these objects are impossible. There's lots of processing going on here, even though Gibson says that processing isn't necessary.

Gibson and Physiology

As we said earlier, Gibson states that perception is best studied psychophysically, and, in view of his feeling that perception occurs without the aid of processing, he would probably not agree with the approach taken in this book, in which we have talked at length about the way the nervous system processes the information that falls on the receptors. In fact, Gibson (1966, p. 5) has stated that the "function of the brain, when looped with its perceptual organs, is not to decode signals, not to interpret messages, not to accept images, not to *organize* the sensory input or to *process* the data, in modern terminology. It is to seek and extract information about the environment from the flowing array of ambient energy."

Interestingly enough, evidence has recently been found for cortical neurons that might be involved in detecting the point at which the flow pattern experienced by a moving observer is invariant. This evidence comes from an experiment by D. Regan and Max Cyander (1979), who have found neurons in the visual cortex of the cat that respond strongly when the sides of a rectangle move away from each other, as in Figure 8.24(a), or toward each other, as in (b), but show little or no response when the sides of the rectangle move in the same direction, as in (c). If you look back at Figure 8.21, which

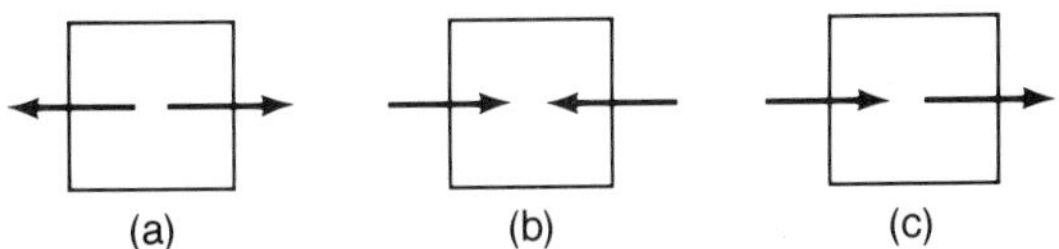

Figure 8.24 Stimuli used by Regan and Cyander (1979) to stimulate a neuron in the visual cortex of the cat that fired when the sides of a rectangle moved away from each other (a) or toward each other (b) but did not fire when the two sides moved in the same direction (c).

shows how the environment flows as an observer moves toward point A, you can see that when the observer is looking at point A, the contours and textures of the environment are moving away from each other, as are the sides of the rectangle in Figure 8.24(a).

In another paper, Regan and K. I. Beverley (1979) suggest that neurons similar to these cat neurons may be present in the human visual system and that their function might be to signal when an observer is looking at the center of a flow pattern like the one in Figure 8.21. They diagram the workings of one of these neurons, as shown in Figure 8.25. The neuron fires to a flow pattern when the center of the flow pattern falls inside the neuron's receptive field (indicated by the square), as in (a) and (b), but does not fire when the center of the flow pattern is outside the receptive field, as in (c). The firing of this neuron, they suggest, could provide a basis for judging the position of the center of a flow pattern. Thus, there may be neurons in the visual system

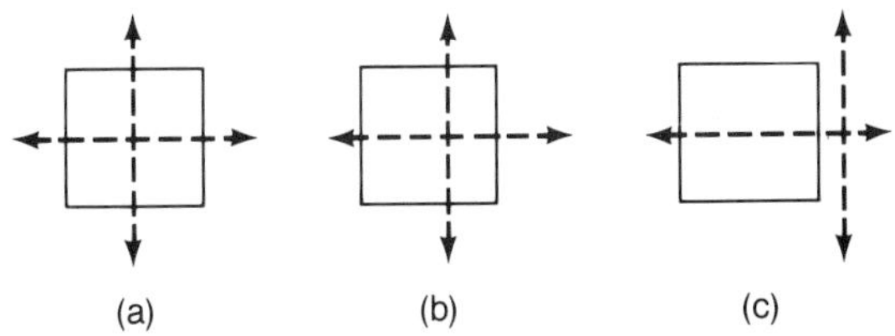

Figure 8.25 The function of neurons that fire to stimuli like those in Figure 8.24 may be to signal when an observer is looking at the center of a flow pattern. Such a neuron would fire when the center of the flow pattern falls inside the cell's receptive field (indicated by the square), as in (a) and (b), but would not fire if the pattern fell outside the receptive field, as in (c). (From Regan & Beverley, 1979.)

that help detect invariant features of the environment experienced by a moving observer, but from what we know about the nervous system (see Chapter 2), these neurons are the end result of much neural processing in the brain.

How Do We Perceive Depth?

In this chapter we have described two different ways of explaining depth perception—the idea of depth cues, and Gibson's idea that an observer picks up information that remains invariant as he or she moves through the environment. As with many so-called opposing views, there are probably elements of truth in both. There is no doubt that many of the depth cues enhance our perception of depth. As I sit here writing this chapter, I can easily tell that the frame of my study window is closer to me than the tree just outside the window, because the window frame covers part of the tree. On the other hand, texture gradients, and perhaps some of the other invariant information proposed by Gibson, may add to my perception of depth, especially when I am moving. It seems to me, however, that whatever information we use to perceive depth, it is unlikely that this information is directly picked up, with no processing involved. As we stated at the beginning of this book: "Perception does not just 'happen.' "

Summary

1. Our perception of the three-dimensional environment depends on depth information on the two-dimensional surface of the retina. Depth cues include overlap, relative size, relative height, atmospheric perspective, familiar size, linear perspective, movement parallax, accommodation, convergence, and binocular disparity.
2. The scattering of light by the atmosphere causes faraway objects and the sky to look blue.
3. The cue of binocular disparity depends on the fact that each eye receives a slightly different view of the world.
4. The horoptor is an imaginary surface that passes through the point of fixation. The images of objects that fall on the horoptor fall on corresponding points on the two retinas, and the images of objects that fall in front of or in back of the horoptor fall on noncorresponding, or disparate, points on the retinas. An object's degree of disparity indicates its distance from the horoptor.
5. Binocular depth cells respond when the retina is stimulated by images with a specific degree of disparity.
6. Depth can be represented in still pictures by using linear perspective and all the depth cues except movement parallax, accommodation, convergence, and binocular disparity.
7. Flatness information is provided by a picture's lack of movement parallax and binocular disparity and by the perception of brush strokes, glare, and the frame of the picture.
8. A convincing illusion of depth can be achieved if a picture which is drawn in linear perspective and uses sufficient depth cues is viewed through a peephole with one eye.
9. Trompe l'oeil artists achieved convincing illusions by painting realistic pictures that contained little depth. A good illusion of depth is achieved by a stereoscope, which duplicates the binocular disparity a person would perceive if he or she were looking at the actual scene.
10. Random dot stereograms show that the cue of binocular disparity alone is sufficient to create an impression of depth.
11. J. J. Gibson approaches depth perception by focusing on the moving, active observer. This approach led to the ground theory of space perception, which states that visual space is determined not by objects that protrude into the air but by information contained on the ground, upon which these objects rest.
12. One example of information contained on the ground is the texture gradient.
13. According to Gibson, certain information remains constant, or invariant, as the observer moves through the environment. Gibson feels that we perceive these invariants directly, without any mental processing.

14. Many researchers agree that it is important to take the moving observer into account when we study perception. Most researchers, however, feel that perception probably does not occur directly, without processing, as Gibson suggests.
15. Neurons have been found in the visual cortex of the cat that might be involved in detecting the point at which a flow pattern experienced by a moving observer is invariant.

Glossary

Accommodation A possible depth cue. Muscular sensations that occur when the eye accommodates to bring objects at different distances into focus may provide information regarding the distance of that object. (213)

Air theories of space perception According to J. J. Gibson, theories of space perception that include depth cues are "air theories," because most of the depth cues depend on objects or groups of objects that are in the air. *See also* Ground theory of space perception. (222)

Alberti's window Used to draw a picture in perspective, Alberti's window is a transparent surface on which an artist traces the scene viewed through the surface. (210)

Atmospheric (or aerial) perspective A depth cue. Objects that are farther away look more blurred and bluer than objects that are closer, because we must look through more air and particles to see them. (206)

Binocular depth cell A neuron in the visual cortex that responds best to stimuli that fall on points separated by a specific degree of disparity on the two retinas. (215)

Binocular disparity When the retinal images of an object fall on disparate points on the two retinas. (213)

Convergence A possible depth cue. Muscular sensations that occur when the eyes move inward (convergence) or outward (divergence) to view objects at different distances may provide information regarding the depth of that object. (213)

Corresponding retinal points The points on each retina that would overlap if one retina were slid on top of the other. (214)

Degree of disparity If the two retinas are stimulated by images that fall on disparate (noncorresponding) points, the degree of disparity is the distance one of the images must be moved so that both images will fall on corresponding points. (215)

Depth cues Information that is correlated with the depth in a scene. (204)

Direct perception J. J. Gibson's idea that we pick up the information provided by invariants directly and that perceptions result from this information without the need for any further processing. (224)

Disparate points *See* Noncorresponding points.

Familiar size A depth cue. Our knowledge of an object's actual size sometimes influences our perception of that object's distance. (208)

Flatness cues Information that indicates a picture is flat. For example, one flatness cue is that movement parallax does not occur in a picture as an observer moves. (217)

Flow pattern The way groups of elements in the environment flow past a moving observer. (224)

Ground theory of space perception J. J. Gibson's idea that our perception of visual space is determined by information contained on the ground. *See also* Air theories of space perception. (222)

Horoptor An imaginary surface that passes through the point of fixation. Objects falling on this surface result in retinal images that fall on corresponding points on the two retinas. (214)

Invariants Environmental properties that do not change as the observer moves. For example, the spacing, or texture, of the elements in a texture gradient does not change as the observer moves on the gradient. The texture of the gradient is, therefore, invariant. (222)

Linear perspective Linear perspective is a method of representing three-dimensional space on a two-dimensional surface. However, when this term is used as a depth cue, it refers to the fact that parallel lines (like railroad tracks) converge as they get farther away, with greater convergence indicating greater distance. (210)

Monocular depth cues Depth cues such as overlap, relative size, relative height, familiar size, linear perspective, movement parallax, and accommodation, which work if we use only one eye. (213)

Movement parallax A depth cue. As an observer moves, nearby objects appear to move rapidly, whereas far objects appear to move slowly. (210)

Noncorresponding (disparate) points Two points, one on each retina, that would not overlap if the retinas were slid onto each other. (215)

Overlap A depth cue (also called interposition). If object A covers object B, then object A is seen as being in front of object B. (204)

Pictorial depth cues Depth cues such as overlap, relative height, and relative size which can be depicted in pictures. (204)

Random dot stereogram A stereogram in which the stimuli are identical pictures of random dots, one of which has a section of the dot pattern shifted slightly in one direction. This shift creates disparity, which causes the perception of depth when the patterns are viewed in a stereoscope. (221)

Rayleigh scattering Sunlight is scattered by small particles in the earth's atmosphere, and the amount of scatter is inversely proportional to the fourth power of the light's wavelength. This means that short-wavelength light is scattered more than long-wavelength light. (209)

Relative height A depth cue. When objects are below the horizon line, objects that are higher in the field of view appear farther away. When objects are above the horizon line, objects that are lower in the field of view appear farther away. (205)

Relative size A depth cue. Objects that take up a small part of the field of view, with everything else being equal, are perceived as farther away than objects that take up a large part of the field of view. (205)

Stereoscope A device that presents pictures to the left and right eyes so that the binocular disparity a person would experience when viewing an actual scene is duplicated. The result is a convincing illusion of depth. (219)

Texture gradient The pattern formed by a regularly textured surface that extends away from the observer. The elements in a texture gradient appear smaller as distance from the observer increases. (222)

Trompe l'oeil "Fool the eye." A school of painters active in the late nineteenth century whose pictures were designed to create the illusion that the viewer was looking not at a two-dimensional painting but at a three-dimensional object. (219)

Plate 1.1 (right) The visible spectrum. See pages 11, 113, and 114 of the text.

Plate 3.1 (below) How the color of a frog's retina changes as the visual pigment in the retina bleaches, as described on page 70 of the text. The top picture was taken immediately after the bleaching light was turned on, so little bleaching has occurred and the retina appears red. When the retina is placed on a flat surface, its edges bend over, causing a double layer of retina and a deeper red color around the edges. The black spots are small pieces of the pigment epithelium, the cell layer on which the retina rests when in the eye. The middle picture was taken after some bleaching so the retina is lighter red, and in the bottom picture, further bleaching results in a light orange appearance. When bleaching is completed, the orange fades and the retina becomes transparent. If this retina were still in the frog's eye, the transparent retina would regain its red color as the pigment regenerates in the dark; however, little regeneration occurs when the retina is dissected from the eye, as in these pictures.

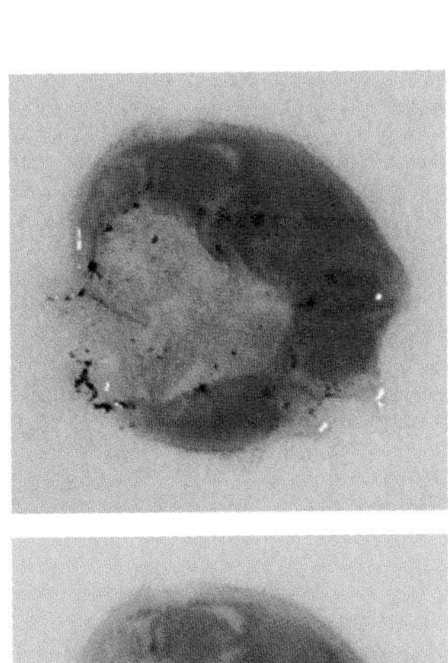

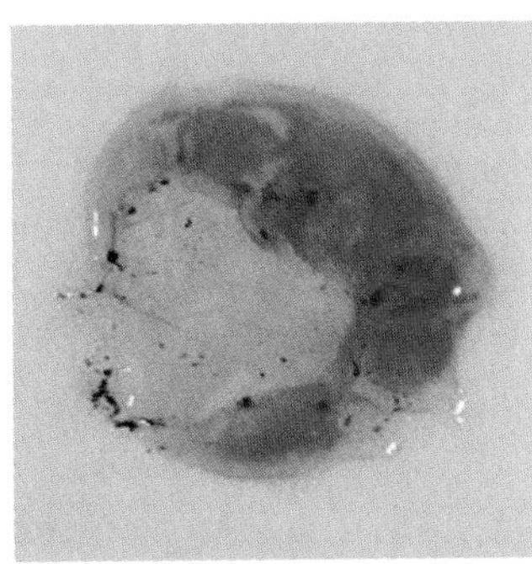

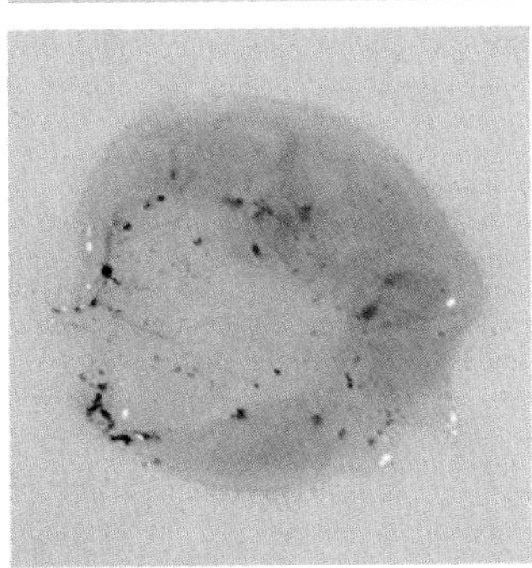

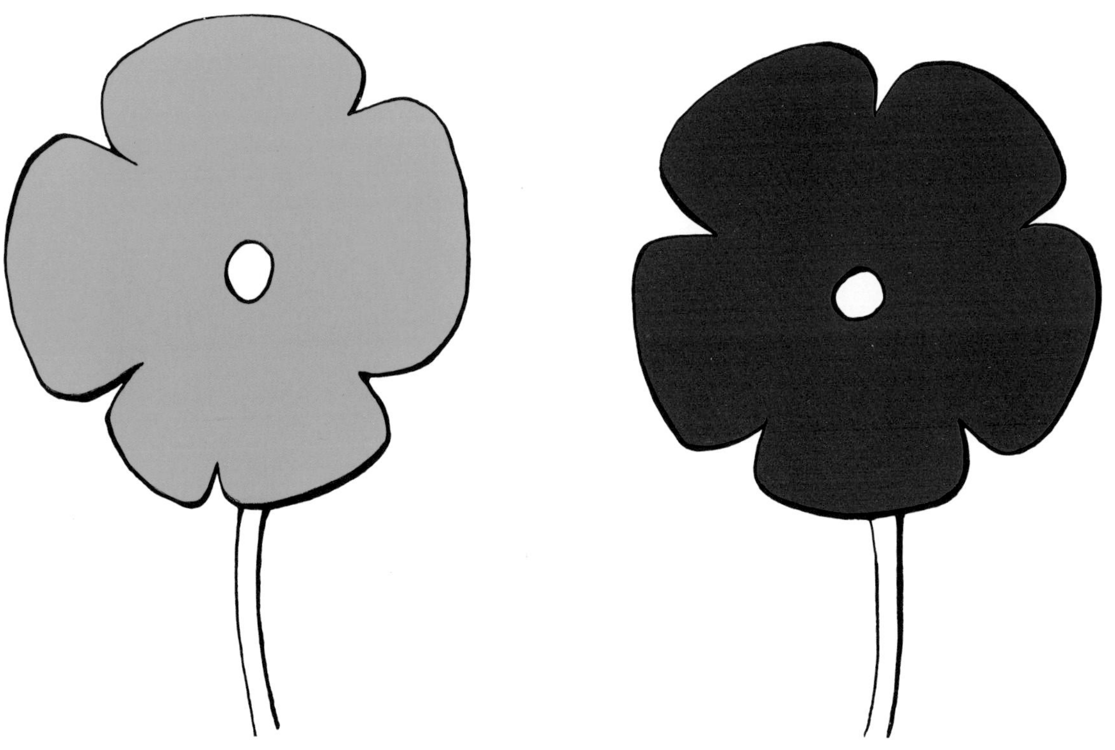

Plate 3.2 Red and blue flowers for the adaptation demonstration described on pages 72–73 of the text.

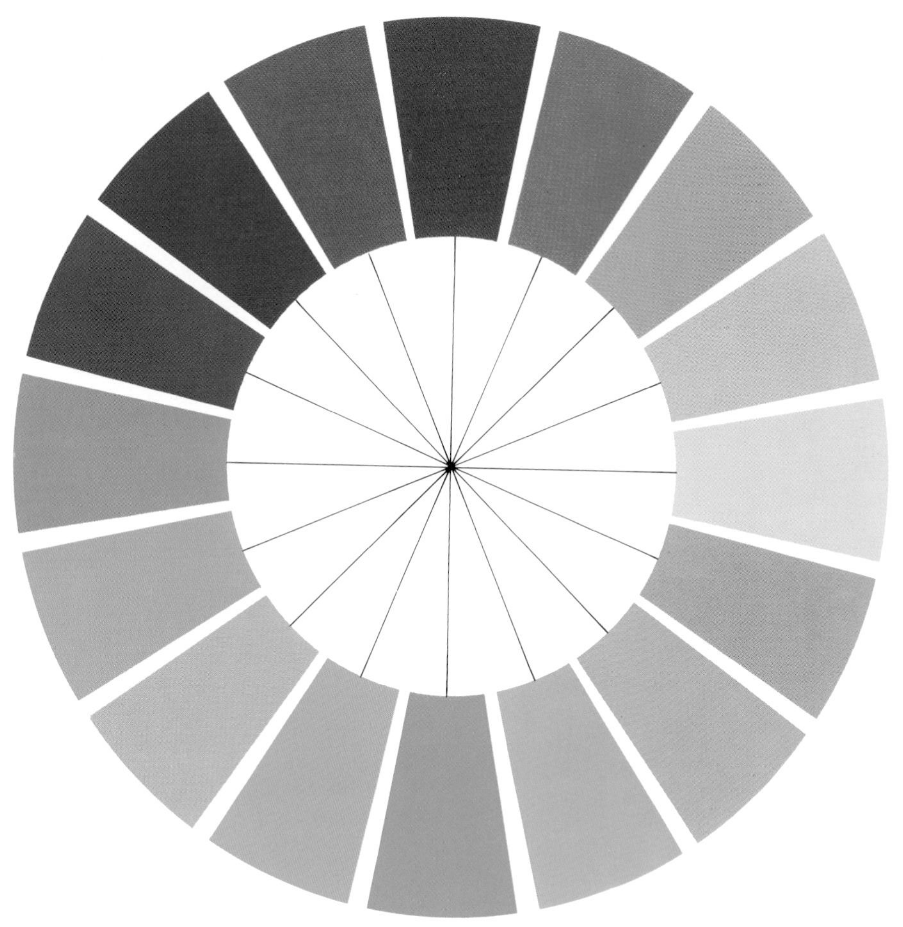

Plate 5.1 The color circle. From Hurvich (1981). See pages 113–114 of the text.

Plate 5.2 A simultaneous contrast demonstration by Joseph Albers (1975), an artist who often uses simultaneous contrast in his paintings. Courtesy of Yale University Press. See pages 118–119 of the text.

Plate 5.3 Field for selective adaptation demonstration. See page 119 of the text.

Plate 5.4 A photograph taken with "daylight" film under daylight illumination provided by sunlight from a window on the left. The colors in this photograph correspond to an observer's perception of the scene. See page 122 of the text.

Plate 5.5 A photograph taken with "daylight" film under tungsten illumination provided by the desk lamp in the upper left of the photograph. The observer's perception of this scene is similar to that depicted in Color Plate 5.4 above, but since the film doesn't have color constancy, this photograph has an orange tint. See page 122 of the text.

Plate 5.6 Field for color constancy and afterimage demonstrations. See pages 122 and 125–126 of the text.

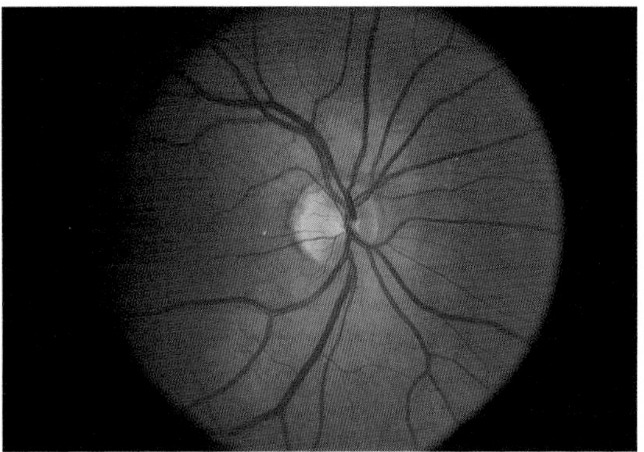

Plate 6.1(a) A normal retina as seen through an ophthalmoscope. The white area in the center is the optic disc. This picture shows only a small area of the retina around the optic disc. The fovea (not visible) is located just past the far left edge of this picture.

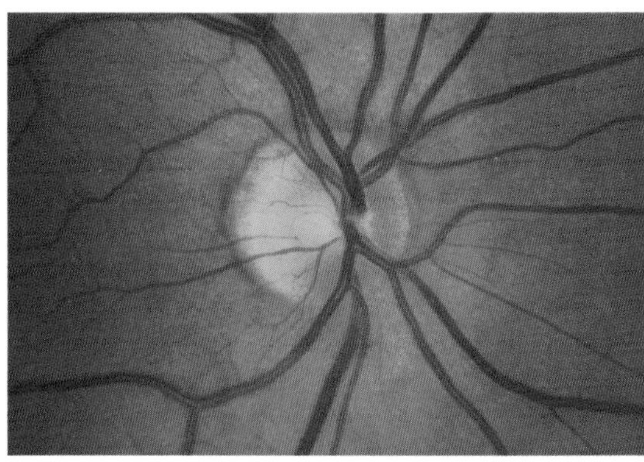

Plate 6.1(b) Close-up of the normal retina in Plate 6.1(a).

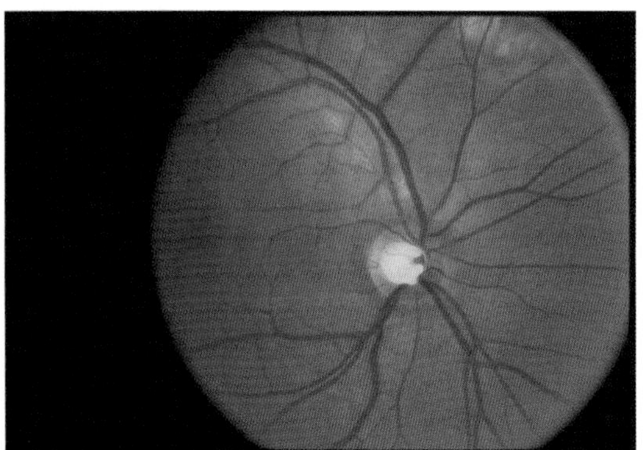

Plate 6.2(a) The retina in an eye with glaucoma. Cupping of the optic disc is indicated by the way the blood vessels vanish over a ridge in the cupped optic disc (see Figure 6.26).

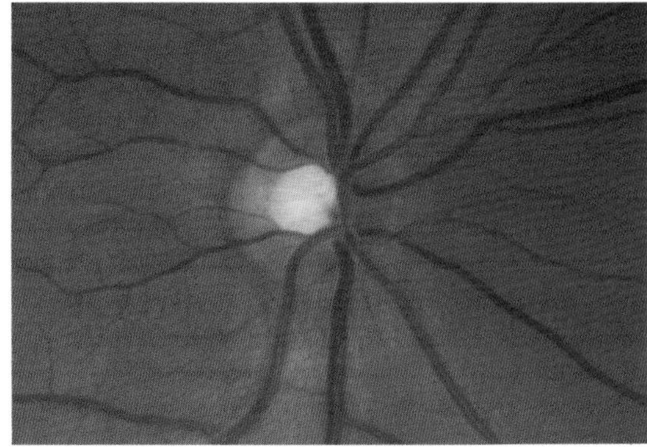

Plate 6.2(b) Close-up of a retina in an eye with glaucoma showing cupping of the optic disc. (Note that this is a different retina than the one in Plate 6.2(a).)

Plate 8.1 The Blue Ridge Mountains of North Carolina. The blueness and fuzziness of the hills is caused by atmospheric perspective. See page 207 of the text. Courtesy of North Carolina Department of Commerce.

Plate 8.2 Gerard David (c. 1460–1523), *Rest on the Flight into Egypt*. See page 207 of the text. Courtesy of the National Gallery of Art, Andrew W. Mellon Collection.

Plate 9.1 It is difficult to tell from this photograph whether the branches sticking out are a lighter green than the other branches or if they are being illuminated by sunlight. See page 258 of the text.

Plate 9.2 This branch reveals that the branches sticking out in Plate 9.1 are a lighter green than the rest of the branches.

Plate 10.1 The spreading effect described on page 272 of the text (from Evans, 1948). Top: The red background appears light on the left and dark on the right, but is actually physically the same all the way across. The white, blue, and black design changes the appearance of the red background. Middle: The red background is the same on the left and in the middle but appears different due to the "spreading effect" of the black and white lines. Bottom: The blue is physically the same all the way across but appears lighter in the middle due to the spreading effect.

Chapter Nine

The Perceptual Constancies

At the end of the last chapter, we introduced the concept of the moving observer and the idea that in everyday life we do much of our perceiving while in motion, whether walking, driving, or simply moving our eyes and head to observe different aspects of the scene around us. The resulting changes in our point of view are accompanied by continual changes in the information presented to our retinas. As my friend Bruce walks toward me his image on my retina becomes larger and larger (chapter-opening illustration); as I walk past my desk, the objects on the desk cast shapes on my retinas that are transformed into new and different shapes as I move past them (Figure 9.2).

For the moment, let's make an assumption about how you perceive the world. Let's assume that your perception is based solely on what is happening on your retina. If this were so, your perceptions would be strange indeed. Your friend John would appear to shrink as he walked away from you; your doorway would at one moment appear to be a rectangular opening in the wall and the next moment a distorted trapezoid constructed by a drunk carpenter; your dinner plate would appear circular as you viewed it from above but would become elliptical as you sat down to eat. In short, you would be living in a confusing world, populated by constantly changing objects whose true sizes and shapes would be difficult to determine.

Fortunately, you are not subjected to the confusion of a world that constantly changes as you move through it. In fact, it is quite the opposite. You perceive John as remaining 5′10″ tall when he walks away, your door is a sturdy rectangle from any point of view, and your plate remains circular throughout dinner. That your perceptions of the properties of objects remain constant in the face of continually changing input is called **perceptual constancy,** and in this chapter we will discuss three of the most important perceptual constancies: size, shape, and lightness.

Size Constancy

Size constancy means that our perception of an object's size remains relatively constant even when we view the object from different distances. To begin our discussion of size constancy, we need to describe what happens to the size of an object's image on our retina as we view the object from different distances. In order to do this, we must introduce the idea of **visual angle.**

Visual Angle

We determine the visual angle of an object by extending one line from the observer's eye to one end of the object and another line from the observer's eye to the other end of the object. The angle between these two lines is the visual angle. Thus, visual angles θ and α, of the person in Figure 9.3, are the angles between lines that extend from the observer's eye to the person's head and feet.

From our definition of the visual angle, you can see that the size of the visual angle depends on two things: (1) the distance between the object and the observer, and (2) the size of the object. Figure 9.3 shows how the visual angle is affected by the object's distance: the closer the object, the larger the visual angle. Figure 9.4 shows how the visual angle is affected by the object's size: the larger the object's size, the larger the visual angle.

Since the visual angle is determined by both the object's size ***and*** its distance from the observer, we cannot determine the visual angle if we know only one or the other. A huge, faraway object can have a small visual angle, and, as illustrated in Figure 9.5, a small close object can have a visual angle equal to a large object that is farther away (see Box 9.3).

Visual angle is so important because an object's visual angle is directly related to the size of that object's image on the retina. You can see this by looking at Figures 9.3, 9.4, and 9.5. When the visual angle is large, the retinal image is large (Figures 9.3 and 9.4), and when two objects have the same visual angle, their images on the retina are the same size (Figure 9.5). Since visual angle and retinal size are so closely related, we will use these terms interchangeably in the remainder of our discussion.

Perceiving Size as Visual Angle Changes

How do we perceive the size of an object as its visual angle changes? To answer this question, consider

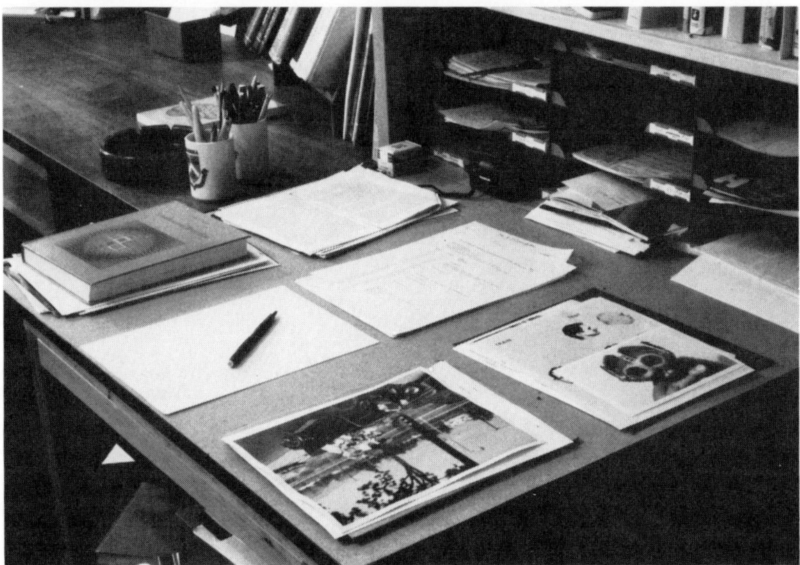

Figure 9.2 The retinal images of the objects on this desk top change as we view the desk from different positions.

the person in Figure 9.3. Assume that, as the observer, you perceive the person to be 6 feet tall when he is standing 4 feet away. When the person moves back to 8 feet, the size of his image on your retina is halved. Does he then look 3 feet tall? Probably not. Most people would perceive him to be about the same size at a distance of 8 feet as at a distance of 4 feet, even though his visual angle and

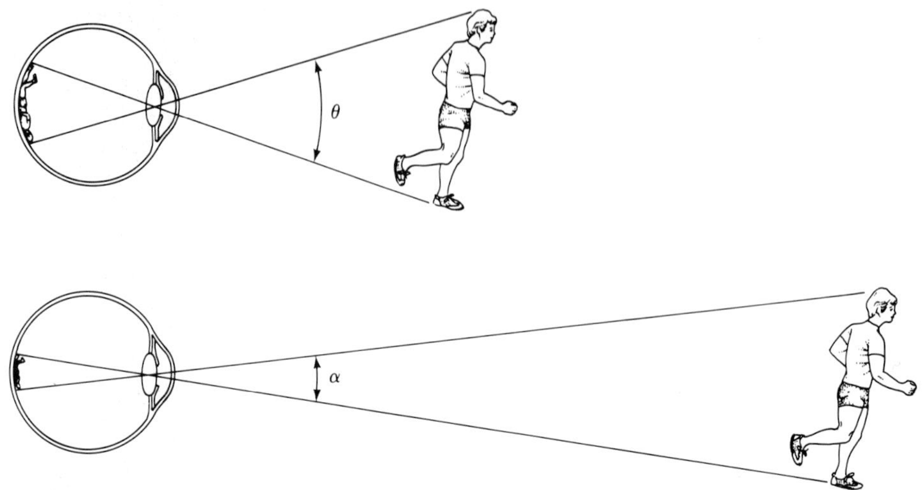

Figure 9.3 Increasing an object's distance decreases the size of its image on the retina and decreases its visual angle.

retinal image are much smaller at 8 feet. In fact, the same result occurs if we replace the person with an unfamiliar stimulus, such as a board. Moving the board away decreases its visual angle but causes little or no change in your perception of its size. That the person and the board appear to stay the same size as they move farther away illustrates size constancy. The **law of size constancy** states that we perceive an object's size as staying constant, no matter what its distance. Thus, even though an object's image on your retina may get smaller, your perception of size must depend on information in addition to the size of the retinal image. In a classic experiment, A. H. Holway and Edwin Boring (1941) showed that size constancy depends on our perception of depth.

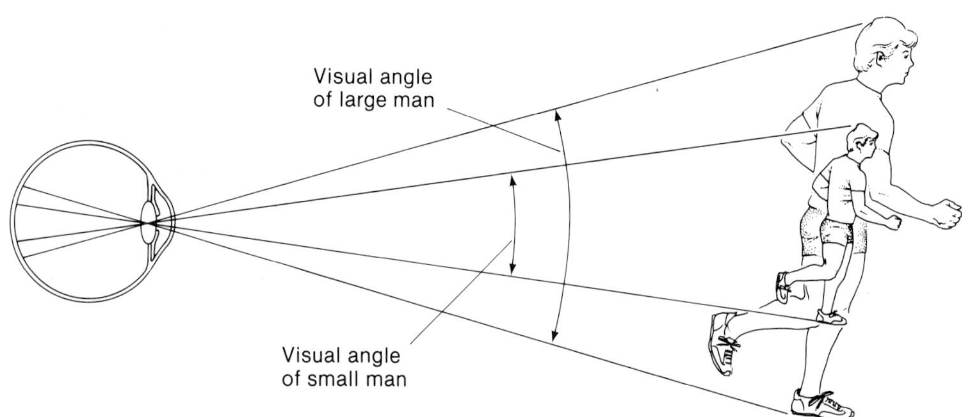

Figure 9.4 If two objects are at the same distance, the larger one will have a larger visual angle.

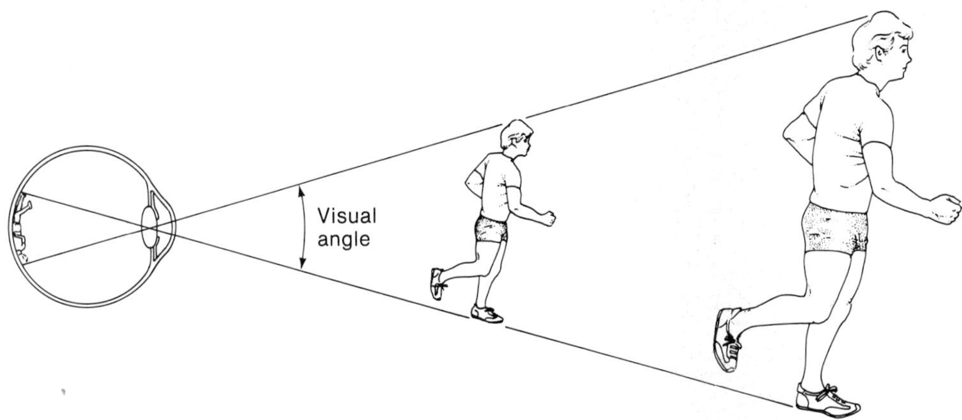

Figure 9.5 Two objects with the same visual angle have the same retinal size.

The Holway and Boring Experiment

The setup for Holway and Boring's experiment is shown in Figure 9.6. The observer sits at the intersection of two hallways so that he sees a luminous test circle when looking down the right hallway and a luminous comparison circle when looking down the left hallway. The comparison circle is always 10 feet from the observer, but test circles are presented at distances ranging from 10 feet to 120 feet. On each trial, the observer's task is to adjust the size of the comparison circle to match that of the test circle. The key to this experiment is that each test circle has a visual angle of one degree. Thus, as shown in the top view of Holway and Boring's setup in Figure 9.7, larger and larger test circles must be used as distance increases, in order to keep the visual angle constant at one degree. Note that in this phase of the experiment, many depth cues are available to the observer.

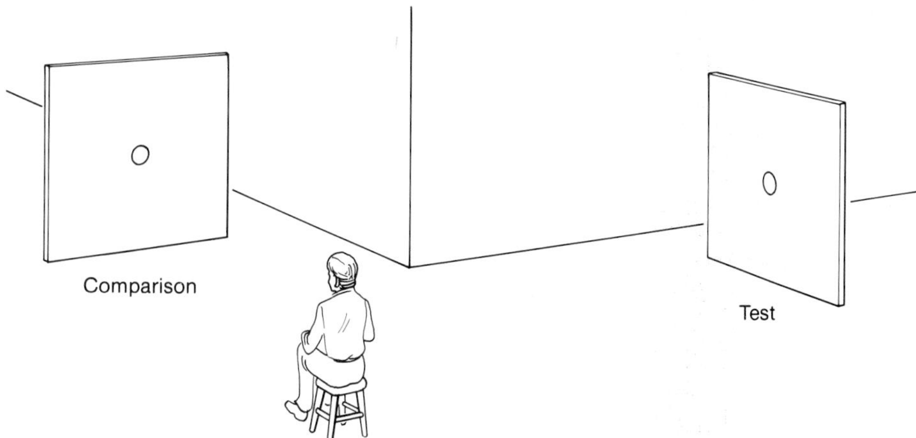

Figure 9.6 Setup of Holway and Boring's (1941) experiment. The observer adjusts the size of the comparison stimulus to match the size of the test stimulus.

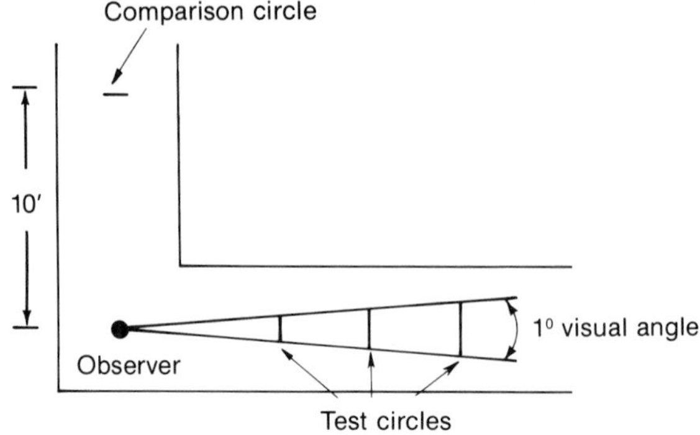

Figure 9.7 Top view of Holway and Boring's experiment. The key feature of this experiment is that each test circle has the same visual angle and therefore casts the same image on the observer's retina. (Adapted from Holway & Boring, 1941.)

The results of this experiment are indicated by line 1 in Figure 9.8. It is clear that the observers based their judgments on the physical sizes of the circles, since large test circles that were far from the observer were matched by large comparison circles, and small test circles that were closer to the observer were matched by small comparison circles. This result occurred even though all test circles had the same visual angle and therefore cast identical images on the retina. This result, therefore, supports the law of size constancy.

Holway and Boring then asked how the presence of depth information affected the observer's perception of size. To determine the role of depth in size perception, Holway and Boring systematically eliminated distance information from the hallway by having the observer view the test circles with one eye (line 2), by having the observer view the

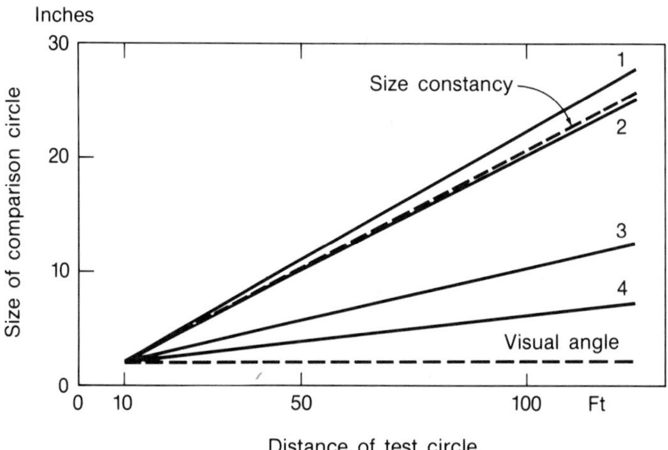

Figure 9.8 Results of Holway and Boring's experiment. The dashed line marked "size constancy" is the result that would be expected if the observers adjust the size of the comparison circle to match the physical size of the test circle. The line marked "visual angle" is the result that would be expected if the observers adjust the size of the comparison circle to match the visual angle of the test circle. (Adapted from Holway & Boring, 1941.)

test circles through a peephole (line 3), and by adding drapes to the hallway to eliminate reflections (line 4). The results of these experiments indicate that, as it becomes harder to determine the distance of the test circles, an observer's judgments cease to follow the law of size constancy. When the observer looks down the draped hallway through a peephole, his judgments fall close to the lower dashed line, which is the result that would be predicted by the **law of visual angle.** The law of visual angle states that our perception of an object's size is determined solely by its visual angle. In a later experiment, similar to Holway and Boring's, all depth cues were eliminated by using screens that permitted the observer to see only the test circles. Under these conditions, size constancy was completely eliminated, and the observer's perceptions followed the law of visual angle (Lichten & Lurie, 1950).

The results of Holway and Boring's experiment indicate the importance of depth information in perceiving size. It has been suggested that a *constancy scaling mechanism* supplements the information available on the retina by taking an object's distance into account (Gregory, 1966). We will call this constancy scaling mechanism **size-distance scaling.** Thus, when a 6-foot-tall person is far away

Box 9.1 Tracing Your Head

Size constancy works when you look into the bathroom mirror. You can demonstrate this by looking in the mirror and estimating how large a circle (or ellipse, depending on the shape of your head) you would have to draw to enclose the image of your head in the mirror. Then trace the outline of your head on the surface of the mirror with a piece of soap. Much to your surprise (even after reading this!), you will see that your tracing is much smaller than you expected. The reason for the small size of the tracing is shown in the figure. The image of your face that you see when you look in the mirror is actually located in back of the mirror, and you base your size estimate on this image. The mirror is actually located halfway between you and your image, and, as you can see from the figure, this means that the image on the surface of the mirror will be half the size of your head. Confirm this for yourself by measuring the diameter of your head and comparing it to the diameter of the tracing in the mirror. The main point of this demonstration is that your *size-distance scaling mechanism* takes into account the distance of the image you see in the back of the mirror, which causes you to see the image of your head in terms of its physical size, not in terms of its real size on the surface of the mirror.

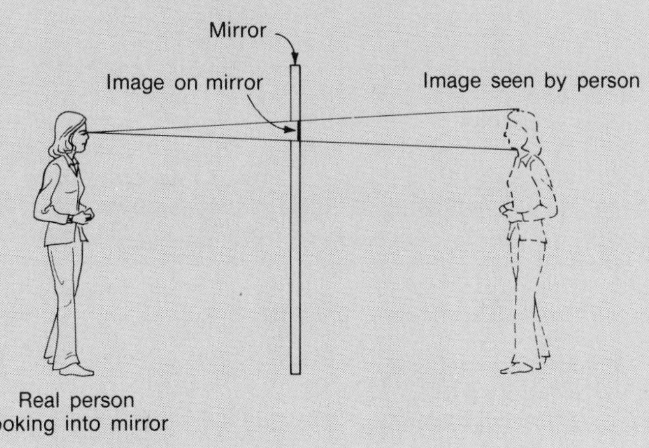

and casts a small image on your retina, the size-distance scaling mechanism takes his distance into account and you still perceive him to be 6 feet tall.

Figure 9.9

Emmert's Law

You can demonstrate size-distance scaling to yourself. Look at the center of the circle in Figure 9.9 for about 60 seconds, then look at the white space to the side of the circle and blink to see the circle's afterimage. Now repeat this procedure, but look at a wall far across the room. Blink to bring back the afterimage if it fades. You should see that the size of the afterimage depends on where you look. If you look at a distant surface, such as the far wall of the room, you see a large afterimage that appears to be far away. If you look at a near surface, such as the page of this book, you see a small afterimage that appears to be close.

The principle underlying this effect, which was first described by Emmert in 1881, is shown in Figure 9.10. Staring at the circle in Figure 9.9 bleaches a small circular area of visual pigment on your retina. This bleached area of the retina determines the retinal size of the afterimage and stays constant. Our perception of the size of the afterimage, as shown in Figure 9.10, is determined by its distance from us. This relationship between the apparent distance of an afterimage and its size is known as **Emmert's law:** the farther away an afterimage appears, the larger it will appear. Stated mathematically, this law is: *P.S.* = *K(R.I.* × *P.D.),* where *P.S.* is the perceived size of the afterimage, *K* is a constant, *R.I.* is the size of the retinal image, and *P.D.* is the perceived distance of the afterimage. Thus, the size of the afterimage gets larger when you view it against a far wall, because viewing it against the wall increases the perceived distance *(P.D.),* but the size of the retinal image *(R.I.)* stays constant.

This same equation can be applied to size constancy—the fact that your perception of a person's size remains constant as the person walks away. As the person walks away, the size of his image on your retina *(R.I.)* gets smaller, but your perception of the person's distance *(P.D.)* gets larger. These two changes cancel each other, and the net result is that your perception of the person's size *(P.S.)* remains constant.

Box 9.2 Perceiving Physical Size and Retinal Size

You can demonstrate *size constancy* to yourself by means of a simple experiment.

Take two small cards or pieces of paper and draw a small circle, about an inch in diameter, in the center of each card. Now hold one card about 6 inches away and the other, just to the side of this card, about 12 inches away. Compare the sizes of the near and far circles. If they appear the same, then size constancy is working and you are perceiving the sizes of the circles based on their *physical sizes,* even though the retinal size of the far circle is half as large as the retinal size of the near circle.

If you repeat this experiment under conditions of poor depth information, you will perceive the circles more in terms of their *visual angles* (or *retinal size*). The best way to eliminate depth information is to turn the lights out and view the circles in the dark. But, in order to see the circles, you must turn them on! You can do this by painting the circles with luminous paint, such as Nite-Lite (Rich Art Color Co., Inc., New York, available at art supply stores). Position one luminous circle about 6 inches away and one about 12 inches away, turn out the lights, and view them with one eye. Do you perceive them in terms of size constancy or visual angle? Since it is difficult to perceive the distance of the circles in the dark, your perception is probably closer to the *law of visual angle* than when you viewed them in the light.

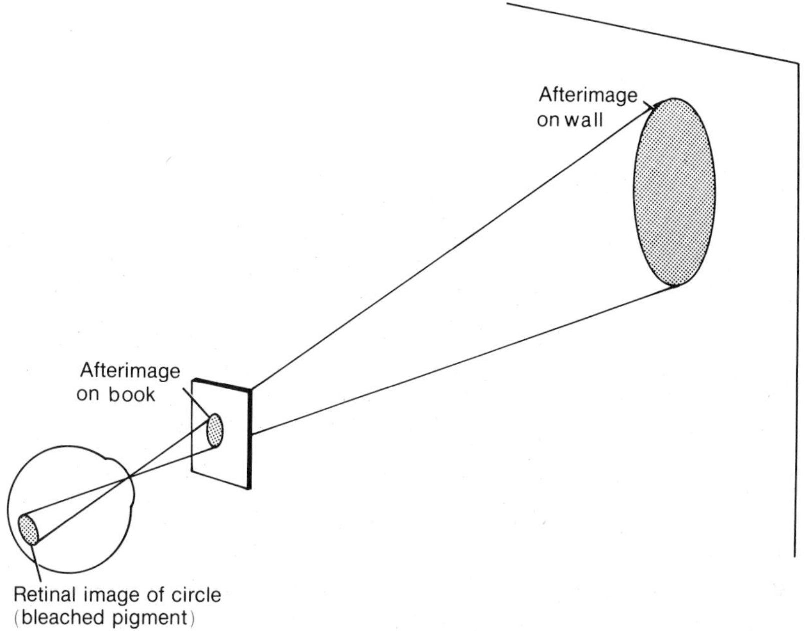

Figure 9.10 The principle underlying the observation that the size of an afterimage increases as the afterimage is viewed against increasingly distant surfaces.

Invariants

If you remember our discussion of J. J. Gibson in the last chapter, you know that he would not agree with the above explanation of size constancy, because it involves a calculation in which the object's retinal size and its distance are taken into account. Things are much simpler than this, according to Gibson, who feels that size constancy can be explained by simply comparing objects to **invariants** of the environment, such as the units of the texture gradient in Figure 8.22. We see immediately that the two poles on this texture gradient are the same size, without having to do any calculations, because the bases of the poles cover the same number of units on the texture gradient.

In fact, texture gradients may sometimes help us perceive the correct sizes of objects; however, given the large amount of evidence linking our perception of size and our perception of distance, it seems likely that the size-distance scaling mechanism described above is also involved in our perception of size.

Can We Perceive an Object's Visual Angle?

You may now be thinking that while you can indeed see a 6-foot-tall person as staying 6 feet tall when he is far away, he does look different than when he is close. You're right. The person's visual angle is smaller when he is far away, and even though the size-distance scaling mechanism causes us to see him at his correct 6-foot size, there is still information available that tells us that his visual angle is small. Perhaps the most obvious information which tells us this is that when the person is far away, he takes up a much smaller fraction of your field of view than when he is close. When a person stands 2 feet from you, he may cover almost your entire field of view, but when he is the length of a football field away, he is just one small object in a large field of view. In fact, experiments have shown that when observers are asked to judge an object's visual angle, they can do so, though they tend to somewhat overestimate the visual angle, probably because they can't completely overcome the tendency to perceive in terms of size constancy when good depth information is available (Gilinsky, 1965).

Though it is possible to estimate the visual angle of an object, our everyday experience is dominated by size constancy. A faraway mountain looks huge, even though its visual angle may be smaller than many nearby objects, and our 6-foot-tall person appears 6 feet tall, no matter where he is. This dominance of size constancy occurs because our every-

Box 9.3 The Visual Angles of the Sun and the Moon

Astronomy was full of such intriguing but meaningless coincidences. The most famous was the fact that, from the earth, both Sun and Moon have the same apparent diameter.

—Arthur Clarke, *2010: Odyssey Two* (1982)

Do the sun and moon appear to be about the same size to you? This is not a particularly easy question to answer, because we usually don't see the sun and moon together, and on the occasions when the moon is visible during the day, it is located far away from the sun in the sky. But there is one time when we see both the sun and moon together—during an eclipse of the sun. Although we can see the flaming corona of the sun surrounding the moon, as shown in the figure above, the moon's disc almost exactly covers the disc of the sun. We perceive the sizes of the sun and moon to be the same, simply because two objects with the same visual angle cast equal images on the retina. If we calculate the visual angles of the sun and moon, the result is 0.5 degrees for both. As you can see in the figure below, the moon is small (diameter = 2,200 miles but close (245,000 miles from earth), while the sun is large (diameter = 865,400 miles) but far away (93 million miles from earth). The situation, therefore, is similar to the one depicted in Figure 9.5, in which a small object that is close casts the same-sized image on the retina as a large object that is far away.

In addition to being an interesting astronomical curiosity, the fact that the sun and moon have both the same visual angle ***and*** the same perceived size indicates that we perceive the sizes of these objects according to the law of visual angle. (If the sizes of the sun and moon were perceived according to the law of size constancy, the sun would appear to be almost 400 times the diameter of the moon.) Our perception according to the law of visual angle is not surprising, since we have no way of judging the relative distances of the sun and the moon; as we saw from the results of Holway and Boring's experiment, when we can't judge an object's distance, our perception of size is determined by the object's visual angle.

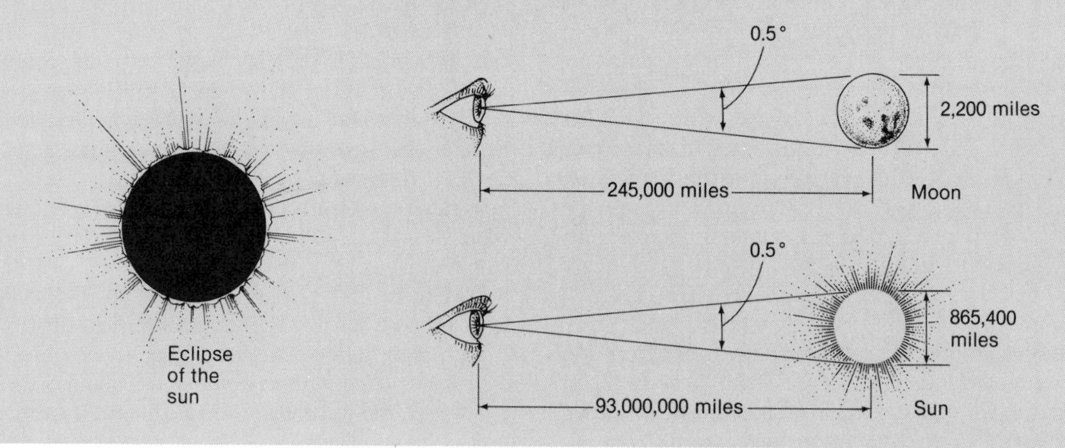

day experience usually includes lots of depth information. In some situations, however, erroneous depth information may lead us to perceive illusions of size.

Illusions of Size

The Ames room. The **Ames room,** which was first constructed by Adelbert Ames, causes two people of equal size to appear very different (Ittleson, 1952). In the photograph of the observer's view of an Ames room in Figure 9.11, you can see that the man on the right looks much bigger than the one on the left. This perception occurs even though the two men are actually the same size. The reason for this erroneous perception of size lies in the construction of the room. Because of the shapes of the wall and windows at the rear of the room, the room looks like a normal rectangular room when viewed from a particular observation point; however, as you can see from the diagram in Figure 9.12, the Ames room is, in fact, shaped so that the left corner of the room is almost twice as far away from us as the right corner.

The greater distance of the man on the left causes him to have a much smaller visual angle than the man on the right. Since we think that we are looking into a normal rectangular room, we assume that both men are at the same distance, and our size-distance scaling mechanism does not correct for the left man's greater depth. We therefore use the only other available information—the visual angles of the two men. Since the man on the right has a larger visual angle than the one on the left, he looks taller. Think about this in another way: if you perceive two people to be the same distance from you, the one who has the larger visual angle will appear larger. This is really a statement of the obvious: when a tall and short person stand next to each other, you per-

Figure 9.11 The Ames room. All three men are actually the same height. (Wittreich, 1959; Photograph courtesy of William Vandivert.)

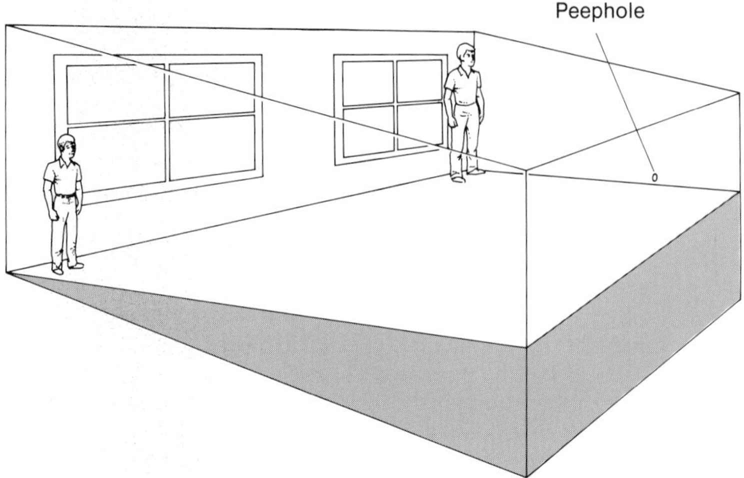

Figure 9.12 The Ames room, showing its true shape. The man on the left is actually almost twice as far away as the man on the right; however, when the room is viewed through the peephole, this difference in distance is not seen. In order for the room to look normal when viewed from through the peephole, it is necessary to enlarge the left side of the room.

ceive the tall person as being taller. The Ames room causes you to think that you are seeing two men at the same distance, which makes the closer one, with the larger visual angle, appear to be taller.

The moon illusion. The **moon illusion** is another perceptual effect that depends on the perception of depth. You may have noticed that when the moon is on the horizon, it appears much larger than when it is directly overhead, at its **zenith.** This difference in the perceived sizes of the horizon and zenith moons, shown in Figure 9.13, is called the moon illusion. People have been aware of this illusion for centuries, and many explanations have been proposed for it. Early explanations of the moon illusion invoked the **apparent-distance theory,**[1] which is based on the idea that an object on the horizon, which is viewed across the filled space of the terrain, should appear to be farther away than an object at the zenith, which is viewed through the empty space of the sky. If a far object has the same visual angle as a near object, the far object will appear larger (as we have seen from the results of Holway and Boring's experiment). The apparent-distance theory, therefore, states that since the horizon and zenith moons have the same visual angles,[2] the farther-appearing horizon moon should appear larger.

Several hundred years after the proposal of the apparent-distance theory, Edwin Boring and Alfred Holway questioned the basis of this theory by asking people to tell them whether the horizon or the zenith moon looked closer. When asked to make this judgment, most people said that the horizon moon looked closer, and when asked why, they said that the horizon moon looked closer because it appeared larger. Thus, while the apparent-distance theory was based on the idea that the horizon moon looked farther away, Boring and Holway's observers said that the horizon moon appeared closer.

[1]A number of writers have attributed this theory to Ptolemy, the second-century astronomer who said that the earth is at the center of the universe, with the sun, moon, and stars revolving around it. Helen and George Ross (1976), however, argue that this attribution of the theory is erroneous and that the apparent-distance theory was not proposed until after Ptolemy.

[2]The moon's physical size (2,200 miles in diameter) and distance from the earth (245,000 miles) are constant throughout the night, so the moon's visual angle is constant. This constancy of the moon's visual angle can be verified by photographing the horizon and zenith moons and measuring the resulting photographs. In the photographs, you will find that the diameters of the horizon and zenith moons are identical.

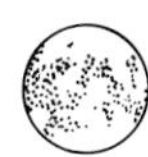

Figure 9.13 An artist's conception of the moon illusion, showing the moon on the horizon and high in the sky simultaneously.

Having rejected the apparent-distance explanation of the moon illusion, Boring and Holway (1940a, 1940b; Boring, 1943) proceeded to do a series of experiments that led them to propose the **eye-elevation hypothesis** of the moon illusion. They projected a small artificial moon onto a screen, 3.5 meters from the observer, then had the observer adjust the size of this artificial moon to match the perceived size of the real moon. However, rather than letting observers tilt their heads up to look at the zenith moon, Boring and Holway had them face forward and elevate their eyes. When observers elevated their eyes to view the zenith moon (Figure 9.14a), they equated the zenith moon with a small artificial moon on the nearby screen. Furthermore, when observers laid on their backs so they could view the zenith moon without elevating their eyes

(a)

(b)

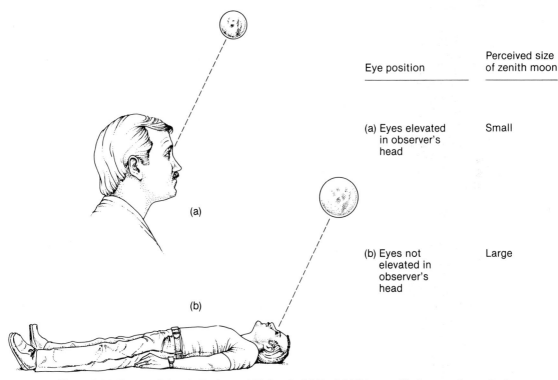

Eye position	Perceived size of zenith moon
(a) Eyes elevated in observer's head	Small
(b) Eyes not elevated in observer's head	Large

Figure 9.14 Two conditions in Boring and Holway's (1940a, 1940b) moon illusion experiment. Boring and Holway concluded that elevation of the observer's eyes was responsible for the illusion, since their observers perceived the zenith moon to be small when they elevated their eyes (top) but perceived it to be large when they laid on their backs and viewed the zenith moon without elevating their eyes (bottom).

(Figure 9.14b), they equated the zenith moon with a large artificial moon. Thus, Boring and Holway proposed that the moon illusion was due not to differences in the apparent distances of the horizon and zenith moons but to the position of the observer's eyes in his or her head.

Boring's eye-elevation hypothesis became the accepted explanation of the moon illusion, despite the fact that Boring himself could think of no reason why elevating the eyes should cause the moon to appear smaller. In 1962, however, Lloyd Kaufman and Irvin Rock (1962a, 1962b; Rock & Kaufman, 1962) questioned the eye-elevation hypothesis for two reasons. First, they saw no significant difference in the size of the moon when they viewed it with their eyes elevated or straight ahead. Second, they questioned Boring's method for determining the perceived size of the moon. Kaufman and Rock felt that it was asking too much of the observers to have them match the size of a faraway object such as the moon with a nearby object, such as an artificial moon only 3.5 meters away. In fact, in the description of his experiment, Boring states that observers found it difficult to match the sizes of the real and artificial moons because of the great distance between them.

Instead of asking observers to match the distant real moon with a nearby artificial moon, Kaufman and Rock built a projection system that enabled observers to match the size of an artificial moon, seen against the zenith sky, by adjusting the size of another artificial moon, seen against the horizon sky. These similar moons greatly simplified the observer's task, and with this new method of measuring the illusion, Kaufman and Rock retested the eye-elevation hypothesis. They found that eye elevation had no essential effect on the perceived size of the moon, concluding that the results on which Boring and Holway based their eye-elevation hypothesis were in error.

Having rejected the eye-elevation hypothesis, Kaufman and Rock returned to the apparent-distance hypothesis, which Boring had rejected because his observers said that the horizon moon looked closer than the zenith moon. Instead of asking observers to judge the distance of the horizon and zenith moons, Kaufman and Rock asked observers to imagine that the moonless sky was a surface and to decide whether the surface seemed farther away at the horizon or at the zenith. When they did this, observers said that the horizon appeared farther away. This result is consistent with observations by other investigators that the **vault of the heavens** appears flattened, as shown in Figure 9.15, and if we assume that the moon is actually perceived to be on the surface of the sky, this result confirms the idea, proposed in apparent-distance theory, that the horizon moon appears farther away than the zenith moon.

After resurrecting the apparent-distance theory, Kaufman and Rock still had to show that the enlarged perceived size of the horizon moon was, in fact, the result of viewing the moon over the terrain, which caused it to appear farther away. They demonstrated this in a number of ways. They found that when the horizon moon was viewed over the terrain, it appeared over 1.3 times larger than the zenith moon;

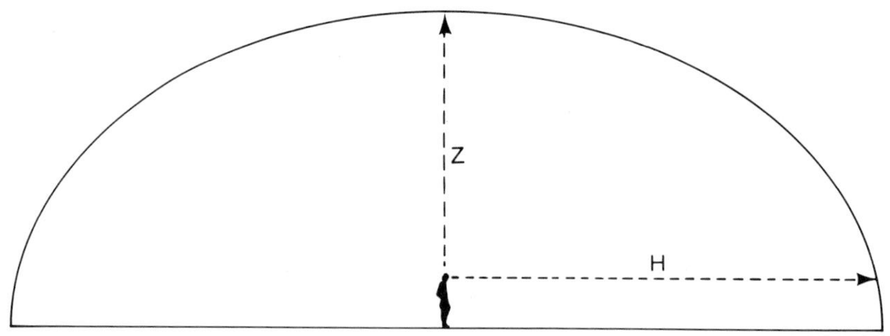

Figure 9.15 When observers imagine that the sky is a surface and then compare the distance to the horizon (H) and the distance to the top of the sky (Z) on a clear, moonless night, they usually say that the horizon appears farther away. The result is a flattened *vault of the heavens,* as shown above.

however, when the terrain was masked off so that the horizon moon was viewed through a hole in a sheet of cardboard, the illusion vanished. When Kaufman and Rock took their apparatus to a place where the visible horizon was about 2 miles away in one direction and only about 2,000 feet away in another direction, they found that the horizon moon appeared much larger when viewed over the far horizon than when viewed over the near horizon. A number of other experiments in which Kaufman and Rock varied the apparent distance to the horizon resulted in the same conclusion: the apparent-distance theory was correct—the horizon moon looks larger because it appears farther away.

The principle involved in the moon illusion is the same one that causes an afterimage to appear larger if it is viewed against a faraway surface. Just as the near and far afterimages of Figure 9.9 have the same visual angle, so do the zenith and horizon moons. The afterimage that appears to be on the wall across the room simulates the horizon moon; the circle appears farther away, so your size-distance scaling mechanism makes it appear larger. The afterimage that appears to be on the page of the book simulates the zenith moon; the circle appears closer, so your scaling mechanism makes it appear smaller.

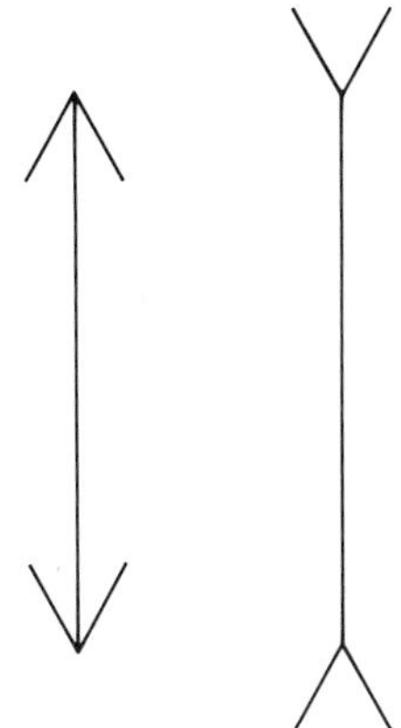

Figure 9.16 The Muller-Lyer illusion. Both lines are actually the same length.

The Muller-Lyer illusion. The **Muller-Lyer illusion,** shown in Figure 9.16, is analogous to the moon illusion. The two central lines are actually equal in length and therefore have the same visual angle, but the line on the right looks longer. Why does this occur? Richard Gregory (1966) has explained this illusion on the basis of what he called **misapplied size constancy.** He points out that size constancy normally helps us maintain a stable perception of objects by taking distance into account. Thus, size constancy causes a 6-foot-tall person to appear 6 feet tall, no matter what his distance. Gregory, however, proposes that this mechanism, which helps us maintain stable perceptions in the three-dimensional world, sometimes creates illusions when applied to objects drawn on a two-dimensional surface. We can see how this works, by comparing the left and right lines of Figure 9.16 to the left and right pictures of Figure 9.17. Gregory suggests that the fins on the right line make this line look like part of the inside corner of a room and that the fins on the left line make this line look like part of the outside corner of a building. Since the inside corner of a room tends to look farther away than the outside corner of a building, we see the right line as being farther away, and our size-distance scaling mechanism causes this line to appear longer.

At this point, you might say that while the Muller-Lyer figures may remind Gregory of the inside corner of a room or the outside corner of a building, they don't look that way to you (or at least they didn't until Gregory told you to see them that way). But, according to Gregory, it is not necessary that you be consciously aware that the Muller-Lyer lines can represent three-dimensional structures; your perceptual system unconsciously takes the depth information contained in the Muller-Lyer figures into account, and your size-distance scaling mechanism causes the left line to shrink and the right line to expand. This theory of visual illusions can also be applied to other illusions that contain depth information, such as the **Ponzo (railroad track) illusion,** shown in Figure 9.18. Here, both horizontal lines have the same visual angle, but the one on top appears farther away and is therefore perceived as larger.

Gregory's theory of visual illusions has not, however, gone unchallenged. Many investigators have proposed illusions, such as the "dumbbell" figure in Figure 9.19, that contain no obvious perspective or depth but still result in an illusion. Thus, although Gregory's explanation seems reasonable

Figure 9.17 According to Gregory (1973), the Muller-Lyer line on the left in Figure 9.16 corresponds to the outside corner of a building and the line on the right corresponds to the inside corner of a room.

for the conventional Muller-Lyer and Ponzo illusions, there are many other illusions which Gregory's theory cannot explain. Unfortunately, while people have found it easy to produce figures such as the one in Figure 9.19, which are difficult for Gregory's theory to explain, a satisfactory alternative to Gregory's theory has yet to be proposed. J. O. Robinson (1972) surveys all the current theories of visual illusions in his book *The Psychology of Visual Illusion* and concludes that "no theory has been able to survive rigorous test." He suggests that there are so many different visual illusions that it is probably unlikely that any one theory can explain them all.

Shape Constancy

One thing we noticed in our walk past the desk of Figure 9.2 is that the shapes of objects on the desk did not appear to change. **Shape constancy** occurs despite large changes in the shapes of the objects on the retina, and we need to ask, as we did for size constancy, what causes our perception of these shapes to remain constant.

Let's start by doing an experiment. Place a penny on your desk, then view it from a height of 5 inches and a distance of 20 inches, as shown in Figure 9.20. While viewing the penny, decide which shape in Figure 9.21 (viewed straight on, as shown in Figure 9.20) most closely matches your perception of the penny's shape at an angle. (Stop! Read no further until you have done this experiment.)

To understand the rationale behind this experiment, look at Figure 9.22. This figure shows what happens to the image that the coin casts on your retina as you view it from different angles. The observer in Figure 9.22(a) is viewing the coin straight on, so the coin's image on her retina is a circle that corresponds to the physical shape of the coin. However, when the observer views the coin at an angle, its image on her retina changes, becoming increas-

Figure 9.18 The Ponzo (railroad track) illusion. The two horizontal rectangles are the same length on the page (measure them), but the far one appears larger.

ingly elliptical as she views it at increasingly acute angles, as shown in Figure 9.22(b) and (c).

The purpose of our experiment was to see how your perception of the coin's shape compared to the shape of the coin's image on your retina. If you picked stimulus number 1 of Figure 9.21, then your perception matches the elliptical shape of the coin's image on your retina. If you picked number 6, then your perception matches the circular physical shape

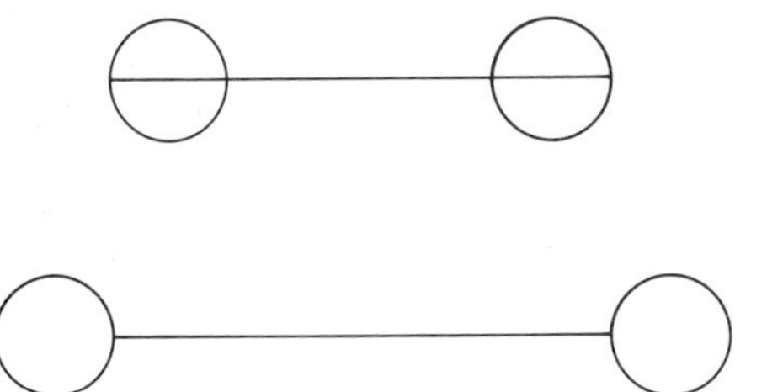

Figure 9.19 The "dumbbell" version of the Muller-Lyer illusion. As in the Muller-Lyer illusion, the two lines are actually the same length.

of the coin. Most people pick number 3, 4, or 5, because they perceive the coin to be elliptical, though not as elliptical as the coin's shape on their retina.

In 1931, Robert Thouless conducted an experiment similar to the one you just did. His observers viewed a circle at a slant and picked the shape that most closely matched their perception. Figure 9.23 shows the results of one of Thouless's experiments. The circle represents the physical shape of the circle, and the shaded ellipse represents the shape of the retinal image when the circle is viewed at an angle. The dashed line shows the shape that Thouless's observers said matched their perception of the circle viewed at an angle. Thouless's observers saw the circle at a slant as elliptical, though not as elliptical as the circle's shape on the retina. Thouless called this result **phenomenal regression to the real object,** because the observer's perception "regresses" away from the elliptical image on the retina toward the true circular shape of the circle. Another way to describe Thouless's result is to say that his observers demonstrated shape constancy—a tendency to see

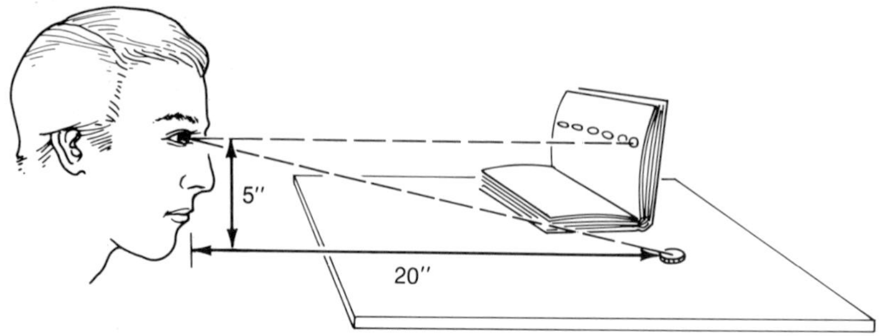

Figure 9.20 Directions for viewing Figure 9.21.

the true physical shapes of objects, even when they are seen in different orientations. (It should be noted, however, that Thouless's observers demonstrated only partial shape constancy. Full shape constancy would require that the perceived shape of the circle match the physical shape of the circle.)

What determines shape constancy? Thouless felt that an important factor must be our ability to perceive the orientation of an object in space and to take that orientation into account when perceiving the object. To test this idea, he placed tilted circles in front of a background of black velvet, then had each observer view them with one eye. Under these viewing conditions, which make it difficult to see the circle's orientation, shape constancy vanishes and we perceive a shape similar to the one the object casts on our retina; but under normal conditions, when orientation is easily perceived, shape constancy works and we perceive the object's physical shape.

Lightness Constancy

Our discussion so far has shown that we tend to perceive two properties of objects, their sizes and shapes, as staying constant, even in the face of large changes in the retinal sizes and shapes of these objects. In this section, we will focus on how we perceive another property of objects—**lightness**—and we will see that we perceive the lightnesses of objects as staying constant, even in the face of large changes in the illumination falling on our retinas. Before we discuss the phenomenon of **lightness constancy,** however, we will begin by defining what we mean by lightness.

What Is Lightness?

Lightness is the property of objects that is related to the percentage of light reflected from an object into your eye. Objects that look black, like the print on this page, reflect about 5 percent of the light falling on them into your eye. Objects that look grey reflect about 10–70 percent of the light (depending on the shade of grey), and objects that look white, like the paper in this book, reflect 80–90 percent of the light. Thus, when we describe something as being black, grey, or white, we are talking about that object's lightness, and this lightness is related to the object's **reflectance**—the percentage of light that the object reflects (see pp. 116–119, in Chapter 5, for a discussion of reflectance). The key word in the previous sentence is *percentage,* because it is the percentage of light reflected, not the *amount,* that determines an object's lightness. To understand what we mean by this, let's consider an experiment in lightness constancy.

An Experiment in Lightness Constancy

Burzlaff conducted a typical lightness constancy experiment in 1931. He prepared two sets of 48 squares, which varied in lightness from extremely white to extremely black, with most being various shades of grey. He mounted one set of squares in

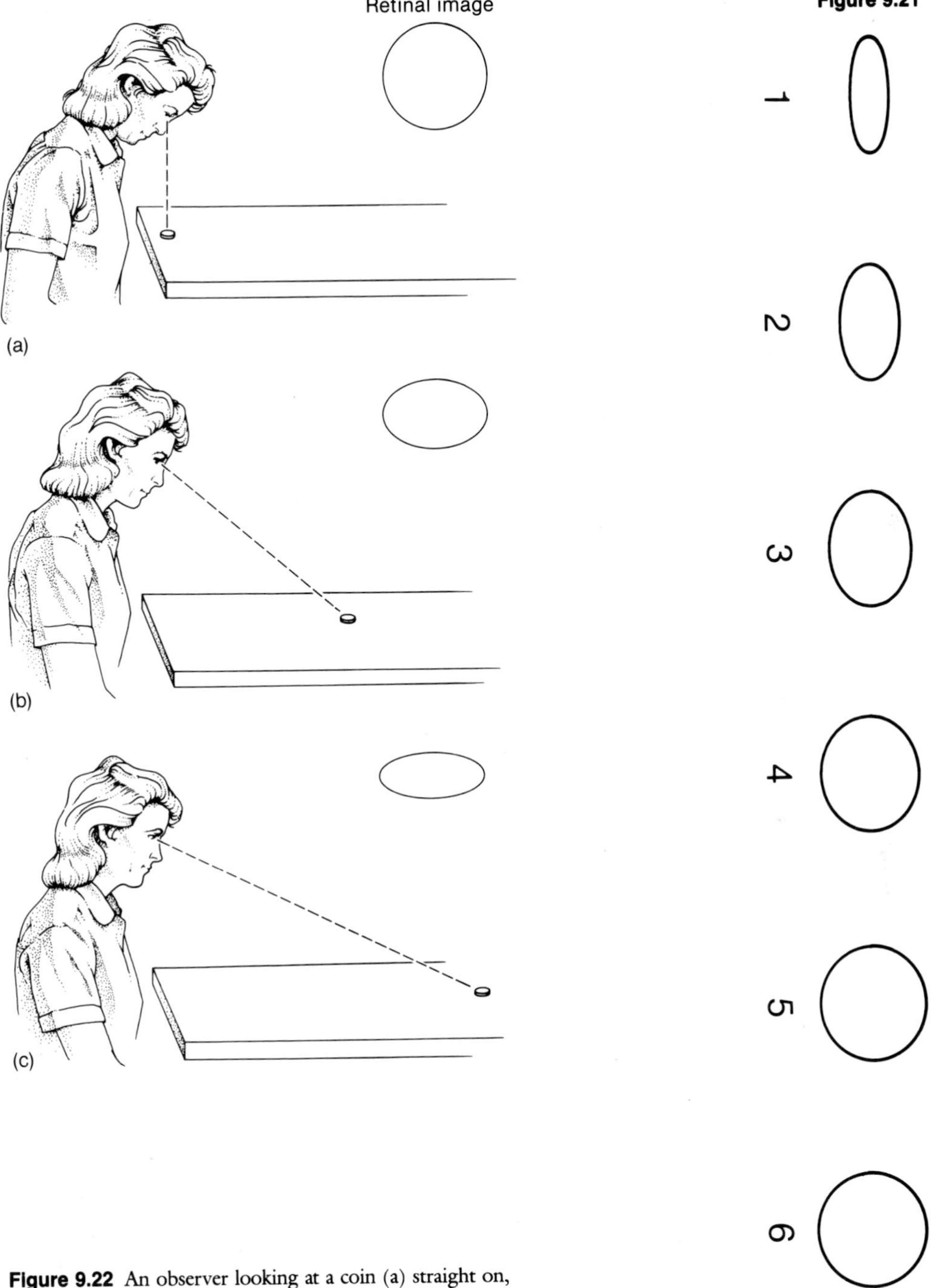

Figure 9.22 An observer looking at a coin (a) straight on, (b) at an angle, and (c) at a more acute angle. The shape of the coin's image on the observer's retina is indicated in the upper right of each picture.

Figure 9.21

1

2

3

4

5

6

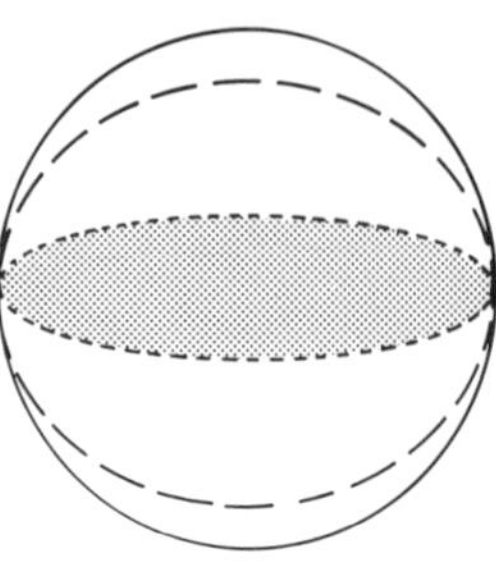

——— Physical shape of circle
— — — Perceived shape of circle viewed at a slant
- - - - - - - - Retinal shape of circle viewed at a slant

Figure 9.23 Results of one of Thouless's (1931) experiments. Observers perceived the circle viewed at an angle to be more circular (dashed line) than the shape of the circle on the observer's retina (shaded ellipse).

order, from white to black, on a large piece of cardboard, then mounted the other set in random order on an identical piece of cardboard and presented the two sets of squares to the observer, as shown in Figure 9.24. The ordered set was mounted on the dimly lit far wall of the room, whereas the random set was located with the observer near the window and was, therefore, exposed to about 20 times more light than the squares on the wall.

The procedure of the experiment was as follows: one square from the brightly illuminated random set was designated the "standard," and the experimenter then pointed to each of the dimly illuminated "comparison" squares on the far wall. On each trial, the observer's task was to indicate whether the comparison square was lighter than, darker than, or the same greyness as the standard. Each comparison square was compared to the standard six times and, using the method of constant stimuli (see p. 8, in Chapter 1), it was possible to determine which comparison square most closely matched the standard square. This procedure, which was repeated for a number of the standard squares, yielded fairly straightforward results. Observers tended to pick a comparison square that matched the reflectance of the standard square. For example, observers said that a comparison square with a reflectance of about 78 percent appeared to be the same greyness as a standard square with a reflectance of about 72 percent.

Let's consider what this result means. The observers matched two squares that were close in reflectance, even though the standard square was exposed to 20 times more illumination than the comparison square. The importance of this finding can be made more clear by calculating the ***amount*** of light reflected from each square. We can't calculate the actual amount of light reflected, since we don't know how much light was coming through Burzlaff's window; however, since we know that there was about 20 times more light hitting the standard squares than the comparison squares, we can calculate the relative amount of light reflected by each square, as follows:

Relative amount of light reflected = reflectance × relative light intensity.
Comparison square = 78 × 1 = 78
Standard square = 72 × 20 = 1,440

Thus, Burzlaff's observers said that two squares appeared to be the same shade of grey when one of them reflected 78 units of light and the other reflected 1,440 units. That the *percentage* of light reflected (what we have been calling "reflectance"), not the ***amount,*** determines lightness is a demonstration of lightness constancy.

Basically, lightness constancy means that we see the true properties of the object no matter what the illumination is. A piece of white paper is seen as white in a dimly lit room or in bright sunlight; and the black print on that paper is seen as black, no matter what the illumination. It's a good thing lightness constancy occurs, because, without it, the lightnesses of the objects around us would be constantly changing. Taking a piece of coal from inside to outside would change it from black to white! Without lightness constancy, it would become meaningless to say "this coal is black" or "this paper is white," because their lightnesses would change each time we changed the illumination.

What is responsible for lightness constancy? We will now consider a few of the things that help keep lightness constant.

Relationships

Evidence that relationships help cause lightness constancy is provided by an effect called **simultaneous contrast,** illustrated in Figure 9.25. In this

Figure 9.24 Burzlaff's (1931) experiment. The observer's task was to judge whether each of the dimly lit comparison stimuli was lighter or darker than one of the brightly lit standard stimuli.

figure, two areas that reflect different amounts of light look the same, because the ratios of their intensities to the intensities of their surroundings are kept constant. Thus, when we take our piece of coal outside, it reflects more light, but so does everything else. Since the ratio of the coal's reflectance to that of the surroundings remains constant, the coal's lightness remains constant. (We will discuss simultaneous contrast in more detail in the next chapter.)

An experiment by Gelb (1929) demonstrates the importance of relationships in the perception of lightness constancy. Figure 9.26, the setup for Gelb's experiment, shows a disc of low reflectance suspended in completely black surroundings. The key feature of this experiment was the presence of a hidden light that illuminated only the disc. When viewed from the observer's position, the disc, which

Figure 9.25 How simultaneous contrast can make two different discs appear identical. If light intensities were as indicated by the numbers in the outer rings and inner discs, the inner discs would appear identical, because the ring-to-disc ratio is 10 to 1 in both cases. (From Wallach, 1963.)

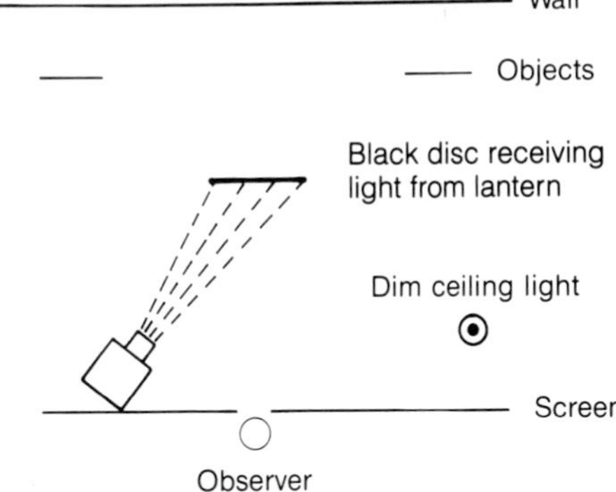

Figure 9.26 The setup of Gelb's concealed illumination experiment. The observer could not see the light on the left, which was projected only onto the black disc. The background, which is also black, was dimly illuminated by the ceiling light. (From Hochberg, 1971.)

would look black in your living room or outdoors, looked white. This result occurred because the only stimulus present, other than the disc, was the black background, which reflected only a small amount of light compared to the secretly illuminated disc. This perception of a black disc as white is consistent with the idea that relationships are important in determining lightness. But Gelb wasn't satisfied just to turn a black disc white; he also wanted to make it turn black again. He did this by placing a small piece of white paper in front of the disc so that it became illuminated by the hidden light. As soon as this piece of white paper was introduced, the disc turned black! This new relationship, with the white paper reflecting much more light than the disc, caused the disc to look dark.

Gelb's experiment shows that lightness constancy breaks down—an ordinarily black object can appear white—if the ordinarily black object has the highest intensity in the field. This effect occurs only under special conditions, such as those used by Gelb: a hidden light and no comparison objects in the field. As soon as a comparison object is placed in the light with the black disc, the relationship between the white paper and the disc reinstates the lightness constancy, and the disc becomes black.

Before we leave Gelb's experiment, let's ask another question: What effect does the observer's knowledge of the situation have on his or her perception? Once the white paper is presented, the observer becomes aware that the disc is really black. You might think that once the truth is known, the disc would always be perceived as black, but this is not the case. When the small piece of white paper is removed, the black disc turns white again, and no amount of knowledge will make it turn black. Knowledge of the situation does not necessarily affect our perception.

Figure 9.27 A shape-sorting box and its shadow.

Shadows

Lightness constancy occurs not only when we bring an object from the low illumination inside to the high illumination outside but also when part of an object is covered by a shadow. When you see shadows on the grass, like those in Figure 9.29, you don't assume that the shadowed grass is dark green and the grass in sunlight is light green. Instead, you assume that the shadowed and unshadowed areas are the same shade of green all over, but that less light falls on some areas than on others.

What makes lightness constancy work in shadows? One reason is the nature of a shadow's contour. Cast a shadow yourself and look at the contour between the shadowed and unshadowed areas. You will see that the contour is fuzzy, as shown in Figure 9.27. This fuzzy area, which is called the shadow's **penumbra,** is responsible for much of the lightness constancy in shadows.

If the penumbra is responsible for lightness constancy, we should be able to decrease lightness constancy by eliminating the penumbra. This is exactly what Ewald Hering (1905) did in his ringed shadow experiment, which you can carry out yourself. Produce a shadow on a piece of white paper with a small object; then draw a dark border along the contour of the shadow, as shown in Figure 9.28. If this border covers the penumbra, you will see the shadowed area change in appearance. Instead of looking like a shadow on a piece of white paper, it looks like a dark spot on the paper. Eliminating the penumbra has decreased lightness constancy so that a change in illumination is perceived as a change in lightness.

Why does the penumbra cause lightness constancy? One reason may be that its presence tells us that a shadow is present, and once we know we are dealing with a shadow, we know that the illumination is changing, not the object's lightness. The

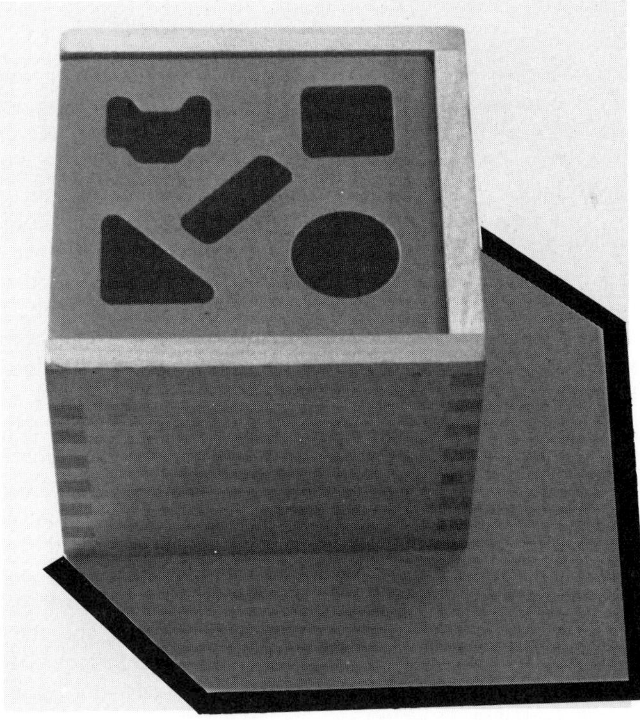

Figure 9.28 The same box and shadow as in Figure 9.27 with the penumbra covered by a black border.

Figure 9.29

penumbra helps us know that shadows are shadows, and so does the shape of the shadow. Shadows are often shaped like trees, people, cars, and other objects in the environment. It is unlikely that the pattern on the grass and building in Figure 9.29 could be anything but the shadow of a tree; therefore, we interpret it that way. It is conceivable that the dark pattern on the house in Figure 9.30 could be due to a strange paint job, but it is much more likely, since the pattern resembles the tree branches the artist has included in the upper left corner, that the pattern results from a shadow cast by the tree branches rather than from a change in lightness. We can be fooled, however, by paintings such as the one in Figure 9.31. In this case, the painter fools us by painting a pattern that looks like a shadow.

Interpretation of How an Object Is Illuminated

A number of experiments have shown that any observer's interpretation of how an object is illuminated affects his or her perception of the object's lightness. We will describe one such experiment in detail in the next chapter, when we discuss contrast, but to illustrate this effect now, we can do our own experiment, based on one first described by Ernst Mach. (Attneave, 1971.)

To do this experiment, you need only a small card or piece of paper. Fold the card as shown in Figure 9.32, then orient it so that the left side is illuminated slightly less than the right (the light should be coming from the right). When viewed at about a 45-degree angle from above, with two eyes, the two sides of the card look about the same lightness. That both sides look white, even though one is more intensely illuminated, is an example of lightness constancy. Now, close one eye and continue viewing the card. Eventually, your perception should "flip" so that the card appears to stand on end like an open book, with the inside toward you, as in Figure 9.33. When this happens, something else also happens. The shadowed left side of the card gets much darker, and the illuminated right side may even appear luminous. Lightness constancy has been eliminated—both sides of the card originally appeared white, but now one side appears dark and the other appears light.

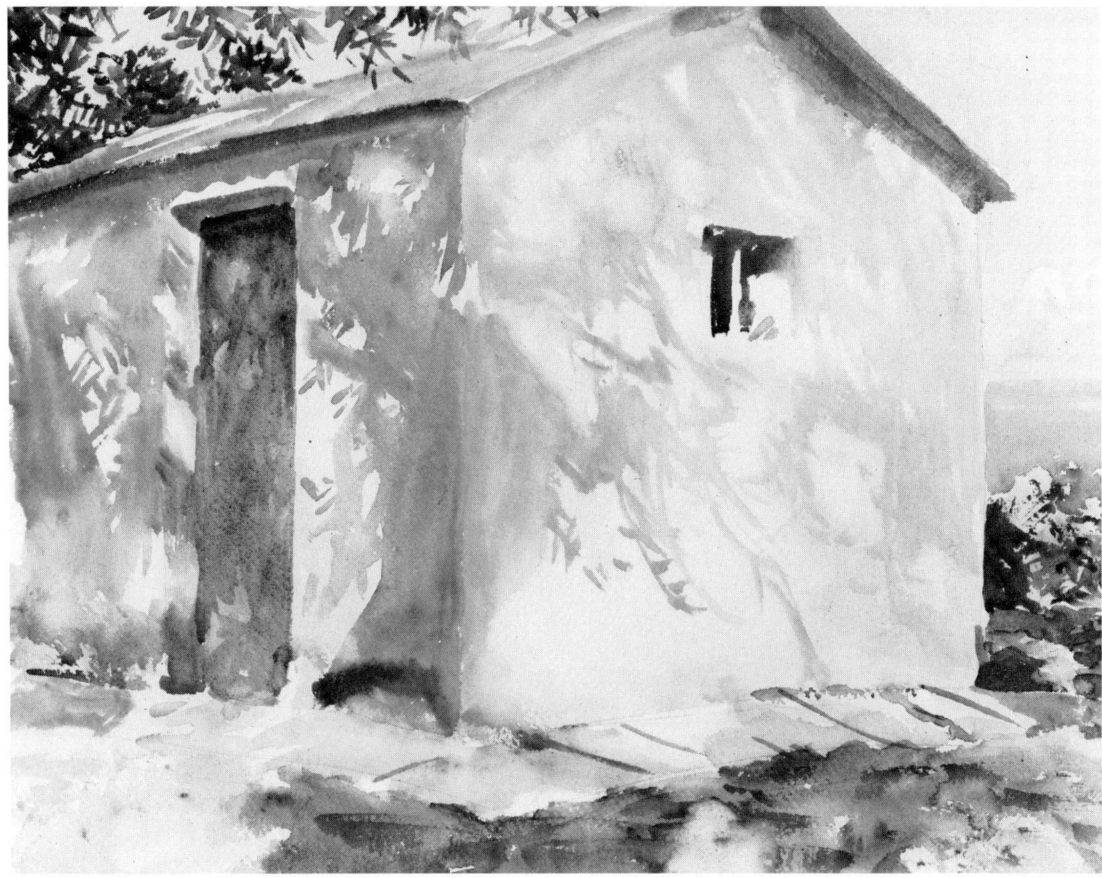

Figure 9.30 *Corfu, Lights and Shadows,* by John Singer Sargent. (Museum of Fine Arts, Boston.)

We can explain this effect by considering how we perceive the illumination relative to the card. Before the card flips, we perceive the right side of the card as being illuminated and the left side as being in shadow. Taking this knowledge of the illumination into account, we conclude that both sides of the card are white. Here, lightness constancy is working. After the card flips, however, the right side of the card no longer appears to be illuminated by the light. The light is still coming from the right, but the illuminated right side of the card now appears to be facing *away* from the light, and the shadowed left side appears to be facing *toward* the light. More light *appears* to be hitting the left side than the right side, when, in reality, the left side is reflecting less light into your eye than the right. How can this be? We could assume that the left side of the card is made of dark grey paper, which reflects little light, and that the right side is made of very white paper, which reflects a lot of light. Apparently, this is what our perceptual system does. Erroneous information about the card's orientation, relative to the light, fools our lightness constancy mechanism into making the left side look darker.

Perception as Hypothesis Testing

We have seen that although the sizes and shapes of the images on our retina are constantly changing as

Figure 9.31 *No. 277* (1968), by Jiro Takamatsu. Many people who look at this fail to notice that the "shadow" is being produced by an invisible key!

we walk through the environment, and although objects are exposed to various conditions of illumination, our perceptual system somehow takes these changes into account so that we perceive a stable environment with constant properties. We have also seen that this constancy sometimes depends on our interpretation of the situation, particularly in the case of lightness constancy. Thus, we interpret the light area on the wall in Figure 9.34 as the result of light coming in through the window rather than as an interesting paint job.

One way to look at this interpretive process is to think of perception as a process of **hypothesis testing.** This is the view of Richard Gregory (1973b), who makes the point that our perceptions are not always certain, and, therefore, "we may think of sensory stimulation as providing *data* for *hypotheses* concerning the state of the external world" (p. 61). You can probably think of situations in which your first impression proved incorrect. You see a shadowy object in the dimly lit corner of a room and think it is a table. Upon closer inspection, however, it turns out to be a chair or, perhaps, just a shadow.

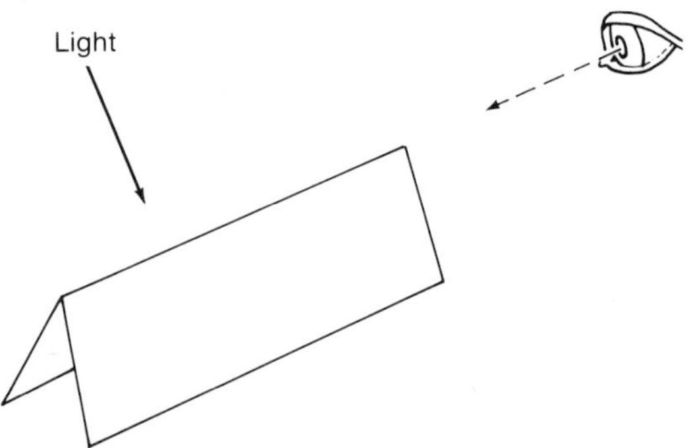

Figure 9.32 How to view the *Mach card.*

Figure 9.33 What the *Mach card* looks like when it perceptually "flips."

Your first hypothesis ("That's a table") was based on the rather indistinct sensory stimulation from the dimly lit corner. After you gain more information about the situation, your third hypothesis ("Oh, I see, that's actually a shadow") turns out to be correct.

We can apply this idea of hypothesis testing to size constancy. We have seen that our perception of size depends on our perception of depth. Therefore, if we misperceive an object's depth, we may also misperceive its size. I remember once looking into a room through a window on which there was a small decal. However, I misperceived the depth of the decal, because I thought it was attached to the far wall of the room rather than to the window. Needless to say, this made the decal look huge; however, as soon as I realized that the decal was

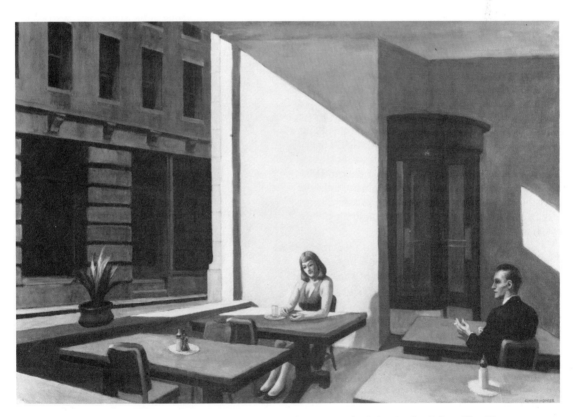

Figure 9.34 *Sunlight in a Cafeteria* (1958), by Edward Hopper. (Yale University Art Gallery, New Haven, Conn.)

actually attached to the window, my perception changed, and I saw what a small decal it actually was. My first hypothesis ("The decal is far away on the wall") caused me to misperceive its size, and only when I became aware of the decal's correct distance ("Oh, I see, it's actually on the nearby window") did I perceive its size correctly.

When there is little stimulus information available, it is difficult to formulate accurate hypotheses. This description of the effect of inclement weather at an Antarctic research base is a good example of a situation in which there is little information to go on in formulating a hypothesis.

> The most treacherous weather phenomenon is something known as a whiteout, in which light is reflected from a thick cloud cover and back up from the snow, obscuring the horizon and surface definition, and surrounding one with a dazzling whiteness. Someone flying a helicopter during a whiteout can't tell up from down; pilots have been known to drop smoke grenades to determine their altitude only to find that they were a few feet above the ground. Others have flown at full power directly into the ice. What one can see is distorted—a discarded matchbox may look like a tent or a vehicle. (*The New Yorker,* March, 1981).

Returning to lightness constancy, we may hypothesize that the light area in Figure 9.34 is due to illumination rather than to an interesting paint job because we can see the window on the left. There's a good chance that this hypothesis is correct, especially since there is a similar pattern of illumination on the far right. But it is *possible* (albeit unlikely) that the same artist who painted the key shadow in Figure 9.31 could have painted "sunlight" onto the walls of this restaurant.

Color Plate 9.1 is an example of a bush that fooled me into the wrong hypothesis. When I first looked at this bush, I thought that the ends of some of its branches looked a lighter green than the rest of the bush because they were sticking out and were therefore being grazed by sunlight. This seemed reasonable until I looked at the branches more closely. As you can see in Color Plate 9.2, they were not, in fact, illuminated more brightly than the rest of the branches: they were actually a lighter green! Had I known anything about the way bushes grow, I probably wouldn't have been fooled. But my incorrect interpretation of the illumination, combined with my ignorance of the principles of bush growth, resulted in a faulty hypothesis, and I mistook a lightness change for a change in the illumination.

According to Gregory, all our perceptions are determined by this process of hypothesis testing. We are, however, usually unaware that this process is occurring, because, in the vast majority of situations, we have enough information available to formulate correct hypotheses. We become aware of hypothesis testing only in situations in which the information is incomplete or misleading, as in the examples above.

Summary

1. The law of size constancy states that we perceive an object's size as staying constant, no matter what its distance.
2. The law of visual angle states that our perception of an object's size is determined solely by its visual angle.
3. Holway and Boring's experiment showed that when depth information is available, the law of size constancy holds, but when depth information is unavailable, the law of visual angle holds.
4. It has been hypothesized that a size-distance scaling mechanism supplements the information available on the retina, by taking an object's distance into account.
5. Emmert's law states that the size of an afterimage depends on the distance of the surface against which it is viewed—the more distant the surface, the larger the afterimage. This effect illustrates size-distance scaling.
6. According to J. J. Gibson, size constancy can be explained by comparing objects to invariant features of the environment, such as the units of a texture gradient.
7. Though it is possible to judge an object's visual angle, our everyday experience is dominated by size constancy.
8. Illusions of size—such as the Ames room, the moon illusion, and the Muller-Lyer illusion—have been explained by the operation of the

size-distance scaling mechanism in the presence of erroneous depth information.

9. Shape constancy occurs when you view an object at an angle and your perception of the object's shape corresponds to its physical shape rather than to the retinal shape of its image. Most people show partial shape constancy; they perceive the shape of an object at an angle to be somewhere between the object's physical and retinal shapes. If we eliminate information that enables us to perceive our viewing angle relative to the object, we decrease shape constancy.

10. Lightness is the property of objects that is related to an object's reflectance—the percentage of the light falling on the object that is reflected. Lightness constancy means that we perceive an object's lightness to be relatively constant, no matter what the illumination.

11. Lightness constancy is influenced by factors such as simultaneous contrast, the penumbra of shadows, and the observer's interpretation of how an object is illuminated.

12. It has been suggested that perception involves hypothesis testing. According to Gregory, "We may think of sensory stimulation as providing data for hypotheses concerning the state of the external world." Our perception of the constancies described above may depend, at least in part, on testing various hypotheses.

Glossary

Ames room A distorted room, first built by Adelbert Ames, that creates an erroneous perception of the sizes of people in the room. The room is constructed so that two people at the far wall of the room appear to stand at the same distance from an observer; in actuality, however, one person is much farther away than the other. (241)

Apparent-distance theory An explanation of the moon illusion, based on the idea that the horizon moon, which is viewed across the filled space of the terrain, should appear farther away than the zenith moon, which is viewed through the empty space of the sky. This theory states that since the horizon and zenith moons have the same visual angle, the farther-appearing horizon moon should appear larger. (242)

Emmert's law States that the size of an afterimage depends on the distance of the surface against which the afterimage is viewed. The farther away the surface against which an afterimage is viewed, the larger the afterimage is perceived to be. (238)

Eye-elevation hypothesis An explanation of the moon illusion; it hypothesizes that the zenith moon looks smaller than the horizon moon because we move our eyes upward to observe the zenith moon. (243)

Hypothesis testing The idea that sensory stimulation forms the basis for hypotheses we make about the environment. The process of hypothesis testing may involve the adoption and rejection of a number of hypotheses before we decide on a final perception of the environment. (256)

Invariants Properties of the environment that remain constant as an observer moves. (See Chapter 8.) (239)

Lightness That property of objects that is related to the percentage of light reflected from an object. Lightness ranges from black, for objects that reflect a small percentage of the light, to white, for objects that reflect a large percentage of the light. (248)

Lightness constancy When our perception of an object's lightness remains constant under different conditions of illumination. (248)

Misapplied size constancy When mechanisms that help maintain size constancy in the three-dimensional world are applied to two-dimensional pictures, an illusion of size sometimes results. (245)

Moon illusion The moon appears to be larger when it is on or near the horizon than when it is high in the sky. (242)

Muller-Lyer illusion An illusion that causes two lines of equal length to appear different lengths because of the addition of outward-facing "arrows" on one line and inward-facing "arrows" on the other. (245)

Penumbra The fuzzy border on many shadows. Note that the fuzziness of a shadow's border depends on how the object is illuminated. Objects illuminated by diffuse light cast very fuzzy shadows (large penumbra), whereas objects illuminated by a point source of light cast sharp shadows (small penumbra). (253)

Perceptual constancy The idea that our perceptions of the properties of objects—such as size, shape, and lightness—remain constant in the face of continually changing input. (232)

Phenomenal regression to the real object The idea that our perception of an object's shape tends to be closer to its physical shape than to the shape of its image on our retina. (247)

Ponzo (railroad track) illusion A size illusion in which two rectangles of equal length, which are drawn between two converging lines, appear to be of different length. (245)

Reflectance The *percentage* of light that an object reflects. Note that this is not the same thing as the *amount* of light reflected. (248)

Shape constancy When our perception of an object's shape remains constant, even when we view the object from different angles. (246)

Simultaneous contrast Our perception of the lightness of an area can be affected by the lightness of the surrounding area. (See Chapter 5.) (250)

Size constancy When our perception of an object's size remains constant, even when we view the object from different distances. (232)

Size constancy, law of States that we perceive an object's size as staying constant, no matter what its distance. (232)

Size-distance scaling mechanism A hypothesized mechanism that helps maintain our perception of size constancy by taking an object's distance into account. (237)

Vault of the heavens Refers to the fact that the sky can be seen as a surface, which most people perceive to be shaped like a flattened bowl, with the top of the sky appearing closer than the sky at the horizon. (244)

Visual angle The visual angle of an object is the angle between two lines that extend from the observer's eye, one to one end of the object and the second to the other end of the object. Note that an object's visual angle is always determined relative to an observer; therefore, an object's visual angle changes as the distance between the object and the observer changes. (232)

Visual angle, law of States that our perception of an object's size is determined solely by its visual angle. (234)

Zenith moon The moon when it is high in the sky. (242)

Chapter Ten

Perceiving Contrast

Winter Scene 1982 by Clifton Page

Look at the scene on the previous page. How do you tell the difference between the various parts of the scene? You might say that different parts of the scene have different shapes. But what enables us to perceive these different shapes? One answer to this question is **contrast.** Our perception of contrast between objects can be caused by differences in their hues; however, as indicated by the black-and-white photograph, we can also perceive contrast in the absence of hue. We perceive contrasts in this scene because of differences in the light reflected from each object; therefore, we can tell the horse from the snow and the snow from the trees. In this chapter, we will ask what factors other than hue influence our perception of contrast.

Before beginning our discussion, we should define exactly what we mean by the term *contrast.* When we say that there is a contrast between the horse and the adjacent snow, we could mean two things: (1) that different amounts of light are *reflected from* the two areas, or (2) that these two areas *look different.* In the first case, we are referring to **physical contrast**; in the second, to **perceptual contrast.** This distinction is analogous to the one we made between light intensity and brightness in Chapter 1. The *amount of light reflected from each area* is a physical property we can measure with a light meter, and *the way each area looks* is a psychological property that a person perceives. In this chapter, we will use the term *contrast* to mean perceptual contrast, and we will use the term *physical contrast* to refer to the physical properties of a stimulus. We make this distinction because it doesn't necessarily follow that good physical contrast results in good perceptual contrast. In fact, many things in addition to physical contrast influence perceptual contrast. Perceptual contrast is influenced by: (1) the observer's state of adaptation, (2) the nature of the contours between adjoining areas, (3) the relationship between the intensities of adjoining areas (simultaneous contrast), (4) an object's apparent position in space, and (5) the size or spatial frequency of the stimulus. (As we will see below, spatial frequency is related to the sizes of the elements of a stimulus—the smaller the elements, the higher the spatial frequency. Thus, extrafine sandpaper has a high spatial frequency and coarse sandpaper has a lower spatial frequency.) We will consider each of these factors, in turn, below.

Adapting the Observer

From Backyard to Basement

To describe how our perception of contrast is influenced by adaptation, let's consider how our perception of contrast changes as we move between the bright backyard and dim basement of Figure 10.2. Suppose you decide to come inside from the bright, sunny backyard of Figure 10.2(a). As you enter the dimly lit basement, your perception corresponds to Figure 10.2(b), and you realize that not only is it darker in the basement than it is outside but you're also having a hard time making out the difference between the dryer and the mittens on top of it. There is a lack of contrast between them. However, as you stay in the basement, you notice that it begins to seem less dark, that you can begin to see the mittens on the dryer, and that you can even begin to see the sink in the corner. This is the familiar process of ***dark adaptation*** we described in Chapter 3, which occurs each time we move from a light place to a darker one. The visual system adjusts its sensitivity to match the lower light level in the basement, and, after 5–10 minutes, you perceive the basement as in Figure 10.3(a).

A similar process occurs when you move from the basement to the backyard. At first you are blinded by the brightness and can see objects only faintly, as in Figure 10.3(b), but within a short time your eyes become adapted to the light, and you see the backyard as in Figure 10.2(a).

Why is this adaptation process necessary? Why must we wait for our eyes to adjust their sensitivity before we can make out the objects in the backyard or the basement? To answer these questions, let's consider what is required of the visual system. We want to be able (1) to see in very dim and very bright light (that is, we want to have a very large **operating range**) and (2) to tell the difference between two things that are very close together in intensity (that is, we want to have high sensitivity to small differences in *physical contrast*). And our visual system can do both things. We can see light levels as low as 7 quanta when we are completely dark adapted (see Box 2.1) and as high as the trillions of quanta reflected by snow on a bright, sunny

Figure 10.2 (a) Left: a sunny backyard. (b) Right: your perception immediately after you enter the basement from the backyard.

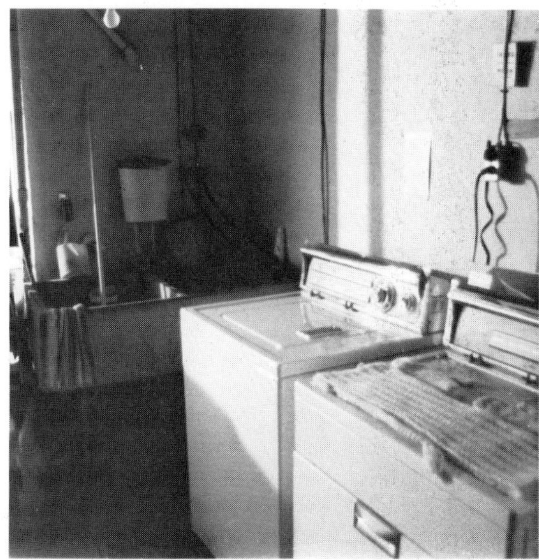

Figure 10.3 (a) Left: your perception after you adjust to the dim light of the basement. (b) Right: your perception immediately after you enter the backyard from the basement.

day. Yet we can also detect the difference between two objects that differ in intensity by less than 1 percent. We can understand how the visual system does this by introducing the concept of *operating curves.*

Operating Curves

An **operating curve** simply describes the relationship between the intensity of a light and how bright that light appears. Figure 10.4 shows a curve that defines a large operating range. The operating range is the sloping portion of the curve from an intensity of about 100 to about 1 billion (10^9). Within this range, changing the intensity causes changes in the brightness of the stimulus (review p. 18, in Chapter 1, for a discussion of the difference between intensity and brightness). For example, if we increase the intensity from A to B, the brightness increases from A′ to B′. Below 100 and above 10^9 the curve becomes horizontal, and changing the intensity does not affect the brightness. It might seem that this would be an ideal operating range for the visual system, because it is large enough to handle intensities ranging from the dimness of your basement to the brightness of your backyard. Unfortunately, there is a problem. To achieve this large operating range, we have sacrificed sensitivity to physical contrast. That is, we would have difficulty telling the difference between two intensities that are close together, because a small intensity change causes only a very small change in the brightness.

For good sensitivity to physical contrast, our operating curve should look like the one in Figure 10.5. This curve represents good physical contrast sensitivity, because a small change in intensity causes a large change in brightness. Increasing the intensity from A to B increases the brightness from A′ to B′, a larger change than for the operating curve of Figure 10.4. However, the problem with the curve in Figure 10.5 is that it represents a very narrow operating range. If this were the operating curve for your visual system, you could see over only a very small range of intensities. For example, if you

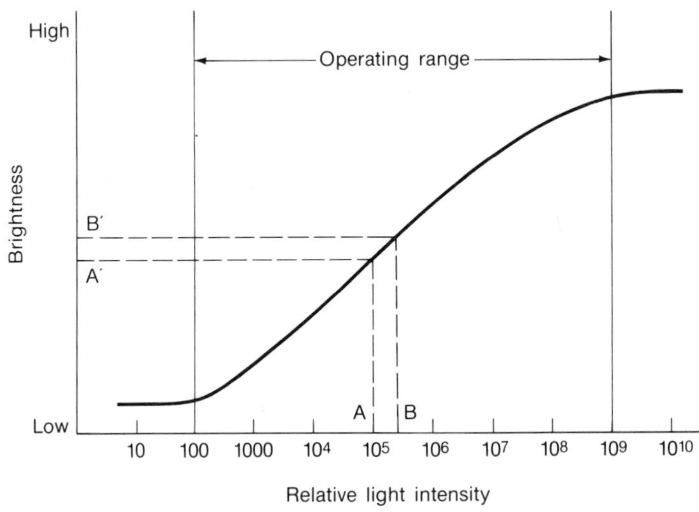

Figure 10.4 An operating curve that results in a large operating range but poor contrast sensitivity.

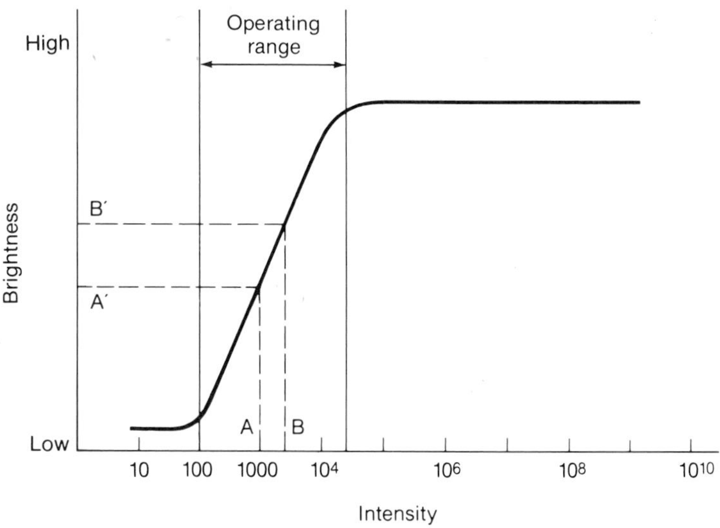

Figure 10.5 An operating curve that results in good contrast sensitivity but a small operating range.

could see well in the low intensities of your basement, you would not be able to distinguish between the objects in the backyard.

How can the visual system achieve good physical contrast sensitivity *and* a large operating range? The visual system achieves this result by using a fairly narrow operating range, such as that in Figure 10.5, and shifting this range to match the level of illumination. Figure 10.6 shows how this works. In dim light, the visual system operates according to curve A; when the light level is increased, the curve shifts to B; and when the level is further increased, the curve shifts to C. In other words, at a particular level of illumination, the visual system works within a fairly narrow operating range that is set to respond at that level of illumination. When the illumination is changed, the operating curve shifts to match the new level of illumination. This shifting of the curve is what is happening during light and dark adaptation. In order to achieve good physical contrast sensitivity *and* a large operating range, we must wait for our visual system to adjust to the level of illumination.

A physiological demonstration of this shift in operating curves is shown in Figure 10.7. These curves were obtained by recording from single neurons in the LGN of the cat. The receptive field of the neuron was located, and then the response to test flashes presented to the center of the receptive field was determined. Curve A shows that when the background illumination is dim, this cell operates in the low-intensity range; when the background illumination is raised, the operating range shifts to higher intensities, as shown by curves B, C, and D. Thus, single nerve cells in the visual system have narrow operating curves that shift as the background intensity is changed.

Staying in the Backyard

Now let's stay in the backyard for a while and consider two problems that confront our visual system as we observe the scene. The first problem occurs as we look from one part of the backyard to another. We look up, and our fovea is exposed to the high intensity of the bright sky, but when we shift our gaze downward, our fovea is exposed to the low intensity of the shadows under some bushes. The

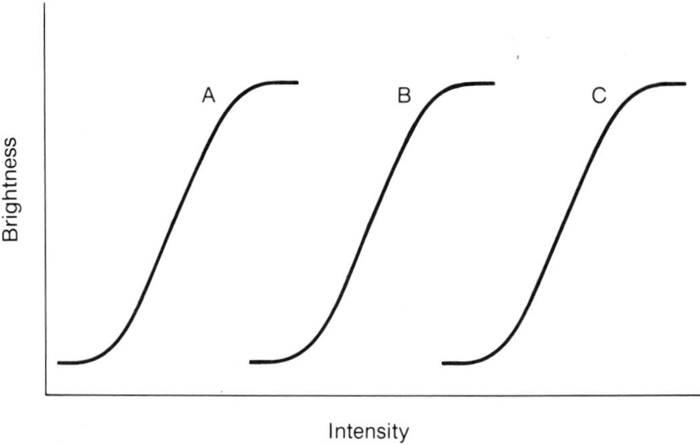

Figure 10.6 A family of operating curves that together cover a large operating range and individually have good contrast sensitivity.

difference between these intensities can represent a range of 1,000 to one or more—a range greater than the range of the visual system's operating curve. The visual system deals with this problem by rapidly adapting to the intensity changes that occur as we shift our gaze from one part of the scene to another. The effect of this **rapid adaptation** is shown in Figure 10.8. The retina shifts its operating curve over a small range within three-tenths of a second after the light level changes; so, as our gaze shifts between light areas and darker areas, the operating curve shifts to partially compensate for these changes in illumination.

The second problem confronting the visual system in the backyard occurs as we look steadily at one part of the scene. When we do this, different areas of the retina are exposed to different intensities—while the fovea is exposed to the intense illumination of the sky, an area of peripheral retina is exposed to the dim illumination from the shadows under the bushes. The visual system deals with this problem by the mechanism of **local adaptation**—different parts of the retina adapt to different levels of illumination. That is, different parts of the retina can set their operating curves at different places, so the retinal area receiving the intense light of the sky is set to operate at high levels of illumination, while the retinal area receiving the dim light from under the bushes is set to operate at lower levels of illumination.

Thus, as we go from basement to backyard, a slow adaptation process sets the general operating curve for the whole eye, and once the general operating curve is set, rapid adaptation and local adaptation help us deal with variations above and below this general level of adaptation.

Simultaneous Contrast

The relative intensities of two adjacent areas are another important influence on perceptual contrast. We saw in Chapter 9 that two areas that reflect *different* amounts of light can appear the *same,* if the ratios of their intensities to the intensities of their surroundings are the same (see Figure 9.24). This effect, which is called **simultaneous contrast,** can also cause two areas that reflect the *same* amount of light to appear *different.* Figure 10.9, which was made by cutting two squares from a piece of grey construction paper and placing one on a dark background and the other on a light background, illustrates this effect. Though both squares reflect exactly the same amount of light, the right one looks light

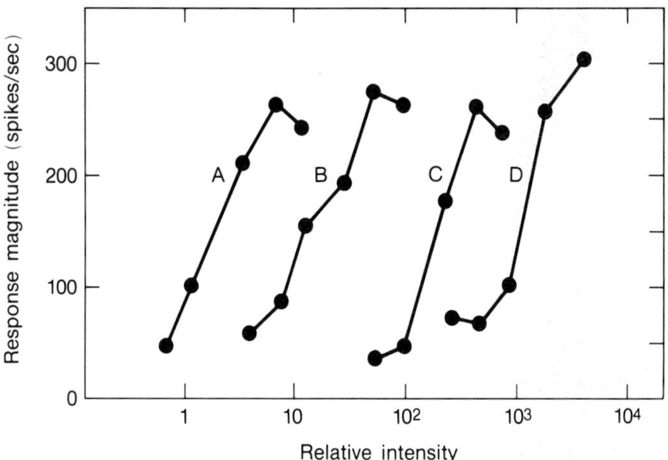

Figure 10.7 Operating curves determined by measuring the relationship between test flash intensity and the firing rate of neurons in the cat's LGN, at four different adapting levels. Curve A was determined by presenting test flashes to the dark adapted retina. Curves B, C, and D were determined by presenting test flashes in the presence of background lights of increasing intensities (B is the least intense, D is the most intense). (From Schweitzer-Tong, 1976.)

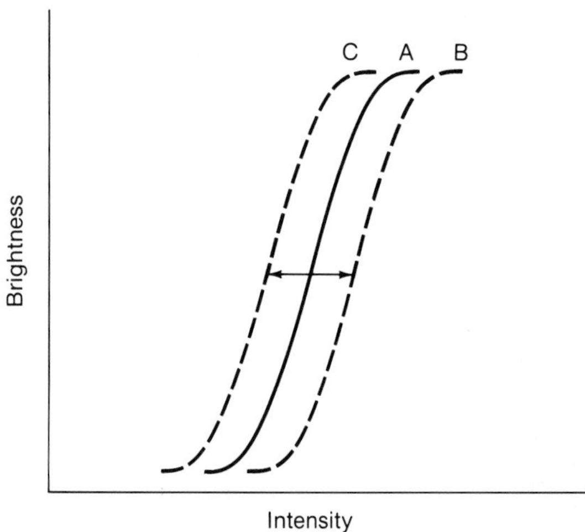

Figure 10.8 Rapid adaptation shifts the operating curves rapidly over a small range as the eye looks at different parts of a scene. Curve B shows how the operating curve shifts up when the eye is exposed to a more intense part of the scene, and curve C shows how the curve shifts down when the eye is exposed to a less intense part of the scene.

Box 10.1 Contrast in Photographs

The two photographs above are of the same face, printed from the same negative, but the one on the left was printed on high-contrast paper and the one on the right on normal contrast paper.

Like human vision, photographic papers have operating curves. The curves for the papers used to print these two photographs are shown below each photograph. The operating curve for the high-contrast paper indicates that all intensities lower than 10 give a white image and all intensities greater than 50 give a black image. Shades of grey occur only at intensities between 10 and 50. Thus, when the photograph is printed on high contrast paper, the gradations of shading in the face are lost and the picture appears mostly as blacks and whites, as in the photograph on the left. Unless you wanted to lose the greys in a picture, you would probably not use high-contrast paper. You would, however, use it if you wanted to enhance the contrast of a scene having a small range of intensities such as might occur in a picture taken in a dimly lit room.

The operating curve for the normal contrast paper indicates that shades of grey occur at intensities between 10 and 250—a much larger operating range than the range of the high-contrast paper. Thus, in the photograph on the right we see the blacks and whites in the face as well as the many shades of grey in between.

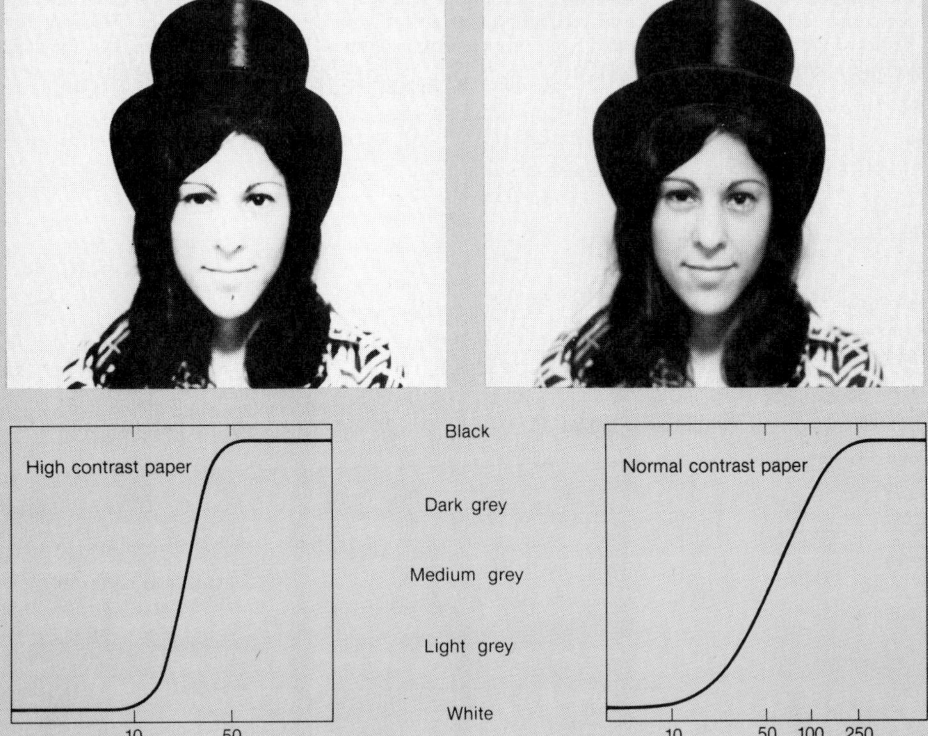

Box 10.1 The same photograph printed on high-contrast paper (left) and normal contrast paper (right). For photographic operating curves, increasing the amount of light presented to the paper increases the ***darkness*** of the image in the photograph. For visual operating curves, increasing the amount of light presented to the observer increases the ***brightness*** the observer perceives.

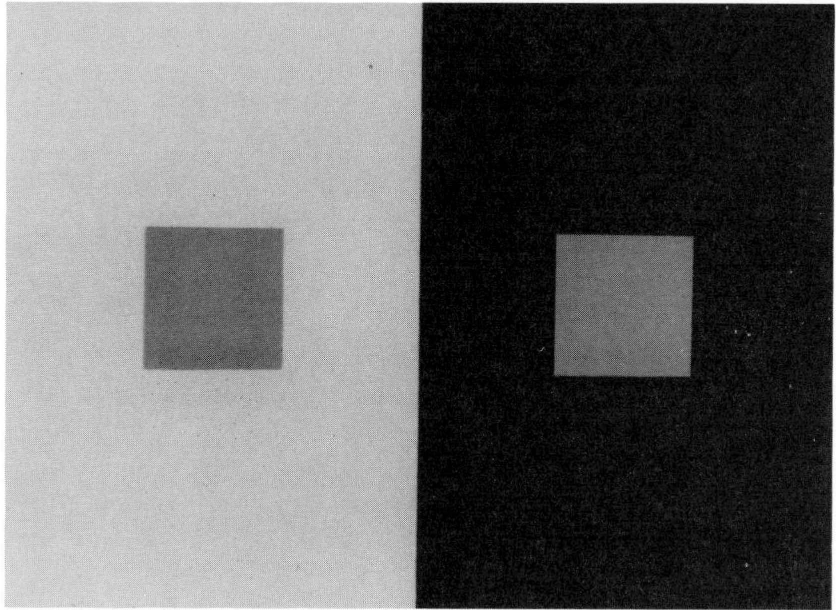

Figure 10.9 Simultaneous contrast. The two center squares reflect the same amount of light into your eyes.

while the left one looks dark. To convince yourself that these two squares really are the same, punch two holes, 2¼ inches apart, in a card or piece of paper and place the holes over the squares. When you do this, the two squares appear identical; but when you remove the card so that the surrounds become visible, the squares again appear different. This simultaneous contrast effect also works for color, as we saw in Color Plate 5.2.

Contours

Contour has been defined as the "narrow region which visually separates something from something else" (O'Brien, 1958). We are particularly interested in contours, not only because they help separate different areas but also because the sharpness of the contour, to a large extent, determines how we perceive the areas on either side of it.

Fuzzy and Sharp Contours

If two areas reflect the same amount of light, but one has a fuzzy contour and the other a sharp contour, the one with the fuzzy contour will look dimmer. As contours between areas become fuzzier, the contrast between them decreases; in fact, if the transition between two areas is very fuzzy, the contrast between them can vanish altogether. If you stare for about 30 seconds at the center of the fuzzy contoured disc in Figure 10.10, you will see the contrast decrease so much that the disc disappears! The contrast has vanished. If you stare at the sharp contoured disc, however, it does not fade—the contrast stays nearly constant.

Box 10.2 Light and Dark in Photographs

Photographs of scenes with a large range of intensities often have areas that are either too light or too dark. This is shown in photographs (a) and (b) below. In picture (a), the hill in the distance is exposed correctly, but the foreground is much too dark. In picture (b), the foreground is exposed correctly but the hill is so light it almost vanishes.

The reason that areas in these two pictures are either too dark or too light is that even low-contrast film with its relatively large operating range cannot handle the large range of intensities in many scenes. Thus, if the photographer exposes the film correctly for the light area, the dark area will be too light; if he or she exposes correctly for the dark area, the light area will be too dark, as shown above. Your eye solves this problem by locally adapting to compensate for very high or very low intensities in parts of a scene.

If film could adapt locally like the eye, then the exposure of each area in the picture could be adjusted independently and the scene would look more like picture (c). In this photograph the darkness of the lighter areas was increased by a darkroom procedure called "burning in," in which the hill in the distance was darkened by exposing it to extra light during the printing process. By using such special techniques we can produce pictures on film that match the perception of light and dark achieved by our visual system.

(a)

(b)

(c)

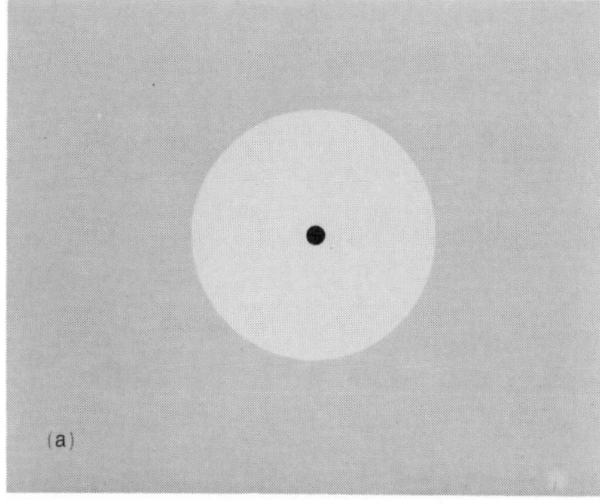

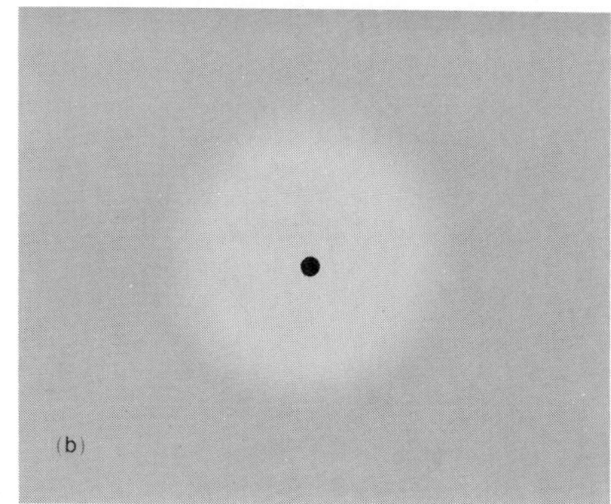

Figure 10.10 Discs with sharp and blurred contours (see text for viewing instructions).

That the fuzzy disc fades, while the sharp disc does not, demonstrates a central principle of visual perception: *the visual system responds well to abrupt changes in the stimulus but poorly to slow changes or no change in the stimulus.* To understand how this principle explains why the fuzzy disc fades and the sharp disc does not, let's consider what happens on the retina when you stare at the discs.

First consider the sharp disc. As you stare at the center of the sharp disc, trying to keep your eyes completely steady, your eyes still move very slightly because of involuntary eye movements,[1] and these movements cause the image of the sharp disc to jiggle on your retina. The jiggling of the sharp disc's image causes the contour of the disc to fall first on some receptors and then on others. The amount of light stimulating the receptors near the sharp contour is therefore constantly changing, and it is this change that keeps the disc visible.

Now let's consider the fuzzy disc. The image of this disc also jiggles on the retina. However, the jiggling of the fuzzy contour causes only slight changes in the amount of light stimulating the receptors near the contour. If you keep your eyes still enough, the small change in stimulation caused by movement of this fuzzy contour is not enough to maintain perception, and the disc fades from view.

[1]You can demonstrate these involuntary eye movements to yourself by staring for about 30–60 seconds at the small black dot in the middle of Figure 10.11 and then looking at the white dot. Even if you try very hard to look steadily at the white dot, you will see an image of the grid pattern jiggling on the top of the figure. This jiggle is due to involuntary eye movements.

Stabilizing the Image

Based on our experience with the fuzzy disc, we might guess that if we could stop the sharp disc's contour from jiggling on the retina, the sharp disc might also fade. But how might we stop this jiggle? We could stop the eye from moving, but that is very difficult. A better way is to let the eye continue to move normally while causing the object at which it looks to move with the eye. If the eye moves one degree to the right and the object simultaneously moves one degree to the right, the object's image will not move on the retina. This technique is called the **stabilized image** technique, because the image is stabilized on the retina. One method of stabilizing the image on the retina is shown in Figure 10.12 (Pritchard, 1961). The observer wears a specially designed contact lens, attached to which is a small projector that beams the stimulus into the observer's eye. Every time the eye moves, the projector system and stimulus move with it; therefore, the resulting image always stimulates the same retinal receptors.

The stabilized image technique helps us find out what happens to the sharp disc when its contour does not jiggle on the retina. When the stabilized

Box 10.3 The Spreading Effect

Look at the middle design in Color Plate 10.1. It appears to contain two fields of red, a dark field on the left and a lighter one in the center. However, in reality, both reds are physically the same. To see that the red is, in fact, the same across the picture, look very closely at the contour between the light and dark. If you concentrate your attention on the red background and ignore the black and white lines, you will see that the red is the same on either side of the contour. In fact, the contour that you see when you look at the picture as a whole vanishes.

The darkening of the red on the left side is due to the presence of the black lines, and the lightening of the red in the center is due to the white lines. It is as though the darkness of the black has spread, making the red on the left darker, and the lightness of the white has spread, making the red on the right lighter. Bezold, who described this effect in 1876, called it the ***spreading effect,*** and later workers have called this effect ***assimilation.*** Note that assimilation has an effect opposite to simultaneous contrast. In simultaneous contrast, adding a lighter ring around an area makes it appear darker. In assimilation, placing light lines inside a homogeneous field makes the field appear lighter.

Although you may think that assimilation is simply an obscure perceptual effect, it is, in fact, one of the basic principles that underlie our perception of pictures such as Mellan's engraving of *Samson and Delilah* below. Compare the shading on the light areas of Delilah's face to the shading of the background. The background looks darker than the light area on the face not because the background is shaded, but because the background contains horizontal lines. The horizontal lines in the background function in the same way as the black lines in the color plate. The darkness of the lines in the background "spreads," making the spaces between the lines, which are actually as white as the face, appear darker.

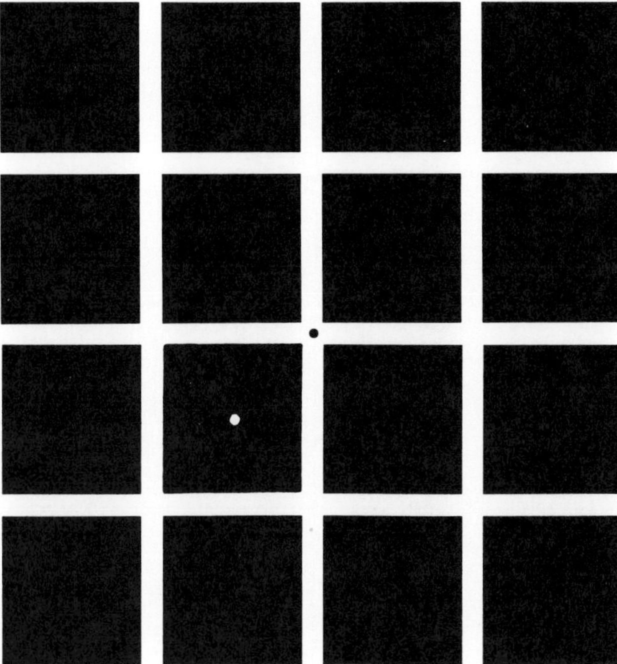

Figure 10.11 Grid pattern for perceiving involuntary eye movements (see text for viewing instructions). (From Verheijen, 1961.)

disc is first presented, the observer sees it, but within about 3 seconds, the disc completely fades from view. By stopping the sharp contour from stimulating new receptors, we eliminate perception of the disc.

Since the stabilized disc fades because of a lack of change in the stimulation of receptors, we might wonder why the center of the sharp disc doesn't fade when viewed under normal (nonstabilized) conditions. You can understand why we might expect the center to fade, by considering what's happening to the receptors under the center of the disc. Although involuntary eye movements cause the disc's center to move along with the contours, this movement causes no change in the amount of light falling on the receptors under the center, because the center of the disc is homogeneous. Therefore, we might expect the center to fade like a stabilized image. However, the center does not fade. Apparently, the center doesn't fade because the sharp contour that surrounds it is still present and jiggling around on the retina.

John Krauskopf (1963) demonstrated that the presence of the sharp contour keeps the center of the disc from fading. In his experiment, the observer looked at a stimulus display like the one in Figure 10.13. The inner disc was red and the outer ring green. Under normal viewing conditions, the observer perceived a red disc inside a green ring. But Krauskopf stabilized the contour between the two discs, while leaving the outer contour unstabilized. Thus, the outer contour of the green ring was jiggling on the retina, as it would under normal viewing conditions, but the contour between the red and green areas was stabilized. The result was that the inner contour and everything it contained disappeared! The red disc vanished and was filled in by green. This dramatic demonstration shows that the jiggling of contours maintains our perception of the area inside those contours. We don't

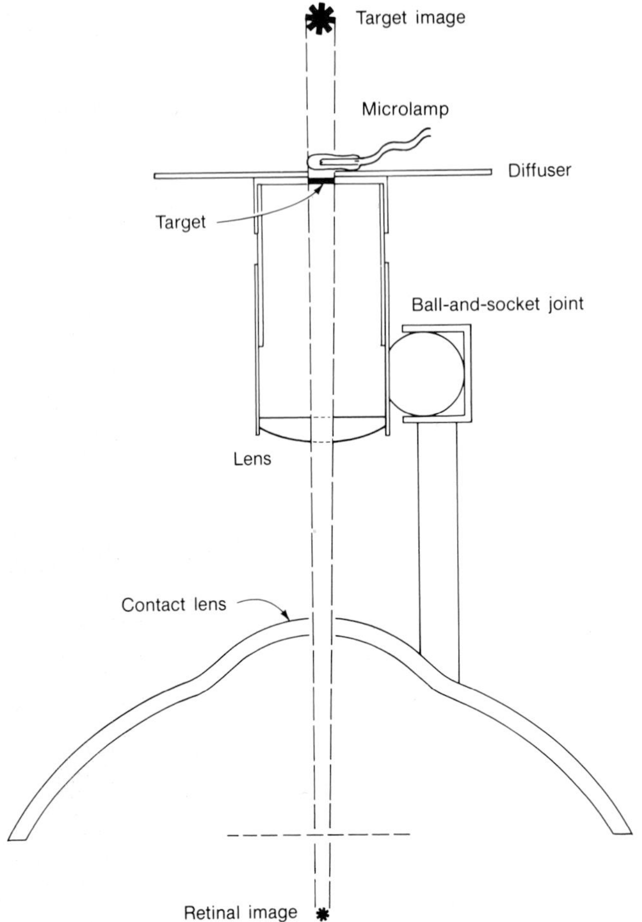

Figure 10.12 Stabilized image device used by Pritchard (1961). Since the contact lens and projector move every time the eye moves, the image projected into the eye always falls on the same point on the retina, as suggested at the bottom of the illustration. The entire optical system weighs only one-quarter of a gram.

know why the jiggling contours keep the inside area from fading, but there is no doubt that without sharp contours, contrast becomes poor or vanishes altogether.

Apparent Position in Space

Alan Gilchrist (1977) has performed an ingenious experiment to show that our perception of contrast can be affected by how we perceive an object in space. Gilchrist took a white card (which we will call the "test" card) and caused it to appear either white or dark grey by changing only the card's *apparent* position in space. His setup is shown in Figure 10.14. The observer looks through a peephole and sees three cards: a black card; the white test card, attached to a doorway inside a dimly lit room; and another white card, attached to the far wall of a brightly lit room. The key to the experiment is how the three cards are perceived in relation to one another. In part one of the experiment, the cards mounted as shown in Figure 10.14 are perceived as shown in Figure 10.15(a). The test card and black card appear to be inside the dimly lit room, with the test card located in front. In part two of the experiment, the actual positioning of the cards is exactly the same, as shown in Figure 10.15(b), but the depth cue of overlap is changed so that the observer perceives the display as shown in Figure 10.15(c). The test card now appears to be in back of the white card on the far wall of the brightly lit room. It is important to remember that in both parts of the experiment, the ***actual*** position of the test card is always the same. What changes is the ***apparent*** position of the test card.

The observer's task in Gilchrist's experiment was to judge the lightness of the test card. The observer did this by matching the test card to one of a series of papers ranging from black (given a value of 2.0) to white (given a value of 9.5). In part one of the experiment, the average lightness, as judged by a number of observers, was 9.0, just slightly less white than the whitest paper available. This makes sense, since the test card is made of white paper.

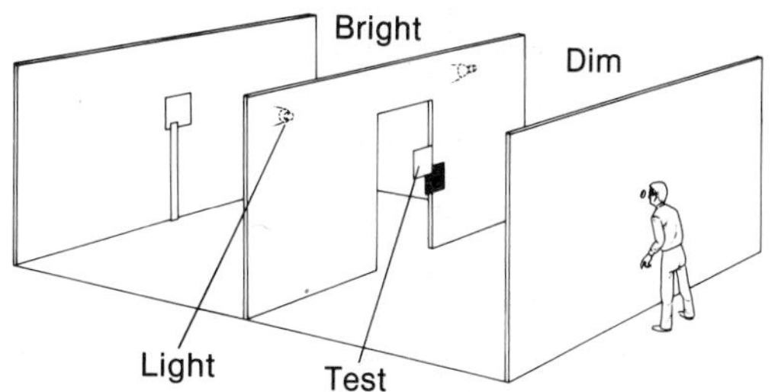

Figure 10.14 The setup used by Gilchrist (1977). The observer looks at the three cards through a peephole. The intensities of light reflected from each card remain constant throughout the experiment. The test card and the card on the far wall are both made of white material, but the card on the far wall reflects much more light than the test card because it is illuminated by lights mounted on the center partition.

The key result of Gilchrist's experiment is that when the apparent position of the test card was changed in part two, the card's appearance also changed. When the test card appeared to be behind the white card in the far room, as in Figure 10.15(c), the average lightness of the test card was judged to be 3.5, a dark grey.

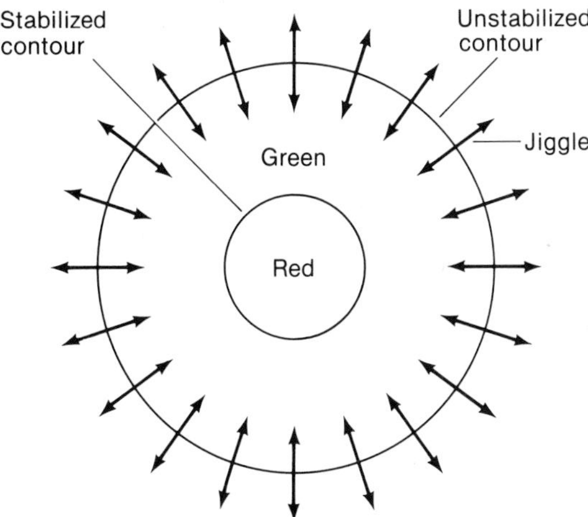

Figure 10.13 The stimulus display used by Krauskopf (1963). In the actual display, the inner disc was red and the outer ring green. The contour between the two colors was stabilized so that it remained stationary on the retina, but the outer contour was not stabilized, so it jiggled on the retina, as indicated by the arrows on the contour.

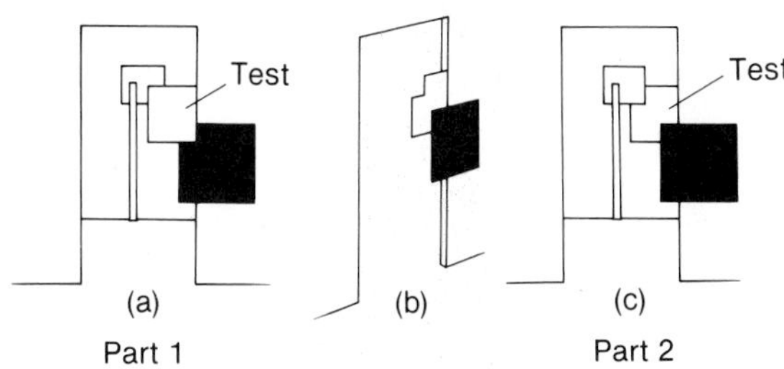

Figure 10.15 (a) What the observer sees in part one of Gilchrist's experiment. When the test card appears to be in front of the black card, it appears white. (b) The arrangement of the cards in part two of the experiment. The test card is now attached to the back of the black card, and its upper left corner is cut out so that it appears as in (c)—located in back of the card on the far wall—when viewed through the peephole. When the test card appears to be in back of the card on the far wall it appears dark grey. Note that the test card's appearance changes, even though both the card's actual position in space and its illumination remain constant throughout the experiment.

Box 10.4 The Ganzfeld, or, What Happens When You Wear Ping-Pong Balls on Your Eyes?

One way to eliminate the movement of contours on the retina is to use the stabilized image technique. Another way is to eliminate the contours by having observers look into a homogeneous field called a **Ganzfeld.** Wolfgang Metzger (1930; described in Koffka, 1935) constructed one of the first Ganzfelds. He had observers sit facing a whitewashed wall that filled their entire field of view. They reported feeling as though they were looking into a fog with a filmy appearance like the sky.

Another way to achieve a Ganzfeld is to have the observer (your author, in this case) wear half a ping-pong ball over each eye (Hochberg et al., 1951). In this situation, the observer perceives a fog like the fog Metzger's observers saw. But more interesting than this fog is the observer's perception when colored lights are projected onto the ping-pong balls. When this is done, some observers at first report seeing the colors, but after 3–6 minutes they say that the colors disappear completely. In most cases observers don't want to believe that the lights are not being dimmed or turned off, even when the experimenter tells them that the colored lights are still present. The effect of a Ganzfeld is similar to the effect of a stabilized image: Elimination of moving contours eliminates the observer's perception of form and color (Cohen, 1957).

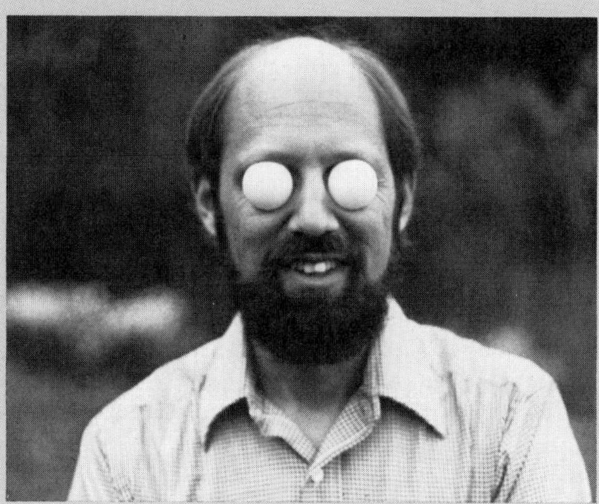

Why do these results occur? In part one of the experiment, the test card is perceived as white because it is seen as being next to the black card. This makes sense, because the white test card reflects much more light than the black card. But in part two of the experiment, Gilchrist succeeds in making the same white card appear dark grey. This occurs because the test card now appears to be located on the rear wall, with the brightly illuminated white card. In this situation, the visual system might reason along the following lines: there are two cards in the far room; since they are in the same room, they are both illuminated by the same light; however, since the test card reflects much less light than the other card, it must be made of much darker material; therefore, the test card should be perceived as dark grey. (Note that the real reason the test card reflects less light is that it is actually in the dimly lit near room. The visual system has been fooled, however, into thinking that the test card is in the brightly lit far room.) This explanation may sound familiar because we proposed a similar one at the end of Chapter 9, when we discussed how our interpretation of the way an object is illuminated can influence our perception of lightness.

Gilchrist's experiment shows that our perception of an object's apparent position in space can influence our perception of contrast. This result, however, is not simply an interesting demonstration of the effect of spatial position on contrast. It has important implications for any theorizing we wish to do about the physiological basis of contrast. We will, therefore, consider this experiment again, at the end of this chapter.

Spatial Frequency

If you look at the two striped patterns on the left of Figure 10.16 from a distance of about two feet, you will probably notice that the contrast of the top pattern is higher; that is, the difference in the lightness of the black and white bars is more pronounced in the top pattern. These two patterns differ in contrast because the **spatial frequency**—the number of bar per unit distance—is lower in the top pattern than in the bottom pattern. That these different patterns have different contrasts has important implications for our understanding of how the visual system works. Before we can understand these implications, however, we need to introduce two important concepts: (1) the *grating stimulus* and (2) the *contrast sensitivity function.* We will consider each of these concepts, in turn, below.

The Grating Stimulus

In our discussion of spatial frequency, we will be concerned with stimuli like those shown in Figure 10.16. These patterns of alternating black-and-white bars are called **gratings,** and we can specify the properties of these gratings, or any other gratings, by specifying the grating's (1) waveform, (2) physical contrast, and (3) spatial frequency.

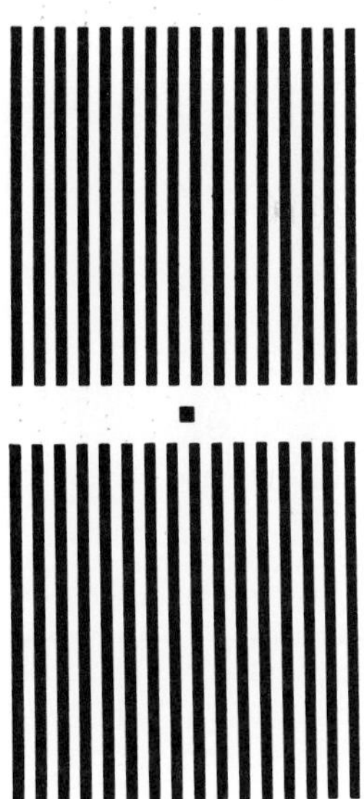

Figure 10.16 The two gratings on the left illustrate the effect of spatial frequency on contrast. When the gratings are viewed from a distance of about 2 feet, the high-spatial-frequency grating on the bottom appears to have less contrast than the low-spatial-frequency grating on the top. These gratings can also be used for a selective adaptation experiment that will be discussed later in the text (From Blakemore & Sutton, 1969.)

Waveform. The waveform of a grating refers to the shape of the grating's intensity distribution. Figure 10.17 shows two gratings and their intensity distributions. The intensity distribution for the grating in Figure 10.17(a) shows that this grating's intensity abruptly alternates between high (for each white bar) and low (for each black bar), and since the distribution looks like a series of squares, this grating is called a *square-wave grating*. The intensity distribution for the grating in Figure 10.17(b) shows that this grating's intensity alternates more gradually between high and low, and since this distribution follows a mathematical function called a sine wave, this grating is called a *sine-wave grating*. There are also rectangle-wave gratings, triangle-wave gratings, and many others, all named by the shape of their intensity distributions, but in our discussion we will concentrate on square-wave and sine-wave gratings.

Physical contrast. A grating's *physical contrast* is equal to its amplitude (A) divided by its mean intensity (M), which is indicated by the dashed line in Figure 10.18. Figure 10.18 shows two gratings with different contrasts. In Figure 10.18(a), the dark bars are very black and the light bars are very white, so the contrast is high; whereas in Figure 10.18(b), the dark bars are dark grey and the light bars are light grey, so the contrast is lower.

Spatial frequency. A grating's spatial frequency is the number of cycles per unit distance along the grating, where one cycle is the unit of the grating that repeats itself. Thus, for the grating in Figure 10.18, one cycle would be a dark bar plus a white bar. Since there are 3½ cycles and the grating is 2 inches wide, we could say that this grating has a spatial frequency of 3½ cycles per 2 inches, or 1¾ cycles per inch. However, spatial frequency is usually not specified in cycles per inch but in cycles per degree of visual angle. (If necessary, see pp. 232–235 of Chapter 9 to review the concept of visual angle.) The advantage of this method of specifying spatial frequency is that it tells us what is happening on the retina.

To understand how specifying spatial frequency in terms of cycles per degree of visual angle tells us what happens on the retina, look at Figure 10.19.

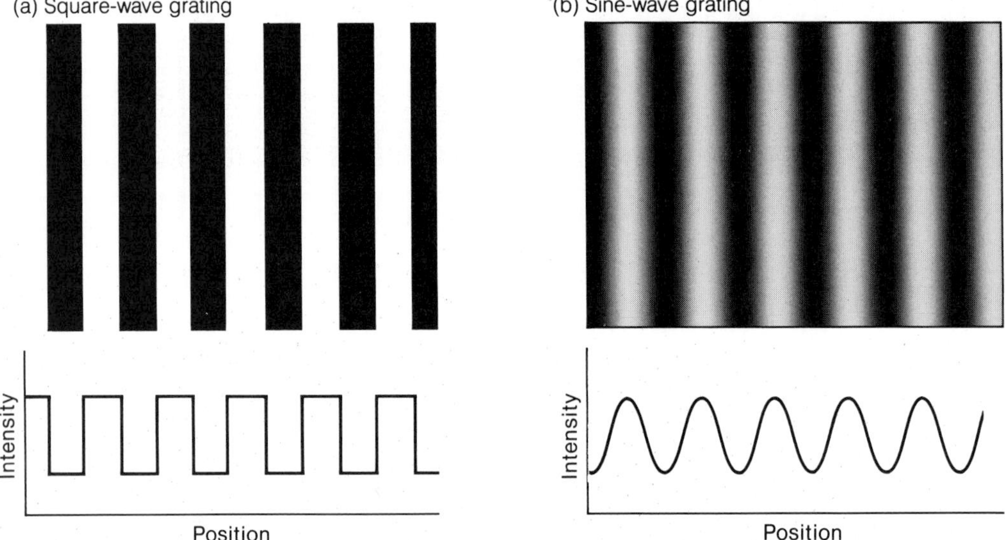

Figure 10.17 (a) Left: a square-wave grating and its intensity distribution. (b) Right: a sine-wave grating and its intensity distribution. The abrupt changes in intensity of the square-wave grating are seen as sharp contours, whereas the more gradual changes in intensity of the sine-wave grating are seen as fuzzy contours.

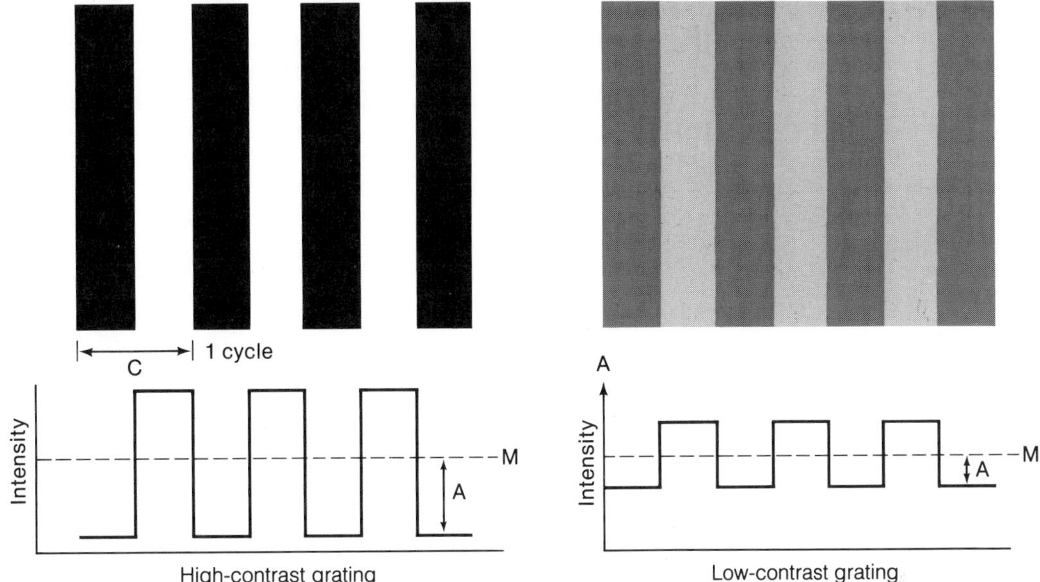

Figure 10.18 A high-contrast, square-wave grating (left) and a low-contrast grating (right). Both gratings have the same mean intensity (M), indicated by the dashed line, but the grating on the left has a larger amplitude (A). The contrast of these gratings can be determined by dividing the amplitude of the grating by its mean intensity. The distance marked C, on the grating on the left, indicates the size of one cycle. Each of these gratings contains 3½ cycles.

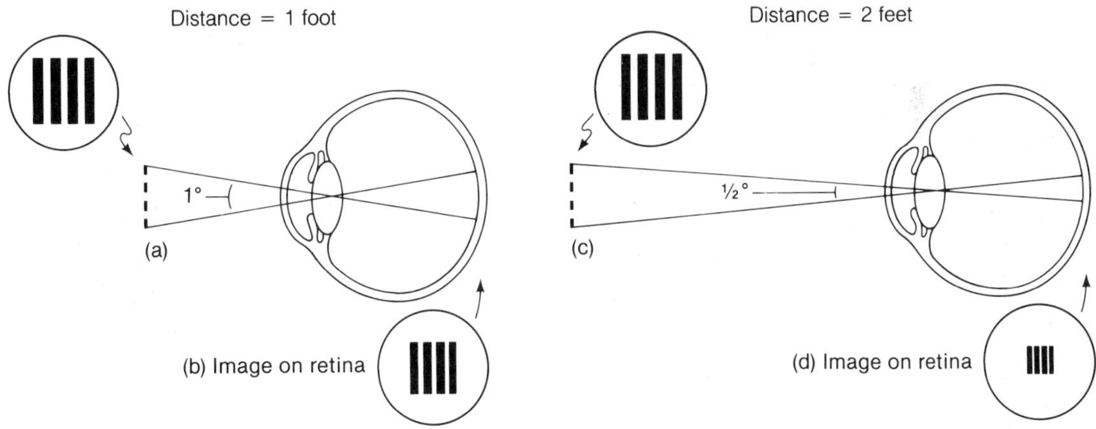

Figure 10.19 (a) A 3½-cycle grating viewed so that the visual angle of the grating is one degree. The spatial frequency of this grating under these viewing conditions is 3½ cycles per degree. (b) The image of the grating from (a) on the retina. (c) The same grating viewed from twice the distance so that the visual angle is now one-half degree. Under these viewing conditions, the spatial frequency of the grating is 7 cycles per degree. (d) The image of the grating from (c) on the retina, showing that moving the grating farther decreases the size of its image on the retina.

When the 3½-cycle grating in Figure 10.19(a) is viewed from a distance of one foot, its visual angle is one degree, and the grating, therefore, covers one degree of visual angle on the retina, as shown in Figure 10.19(b). Thus, the spatial frequency of this grating is 3½ cycles per degree. However, if we move farther away and view the grating from a distance of 2 feet, as shown in Figure 10.19(c), the visual angle becomes ½ degree; so the spatial frequency of the grating becomes 3½ cycles per ½ degree, as shown in Figure 10.19(d), or 7 cycles per degree. Thus, the spatial frequency of a grating depends on both the size of the grating's bars and the distance from which the grating is viewed. Making the bars smaller *or* increasing the viewing distance increases spatial frequency.

The Contrast Sensitivity Function

We saw in Figure 10.16 that the low-frequency grating (wide bars) has more contrast than the high-frequency grating (narrow bars). But these are just two gratings. What would be the result if we looked at others? Is the contrast of low-frequency gratings always higher than that of high-frequency gratings? To answer this question, we must systematically measure the contrast of gratings over a wide range of frequencies. We need to determine the **contrast sensitivity function (CSF).**

The contrast sensitivity function is a plot of the physical contrast needed to see a grating versus the grating's spatial frequency. To measure the CSF, we start with a grating of very low frequency (wide bars) and physical contrast so low that the grating cannot be seen—that is, it appears to be a homogeneous grey field. We then slowly increase the physical contrast of the grating until the observer reports that he or she can just barely see its bars. This level of physical contrast is called the *threshold* for seeing the bars. To plot the CSF, we convert the threshold into **contrast sensitivity** by the relationship contrast sensitivity = 1/threshold, just as we did for the spectral sensitivity curves we determined in Chapter 1 (see Figures 1.8 and 1.9). The result of this determination is point A in Figure 10.20.

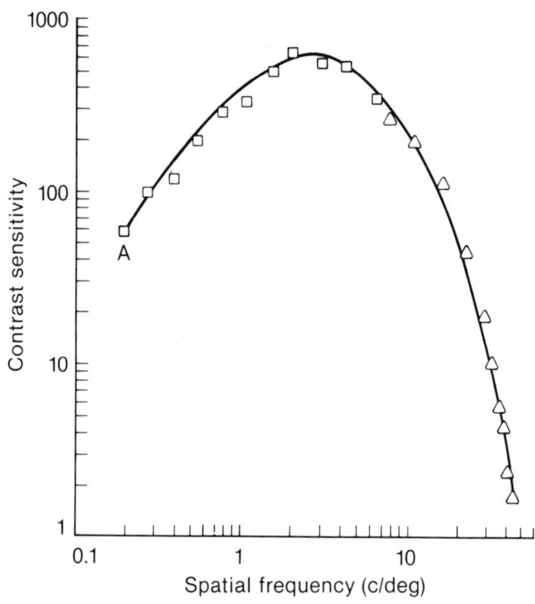

Figure 10.20 A contrast sensitivity function (CSF) for a sine-wave grating, as measured by Campbell and Robson (1968).

Next, we increase the grating's spatial frequency by narrowing the bars and then repeat the above procedure, determining how much physical contrast enables the observer to just barely see the bars. If we continue this procedure for gratings with higher and higher spatial frequencies, we get the curve in Figure 10.20, which is the contrast sensitivity function for a sine-wave grating (Campbell & Robson, 1968). This CSF tells us that the visual system is most sensitive to sine-wave gratings with spatial frequencies of about 3 cycles per degree. (You may wonder why Campbell and Robson used sine-wave rather than square-wave gratings. They did so because sine waves provide the basis for a mathematical technique called *Fourier analysis,* which tells us some important things about the visual system. If you are interested in Fourier analysis, see Appendix C.)

The CSF in Figure 10.20 tells us that our ability to detect a grating depends on the grating's spatial frequency. Rather than stop at this point, however, many investigators wondered what mechanism might underlie this function. One idea is that the contrast sensitivity function reflects the activity of a number of *detectors,* or *channels,* each of which are sensitive to a narrow range of spatial frequencies.

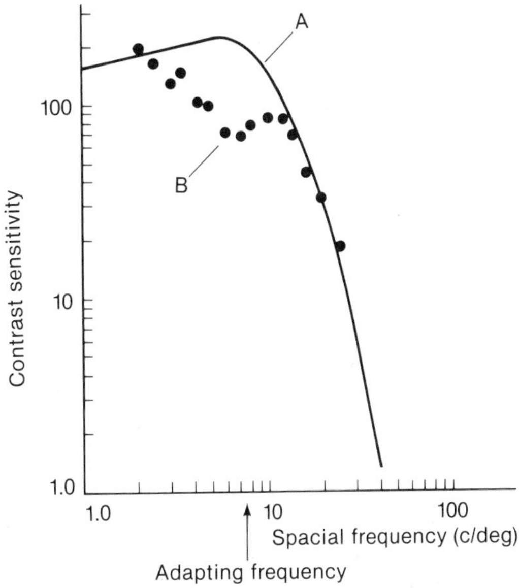

Figure 10.21 The results of a selective adaptation experiment. The solid curve (A) indicates the CSF determined prior to adaptation. The data points (curve B) indicate the CSF determined after adaptation to a 7½-cycle/degree grating. Note that the adaptation causes a maximum decrease in contrast sensitivity at a spatial frequency of 7½ cycles/degree. (From Blakemore & Campbell, 1968.)

Spatial Frequency Channels in the Visual System

The idea of **spatial frequency channels**—channels in the visual system that are sensitive to narrow ranges of spatial frequencies—is supported by experiments in which a procedure called selective adaptation is used. A typical selective adaptation experiment would be done as follows:

1. Determine the contrast sensitivity function (curve A in Figure 10.21).
2. Adapt a person by having him look at a 7½-cycle/degree grating for 1–2 minutes.
3. Redetermine the contrast sensitivity function. The resulting CSF, curve B of Figure 10.21, shows decreased sensitivity only in the frequency range around the adapting frequency of 7½ cycles/degree. If we repeated this experiment with a different adapting stimulus, we would get the same result except that the CSF would show decreased sensitivity only near the frequency of the new adapting stimulus.

The results of this selective adaptation experiment (and many similar experiments) support the idea that the CSF consists of a number of channels, each of which are sensitive to a narrow range of spatial frequencies. Many researchers believe it likely that these channels correspond to neurons in the cortex. The adaptation observed in our experiment is explained by assuming that inspection of the adapting grating fatigues those neurons sensitive to a narrow range of frequencies around the adapting frequency. When we redetermine the CSF, the response of these neurons is decreased, which causes the decreased sensitivity around the adapting frequency.

An adaptation experiment that you can perform yourself is shown in Figure 10.16—a stimulus that was used in experiments by Colin Blakemore and Peter Sutton (1969). Move your eyes back and forth along the horizontal line between the two adaptation patterns on the left, for about 60 seconds. This adapts you to the wide (low-frequency) bars above the line and to the narrow (high-frequency) bars below the line. After this adaptation, shift your gaze to the dot between the two gratings on the right and compare the spacing between the lines of the top and bottom gratings. The lines of the top grating probably will appear more closely spaced than those of the bottom grating, even though the spacing of the bars is actually the same.

Blakemore and Sutton say that this change in our perception of the bars results from the fatiguing, during adaptation, of neurons that respond to wide bars (or low spatial frequencies) in the area of the upper grating and to narrow bars (or high spatial frequencies) in the area of the lower grating. We won't go into the details here, but the idea of channels tuned to specific spatial frequencies predicts (1) that adaptation to low spatial frequencies should shift our perception of the grating on the upper right to higher frequencies (causing the lines in this grating to appear closer together) and (2) that adaptation to high spatial frequencies should shift our perception of the grating on the lower right toward lower frequencies (causing the lines in this grating to appear farther apart).

Contrast Sensitivity and Visual Acuity

Before the idea of spatial frequencies was introduced, most work on the resolving power of the visual system was limited to measuring visual acuity (see pp. 79 and 153). Most visual acuity experiments, however, study only a small portion of our ability to resolve details. To illustrate this, let's consider an experiment in which visual acuity is measured by using a grating stimulus. When using a grating to measure acuity, the experimenter usually asks what the finest grating is that a person can detect, and this detection task is usually carried out with a high-contrast grating made up of very fine (high-spatial-frequency) lines. Although such an experiment does measure the maximum resolving power of the visual system, we find only how well we can resolve stimuli with high contrasts and high spatial frequencies. In so doing, we ignore the vast majority of our visual experience, because our everyday experience consists of stimuli with a wide range of spatial frequencies and contrasts. Seeing fine details (reading a book, threading a needle) involves high spatial frequencies, whereas seeing larger objects (a nearby car, a person's face, a whole person) involves low spatial frequencies. When you read a book under good lighting conditions, you are dealing with high spatial frequencies and high contrast, but when you try to find a seat in a dark movie theater without bumping into people, you are dealing with low spatial frequencies and low contrast.

The idea of spatial frequencies and the contrast sensitivity function help us better understand how we see the wide range of stimuli with which we daily come in contact. An experiment that compared the CSFs of a group of 73-year-old observers to those of a group of 18-year-old observers provides a good example of the application of spatial frequency analysis. When these two groups were given a standard visual acuity test, both groups showed essentially the same visual acuity. However, the CSFs of the two groups were a different story. Though the ability to see narrow (high-frequency) gratings was the same for both groups (as would be expected from their similar acuities), the older observers required three times more contrast to see the wide (low-frequency) gratings (Sekuler, Hutman, & Owsley, 1980). Sekuler et al. suggest that the older observers' insensitivity to low spatial frequencies may explain why older people often have difficulty recognizing faces and many other objects that require low-spatial-frequency information.

Another demonstration of the value of the spatial frequency approach is illustrated by the picture in Figure 10.22. When you look at this picture from a distance of 2 or 3 feet, you should be able to see a faint white border between the grey shadow on the right side of the container and the grey background. But something interesting happens as you move closer to the picture. As you move closer and closer, the border becomes less and less distinct, until when you are very close (6–12 inches) the border may even vanish! This phenomenon can't be understood in terms of visual acuity, because as we move closer, we should be able to see details better. However, we can easily understand this in terms of spatial frequency. By moving closer, we decrease the spatial frequency of the border (see Figure 10.19);

Figure 10.22 *Requiem* (detail), pastel and acrylic, by Tom McDonald, 1982. When viewed from a distance of about 3 feet, the low-contrast border on the upper right of the container is visible. However, by moving closer to the picture, you decrease the spatial frequency of the border, and if you move still closer, the border becomes less distinct and may even vanish.

and, since our sensitivity to contrast drops off at low spatial frequencies (see the CSF in Figure 10.20), moving closer causes us to lose our ability to detect the faint, low-contrast white border.

The spatial frequency approach, therefore, tells us much more than a simple measure of visual acuity. And, from all the evidence accumulated to date, it appears that there are both channels sensitive to narrow frequency ranges and neurons in the visual system tuned to respond to a narrow range of spatial frequencies.

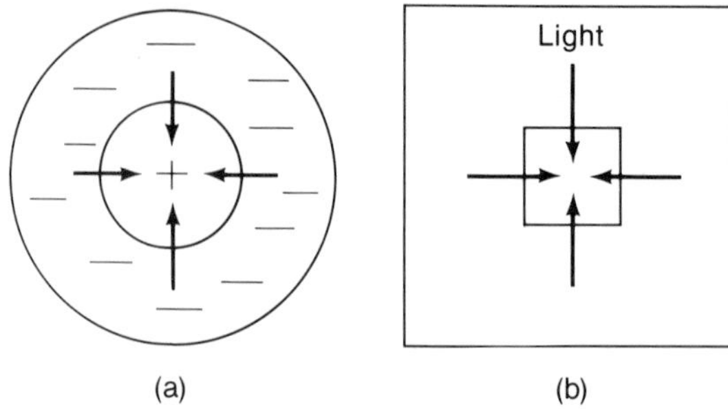

Figure 10.23 (a) A center-surround receptive field with an excitatory center and an inhibitory surround. Stimulation of the surround inhibits the center via lateral inhibition, as indicated by the arrows, and decreases the ability of the receptive field's center to cause the cell to fire. (b) The image cast on the retina by the left side of the simultaneous contrast demonstration of Figure 10.9. The light surround stimulates receptors surrounding the dark square, and this stimulation sends lateral inhibition to the area stimulated by the square, as indicated by the arrows. This inhibition decreases the firing caused by the square, which makes the square appear darker.

The Physiological Bases of Contrast

It appears likely that neurons in the visual system, perhaps the simple or complex cortical neurons described in Chapter 2, are responsible for the spatial frequency channels described above. The involvement of neurons in contrast perception is also suggested by the effect of simultaneous contrast, as shown in Figure 10.9. In this figure, the light surround on the left darkens the square in the center. This is similar to what happens to cells with center-surround receptive fields (Figure 2.26), in which stimulation of the inhibitory surround can inhibit the response of the excitatory center via lateral inhibition (Figure 2.27). This analogy between center-surround receptive fields and simultaneous contrast, illustrated in Figure 10.23, suggests that lateral inhibition is responsible for darkening the center square on the left of Figure 10.9.

Though lateral inhibition plays an important role in determining our perception of contrast, it cannot explain all contrast phenomena. Let's consider, for example, how we would expect lateral inhibition to influence our perception of the grey triangles in Figure 10.24. Since both triangles are bounded on two sides by black and on one side by white, we would expect the amount of lateral inhibition coming from the areas surrounding the triangles to be identical. However, most people see the triangle in the upper part of the cross as lighter than the triangle in the lower part, a result which is difficult to explain in terms of lateral inhibition.

Perhaps the most impressive evidence against the idea that all contrast phenomena can be explained by lateral inhibition are the results of the Mach card demonstration, described in Chapter 9 (Figures 9.31 and 9.32), and Alan Gilchrist's experiment, described in this chapter (Figures 10.14 and 10.15). Consider what happens to the Mach card's image on the retina when it flips from one orientation to another. Since the card never actually moves, the perceptual flip is not accompanied by any change in the pattern of light and dark on the retina. Because lateral inhibition depends solely on the pattern of light and dark on the retina, it cannot explain the change in lightness seen in the Mach card demonstration. Similarly, in Gilchrist's experiment, a very small change in the pattern of light and dark on the retina (see Figure 10.15) is accompanied by a large change in the appearance of the test card, which cannot be explained by lateral inhibition.

So, while we can provide physiological explanations for some things, we are still unable to explain many perceptual phenomena in terms of physiology. Though we can explain simultaneous contrast in terms of lateral inhibition, we cannot explain why such stimuli as the Mach card and Gilchrist's test card change their appearance when they change their apparent positions in space. This, of course, does not mean that physiological explanations do not exist—something happens in our brain when the

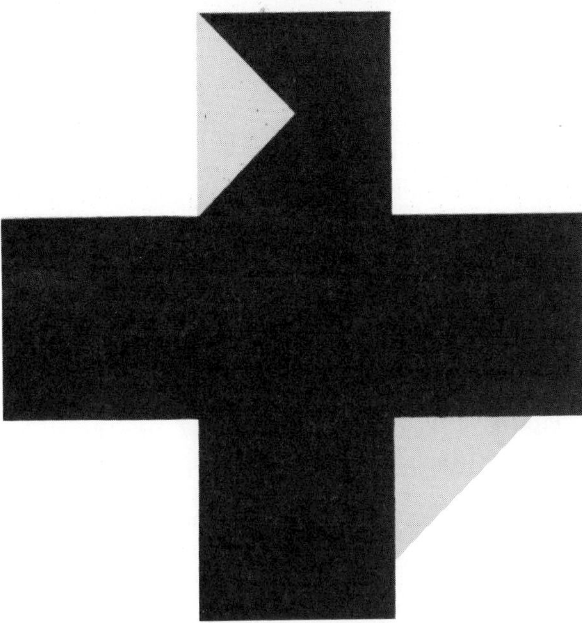

Figure 10.24 The Wertheimer-Benary demonstration. The two grey triangles reflect the same amount of light, but the one in the upper part of the cross looks slightly lighter.

Mach card "flips" or when Gilchrist's card changes to a new position; it is just that we are only now beginning to be able to explain perception physiologically.

Summary

1. The visual system must be able to work over a wide range of intensities while still maintaining good contrast sensitivity. It accomplishes this by working within a fairly narrow operating range that matches the average intensity of the scene. If a large change occurs in the average intensity of a scene, the operating range is shifted by the process of light or dark adaptation to match the new average intensity. This shift in operating curves with changes in illumination levels has been demonstrated physiologically.
2. Like human vision, photographic papers have operating curves. These curves differ for high- and low-contrast paper.
3. In many scenes, especially outdoor scenes with bright skies and dark shadows, the range of intensities is larger than the visual operating range. The retina can extend the operating range slightly by rapid adaptation, a process that causes small but rapid changes in the sensitivity of the retina as we look at different parts of the scene.
4. Because the operating range of film is insufficient to handle the large range of intensities in many scenes, unmanipulated photographs of such scenes will have areas that are too light or too dark.
5. The contrast between two adjacent areas depends on the relationship of the intensities of the two areas. This principle, which is called simultaneous contrast, shows that intensity alone does not determine the contrast between areas or the brightness of individual areas.
6. A process called the spreading effect, or assimilation, can change our perception of the lightness of an area. Placing light lines inside a homogeneous field makes the field appear lighter.

7. Sharp contours result in greater contrast between areas than do fuzzy contours.

8. Involuntary eye movements keep the eye in constant motion so that contours continually stimulate different areas of the retina. That we need this continual change in stimulation to maintain perception of the contour is demonstrated by stabilized image experiments. These experiments show that when contours do not move on the retina, the contours and everything inside them fades from view.

9. Contour movement on the retina can be eliminated by having an observer look into a homogeneous field called a Ganzfeld. The effect of the Ganzfeld is similar to the effect of a stabilized image.

10. Our perception of contrast can be affected by how we perceive an object in space.

11. Our perception of contrast is affected by a pattern's spatial frequency. The contrast sensitivity function—a plot of the sensitivity for seeing a grating versus the grating's spatial frequency—indicates that we are maximally sensitive to frequencies of about 3 cycles per degree.

12. The results of selective adaptation experiments support the idea that the contrast sensitivity function reflects the activity of a number of detectors, or channels, each of which are sensitive to a narrow range of spatial frequencies. Many researchers believe it likely that these channels correspond to neurons in the cortex.

13. Most visual acuity experiments study only our ability to resolve stimuli with high contrasts and high spatial frequencies. In such experiments, we ignore the vast majority of our visual experience, because our everyday experience consists of stimuli with a wide range of spatial frequencies and contrasts. The contrast sensitivity function and the idea of spatial frequencies help us better understand how we see the wide range of stimuli with which we daily come in contact.

14. Though lateral inhibition plays an important role in determining our perception of contrast, it cannot explain all contrast phenomena. For example, lateral inhibition cannot explain why our perception of contrast is influenced by an object's apparent position in space.

Glossary

Assimilation *See* Spreading effect. (272)

Contour A narrow region that visually separates two areas. (269)

Contrast The physical contrast of a grating stimulus is the grating's amplitude divided by its mean intensity. (262)

Contrast sensitivity Sensitivity to physical contrast. Contrast sensitivity is usually measured by taking the reciprocal of the minimum physical contrast that a grating must have for the observer to barely see the bars of the grating. (280)

Contrast sensitivity function (CSF) A plot of contrast sensitivity versus the spatial frequency of a grating stimulus. (280)

Ganzfeld A totally homogeneous field. (276)

Grating A stimulus of alternating light and dark bars that is used to measure visual acuity and is often used in experiments in which contrast sensitivity is measured as a function of spatial frequency. (277)

Local adaptation An increase or decrease in the eye's sensitivity in a small area of the retina. (266)

Operating curve A function relating the psychological response of brightness to a light's physical intensity. (264)

Operating range The range of intensities over which increases in light intensity cause increases in the perceived brightness of the light. (262)

Perceptual contrast The perception of differences in lightness in adjacent areas. (262)

Physical contrast Differences in light intensity in adjacent areas. (262)

Rapid adaptation An increase or decrease in the eye's sensitivity to light that occurs during the first third of a second after the intensity of light reaching the eye decreases or increases. (266)

Simultaneous contrast Our perception of the lightness of an area can be affected by the lightness of the surrounding area. (266)

Spatial frequency In a grating stimulus, spatial frequency refers to the frequency with which the grating repeats itself per degree of visual angle.

For more natural stimuli, high spatial frequencies are associated with fine details and low spatial frequencies are associated with grosser features. (277)

Spatial frequency channels Hypothesized channels in the visual system that are sensitive to narrow ranges of spatial frequencies. (281)

Spreading effect (or assimilation) Adding fine lines to a homogeneous field affects the lightness of the field. Light lines lighten the field and dark lines darken the field. (272)

Stabilized image An image that is optically stabilized on the retina, so that when the eye moves, the image stays imaged at the same place on the retina. (271)

Chapter Eleven

Perceiving Movement

A Passing Umbrella by Kenneth Antol, 1983

Everyone is familiar with movement because movement is all around us, but you may not realize that there are a number of different ways to cause the perception of movement. To introduce movement perception, we will look first at five different ways that we can make a spot of light appear to move and then consider some of the mechanisms proposed to explain these different types of movement.

Five Ways to Make a Light Appear to Move

If you wanted to make a small spot of light appear to move, it would be logical to simply move the spot of light across an observer's field of view. This situation, represented by Figure 11.2(a), is called **real movement,** since the light is really moving. As Figure 11.2 indicates, however, there are four other ways to make an observer say "the light is moving." These four ways to achieve the perception of movement do not, however, involve real movement, as in (a), but are illusions of movement, because in all four cases the light appears to move, even though it is actually stationary.

Figure 11.2(b) shows that we can create an illusion of movement between two lights by flashing one light on and off, waiting about 60 msec (1 msec = 1/1,000 sec), and then flashing the other light on and off. The movement that is perceived between them is called **stroboscopic movement.** This is the type of movement that Max Wertheimer was studying when he founded Gestalt psychology (see Chapter 7), and it is the movement you perceive in a film, which is actually a series of still pictures flashed one after another.

Another way to move the spot is to surround it with another object and then move this other object. Figure 11.2(c) indicates that moving the rectangle to the left causes the dot to appear to move to the right. This effect is called **induced movement.** You've experienced induced movement if you've seen the moon racing though the clouds on a windy night. The moving clouds induce movement in the (relatively) stationary moon.

Perhaps the simplest way to make the light appear to move is to turn out all the room lights, as indicated in Figure 11.2(d). When the surrounding framework of the room is not visible, the small stationary light begins moving, usually in a rather erratic path. This illusion is called **autokinetic movement.**

Finally, if an observer first views a pattern that is moving in one direction, such as the moving belt of stripes shown in Figure 11.3, and then views the spot of light, the spot (and its surroundings) will appear to move in a direction opposite to the movement of the stripes. This is called an **aftereffect of movement.**

Thus, when we talk about perceiving movement, we are talking about a perception that can be achieved in at least five different ways, four of which result in illusions of movement and one of which results in real movement.

Real Movement

Much of the research on real movement has focused on determining which factors influence our threshold for perceiving movement and our perception of the velocity of movement. You can just barely perceive the movement of a spot in a homogeneous field when it is moving with a velocity of about one-sixth to one-third of a degree of visual angle per second (Aubert, 1886). If the spot in Figure 11.4 is viewed from a distance of one foot, it would take about 14 seconds to move from A to B at a velocity of one-third of a degree per second, and at that velocity you would just barely be able to perceive its movement. If, however, we added some vertical lines to the space between A and B, you could perceive its movement even at velocities as low as one-sixtieth of a degree of visual angle per second. Since adding the lines enhances our sensitivity to movement, our perception of movement cannot be explained simply by considering the moving dot. We must also take the surroundings into account.

J. F. Brown (1931a) did a series of experiments which showed that our perception of an object's velocity is influenced by its surroundings. When an observer fixates on a string, in a display like the one in Figure 11.5, and then watches a small object move from the bottom to the top of the rectangle at a constant speed, he or she reports that the object appears to accelerate when near the bottom or top of the rectangle or when near the fixation string at the center of the rectangle.

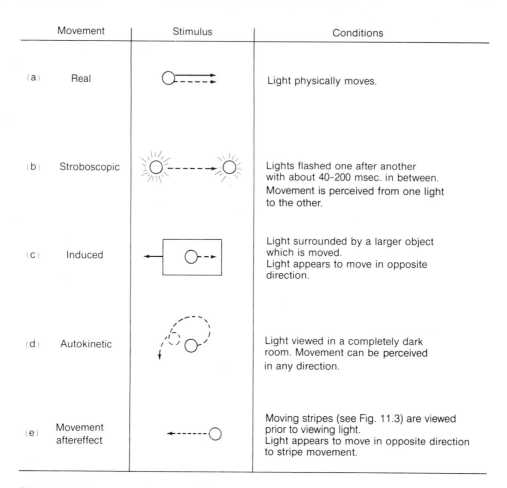

	Movement	Stimulus	Conditions
(a)	Real		Light physically moves.
(b)	Stroboscopic		Lights flashed one after another with about 40–200 msec. in between. Movement is perceived from one light to the other.
(c)	Induced		Light surrounded by a larger object which is moved. Light appears to move in opposite direction.
(d)	Autokinetic		Light viewed in a completely dark room. Movement can be perceived in any direction.
(e)	Movement aftereffect		Moving stripes (see Fig. 11.3) are viewed prior to viewing light. Light appears to move in opposite direction to stripe movement.

Figure 11.2 Five ways to make a spot of light appear to move. Solid arrows indicate actual movement and dashed arrows indicate the perceived movement of the light. Note that the light physically moves only in (a). In all other cases, perceived movement occurs in the absence of physical movement of the spot.

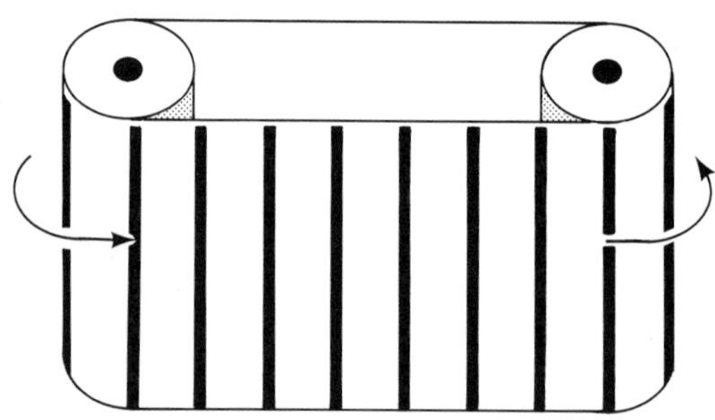

Figure 11.3 Stimulus for the movement aftereffect of Figure 11.2(e).

In another experiment, Brown (1931b) found that both the size of the object and the rectangle through which it moves influence the observer's perception of velocity. He had an observer sit in a dimly lit room between a small rectangle and a large rectangle, like those shown in Figure 11.6. He then asked the observer to equalize the speed of a large dot moving across the large rectangle with the speed of a small dot moving across the small rectangle. Brown found that when the large rectangle was ten times larger than the small one, the large dot had to move seven times faster than the small one for them appear to move at the same speed. In other

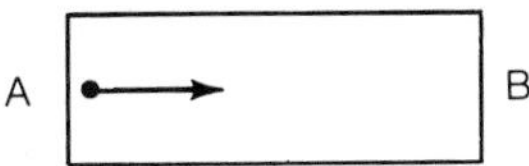

Figure 11.4

words, an elephant in a large cage must move much faster than a mouse in a small cage if they are to appear to move at the same speed! This effect, which is called **velocity transposition,** shows that two images moving across the visual field at different speeds can be perceived to be moving at the same speed.

Velocity transposition plays a role in our perception of film. Imagine that you are viewing a film in which a car drives from the left to the right side of the screen in 3 seconds. If you then move the projector back so that the size of the image on the screen increases, the car will still move across the greater distance in 3 seconds. (If this weren't so, films with larger images would take longer!) However, according to the principle of velocity transposition, we would perceive the car to be moving at about the same speed in both cases. Though no one has done Brown's velocity transposition experiment with films, it seems unlikely that, say, tripling the size of the film image would triple the perceived velocity of the car. A car traveling at 50 miles per hour on a small screen will not appear to be traveling at 150 miles per hour on a larger screen.

Brown further demonstrated a lack of correspondence between the velocity of the image moving across the retina and perceived velocity, by increasing the distance between his moving dots and the observer. Increasing distance decreases the visual angle through which the dots travel (see p. 232) and therefore decreases the speed with which the dots move across the observer's retina. Brown showed that increasing the distance by a factor of 20 decreases the perceived velocity by less than half. A large change in retinal velocity is accompanied by only a small change in perceived velocity. This effect is called **speed constancy.**

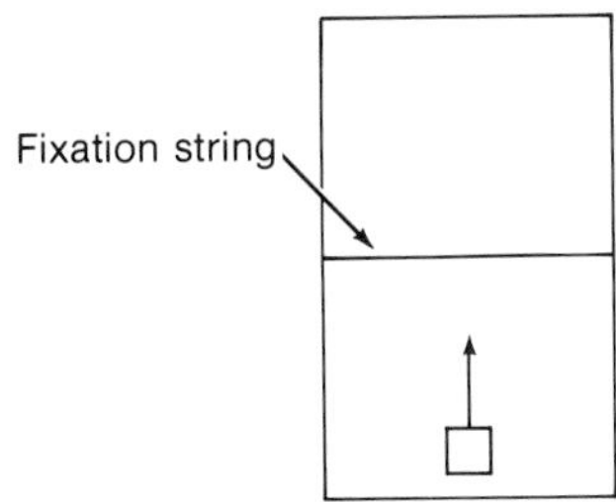

Figure 11.5

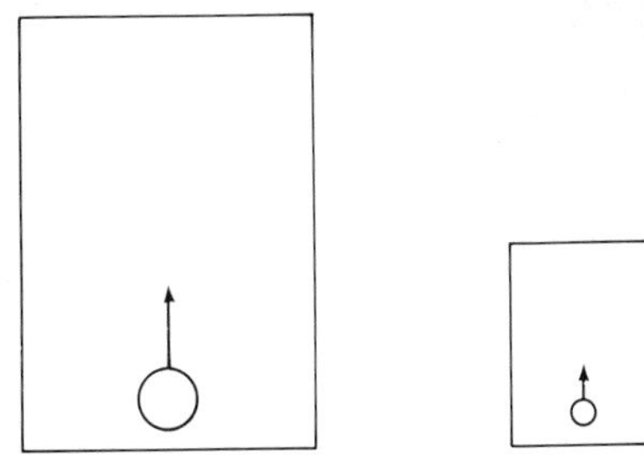

Figure 11.6 Velocity transposition. The large circle must move faster than the samll circle to appear to move at the same speed.

The lack of correlation between retinal and perceived velocity also occurs when an observer follows a moving object with his eyes. When a person fixates on a moving object, the object's image does not move on the retina, yet it appears to be moving about one and a half to two times *faster* than when the eyes are stationary and the object's image moves across the retina! Clearly, the perception of real movement does not depend on the movement of an image across the retina. What, then, is responsible for the perception of real movement?

Mechanisms for the Perception of Real Movement

Movement Detectors

In discussing the mechanisms of real movement perception, we must consider that we perceive movement (1) when the eyes are stationary, so the image of the stimulus moves across the retina, and (2) when the eyes are tracking the moving stimulus, so its image stays stationary on the retina. We will first consider physiological mechanisms that operate when the eye is stationary.

When an image moves across the retina, it stimulates a series of receptors, one after another. The brain reads the message from these receptors by means of a **movement detector,** such as the one described in Chapter 2. We saw in that chapter that signals from a number of receptors can feed into a single cell so that the cell fires only when movement occurs in a particular direction. We also saw that some cells in the cat's cortex respond only to movement in a specific direction, and Figure 11.7 shows how the magnitude of a complex cell's response varies with the direction of a bar's movement (Blakemore & Tobin, 1972). When the bar is oriented at about +20 degrees, the cell fires 53 impulses per presentation, but the response drops rapidly to the cell's spontaneous firing level on either side of this orientation. Thus, a bar of light oriented at 20 degrees will cause a large burst of firing, and this will signal the presence of a bar moving in that direction.

But simply monitoring the firing rate of this cell does not provide enough information to determine the direction of movement, because the cell's firing rate can be affected both by the bar's direction ***and*** by its intensity. So, if we increase the bar's intensity, we might find that the cell fires at 53 impulses per second, even when the bar is not oriented at +20 degrees. Fortunately, however, the bar causes many nerve cells to fire as it moves across the retina, and the brain can determine the direction of movement by taking the responses of all these cells into account. As a bar oriented at +20 degrees moves across the retina, it will cause large bursts of firing in cells that prefer this orientation and smaller bursts in cells that prefer other orientations. By analyzing the overall pattern of responses from many of these cells, the brain can determine the direction of movement. This is the same idea we introduced on page 60 of Chapter 2, when we suggested that the brain probably determines the properties of a stimulus by looking both at the responses of individual feature detectors and at the overall firing pattern of many of these feature detectors.

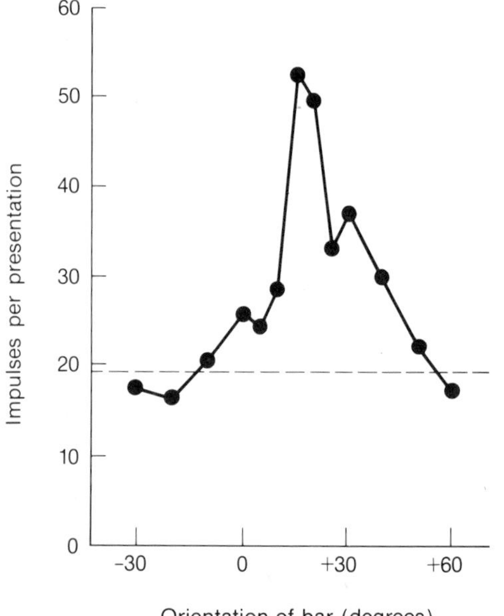

Figure 11.7 "Directional tuning curve," showing the relationship between the orientation of a moving bar and the response of a complex cell in the cat's cortex. The cell responds best when the bar is oriented at about 15–20 degrees. The dashed line indicates the rate of spontaneous firing. (From Blakemore & Tobin, 1972.)

The *velocity* of movement may be signaled in a similar fashion. Just as there are movement detectors tuned to respond best to different directions of movement, so there are cells in the visual system tuned to respond best to different velocities. Figure 11.8 shows **velocity tuning curves** for two cells in the cat's LGN. These curves indicate that cell A responds best to velocities of about 8 degrees of visual angle per second, while cell B responds best to velocities of about 60 degrees of visual angle per second.

So far, the brain's detection of movement seems fairly straightforward. Movement detectors, which fire as the stimulus moves across the retina, provide plenty of information; however, movement detectors cannot explain your perceptions in cases when (1) you perceive movement when there is *no* movement on the retina and (2) you perceive no movement when there *is* movement on the retina. In the first case, you perceive movement in the absence of movement on the retina when you follow a moving object with your eyes. Your eye movements keep the object's image stationary on your fovea, but you still perceive the object as moving. In the second case, you perceive no movement when there is movement on the retina as you move your eyes to look at different parts of a scene or as you walk through a scene. Though the image of the scene moves across your retina, you do not perceive the

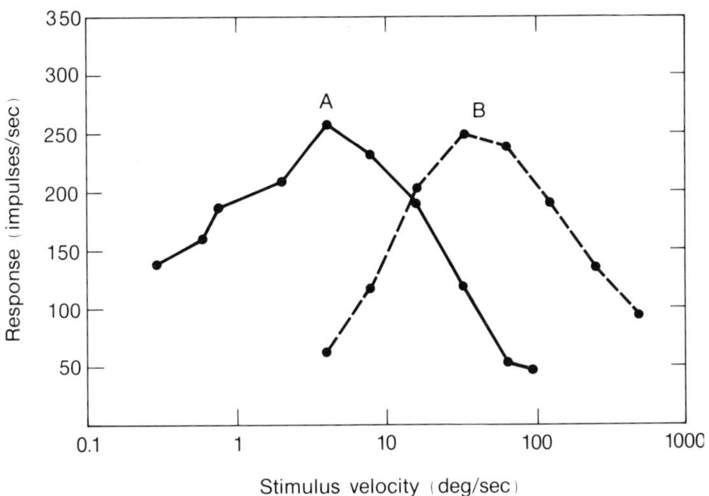

Figure 11.8 "Velocity tuning curves" of two cells in the cat's lateral geniculate nucleus (LGN). Cell A responds best to slow movement of the bar across the retina, while cell B responds best to rapid movement of the bar across the retina. (From Frishman, 1979.)

scene as moving. Therefore, any mechanism capable of dealing with these situations must be able to tell whether retinal stimulation results from movement of the stimulus, movement of the observer, or both. We will now consider two responses to our need for such a mechanism: J. J. Gibson's theory and the corollary discharge theory.

J. J. Gibson: Information in the Scene

When we discussed J. J. Gibson's approach to perception in Chapter 8, we saw that he avoids physiology. Thus, Gibson would not find appealing an explanation of movement perception based on movement detectors. Instead, he looks for information in the scene that tells us whether the stimulus or the observer is moving. To understand Gibson's thinking, let's look at what happens in three different situations.

1. A person walks past a stationary observer. This is the case most easily handled by movement detectors, since an object (our walking person) is sweeping across the retina, as shown in Figure 11.9. Gibson would say that the walking person provides information about movement by moving *relative to the background*—he covers and then uncovers parts of the background as he walks by. This case is not as interesting to Gibson as the two below, because here the observer is stationary. Remember from our discussion on pages 220–228, in Chapter 8, that

Figure 11.9 A person moving from left to right past a stationary observer. In this situation, the person moves across the observer's field of view, but the background remains stationary.

Box 11.1 What's Moving in a Film?

What's moving in the picture below? Most people would say that the man and the car are moving, even though the background is blurred as if *it* is moving. We often see images like this in films. Our hero is madly racing somewhere, but no matter how fast he moves he stays in sharp focus and, in addition, never leaves the screen. Images such as this are achieved by means of a **tracking shot,** in which the camera moves along with the object that is moving.

When you see a shot like the one below, why do you assume that the man and the car are moving and not the background? For one thing, you know that men and cars are much more likely to move than cement walls. Also, the man's appearance (he *looks* as if he is running) indicates that he is running. Finally, from your long experience in seeing films, you are familiar with tracking shots. If you had never seen a film before, a tracking shot might fool you into thinking that the man was stationary and the background was moving. Your assumptions about what is moving in a film, therefore, are based largely on your past experiences in seeing films and on your knowledge of the nature of the environment.

The importance of your past experience with film is also illustrated by your interpretation of the results of a **pan shot,** in which the camera stays at one location and smoothly scans a scene. For example, when the camera pans across a landscape from left to right, the resulting film shows the landscape moving across the screen from right to left. Having seen this effect in many films, you do not think the landscape is moving; instead, you realize that a moving camera is showing you what a stationary landscape looks like. (Or, if the film shows a person beginning to look from left to right in the shot immediately preceding, you assume that you are being shown what the person is seeing.)

Another familiar scene shows people inside a car and changing scenery moving past the car window. From our past experience in moving cars, movement of the entire scene outside the window usually indicates that the car is moving, so we assume that we are watching people in a moving car. This impression of movement, however, may simply be a creation of the filmmaker, since this type of shot is often accomplished by filming the interior of a stationary car inside a studio and later adding images of a moving scene to the windows.

Thus, in film, things that move across the screen are often stationary, and stationary things on the screen are often moving. Our decision as to what's moving and what isn't is usually based not only on the physical movement on the screen but also on what seems reasonable, based on our experience with moving objects in the world and on our past experiences in watching films.

Gibson is most interested in situations in which the *observer* is moving.

2. A person walks past the observer, who moves his eyes to follow the person. In this situation, shown in Figure 11.10, the image of the moving person remains stationary on the observer's retina, but the background image moves across the retina in a direction opposite to the person's movement. We perceive movement even though the walking person does not move on our retina, because the walking person moves *relative to the background*. According to Gibson, in both this situation and the one above, the walking person's movement relative to the background is the crucial information we need to perceive the person as moving.

3. The observer walks past a stationary person. In this situation, shown in Figure 11.11, both the person and the background sweep across the observer's retina. That the person and background do not move relative to one another provides information that the observer is moving, not the person or the background. In this situation we perceive no movement, despite much movement on our retina, because there is no movement relative to the background.

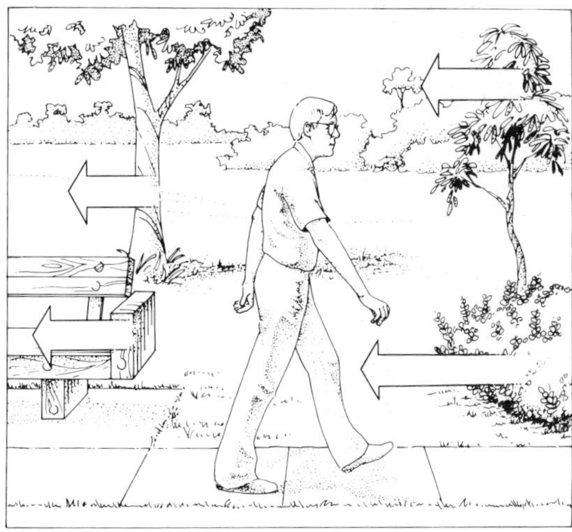

Figure 11.10 A person moving from left to right, as in Figure 11.9, but the observer follows the person with her eyes. This causes the image of the moving person to remain stationary, while the background flows from left to right.

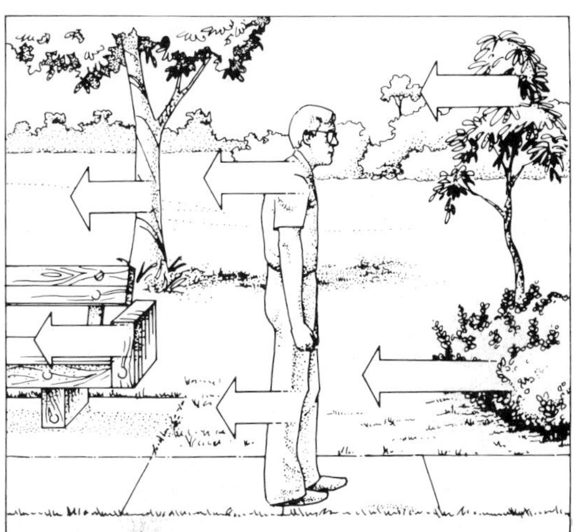

Figure 11.11 The observer moves past a stationary person from left to right, causing the image of the person and the background to move from right to left across the observer's field of view.

Gibson's explanation works well when we can see both the object and background. However, some researchers have noted that Gibson cannot explain how we can perceive movement when movement relative to the background is not visible, as in the case when a spot of light is seen in the dark or when an object is seen against a completely textureless background. In these cases, the background cannot provide the information we need to decide whether the object is moving or we are moving.[1] To deal with this situation, we must turn to corollary discharge theory.

The Corollary Discharge

The idea underlying **corollary discharge** theory is that information about the observer's movement is provided not only by information in the stimulus array, as Gibson suggests, but also from signals gen-

[1]We should note that Gibson would not be bothered by his theory's inability to deal with these situations, because he would consider them artificial situations that might occur in perception laboratories but would be extremely rare in real life. Remember that the motivation behind Gibson's theory is to explain perception for real-life situations in which the observer moves through the environment (see Chapter 8).

erated inside the observer (von Holst, 1954; Teuber, 1960; Gyr, 1972). Figure 11.12 shows the model proposed by this theory. Assume that an observer decides to move his eyes to the left. A motor signal (M) is sent from the motor area of the brain to the eye muscles, which activates the muscles and causes the eye to move to the left. The eye movement causes the image on the retina to move to the left, which results in a **sensory movement signal** (S) in the optic nerve. (We call this a "sensory movement" signal to differentiate it from the sensory signal present when the eye is stationary. Thus, sensory movement refers to the signal generated by the *movement* of an image across the retina.)

The sensory movement signal indicates that an image has moved across the retina, and it will cause us to perceive the scene as moving when it reaches the visual receiving area. This, of course, is undesirable because the eye has moved and not the scene, and it is here that the corollary discharge (C) comes into play. The corollary discharge is the same as the motor signal (M) sent from the brain to the eye muscles; therefore, it carries information that a signal to move left has been sent from the brain to the eye. This corollary discharge cancels the sensory movement signal at a site called the **comparator,** thereby causing the scene to remain stationary.

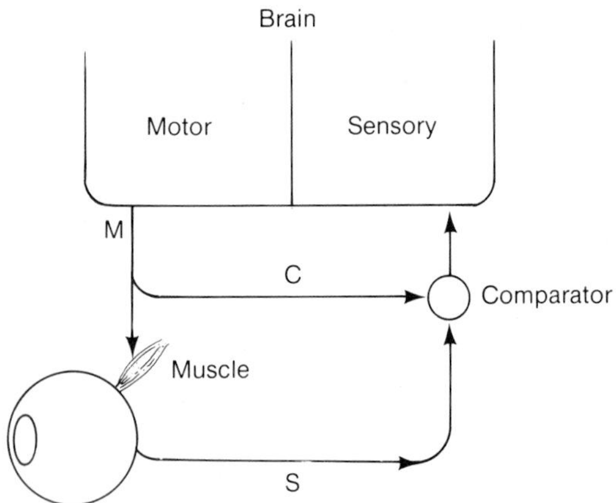

Figure 11.12 Diagram of the corollary discharge model. (From Teuber, 1960.) The brain is divided into two areas: the motor area, which sends motor signals to muscles, and the sensory area, which receives sensory signals from the sense organs. The exact location of the comparator is not specified.

This model makes two predictions that can be tested. First, it predicts that if the eye moves without corollary discharge, then the sensory movement signal will not be canceled, and the scene, therefore, should appear to move. You can demonstrate this to yourself by gently pushing on the side of your eyelid, as shown in Figure 11.13, so that your eye moves. Moving your eye with your finger in this way eliminates the corollary discharge, because the eye moves without a motor signal being sent from the brain to the eye muscles. When you do this, you will notice that the scene appears to jiggle back and forth as you move your eye, just as the model predicts.

The model also predicts that the scene should appear to move if there is a corollary discharge but no sensory movement signal to cancel it. This is more difficult to demonstrate. To do so, we must paralyze the eye so that when the observer tries to move his or her eyes, the motor signal sent from the brain to the eye muscles will result in a corollary discharge but—since the paralyzed eye will remain stationary—cause no sensory movement signal.

John Stevens and a group of researchers (1976) recently carried out this experiment, using the setup shown in Figure 11.14. Stevens was temporarily paralyzed by a paralytic drug injected into his circulation, and he reported his perceptions when he tried to move his eyes. This is a difficult experiment

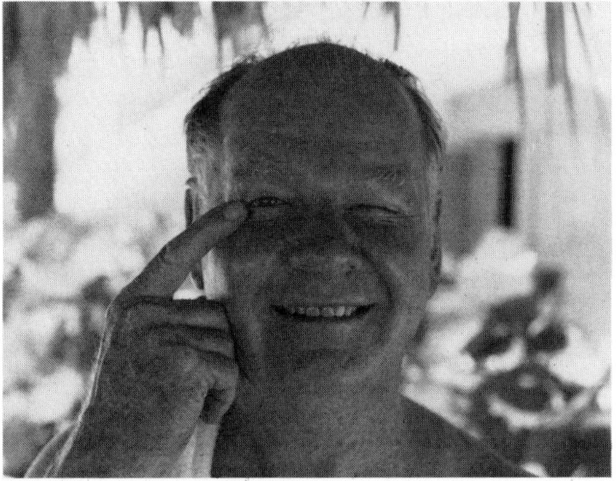

Figure 11.13 Why is this man smiling? Because every time he moves his eyeball by pushing on his eyelid, he sees the world jiggle.

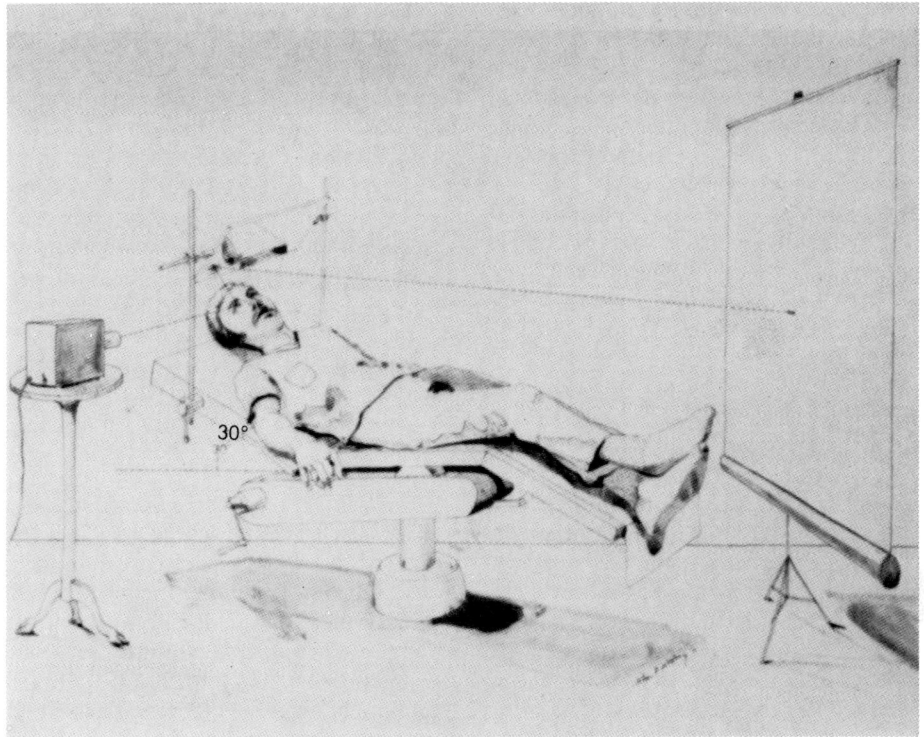

Figure 11.14 Setup for the Stevens et al. (1976) total paralysis experiment. The observer reclines on an operating table and views the screen through a mirror. The projector illuminates a small mirror mounted on a contact lens in the observer's eye, which produces a dot on the screen that follows the observer's eye movements. Since the observer was totally paralyzed, no eye movements were detected. (The projectors used to present stimulus patterns are not shown.)

to do, not only because of the possible dangers of being even temporarily paralyzed (Stevens had to be artificially respirated, since the drug also paralyzed the muscles used in breathing) but also because of the difficulty in communicating perceptions when the observer can't talk or move! To solve this problem, a tourniquet was applied to Stevens' right arm to cut off the circulation and keep the paralyzing drug from acting on his arm. This enabled Stevens to signal "yes," "no," "skip to the next experiment," or "stop the experiment" with the fingers of his unparalyzed right hand. Besides demonstrating the dedication of the experimenter, this experiment also confirmed the corollary discharge model. When Stevens tried to move his eyes, the scene became displaced from its original position, as the model predicts.

Let's now consider what happens when an observer tracks a moving car as it drives past. Since the eye moves to follow the car, the car's image remains stationary on the retina and no sensory movement signal occurs. But since the eye is moving, a corollary discharge reaches the comparator, and because it is not canceled by a sensory movement signal, we perceive the car to be moving. But what about the rest of the scene? As we follow the car with our eyes, the image of the rest of the scene sweeps across our retina, which generates a sensory movement signal; however, this sensory movement signal is canceled by the corollary discharge due to the eye movement, and we therefore perceive everything but the car as stationary.

Corollary discharge theory explains many of the facts of movement perception and has been supported by some recent single-cell recording experiments. Cells have been found in the monkey's superior colliculus (a visual center in the midbrain that plays an important role in controlling eye movements) that increase their firing rate when the eye is stationary and a bar moves across the cell's receptive field, as shown in Figure 11.15(a), but decrease their firing rate when the eye moves so that the receptive field moves across a stationary bar, as shown in Figure 11.15(b) (Robinson & Wurtz, 1976). Note that in both cases, the bar traverses the receptive field; but when the eye is stationary, the cell fires, and when the eye is moving, the cell does not fire.

According to corollary discharge theory, the cell should fire when the bar moves across the receptive field, because a sensory movement signal is elicited by the moving bar and there is no corollary discharge. However, the cell should not fire when the eye moves, because the corollary discharge generated by the motor signal that moves the eye cancels the sensory movement signal generated when the bar sweeps across the receptive field. The behavior of these superior colliculus cells, therefore, supports the idea that a corollary discharge inhibits firing when the eye moves, thereby enabling the visual system to differentiate between retinal movement that results from movement of a stimulus and retinal movement that results from movement of the eyes.

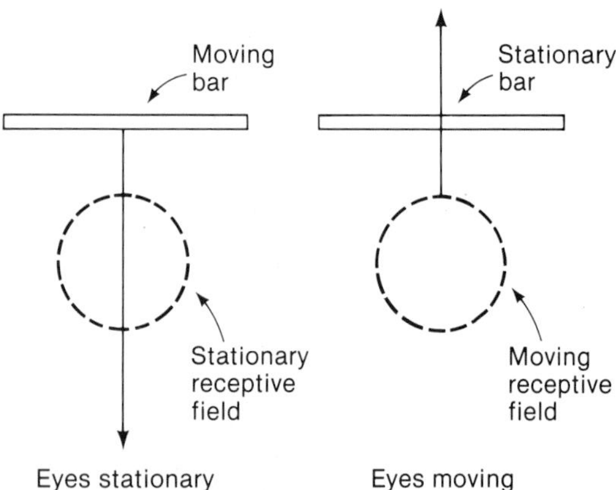

Figure 11.15 The two conditions in the experiment in which Robinson and Wurtz (1976) recorded from single cells in the monkey's superior colliculus. In the first condition, the monkey's eyes remain stationary and a bar moves across the cell's receptive field. In the second condition, the bar remains stationary and the monkey moves its eyes so that the cell's receptive field moves across the bar.

Though we see real movement much more often than illusions of movement in everyday life, most research on the perception of movement has been concerned with illusions, especially with stroboscopic movement. We will next consider these illusions, beginning with stroboscopic movement.

Illusions of Movement

Stroboscopic Movement

Movement between two lights. Stroboscopic movement was first demonstrated in 1875 by Exner, who showed that when two electrical sparks discharged next to each other are briefly separated in time, movement appears to occur across the space between them. However, it wasn't until Wertheimer's paper of 1912 (see p. 166) that research on stroboscopic movement began in earnest. Wertheimer and later workers found that the nature of the movement that occurs between two flashing lights depends on both the timing between the flashes and the space between the lights.

Figure 11.16 shows how our perception of two flashes of light changes as the time interval between them is increased (Graham, 1965). When the time between the two flashes is less than about 30 msec, they are perceived to flash on and off simultaneously. As the interval is increased above 30 msec, **partial movement** is perceived between the two lights; and at a separation of about 60 msec, the lights appear to move continuously from one to the other. This continuous movement is called **optimal movement,** because it looks just like real movement. At intervals between about 60 and 200 msec, a type of movement called **phi movement,** or **objectless movement,** is perceived between the two lights. It is called objectless movement because, while movement appears to occur between the two lights, it is difficult to actually perceive an object moving across the space between them. Finally, at time intervals above about 200–400 msec, *no* movement is perceived between the two lights; they appear

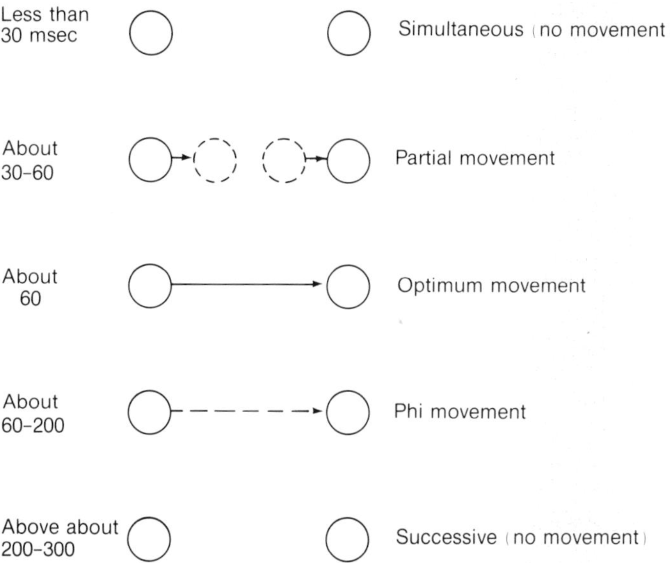

Figure 11.16 The perception of stroboscopic movement depends on the time interval between two flashing lights. As the time interval is increased, the observer's perception goes through the stages shown above.

successively, with first one flashing on and off, and then the other.

The distance between the two lights also affects the perception of stroboscopic movement. As the distance between the two lights increases, it is necessary to increase either the time interval between the two flashes or the intensity of the flashes, to maintain the same perception of movement.

Movement in complex displays. Most of the work on stroboscopic movement has used simple displays, such as the two lights shown in Figure 11.16. However, some investigators have shown that stroboscopic movement also occurs when they present more complex displays, which often result in interesting movement effects. In 1926, J. Ternus did an experiment in which he showed that the nature of the movement resulting from a stroboscopic presentation depends on the overall configuration of the stimulus.

To understand Ternus's demonstration, let's first consider what happens when we flash the two lights in Figure 11.17(a) on and off simultaneously and then, after a brief time interval, flash them both on and off again. When we do this, we simply see lights B and C flashing on and off twice, with no movement between them. Ternus added lights A and D to this display, as shown in Figure 11.17(b). He first flashed the group A-B-C, then, after a brief time interval, flashed the group B-C-D. Flashing the lights in this way creates the perception that each light moves one space to the right, so that the light at A appears to move to position B, B appears to move to C, and C appears to move to D. Notice that in this situation, lights B and C are flashing on and off just as they did in Figure 11.17(a), but

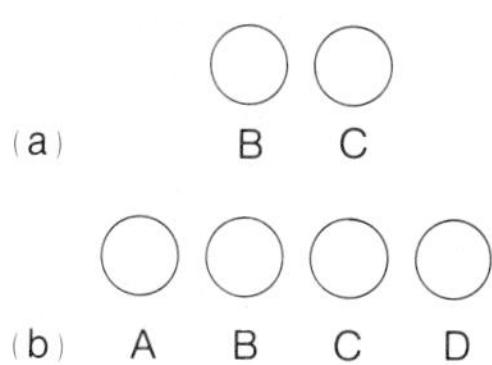

Figure 11.17 The stimuli used in Ternus's (1926) stroboscopic movement experiment that demonstrated *phenomenal identity.*

flashing the lights as in (b) causes them to appear to move. This movement demonstrates what Ternus called **phenomenal identity,** because the group A-B-C retains its identity; the three lights are seen to move together as a whole, even though lights B and C are simply flashing on and off in the same position. Ternus's result supports the Gestalt principle, discussed in Chapter 6, that the whole is more than the sum of its parts.

Paul Kolers (1972) used rectangular stimuli to show that the shapes of objects in complex displays may influence the stroboscopic movement between these objects. Figure 11.18 illustrates one of his experiments. In Figure 11.18(a), the center rectangle, A, is flashed, followed by the two side rectangles, B and C, which are flashed on and off together. When this is done, rectangle A appears to split and move simultaneously to B and C. In 11.18(b), the center rectangle splits, and its parts rotate in opposite directions to move to new orientations at positions B and C. Thus, in stroboscopic movement, the vertical rectangle will move easily to either vertical or horizontal rectangles. However, if the vertical rectangle is placed between a vertical and a horizontal rectangle, as shown in 11.18(c), movement occurs only to the more similar (but also more distant!) rectangle, C, and horizontal rectangle B blinks on and off. Kolers calls this effect **figural selection.**

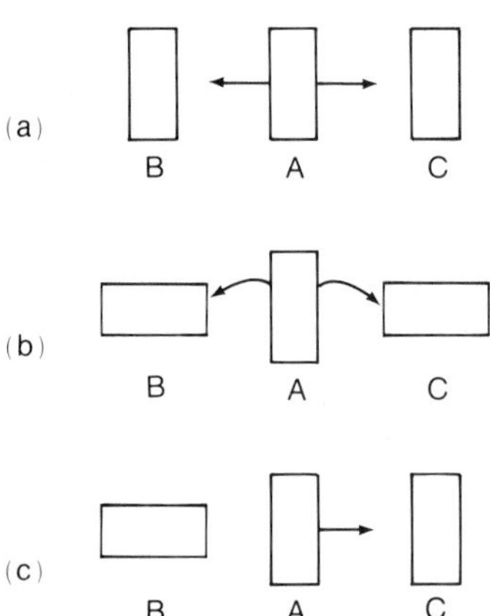

Figure 11.18 The stimuli used in Koler's (1972) stroboscopic movement experiments. A is flashed first, followed by B and C simultaneously. The direction of A's movement, indicated by the arrows, depends on the orientation and distance of objects B and C.

The movement perceived in film is the most familiar example of stroboscopic movement in complex displays. Twenty-four pictures are flashed on the screen per second, with a dark interval between each picture and with each picture slightly different from the next. Film has a lot going for it: at 24 pictures per second, there are 42 msec between each picture, approximating the range in which optimal movement takes place; the individual pictures are usually very similar to each other, as you can see in Figure 11.19, and the pictures are usually meaningful, thereby facilitating smooth stroboscopic movement.

Effect of past experience. A number of experiments have shown that the observer's past experience affects stroboscopic motion. One of the earliest of such demonstrations was Max Wertheimer's (1912) famous experiment that inaugurated Gestalt psychology (see p. 166). He flashed two lines, A and B, one after another, so that line A appeared to move downward through the 60-degree angle to B, as shown in Figure 11.20(a). This is the usual result observed when two lines at an angle are presented; movement occurs through the smaller 60-degree angle rather than through the larger 120-degree angle. However, when the arrangement of Figure 11.20(a) is preceded by the lines shown in Figure 11.20(b) and (c), then line A is perceived to move through the larger 120-degree angle, as shown in Figure 11.20(d). Thus, Wertheimer showed that stroboscopic movement can be affected by the observer's previous experience.

What mechanism is responsible for stroboscopic movement? Numerous explanations have been proposed, including the idea that the observer moves his or her eyes between the two stimuli as they are flashed. This idea, however, cannot be correct, because it is possible to see stroboscopic movement in two directions at once, as shown in Figure 11.18, but impossible to move the eyes in two directions at once. Furthermore, in complex displays such as those seen in films, movement occurs in many directions at once. So far, all proposed explanations have been subsequently disproven. Thus, the mechanism responsible for stroboscopic movement remains unknown.

Figure 11.19 Seven frames from Edwin S. Porter's 1903 film *The Great Train Robbery.* This sequence lasts about four-tenths of a second when projected.

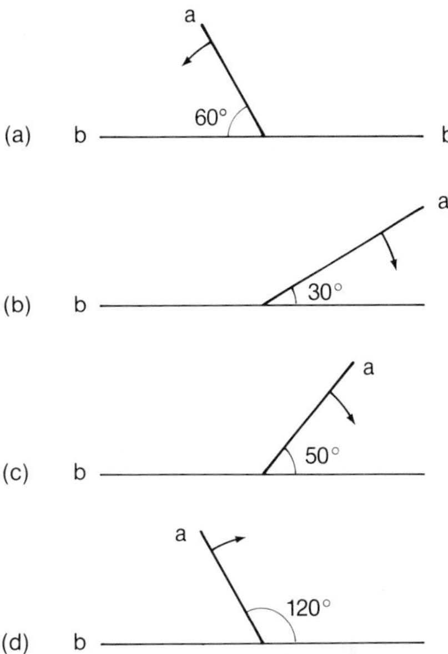

Figure 11.20 Stimuli used in Max Wertheimer's (1912) stroboscopic movement experiment. The tilted line is flashed first, followed by the horizontal line.

Induced Movement

One example of induced movement, mentioned earlier, is the perception that the moon is racing through the clouds when really the clouds are moving and not the moon. You also may have experienced an induced movement effect while sitting in your car at a stoplight. As you feel your car moving backward, you jam on the brakes, only to realize that your car is standing still and the one next to you is moving forward. Another example of induced movement is the way a pigeon's head appears to move when the pigeon walks. When asked to describe how a pigeon's head moves, most people say that the head moves forward and then backward every time the pigeon takes a step. But films of pigeons walking show that this isn't so; the pigeon's head does move forward, but then the pigeon's body moves forward under the head, making the pigeon's head appear to move backward, as shown in Figure 11.21.

In two of the above examples, a small object (the distant moon, the pigeon's head) appears to move because of the movement of a large object (the clouds, the pigeon's body). This general characteristic of induced movement was described by Karl Duncker in 1929. Duncker had observers sit in a darkened room and observe a small luminous circle inside a luminous rectangle, as shown in Figure 11.22. When Duncker moved the rectangle to the right, his observers reported that the circle appeared to move to the left.

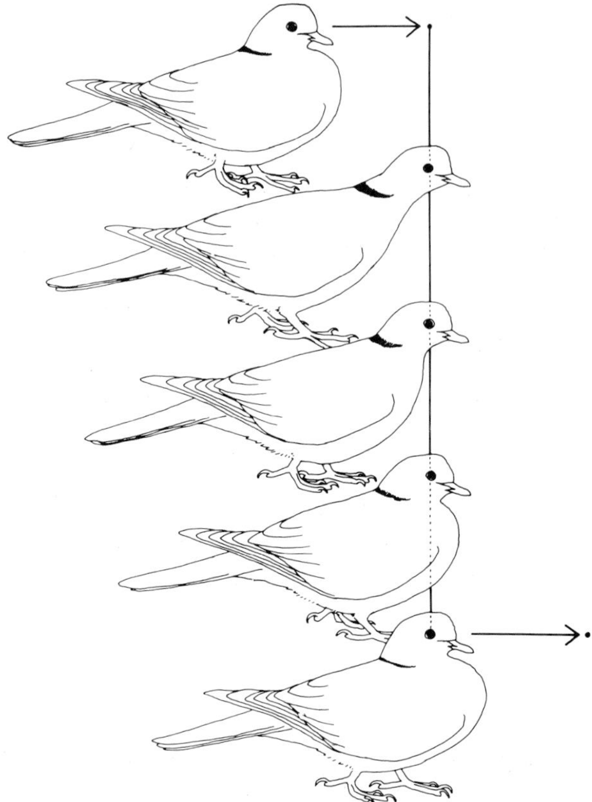

Figure 11.21 How a pigeon walks. These pictures, which were taken from a film of a pigeon walking, show that a pigeon moves its head forward and then moves its body forward while keeping its head stationary. The pigeon's head never moves backward. (Figure courtesy of Mark Friedman; see Friedman, 1975.)

You can demonstrate induced movement to yourself by sticking a small dot of paper to the screen of your television set, as shown in Figure 11.23,

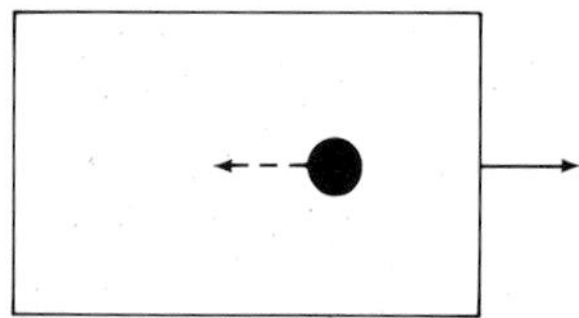

Figure 11.22 Duncker's (1929) induced movement demonstration, as described by Wallach (1959). When the rectangle is moved to the right, as indicated by the solid arrow, the disk inside the rectangle appears to move to the left, as indicated by the dashed arrow.

and tuning in a program in which the television camera pans back and forth across a scene, or in which the camera tracks (follows) a moving person or car (a football game is particularly good). These camera movements cause the entire TV image to move across the screen, which will induce movement in the dot you have stuck to the screen. The movement you see, however, will not be as impressive as that observed by Duncker's observers, because the stationary border of the TV screen exerts a stabilizing influence on the dot.

A recent experiment by Sakata and co-workers (1977) presents evidence for a neuron that may be involved in the perception of induced movement. This neuron, located in the posterior parietal association cortex—an area between the occipital and

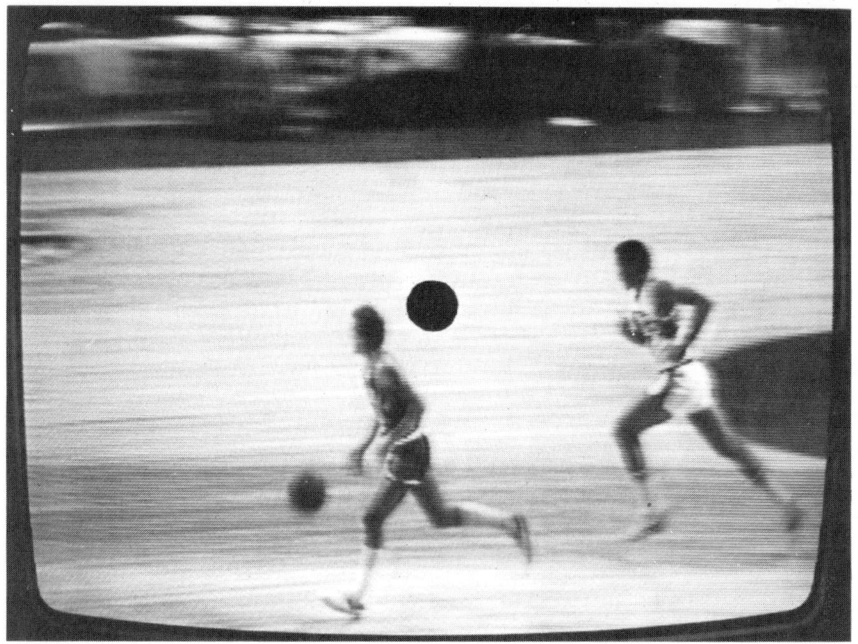

Figure 11.23 As these basketball players race down the court, the dot stuck to the center of the TV screen races with them!

parietal lobes (see Figure 2.11)—increases its firing rate as a monkey follows a spot of light moving downward and decreases its firing rate when the spot moves upward (Figure 11.24a). The interesting feature of this cell, in terms of induced movement, is that it increases its firing rate when a frame

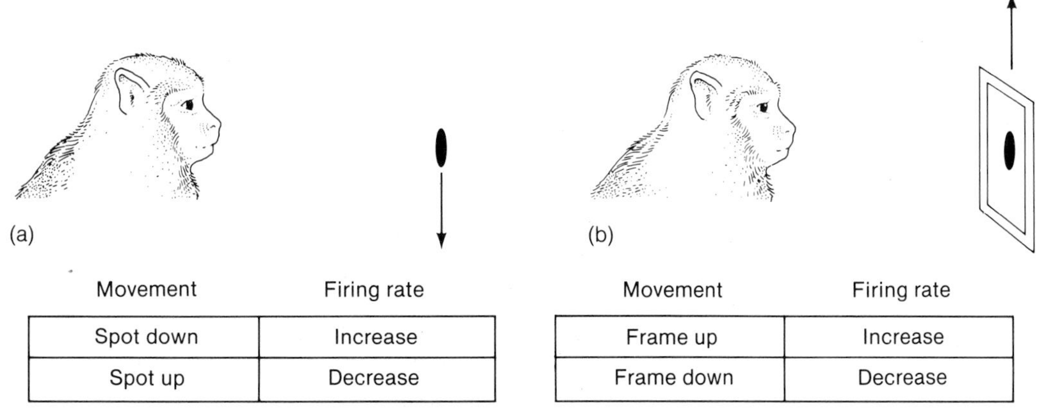

Movement	Firing rate
Spot down	Increase
Spot up	Decrease

Movement	Firing rate
Frame up	Increase
Frame down	Decrease

Figure 11.24 The response of a neuron that may be involved in the perception of induced movement. This neuron increases its firing rate when the spot moves down (left) or when the frame moves up (right). According to Duncker's result (Figure 11.22), upward movement of the frame should make the spot appear to move down.

surrounding a stationary light is moved up and decreases its firing rate when the frame is moved down (Figure 11.24b). The important point here is that in induced movement, movement of a frame in one direction will make a spot appear to move in the opposite direction, which is exactly how this cell responds: it increases its firing when the spot moves down *or* the frame moves up, and it decreases its firing when the spot moves up *or* the frame moves down.

Autokinetic Movement

I first became aware of autokinetic movement while I was looking up at stars on a dark night. I noticed that a star which was separated somewhat from the others appeared to be moving. "That must be an airplane," I thought. Although it continued to move as I watched, it didn't fly away; it "moved" but stayed in about the same area of sky. I then realized that the "airplane" was a star and I was experiencing an illusion. Later, I found that when I observed a small stationary spot of light in a dark room, the spot of light appeared to move. This movement is called autokinetic movement, or the autokinetic effect. You can demonstrate this effect to yourself by looking at a lighted cigarette from across a completely dark room.

One particularly interesting feature of the autokinetic effect is that it can be influenced by suggestion. As a graduate teaching assistant at Brown University, I demonstrated this to my students by presenting a small stationary spot of light in a dark room and telling them they would see a spot of light that was being moved by a motor. (Motor noises were provided to make this more convincing.) Their task was to tell me whether the spot was moving to the left or to the right.

All the students saw the spot move; then, after determining how many saw it move to the left and how many to the right, I told them that we would look at it again and that this time it would be moving to the right. After the second presentation, many of the students who had seen it move left at first said it was now moving to the right. Thus, suggesting the direction that the spot should move caused a change in the perception of its movement.

This result was not an original one. In 1935, social psychologist Muzafer Sherif did an experiment in which he instructed observers as follows: "When the room is completely dark I shall give you the signal 'ready' and then show you a point of light. After a short time the light will start to move. As soon as you see it move, press the key. A few seconds later the light will disappear. Then tell me the distance it moved."

Sherif's experiment was run both for individual observers and for groups of two or three at a time, and the results depended on whether the observers were run individually or in groups. When run individually, observers reported that the dot moved anywhere from 0.8 to 7.4 inches, but when run in groups of three, all observers reported after a few trials that the dot moved about 4 inches. When run together, the observers apparently influenced each other, and their perceptions became the same!

Because the autokinetic effect is so open to suggestion, Allan Rechtschaffen and Sarnoff Mednick (1955), two clinical psychologists, were able to turn the effect into a personality test. To administer this test, which they called the **autokinetic word technique,** they had the observers view a spot of light in a dark room. The observers were told that they were being tested on their ability to see words written by a point of light and should report any words or letters they saw to the experimenters. All observers reported that words were written by the point of light, showing that the experimenters' suggestion was effective, since most observers do not spontaneously report seeing words. Nine observers produced a total of 122 words during the series of tests, from a minimum of 2 words to a maximum of 43. Though many of the reported words were simple ones, such as "and," "on," and "the," a number of subjects gave long, rather revealing responses. One subject, after giving a number of responses of a highly personal nature, indignantly asked the experimenter, "Where did you get all of that information about me?" A female subject produced the following paragraph:

"When men are tired and depraved, they become mean and callous individuals. When men learn to master their souls, the world will be a more humane and tolerant place in which to live. Men should learn to control themselves."

Aftereffects of Movement

Figure 11.25 shows a picture of the stimulus for an illusion of movement unsurprisingly called the **waterfall illusion.** If you stare for about 30–60 seconds at a real waterfall that fills only part of your field of view and then look away at some other part of the scene, you will see the scene move up (assuming that the waterfall was moving down!). This is called an aftereffect of movement, because the

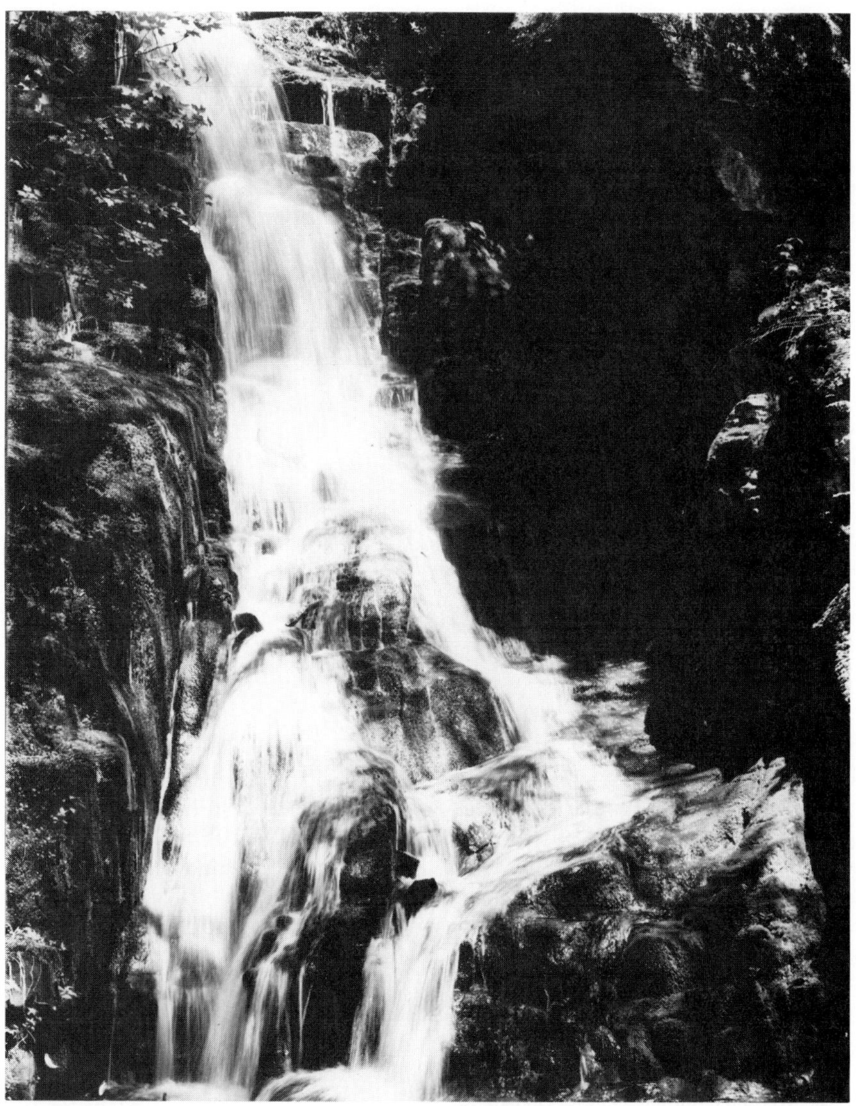

Figure 11.25 To see the waterfall illusion, stare for 30–60 seconds at one spot on a real waterfall and then look off to the side. The effect works better with small waterfalls that fill only a small part of your field of view.

Box 11.2 A Long-Lasting Movement Aftereffect

Most aftereffects of movement are brief, lasting only seconds or minutes at the most. However, Richard Masland (1969) has shown that the spiral aftereffect can be perceived as long as 20 hours after viewing a rotating spiral. He studied this long-lasting effect with three groups of observers. The two experimental groups viewed the center of a rotating spiral for 15 minutes, and a control group viewed a stationary spiral for 15 minutes. After viewing the rotating spiral, observers in one of the experimental groups looked at a stationary spiral for 10 minutes. These observers saw the normal spiral aftereffect: the stationary spiral appeared to rotate in the direction opposite the original rotation of the spiral. The observers in the other experimental group were prevented from seeing the normal spiral aftereffect by sitting in the dark for 10 minutes after viewing the rotating spiral.

All observers returned between 20 and 26 hours later for a second session and were asked to look at the stationary spiral. Observers who had observed the aftereffect in the first session would typically exclaim, "It's still moving!" upon seeing the stationary spiral, and observers who sat in the dark at the end of the first session also reported that the spiral appeared to be moving. The perception of the aftereffect by observers who originally sat in the dark shows that it is not necessary to have seen the normal aftereffect in order to see the long-term aftereffect. The control group saw no movement of the spiral during the first or second sessions, indicating that it was necessary to have viewed the original movement of the rotating spiral to see the aftereffect.

Masland also showed that this aftereffect occurs only if the stationary spiral is imaged on the retinal area that experienced the original rotation. Apparently, looking at a rotating spiral for 15 minutes causes a long-lasting change in a local area of the visual system. However, this local change has little or no effect on perception of the everyday environment, since the observers reported that their vision was completely normal during the time between the first and second sessions. A perceptual effect occurred only when the retinal area exposed to the rotating spiral was exposed to a stationary version of this spiral.

What is the physiological mechanism responsible for this effect? The answer to this question is not known, but one possibility is that the 15-minute exposure to the rotating spiral which causes the aftereffect could cause a long-lasting effect on movement-sensitive neurons in the cortex. Electrophysiological experiments on the effect of prolonged stimulation on movement-sensitive cortical neurons might help us explain Masland's long-term movement aftereffect.

observer must first view an inducing stimulus, such as the waterfall, to get the effect. Another such effect, called the **spiral aftereffect,** can be observed by placing a spiral such as the one in Figure 11.26 on the turntable of your record player. Set the turntable for a speed of 33⅓ and look at the center of the spiral for about 30–60 seconds. The spiral should look as though it is expanding as you observe it, and when you look away from the spiral at another object, that object should appear to shrink.

Stuart Anstis and Richard Gregory (1964) showed that the waterfall illusion depends on the movement of the inducing stimulus across the retina. Instead of having observers view a waterfall, they had them view a belt of horizontally moving, vertical black and white stripes, similar to that in Figure 11.3. The observers viewed these moving stripes either with their eyes stationary, so the pattern moved across the retina, or with their eyes tracking the moving stripes, so the pattern remained stationary on the retina. In both the "eyes stationary" and "eyes tracking" conditions, the observers perceived the movement of the stripes, but an aftereffect of movement occurred only after the "eyes stationary" condition. Thus, the important factor in determining this aftereffect of movement is not the perception of the stripes' movement but the movement of the stripes across the retina.

That the waterfall illusion occurs only if the inducing stimulus moves across the retina supports the idea that movement detectors, which respond only to movement across the retina, play a role in

Figure 11.26

this illusion. In fact, Horace Barlow and Robert Hill (1963) have found electrophysiological evidence that movement detectors *are* involved in the waterfall illusion. They recorded from a directionally selective cell in the rabbit's retina, during and after stimulating the cell in its preferred direction of movement. Figure 11.27 shows their results. They found that when the stimulus was moved across the receptive field, the cell's firing rate increased to above its spontaneous level, and when the stimulus was turned off, the cell's firing rate fell to below its spontaneous level. Barlow and Hill hypothesize that this cell (which we will call cell no. 1) is paired with another cell (cell no. 2), which is directionally selective in the opposite direction. After stimulation of cell no. 1 is stopped, its firing rate drops to below its spontaneous level; therefore, cell no. 1 is firing at a lower rate than cell no. 2, which is still firing at its spontaneous level. So we perceive movement in the preferred direction of cell no. 2, because it is firing at a greater rate than cell no. 1. Thus, according to Barlow and Hill, aftereffects of movement result from temporary imbalances of the discharges of cells that respond in opposite directions.

Some Consequences of Movement

Now that we have described five different ways that the perception of movement can occur, in the remainder of the chapter, we will look at a few consequences of movement. We will see that movement can (1) cause us to perceive that one thing causes another, (2) give human or animal characteristics to geometrical objects, (3) cause us to perceive the location of an object, even though it is hidden from view, and (4) play an important role in linking together successive shots of a film.

The Perception of Causality

When we see a hammer driving a nail into a board or a knife cutting bread, we are perceiving causality: the hammer causes the nail to go into the board, and the knife causes the bread to be cut. The perception of movement is one important component of these and many other situations in which we perceive causality. While in some situations, such as a match causing a piece of paper to burn, we may conclude that one event causes another in the absence of movement, the majority of examples of the precept of causality involve movement. One researcher in particular, Albert Michotte (1963), in his book *The Perception of Causality,* concentrates his attention on situations in which our perception of causality is linked to our perception of movement.

Timing is the key word in describing the results of Michotte's experiments on causality. The most important factor in determining whether we perceive event A as causing event B is the timing between them. Michotte illustrates this by pointing out that, if a gust of wind blows a door shut and a light goes on at the other end of the corridor simultaneously, the impression of a causal relationship between the door closing and the light going on is forced upon us. Even though we may think it unlikely that shutting a door would turn on a light (although this is certainly not impossible, since shutting a refrigerator door turns *off* a light), the timing between the door and light may, as Michotte says, *force* an impression of a causal relationship upon us.

In order to experimentally study the effect of timing on the perception of causality, Michotte uses stimuli such as squares A and B in Figure 11.28.

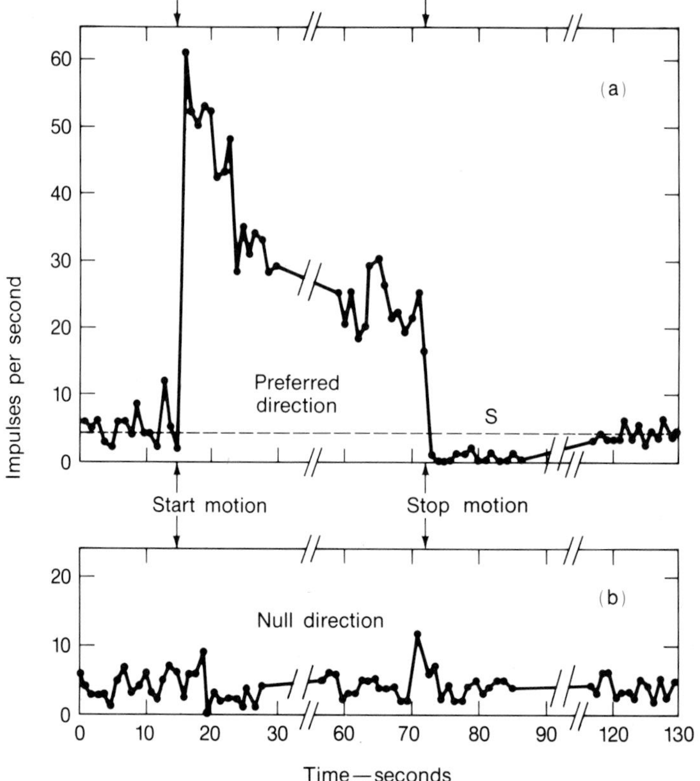

Figure 11.27 Response of a directionally selective cell in the rabbit's retina to a stimulus moving in its preferred direction. In (a) we see that during 60 seconds of continuous stimulation, the rate of nerve firing stays above the spontaneous level, S. After the stimulation is stopped, firing decreases to below the spontaneous level for about 30 seconds. (b) The same stimulus conditions as in (a) but in the cells' "null direction" (opposite to the preferred direction), showing that stimulation in the null direction has no effect on the response of this cell. (From Barlow & Hill, 1963.)

Square A moves toward square B; then, after A either reaches B or stops before getting to B, B moves away from A. By varying the timing between the movement of A and B, Michotte has identified the conditions that result in what he calls the **launching effect.**

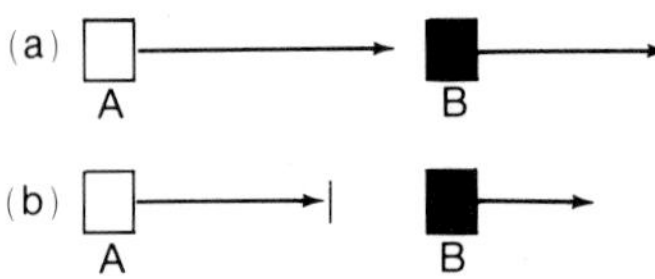

Figure 11.28 Two of Michotte's (1963) demonstrations of the launching effect. Square A moves first and stops; then B moves.

The launching effect. Figure 11.28(a) illustrates an experiment in which launching was observed. A moves to B and stops, then B almost immediately begins to move in the same direction as A. Observers report that object A appears to "launch" object B. The interval between the time A reaches B and B moves is crucial: when the interval between A and B is greater than about one-fifth of a second, the impression of launching disappears. Observers no longer perceive that event A causes event B; instead, they perceive two separate events.

The launching effect can occur even if A stops before reaching B, as shown in Figure 11.28(b), but the speed of A becomes more important if a space is introduced. For example, if there is a space of 20 mm between A and B, and A is moving at 20 cm/second, launching is not perceived; but launching can be perceived, even at gaps above 50 mm, if A is traveling at 90 cm/second.

The major significance of Michotte's launching experiments is his conclusion that the impression of causality experienced by his subjects is a *direct* perception. That is, the subject does not say to himself, "A hit B, and B moved, which must mean that A caused B to move." If the conditions of timing, speed, and distance are correct, causality is perceived without any intervening reasoning on the part of the subject. Michotte cites the example of stroboscopic movement to emphasize this point. When stroboscopic movement occurs, we do not *decide* that since light A flashed on and off and then light B flashed on and off, there must be movement between them. Instead, we simply *see* movement from A to B. Causality works in the same way. If the conditions are right, we perceive that the movement of A causes the movement of B *directly,* with no intervening reasoning process.

Bringing a Triangle to Life

Movement can also give "life" to inanimate objects, because a major property of living things is mobility. While this hardly means that we conclude that all moving things are alive, Fritz Heider and Marianne Simmel (1944) have shown that movement can give personalities, feelings, and motives to geometrical figures. They showed a two-and-one-half-minute film, the cast of which appears in Figure 11.29: a "house" inhabited by a large triangle, a small triangle, and a disc. In the film, these geometrical figures move and interact with each other in various ways. For example, the large triangle might bump into the smaller one, or the disc might move inside the house and then outside again. The observer's task was simply to watch the film and write down what happened. Thirty-three of the 34 observers interpreted the film in terms of animate beings. That is, they gave human or animal properties to each geometrical figure on the basis of the figure's movements. When asked specifically about the figures, observers showed no hesitation in assigning personality characteristics to them. Everyone disliked the big triangle, since it picked on the smaller triangle. The small triangle, on the other hand, was perceived as being "heroic, brave, timid, cagey, and sly." Thus, movement can not only establish cause and effect relationships between geometrical figures, it can also give them qualities usually associated with living things. As we will see in the next section, movement can also give substance to an object that can't be seen.

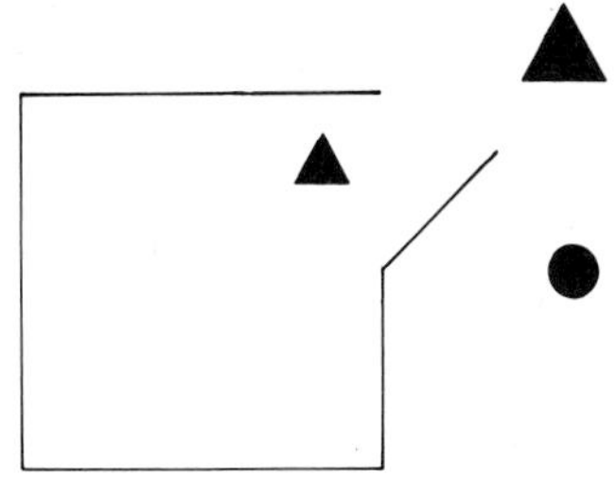

Figure 11.29 A scene from Heider and Simmel's (1944) film.

The Tunnel Effect

You have probably watched a moving object disappear behind an obstruction, such as a bush or a building, and then reappear on the other side. When the object disappears, sometimes it doesn't really seem to disappear. You know that it still exists behind the obstruction and have a general sense of where it is while it is hidden, so you can predict when it will reappear (assuming that its speed stays fairly constant while obscured). An effect similar to this has been called the **tunnel effect** by Luke Burke (1952).

Some of Burke's stimuli are shown in Figure 11.30(a) and (b). An object travels along a path, disappears into a "tunnel," and comes out the other end. The tunnel effect occurs when an impression of continuous movement inside the tunnel is produced, even though the object is not visible when in the tunnel. This effect works best when the tunnel is short and the object is moving rapidly. For example, in the experiment in Figure 11.30(a), a

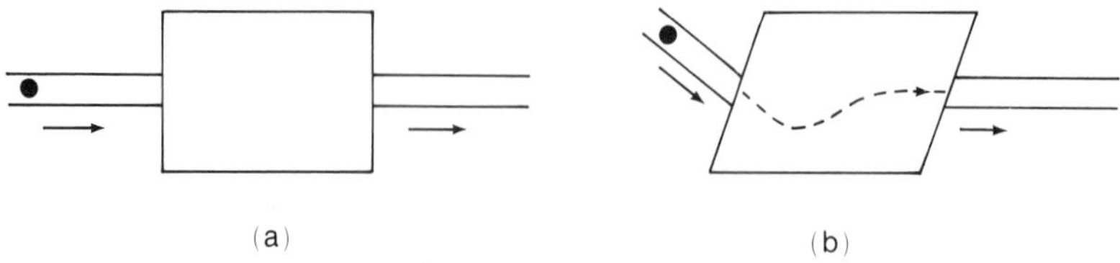

Figure 11.30 Two of Burke's (1952) stimuli for demonstrating the tunnel effect.

strong impression of movement inside the tunnel is created when the tunnel is 40 mm long and the object goes through it in 15 msec; however, if the length of the tunnel, or the amount of time the object spends inside it, is increased, the impression of movement through the tunnel is decreased.

An interesting variation on this effect is shown in Figure 11.30(b). If the entry and exit to the tunnel form an angle, the object appears to curve inside the tunnel. The tunnel experiment, therefore, illustrates that we can sense the path of a movement, even when the moving object is hidden. This effect is related to the law of good continuation, illustrated in Figure 7.16. Even though parts of the smokestack in Pissaro's painting are hidden by smoke, we perceive them as continuing behind the smoke. Similarly, we can perceive the movement of an object as continuing behind a tunnel or other barrier.

Linking Shots in Film

One of film's most important properties is that successive shots often become linked together in the viewer's mind (Isenhour, 1975). A familiar example of this occurs when a shot of a cowboy firing his gun is followed by a shot of another cowboy falling off his horse. We link the two shots together in our mind and interpret the sequence as a continuous event, even though we may never see the two cowboys together. In this example, the two shots can become linked even though there is no movement (both cowboys can be stationary), but in some cases, movement plays an important role in linking consecutive shots.

Two shots from a film that show a man hammering a nail into a board are reproduced in Figure 11.31. The first is a medium shot, which shows the man bringing the hammer down toward the nail, and this shot is followed by a closeup of the hammer hitting the nail. (The slight blur of the hammer is due to its movement.) Though we do not see the entire movement of the hammer, we perceive this sequence as being linked together, so that the hammer hitting the nail in shot two is assumed to result from the downward path of the hammer begun in shot one.

You may say that this effect depends not on movement but on showing two pictures of the same event from different viewpoints: one picture just happens to be a medium shot and the other a closeup. However, we can illustrate the importance of movement by changing shot two of Figure 11.31 to a new shot two, shown in Figure 11.32. This shot is identical in terms of movement, but we have replaced the original hammer from shot one with a much different hammer in shot two. No one could fail to perceive the difference in hammers; yet, when we view the film, the movement between shots one and two creates a strong link between the two shots. While it does seem strange that the hammer has apparently changed, we still perceive a continuous movement between the two shots. Movement links the two shots together in spite of the different hammers.

Summary

1. There are five ways to make a spot of light appear to move: (1) make the spot really move (real movement); (2) flash two lights in different positions on and off, one after the other (stroboscopic movement); (3) move a large object that surrounds the spot (induced movement); (4) view the spot in a completely dark room (autokinetic movement); and (5) view

Figure 11.31 Even though there are slight differences between some of the details in these two shots (can you find them?), the movement of the hammer helps link these two shots together.

the spot after viewing a moving pattern, such as a belt of vertical stripes (movement aftereffect).

2. The threshold for real movement depends on the background. Movement is more easily seen if the object moves across a structured background.

3. Perception of velocity depends on the surroundings. The phenomena of velocity transposition and speed constancy indicate that perceived velocity does not depend on retinal velocity.

4. Motion detectors, tuned to respond to movement in a specific direction, provide a mecha-

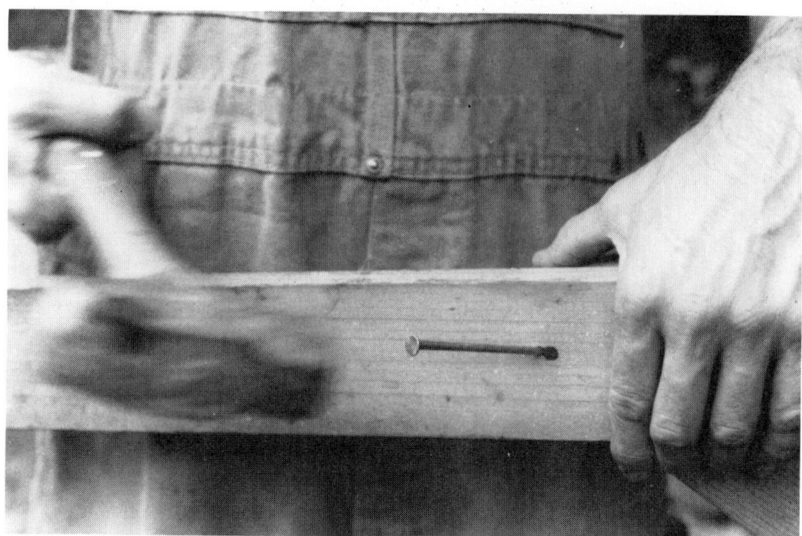

Figure 11.32 Even when the change between the two shots is great, as in this case where the hammer is different in the closeup, movement still links the two shots together.

nism to explain how we perceive the movement of a stimulus across the retina but cannot deal with situations such as tracking a stimulus, in which movement is perceived in the absence of movement across the retina, or situations such as walking through a scene, in which movement is not perceived, even though stimuli move across the retina.

5. We need a mechanism to determine when stimulation results from movement of the stimulus, movement of the observer, or both. Gibson has suggested that we can determine this by observing whether or not an object is displaced relative to the background. This idea, however, cannot explain our perception of movement when no structured background is present.

6. Our perception of the movement of one object relative to another, in film, is influenced not only by the physical movement on the screen but also by our past experience with moving objects in the environment and our past experience in watching films.

7. The corollary discharge provides a mechanism to differentiate between stimulation due to observer movement and stimulus movement; and, although the corollary discharge is hypothetical, there is neurophysiological evidence for its existence.

8. Stroboscopic movement is affected by the time interval between two flashes. As time between flashes is increased, observers first see the lights flash on and off simultaneously (no movement), then see partial movement, optimal movement, and phi movement between the lights, and at long time intervals see the lights flash on and off successively. Stroboscopic movement is also affected by the space between the stimuli and the intensity of the stimuli.

9. The principle of phenomenal identity, first demonstrated by Ternus, shows that complex displays often move together as a whole in stroboscopic movement. Figural selection is another example of how movement occurs in complex displays.

10. Perception of stroboscopic movement can be influenced by the observer's past experience.

11. Stroboscopic movement cannot be due to the observer's eye movements. The mechanism responsible for stroboscopic movement is still not understood.

12. Movement is induced in a small object when it is surrounded by a larger object that is moving. Recently, a neuron has been discovered that may be involved in the perception of induced movement.

13. Autokinetic movement is the illusory movement of a stationary spot of light in dark surroundings. This illusion can be modified by suggestion.

14. The waterfall illusion and the spiral aftereffect are aftereffects of movement. They occur only if the inducing pattern moves on the retina. The spiral aftereffect can be perceived as long as 20 hours after viewing a rotating spiral.

15. There is no good explanation for the autokinetic effect, but the action of directionally selective movement detectors can explain the waterfall illusion.

16. Michotte's launching effect demonstrates that motion can result in a direct perception of causality.

17. Movement can give human characteristics to geometrical objects, and it can maintain our perception of objects if they briefly disappear behind an obstruction and then reappear (the tunnel effect). Movement can also help link successive shots in film.

Glossary

Aftereffect of movement Illusory movement of a stationary object that occurs after an inducing stimulus in motion has been viewed for 30–60 seconds. The spiral aftereffect and the waterfall illusion are examples of aftereffects of movement. (289)

Autokinetic movement Illusory movement of a stationary spot of light that occurs when the light is viewed in the dark, so that the surroundings are not visible. (289)

Autokinetic word technique A test in which observers are told that a spot of light viewed in a dark room will move to spell letters or words. In actuality, the light is stationary; but the autokinetic effect, combined with the suggestion that letters or words will be perceived, causes many observers to perceive a moving spot that spells letters or words. (304)

Comparator A structure hypothesized by the corollary discharge theory of movement perception. The corollary discharge signal and the sensory movement signal meet at the comparator. (296)

Corollary discharge A copy of the signal sent from the motor area of the brain to the eye muscles that activates the eye muscles and causes the eye to move. According to the corollary discharge theory of movement perception, this corollary discharge signal is sent not to the eye muscles but to a structure called the "comparator." (295)

Figural selection When one object is flashed on and off, followed by two or more other objects located at approximately the same distance from the first object, stroboscopic movement will occur to the object most similar in shape to the first object. (300)

Induced movement Illusory movement of one object that is caused by the movement of another object nearby. (289)

Launching effect When one shape moves toward another shape and stops, then the other shape moves immediately or after a brief time interval, it appears that the first shape has "launched" the second shape into motion. (308)

Movement detectors Neurons that selectively respond to images moving across the retina in a particular direction. (292)

Optimal movement Stroboscopic movement that looks identical to real movement. (298)

Pan shot In film, a shot in which the camera stays in one location and smoothly scans a scene. (294)

Partial movement Stroboscopic movement in which the illusion of movement between two objects is not complete, so that one object appears to move only partway across the space between them. (298)

Phenomenal identity A stroboscopic movement effect that occurs when a group of lights appears to move as a whole to a new position. (300)

Phi (or objectless) movement Stroboscopic movement in which movement appears to occur between two objects, although it is difficult to actually perceive an object moving across the space between them. (298)

Real movement Physical movement of a stimulus. (298)

Sensory movement signal The electrical signal generated by movement of an image across the retina. This is one of the signals that plays a role in the corollary discharge theory of movement perception. (296)

Speed constancy Our perception of an object's speed stays fairly constant, even when we view the object from different distances, thereby changing the speed at which the object's image moves across the retina. (291)

Spiral aftereffect An aftereffect of movement. When we view objects immediately after viewing a rotating spiral for 30–60 seconds, the objects appear to shrink or expand. (306)

Stroboscopic movement An illusion of movement that occurs between two objects separated in space when the objects are flashed on and off, one after another, separated by a time interval of about 50–100 msec. (289)

Tracking shot In film, a shot in which the camera follows a moving object, usually a person. (294)

Tunnel effect Under certain conditions, when a moving object disappears into one end of a "tunnel" and, after a brief time interval, reappears at the other end, observers perceive the course of the object's movement inside the tunnel, even though they do not actually see the object. (309)

Velocity transposition A large object moving across a large space must move faster than a small object moving across a small space for the two objects to appear to move at the same speed. (291)

Velocity Tuning Curve A function relating a cell's firing rate to the velocity of a moving stimulus. (292)

Waterfall illusion An aftereffect of movement. When we view objects immediately after viewing a waterfall for 30–60 seconds, the objects appear to move up. (305)

Chapter Twelve

Perceptual Development

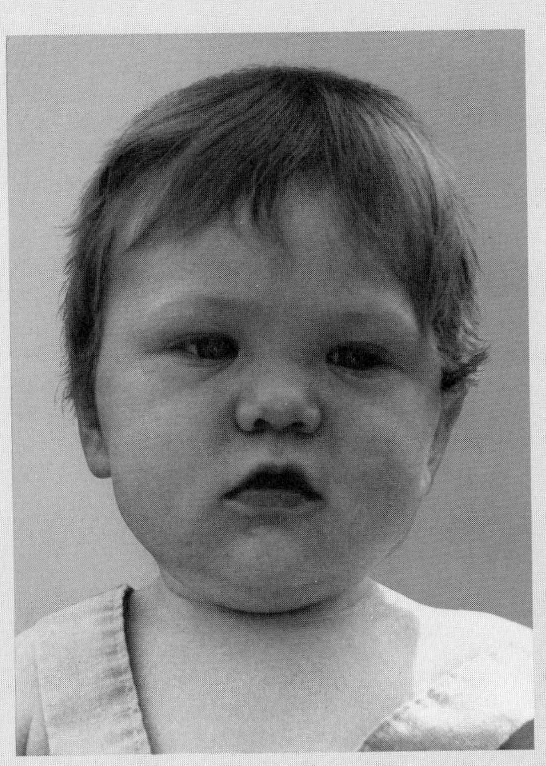

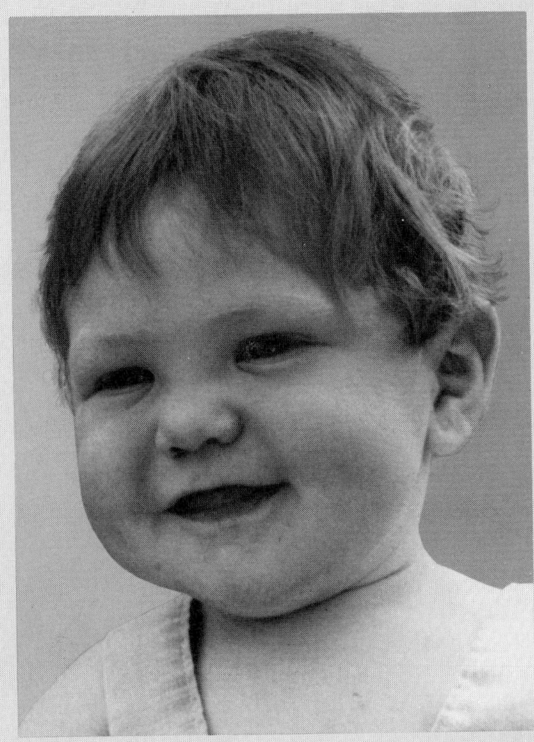

We have seen that the complex network of neurons called the visual system endows us with truly amazing capacities. We can see fine details and keep them in focus when an object moves from close to far away. We see something move and can follow the moving object with our eyes, keeping its image on our foveas so we can see the object clearly. We perceive the depths and sizes of things in the world and are fortunate enough to have a visual system that colors these objects with thousands of different hues. And these objects are not simply meaningless shapes; they are recognizable things, to which we attach meanings.

Our visual system does all these things and more, and as we mentioned at the beginning of this book, it accomplishes these things with such apparent ease that we take perception for granted. But has it always been this way? Were we born with the abilities to see fine details, follow moving objects, and see all the colors of the spectrum? William James, one of the first American psychologists, answered this question negatively, by describing the newborn's perception as a "great blooming buzzing confusion." That is, James felt that the newborn either perceives nothing or can make little sense of what it does perceive.

We can begin our discussion by stating that James' idea has been proved wrong: the newborn's world is far from a blooming, buzzing confusion. We will see, however, that while newborns can perceive a good deal more than William James gave them credit for, they still have a long way to go before reaching adult standards of perception. In this chapter, we will describe research, most of it done during the past two decades, that shows how our perceptual abilities develop from birth to adulthood.

Measuring Infant Perception

We saw in Chapter 6 that a routine part of an eye examination is the visual acuity test, in which the examiner asks you to read the letters on an eye chart, and you respond to the best of your ability. It's not so easy, however, to test the vision of a newborn or even that of a one-year-old infant, who not only can't read the letters on an eye chart but also has an extremely limited repertoire of other behaviors. Our problem in measuring infant perception, therefore, is how to use their limited behavioral abilities to help us assess their visual ability.

What can an infant do? Infants move their eyes to look at things and will try to touch an object that appears to be within reach. In addition to these two behaviors, we can also measure a physiological response called the visual evoked response. We will describe how each of these behaviors has been used to measure perception.

Looking

One of the most widely used techniques to measure infant perception is called the **preferential looking technique.** The basic principle underlying this procedure is simple: two stimuli are presented to the infant, and the experimenter watches the infant's eyes to see whether the infant looks at one of the stimuli more than the other. If the infant does look at one stimulus more than the other, we conclude that he or she can tell the difference between them. In pioneering work done in the 1960s, Robert Fantz showed that an infant will choose to look at an object with contours, such as the one in Figure 12.2(a), over one that is homogeneous, such as the one in Figure 12.2(b) (Fantz et al., 1962). This discovery enabled Fantz, and others who followed him, to measure an infant's visual acuity, as we will see below.

We can also assess an infant's vision by determining how long the infant will look at an object before looking away. One technique that makes use of this measure is called the **habituation procedure.** Let's consider an experiment that uses this procedure: an infant is presented with a patterned

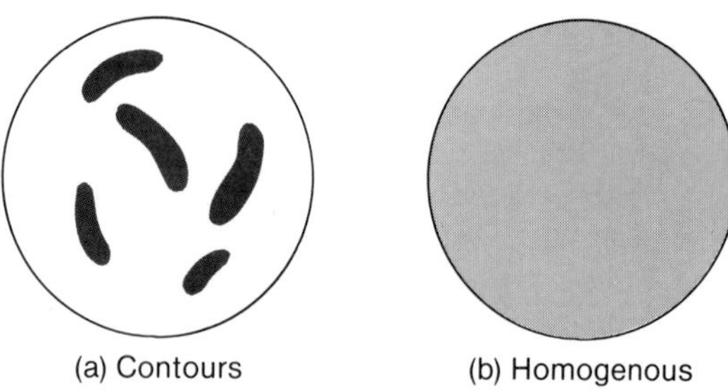

Figure 12.2 Given a choice, infants will look more at contours than at a homogenous field.

stimulus, and we measure how long he or she looks at the stimulus before looking away. We then continue to present this same stimulus, measuring the infant's looking time on each presentation. The usual result of this procedure is shown by the filled data points in Figure 12.3: the infant looks at the stimulus less and less each time it is repeated. This decrease in looking time with repeated presentations is called **habituation.**

To determine whether the infant can tell the difference between the pattern we have been presenting and a different pattern, we present the new pattern and measure looking time. If the infant can tell the difference between the original stimulus and the new one, it will increase its looking time, as shown by the open circles in Figure 12.3. This increase in looking time, with the presentation of a new stimulus, is called **dishabituation**, which follows from the fact that infants older than about 3 months will look longer at a novel stimulus than at one they have seen before (Fagan, 1976). If, however, the infant cannot tell the difference between the original stimulus and the new one, it will continue to habituate to the new stimulus, as shown by the open squares in Figure 12.3.

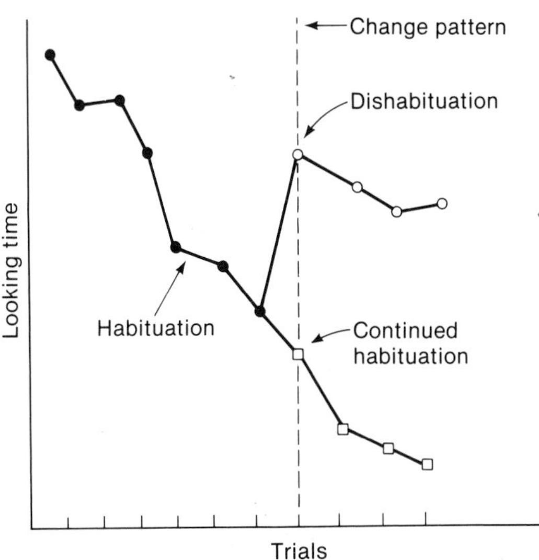

Figure 12.3 In the habituation procedure, the amount of time that the infant looks at a stimulus decreases during habituation. When the stimulus is changed (at the dashed vertical line), the infant either continues to habituate (indicating that the new stimulus appears similar to the old one) or dishabituates (indicating that the new stimulus appears different from the old one).

Reaching

Infants older than about 5 months will reach for an object they perceive to be within reach but will not reach for an object they perceive to be out of reach (Yonas, Petterson, & Granrud, 1982). We will see below that this behavior is useful in testing infants' depth perception.

Visual Evoked Potential

The **visual evoked potential (VEP)** is recorded by disc electrodes placed on the back of the head, over the visual cortex. The infant looks at a grey field, which is briefly replaced by a field of alternating black and white stripes. If the stripes are thick enough to be resolved by the visual system, an electrical response is generated in the visual cortex; however, if the stripes are too thin, no response is generated. Thus, the VEP provides an objective measure of the resolving power of the visual system and is, therefore, well suited for studying the development of visual acuity.

How Does Perceptual Development Proceed?

An important principle governing the development of perception is that certain basic capacities must be present before other capacities can appear. Perhaps the most obvious illustration of this principle is that an infant must be able to see some details before such capacities as depth and form perception can develop. Keeping this principle in mind as we discuss perceptual development, we will start with such basic capacities as visual acuity and then describe more complex capacities, such as the perception of depth and form.

Seeing Details

Visual acuity. Before describing psychophysical experiments that measure visual acuity in infants, let's reconsider the physiological basis for visual acuity. Remember that the fovea is the area in the retina with the highest acuity, largely because of the wiring and close packing of the foveal cones. The foveal cones, not fully developed at birth, continue their development during the first months of life (Mann, 1964). On the basis of this alone, we would expect the infant's acuity to be less than an adult's, but we should also consider the development of the visual cortex. Figure 12.4 shows the state of cortical development at birth, three months, and six months (Conel, 1939, 1947, 1951). These pictures indicate that the visual cortex is only partially developed at birth and becomes more developed at three and at six months. Most significant about these pictures is the large jump in development between birth and about three months. We will see below that during this time, visual acuity and other visual capacities develop very rapidly.

The preferential looking technique has been successfully used to measure the acuity of infants as young as one month of age. To determine acuity with this technique, the infant is presented with two cards, one with alternating black and white stripes and a grey card that reflects the same amount of light that the striped card would reflect if the stripes were smeared out evenly over the whole card. One card is presented on the left and one on the right, and the experimenter determines how long the infant looks at each card, by noting the position of the infant's eyes. If the stripes are thin and closely spaced, so the infant can't see them, both cards appear iden-

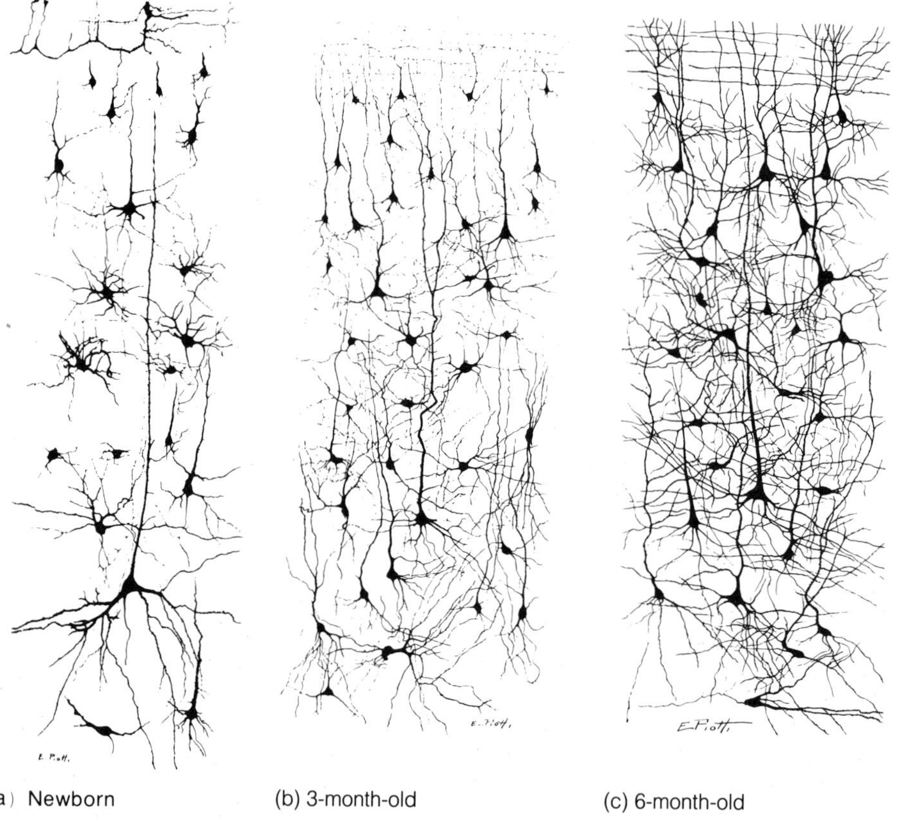

Figure 12.4 Drawings of neurons in the visual cortex of the newborn, 3-month-old, and 6-month-old human infant. (From Conel, 1939, 1947, 1951.)

tical to the infant, who gives them equal attention. If, however, the infant can see the stripes, he or she will look more often at the striped card. Thus, the narrowest stripe width that results in preferential looking indicates the infant's visual acuity.

In 1962, Robert Fantz and co-workers applied this technique to one-month, 5-month, and 6-month-old infants and found that the one-month-old infant can resolve a stripe measuring 40′ (40′ = 40 minutes of visual angle; 60 minutes of visual angle equals one degree). Compared with the adult's acuity of about one minute of visual angle, this is not impressive, but it means that the infant can see ⅛-inch-wide stripes at a distance of 10 inches. According to Fantz's measurements, acuity reaches about 5′–7′ of visual angle by the age of 6 months (see also Fantz, 1961).

Later investigators have found acuity values slightly higher than this but in the same general range (Harris et al., 1976; Salapatek et al., 1976; Banks & Salapatek, 1978; Dobson & Teller, 1978), and have also found an increase in acuity over the first 6 months, a nice example of which is shown in Figure 12.5 (Teller et al., 1974). Each curve in this figure represents a function measured by using the preferential looking technique at a different age. The vertical axis indicates the percent of trials on which the infant looked at the striped (as opposed to the grey) card. As the infant gets older, its attention is attracted by stripes with finer and finer widths. For example, the stripe width must be 128′ to attract a 1½-month-old infant's attention on 70 percent of the trials but needs to be only about 6′ to attract a 6-month-old infant's attention on 70 percent of the trials.

The increase in visual acuity with increasing age is shown in Figure 12.6. This graph shows how acuity, measured using the visual evoked potential, increases over the first 6 months of age for a number of different infants. Notice that although acuity increases from worse than 20/200 at 2 months (see Chapter 6 for a description of this way of indicating acuity) to 20/40 by 6 months, adult acuity of 20/20 is not reached at even one year of age. Apparently, the rapid improvement of acuity over the first 6 months is followed by a leveling off period, and full adult acuity is not reached until sometime after one year of age.

Contrast sensitivity. Visual acuity, which is typically measured with high-contrast, black-and-white stimuli, indicates the visual system's capacity to resolve fine details under optimum conditions. Acuity tells us little, however, about how well we can see under lower contrasts and how well we can see forms larger than fine details. As we saw in Chapter 10, we can determine the visual system's ability to see forms of different sizes at a wide range of con-

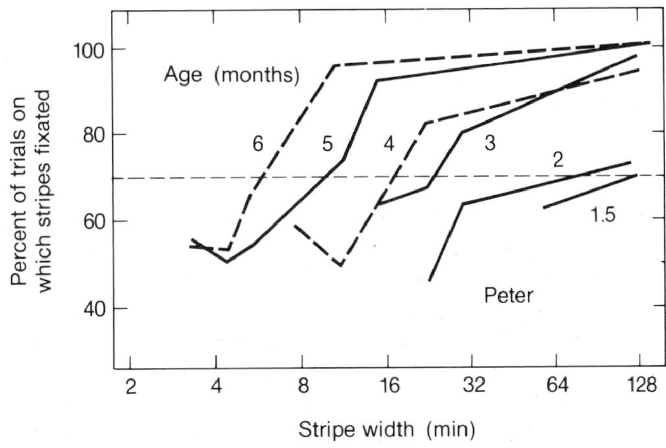

Figure 12.5 A series of psychophysical functions obtained by using the preferential looking technique for a single subject at ages 1.5–6 months. (From Teller et al., 1974.)

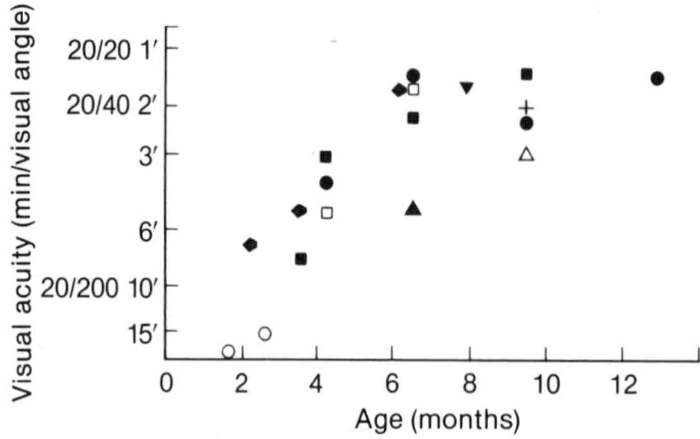

Figure 12.6 The improvement of acuity over the first year of life, as measured by the visual evoked potential. The numbers on the vertical axis indicate the smallest stripe width in minutes of visual angle that results in a detectable evoked response. Snellen acuity values (see Chapter 6) are also indicated on this axis. The different symbols represent measurements on different subjects. (Pirchio et al., 1978.)

trasts, by measuring the contrast sensitivity function (CSF). We measure this function in infants in the same way that we measure acuity, but we present sine-wave gratings of different contrasts to the infant instead of the high-contrast, black-and-white gratings used to measure acuity. (See pp. 280–284, in Chapter 10, for a description of the CSF.)

Contrast sensitivity functions for one-, 2-, and 3-month-old infants and for adults, all determined with the preferential looking technique, are shown in Figure 12.7 (Salapatek & Banks, 1978; Banks & Salapatek, 1978, 1981; Banks, 1982). Similar results have been obtained by using the visual evoked potential, also indicating that the contrast sensitivity of 6-month-olds is much better than that of 3-month-olds, but still slightly below adult sensitivity (Pirchio et al., 1978). Comparing the infant curves with the adult curve indicates that: (1) the infant's contrast sensitivity is much lower than the adult's at all frequencies; (2) what sensitivity the infant does have is restricted to lower frequencies; and (3) the infant can see little or nothing at frequencies above about 2–3 cycles per degree, the frequencies to which the adult is most sensitive.

What does the young infant's depressed CSF tell us about its visual world? Clearly, the infant is sensitive to only a small fraction of the pattern information available to the adult. At one month, the infant can see no fine details and can see only relatively large objects with high contrast. The vision of infants at this age is slightly worse than adult night vision (Fiorentini & Maffei, 1973; Pirchio et al., 1978).

We should not conclude from the young infant's poor vision, however, that it can see nothing at all. At very close distances, a young infant can make out some gross features, as indicated in Figure 12.8, which simulates how one-, 2-, and 3-month-old infants perceive a woman's face from a distance of

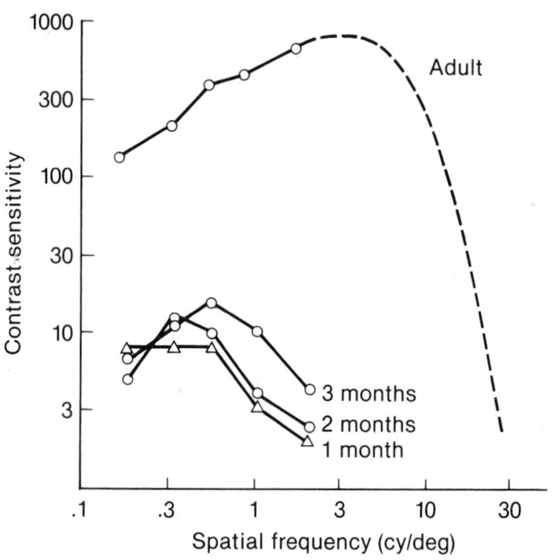

Figure 12.7 Contrast sensitivity functions for an adult and for infants tested at one, 2, and 3 months of age.

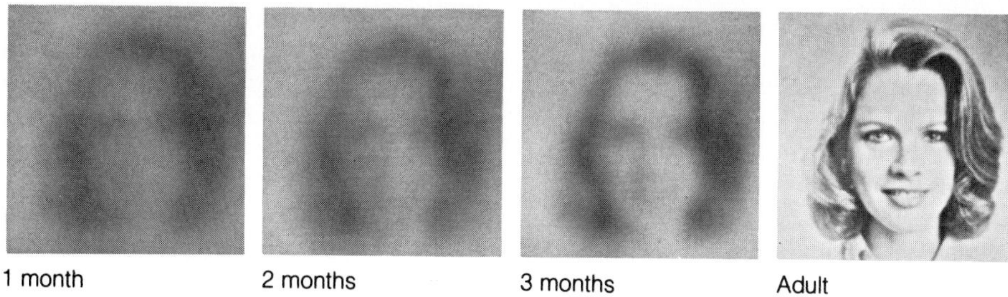

Figure 12.8 Simulations of what one-, 2-, and 3-month-old infants see when they look at the woman's face from a distance of about 6 inches. These pictures were obtained by using a mathematical procedure that applies infant contrast sensitivity functions to the photograph on the right, which depicts what an adult perceives. (From Ginsburg, 1983).

6 inches. At one month, the contrast is so low that it is difficult to make out facial expressions, but it is possible to see very high contrast areas, such as the contour between the woman's hairline and forehead. By 3 months, however, the infant's contrast perception has improved enough so that the perception of facial expressions is possible, and behavioral tests indicate that by 3–4 months of age, infants can, in fact, tell the difference between a face that looks happy and faces that look surprised, angry, or neutral (LaBarbera et al., 1976; Young-Browne et al., 1977). In Figure 12.9, the contrast in Figure 12.8 is enhanced to make it easier to see the improvement in vision that occurs between one and 3 months.

The improvement in the perception of details and contrast, which begins almost at birth and brings the infant to nearly adult levels by 6 months of age, makes possible the development of accommodation, the mechanism that enables the infant to adjust its focus to see near and far objects.

Accommodation. We saw in Chapter 6 that adults have the ability to accommodate—to change the shape of their lens—so they can see both near and far objects clearly. This capacity, however, does not exist at birth, and for good reason: the purpose of accommodation is to bring out-of-focus vision into focus, but if everything is out of focus, accommodation clearly can't work. But as the infant's world becomes more and more detailed, the need for accommodation, and the possibility that it might work, increases. In fact, Martin Banks (1980) has shown that infants as young as one month old have the ability to accommodate slightly and that by 3 months they can accommodate nearly as well as adults.

Banks measured infants' ability to accommodate, by using a retinoscope (see p. 154, Chapter 6). This device, which enables an examine to determine how well a person's eye focuses light, was used to determine the infant's ability to focus on a high-contrast checkerboard pattern placed at different distances

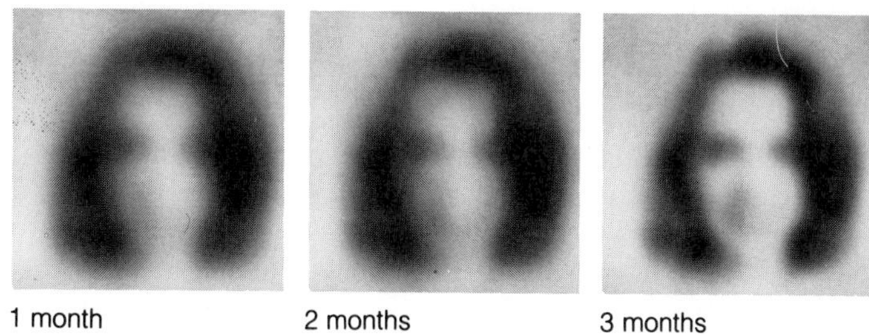

Figure 12.9 The infant perceptions from Figure 12.8, with the contrast enhanced to make it easier to see the improvement in vision that occurs between one and 3 months. (From Ginsburg, 1983.)

from its eye. Banks found that by 3 months of age, infants will change their focus as the checkerboard is moved to different distances, in much the same way as adults. Thus, infants as young as 3 months of age have the capacity to accommodate to very high contrast targets. Though infants may not be able to use this capacity to accommodate to low-contrast targets they cannot see, as their vision becomes clearer, their capacity to accommodate enables them to bring more and more of their visual world into focus at different distances.

Depth Perception

Just as we cannot accommodate if everything in the world is blurred, we cannot perceive depth until we can see clearly. We will see below that some of the mechanisms of depth perception begin to appear at about 3 months of age, but that full depth perception is not established until about 6 months. We will consider the development of depth perception by first considering binocular depth perception and then looking at monocular depth perception (see pages 204–216, in Chapter 8, for a review of binocular and monocular depth perception).

Binocular depth perception. We see the world with two eyes that have different points of view, about three inches apart. This fact, discussed in Chapter 8, gives rise to binocular disparity information that enables us to see the world in depth (review binocular disparity on pp. 213–216). Before binocular disparity can work, however, both eyes must be able to binocularly fixate—to direct their foveas to exactly the same place. At birth, the capacity to binocularly fixate is not present; the infant's eyes are relatively uncoordinated, so that one eye might be directed toward one place, while the other eye is directed somewhere else.

To determine when the capacity to binocularly fixate appears, Richard Aslin (1977) did a simple experiment. He filmed infants' eyes while moving a target between a near point, 12 cm away, and a far point, 57 cm away. If the infant directs both eyes at the target, then the eyes should diverge (rotate outward) as the target moves away, as shown in Figure 12.10(a), and should converge (rotate inward) as the target moves closer, as shown in Figure 12.10(b). Aslin's films indicate that while some divergence and convergence does occur in one- and 2-month-old infants, these eye movements do not reliably point both eyes at the target until about 3 months of age.

Although **binocular fixation** may be present by 3 months of age, this does not guarantee that the infant can use the resulting disparity information to perceive depth. To determine when infants can use this information to perceive depth, Robert Fox and co-workers (Fox et al., 1980; Shea et al., 1980) presented random dot stereograms to infants ranging in age from 2½ to 6 months. Before describing Fox's experiment, let's briefly review the idea behind stereograms (for a more detailed description of stereograms, see p. 219, in Chapter 8).

A stereogram consists of two pictures like those in Figure 8.17, one made from the point of view of each eye. When we use a special viewer to present the left picture to the left eye and the right picture to the right eye, the disparity information provided by the different pictures results in a striking perception of depth. As we saw in Chapter 8, however, the depth we see in stereograms like Figure 8.17 may be due not only to the disparity between the two pictures but also to monocular depth cues such as overlap, perspective convergence, and relative height. One way to eliminate these monocular cues is to use random dot pictures, like the ones in Box 8.2 (see p. 221 for a description of how random dot stereograms work).

The beauty of a random dot stereogram is that its disparity information results in a perception of depth only if: (1) the stereogram is observed with a viewer that presents one picture to the left eye and the other picture to the right eye, and (2) the observer's visual system can convert the picture's disparity information into an impression of depth. Thus, if we present a random dot stereogram to an infant whose visual system is not yet able to use disparity information, all he or she will see is a random collection of dots.

In Fox's experiment, a child wearing special viewing glasses was seated in its mother's lap in front of a television screen, as shown in Figure 12.11. The child viewed a random dot stereogram that looked, to an observer sensitive to disparity information, like a rectangle in depth moving either to the left or to the right. Fox's premise was that an

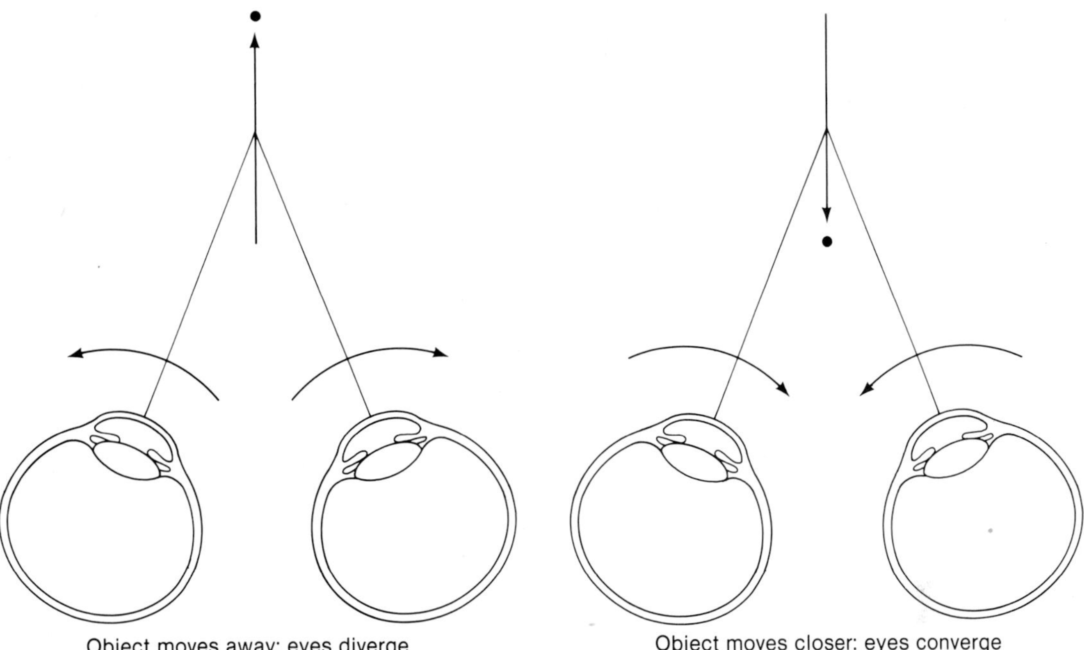

Figure 12.10 If an infant fixates on a moving object, its eyes (a) diverge (rotate outward) as it follows an object that moves away and (b) converge (rotate inward) as it follows an object that moves closer.

Figure 12.11 The setup used by Fox et al. (1980) to test infants' ability to use binocular disparity information. If the infant can use disparity information to see depth, he or she sees a rectangle moving back and forth in front of the screen.

infant sensitive to disparity will move his or her eyes to follow the moving rectangle. He found that infants younger than about 3 months of age would not follow the rectangle, but infants between 3½ and 6 months of age would follow it. He therefore concluded that the ability to use disparity information to perceive depth emerges sometime between 3½ and 6 months of age.

The infant's ability to use binocular information to perceive depth has also been demonstrated with an entirely different procedure, by Carl Granrud, Albert Yonas, and Linda Pettersen (1982a). They used the knowledge that when infants older than about 5 months are given a choice between an object within reaching distance and one beyond their reach, they will reach out for the nearer object. When 5- and 7-month-olds were given a choice between an object within reach and another object just out of reach, they chose the near object 96 percent of the time. If, however, the infants had one eye covered, thereby eliminating binocular information, they reached for the near object only 58 percent of the time. Thus, at 5 months of age, the presence of binocular information greatly improves the infant's perception of depth.

The result of Granrud et al.'s experiment seems to indicate that 5- and 7-month-old infants perceive little depth with only one eye. Does this mean that these infants can't use monocular depth information? Apparently not. Some experiments show that 5½-month-old infants do use monocular depth cues to perceive depth.

Monocular depth perception. Evidence that 6-month-old infants can see depth with one eye was obtained by using a piece of apparatus that has become a classic: the **visual cliff** of Elinor Gibson and Richard Walk (1960). The visual cliff, shown in Figure 12.12, consists of a center board laid across a sheet of glass, with a surface of patterned material located directly under the glass on the shallow side, and at a distance of a few feet below the glass, on

Figure 12.12 A mother calling to her child from across the deep side of the visual cliff. Despite the presence of the glass surface covering the cliff, the child refuses to cross over to the mother. (From Gibson & Walk, 1960. Photograph courtesy of William Vandivert.)

the deep side. Gibson and Walk found that a young child placed on the center board will crawl across the shallow side to get to his or her mother but will not crawl across the "cliff," or deep side. Thus, when the infant is old enough to crawl (at about 6 months), depth perception is sufficiently developed to enable the infant to differentiate between the deep and shallow sides of the cliff. For our purposes, the important result is that infants with one eye patched can detect the visual cliff's depth as well as infants using two eyes (Walk & Dodge, 1962; Walk, 1968).

It appears from Walk's results that infants can use monocular vision to detect depth when they are on a visual cliff. Apparently, however, monocular vision is not as well suited for detecting depth when fine spatial behavior such as reaching is involved, as in Granrud's experiments.

But there is evidence that infants can use information taken in through one eye to detect depth in situations other than the visual cliff. For example, Albert Yonas and co-workers (1982) found that the monocular depth cue of relative size can result in a perception of depth in 5½-month-old infants. They demonstrated this by having infants monocularly view pairs of cardboard objects (triangles, squares, or diamonds), one large and one small, located at the same distance. When adults viewed this display with one eye, the depth effect was striking; they reported that the larger object appeared closer on 80 percent of the trials and that the two objects appeared to be at the same distance on 20 percent of the trials. Apparently, 5½-month-old infants also experience this depth effect, because, when given a choice between the two objects, they reach for the large one more often than the small one. Yonas did not get this result for 5-month-old infants (who reached equally for both objects); therefore, the monocular depth cue of relative size apparently does not become effective for infants until about 5½ months of age.

Color Vision

Color perception is another basic capacity that appears to develop during the first half year of life. The question most investigators have asked is: Are infants monochromats, dichromats, or trichromats? (See pp. 132–134, in Chapter 5, to review these terms.) Though claims have been made that 3-month-old infants are trichromats (Bornstein, 1976; Bornstein et al., 1976), some investigators are not convinced (Werner & Wooten, 1979). There is good evidence, however, that 2-month-old infants are at least dichromats.

An experiment by David Peebles and Davida Teller (1975) shows that 2-month-old infants have color vision. They reasoned that if an infant can discriminate a colored object from a white one, based *only* on a difference in wavelength, then the infant can perceive color. The secret to the success of such an experiment is to make certain that the colored and white objects have the same brightnesses. Peebles and Teller accomplished this (with a procedure we will not go into here) and found that when a red bar was superimposed on a white background, the infant looked at the red bar. In a later, more extensive experiment, Teller, Peebles, and Michael Sekel (1978) presented colors from all parts of the spectrum on the white background. They found that infants could tell the difference between white and blue, greenish blue, orange, and red but could not discriminate between white and yellow-green and white and purple. Infants, therefore, definitely have color vision, but at 2 months of age it seems to be less developed than that of adults.

Form Perception

So far we have seen that during the first 6 months of life, infants develop good detail vision. But does this mean that they can perceive forms? Many experiments have shown that newborns and older infants look at some forms more than others. For example, when given a choice between curved and straight contours, newborns look more at the curved contours (Fantz et al., 1975); however, while this result tells us that newborns can tell the difference between two different forms, it doesn't tell us what they are perceiving. Of particular interest to us is whether an infant perceives a form in terms of its individual parts or in terms of the whole form. The available evidence indicates that early perception is in terms of parts; only later are whole forms perceived.

One way to investigate the problem of the perception of parts versus wholes is to measure the fixation patterns of infants as they view patterns. Philip Salapatek (1975) measured the visual scanning of one- and 2-month-old infants by filming the infants' eyes as they looked at triangles and other geometrical objects. His results, shown in Figure 12.13, indicate that one-month-old infants tend to look at a single vertex of a triangle, whereas 2-month-old infants are more likely to scan more of the triangle. A similar situation occurs when infants look at a face or a picture of a face. The one-month-old infants either don't look at the face at all or look at only a limited portion of it, usually near the perimeter; 2-month-olds, however, look at the face more often, and when they do, they scan more broadly and often look at the details inside the face (Maurer & Salapatek, 1976). Thus, these experiments indicate that at the age of about 2 months, infants begin to scan the pattern more as a whole.

This more extensive scanning at about 2 months, however, does not tell us whether the infant *perceives* the form as a whole. The infant may be fixating the individual parts of a form, without combining or integrating them into the perception of the form as a whole. One approach to investigating this problem is to present two forms that have the same parts but are arranged differently. Such experiments show that newborns look equally often at two pictures of faces, one of which has normally arranged features and the other of which has its features reorganized so that the eyes, nose, mouth, and other parts of the face are not in their usual positions (Figure 12.14). Four-month-old infants, however, prefer to look at the normal faces (Kagan et al., 1966; Fantz et al., 1975). This result suggests that the older infants may be perceiving the faces as wholes rather than as individual features.

Figure 12.14 Stimuli from Fantz's experiments, in which he showed that newborns spend almost equal time looking at the normally arranged and scrambled faces but that 4-month-olds prefer to look at the normally arranged face.

Recent experiments support the idea that as infants get older they tend to respond to forms more as wholes. Mark Strauss and Lynne Curtis (1983) recently used the habituation procedure to determine whether infants could distinguish different arrangements of dots. They used arrangements of dots like those in Figure 12.15, which had been previously classified by adults as being "good," "intermediate," or "poor" forms (see p. 170, in Chapter 7, to review the Gestalt idea of Pragnanz, or pattern goodness).

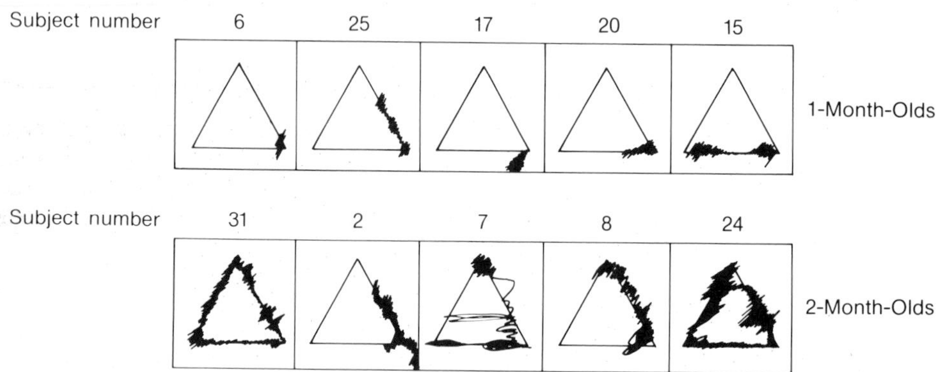

Figure 12.13 How one- and 2-month-olds look at triangles. (From Salapatek, 1975.)

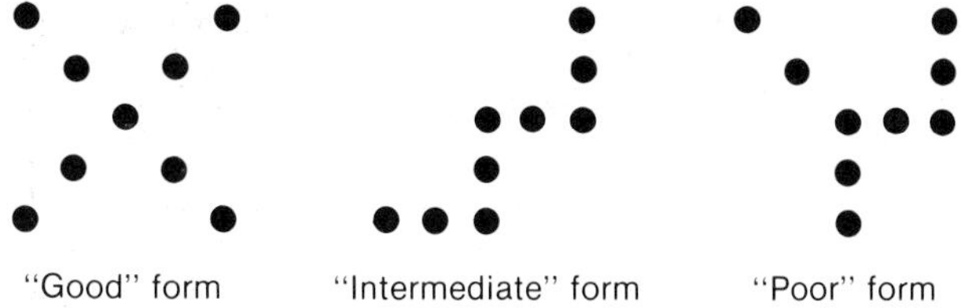

Figure 12.15 Some of the stimuli used in the experiment that led Strauss and Curtis (1983) to conclude that between the ages of 3 and 5 months, infants develop the ability to "put together" complex forms.

Strauss and Curtis repeatedly presented one of the forms, measuring the amount of time the infant looked at the form on each trial, until the looking time on each trial had decreased to half of the time on the initial trials. After this habituation, they substituted another form from the same group (if they initially presented a "good" form, they substituted another good form) and measured the amount of time the infant looked at this new form. They found that 3-month-old infants would increase their looking time to a new good form, indicating that they could distinguish two different good forms, but did not increase their looking time to a new intermediate or poor form, indicating that they could not distinguish different intermediate or poor forms. Four-month-old infants, on the other hand, could distinguish two good or intermediate forms but could not distinguish two poor forms, whereas 5-month-olds could tell the difference between any of the forms, no matter what their pattern goodness.

What conclusion can we draw from these results? We might argue that the infants were discriminating between the different patterns, not by looking at the overall pattern but by looking at single elements of the pattern. Strauss and Curtis, however, reject this idea, arguing that if the infants based their looking on single elements, the pattern type would have made no difference. It appears that 3-month-olds can "put together" the elements of a good pattern into a "whole" perception but cannot do this for poorer, more complicated patterns. As the infants get older, however, they become able to put together the more complex patterns.

Increasing age brings more advanced capacities for form perception. By the age of 5–6 months, infants can not only recognize a person's face but can generalize from one facial pose to another. Joseph Fagan habituated 7-month-old infants to the training face in Figure 12.16(a) by presenting it for 40 seconds. When he then presented the training face in a different pose and paired it with a new face, as shown in Figure 12.16(b), the infants indicated that they recognized the original face by looking more at the new face. The conclusion that the infants rec-

Figure 12.16 Some of the stimuli used in Fagan's (1976) experiment, in which he showed that after seeing one pose of a face, 7-month-old infants can recognize this face when it is seen in a different pose.

Box 12.1 Sensory-Motor Coordination

Although you may often sit in one place to watch a film, a television program, or even a lecture on perception, much of your visual experience occurs as you interact more actively with your environment. This active interaction with the environment—which ranges from simple actions, such as turning the pages in this book, to more complex actions, such as figure skating or gymnastics—involves **sensory-motor coordination.** Although many of your day-to-day tasks may seem easy to you now, you originally had to learn to coordinate your movements with your perceptions to do even the simplest things. How did you develop this ability?

Richard Held (1965) has suggested that a person must actively interact with the environment to develop sensory-motor coordination. To support this idea, Held did an experiment in which he disrupted sensory-motor coordination by having a person wear prism goggles that shift perception to the left or right. A person wearing the goggles often has trouble picking up things and often bumps into things, because they are not where they appear to be. Eventually, however, the person adapts to the displaced vision and can function while wearing the goggles.

That a person can adapt to displaced vision is nothing new—psychologists have been putting prism goggles on people (and on themselves) since before the turn of the century—but Held added something new. He had one person wear the goggles while walking along an outdoor path and another person wear them while being pushed in a wheelchair along the same path. Thus, both people were exposed to the same visual stimulation, but the walking person was active whereas the other was passive. After this trip along the path, Held tested the extent of adaptation to the goggles and found that the active person adapted to the goggles but the passive person did not. This result supports the idea that active or **self-produced movement** is necessary to adapt to the displaced vision caused by prism goggles.

To show that self-produced movement is important not only for the sensory-motor coordination involved in an adult's adaptation to prism goggles but also for a newborn's development of sensory-motor coordination, Held and Alan Hein (1963) did an experiment in which two dark-reared kittens were given their first visual experience in the "kitten carousel" shown in the figure. As the active kitten walked, it transported the passive kitten riding in the gondola. Just as in the goggle experiment described above, both kittens received the same visual stimulation, but this stimulation was caused by self-produced movement only for the active kitten. As predicted, the active kitten developed good sensory-motor coordination, as indicated by its ability to blink at an

ognized the test face, even though it was in a different pose, follows from the fact that, given a choice, an infant familiar with a stimulus will look longer at a new, unfamiliar stimulus.

That infants can recognize different views of the same face indicates that they can perceive invariance across transformations. That is, even though the face is transformed by changing its position, things such as the relationships between the eyes, nose, and mouth remain constant, or invariant, and the infant apparently can recognize these invariant relationships. DeLoache, Strauss, and Maynard (1979) also demonstrated the infant's ability to recognize invariance. When 5-month-olds were shown a doll for 60 seconds and then given a choice between a *photograph* of the same doll and a photograph of a novel doll, they looked more at the photograph of the novel doll. Thus, the child can tell that the real doll and the photograph share some properties in common, even though one is three dimensional and the other two dimensional.

The above descriptions of the infant's ability to perceive forms indicates that the infant's perception comes a long way during the first 6 months of life. In fact, 6–8-month-old infants can not only recognize the invariant features of faces but can recognize similarities between a sequence of light flashes and a similarly timed sequence of tones (Allen et al., 1977), and can identify the shape of a visually presented object they had previously felt (Bryant et approaching object, to put out its paws to ward off collision when carried downward toward a surface, and to avoid the deep side of a visual cliff; the passive kitten, however, had poor sensory-motor coordination, as indicated by its inability to do any of these things.

Thus, to develop sensory-motor coordination, it is necessary not only to be exposed to changing visual stimulation but also to cause the scene to change by means of self-produced movement. It is this interaction between changes in visual stimulation and the movement which produces these changes that helps you to coordinate what you do with what you see.

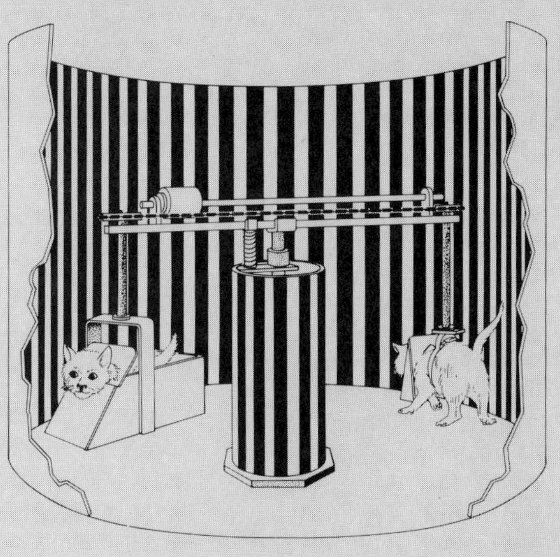

al., 1972). Just as acuity increases rapidly over the first 6 months of life, so does the ability to perceive forms.

Why Does Perception Develop?

We've seen that the infant possesses some perceptual capacities at birth and that perception improves rapidly during the first 6 months of life. Why does this improvement occur? Do the infant's increased perceptual capacities result from genetically programmed development that proceeds independent of the infant's experience with its environment? Or does this improved perception result primarily from the infant's experience with its environment? These two possibilities represent the extremes of what has been called the nature versus nurture debate, and, as is usually the case when dealing with extremes, the correct answer lies somewhere between these two. As Richard Aslin (1981) states in a recent paper on perceptual development, "There can be little doubt that development is determined by a combination of genetic and environmental factors operating in a complex manner." Much of the evidence that led Aslin to the conclusion that both genetics and the environment play a role in perceptual development has come from **deprivation experiments,** in which the effect of the environment is determined by depriving a human or animal of contact with the environment.

The First Deprivation Experiments

One of the first deprivation experiments was done by Austin Riesen in 1947, the purpose of which was to determine the role of learning in the development of perception. He attempted to accomplish this by raising two groups of chimpanzees: one group was raised in a normal, lighted environment and was, therefore, able to learn by looking at the environment; the other group was raised in the dark and was, therefore, deprived of the ability to learn by looking at the environment. Riesen's idea was that if learning is necessary for perception, animals reared in the dark, and thus prevented from learning, would perceive poorly or not at all when tested later, whereas animals reared in the light would perceive well when tested later. Riesen assumed that, at the time of testing, each group of monkeys would be identical *except* for their amount of learning.

The results of these experiments turned out as expected: two chimpanzees, reared in the dark from birth to 16 months, could turn their heads toward a light source but otherwise behaved as though completely blind. In contrast, chimpanzees reared in the light could see normally. While these results seemed to indicate that learning was important for the development of perception, this conclusion does not actually follow from Riesen's experiment, because his initial assumption—that each group of monkeys would be identical except for the amount of learning done—was later shown to be invalid.

The flaw in Riesen's reasoning was that **dark rearing** not only prevents animals from learning, it also destroys their visual system! The visual systems of animals reared in the dark degenerate, so that when the animals are tested after their period of dark rearing, they are often almost blind. Their poor perception, originally thought to result from a lack of learning, was probably due to the damage the light deprivation caused to their visual system.

Although these early experiments failed to determine the role of learning in the development of perception, they did show something else: stimulation is necessary for the development and maintenance of the visual system. This conclusion formed the basis of a new generation of deprivation experiments, which asked two basic questions: (1) How does the *type* of deprivation affect both the functioning of the visual system and perception? and, (2) How does the *timing* of deprivation affect the functioning of the visual system and perception? As we describe these experiments below, we will see that the effects of deprivation depend on both *how* the deprivation is carried out and *when* the deprivation occurs in the life of the animal. We will first consider some experiments that have looked at the visual systems of newborn cats and monkeys and have asked how rearing these animals in the dark affects these newborn visual systems.

Newborn Cats and Monkeys

We saw above that the infant's visual system is not totally developed at birth. Experiments on cats and monkeys (who have been the main subjects of deprivation experiments) show that the visual systems of these animals, while not totally mature at birth, do have many adultlike properties.

To determine the state of the visual system of newborn cats and monkeys, animals are kept in the dark until they are old enough to be tested, and then the responses of neurons in the cortex are measured. The first study of this kind was done by Hubel and Wiesel, on kittens in 1963. (Remember from Chapter 2 that Hubel and Wiesel were also the first investigators to determine the characteristics of simple, complex, and hypercomplex cells in the cat's cortex.) To be sure that their kittens had no visual experience before they were tested, Hubel and Wiesel either tested them before they opened their eyes or put occluders (which eliminated all patterned stimuli) on the kittens' eyes as soon as they opened, at 8–10 days, and tested the kittens shortly afterward. Surprisingly, Hubel and Wiesel found that 8–16-day-old kittens who have never seen patterned light have receptive fields very similar to those of adult cats. That is, they found cells in the cortex of these visually inexperienced kittens that correspond to the simple, complex, and hypercomplex cells seen in the adult. Furthermore, they found that most cells, as in the adult, respond to stimulation of both eyes, and they also found evidence of columns of cells with the same receptive field orientation. The major difference between the cells of a kitten and an adult cat is that the response of the kitten's cells is more sluggish.

Following Hubel and Wiesel's report that there is little difference between cells in the kitten's cortex and those of the adult cat, other experiments have confirmed this result in both the kitten (Sherk & Stryker, 1976) and monkey (Wiesel & Hubel, 1974). Not all investigators, however, agree with Hubel and Wiesel's result. John Pettigrew (1974) reports that there are few orientation-selective cells in the newborn kitten and finds that not until 4–5 weeks of age do the kitten's cortical cells reach their adult state. A number of other investigators (Buissert & Imbert, 1976; Bonds, 1978; Imbert, 1979) report results between those of Hubel and Wiesel and those of Pettigrew. They find that about 25–40 percent of cells in the newborn kitten are orientation-selective and that, by 5–6 weeks of age, most cells have adult properties. Although there is some disagreement about the state of the kitten's visual system at birth, it seems safe to conclude, taking all these studies into account, that a large number, but not all, of the cells in the newborn kitten are selective for orientation, but it is not until 4–6 weeks that most of the cells reach adult standards.

The results regarding the **binocularity** of cells in the newborn kitten are more clear. Most investigators agree with Hubel and Wiesel's finding that most cells in the newborn respond to stimulation of both eyes. That alone, however, does not mean that true binocular vision is present. For the visual system to make use of binocular vision to perceive depth, the eyes must be precisely aligned so that small disparities between images that fall on the two retinas can be detected (see p. 213, in Chapter 8, to review retinal disparity). Pettigrew (1974) finds that although most cells in the newborn kitten can respond to stimulation of both eyes, the eyes are poorly aligned; and not until about 5 weeks of age are the eyes aligned so that the kitten can make use of binocular disparity information.

Of the numerous studies indicating that the kitten's visual cells do not reach adult standards until about 4–6 weeks after birth, a few have reared some of the kittens in the dark for their first 4–6 weeks and then looked at their cells. The usual result is that after 4–6 weeks of dark rearing, the kitten's cells show little or no development beyond their newborn state. So it appears that experience in the light is necessary in order for normal development to occur during the first 4–6 weeks of life (Pettigrew, 1974; Bonds, 1978).

Deprivation of light for the first 4–6 weeks retards normal development. But what happens if we deprive animals of light for longer periods of time? Many experiments indicate that longer periods of deprivation not only retard development but can cause drastic changes in the visual system. We will now look at the results of these experiments.

How Deprivation Affects Acuity

If a kitten or monkey is deprived of light by dark rearing or by suturing both eyes closed, acuity decreases, and the neurons that would usually respond to stimulation either cease to respond or respond abnormally. Similar results occur if deprivation is limited to one eye. The longer the monocular deprivation, the worse the animal's acuity becomes, until, for long periods of deprivation, the animal becomes essentially blind in the deprived eye but still sees normally in the undeprived eye (Hubel & Wiesel, 1963; Dews & Wiesel, 1970; Baker et al., 1974; Berkeley, 1981; Mitchell, 1981).

An important consequence of the decreased acuity in the deprived eye, which occurs because of monocular rearing, is a decrease in the animal's capacity for binocular vision. Although about 80 percent of cells in the visual cortex of the adult cat respond to stimulation of both eyes, none of the cells of monocularly reared kittens respond to stimulation of both eyes. This finding has led to much research on how **monocular rearing** affects binocularity.

How Monocular Rearing Affects Binocularity

The effect of monocular rearing on binocularity is illustrated most clearly by **ocular dominance histograms,** such as those shown in Figure 12.17. These histograms are determined by recording from a large number of cells and then rating each cell's ability to respond to stimulation of both the **contralateral eye** (the eye on the opposite side of the head from the cell) and the **ipsilateral eye** (the eye on the same side as the cell). Each cell is placed in one of the following categories, according to the degree of **ocular dominance**:

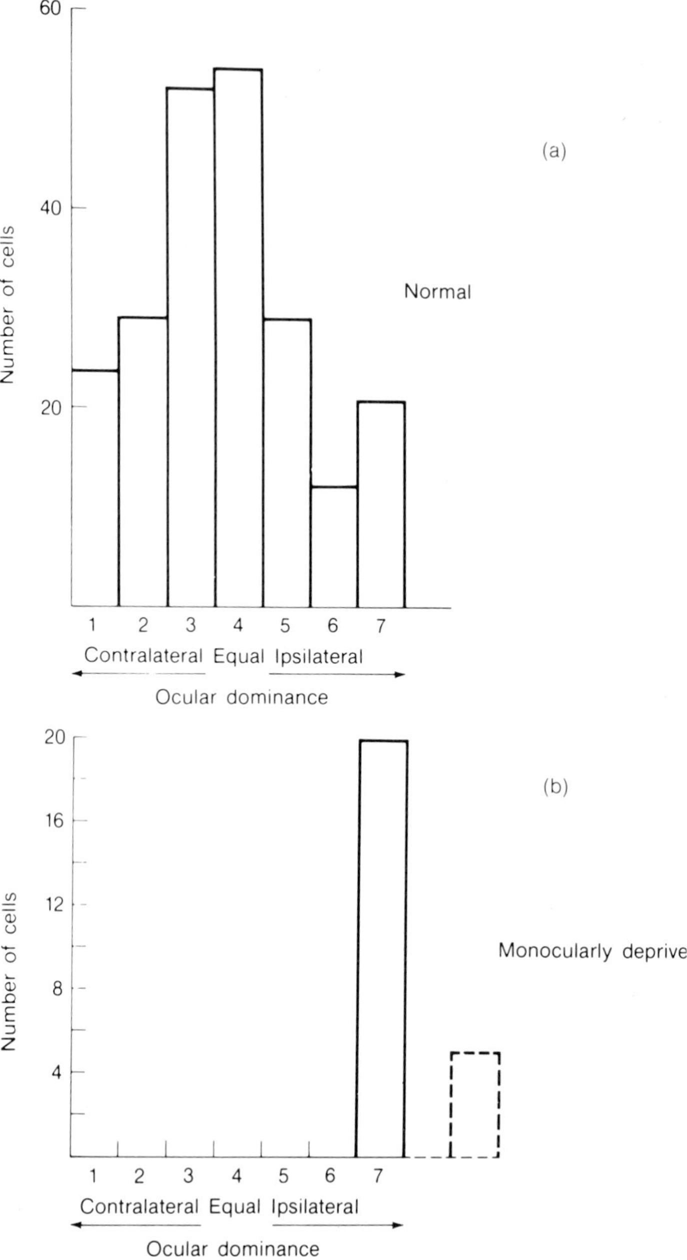

Figure 12.17 (a) Ocular dominance histogram for 223 cells recorded from the visual cortex of adult cats. Note that a large number of cells responded to stimulation of both eyes. (b) Ocular dominance histogram of 25 cells, recorded from the visual cortex of a 2½-month-old kitten that was reared with its right eye sutured shut until the time of the experiment. The dashed bar on the right indicates that five cells did not respond to stimulation of either eye. The solid bar indicates that all 20 cells which responded to stimulation responded only to the eye that was opened during rearing. (From Wiesel & Hubel, 1963.)

Category	Description
1	Cell responds only to stimulation of the contralateral eye. Thus, if the cell is in the right hemisphere, it responds only to stimulation of the left eye.
2	Cell responds much more to stimulation of the contralateral eye than to stimulation of the ipsilateral eye.
3	Cell responds slightly more to stimulation of the contralateral eye.
4	Cell responds equally to stimulation of each eye.
5	Cell responds slightly more to stimulation of the ipsilateral eye.
6	Cell responds much more to stimulation of the ipsilateral eye.
7	Cell responds only to stimulation of the ipsilateral eye.

The histograms in Figure 12.17 show the striking effect of monocular deprivation on the way the kitten's cells respond to stimulation of each eye. Whereas most of the cells in the normal cat fall in the center of the histogram (categories 3, 4, and 5), indicating that they respond to stimulation of both eyes, all the cells in the deprived kitten respond only to the undeprived eye.

Hubel and Wiesel found that the longer the time kittens are monocularly deprived from birth, the greater the abnormalities in their ocular dominance histograms; if adult cats are monocularly deprived, however, even for long periods of time, their ocular dominance histograms are unaffected. This finding led Hubel and Wiesel to propose a **critical period,** early in the kitten's life, during which suturing one eye has a large effect; once this period is past, however, suturing has little effect.

To investigate this idea, Hubel and Wiesel (1970a) did an experiment to determine when the critical period occurs, by monocularly depriving kittens at various times after birth. They found that deprivation for only 3 days between the fourth and fifth week causes a large change in the ocular dominance histograms; when deprivation was started past about the eighth week, however, much smaller effects were observed, until by 4 months, even long periods of deprivation caused no effect. Hubel and Wiesel concluded that the critical period for susceptibility to monocular deprivation is between about 4 and 8 weeks.

Many investigators have found that extremely brief periods of deprivation during the critical period can cause large effects on the kitten's occular dominance. For example, C. R. Olson and Ralph Freeman (1975) found that suturing one eye of a 4-week-old kitten for only one day causes the large effect on the ocular dominance histogram shown in Figure 12.18.

The large effects of monocular deprivation on the kitten's visual system led researchers to investigate the effects of other conditions that affect the coordination between the two eyes. In one such condition found in humans, called **strabismus,** the coordination between the two eyes is upset because of an imbalance in the eye muscles. This inbalance in the eye muscles causes the eyes to be misaligned, so the image formed in one eye does not fall on the corresponding area of the other eye. We will see below that this misalignment causes a decrease in binocular vision in humans, but first let's consider some experiments that investigate the effects of strabismus on monkeys and kittens.

How Strabismus Affects Binocularity

The effects of strabismus can be duplicated in animals by either cutting the eye muscles or by fitting the animal with a helmet that contains small optical

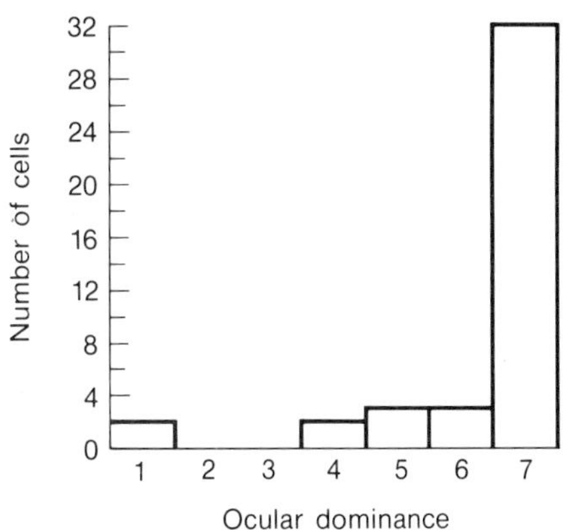

Figure 12.18 Ocular dominance histogram of a kitten that had one eye sutured shut for 24 hours, following 4 weeks of normal vision. (From Olson & Freeman, 1975.)

prisms. Both procedures cause misalignment of the images in the two eyes; cutting the eye muscles causes the eyes to become misaligned, as shown in Figure 12.19, and optical prisms, shown in Figure 12.20, change the direction of the light entering the eyes. Each way of producing artificial strabismus causes effects similar to that of monocular deprivation—a large decrease in the number of cortical cells that respond to stimulation of both eyes.

Hubel and Wiesel (1965b) found that whereas 80 percent of cortical cells in normal cats respond to stimulation of both eyes, only 20 percent of the cells in the strabismus cats responded to stimulation of both eyes. Similarly, M. L. J. Crawford and G. K. von Noorden (1980) found that 70 percent of cortical cells in normal monkeys respond to stimulation of both eyes, but less than 10 percent of the cells in monkeys that had worn the prism helmets for 60 days responded to stimulation of both eyes.

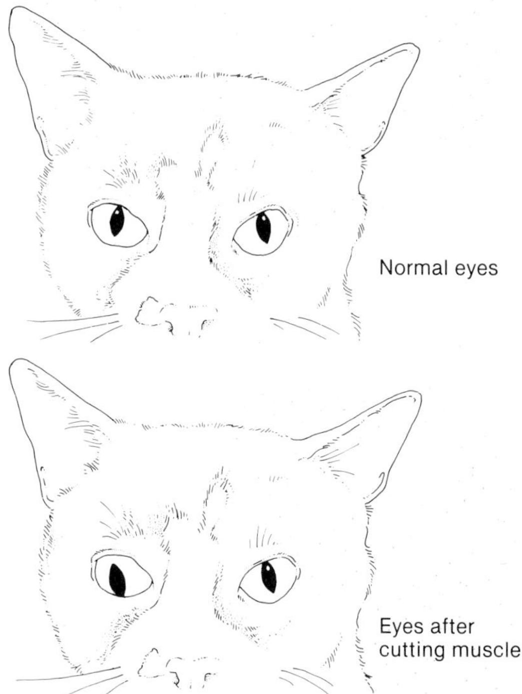

Figure 12.19 The appearance of a normal cat's eyes and the eyes of a cat whose eyes are misaligned due to cutting of its eye muscles.

Figure 12.21 shows that the number of cells responding to both eyes decreases as the prisms are worn for longer periods of time (see also Smith et al., 1979).

In all the experiments described so far, the functioning of cortical cells is affected either by depriving the animal of all pattern vision or by causing a misalignment of the images falling on the two eyes. The results of these experiments led a number of investigators to wonder what would happen if, instead of depriving animals of all pattern vision, as was the case in the lid-suturing experiments, animals were deprived of some patterns but not others. These experiments, which are called **selective rearing** experiments, show that the response of cortical cells is greatly influenced by the animal's visual environment.

The Effects of Selective Rearing

In the first selective rearing experiments, kittens were exposed to either vertical or horizontal stripes, in two ways, by two different groups of researchers. Colin Blakemore and Grahame Cooper (1970) placed kittens in striped tubes, like the one in Figure 12.22, while Helmut Hirsch and D. N. Spinelli (1970, 1971) fitted kittens with goggles that presented vertical stripes to one eye and horizontal stripes to the other, as shown in Figure 12.23.

Blakemore and Cooper's kittens were kept in the dark from birth to 2 weeks of age, at which time they were placed in the tube for 5 hours a day; the rest of the time, they remained in the dark. Since the kittens sat on a Plexiglas platform and the tube extended both above and below them, there were no visible corners or edges in their environment, other than the vertical or horizontal stripes on the sides of the tube. The kittens wore a neck ruff to prevent them from turning vertical stripes into oblique or horizontal stripes by turning their heads; however, according to Blakemore and Cooper, "The kittens did not seem upset by the monotony of their surroundings and they sat for long periods inspecting the walls of the tube."

After 5 months, the selective rearing was stopped and the kittens were placed in the dark, except for brief sessions in which their vision was tested. This testing uncovered a number of defects in their visual behavior. Their head movements were jerky when

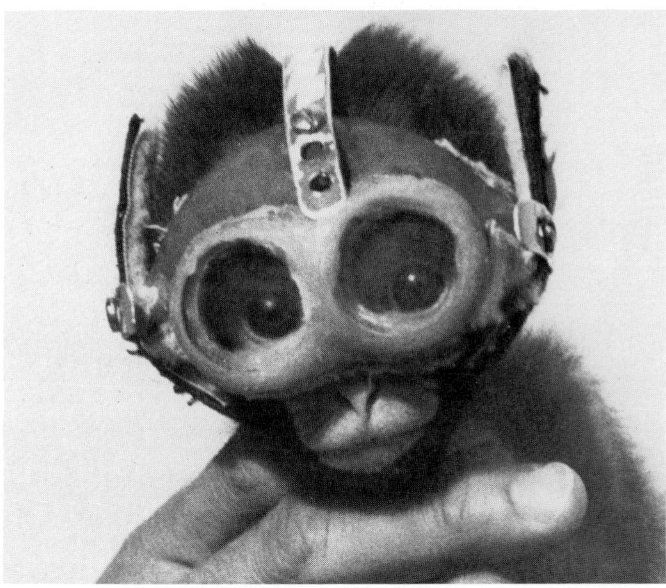

Figure 12.20 A monkey wearing an optical prism-helmet, which causes a misalignment of the images in the two eyes. (From Crawford & von Noorden, 1980.)

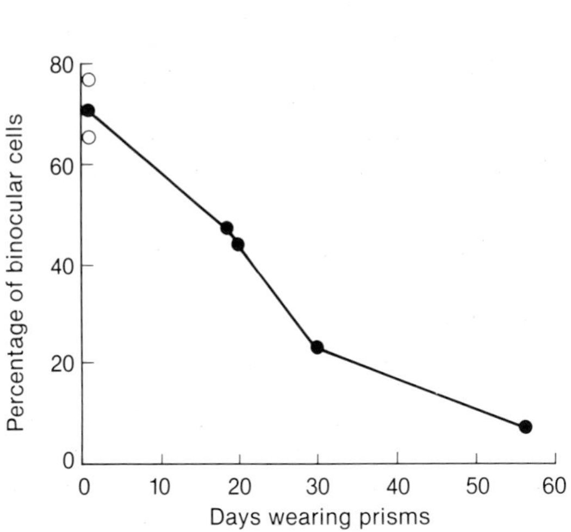

Figure 12.21 The percentage of cells that respond to stimulation of both eyes starts out at about 70 percent in normal monkeys, but then decreases to less than 10 percent after wearing a prism helmet for 60 days. (From Crawford & von Noorden, 1980.)

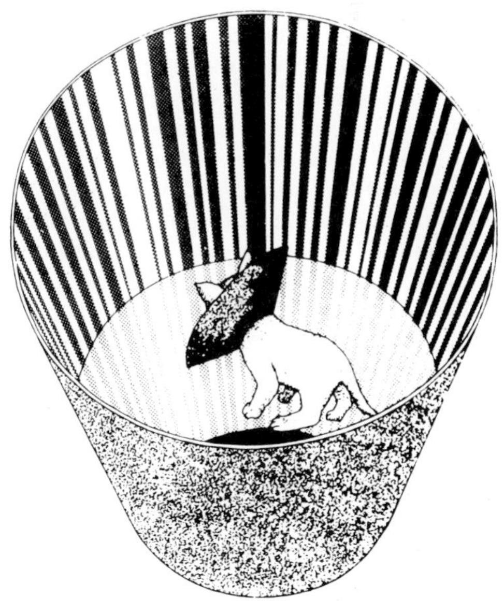

Figure 12.22 Blakemore and Cooper's (1970) striped tube. The kitten wore a black ruff to mask its body from its eyes and stood on a glass platform in the middle of the cylinder. A spotlight (not shown) illuminated the walls from above.

Figure 12.23 One of Hirsch and Spinelli's (1971) cats wearing goggles. The vertically and horizontally striped stimulus patterns are mounted on the inside surface of the black rectangular sheet on the front of the goggles. The neck ruff, which the cats normally wore, is not shown.

following moving objects; they tried to touch moving objects that were across the room, far from their reach; and they often bumped into things. Most important, however, these kittens seemed blind to stripes orthogonal (at 90 degrees) to the orientation of the stripes in the environment in which they were reared. In one test, Blakemore and Cooper held a rod in front of two kittens, one of which had been raised in a vertical environment and the other in a horizontal environment. When the rod was held in a vertical position and shaken, the vertically reared kitten played with it, while the horizontally reared kitten ignored it. When the rod was changed to a horizontal position, the kittens traded roles: the horizontally reared kitten played with the rod, while the vertically reared kitten ignored it.

Following these behavioral tests, Blakemore and Cooper recorded from cells in the visual cortex and determined the stimulus orientation that caused the largest response from each cell. Their results are shown in Figure 12.24. These plots, in which each line represents the optimum orientation for a single cell, show that many of the cells of the horizontally reared cat respond best to horizontal stimuli, but none responds to vertical stimuli. The cells of the vertically reared cat, on the other hand, respond best to vertical stimuli, but none responds to horizontal stimuli. These results, combined with the behavioral results described above, indicate a correspondence between the directional selectivity of cortical neurons and the cat's ability to perceive stimuli in different orientations. Other investigators have found similar connections between behavior and cortical physiology (Hirsch, 1972; Muir & Mitchell, 1975; Blasdel et al., 1977).

The results of Hirsch and Spinelli's experiments, in which kittens wore goggles instead of being reared in a tube, were even more striking: they found few cells that deviated from the horizontal (for cells connected to the eye exposed to horizontal stripes) or vertical (for cells connected to the eye exposed to vertical stripes) by more than 5–10 degrees. Thus, Hirsch and Spinelli's goggle-rearing results show that cells respond to orientations very close to the orientations seen during rearing.

In one of the most amazing results of all the selective rearing experiments, Colin Blakemore and Donald Mitchell (1973) demonstrated that *one hour*

Box 12.2 The Development of Birdsong: An Example of a Critical Period

The idea that a critical period exists for development applies not only to the development of the visual system but to that of other things as well. For example, many experiments have shown that some birds' ability to sing the songs characteristic of their species depends on hearing their species' song during a critical period of their development. A favorite subject of these birdsong experiments is the chaffinch, a small bird found in western Europe, northern Africa, and central Asia.

Just as we can deprive a cat or monkey of visual experience, we can keep a chaffinch from hearing both other chaffinches and its own song. If reared in isolation, away from the songs of other birds, the chaffinch develops a song of about the right length and number of notes but with a lower than normal pitch and without the normally distinctive rhythmic patterning.

If a wild chaffinch hears adults singing during its first 4 months of life and is then isolated, it will develop the correct adult song when about 10–12 months old. Such observations have led to the concept of a critical period for song learning in the chaffinch. The chaffinch normally develops its adult song pattern between about 3 and 10 months of age, and whatever song it sings at about 10 months is the one it sings for the rest of its life. The bird's first 10 months, therefore, are considered to constitute the critical period of song development. If a bird is isolated during this period, it never develops the characteristic chaffinch song, even if it begins hearing other adults after it is 10 months old.

In addition to the influence of other birds, song development is also influenced by the chaffinch's ability to hear its own sound. Birds deafened at about 3 months of age, before any song development has taken place, develop an extremely abnormal song, sometimes resembling a screech. Birds deafened between about 3 and 10 months, the normal period of song learning, develop songs resembling those they had sung until the time of deafening. Deafening a year-old bird that has developed its adult song also has an effect—the bird will regress to an earlier stage of song development. However, once a chaffinch has sung for a year, deafening has no effect on its singing. By this time the bird has learned its song well; the song has become a permanent part of the bird's behavior, continuing even if the bird can't hear its own song (Thorpe, 1958; Nottebohm, 1970).

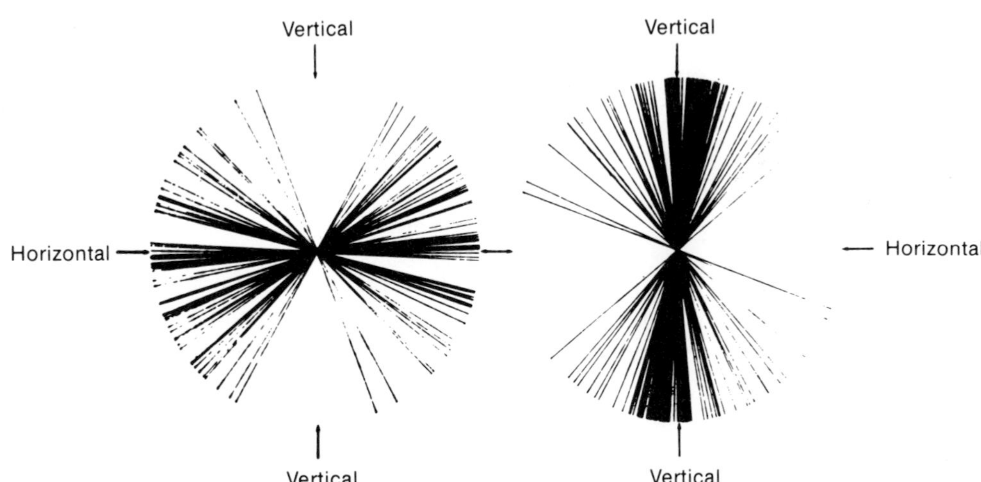

Figure 12.24 Distribution of optimal orientations for 52 cells from a horizontally experienced cat, on the left, and for 72 cells from a vertically experienced cat, on the right. (From Blakemore & Cooper, 1970.)

of exposure to the striped tube could drastically change the cells in the kitten's cortex. They kept a kitten in the dark until 28 days of age, placed the kitten into a tube with vertical stripes for one hour, and then put the kitten back into the dark until recording was carried out, at about 42 days of age. The result of this one-hour exposure to an environment of vertical stripes, shown in Figure 12.25, is a transformed cortex! As in the kittens exposed to vertical stripes for much longer periods of time, most cells respond best to vertical or near vertical orientations.

These large effects on the properties of cortical cells, caused by vertical or horizontal rearing, stimulated a large number of experiments in which animals were exposed to many different environments. In general, their results paralleled those of vertical and horizontal rearing experiments, in that the properties of the kitten's receptive fields tended to resemble the environment to which the kitten was exposed. The results of some of these experiments are described as follows:

Rearing stimulus	*Cortical cells*
1. Moving white spots (Van Sluyters & Blakemore, 1973).	Most cells respond as well to spots as to lines (normally, lines are preferred). Many cells respond best to moving spots of about the same size as those seen during rearing.
2. Random array of point sources of light, like bright stars on a dark sky (Pettigrew & Freeman, 1973).	Many cells are "spot detectors," which respond best to very small moving targets and respond poorly to linear contours.
3. Strobe light flashing at 2 flashes per second (Olson & Pettigrew, 1974).	Cells show little preference for line over spot stimulus. Only 45 percent of cells are orientation specific, compared with 86 percent in the normal cat.
4. Stripes moving in one direction (Tretter et al., 1975).	More cells respond to lines moving in the direction of movement experienced during rearing.

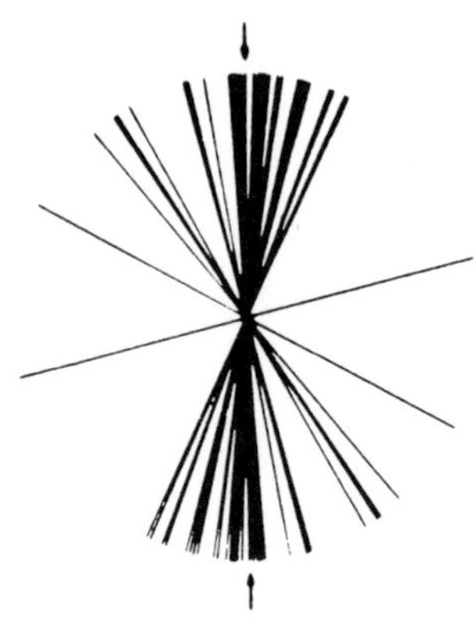

Figure 12.25 The effect of spending one hour in an environment of vertical stripes, at 28 days of age, on the optimal orientation of cortical cells. (From Blakemore & Mitchell, 1973.)

What causes these impressive effects? We have seen that the cat's cortical cells respond to specific orientations early in life (at birth, according to Hubel and Wiesel, and by no later than 4–5 weeks, according to other investigators). It appears that the adult wiring, which the kitten begins with early in life, is modified by the environment. But how does this modification occur? There are two ideas as to the nature of this modification: (1) the **degeneration hypothesis** (some cells degenerate, or simply become unresponsive) and (2) the **rewiring hypothesis** (some cells change their connections). Let's consider each of these ideas in turn.

The problem with which we are dealing can be stated in terms of a horizontal rearing experiment. When a kitten is exposed to only horizontal stripes, the kitten's cortical cells respond only to horizontal, or nearly horizontal, stripes. The question is: What happens to the cells that would respond under normal rearing conditions to oblique and vertical stripes? The degeneration hypothesis states that in horizontally reared kittens, cells sensitive to oblique and vertical orientations degenerate or become unresponsive, because they are not used. This hypothesis is supported by the results of experiments done by Michael Stryker and co-workers (1978), who raised kittens with vertical/horizontal goggles like those shown in Figure 12.23. They found that the orientation selectivity of the cat's cortical cells was determined by the orientations the cat viewed during rearing. However, they also found that many cells responded abnormally or were completely unresponsive, with about half of the cells being unselective for orientation. The researchers concluded that cortical neurons which receive appropriate stimulation during early life maintain innate orientation preferences and that the remaining cells lose either their responsiveness or their orientation selectivity.

The rewiring hypothesis states that horizontal rearing causes cells that normally would have responded to oblique or vertical orientations to be rewired so that they respond to horizontal orientations. Blakemore and Cooper (1970) argue for this idea, primarily because they found no cortical areas with unresponsive cells. They argue that if all the vertically responsive cells degenerated, then the cortical columns that respond to vertical orientations (see Chapter 2) should degenerate, and "silent" columns should be observed. Since they found no such silent columns, they argue against the degeneration hypothesis and in favor of the rewiring hypothesis. (See Blakemore & Mitchell, 1973; Blakemore & Van Sluyters, 1975; Blakemore, 1974, 1976, 1977.)

Which of the two hypotheses is correct? It is difficult to decide, because there appears to be a conflict in the data. Stryker finds large numbers of abnormal and unresponsive cells, while Blakemore does not. The question, therefore, remains unsettled. In a recent review of all the evidence, however, Anthony Movshon and Richard Van Sluyters (1981) concluded that the available evidence tends to favor the degeneration hypothesis over the rewiring hypothesis.

The demonstration that large physiological and behavioral changes occur in monocularly and selectively reared cats and monkeys has caused numerous investigators to look at analogous cases in humans. Scientists, of course, are not rearing human babies with one eye occluded or in vertically or horizontally striped tubes; however, some very young children have one eye patched after an eye operation, and others are exposed to an image in which horizontals or verticals are out of focus on the retina because of a condition called **astigmatism** (see Chapter 6). In considering early patching of one eye and astigmatism, we will see that these conditions do, in fact, result in changes in perception later in life that are analogous to the changes in physiology and perception observed in monocularly deprived or selectively reared cats and monkeys.

The Effects of Visual Deprivation on Humans

Early eye patching affects acuity. In Hubel and Wiesel's monocular rearing experiments, cats that had one eye occluded between 4 and 8 weeks of age essentially lost the use of that eye, as indicated behaviorally and by the fact that no cortical cells would fire to stimulation of the previously occluded eye. There is increasing evidence that **amblyopia**—a large reduction in the visual acuity in one eye—may sometimes occur in humans who, as young children, had reduced use of one eye due to patching following an eye operation. This evidence has been provided by Shinobu Awaya and co-workers (1973), who investigated the histories of 19 patients with amblyopia and found that all had had their amblyopic (low visual acuity) eye closed early in life, following an eye operation, with most of the closures occurring during the first year. This type of amblyopia has therefore been called **stimulus deprivation amblyopia,** to distinguish it from amblyopia due to other causes (von Noorden & Maumanee, 1968). It seems likely that the same mechanisms are responsible for stimulus deprivation amblyopia and the loss of vision in Hubel and Wiesel's monocularly reared kittens.

Early strabismus affects binocularity. Another cause of reduced vision in one eye is *strabismus,* in which an imbalance in the eye muscles upsets the coordination between the two eyes. We saw that artificially produced strabismus in animals causes a loss of cortical cells that respond to stimulation of both eyes. Numerous investigators have recently found evidence of a similar lack of binocularly driven cells in people who had strabismus as young children. Though strabismus can be corrected by a muscle operation that restores the balance between the two eyes, this operation is usually not performed until 3 to 5 years of age. This is apparently too late, however, to prevent permanent cortical damage similar to that observed in monocularly deprived cats or cats with artificially produced strabismus.

Box 12.3 The Case of S.B.: Recovery from Lifelong Blindness

Richard Gregory and Jean Wallace (1963) tell the story of S.B., a 53-year-old man blind since the age of 10 months, who had a corneal transplant operation (see Chapter 6, p. 145) in an attempt to restore his sight. Before the operation, S.B. could see light and dark and had very rudimentary pattern vision, being able to see fingers at a distance of about 9 inches. S.B.'s first visual experience, immediately after the operation, was a blurred perception of the surgeon's face, which S.B. knew was a face only because he heard the surgeon's voice and knew that voices come from faces.

When Gregory and Wallace examined S.B., 48 days after the operation, they found that he did not look at the objects around him as normally sighted people do. He could name objects only when they were called to his attention, and even though he could recognize large letters, he had difficulty recognizing faces and appeared unaware of facial expressions. He also experienced distortions of depth; for example, when looking down from a window 30–40 feet above the ground, he thought he could safely lower himself down with his hands. Only after seeing the same window from the outside did he realize that this would be impossible.

When Gregory and Wallace visited S.B. at his home, about 6 months after the operation, they found that his vision had improved considerably. He could recognize the faces of friends from about 15 feet away, cross streets confidently, and draw fairly detailed pictures of objects in his environment.

This case is one of the more successful reports of recovery from blindness. S.B.'s ability to perceive details indicates that his long deprivation of form vision did not cause the extensive permanent damage to his visual system experienced by Riesen's dark-reared monkeys (see p. 330) who were totally blinded by their early light deprivation. Apparently, enough patterns were imaged on S.B's retinas to keep his cortical cells from becoming completely inactive, which enabled him to regain some form perception.

Most people would regard the regaining of sight experienced by S.B. to be a happy event. Strangely enough, however, a common reaction to the regaining of sight is depression and unhappiness. Though S.B.'s sight had improved enormously when Gregory and Wallace visited him 6 months after he left the hospital, they noticed that he appeared dispirited. Before the operation, S.B. was a cheerful and outgoing person, but as time progressed after the operation, he became more and more depressed.

What causes this depression? One theory, proposed by Alberto Valvo (1968), is that it is difficult to deal with the dramatic change from the world of touch to the world of vision, where everything is done differently. Consider this entry in the diary of a 35-year-old man who had an operation similar to S.B.'s: "Paradoxically, when my sight started improving I began to feel depressed. I often experienced periods of crying. . . . In the evening I preferred to rest in a dark room. Some days I felt confused: I did not know whether to touch or to look. . . . Recovery of vision has been a long and hard road for me, like entering a strange world. In these moments of depression I sometimes wondered if I was happier before. . . ."

Despite his depression, this man expresses hope for the future, stating that, "I know that there is still room for improvement and I am determined to do my best to accomplish it." S.B., however, never regained the cheerfulness he once possessed. His increasing depression led him to withdraw from active life, and he died 3 years after the operation.

Since ethical considerations prevent us from recording from single neurons in the human cortex, how is it possible to determine whether people who had early strabismus lack binocularly driven cells? One approach involves the measurement of a perceptual effect called the **tilt aftereffect.** You can illustrate this aftereffect to yourself, by staring for about 60 seconds at the adaptation lines on the left of Figure 12.26 and then transferring your gaze to the test lines on the right. If the aftereffect is suc-

Figure 12.26 Stimuli for measuring the tilt aftereffect. Stare at the inspection pattern on the left for about 60 seconds and then transfer your gaze to the test lines on the right. If you see the test lines as tilted, you are experiencing the tilt aftereffect.

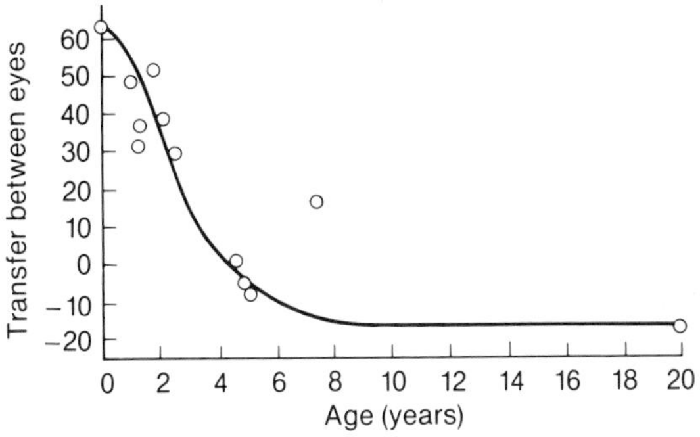

Figure 12.27 The degree of interocular transfer of the tilt aftereffect as a function of the age at which surgery was performed to correct strabismus. (From Banks, Aslin, & Letson, 1975.)

cessful, the lines on the right will appear to be slightly tilted, even though, in reality, they are vertical.

The tilt aftereffect can be used to measure binocularity because of the phenomenon of **interocular transfer.** If an observer looks at the adaptation lines with one eye and then looks at the test lines with the other eye, the aftereffect will transfer between the eyes. This transfer, which causes an effect about 60–70 percent as strong as the effect that occurs if the adaptation and test lines are viewed with the same eye, indicates that information from one eye must be being shared with the other. Since the first place that neurons from the left and right eyes meet is the visual cortex (little or no interaction between the eyes occurs in the lateral geniculate nucleus), this information sharing between the two eyes must take place at the level of the visual cortex, or higher. The degree of transfer of the tilt aftereffect, therefore, can be used to assess the state of binocularly driven cells in the cortex (Mitchell & Ware, 1974; Ware & Mitchell, 1974; Mitchell et al., 1975; Aslin & Banks, 1978).

Armed with the tilt aftereffect, Martin Banks, Richard Aslin, and Robert Letson (1975) measured the degree of interocular transfer in people who had strabismus early in life. Figure 12.27 plots the magnitude of interocular transfer as a function of the age at which 12 people born with strabismus had corrective surgery. When the surgery was carried out early in the person's life, interocular transfer is high, indicating good binocular function, but if surgery was delayed, interocular transfer is poor, indicating poor binocular function. Based on the results in Figure 12.27, other data from their experiments, and data from similar experiments by A. Hohmann and Otto Creutzfeldt (1975), Aslin and Banks (1978) concluded that a critical period for binocular development begins during the first year of life, reaches a peak during the second year, and decreases by 4–8 years of age.

Early astigmatism affects sensitivity to orientation. Another human analogue of the animal deprivation experiments is provided by people who have **astigmatism** early in life. Astigmatism, which is caused by a distortion of the cornea of the eye, results in an image that is out of focus, either in the horizontal or vertical, as shown in Figure 12.28 (see Chapter 6, p. 144). Thus, a person who has an astigmatism at an early age is exposed to an environment in which lines in one orientation are imaged sharply on the retina but lines 90 degrees from this orientation are out of focus.

Ralph Freeman and John Pettigrew (1973) showed that cats reared with an artificial astigmatism created by wearing a mask containing astigmatic lenses, develop cortical cells that favor whichever orientation is in sharp focus during rearing. This result in cats resembles a condition known as **meridional amblyopia** in humans. People with this condition have astigmatisms that cannot be optically corrected. That is, even if these people wear glasses that compensate for their distorted corneas so that all orientations are sharply imaged on the

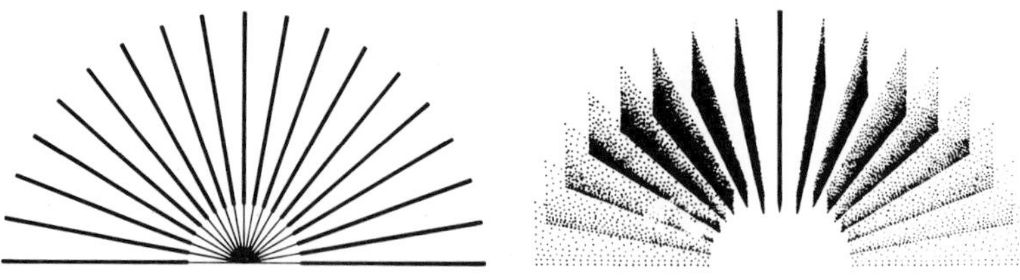

Figure 12.28 Left: astigmatic fan chart used to test for astigmatism. Right: an astigmatic patient will perceive the lines in one orientation (in this case vertical) as sharp and the lines in the other orientation as blurred. (From Tevor-Roper, 1970.)

retina, they still have impaired acuity for objects in the orientation originally blurred by their astigmatism.

To show that a person with meridional amblyopia has decreased visual acuity in one orientation, even when his or her vision is optically corrected so that the retinal image is sharp, Donald Mitchell and Frances Wilkinson (1974) carefully measured the optically corrected vision of a person with meridional amblyopia and obtained the top curve in Figure 12.29. This observer has an astigmatism that blurs horizontal images (orientations = 0 and 180 degrees), and the curve indicates that this observer's acuity is lowest at these orientations and is best at the vertical orientation of 90 degrees.

Anticipating arguments that the results in the upper curve of Figure 12.29 could be due to an imperfect optical correction, Mitchell and Wilkinson used a laser to present a sharp image to the observer's retina. This laser bypasses the observer's distorted cornea and therefore ensures that the image is focused sharply on the retina. The results of this method of stimulus presentation, shown by the lower curve in Figure 12.29, indicate that the differences

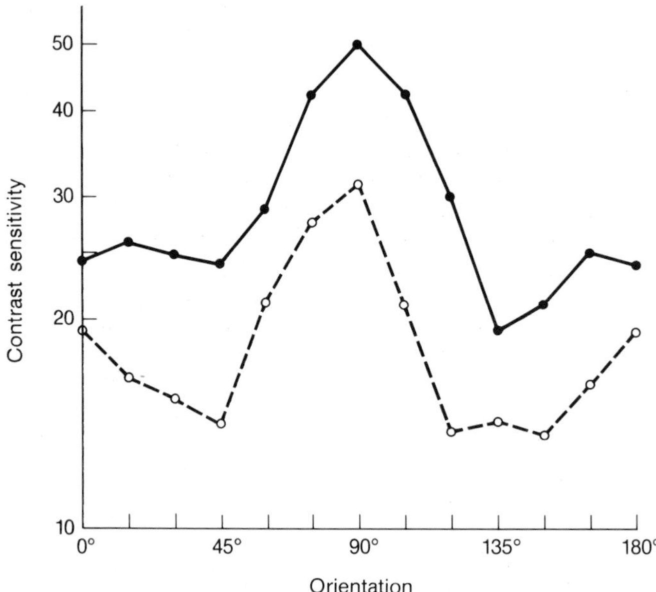

Figure 12.29 A plot of contrast sensitivity for different orientations (see text for details). (From Mitchell & Wilkinson, 1974.)

in acuity for horizontal and vertical orientations (observed in the upper curve) remain.

The results of Figure 12.29 indicate that the decreased acuity for horizontal orientations must result not from the way the image is focused on the retina but, probably, from changes that have taken place in the observer's brain. Just as the neurons of Freeman and Pettigrew's astigmatic cats respond less well to orientations blurred by the astigmatism, so the neurons of the observer in Figure 12.29 may respond less well to lines oriented at 0 and 180 degrees. This idea is further supported by other findings: in astigmatic observers with optically corrected vision, the visually evoked potential is lowest in response to stimuli oriented in the direction originally blurred by the astigmatism (Freeman & Thibos, 1973). Apparently, the selective rearing effects observed in cats can also affect the vision of humans.

Back to Our Original Question: Genetics or the Environment?

Remember the question posed at the beginning of this section: Why does perception develop? We asked whether the increase in perceptual ability seen in infants during the first year of life results from genetically programmed development which proceeds independently of experience, or whether the infant's improved perception results primarily from experience with the environment.

That certain cortical cells of the newborn cat and monkey are similar to cells found in adult animals indicates that some of the basic mechanisms for perception are innate; that is, some perceptual mechanisms are "wired in" at birth, before any experience can occur. The visual systems of cats and monkeys do not reach full adult levels, however, until at least 4–6 weeks of age, and this development is delayed if the animals are deprived of stimulation by dark rearing. Further, experiments have shown that the nature of the environment during the critical period can change later perception by changing the properties of cortical neurons.

The strongest argument for the role of experience in the development of perception comes from a consideration of the development of binocular vision. For the visual system to make use of binocular vision to perceive depth, it must be able to detect small disparities between the images that fall on the retina. Many investigators feel it inconceivable that the neural wiring necessary for this ability could be genetically programmed with sufficient precision to detect these small disparities, especially since the exact determination of retinal disparity depends on the distance between the eyes, which changes as the organism grows. It makes sense, therefore, to suggest that experience plays an important role in shaping our ability to use binocular information to perceive depth.

Taken together, the results of all the deprivation experiments confirm Richard Aslin's (1981) statement, quoted at the beginning of this section: "There can be little doubt that development is determined by a combination of genetic and environmental factors operating in a complex manner."

Summary

1. There are a number of ways to measure infant perception: (a) the preferential looking technique, (b) the habituation procedure, (c) measuring reaching behavior, and (d) the visual evoked potential.
2. The visual acuity of human infants can be measured by both the preferential looking technique and the evoked potential technique. Both techniques indicate that 1–2-month-old infants have poor visual acuity but that their acuity improves rapidly over the first 6 months of life. Acuity approaches adult levels by one year, but adult levels are not achieved until sometime after one year of age.
3. The infant's contrast sensitivity is much lower than the adult's at all spatial frequencies. What sensitivity the infant does have is restricted to lower frequencies. By 6 months of age, the infant's contrast sensitivity has considerably improved but is still below adult levels.
4. Infants as young as one month old have the ability to accommodate slightly, and by 3 months they can accommodate nearly as well as adults.
5. Reliable binocular fixation does not occur until about 3 months of age. The ability to use disparity information to perceive depth emerges sometime between 3½ and 6 months of age.

6. Six-month-old infants can use monocular vision to detect depth on a visual cliff. By the age of 5½ months, infants can use the monocular depth information provided by relative size.

7. Two-month-old infants have at least dichromatic color vision.

8. Very young infants tend to see forms in parts, but as they get older they perceive more in terms of wholes. Increasing age brings more advanced capacities for form perception, so that by the age of 5–6 months, infants can not only recognize a person's face but can generalize from one facial pose to another.

9. To develop sensory-motor coordination, it is necessary not only to be exposed to changing visual stimulation but also to cause the scene to change by means of self-produced movement.

10. The first visual deprivation experiments were motivated by an attempt to determine whether perception is innate or whether we must learn to perceive. These experiments could not answer this question, because eliminating the opportunity to learn by dark rearing causes the visual system to degenerate.

11. A large number (but not all) of the cortical cells of the newborn kitten are selective for orientation, but it is not until 4–6 weeks of age that most of these cells reach adult standards of orientation selectivity.

12. Most cells in the newborn kitten respond to stimulation of both eyes. It is not until about 5 weeks of age, however, that the kitten's eyes are aligned so that it can make use of binocular disparity information. Deprivation experiments indicate that experience in the light is necessary in order for normal development to occur during the first 4–6 weeks of life.

13. Monocular light deprivation causes a decrease in acuity in the deprived eye, with long periods of deprivation resulting in blindness. Monocular deprivation also causes a large decrease in binocularity.

14. The critical period for susceptibility to monocular deprivation is between about 4 and 8 weeks. Deprivation for even one day during the critical period can have a large effect.

15. Critical periods occur for the development not only of the visual system but also for other capacities, such as a bird's ability to sing the song characteristic of its species.

16. Artificially produced strabismus in cats results in a large decrease in the number of cells that respond to stimulation of both eyes.

17. Kittens reared in all horizontal- or all vertical-environments have cortical neurons that respond primarily to the orientation present during rearing. Exposure for as little as one hour during the critical period has a large effect. These physiological changes are accompanied by behavioral indications of severely reduced vision for orientations orthogonal to the rearing orientation.

18. Rearing in environments consisting of moving white spots, point sources of light, strobe lights, or stripes moving in one direction results in cortical cells that respond preferentially to stimuli resembling the stimuli present during rearing.

19. The physiological bases of these selective rearing effects is a matter of controversy. One idea is that selective exposure to one orientation causes cells originally unresponsive to that orientation to become "rewired," so they become responsive to the new orientation. Another idea is that selective exposure to one orientation causes cells unresponsive to that orientation to degenerate or simply become unresponsive. Available evidence tends to favor the degeneration hypothesis over the rewiring hypothesis.

20. Children who have one eye patched early in life, due to an eye operation, often develop stimulus deprivation amblyopia, a loss of visual acuity in the deprived eye. This amblyopia may be caused by the same mechanisms that impair vision in monocularly deprived kittens.

21. Children who develop squint from early strabismus often develop, in turn, an inability to use disparity information from the two eyes to see depth. There appears to be a critical period for binocular development that begins during

the first year of life, reaches a peak during the second year, and decreases by 4–8 years of age.

22. Meridional amblyopia, a loss of acuity for stimuli of a particular orientation, may result from an early astigmatism that causes a loss of cortical cells responsive to that orientation.

23. In some cases of prolonged deprivation of patterned stimulation, due to an opaque cornea, vision has been restored by transplanting a new cornea. This restoration of vision occurs only gradually and is sometimes accompanied by an emotional reaction, perhaps caused by the difficulty in moving from the world of the blind to the world of the sighted.

24. The above evidence supports the idea that some perception is present at birth and that both the maintenance and further development of this perception depend on experience during an early critical period. Development is determined by a combination of genetic and environmental factors operating in a complex manner.

Glossary

Amblyopia A large reduction in the visual acuity in one eye. (339)

Astigmatism A condition in which vision is blurred in some orientations because of a misshapen cornea. (341)

Binocular fixation Fixating on an object with both eyes simultaneously. (322)

Binocularity The ability of a neuron to be activated by stimulation of both eyes. (331)

Contralateral eye The eye on the opposite side of the head from a cortical recording electrode. (331)

Critical period A short period of time, usually early in an organism's life, during which changes in the environment have a large effect on the organism's physiology or behavior. (333)

Dark rearing Rearing an animal in total darkness. (330)

Degeneration hypothesis The idea that selective rearing causes cells sensitive to patterns absent during rearing to degenerate. According to the degeneration hypothesis, cells sensitive to vertical lines will degenerate if an animal is exposed to an environment consisting only of horizontal lines. (338)

Deprivation experiments An experiment in which an animal (or human) is deprived of some aspect of environmental contact, such as visual experience during rearing, and, following this deprivation, its effect on the animal's (or human's) behavior and/or physiology is assessed. (329)

Dishabituation After a period of habituation, in which one stimulus is presented on repeated trials, presentation of another stimulus, which is perceived as different, causes an increase in the time that an infant looks at the new stimulus. (317)

Habituation When the same stimulus is repeatedly presented, infants look at the stimulus less and less on each succeeding trial. (317)

Habituation procedure An infant is first habituated to a stimulus and is then tested to see if dishabituation occurs when a new stimulus is presented. (316)

Interocular transfer When presenting an adaptation stimulus to one eye results in an aftereffect in the other eye. (341)

Ipsilateral eye The eye on the same side of the head as a cortical recording electrode. (331)

Meridional amblyopia An astigmatism that cannot be completely corrected with glasses. (341)

Monocular rearing Rearing an animal with one eye occluded, so that the animal receives visual input only through the unoccluded eye. (331)

Ocular dominance The degree to which a neuron is influenced by stimulation of each eye. A neuron has a large amount of ocular dominance if it responds only to stimulation of one eye. There is no ocular dominance if the neuron responds equally to stimulation of each eye. (331)

Ocular dominance histogram A histogram that indicates the degree of ocular dominance of a large population of neurons. (331)

Preferential looking technique A technique used to measure perception in infants. Two stimuli are presented, and the infant's looking behavior is monitored to determine the amount of time the infant spends viewing each stimulus. (316)

Rewiring hypothesis The idea that selective rearing causes cells sensitive to patterns absent during rearing to become rewired, so they become sensitive to the pattern that is present. According to the rewiring hypothesis, cells sensitive to vertical lines will become sensitive to horizontal lines if an animal is exposed to an environment consisting only of horizontal lines. (338)

Selective rearing Rearing an animal in an environment that contains only one kind of pattern, such as vertical or horizontal stripes. (334)

Self-produced movement Movement produced by an organism, such as walking through the environment rather than being pushed through it in a wheelchair. (328)

Sensory-motor coordination Coordination between perception and movement. For example, picking up an object involves coordination between seeing the object and the movement necessary to reach for it. (328)

Stimulus deprivation amblyopia Amblyopia due to early closure of one eye. (339)

Strabismus A condition in which an imbalance in the eye muscles causes the eyes to be misaligned, thereby upsetting the coordination between them. (333)

Tilt aftereffect By staring at an adapting field of lines that are tilted from the vertical and then looking at vertical lines, we cause the vertical lines to appear to be tilted in a direction opposite to that of the adapting field. (340)

Visual cliff An apparatus used to test depth perception in infants, in which a visual drop-off is covered by a sheet of glass so that, although the drop can be seen, it is not possible to fall off the "cliff." If an infant will not venture over the cliff onto the glass, it is assumed that the infant can perceive depth. (324)

Visual evoked potential (VEP) An electrical response to visual stimulation, recorded by placing disc electrodes on the back of the head. This potential reflects the activity of a large population of neurons in the visual cortex. (317)

Chapter Thirteen

Basic Mechanisms of Hearing

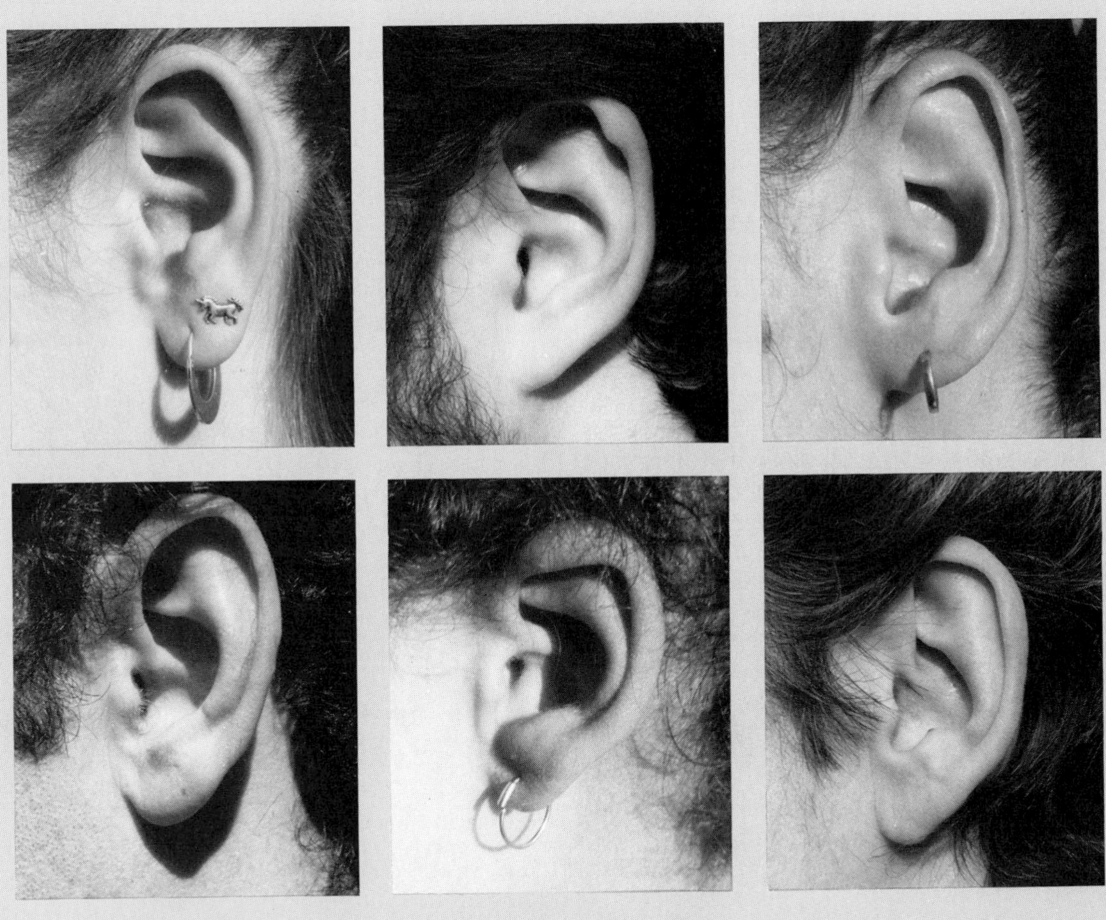

So far, we have focused our attention on the sense of vision, briefly digressing to discuss the skin senses in Chapter 4 and the organization of sounds in Chapter 7. We end this book by discussing the sense of hearing in this chapter and the next, and the senses of smell and taste in the final chapter. Why have we waited so long to discuss hearing? Is it less important than vision? Though assigning relative degrees of importance to the various senses may be a meaningless exercise, most people, at one time or another, have asked themselves the following question: "If I had to be either blind or deaf, which would I pick?" Certainly, neither possibility is attractive, but how would you answer this question?

The thought of living in a world of darkness, unable to see the beauty of the world around you, is a rather depressing idea, yet so is the thought of living in a world of silence, unable to hear other people talking or, more important for many of us, unable to enjoy music. I hope you will never have to deal with either possibility, but thinking about them has helped me realize that any answer to the question "Which sense is more important?" is a rather personal one that will be different for different people. (Perhaps touch should also be considered here. Being able to feel someone else touching you may well rank high on your list of things you would not want to live without.)

One reason for discussing vision first is that we know more about vision than about hearing. Also, in discussing vision, we have established many basic principles of sensory functioning that also hold for hearing. Finally, we have waited to discuss hearing because of the complexity of the auditory system. Though we can easily talk about how light enters the eye and stimulates the rod and cone receptors, the stimulus for sound must pass through a complicated chain of structures before reaching the receptors for hearing. We will begin this chapter, therefore, by first describing the sound stimulus and then describing its journey from the ear's entrance to receptors deep inside the ear.

Sound as Vibrations of the Air

To begin our discussion of hearing, let's consider your radio or stereo system's loudspeaker, which is really a device for producing vibrations to be transmitted to the surrounding air. People have been known to turn their stereos up loud enough so these vibrations can be felt through the floor, but even at softer levels, these vibrations are there. (Turn on your radio or stereo and feel the vibrations by placing your hand on the speaker. This technique is often used by deaf people to "listen" to music.)

The vibrations you feel when you place your hand on the speaker affect the surrounding air, as shown in Figure 13.2. When the diaphragm of the speaker moves out, it pushes the surrounding air molecules together and increases the density of molecules near the diaphragm; then, when the speaker diaphragm moves back in, it creates a partial vacuum, decreasing the density of molecules near the diaphragm. By repeating this process many hundreds or even thousands of times a second, the speaker creates a pattern of alternating high and low pressure in the air that travels outward from the speaker, in much the same way that ripples travel outward from a pebble dropped in a quiet pool of water. This pattern of air pressure changes is called a **sound wave**; we will see later in this chapter and in the next that the nature of the sounds we hear, particularly a sound's pitch and loudness, is related to the form of this sound wave.

Here we will be concerned with a very simple kind of sound wave called a pure tone. Pure tones are not often found in our everyday environment

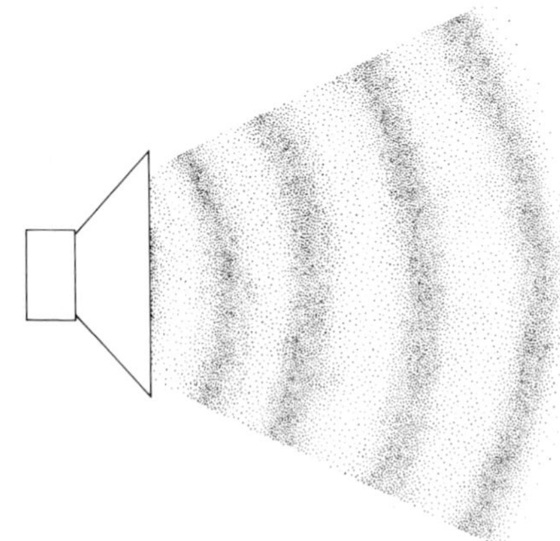

Figure 13.2 The effect of a vibrating speaker diaphragm on the surrounding air. Dark areas represent regions of high air pressure and light areas represent areas of low air pressure.

but are used extensively in the laboratory to study the basic mechanisms of hearing. One way to produce a pure tone is to connect an electronic device called an oscillator to our loudspeaker. This oscillator causes the speaker's diaphragm to vibrate in and out with a sine-wave motion, as shown in Figure 13.3. We can adjust the oscillator so that it causes the diaphragm of the speaker to vibrate with a certain **amplitude**—the distance the diaphragm moves from its rest position—labeled A in Figure 13.3. We can also adjust the oscillator so that it causes the speaker to vibrate with a certain **frequency**—the number of times per second that the speaker diaphragm goes through the cycle of moving out, back in, and then out again, as shown in the figure.

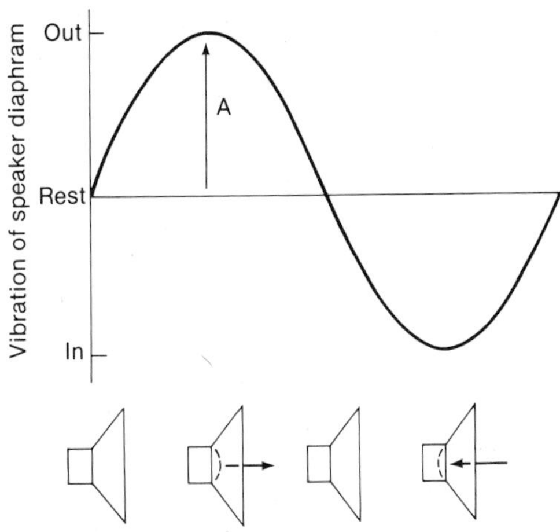

Figure 13.3 The motion of a speaker diaphragm in response to a sine-wave stimulus from an oscillator. The sine-wave motion of the diaphragm results in a pure tone. The amplitude (A) represents the maximum deflection of the speaker diaphragm from its rest position.

The sine-wave vibration of the diaphragm is transmitted to the surrounding air and results in changes in the air pressure, as shown in Figure 13.4. This figure shows that the pressure first increases above atmospheric pressure and then decreases below atmospheric pressure and that this increase and decrease follow a sine wave, just as the vibration of the speaker diaphragm follows a sine wave. This sinusoidal change in pressure results in what we call a pure tone, and we describe a particular pure tone by indicating its frequency in units called **Hertz (Hz),** where one Hertz is the same as one cycle per second. Thus, a 1,000-Hertz tone is a pure tone that goes through 1,000 cycles per second.

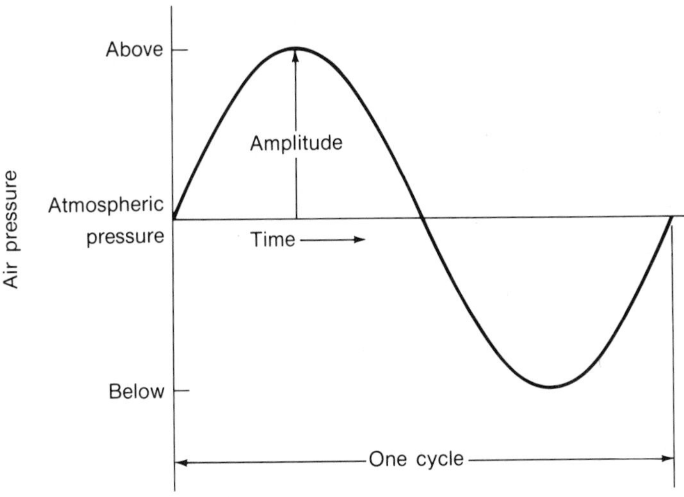

Figure 13.4 The sinusoidal vibration of the speaker diaphragm results in a sinusoidal change in the air pressure, as shown above.

Stimulating the Receptors for Hearing

Knowing now that when we talk about sound we are actually talking about air pressure changes, we will ask an important question: How are these pressure changes—or vibrations—transformed into electrical energy that the nervous system can understand? Transformation of air vibrations into electrical energy is accomplished by the ear, the complex structure shown in Figure 13.5. Deep inside the ear is a snail-shaped structure called the **cochlea,** which is filled with liquid and contains receptors called **hair cells.** These hair cells, shown in Figure 13.6, contain tiny structures called cilia, which are bent when the liquid inside the cochlea vibrates. This bending of the cilia of the hair cells generates electrical signals that are sent down the auditory nerve toward the brain. Our problem, then, is this: How can sound vibrations, which are carried through the air, cause the liquid inside the cochlea to vibrate?

To answer this question, we will begin with sound waves entering the ear and follow their effect as they travel through the ear's various structures. Sound waves first encounter the **outer ear.**

The Outer Ear

When we talk about the "ear" in everyday conversation, we usually refer to the funny-looking structure that sticks out from the sides of our head, shown in the chapter-opening illustration. While this most obvious part of the ear, called the **pinna,** is of some importance in helping us locate sounds and is of great importance for those of us who wear eyeglasses or earrings, it is the part of the ear we could most easily do without. The major workings of the ear are found inside the head, hidden from view.

It is to these hidden places that sound waves must travel before they are heard, and in the first stage of their journey they pass through the **outer ear,** which consists of the pinna and the auditory canal (Figure 13.5). The **external auditory meatus** (or **auditory canal**) is a tubelike structure about 3 cm long, whose function is to protect the delicate structures of the middle ear from the hazards of the outside world. The auditory canal's 3-cm recess, along with its wax, which has an apparently unpleasant effect on curious insects (Schubert, 1980), protects the delicate **tympanic membrane,** or eardrum, at the end of the canal and helps keep this membrane

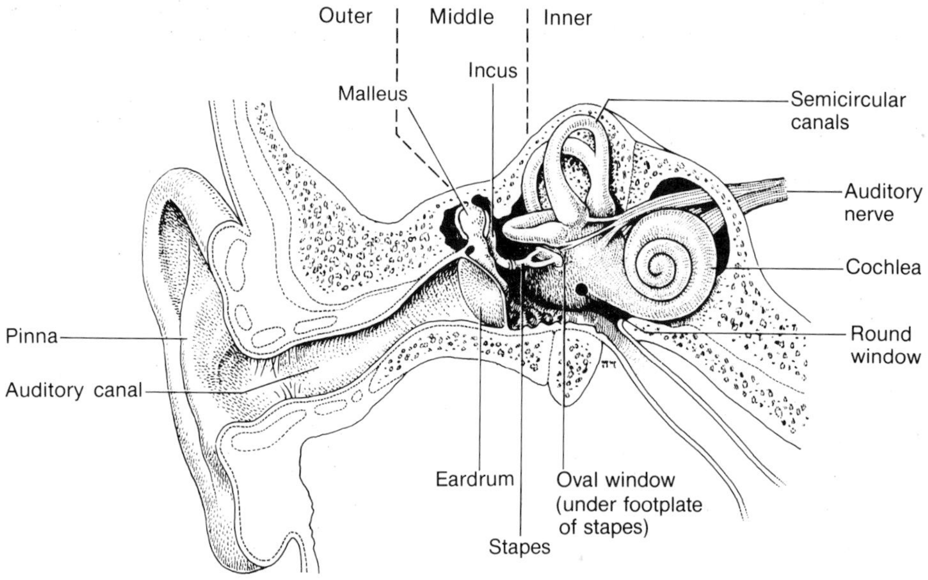

Figure 13.5 The ear, showing its three subdivisions—outer, middle, and inner.

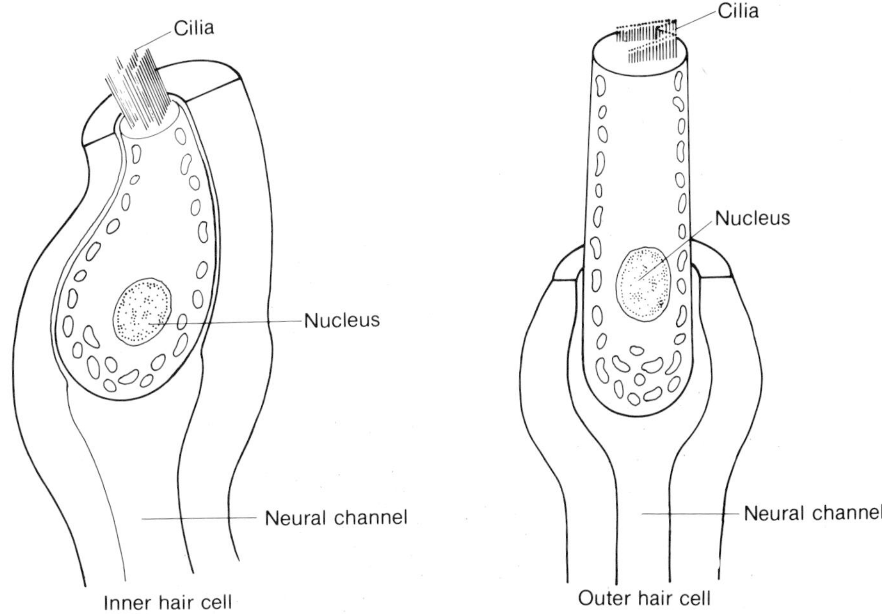

Figure 13.6 The inner and outer hair cells. Vibration of the cilia, or hairs, generates an electrical signal. (Adapted from Gulick, 1971.)

and the structures in the middle ear at a relatively constant temperature.

Before leaving the outer ear, we should note that, in addition to its protective function, it enhances the intensities of some sounds by means of a mechanism called **resonance.** Resonance occurs when sound waves near the **resonant frequency** of the auditory canal are reflected from the closed end of the canal and reinforce incoming sound waves of the same frequency. The resonant frequency of the auditory canal, which is determined by the length of the canal, is about 3,400 Hz, and measurements of the sound pressures inside the ear indicate that the auditory canal has a slight amplifying effect on frequencies between about 2,000 and 5,000 Hz.

The Middle Ear

Our airborne sound waves reach the **middle ear** when they hit the tympanic membrane, or eardrum, at the end of the auditory canal. The middle ear is a small cavity, about 2 cubic cm in volume, bounded at one end by the tympanic membrane and at the other end by a bony structure called the cochlea. It is in the middle ear that we confront the problem posed earlier: How can airborne sound vibrations cause the liquid inside the cochlea to vibrate? To understand why this is a problem, we must introduce the idea of **impedance.**

Every material has a characteristic impedance, or resistance, to the passage of vibrations, and the ability of a vibration to pass from one material to another is determined by the impedances of the two materials. If the impedances are similar, there is no problem—the vibration passes easily from one material to the other. If the impedances of the two materials are different, however, as is the case for air and liquid, there is an **impedance mismatch,** and the vibrations are poorly transmitted from one material to the other. In the case of the ear, if airborne vibrations had to pass directly from the air to the cochlear liquid only about 3 percent of the vibrations would be transmitted (Durrant & Lovrinic, 1977). Fortunately, these vibrations do not pass directly from the air to the cochlea; instead, they first pass through the middle ear, which helps solve the problem created by the impedance mismatch between air and liquid.

To understand how the middle ear solves the problem of impedance mismatch, let's look at the structure of this part of the ear, shown in Figure 13.7. When air vibrations reach the end of the auditory canal, they cause the tympanic membrane to vibrate. This conical membrane, which is shaped very much like the diaphragm of a loudspeaker, transmits the vibration to the **malleus** (or **anvil**), the first of a sequence of three bones called the **ossicles,** which are the main structures found inside the middle ear cavity. The malleus then transmits the vibrations to the **incus** (or **hammer**), which, in turn, causes the last of the ossicles, the **stapes** (or **stirrup),** to vibrate. These three bones, which are the smallest in the body, solve the impedance mismatch problem in two ways.

The first solution to the impedance mismatch problem involves a comparison of the areas of the tympanic membrane and the stirrup. The tympanic membrane has an area of about 0.6 square cm, whereas the stirrup has an area of about 0.032 square cm—a ratio of about 17 to one. Concentrating the vibration of the large tympanic membrane onto the smaller stapes, as shown in Figure 13.8, increases the pressure per unit area in the same way that a 110-pound woman, wearing shoes with 1-cm^2 spiked heels, can generate a pressure of 110,000 pounds per square foot by concentrating all her weight on one heel.

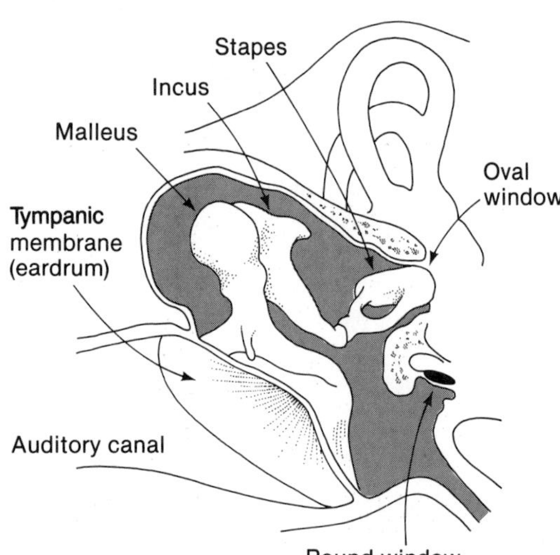

Figure 13.7 The middle ear. The three bones of the middle ear transmit the vibrations of the tympanic membrane to the inner ear.

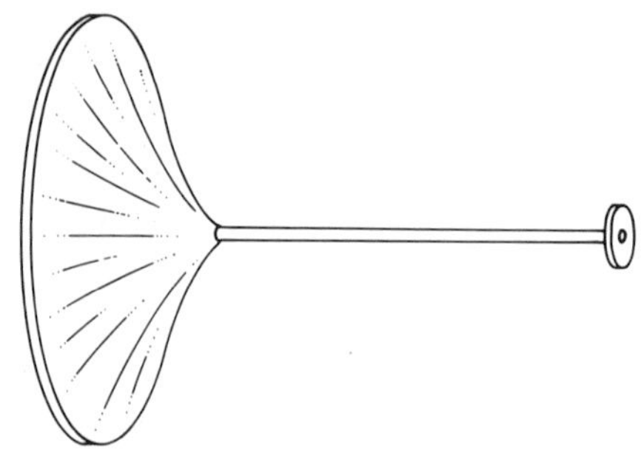

Figure 13.8 A diagrammatic representation of the tympanic membrane and the stapes, showing their difference in size. (From Schubert, 1980.)

The second solution of the impedance mismatch problem makes use of the lever principle, as illustrated in Figure 13.9. This figure shows that if a board is balanced on a fulcrum, a small weight on the long end of the board can overcome a larger weight on the short end. Though it is not obvious from looking at the ossicles, they are hinged so that they increase the vibration, by a factor of about 1.3, by means of this lever principle.

The ossicles' two solutions to the impedance mismatch problem increase the vibrations by a factor of at least (1.3 × 17) = 22 (Durrant & Lovrinic, 1977), with some calculations setting this value as high as a factor of 100 (Schubert, 1980). In any case, without the middle ear it would undoubtedly be much more difficult for us to hear. In fact, the

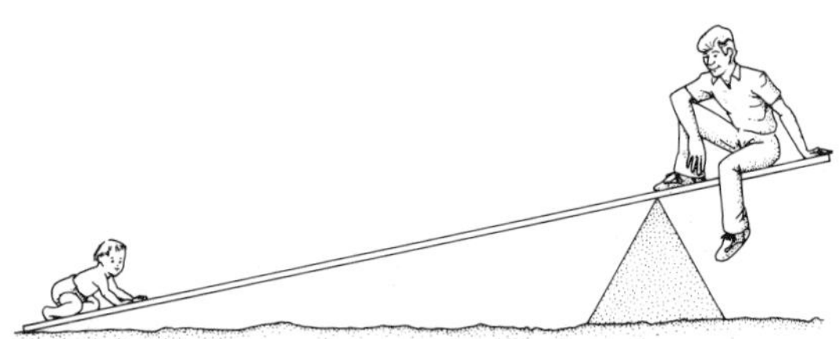

Figure 13.9 The lever principle. The baby on the long end of the board can overcome the weight of the man on the short end. (The baby, however, will be in for a surprise if it crawls very far toward the man.)

effect of losing the ossicles has been measured in patients whose ossicles have been damaged beyond surgical repair. In such cases, an operation is sometimes performed so that sound is transmitted directly to the cochlea through the air. When the ossicles are absent, the sound pressure must be increased by a factor of 10–50 to achieve the same hearing ability as when the ossicles were present.

The Inner Ear

Our vibrations, which have been transformed from the airborne vibrations that entered the outer ear into the mechanical vibrations of the stapes, now enter the liquid-filled cochlea of the **inner ear,** through a membrane called the **oval window.** The cochlea, which is a bony, snail-like structure, is difficult to visualize because it is rolled into 2¾ turns. But if we uncoil the cochlea so it becomes a long straight tube, as in Figure 13.10(a) and (b), we can more easily describe the structure inside. The most obvious feature of the uncoiled cochlea is a structure called the **cochlear partition,** extending almost the entire length of the cochlea except for a small opening at the end, called the **helicotrema,** which connects the top and the bottom of the cochlea. (It should be noted that diagrams such as this one, which are not to scale, do not indicate the cochlea's true shape. In reality, the diameter of the uncoiled cochlea forms a cylinder 2 mm in diameter and 35 mm long.)

The cochlear partition is best seen if we look at the cochlea end-on and in cross section, as in Figure 13.11. When we look at the cochlea in this way, we see that it is divided into three compartments—the **scala vestibuli,** the **scala tympani,** and the **scala media**—and that the cochlear partition contains a large structure, which is called the **organ of Corti.** Details of the organ of Corti are shown in Figure 13.12, its three structures of primary importance are the **basilar membrane,** the **tectorial membrane,** and the hair cells. The hair cells, which are

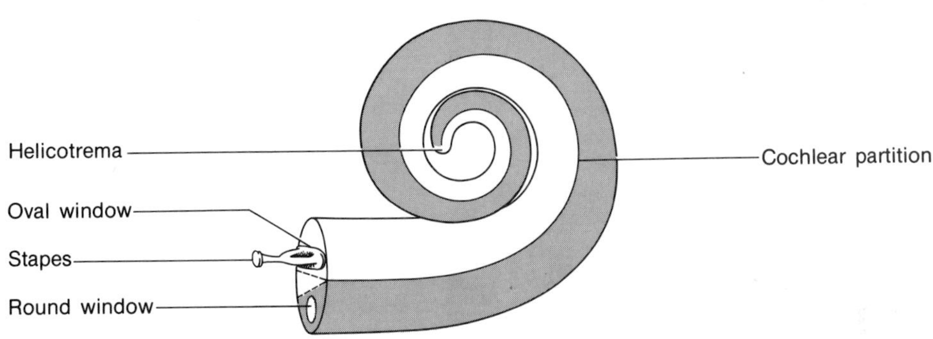

(a) Partially uncoiled cochlea

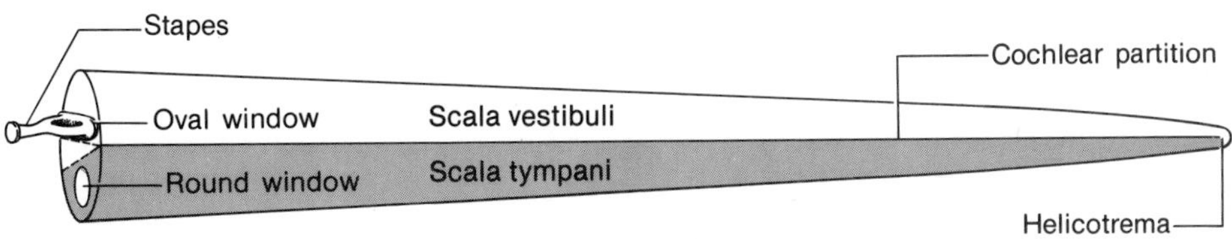

(b) Fully uncoiled cochlea

Figure 13.10 (a) A partially uncoiled cochlea. (b) A fully uncoiled cochlea.

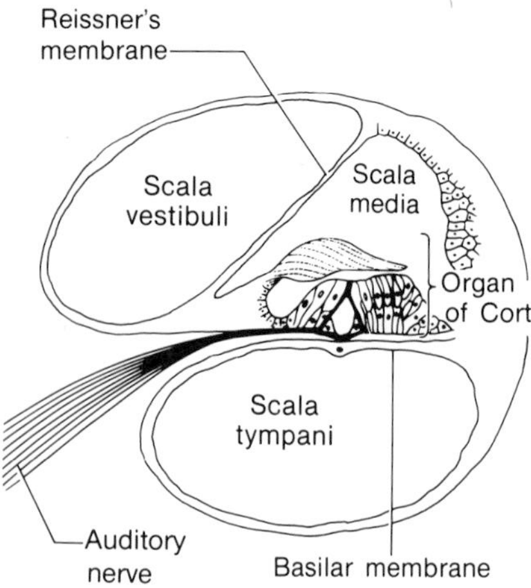

Figure 13.11 A cross section of the cochlea.

the receptors for hearing, are shown close-up in Figure 13.6. From this picture we can see that there are two types of hair cells—inner and outer hair cells—and, like other cells in the nervous system, the hair cells have a cell body and a nerve fiber. The unique feature of these receptors is the small cilia (or hairs) that protrude from the cell body. These hairs are the target of the vibrations we have been following through the ear: when the hair cells are bent, they generate electrical signals that are transmitted by the cell's nerve fiber, via the auditory nerve, toward the brain.

Now that we know what's inside the cochlea, let's return to the oval window, where the stapes is vibrating. When the stapes pushes in on the oval window, it transmits pressure to the liquid inside the cochlea. From Figure 13.10(b), we might think that this pressure would be transmitted down the scala vestibuli, around the opening at the helicotrema, and down the scala tympani to the **round window.** In fact, very little pressure is transmitted around the end of the cochlear partition; the helicotrema acts almost as if it is closed. Rather than transmit pressure through the helicotrema, the liquid in the scala vestibuli pushes on the cochlear partition. This push, which causes the elastic cochlear partition to move downward, is followed by a pull that causes the cochlear partition to move upward. This pull occurs when the stapes pulls back from the oval window, decreasing the pressure inside

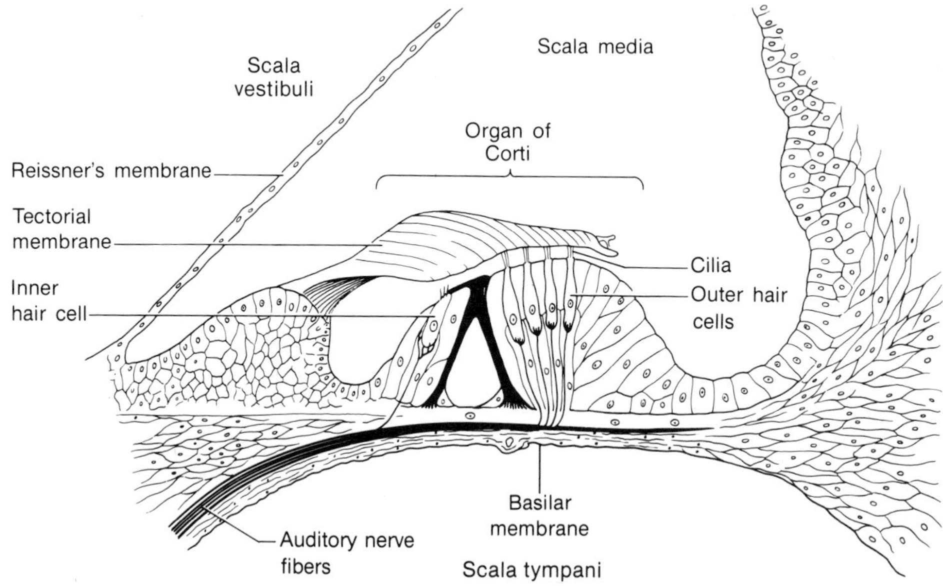

Figure 13.12 The organ of Corti. (Adapted from Gulick, 1971.)

the scala vestibuli. This pushing and pulling on the cochlear partition sets it into motion. It begins to vibrate with exactly the same frequency as the stapes.

It has been a long trip from the outer ear, but the cochlear partition is finally vibrating, and this vibration causes the hair cells to bend. We can understand how this occurs by looking at Figure 13.12. Vibration of the cochlear partition sets the organ of Corti into an up-and-down motion, which causes the hair cells to rub against the tectorial membrane. It is this contact with the tectorial membrane, plus the movement of the liquid in the scala vestibuli, that bends the hair cells and leads to the generation of electrical signals.

Now that we have succeeded in bending the hair cells, we come to an important question: How do the electrical signals that result from bending the hair cells cause us to perceive the various qualities of sound? Numerous theories have been proposed to answer this question, and they have focused on explaining how the workings of the auditory system enable us to perceive a tone's **pitch.**

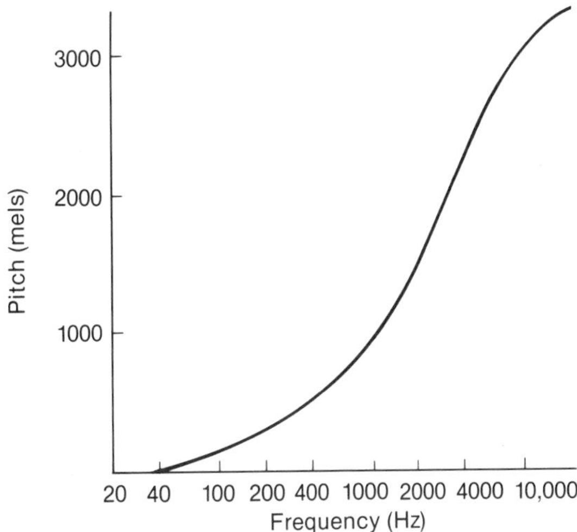

Figure 13.13 The relationship between frequency and pitch. The pitch scale on the left is in mels. A 2,000-mel tone sounds twice as high in pitch as a 1,000-mel tone. (Stevens & Volkman, 1940.)

Theories of Pitch Perception

Before describing some theories of pitch perception, we must establish an important fact, central to all these theories: the perception of pitch is determined, largely, by frequency. (Remember that pitch refers to what you hear and is, therefore, psychological, whereas frequency refers to the vibrations of the air and is, therefore, a physical measure.) This relationship between pitch and frequency is illustrated in Figure 13.13, which shows that as frequency increases, pitch increases. The frequency of the lowest note on the piano is 27.5 Hz, and the frequency of the highest note is 4,186 Hz. Though a tone's amplitude can slightly influence its pitch, and though the pitches of complex sounds, such as those of speech and music, are sometimes influenced in a complicated way by frequency, it is correct to say that the frequency of a pure tone is the major determinant of the tone's pitch. This being the case, all theories of pitch perception described below propose mechanisms by which a tone's frequency can be coded by the firing of nerve fibers in the auditory system.

Helmholtz's Resonance Theory

Hermann von Helmholtz (1863), who also championed the trichromatic theory of color vision (Chapter 5) and invented the ophthalmoscope (Chapter 6), proposed that the basilar membrane is made up of a series of transverse fibers, each tuned to resonate to a specific frequency. Thus, a particular frequency would stimulate only the fiber sensitive to this frequency, which would cause nerve fibers innervating this area of the basilar membrane to fire. **Resonance theory** has been rejected, however, because it has been shown that the basilar membrane fibers are connected to each other in such a way that it is impossible for one to resonate independently of the others, as Helmholtz proposed. As we will see below, large portions of the basilar membrane vibrate in response to sound.

Rutherford's Frequency Theory

In 1886, Rutherford proposed that the basilar membrane vibrates as a whole, as shown in Figure 13.14, and that the rate of this vibration matches the frequency of the stimulus. According to the **frequency theory,** the frequency of the stimulus is

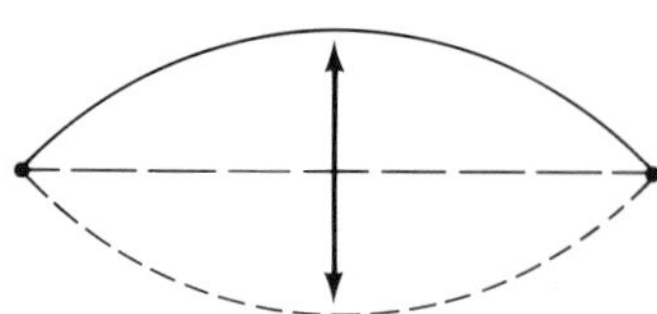

Figure 13.14 Rutherford's conception of how the basilar membrane vibrates. The horizontal line indicates the resting level of the membrane, and the curved lines show the membrane at its maximum up position and maximum down position.

signaled by the frequency of nerve firing. Thus, if a 10,000-Hz tone causes the basilar membrane to vibrate 10,000 times per second, this vibration would cause nerve fibers in the auditory nerve to fire at 10,000 impulses per second.

Though later work showed that the basilar membrane does not vibrate in exactly the way Rutherford proposed, this is not a serious problem for frequency theory, because if we observe one point on the basilar membrane during vibration, we see that the frequency of vibration of that point on the membrane does match the frequency of the stimulus. A 400-Hz tone causes the membrane to move up and down 400 times a second, a 3,000-Hz tone causes the membrane to move up and down 3,000 times a second, and so on. The flaw in Rutherford's theory, however, is that nerve fibers have a refractory period, which limits their maximum firing rate to about 1,000 impulses per second (see p. 37, in Chapter 2). Thus, while the membrane may vibrate up and down 3,000 times in response to a 3,000-Hz tone, nerve fibers cannot fire at 3,000 impulses per second. In order to deal with this problem, Ernest Wever (1949) proposed a modification of the frequency theory, called the **volley principle.**

Wever's Volley Principle

Ernest Wever's (1949) volley principle states that high rates of nerve firing can be accomplished if nerve fibers work in the manner illustrated in Figure 13.15. In this illustration, five fibers work together, with each one firing every fifth period of the sound wave. Fiber ***a*** fires to the first period and then becomes refractory. While ***a*** is refractory, fibers ***b***, ***c***, ***d***, and ***e*** fire to the second, third, fourth, and fifth periods, respectively; then ***a***, which has now recovered from being refractory, fires to the sixth period, and so on. Thus, while the firing rate of

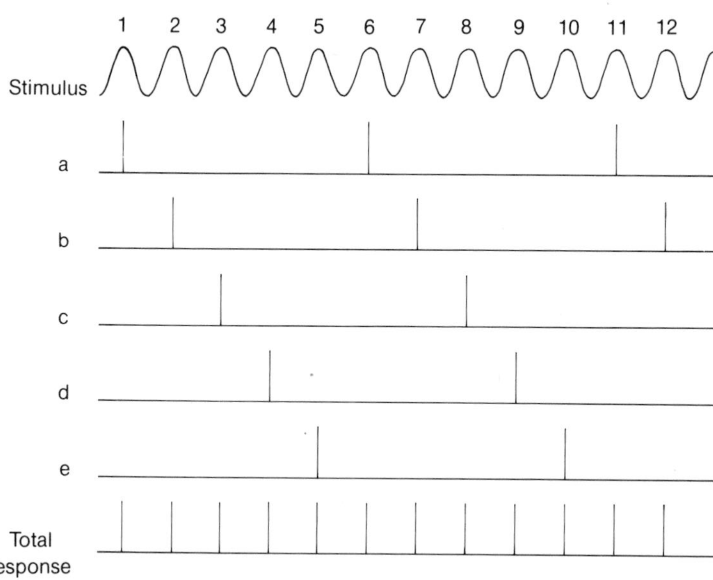

Figure 13.15 How a number of nerve fibers work together, according to Wever's volley principle.

individual fibers is limited by the refractory period, groups of fibers can work together to cause high rates of nerve firing, as indicated by the bottom record of Figure 13.15. Though research has failed to demonstrate that nerve fibers take turns firing in the orderly way proposed by Wever, there is evidence that something similar to Wever's volley principle does operate in the auditory system.

Jerzy Rose and co-workers (1967) have demonstrated that fibers in the auditory nerve fire in synchrony with the stimulus. This is illustrated in Figure 13.16, which shows the relationship between a pure tone stimulus and the firing of three auditory nerve fibers. Looking at the response of fiber *a*, we can see that it fires in an irregular manner (not regularly, as Wever proposed), but when it does fire, it fires only when the pure tone stimulus is at its peak. This synchronization of nerve firing with the peak of a pure tone stimulus is called **phase locking.** Similar results for two more fibers are also shown in this figure. Note that while the firing rates and patterns are different for each fiber, when they do fire, they are phase-locked to the stimulus. Thus, groups of fibers working together could signal pitch, as proposed by the volley principle, although the fibers do not "work together" in quite the orderly way proposed by Wever.

Most of the evidence that phase locking is important in signaling the frequency of the stimulus comes from records, like those in Figure 13.16, obtained from auditory nerve fibers. The evidence for phase locking becomes weaker, however, at higher centers in the auditory system, because as we move toward the cortex, it becomes harder to find neurons that will phase lock to frequencies above about 1,000 Hz. And even in the auditory nerve, phase locking works well only up to about 5,000 Hz. Thus, some other mechanism, in addition to phase locking, is needed to signal the frequency of the auditory stimulus. This other mechanism is provided by Békésy's **place theory.**

Békésy's Place Theory

George von Békésy's solution to the problem of signaling frequency is shown very diagrammatically in Figure 13.17. This figure shows an uncoiled cochlear partition, stretching from the stapes at one end of the cochlea to the helicotrema at the other. The hair cells inside the cochlear partition also stretch from the stapes to the helicotrema, and Békésy proposed that each frequency maximally stimulates different hair cells. Low-frequency tones stimulate hair cells near the helicotrema, whereas high-frequency tones stimulate hair cells near the stapes. Frequency is therefore signaled by the *place* along the cochlear partition that is maximally stimulated.

This may sound similar to Helmholtz's resonance theory, because both theories postulate that a specific frequency stimulates a specific place along the cochlear partition. The two theories differ, however, in the mechanisms they propose to explain how these specific places are stimulated. Whereas Helmholtz proposed that different places were stimulated because of the existence of tuned resonators along the basilar membrane, Békésy proposed that different places were stimulated because of the way the basilar membrane vibrates.

The traveling wave. Békésy, who won the Nobel Prize in 1961 for his pioneering work on the functioning of the ear, first determined that the vibra-

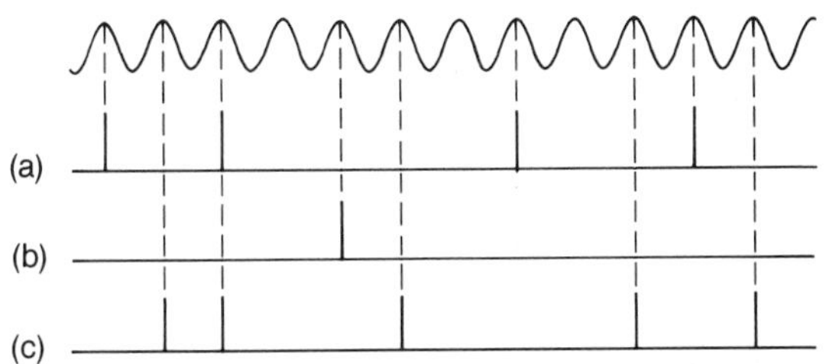

Figure 13.16 The response of three nerve fibers that are phase-locked to the stimulus.

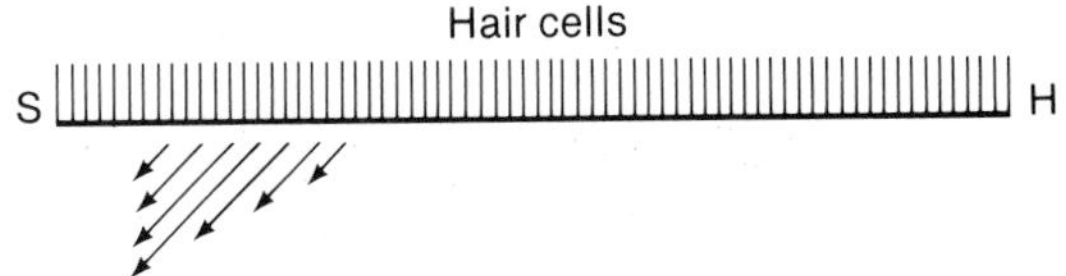

Figure 13.17 The principle underlying place theory. Hair cells line the cochlear partition from the stapes to the helicotrema. According to place theory, a given frequency causes maximal stimulation of the hair cells at a particular place along the cochlear partition. In this figure, the arrows indicate that a high-frequency tone is stimulating hair cells near the stapes.

tion of the cochlear partition is controlled largely by the properties of the basilar membrane (notice, in Figure 13.12, that the organ of Corti sits on top of the basilar membrane). He then analyzed the properties of the basilar membrane, taking note of two important facts: (1) the basilar membrane is three or four times wider at the helicotrema end than at the stapes end, and (2) it is about 100 times stiffer at the stapes than at the helicotrema (see Figure 13.18). Using these facts, Békésy constructed models of the cochlea, which enabled him to show that the pressure waves in the cochlear fluid set up a **traveling wave** on the basilar membrane. He later observed this traveling wave by drilling a hole in the cochlea of a human cadaver, which enabled him to observe the vibrations of the basilar membrane with a microscope (Békésy, 1960).

Figures 13.19 and 13.20 show what a traveling wave looks like. The horizontal line in Figure 13.20 represents the basilar membrane at rest, with the end marked S being near the stapes and the end marked H being near the helicotrema. Curve 1 shows the position of the basilar membrane at one point in time during its vibration, and curves 2 and 3 show the position of the membrane at two later instants. Figure 13.19 shows a perspective view of the traveling wave at one point in time. In both figures, a wave is traveling down the basilar membrane from the stapes to the helicotrema.

Since the shape of the traveling wave changes with each instant of time, it is difficult to visualize its overall effect on the basilar membrane. We can, however, determine its overall effect, by determining the maximum displacement that the wave causes at each point along the membrane. This maximum displacement, which is indicated by the dashed line of Figure 13.20, is called the **envelope of the traveling wave.** The envelope helps us determine the effect of the basilar membrane's vibration on the

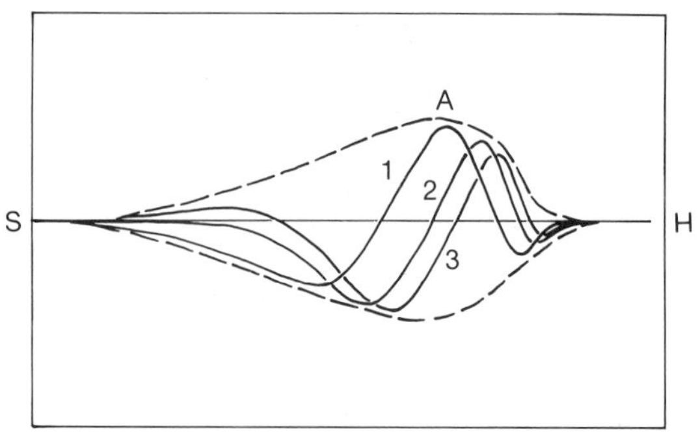

Figure 13.20 Vibration of the basilar membrane, showing the position of the membrane at three points in time, indicated by the solid lines, and the envelope of the vibration, indicated by the dashed lines. (Adapted from Békésy, 1960.)

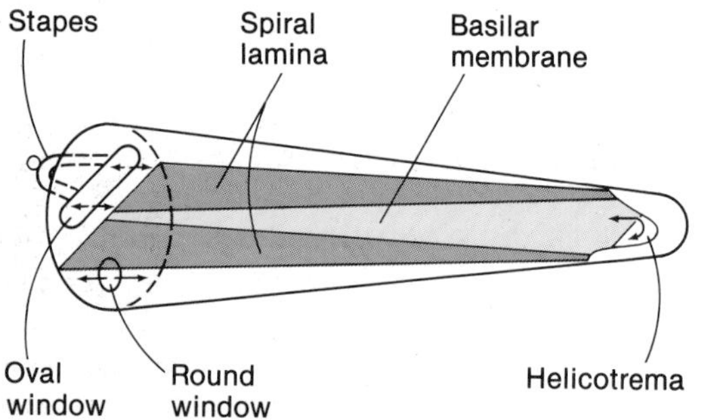

Figure 13.18 A perspective view of an uncoiled cochlea, showing how the basilar membrane gets wider at the helicotrema end of the cochlea. The spiral lamina is a supporting structure that makes up for the basilar membrane's difference in width at the stapes and helicotrema ends of the cochlea. (From Schubert, 1980.)

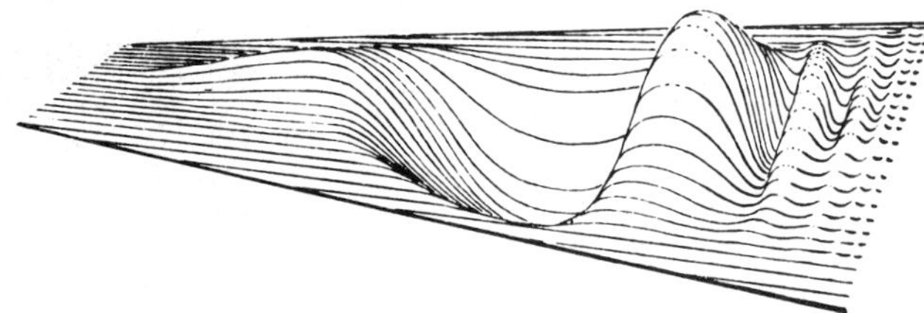

Figure 13.19 A perspective view, showing the traveling wave of the basilar membrane. (From Tonndorf, 1960.)

hair cells, because the degree to which the hair cells are bent, and the resultant rate of firing in the fibers of those hair cells, depends on the amount that the basilar membrane is displaced, with greater displacement resulting in greater firing rates.

Békésy's (1960) observations of the basilar membrane's vibrations led him to conclude that the envelope of the basilar membrane has two important properties. (1) The envelope is peaked at one point on the basilar membrane. The envelope in Figure 13.20 indicates that point A on the basilar membrane is displaced the most by the traveling wave, which means that hair cells near point A will send out stronger signals than those near other parts of the membrane. (2) The position of this peak on the basilar membrane is a function of the frequency of the sound. We can see in Figure 13.21, which shows the envelopes of vibration for stimuli ranging from 25 to 1,600 Hz, that low frequencies cause maximum vibration near the helicotrema, while high frequencies cause maximum vibration near the stapes.

The change in the peak of the basilar membrane displacement with frequency means that when we present a low-frequency tone, there will be greater activity in the hair cells near the helicotrema (note, however, that at low frequencies, most of the membrane vibrates), and as we increase the frequency, maximum hair cell activity moves toward the stapes. The correspondence between the frequency of the stimulus and the place in the cochlea where hair cells are maximally stimulated is shown in Figure 13.22. This map of the cochlea was constructed by placing electrodes at different locations on the cochlea and determining the stimulus frequency that caused the largest response at each location (Culler et al., 1943).

The relation between position on the cochlea and stimulus frequency has also been demonstrated by **stimulation deafness** experiments, in which the structures of the cochlea are examined after an animal has been exposed to loud tones. The results of such an experiment are shown in Figure 13.23. In this experiment, guinea pigs were exposed to high-intensity tones for 4 minutes, the animals were sacrificed, and their cochleas were examined. In Figure 13.23, the light areas indicate the extent of damage to the organ of Corti, for tones of different frequencies. The 300-Hz tone causes damage to a large area near the helicotrema, and, as the frequency of the tone is increased, the damage moves toward the stapes and also becomes more localized, with high-frequency tones causing damage to much smaller areas than low-frequency tones (Smith, 1947).

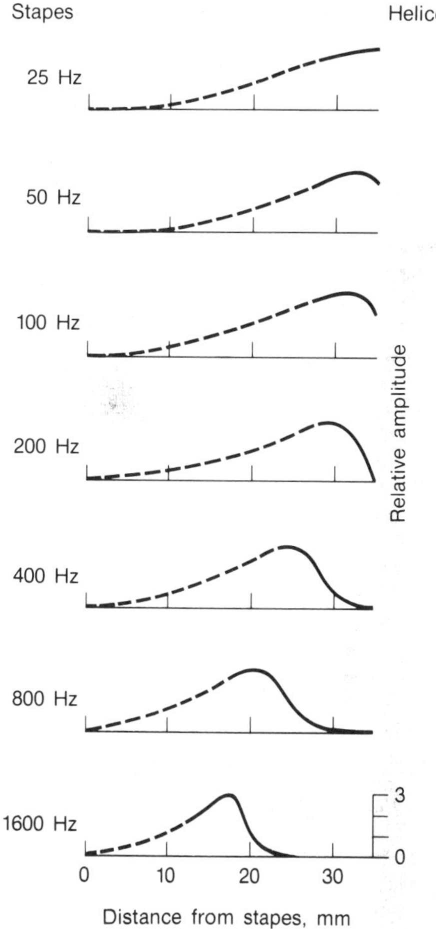

Figure 13.21 The envelopes of basilar membrane vibration at frequencies ranging from 25 to 1,600 Hz. (From Békésy, 1960.)

Békésy's observations of the traveling wave, the map of the cochlea in Figure 13.22, and the stimulation deafness experiments of Figure 13.23 all indicate a correspondence between stimulus frequency and the maximally stimulated place on the cochlea. However, for a place code such as this to work, the place information contained in the cochlea must be transmitted to more central stations in

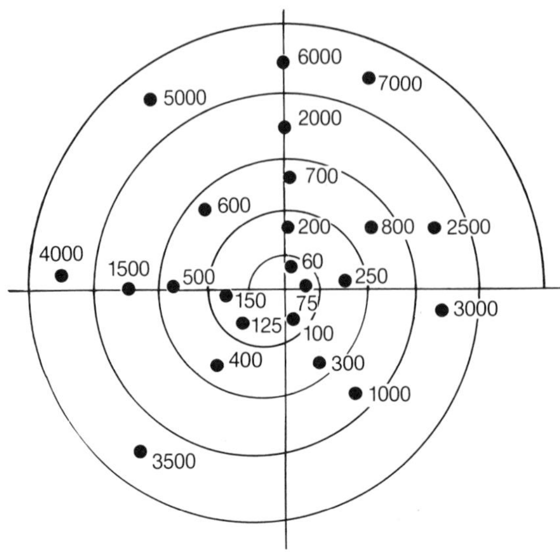

Figure 13.22 Map of the cochlea. Low frequencies cause the largest response near the helicotrema, and high frequencies cause the largest response near the stapes. (From Culler et al., 1943.)

the auditory system. We can show that this does, in fact, occur, by looking at how neurons on these more central structures respond to different frequencies. Before we do this, however, we should identify these more central structures.

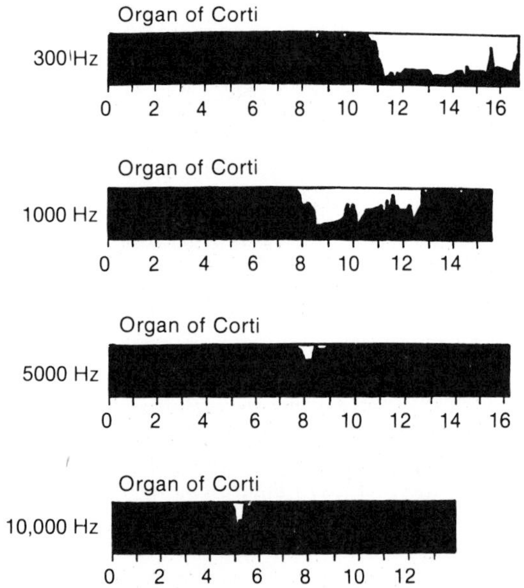

Figure 13.23 The effects of overstimulation on the organ of Corti. Degeneration of the organ of Corti is indicated in white. (From Smith, 1947, and Smith & Wever, 1949.)

Place Information Past the Cochlea

Figure 13.24 is a simplified diagram of the auditory pathways. We should emphasize that the route traveled between the cochlea and the auditory cortex is quite complex, and we do not yet know many of its details. Figure 13.24 does, however, identify the most important structures through which signals pass on their way to the cortex. Nerve fibers from the cochlea first synapse in the **cochlear nucleus,** then in the superior olivary nucleus, and finally in the inferior colliculus of the midbrain, before reaching the medial geniculate nucleus of the thalamus. (Remember that neurons from the visual system synapse in the nearby lateral geniculate nucleus of the thalamus.) From the medial geniculate nucleus, fibers then go to the primary **auditory receiving area,** which is located in the temporal lobe of the cortex.

The complexity of the auditory system becomes apparent when we consider that, in addition to the pathway from the cochlea to the cortex, there are also connections between nuclei on the opposite sides. For example, the cochlear nucleus of the right

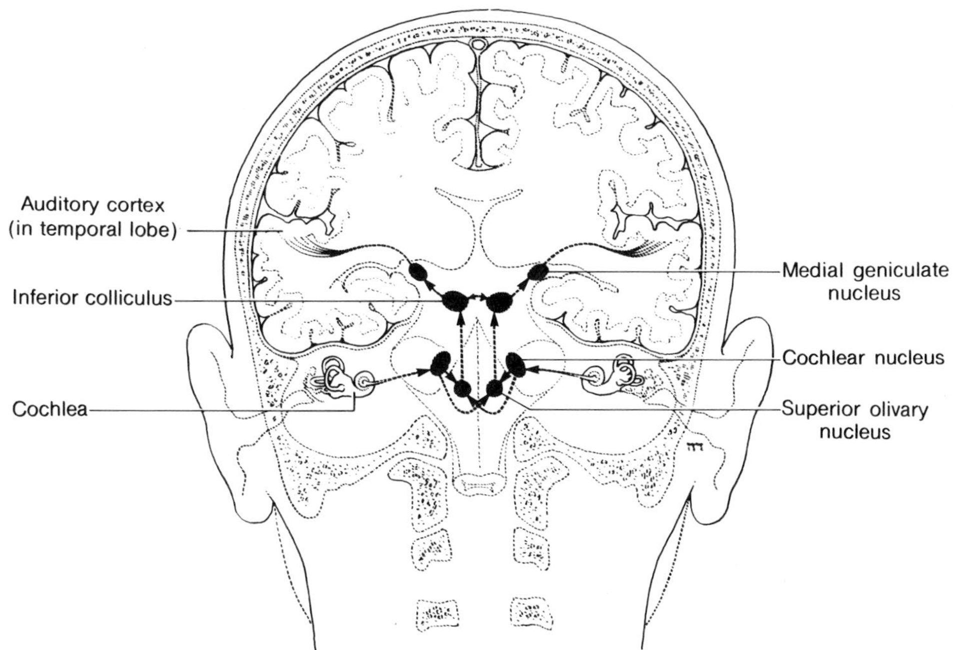

Figure 13.24 Simplified diagram of the auditory pathways. (Adapted from Wever, 1949.)

ear sends axons to the superior olivary nucleus and the inferior colliculus of the left ear, and the left and right inferior colliculi communicate with each other. In addition to these fibers, which send signals from the cochlea toward the brain, other fibers send signals from the brain back to the cochlea.

We are specifically interested in determining whether a **tonotopic map** exists in the nuclei along the auditory pathway. That is, we want to know if neurons that respond to the same frequency are grouped together in the nuclei and if neurons that respond to nearby frequencies are found near each other. To determine the frequencies to which a neuron responds, we determine the neuron's **tuning curve** by measuring the intensity necessary to elicit a threshold response at different frequencies along the audible range. Figure 13.25 shows tuning curves for three auditory nerve fibers. The frequency at which each neuron has the lowest threshold, indicated by the arrows, is called the **characteristic frequency,** or "best frequency," of the neuron.

To determine a tonotopic map, we determine a neuron's characteristic frequency and its location. Figure 13.26 shows the result of such determinations in part of the auditory cortex of the cat. The characteristic frequencies of neurons in this cortical area are arranged in an orderly way, with neurons responding best to high frequencies located to the left and neurons responding to lower frequencies to the right. In addition to the surface map shown in Figure 13.26, there is also a **columnar arrangement,** similar to that observed in the visual system (see p. 51, in Chapter 2). If we record along an electrode track that is perpendicular to the surface of the cortex, we find neurons with the same characteristic frequency (Abeles & Goldstein, 1970).

This type of tonotopic map has been found in all the nuclei shown in Figure 13.24, and the presence of such maps supports the idea that the frequency of a tone can be indicated by the place where activity is occurring. Once the tonotopic map is known, we need only know which neurons are firing the most to know which frequency is being presented to the ear.

We can summarize the evidence for Békésy's place theory as follows: (1) the maximum displacement of the traveling wave generated by sound moves from the helicotrema to the stapes end of the basilar

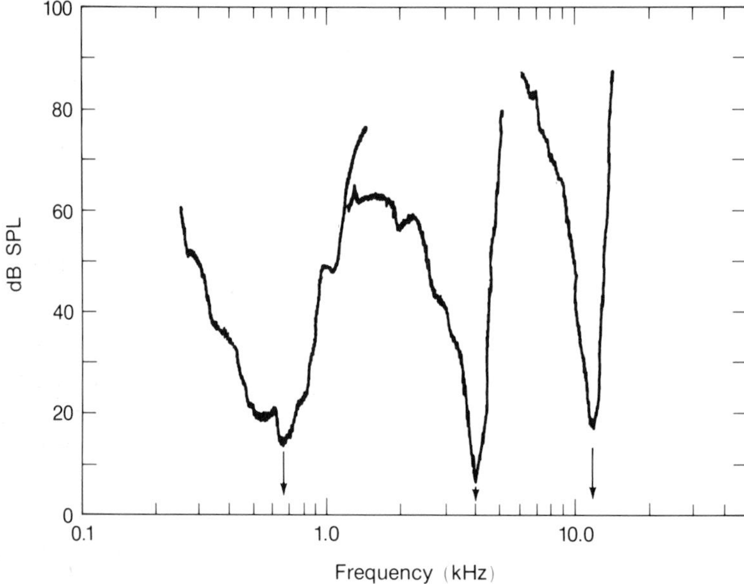

Figure 13.25 Tuning curves of three auditory nerve fibers in one animal. The characteristic frequency of each fiber is indicated by the arrows along the frequency axis. (From Kiang, 1975.)

membrane, as the frequency of the stimulus is increased; (2) maps determined by recording the electrical response of the cochlea show that low-frequency tones generate a larger response near the helicotrema and high-frequency tones generate a larger response near the stapes; (3) stimulation deafness experiments show a similar separation of high- and low-frequency tones along the cochlea; and (4) there are tonotopic maps in the central structures of the auditory system.

Evaluating the Theories

We have seen that neither Helmholtz's nor Rutherford's theories are still taken seriously as viable theories of pitch perception. But we have also seen evidence to support both a modified form of volley theory (which we will, henceforth, call the "timing mechanism") and Békésy's place theory. Each of these theories, however, is not without problems.

A major problem with place theory is that it can't explain how we can make very fine discriminations between frequencies. The just noticeable difference for a 100-Hz tone is about 3 Hz, which means that we can tell the difference between a 100- and a 103-Hz tone. The problem for place theory is that, although we can tell the difference between 100- and 103-Hz tones, the envelopes of the vibration caused by these low-frequency tones are quite broad—covering the entire basilar membrane—and there is little difference between the peaks of these envelopes. It is difficult, therefore, to explain our ability to discriminate between two low-frequency tones on the basis of the vibrational pattern of the basilar membrane. It appears, however, that the nervous system at least partially solves this problem, because neural tuning curves, like those in Figure 13.25, are narrower than the envelope of basilar membrane vibration. Apparently, some process, which occurs between basilar membrane vibration and generation of the neural response, "sharpens" the neural tuning curves, but the nature of this process is still unknown. In any case, even the neural tuning curves are too broad to explain our ability to distinguish nearby frequencies.

The problem with the idea that the timing of nerve impulses signals the stimulus frequency is one we have mentioned earlier. The upper frequency

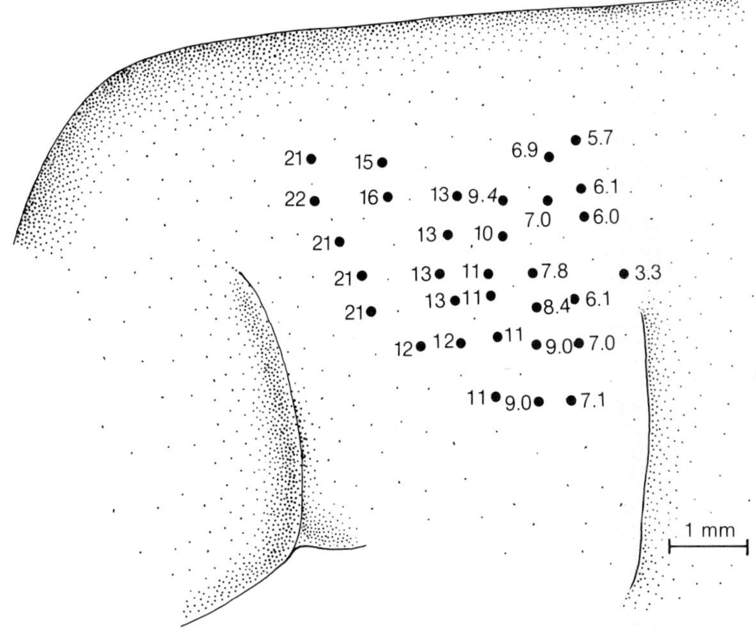

Figure 13.26 Tonotopic map on the surface of the auditory cortex of the cat. Each large dot represents a single neuron, and the number beside each dot represents the characteristic frequency of that neuron in thousands of Hz. (From Abeles & Goldstein, 1970.)

limit for phase locking of the response of fibers in the auditory nerve is about 4,000–5,000 Hz, and phase locking holds only up to about 1,000 Hz in structures nearer the cortex.

Thus, while there is evidence for both the place and timing mechanisms, each one has its drawbacks. Given the above, which mechanism is correct? To answer this question, let's draw an analogy between the situation for the place and timing mechanisms of hearing and the situation for the trichromatic and opponent-process theories of color vision, which we discussed in Chapter 5. The trichromatic and opponent-process theories were competitors; if you were a color vision researcher before about 1955, you believed in either one theory or the other, but not in both, with most researchers believing in the trichromatic theory. Similarly, most early researchers in hearing were partial to either place theory or timing theory, but not to both.

Presently, in both hearing and color vision, few researchers fail to recognize that the previously competing theories actually complement each other. This change occurred in color vision with the discovery of single neurons that respond in an opponent fashion to different wavelengths. This discovery made it impossible for researchers in the trichromatic camp to ignore opponent-process theory. Similarly, in hearing, the finding that some cells phase lock to stimulus frequency—combined with place theory's inability to explain how we discriminate between low-frequency tones—made it difficult for proponents of place theory to ignore the possibility that the timing of nerve impulses may play a role in our perception of pitch.

We can see how the place and timing mechanisms may work together, by considering how they operate in different frequency ranges. Place mechanism is weak at frequencies below 1,000 Hz because of the broad pattern of basilar membrane vibration at these frequencies; however, the timing mechanism works best at these frequencies, because fibers can phase lock most easily below 1,000 Hz. On the

Box 13.1 Environmental Noise and Hearing Loss

The results of studies such as those presented in Figure 13.23, show that continuous exposure to high-intensity tones can damage the cochleas of animals. Does this mean that environmental noise might damage the cochleas of people, resulting, perhaps, in permanent hearing loss? The answer to both parts of this question appears to be "yes."

Some people who have worked in noisy environments have willed their ear structures to medical research, and, in a number of these cases, clear damage to the organ of Corti has been observed. For example, examination of the cochlea of a man who worked in a steel mill indicated that the organ of Corti had collapsed and that no receptor cells remained (Miller, 1974).

There are also psychophysical measurements of the hearing of people who work in noisy environments. One study found that jute weavers exposed to mill noises of 98 decibels (dB), 8 hours per day for 10 years or more, experienced a 35-dB rise in their threshold for hearing a 4,000-Hz tone.

The permanent hearing loss suffered by the jute weavers was caused by long-term exposure to noise; however, hearing can also be permanently impaired by impulsive noises intense enough to rip or tear the structures of the inner ear. One example is provided by a 21-year-old college student who was in the process of raiding a rival fraternity house when a firecracker exploded in his hand, 15 inches from his right ear. As shown in the figure this mishap caused a rise in his threshold of over 50dB, at frequencies between 3,000 and 8,000 Hz. But even more serious than this large rise in threshold, the student also experienced a ringing sensation in his ear that was still present 2 years after the accident (Ward & Glorig, 1961).

Ringing in the ears, which is known as **tinnitus** (ti-NEYE-tus, from the Latin for "tinkling"), affects more than 36 million Americans, nearly 8 million of them severely. The most common cause of tinnitus is exposure to loud sounds, although this condition can also be caused by certain drugs, ear infections, or food allergies. Whatever the cause, tinnitus is an extremely debilitating condition. According to Dr. Jack Vernon, director of the Kresge Hearing Research Laboratory at the University of Oregon, tinnitus is the third worst thing that can happen to us, ranking only below intractable severe pain and intractable severe dizziness. In its most serious form, the constant noise of tinnitus is totally incapacitating, making it impossible for people to maintain their concentration long enough to complete a task, and in some cases even driving people to suicide.

Is there a cure for this condition? Unfortunately, for most people the answer to this ques-

other hand, timing is weak at frequencies above about 5,000 Hz, because cells lose their ability to phase lock above this frequency; however, the place mechanism works best at these frequencies, because the basilar membrane's vibration pattern is more narrowly tuned at high frequencies.

Thus, numerous results suggest that the timing of nerve impulses is important at low frequencies (below 500–1,000 Hz), that place is important at high frequencies (above 4,500–5,000 Hz), and that both mechanisms operate at frequencies in between (see Figure 13.27). An interesting fact, which supports the idea of a change in the mechanism of pitch perception at about 4,000—5,000 Hz, is that tones above 4,500–5,000 Hz lack the musical quality of tones below that frequency. That is, a sequence of tones with frequencies above 5,000 Hz does not result in a sense of melody (Attneave & Olson, 1971). (Remember that the highest note on the piano has a frequency of 4,186 Hz.)

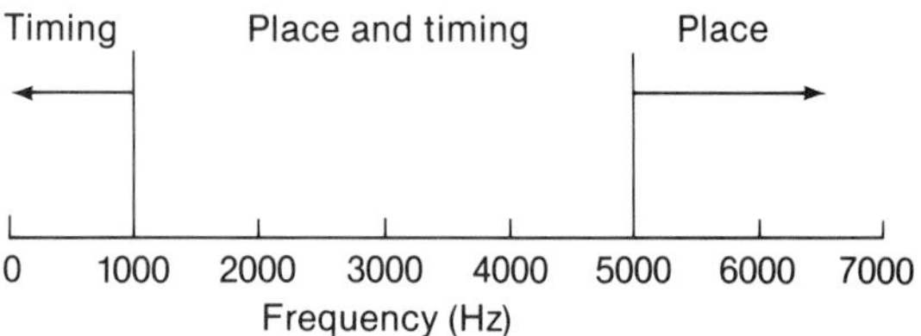

Figure 13.27 Pitch perception is determined by the timing of nerve firing below 1,000 Hz, by the place of stimulation along the basilar membrane at above 5,000 Hz, and by both timing and place mechanisms between 1,000 and 5,000 Hz.

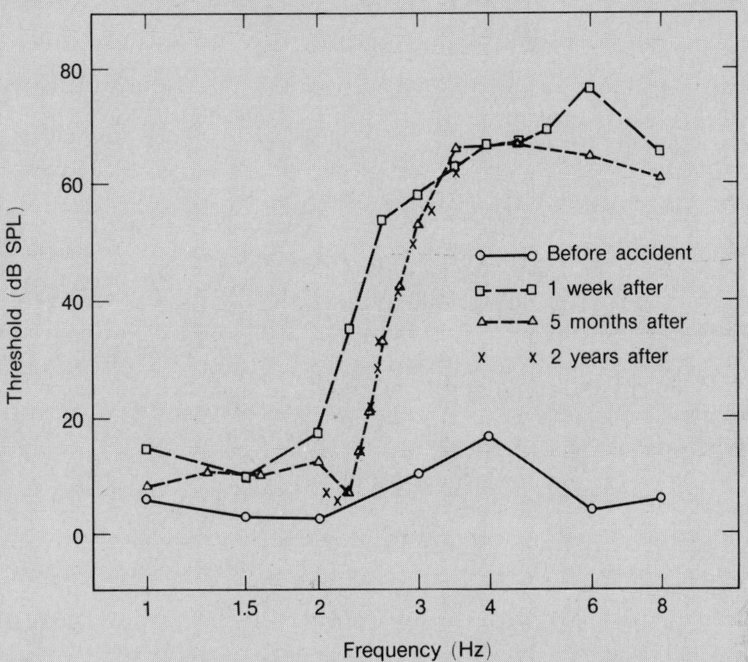

tion is "no." Some people, however, can gain relief by using a device called a **tinnitus masker.** The masker, which is worn in the ear like a hearing aid, produces a sound like a waterfall or the hiss of an FM radio tuned between stations. This externally produced noise masks the internal noise of tinnitus, making life bearable for some tinnitus sufferers.

Although the combination of the place and timing mechanisms of pitch perception seems to explain what we know about pitch perception better than either mechanism can alone, this does not mean that we have solved all the problems of pitch perception. The mechanism that enables us to distinguish two closely spaced tones is still not solved, and numerous questions about hearing that we have not mentioned here remain to be explained.

The Role of the Auditory Cortex

You may have noticed that our discussion of pitch perception has focused primarily on events in the cochlea and auditory nerve. We have said little about the cortex, except to note that there is a tonotopic map on the cortex (Figure 13.26) and that cells with the same characteristic frequency are organized in cortical columns. One reason for our apparent neglect of the cortex is that much of the research on the auditory system has focused on the cochlea and on the many structures through which signals from the cochlea must pass on their way to the cortex (Figure 13.24). That signals generated in the cochlea pass through many structures on their way to the cortex has even led to the following statement in a recent textbook on hearing: "Given the extent to which information is processed in the brainstem, it is not unreasonable to question what aspects of auditory function depend on cortical processing and, indeed, whether the auditory cor-

Box 13.2 Sonar System of the Blind

In 1749, Diderot reported the "amazing ability" of a blind acquaintance to perceive the presence of objects and their distance from him. Since that first published report, many people have confirmed this phenomenon and have speculated as to how it might occur. Explanations for this effect have ranged from **facial vision**—a hypothesized ability of blind people to detect obstacles by sensing pressure or temperature changes on their face—to mystical explanations depending on magnetism, electrical fields, or the subconscious. Recent experiments, however, have shown that the primary mechanism appears to be auditory; blind people can judge the presence of objects by paying attention to the sounds of their own footsteps or vocalizations.

In an ingenious experiment, which showed that the sound of a person's footsteps can be used to detect his approach to an object, the experimenter carried a microphone at shoulder height and walked toward a wall. The subjects, who were isolated in a soundproof room and could hear only the sounds picked up by the microphone, were told to state when they first "perceived" the wall. Because the pitch of the experimenter's footsteps appeared to rise as he approached the wall, the subjects in the booth were able to perceive the wall at distances between 3 and 10 inches (Supa et al., 1944).

In another experiment, blindfolded subjects walked toward an obstacle positioned at a distance of 6, 12, 18, 24, or 30 feet, until they perceived it (and stopped) or collided with it. With some practice, all these subjects were able to stop before colliding with the obstacle; however, if they were both blindfolded ***and*** wore earplugs, their performance decreased and they collided with the object more frequently (Ammons et al., 1953).

Perhaps the most impressive demonstration of how sound can be used to detect objects is provided by an experiment inspired by the way bats and dolphins use sonar, or "echo ranging," to determine the distances and sizes of objects. It was reasoned that if a dolphin can judge an object's distance by emitting a sound and sensing the echo reflected from the object, perhaps people can do the same thing. Two blind college students were asked to judge which of two objects was farther away. They were told that to aid them in making this judgment, they could produce any sound they wished. The subjects produced sounds in a variety of ways. They snapped their fingers, hissed, whistled, and, most often, repeated words such as "now, now, now. . ." By judging the echo produced by these sounds, they were able to tell which of the two objects was closer. In fact, their performance was so impressive that it was possible to vary the separation between the objects and, using the method of constant stimuli, to determine the psychophysical function in the figure. This function, which looks very much like other functions determined by the method of constant stimuli (see Figure 1.7), is an impressive demonstration of the capacity of blind people to "see" with their ears (Kellogg, 1962).

---

tex is even necessary for hearing!" (Durrant & Lovrinic, 1977, p. 133).

After making this interesting observation, Durrant and Lovrinic point out that the role of the cortex for various auditory tasks has usually been evaluated by training animals (usually cats) to perform a task, then removing the auditory cortex on both sides, and, finally, after allowing some time for recovery from the operation and perhaps administering some additional training, seeing how well the animals can perform the task.

The general results of this type of experiment have led to the conclusion that the following tasks can be performed without an auditory cortex:

1. Responding to the onset of a sound.
2. Responding to changes in the intensity of a tone.
3. Responding to changes in the frequency of a tone.

This last capability is perhaps the most surprising, because it is related to the perception of pitch. Apparently, the cortex is not necessary for discriminating between different frequencies, which suggests that our ability to perceive pitch may, in fact, not be determined by the auditory cortex. This does not mean, of course, that the auditory cortex is not

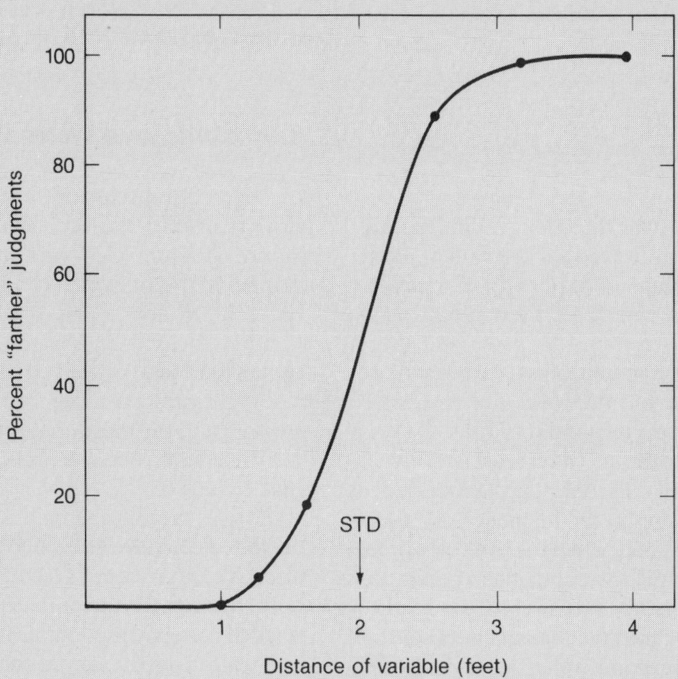

Box 13.2 The results of an experiment in which a blind observer was presented with two one-foot diameter plywood discs, a standard disc which was always two feet away and a variable disc which was either closer or farther than the standard. The observer judged whether each variable was closer or farther than the standard, making 100 judgments for each disc. That this blind observer was able to judge distance based on echo ranging is indicated by the fact that changing the distance of the variable by less than a foot (from 1.59 to 2.55 feet) resulted in a change from 19 to 89 percent "farther" responses. (Graph plotted from data in Kellog, 1962)

important for hearing. A number of tasks are affected by removal of the auditory cortex:

1. Discriminating the pattern of tones.
2. Discriminating the duration of a sound.
3. Localizing sounds in space.

To clarify what we mean by saying that the cortex is necessary for discriminating the pattern of tones, let's consider an experiment by Irving Diamond and Dewey Neff (1957). Diamond and Neff trained cats to perform the discrimination diagramed in Figure 13.28. In this discrimination, the cat had to learn to distinguish between a sequence in which the pattern was 800-1,000-800 (low-high-low) and a sequence in which the pattern was 1,000-800-1,000 (high-low-high). Although cats can distinguish these two patterns before their cortex is removed, they can't relearn this task after removal of the cortex.

From the limited research completed on the upper levels of the auditory system, it appears that we can draw an analogy between the auditory and visual systems. Remember that cells early in the visual system respond primarily to simple stimuli, such as spots of light, whereas cells in the visual cortex respond to more complex stimuli, such as corners

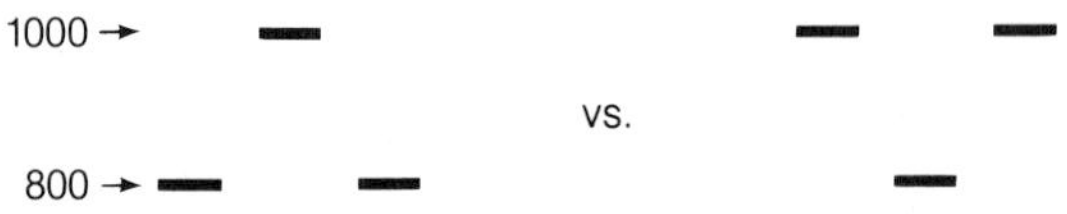

1000 → — — —

vs.

800 → — — —

Figure 13.28 Cats can distinguish these two patterns of stimulation before their cortex is removed, but they can no longer discriminate between them after removal of their cortex.

that move in a particular direction. A similar situation apparently exists in the auditory system. Early in the system, cells respond to pure tones with specific frequencies; as we move up the auditory pathways, however, cells respond to more and more complex stimuli. For example, cells have been found that respond neither to pure tones nor to combinations of tones but do respond to noises like keys jangling or paper tearing. Whitfield and Evans (1965) found cortical cells in the cat that responded only to smooth changes in the frequency of a tone: some cells responded only when the tone was swept from low to high frequencies, and others responded when the tonal frequency was swept from high to low. These cells are called **frequency sweep detectors,** because they respond well to changes in frequency but poorly or not at all to steady tones of a single frequency.

It appears, therefore, that the auditory cortex does have something to do with hearing, and Durrant and Lovrinic (1977) point out that "the greater the complexity of the sound and the more information contained within the sound, the greater the extent to which the cortex is expected to be involved in the processing of auditory information" (p. 134). Undoubtedly, the auditory cortex is heavily involved in the perception of speech—a type of complex sound we will discuss in the next chapter—and cortical areas beyond the primary auditory cortex are involved in dealing with the complexities of meaning and memory, critical components for the accurate perception of speech.

Auditory Sensitivity and the Perception of Loudness

Having described the basic physiology of the auditory system, we will now look at the results of some psychophysical experiments that describe how the **loudness** of a tone increases as we increase the tone's amplitude and how our sensitivity to sound varies as we change a tone's frequency.

Amplitude and Decibels

We began our discussion of sound by showing that movement of a speaker diaphragm in a sine-wave pattern (Figure 13.3) sets up sine-wave pressure changes in the air, which we call a pure tone (Figure 13.4). Until now, our discussion of pitch perception has focused on the tone's frequency, but to discuss loudness, we must consider the tone's amplitude—the pressure difference between atmospheric pressure and the maximum pressure reached during the sinusoidal pressure cycle, as shown in Figure 13.4.

As we increase the amplitude of a 1,000-Hz tone, the tone becomes louder and louder. If we start near threshold, so we can barely hear the tone, and continue to increase the amplitude until the tone has reached ear-splitting loudness, we will find that we have increased the amplitude by a factor of about 10 million! Since it is rather unwieldy to deal with such large numbers for a tone's amplitude, auditory researchers have developed a scale that converts amplitude to a much more manageable quantity, called the **decibel.**

Decibels are defined by the following equation:

$$dB = 20 \log(p/p_o)$$

where p is the amplitude of the sound wave, and p_o is a reference pressure set by the experimenter. Most researchers set the reference pressure as 0.0002 dynes/cm^2, the pressure at the threshold for hearing in the most sensitive frequency range (1,000–4,000 Hz); to indicate that this is the chosen reference pressure, we use the term **sound pressure level (SPL).** Thus, in our discussion below, when we say that the SPL of a tone is 50 dB, you will know that this value was calculated based on a reference pressure of 0.0002 dynes/cm^2.

To move decibels from the realm of abstract mathematics into real life, look at Table 13.1, which shows sound pressure levels in decibels for sounds ranging from threshold to a jet engine at takeoff.

The nice thing about the decibel scale is that it

has converted a sound pressure range of 0.0002 (the pressure at threshold) to 2,000 (the pressure of a jet at takeoff) into the much more manageable range of sound pressure levels of 0 to 140 dB.

Loudness

Though loudness is difficult to define, we all know what it means to say that a jet plane taking off is loud or that a whisper is soft. Although it is tempting to equate loudness with SPL, especially when we look at Table 13.1, we should not fall into the trap of confusing the two. It is important to remember that SPL is a *physical quantity* that depends on the pressure of the sound, whereas loudness is a *psychological response* to the sound, and that while increasing the SPL often increases a tone's loudness, SPL and loudness are not the same thing.

If we use Stevens' magnitude estimation procedure to determine the relationship between loudness and sound pressure, we find no one-to-one relation between the two. At moderate intensities, a power law with an exponent of about 0.4–0.6 (depending on the conditions of measurement and the frequency of the tone) relates the two. This means that in hearing, as in vision, response compression occurs in the relationship between perception and the physical measurement of the stimulus (see p. 14, in Chapter 1). That is, large increases in sound pressure cause small increases in loudness. Increasing the sound pressure by a factor of 10 (which is the same as increasing SPL by 20 dB) increases the loudness by only a factor of about 2.5–4.0.

Another way to differentiate between the physical and psychological properties of sound is to consider the **auditory response area,** shown in Figure 13.29.

Table 13.1
Some common sound pressure levels (in decibels)

Sound	*SPL (dB)*
Barely audible sound (threshold)	0
Leaves rustling	20
Quiet residential community	40
Average speaking voice	60
Loud music from radio/heavy traffic	80
Subway	100
The Rolling Stones	120
Jet engine at takeoff	140

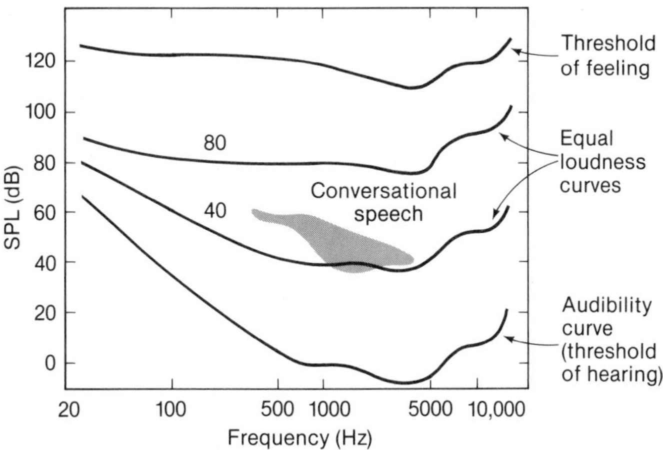

Figure 13.29 The auditory response area. Hearing functions between the lower curve, which represents the threshold for hearing, and the upper curve, which represents the threshold for feeling. Tones with SPLs below the threshold curve cannot be heard; tones with SPLs above the feeling curve result in pain and eventually cause damage to the ear. The shaded area indicates the frequency and intensity range for conversational speech. (From Fletcher & Munson, 1933.)

Box 13.3 Infrasound Detection by the Homing Pigeon

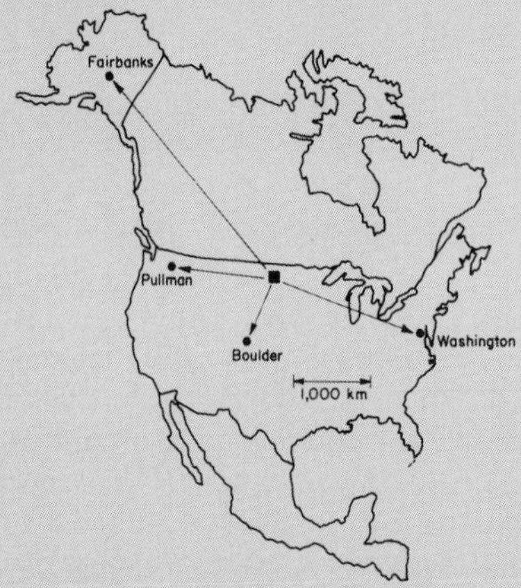

Just as we can see only a limited band of the electromagnetic spectrum, so we can hear only a limited band of frequencies. We can hear the vibrations we call sound in the frequency range from about 20 Hz to 20,000 Hz. Vibrations occurring below 20 Hz and above 20,000 Hz are silent to us, though some animals can hear these sounds. Dogs, for example, can hear higher frequencies than we can. Blowing a dog whistle has little effect on us but may get the attention of every dog on the block. At the other end of the frequency spectrum, below about 10 Hz, are sounds called **infrasounds,** which we can't hear but which are clearly audible to homing pigeons.

Infrasounds are fascinating because they are very prevalent and travel over long distances. Thunderstorms, earthquakes, ocean waves, and the wind coursing through mountain ranges produce infrasounds that can travel for hundreds or even thousands of miles, because low-frequency sounds are attenuated only slightly by the atmosphere (Cook, 1969; Gossard & Hooke, 1975). An example of the ability of infrasounds to travel long distances is shown in the figure above, which shows the locations of four tracking stations (circles) that picked up infrasounds generated by a severe thunderstorm (square).

Melvin Kreithen and Douglas Quine (1979) became interested in infrasound, because it had been suggested that birds might use these sounds as an aid to navigation (Griffin, 1969). They measured the bird's ability to detect infrasounds, by using a behavioral technique called *cardiac conditioning*. A 10-second burst of infrasound, followed by a mild shock, was presented at random intervals to a bird. After a number of these sound-shock presentations, the bird's heart rate speeds up when it hears the sound. Thus, by presenting sounds and monitoring the bird's heart rate, the investigators could tell when the bird heard a sound. Using this method, Kreithen and Quine found, much to their surprise, that homing pigeons can detect sound vibrations as low as 0.05 Hz—0.05 cycles of vibration per second, or 3 cycles of vibration per *minute*!

By listening to these infrasounds, homing pigeons may be able to detect oncoming weather patterns or even use the sounds generated by faraway mountains and valleys to locate their position as they fly. Whether the pigeons actually use this information is unknown, but it is fascinating to think that a bird flying far overhead may, as it flys, be listening to a thunderstorm hundreds of miles away.

The Auditory Response Area

The area between the bottom and top curves of Figure 13.29 is called the auditory response area, because this area defines the frequencies and the SPLs over which hearing functions. The bottom curve, marked "audibility curve," indicates the threshold SPL for frequencies throughout the range of hearing, whereas the top curve, marked "threshold of feeling," indicates the SPL at which sound is felt rather than heard. It is between these two extremes that we experience sound: at SPLs below the audibility curve, we can't hear sound; at SPLs above the threshold of feeling, we experience pain, and continued exposure to SPLs above this level is damaging to the ear.

The **audibility curve** shows the minimum sound pressure level in decibels needed to just detect a tone, as a function of the tone's frequency. The audibility curve is analogous to the spectral sensitivity curve for vision, which we measured in Chapters 1 and 3. Remember that we determined the spectral sensitivity curve by measuring the light intensity necessary to just see a light, at wavelengths across the spectrum. We determine the audibility curve by measuring the sound pressure level necessary to just hear a tone, at frequencies across the range of hearing. The audibility curve indicates that when an observer adjusts a 30-Hz tone to an SPL of about 65 dB, he or she can just hear it—it is at threshold. As we increase the frequency above 30 Hz, the threshold decreases until it reaches a minimum of about 2,000–4,000 Hz; above 4,000 Hz, the threshold increases as frequency increases. It is interesting to note that the frequency range between about 400 and 3,000 Hz falls near the range of frequencies to which we are most sensitive and is also the one most important for understanding speech.

The audibility curve tells us some interesting things about the relationship between SPL and our psychological response to pure tones. For example, different sound pressure levels (physical property) can result in the same loudness (psychological response). We can see how this works by looking up the thresholds for hearing a 30-Hz tone and a 1,000-Hz tone. The audibility curve indicates that the threshold for hearing the 30-Hz tone is 65 dB SPL and the threshold for hearing the 1,000-Hz tone is zero dB SPL. Thus, while these tones have vastly different SPLs, their loudnesses are the same—near zero—since these tones are both at threshold.

That different sound pressure levels can result in the same loudness is also indicated by the curves marked "40" and "80." These curves are **equal loudness curves,** which are determined by finding the SPL that causes the same loudness at each frequency. We do this by setting the 1,000-Hz tone as a standard and matching the loudness of all other tones to it. For example, the curve marked "40" in Figure 13.29 is the result of matching the loudness of all other frequencies to a 40-dB-SPL–1,000-Hz tone. It is obvious from these curves that different sound pressure levels result in the same loudness. For example, a 30-Hz tone must have an SPL of 80 dB in order to match the loudness of the 40-dB-SPL–1,000-Hz tone.

The audibility curve also tells us that two tones of the *same sound pressure level* can have quite *different loudnesses.* A 70-dB-SPL tone is very soft if it has a frequency of 30 Hz, since it is just barely above threshold, but it is very loud if it has a frequency of 3,000 Hz, since it is over 70 dB *above* threshold. The above examples should convince you that although increasing SPL at a given frequency does increase loudness, SPL and loudness are not the same thing.

Notice that the equal loudness curve marked "40" looks similar to the audibility function, in that it curves up at low frequencies: higher SPLs are needed for low-frequency tones to have the same loudness as a 1,000-Hz tone. However, the equal loudness curve marked "80" is considerably flattened, indicating that at 80 dB, all tones from 30 to 5,000 Hz have about the same loudness. The difference between these two equal loudness curves explains something that happens as you adjust the loudness control on your stereo system.

If you are playing music at a fairly loud level, say, 80 dB SPL, you should be able to easily hear all the frequencies in the music, because at 80 dB SPL, all frequencies from 30 to 15,000 Hz are well above threshold. What happens, however, when you turn down the loudness so that the music is fairly soft, say, 20 dB? From the audibility curve, you can see that if the SPL is 20 dB, you will not be able to hear any frequencies below about 200 Hz. (Be sure you understand how to determine this. Find 20 dB on the SPL scale and draw a horizontal line across to the right. You should notice that the 20-dB line intersects the audibility curve at a frequency just slightly over 200 Hz and that the thresholds of frequencies below 200 Hz fall above the 20-dB line, which means that these frequencies will not be heard if the SPL is 20 dB.) This is certainly a bad situation, because it means that when you play music softly, you won't hear the low pitches. Fortunately, most stereo receivers have a button or switch labeled "Loudness" that, when activated, boosts the level of low frequencies so that you can hear them, even when your next-door neighbor asks you to turn down your stereo.

Auditory Space

Standing on a hill overlooking a neighborhood in Pittsburgh, at the beginning of our discussion of

Box 13.4 The Precedence Effect

The reverberation that occurs when you listen to music, or to someone talking in an enclosed room, means that your ears first receive sound waves directly from the sound source and then receive indirect sounds, which are reflected from the ceiling, floor, and walls of the room. Since your ears receive a sequence of sounds, why do you perceive only a single sound? The answer to this question is that, for reasons still not completely understood, your auditory system suppresses the sound waves that reach your ears indirectly and attends only to the first sound waves reaching your ears. This effect, which is called the **precedence effect,** was extensively studied by Hans Wallach and co-workers (1949).

Wallach demonstrated the precedence effect by having a subject listen to music coming from two speakers located an equal distance away. When the music came from both speakers simultaneously, the subject heard the music coming from a point between the two speakers. However, if Wallach caused the sound from one speaker to precede the sound from the other by having two phonograph pickups play the same record—the needle of one pickup following in the same groove as the needle of the other—the subject reported that the sound appeared to come only from the speaker that first produced the sound. On the basis of this result and those of other experiments, Wallach concluded that the first sound reaching our ears is heard, and sounds arriving within about 70 msec of this first sound are suppressed.

To demonstrate the precedence effect to yourself, turn your stereo system to monaural (or "mixed") so that both speakers play the same sounds, and position yourself between the speakers, so you hear the sound coming from both speakers or from a point between them. Then move a small distance to the left or right. When you do this, the sound suddenly appears to be coming from only the nearer speaker. You might think that this effect is due to the fact that moving toward one speaker makes the sound from that speaker louder. However, Wallach showed that the small increase in loudness that would occur from moving slightly closer to one speaker cannot cause you to hear only that speaker; you hear only the nearer speaker because the sound from that speaker reaches your ears first.

When you hear the sound coming from the near speaker, does this mean you no longer hear the far speaker? You can answer this question by positioning yourself closer to one speaker and having a friend disconnect the other speaker. When this happens, you will notice a difference in the quality of the sound. Even when you think you are listening to only the near speaker, you are also hearing the far speaker, and the contribution from this speaker gives the sound a fuller, more expansive quality (Green, 1976).

depth perception in Chapter 8, we were able to see from the cars and houses directly in front of us to the houses and trees lining a ridge in the distance. Our ability to see objects in the visual space around us is something we are usually much more aware of than the other kind of space that surrounds us—the auditory space of trees rustling in the wind, traffic, people talking, and dogs barking. We can think of these sounds as making up an auditory space, because, when we hear them, we can usually tell where they are coming from. Traffic approaching on the right, people talking behind you, and an airplane flying overhead are common perceptions that depend on your ability to localize sounds in space.

In Chapter 8, we saw that we can perceive depth with just one eye by using monocular depth cues; depth perception is improved, however, if we are able to make use of the depth information provided by binocular disparity. In hearing, the use of two ears is very important if we are to accurately localize sounds in our environment. You can prove this to yourself by blocking the sound from one ear and noticing how well you can tell where the sounds around you are coming from. You will probably notice that it is much more difficult to localize sounds with one ear than it is with two, and that you end up moving your head around a lot to compensate for the loss of information from the blocked ear. Sounds are localized much less accurately with

monaural (one-eared) **hearing** than with **binaural** (two-eared) **hearing.**

Just as we can locate objects in visual space because our two eyes receive slightly different images, sound **localization** in auditory space depends on our having two ears that receive slightly different sounds. In the remainder of this chapter, therefore, we will describe how information we take in with both ears helps us to localize sounds.

Interaural Time Difference

The basis for the idea that the two ears receive different sounds is illustrated in Figure 13.30. We can see from this figure that when a sound originates from directly in front of the listener, at A, the distance to each ear is the same, but if a sound originates from the side, as in B, the sound must travel farther and, therefore, takes longer to get to the left ear than to the right ear. We can measure this **interaural time difference** by placing microphones in a person's ears and measuring the arrival time of the sound from a source located at different positions in space relative to the person. The results of these measurements indicate that there is no difference in the arrival time of a sound when the source is directly in front of or directly behind the listener; however, as the source is moved to the side, there is a delay between the time the sound reaches the near ear and the time it reaches the far ear, with this difference reaching a maximum of about 600 microseconds (1,000 microseconds = 1/1,000 second) when the sound is located directly opposite one of the ears, as in B of Figure 13.30 (Feddersen et al., 1957). Although time differences on the order of microseconds are very small, it has been shown that we can detect differences in arrival time as short as 10 microseconds (Durlach & Colburn, 1978).

While the interaural time difference provides information about the location of a tone, it does not do so unambiguously, because a number of points in space are located at the same distance from both ears and, therefore, result in the same interaural time difference. In fact, a surface called the **cone of confusion,** shown in Figure 13.31, is defined by all the points in space that are the same distance from both ears. Any point lying on this cone will be equidistant from both ears, so it is difficult to tell exactly

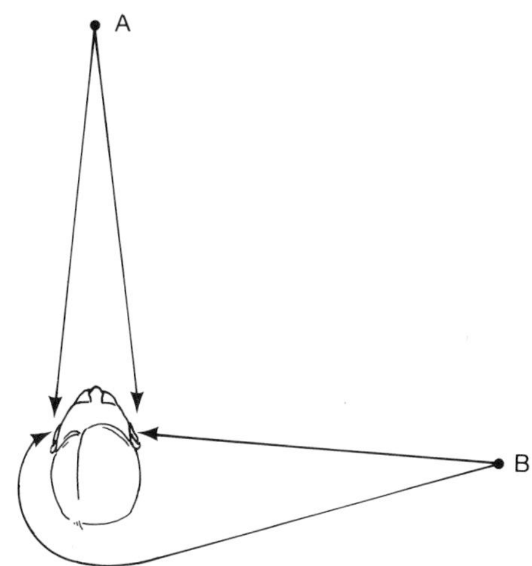

Figure 13.30 The principle underlying interaural time difference. The tone directly in front of the listener, at A, reaches the ears at the same time. However, if the tone is off to the side, as at B, it reaches the listener's right ear before it reaches his left ear.

where on the cone a sound is coming from, based only on the interaural time difference. The solution to this problem is simple: the observer moves his or her head and finds that tones which were difficult to localize with the head stationary can be localized much more easily. Our ability to localize tones in everyday experience can be largely attributed to the effect of these head movements.

Interaural Intensity Difference

In addition to a difference in the arrival time of sound at the two ears, there is also a difference in the intensity of the sound reaching the two ears. This occurs for high-frequency tones because the head casts a "shadow," which decreases the intensity of the sound reaching the far ear. This difference in the intensity at the two ears, which is called the **interaural intensity difference**, has been measured by recording the sound intensity reaching each ear with microphones and a movable sound source. The results of these measurements indicate that the effect of this shadow depends on the frequency of the tone. There is essentially no shadow for low-frequency tones, but there is a large shadow

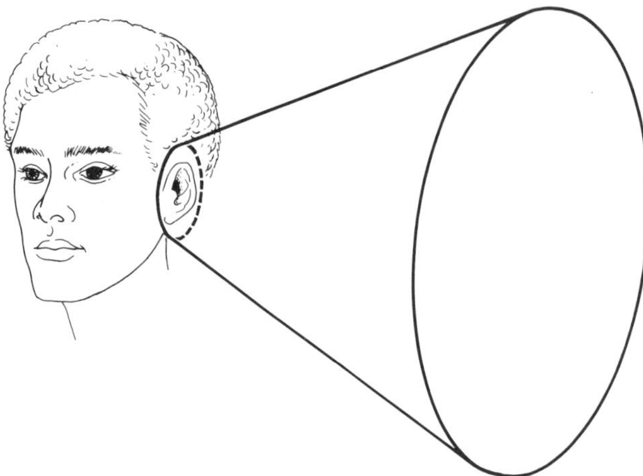

Figure 13.31 The "cone of confusion." Without moving the head, it is difficult to localize tones originating from locations on the surface of this cone.

Box 13.5 Perceiving Sound in Rooms: Reverberation Time

We've seen that your perception of light depends not only on the nature of the light source but also on what happens to the light between the time it leaves its source and the time it enters your eyes. If light encounters haze on its way from an object to your eyes, the object may seem bluer or fuzzier than it would if the haze were not there. If the light encounters some raindrops, it may turn into a rainbow. In a similar way, your perception of sound also depends not only on the sound produced at the source but also on what happens to the sound between the time it leaves the source and the time it enters your ears.

What happens to a sound between the time it is produced and the time it reaches your ears? We can see from the figure that the answer to this question depends on the environment in which you hear the sound. If you are sitting outdoors next to someone playing a guitar, most of the sound you hear travels in a straight line and reaches your ears directly. If, however, you are listening to the same guitar in an enclosed room, then only some of the sound you hear travels directly to your ears; the rest of the sound you hear travels from the guitar to the room's walls, ceiling, and floor before reaching your ears. The sound reaching your ears directly, along path A, is called **direct sound,** and the sound reaching your ears later, along paths like B and C, is called **indirect sound.**

The science of architectural acoustics is largely concerned with how this indirect sound changes the quality of the sounds we hear in rooms. The major factor affecting indirect sound is the amount of sound absorbed by the walls, ceilings, and floors of the room. If most of the sound is absorbed, then there are few sound reflections and we hear little indirect sound. If little of the sound is absorbed, however, then there are many sound reflections and we hear much indirect sound. The amount of indirect sound produced by a room is expressed as the **reverberation time** of the room, where reverberation time is the time it takes for the sound to decrease to one-thousandth its original pressure.

What is the relationship between reverberation time and perception of music? If the reverberation time is short, music will sound "dead," because most of the sound is absorbed by the room and it is difficult to produce sounds of very high intensity. If the reverberation time is long, music sounds "muddled," because most of the sound is reflected by the room and the sounds overlap each other. Thus, the job of the acoustical engineer is to design a room in which the reverberation time is neither too short nor too long.

for high-frequency tones. Thus, when a 200-Hz tone is moved to different locations, the sound intensities reaching both ears stay equal, but when a 6,000-Hz tone is moved, the intensity reaching the far ear is up to 20 dB less than the intensity reaching the near ear.

The difference between the interaural intensity differences for high and low frequencies is caused by differences in the wavelengths of the tones. The wavelength of the 200-Hz tone is large compared to the size of the head, as shown in Figure 13.32(a); so the head does not interfere with the sound wave, and the intensity is unaffected. The wavelength of the 6,000-Hz tone, however, is very small compared to the size of the head, as shown in Figure 13.32(b); so the wave casts a shadow on the far side of the head, and the intensity at the far ear is decreased. Because of this effect of the tone's wavelength, the interaural intensity difference is an effective cue for sound location only at high frequencies.

Sound Reflections by the Pinna

In describing the outer ear at the beginning of this chapter, we noted that while the pinna's major importance to some people is in helping hold on their eyeglasses or earrings, it does play a role in helping us to localize sounds. This function of the pinna has been studied by Gardner and Gardner (1973), who smoothed out the irregularities of the pinna by inserting plugs of various shapes into people's ears. They found that as they increasingly smoothed out the pinna by inserting different plugs, their listeners had more and more difficulty in localizing sounds. One possible reason for this result is that high-frequency tones are reflected back and forth

The optimal reverberation time for a room depends on the size of the room, with most average-sized concert halls needing a reverberation time of about 1.5–2.0 seconds.

However, reverberation time is apparently not the only factor that affects our perception of music in concert halls. This is illustrated by the problems associated with the design of New York's Philharmonic Hall. When it opened in 1962, Philharmonic Hall had a reverberation time of close to 2.0 seconds, a value comparable to the reverberation times of many of the most successful concert halls in the world. Even so, the hall was criticized for sounding as though it had a short reverberation time, and musicians in the orchestra complained that they could not hear each other. These criticisms resulted in a series of alterations to the hall, made over many years, until eventually, when none of the alterations proved satisfactory, the entire interior of the hall was destroyed and the hall was completely rebuilt. Finally, in 1976, 14 years after it opened, Philharmonic Hall had good acoustics. Based on this experience with Philharmonic Hall, it is safe to say that the acoustics of concert halls is not an exact science (Backus, 1977).

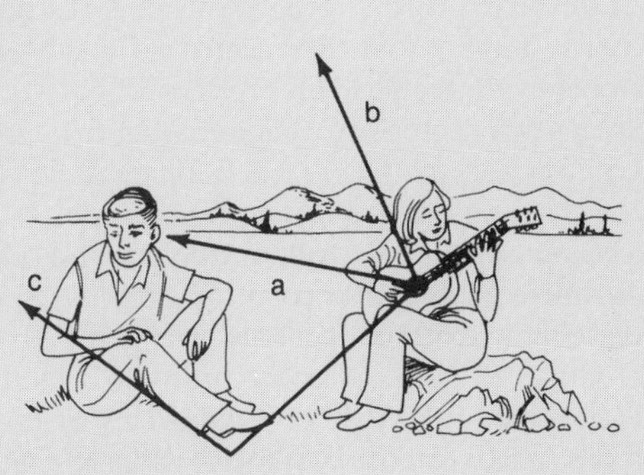

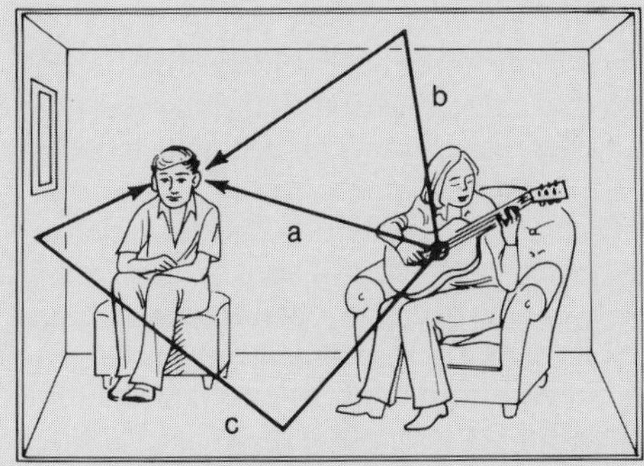

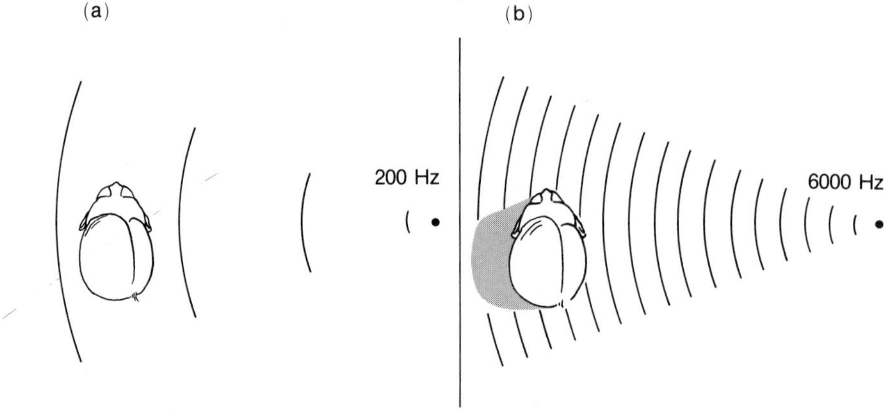

Figure 13.32 The principle underlying interaural intensity difference. Low-frequency tones are not affected by the listener's head, so the intensity of the 200-Hz tone is the same at both ears. High-frequency tones are affected by the presence of the listener's head, resulting in a sound "shadow" that decreases the intensity of the tone reaching the listener's far ear.

inside the whorls of the pinna, causing echoes with different patterns for different distances and directions of the sound source (Batteau, 1967; Scharf, 1975).

Physiological Mechanisms of Localization

We have noted that one effect of removing an animal's auditory cortex is a decreased ability to localize sounds. The auditory cortex, therefore, plays an important role in the localization of sound, and recent electrophysiological studies have identified cells in the auditory cortex of the monkey that respond best to specific interaural time differences (Brugge & Merzenich, 1973). For example, one of these cells fires best when a sound reaches the left ear 800 microseconds before it reaches the right ear, or when a sound reaches the right ear 1,200 microseconds before it reaches the left ear. This cell, which could be called an **interaural time difference detector,** is similar to the binocular depth cells described in Chapter 8, that respond best to specific degrees of disparity between the two eyes. These interaural time difference cells have been recorded not only from the cortex but also from nuclei as early in the auditory system as the superior olivary nucleus, the first nucleus in the system to receive inputs from both ears (Hall, 1965).

Perhaps the most impressive demonstration of cells which provide information about sound location are cells that respond only to sounds which originate in limited areas of space. These cells, located in the owl's mesencephalicus lateralus dorsalis (MLD)—a nucleus equivalent to the inferior colliculus of mammals—have been studied by Eric Knudsen and Masakazu Konishi (1978a, b), using the apparatus shown in Figure 13.33. By recording from a cell while stimulating from different positions in space, they found cells that respond only when the sound originates from a small elliptical area in space, the receptive field of the cell. Furthermore, they found that some of these receptive fields have excitatory centers and inhibitory surrounds; so an excitatory response, elicited by sound in the center of the receptive field, could be inhibited by another sound, presented to the side or above or below the center. This property of the MLD cells means that center-surround receptive fields exist not only on the retina (Figures 2.25 and 2.26) and on the skin (Figure 4.16) but also in space!

Knudsen and Konishi not only found cells with receptive fields at particular locations in space, they discovered that these cells are arranged so that there is a map of auditory space on the MLD. That is, each cell on the MLD responds to a specific area in space (relative to the position of the head), and adjacent cells respond to adjacent areas of space. We can

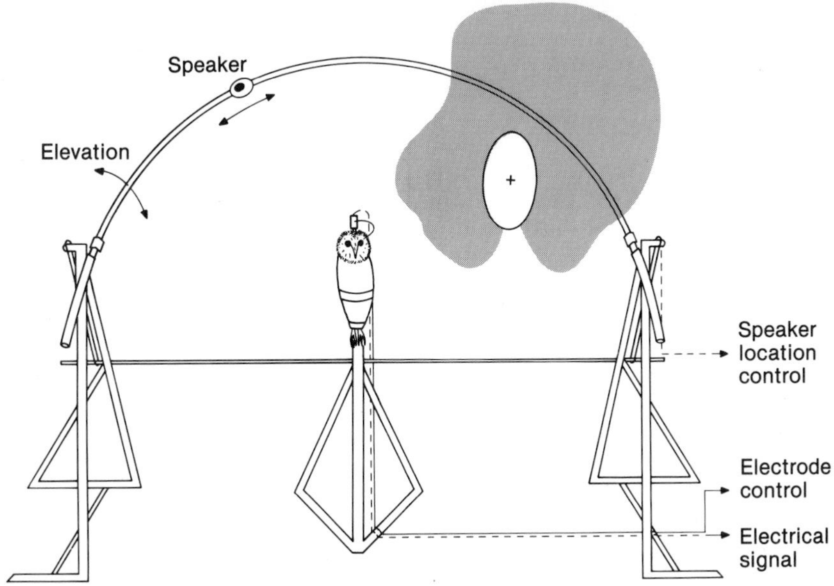

Figure 13.33 The apparatus used by Knudsen and Konishi (1978 a, b) to map auditory receptive fields in space. The speaker can be moved to different positions in space by sliding the speaker along the curved rod or by moving the rod around the owl. The elliptical area marked with a plus is the excitatory area of a typical receptive field, and the shaded area is the inhibitory area.

compare this mapping of space on the MLD to other maps in the nervous system: each point on the cochlea is represented by a small area on the auditory cortex (Figure 13.22); each point on the retina is represented by a small area on the visual cortex; and each point on the skin is represented by a small area on the sensory cortex (Figure 4.15). In each of these situations, sequences of neurons travel from the receptor surfaces of the cochlea, retina, and skin to points on the auditory, visual, and sensory areas of the cortex, respectively. We cannot think in terms of sequences of neurons that travel from a receptor surface to points on the MLD, however, because each point on the MLD represents a point not on a receptor surface but, rather, in space relative to the position of the head.

Although a precise mapping of auditory space, like that seen in these owl MLD cells, has not yet been demonstrated in mammals, cells have been found in the cat's cortex that respond to sounds located in specific positions in space and to sounds which move in specific directions. Anssi Sovijarvi and Johani Hyvarinen (1974) recorded from cells in the cat's auditory cortex that respond with a large burst of firing to movement of a sound in one direction and with no response or inhibition to movement in the opposite direction. In addition to these directionally sensitive cells, which are similar to the directionally sensitive cells in the visual and cutaneous systems, described in Chapters 2 and 4, they also found some cells that respond best to stationary sounds located in a particular region of space. These results suggest that a mapping of space similar to that found in the owl's MLD may also exist in the auditory system of mammals.

Summary

1. An object generates sound when its vibrations result in pressure waves in the medium surrounding the object. When these vibrations are sinusoidal, a pure tone results. Two basic characteristics of pure tones are the frequency and amplitude of the wave.

2. The ear consists of three divisions. (1) Outer ear—pinna, auditory canal, tympanic membrane. The tympanic membrane vibrates in response to sound. The outer ear amplifies frequencies between about 2,000 and 5,000 Hz, by resonance. (2) Middle ear—ossicles: malleus, incus, and stapes. The lever action of the ossicles and the difference in area between the tympanic membrane and the footplate of the stapes compensate for the impedance mismatch between the outer and inner ear. (3) Inner ear—cochlea, cochlear partition, helicotrema, organ of Corti, basilar membrane, tectorial membrane, hair cells. Vibration is transmitted from the cochlear fluid to the basilar membrane and hair cells. The bending of the hair cells against the tectorial membrane, which occurs in response to vibration, causes transduction.

3. Helmholtz's resonance theory of pitch perception proposed that fibers on the basilar membrane act like independently tuned resonators. This idea was later shown to be incorrect.

4. Rutherford proposed that the basilar membrane vibrates as a whole and that the stimulus frequency is signaled by the firing frequency of single nerve fibers. This idea cannot be correct, however, because nerve fibers have a refractory period that limits their firing rate to about 1,000 impulses per second.

5. Wever's volley principle states that stimulus frequency is signaled by groups of fibers firing in orderly volleys. Later research showed that, while they do not fire in orderly volleys, fibers in the auditory nerve do fire in synchrony with the stimulus. This synchronization of nerve firing with the peak of a pure tone stimulus is called phase locking.

6. Békésy showed that the basilar membrane vibrates in a traveling wave. The peak of the envelope of the traveling wave depends on frequency, with low frequencies causing peak vibration near the helicotrema and high frequencies causing peak vibration near the stapes. This correlation between frequency and the peak of basilar membrane vibration is the basis of Békésy's place theory of pitch perception.

7. Additional evidence for place theory is provided by electrical maps of the cochlea, stimulation deafness experiments and the presence of tonotopic maps in the nuclei of the auditory system. Tonotopic maps are determined by measuring tuning curves to determine a neuron's characteristic frequency, and then mapping the locations of each characteristic frequency onto the surface of each nucleus.

8. Noise in the environment can damage the cochlea and cause permanent hearing loss. Loud noise and other causes can result in a condition called tinnitus.

9. Place theory can't explain how we can make very fine discriminations between low frequencies, because of the broadness of the envelopes of vibration for low frequency tones. The timing mechanism can't explain how we perceive high-frequency tones, because the upper limit for the phase locking of neurons in the auditory nerve is about 4,000 Hz, and phase locking holds only up to about 1,000 Hz in structures nearer the cortex.

10. Place and timing mechanisms probably work together to determine pitch perception, with the timing mechanism operating below 500–1,000 Hz, place and timing working together between 1,000 and 5,000 Hz, and place operating exclusively above 5,000 Hz.

11. The auditory cortex is important for discriminating patterns of tones, for discriminating the duration of a sound, and for localizing sounds in space.

12. Blind people can judge the presence of objects by paying attention to the sounds of their own footsteps or vocalizations.

13. The unit used to designate the amplitude of a tone is the decibel (dB). $dB = 20 \log (p/p_o)$. When the reference pressure, p_o, is set at .0002 dynes/cm^2, this amplitude measure is called sound pressure level (SPL).

14. Loudness is closely related to SPL. The power function relating loudness and pressure has an exponent of 0.4–0.6, depending on the frequency and the conditions of measurement.

15. The auditory response area defines the fre-

quencies and SPLs over which hearing functions. The audibility curve indicates the threshold SPL for frequencies throughout the range of hearing. The range of hearing extends from 20 to 20,000 Hz, with the lowest threshold at 2,000–4,000 Hz. The audibility curve tells us that two tones with different SPLs can both be at threshold.

16. An equal loudness curve is a plot of the SPL that results in the same loudness as a 1,000-Hz reference tone, for frequencies across the range of hearing. Equal loudness curves tell us that two tones with the same SPLs can result in different loudnesses and that two tones with different SPLs can result in the same loudness.

17. Homing pigeons can detect infrasounds—frequencies below 10 Hz. It has been hypothesized that this ability may be used as an aid in navigation.

18. The auditory system suppresses sound waves that reach your ears indirectly. This is called the precedence effect.

19. The quality of sound heard in rooms depends on the amount of sound absorbed by the surfaces in the room. Concert halls with short reverberation times can cause music to sound "dead," whereas concert halls with long reverberation times can cause music to sound "muddled."

20. Sound is localized by means of interaural time and intensity differences and by head movements. Cells have been found at various levels of the auditory system that respond best to specific interaural time differences, and some cells have been found that respond to sounds located at specific positions in space.

Glossary

Amplitude In the case of a repeating sound wave, such as the sine wave of a pure tone, amplitude represents the pressure difference between atmospheric pressure and the maximum pressure of the wave. (349)

Audibility curve A curve that indicates the sound pressure level (SPL) at threshold for frequencies across the audible spectrum. (369)

Auditory canal *See* External auditory meatus. (350)

Auditory receiving area The area of the cortex, located in the temporal lobe, that is the primary receiving area for hearing. (360)

Auditory response area The area that defines the frequencies and SPLs over which hearing functions. This area extends between the audibility curve and the curve for the threshold of feeling. (368)

Basilar membrane A membrane that stretches the length of the cochlea and controls the vibration of the cochlear partition. (353)

Binaural hearing Hearing with two ears. (371)

Characteristic frequency The frequency at which a neuron has its lowest threshold. (361)

Cochlea The snail-shaped, liquid-filled structure that contains the structures of the inner ear, the most important of which are the basilar membrane, the tectorial membrane, and the hair cells. (350)

Cochlear nucleus The nucleus where nerve fibers from the cochlea first synapse. (360)

Cochlear partition A partition in the cochlea, extending almost its full length, that separates the scala tympani and the scala vestibuli. (353)

Columnar arrangement Neurons in the auditory cortex are arranged in columns, with neurons in each column having the same characteristic frequency. (361)

Cone of confusion The cone-shaped surface defined by all the points in space that are the same distance from both ears. (371)

Decibel (dB) A unit that indicates the presence of a tone relative to a reference pressure. $dB = 20 \log (p/p_o)$ where p is the pressure of the tone and p_o is the reference pressure. (368)

Direct sound Sound that is transmitted directly to the ears from a sound source. (374)

Eardrum *See* Tympanic membrane. (350)

Envelope of the traveling wave A curve that indicates the maximum displacement at each point along the basilar membrane caused by a traveling wave. (358)

Equal loudness curve A curve indicating the SPLs that cause the same loudness at frequencies across the audible spectrum. (369)

External auditory meatus (auditory canal) The canal through which air vibrations travel from the environment to the tympanic membrane. (350)

Facial vision A hypothesized ability of blind people to detect obstacles by sensing pressure or temperature changes on their face. (366)

Frequency In the case of a repeating sound wave, such as the sine wave of a pure tone, frequency is the number of times per second that the wave repeats itself. (349)

Frequency sweep detector A neuron in the auditory cortex that fires only when frequencies are smoothly increased or decreased. (368)

Frequency theory Rutherford's theory of pitch perception, which proposes that the basilar membrane vibrates as a whole and that the rate of this vibration matches the frequency of the stimulus. (355)

Hair cells Small hairs, or cilia, that are the receptors for hearing. There are two kinds of hair cells—inner and outer hair cells. (350)

Helicotrema A small opening at the end of the cochlear partition that connects the scala vestibuli and the scala tympani. (353)

Hertz (Hz) The unit for designating the frequency of a tone. One Hertz equals one cycle per second. (349)

Impedance In the auditory system, impedance refers to resistance to the passage of vibrations. (351)

Impedance mismatch Occurs when there is a large difference in the impedances of two adjacent materials, such as the air of the outer and middle ear and the liquid of the inner ear. (351)

Incus (hammer) The second of the three ossicles of the middle ear. It transmits vibrations from the malleus to the stapes. (352)

Indirect sound Sound that reaches the ears after being reflected from a surface, such as a room's walls. (374)

Infrasounds Vibrations below 10 Hertz. (370)

Inner ear The innermost division of the ear, containing the cochlea. (353)

Interaural intensity difference When a sound source is positioned closer to one ear than to the other, the intensity of the sound is greater at the closer ear. This effect is most pronounced for high-frequency tones. (373)

Interaural time difference When a sound source is positioned closer to one ear than to the other, the sound reaches the close ear slightly before reaching the far ear. (373)

Interaural time difference detector A neuron that fires only when a stimulus is presented first to one ear and then to the other ear, with a specific delay between stimulation of the two ears. (375)

Localization In audition, the capacity to locate a sound in space. (373)

Loudness The quality of sound that ranges from soft to loud. For a tone of a particular frequency, loudness usually increases with increasing decibels. (368)

Malleus (anvil) The first of the ossicles of the middle ear. It receives vibrations from the tympanic membrane and transmits them to the incus. (352)

Middle ear The small, air-filled space between the auditory canal and cochlea that contains the ossicles. (351)

Monaural hearing Hearing with only one ear. (373)

Organ of Corti The major structure of the cochlear partition—the organ of Corti contains the basilar membrane, the tectorial membrane, and the receptors for hearing. (353)

Ossicles Three small bones in the middle ear that transmit vibrations from the outer to the inner ear. (352)

Outer ear The pinna and the external auditory meatus. (350)

Oval window A small, membrane-covered hole in the cochlea that receives vibrations from the stapes. (353)

Phase locking Occurs when nerve firing is synchronized with the peak of a pure tone stimulus. (357)

Pinna The part of the ear that is visible on the outside of the head. (350)

Pitch That quality of sound, ranging from low to high, that is most closely associated with the frequency of a tone. (355)

Place theory Békésy's theory, which states that the frequency of a tone is signaled by the place along the cochlear partition that is maximally stimulated. (357)

Precedence effect If two identical or very similar sounds reach your ears, separated by a time interval of less than about 50–100 msec, you hear the sound that first reaches your ears, and the auditory system suppresses other similar sounds that reach your ears within this 50–100-msec time interval. (372)

Resonance A mechanism that enhances the intensity of certain frequencies, due to reflection of sound waves in a closed tube. (351)

Resonance theory Helmholtz's theory of pitch perception, which proposes that the basilar membrane is made up of a series of transverse fibers, each tuned to resonate to a specific frequency. (355)

Resonant frequency The frequency that is most strongly enhanced by resonance. The resonance frequency of a closed tube is determined by the length of the tube. (351)

Reverberation time Reflection of sound by the walls, ceiling, or floor of a room increases the duration of the sound. The reverberation time of a room is the time it takes for a sound to decrease to 1/1,000 of its original pressure. (374)

Round window A small membrane-covered opening at the end of the scala tympani. (354)

Scala media One of the liquid-filled compartments in the cochlea (see Figure 13.11). (353)

Scala tympani (also called the tympanic canal) The liquid-filled compartment of the cochlea that stretches from the helicotrema to the round window and is separated from the scala vestibuli by the cochlear partition. (353)

Scala vestibuli (also called the vestibular canal) The compartment of the cochlea that stretches from the oval window to the helicotrema and is separated from the scala tympani by the cochlear partition. (353)

Sound pressure level (SPL) A designation used to indicate that the reference pressure used for calculating a tone's decibel rating is set at 0.0002 dynes/cm^2, the threshold in the most sensitive frequency range for hearing. (368)

Sound waves A pressure change in a medium. Most of the sounds we hear result from air pressure changes. (348)

Stapes (stirrup) The last of the three ossicles in the middle ear. It receives vibrations from the incus and transmits these vibrations to the oval window of the inner ear. (352)

Stimulation deafness Deafness caused by intense auditory stimulation that damages structures in the cochlea. (359)

Tectorial membrane A membrane that stretches the length of the cochlea and is located directly over the hair cells. Vibrations of the cochlear partition cause the tectorial membrane to stimulate the hair cells by rubbing against them. (353)

Tinnitus A persistent ringing in the ears, often caused by exposure to loud sounds. (364)

Tinnitus masker A device that produces a hissing sound, which, in some patients, masks, or covers up, the ringing produced by tinnitus. (364)

Tonotopic map When neurons with the same characteristic frequency are grouped together and neurons with nearby characteristic frequencies are found near each other. (361)

Traveling wave The basilar membrane vibrates in a traveling wave, in which the peak of the membrane's vibration travels from the stapes to the helicotrema. (358)

Tuning curve A curve that indicates the intensity necessary to elicit a threshold response from a neuron, at different frequencies along the audible range. (361)

Tympanic membrane (eardrum) A membrane at the end of the external auditory meatus that vibrates in response to vibrations of the air and transmits these vibrations to the ossicles in the middle ear. (350)

Volley principle Wever's idea that groups of nerve fibers fire in volleys, with some fibers firing while others are refractory. In this way, groups of fibers can effect high rates of nerve firing. (356)

Chapter Fourteen

Perceiving Speech

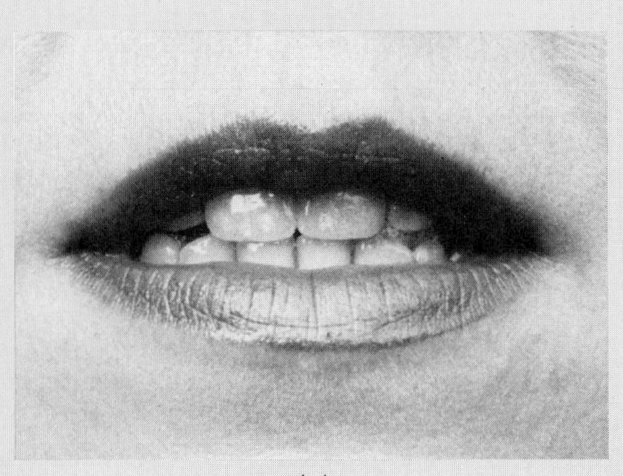

/s/

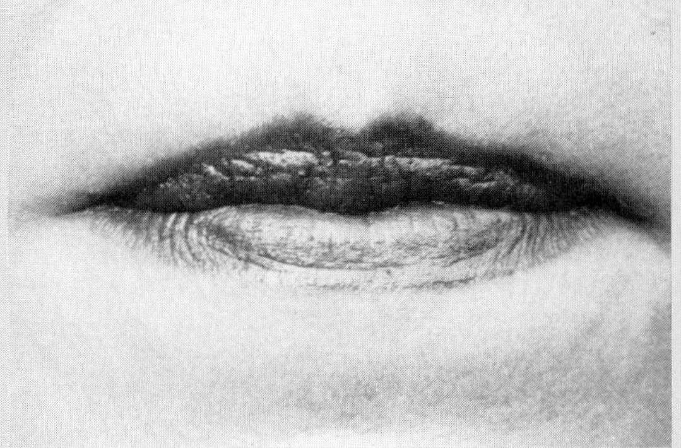

/p/

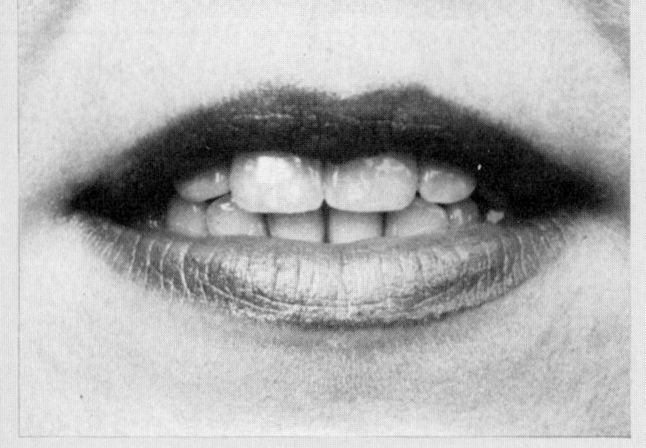

/i/

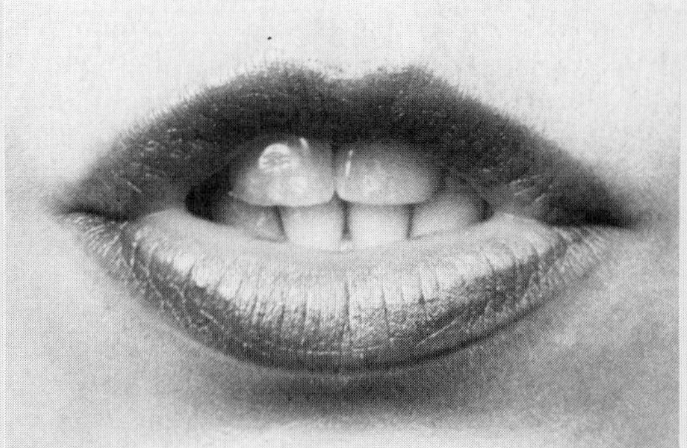

/č/

In the last chapter, we asked how we perceive individual pure tones, which produce only flat-sounding sensations of pitch. In this chapter, we ask how we perceive the much richer, more varied, and more meaningful stimuli of speech. Although the complexity of a stimulus such as "Good morning, how are you?" may not be that obvious, you will see that perceiving speech is vastly more complex than perceiving a pure tone. "Good morning, how are you?" contains not one frequency but many frequencies occurring both simultaneously and consecutively. Yet, despite the complexity of the speech stimulus, we can easily make sense of this rapid-fire jumble of frequencies and reply quite rapidly with speech of our own.

The amazing thing about our ability to understand speech is that the stimulus is both complex and extremely variable; that is, different people pronounce words very differently, speak in different pitch ranges, and speak at different speeds. Nevertheless, speakers of English usually have little trouble understanding other speakers of English.

We begin our discussion of speech by describing the stimulus. But rather than starting with something as complicated as "Good morning, how are you?", we will start by considering a much smaller unit of speech, called the **phoneme.**

Table 14.1
Major consonants and vowels of English and their phonetic symbols

Consonants				*Vowels*	
p	*p*ull	s	*s*ip	i	h*ee*d
b	*b*ull	z	zip	I	h*i*d
m	*m*an	r	*r*ip	e	b*a*it
w	*w*ill	š	*sh*ould	ɛ	h*e*ad
f	*f*ill	ž	plea*s*ure	æ	h*a*d
v	*v*et	č	*ch*op	*u*	wh*o*'d
θ	*th*igh	ǰ	*g*yp	U	p*u*t
ð	*th*y	y	*y*ip	ʌ	b*u*t
t	*t*ie	k	*k*ale	o	bo*a*t
d	*d*ie	g	*g*ale	ɔ	b*ou*ght
n	*n*ear	h	*h*ail	a	h*o*t
l	*l*ear	ŋ	si*ng*	ə	sof*a*
				ɨ	man*y*

The Stimuli for Speech

The Phoneme

A phoneme is defined as "the shortest segment of speech which, if changed, would change the meaning of a word." The phonemes of English are listed in Table 14.1. Each phoneme is represented by a phonetic symbol that stands for a speech sound, with 15 phonemes having vowel sounds and 24 phonemes having consonant sounds. To illustrate our definition of phoneme, consider the word "bit," which contains the phonemes /b/, /I/, and /t/.[1] We know that /b/, /I/, and /t/ are phonemes, because we can change the meaning of the word by changing each phoneme individually. Thus, "bit" becomes "pit" if the /b/ is changed to /p/, it becomes "bet" if the /I/ is changed to /ϵ/, and it becomes "bid" if the /t/ it changed to /d/.

Phonemes, then, stand for specific sounds, and these sounds are made up of various frequencies that occur both simultaneously and consecutively. The pattern of frequencies that make up a phoneme, or any other sound, is called the sound's **acoustic signal.**

The Acoustic Signal

The sound spectrogram. One way to visualize the pattern of frequencies that make up a sound is by means of a **sound spectrogram,** like the one shown in Figure 14.2. In this figure, which is a spectrogram of the words "shoo cat," frequency is plotted on the vertical axis and time on the horizontal axis, with the amount of sound energy indicated by the degree of darkness.

The best way to understand the spectrogram is to read it from left to right, trying to correlate the sound produced at each point on the time axis with the frequencies indicated above those points. Starting at the left of Figure 14.2, we first encounter the /š/ sound (sh) of the word "shoo." Notice that the /š/ lasts about 0.2 seconds, and, during that time, it

[1]Single phonemes and pairs of phonemes are set off from the text by slashes.

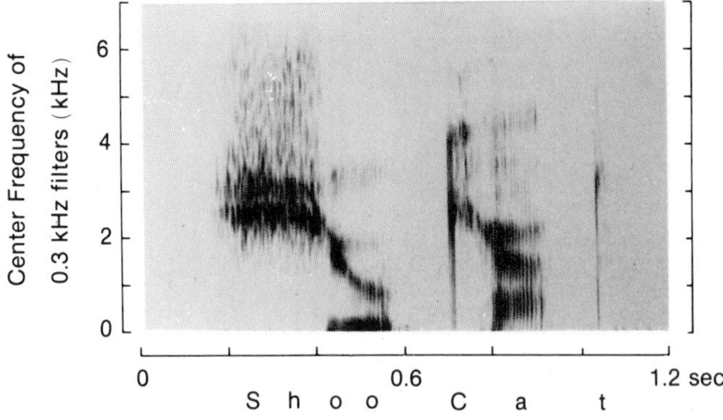

Figure 14.2 A sound spectrogram of the words "shoo cat." (From Kiang, 1975.)

generates a lot of energy between 2,000 and 3,500 Hz (indicated by the dark area on the spectrogram) and also some energy between 3,500 and 6,000 Hz. The high pitch of the sound /š/ is indicated by the fact that this sound consists only of frequencies above about 2,000 Hz.

The lower pitch of the /u/ sound (oo) that follows the /š/ is indicated by the fact that this sound contains energy only below 2,000 Hz. The energy caused by /u/ occurs primarily in two bands, one at the very bottom of the spectrogram, below 500 Hz, and the other at about 1,000 Hz. These horizontal (or nearly horizontal) bands of energy, called **formants,** are characteristic of vowels. The band with the lowest frequency is called the first formant; the next highest frequency, the second formant; and so on. Notice that three formants are visible for the /æ/ sound of "cat."

The short-term spectrum. The sound spectrogram shows the pattern of frequencies during the time course of a whole phoneme, or, in the case of Figure 14.2, two words consisting of five phonemes. Another way to describe the frequencies in a sound is to plot a **short-term spectrum,** showing in detail which frequencies are produced during a fairly short period of time. A short-term spectrum for the sound /ga/ is shown in Figure 14.3, along with the sound spectrogram for /ga/. The short-term spectrum indicates which frequencies occur during the first 26 msec of the sound /ga/.

Notice that the short-term spectrum in Figure 14.3(a) indicates a peak of energy between 1,000 and 2,000 Hz. This peak in the short-term spectrum corresponds well with the dark area between 1,000 and 2,000 Hz in the first 26 msec of the spectrogram in Figure 14.3(b). Also notice that there is a minimum in the short-term spectrum, just below 3,000 Hz, which is visible as the light area below 3,000 Hz in the first 26 msec of the spectrogram. One advantage of the short-term spectrum over the spectrogram is that it indicates with much more precision exactly how much energy is present at each frequency. The disadvantage of the short-term spectrum is that it gives us information only about the frequencies present during a very brief period of time. As we discuss some of the proposed explanations for how we perceive speech, we will see that both the spectrogram and the short-term spectrum provide valuable ways to specify the speech stimulus.

How Do We Perceive Phonemes?

Acoustic Cues and the Problem of Invariance

Now that we have some appreciation for the complexity of the speech stimulus, let's ask how we perceive a sound, beginning with the pattern of frequencies that constitute the sound. One clue to how we perceive a phoneme might be found in the

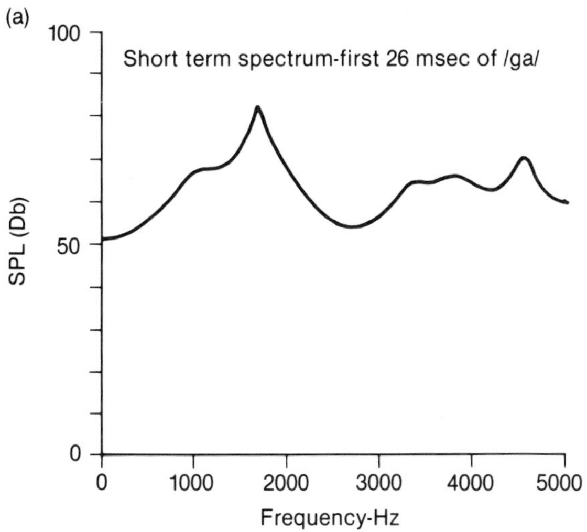

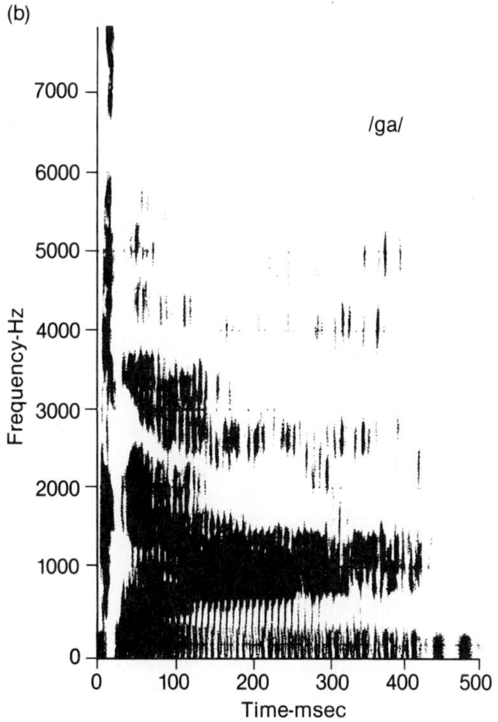

Figure 14.3 (a) A short-term spectrum of the acoustic energy in the first 26 msecs of the phoneme /ga/. (b) Sound spectrogram of the phoneme /ga/. (Courtesy of James Sawusch.)

acoustic signal—the pattern of frequencies-over-time indicated by the spectrogram. Looking at the acoustic signal, we could hypothesize that each phoneme is signaled by a particular **acoustic cue**—a pattern of frequencies-over-time associated with that phoneme. If this were true, speech perception could be explained rather easily: when the acoustic cue that stands for a particular phoneme is present, we perceive that phoneme. Thus, if the auditory system detects the acoustic cue for, say, the phoneme /d/, we hear the sound /d/. If that cue is followed by the cues for /I/ and /g/, the auditory system causes us to hear these phonemes, and, putting all three phonemes together, we hear the word "dig."

Unfortunately, things aren't that simple, because our hypothesis—that each phoneme is signaled by an acoustic cue which is always associated with that phoneme—is not true. This hypothesis is disproved by the effect of context—the pattern of frequencies associated with a particular phoneme is often influenced by other phonemes. An example of the effect of context is shown in Figure 14.4, which shows idealized spectrograms for the sounds /di/ and /du/. We say that these spectrograms are idealized because they are hand-drawn and do not show many of the irregularities obvious in spectrograms like those in Figures 14.2 and 14.3. These hand-drawn spectrograms do, however, accurately show two of the important characteristics of the sounds /di/ and /du/: the formants and the formant transitions. The formants are the horizontal bands of energy at about 200 and 2,600 Hz for /di/ and at 200 and 600 Hz for /du/. Remembering that formants are characteristic of vowels, we conclude that the formants at 200 and 2,600 Hz are the acoustic cue for the sound /i/ and the formants at 200 and 600 are the acoustic cue for the sound /u/.

The rapid shifts in frequency preceding each formant are called **formant transitions.** The formant transitions are the acoustic cues for the sound /d/. We can see that the formant transitions associated with the first formants of /di/ and /du/ are the same. However, the formant transition for the second formant in /di/ is different from the formant transition for the second formant in /du/, even though in each case we hear the same /d/ sound. This is an illustration of the effect of context. The acoustic cue that signals the consonant /d/ depends on the vowel following the /d/.

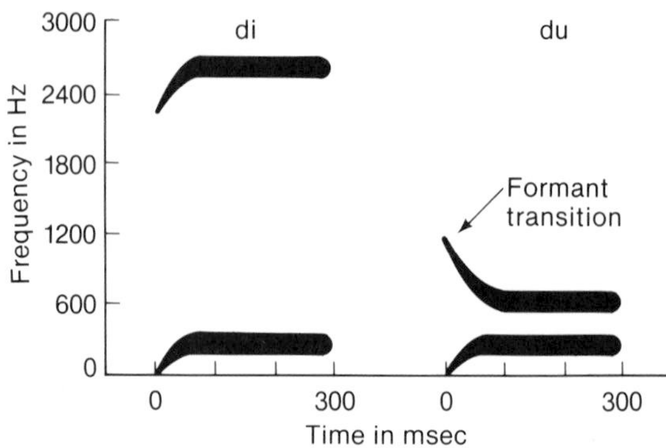

Figure 14.4 Hand-drawn spectrograms for /di/ and /du/. (From Liberman et al., 1967.)

The important thing about the effect of context is that, although the acoustic cues for the /d/ change in different contexts, the sound /d/ remains **invariant**; that is, the sound we hear stays constant. This invariance of the listener's perception of the sound in the face of variable acoustic cues is a central problem in speech perception, and much of the research in speech perception has been dedicated to solving it. One attempt to solve this problem is known as the **motor theory of speech perception.**

The Motor Theory of Speech Perception

The problem of invariance. The motor theory of speech perception is described in a now classic paper by Alvin Liberman and co-workers (1967), called "Perception of the Speech Code." At the beginning of this paper, Liberman describes the /di/ /du/ problem of Figure 14.4 and asks how our perception of /d/ can remain invariant, even though the acoustic cues for /d/ are different for /di/ and /du/. He concludes that the invariance in our perception of these consonants cannot be explained by looking at the acoustic signal, because the acoustic cues for many consonants depend on the context in which these consonants are found. What we must do, says Liberman, is look for some aspect of the phonemes that remains invariant when context is changed. And he suggests that what does remain invariant is the way each phoneme is *produced.* Before continuing our description of the motor theory of speech perception, therefore, let's consider how the sounds of speech are produced, focusing on the consonants.

The production of consonant sounds. We will describe how we produce consonants, by focusing on the sounds /d/ and /f/. (Those interested in descriptions of how we produce the rest of the consonants should consult Appendix D.) As you make these sounds, notice what your tongue, lips, and teeth are doing. To produce the sound /d/, you place your tongue against the ridge above your upper teeth (the alveolar ridge of Figure 14.5) and then release a slight rush of air as you move your tongue away from the alveolar ridge (try it). As you produce the sound /f/, you place your bottom lip against your upper front teeth and then push air between the lips and the teeth. These events can be described in terms of (1) **place of articulation** and (2) **manner of articulation.**

The place of articulation refers to the fact that the airstream is obstructed in some way during the production of all consonants. The place at which this obstruction occurs is called the place of articulation. For the sound /d/, the place of articulation is the alveolar ridge; therefore, the place of articulation for /d/ is called *alveolar.* For the sound /f/, the place of articulation—the bottom lip and the upper front teeth—is called *labiodental.*

The manner of articulation refers to the mechanical means by which the consonants are produced and most often refers to the way air is pushed through an opening. To produce the sound /d/, we completely close off the place of articulation, by placing the tongue on the alveolar ridge, and then release a slight rush of air. This manner of articulation is called *stop.* To produce the sound /f/, we push air between the small space between the lips and the upper teeth. This manner of articulation is called *fricative.*

In addition to the place and manner of articulation, we can also describe consonant production in terms of **voicing,** that is, whether or not producing the sound causes the vocal cords (see Figure 14.5) to vibrate. Place your fingers on either side of your neck and say the words "sip" and "zip." The vibration you feel when you say the /z/ of "zip" is due to vibration of the vocal cords. That you feel no vibration when you say the /s/ of "sip" means that the vocal cords are not vibrating. Consonants that cause vibration of the vocal cords are called *voiced,* whereas consonants that cause no vibration are called *unvoiced.* The consonant /d/ is voiced, and the consonant /f/ is unvoiced.

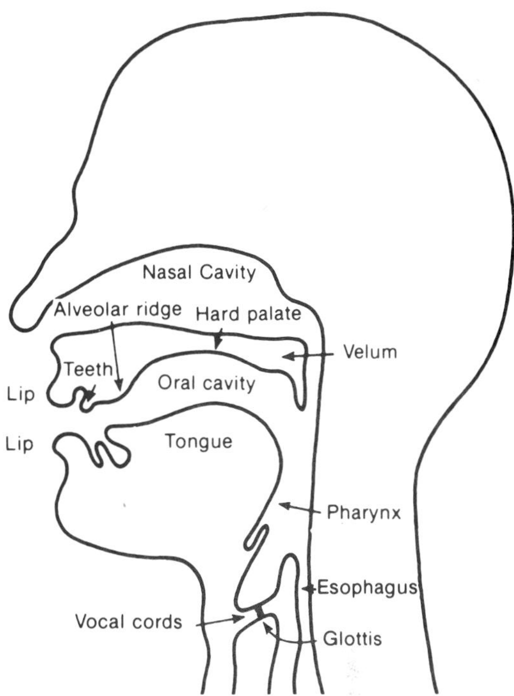

Figure 14.5 The vocal tract. (From Clark & Clark, 1977.)

The important thing about how consonants are produced is that each consonant has a unique combination of place of articulation, manner of articulation, and voicing. For example, we can describe /d/ as a *voiced, alveolar, stop,* and we can describe /f/ as an *unvoiced, labiodental, fricative,* and if we were to consider all the other phonemes, we would see that each one has its own unique **pattern of articulation.**

Now that we know something about how consonants are produced, let's return to the problem of invariance—the problem that our perception of a phoneme remains invariant, even though context can change the acoustic cues associated with that phoneme. Liberman suggests that each phoneme's unique pattern of articulation may offer a solution to the problem of invariance. Each phoneme can be identified by its pattern of articulation, and, most important as far as Liberman is concerned, this pattern of articulation remains constant even in different contexts. That is, the pattern of articulation of /d/ is always voiced, alveolar, stop, no matter what its context. That our *perception* of a phoneme ***and*** the way we ***produce*** the phoneme remains constant, regardless of context, suggests to Liberman a link between *perception* and *production* that can explain how we perceive speech. Before defining the link between our *perception* and *production* of a sound, let's first look at another piece of evidence that Liberman presents to demonstrate this link. This evidence is provided by a phenomenon called **categorical perception.**

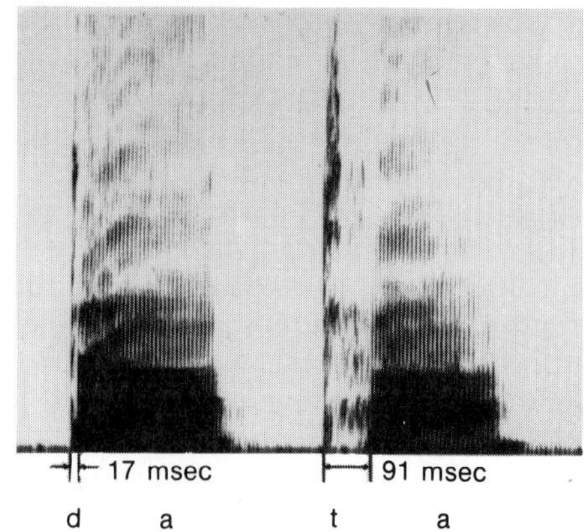

Figure 14.6 Spectrograms for /da/ and /ta/. The time between the beginning of the sound and voicing is indicated at the beginning of the spectrogram for each sound. (Spectrogram courtesy of Ron Cole.)

Categorical perception. To understand categorical perception, let's consider the consonants of the two stimuli /da/ and /ta/. The consonants /d/ and /t/ differ in voicing; /d/ is voiced, and /t/ is unvoiced. This difference between /d/ and /t/ causes an acoustic characteristic called **voice onset time (VOT)**—the time delay between the beginning of a sound and the beginning of voicing—to differ for /da/ and /ta/.

The difference in VOT for /da/ and /ta/ is illustrated by the spectrograms in Figure 14.6. We can see from these spectrograms that the time between the beginning of the sound /da/ and the beginning of voicing (indicated by the presence of vertical striations in the spectrogram) is 17 msec for /da/ and 91 msec for /ta/. Thus, the voiced /d/ causes /da/ to have a short VOT, and the unvoiced /t/ causes /ta/ to have a long VOT.

In a typical categorical perception experiment, a computer is used to synthesize sounds corresponding to two consonant-vowel pairs, such as /da/ and /ta/. The computer varies the VOT in small steps between about 0 and 80 msec, and the listener's task is to indicate whether a /da/ or a /ta/ is heard at each step. The results of such an experiment are shown by the solid line in Figure 14.7 (Eimas & Corbit, 1973). When the VOT is 0 msec, 100 percent of the stimuli are identified as /da/, and increasing VOT has no effect until the VOT reaches about 35 msec. At this point, which is called the **phonetic boundary,** listeners suddenly begin hearing /ta/; when the VOT is increased just a little more, to 40 msec, most of the stimuli are identified as /ta/. This phenomenon of hearing /da/ on one side of the phonetic boundary and /ta/ on the other side is called categorical perception. Even though the VOT is changed in many steps, the listener perceives only two categories, /da/ and /ta/.

We can also demonstrate this perceptual categorization by seeing how well a listener can discriminate between two stimuli that differ in VOT. When we do this, we find that a listener cannot tell the difference between two stimuli on the same side of the phonetic boundary but can tell the difference between two stimuli on different sides of the boundary. For example, a listener can't tell the difference between two stimuli with VOTs of 0 and 30 msec (both are perceived as /da/) but can tell the difference between two stimuli with VOTs of 30 and 50 msec (one is perceived as /da/, the other as /ta/).

The importance of categorical perception, as far as Liberman is concerned, is that it illustrates a link between perception and production of a sound. Even when the VOT varies over a large range, we perceive /da/ in only one way; then, at the phonetic boundary, our perception suddenly changes to /ta/, which we also perceive in only one way. That we perceive /da/ and /ta/ in only one way is paralleled by the way we produce these sounds: in natural speech, there is only one way to produce a /d/ and only one way to produce a /t/.

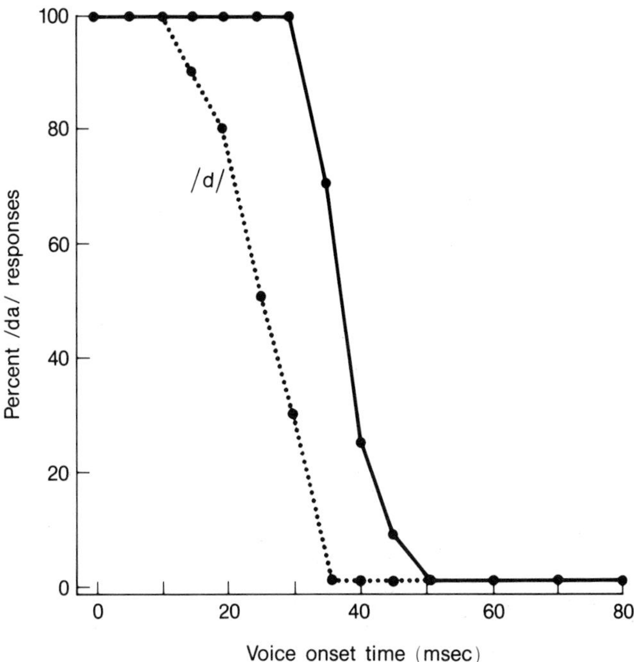

Figure 14.7 The results of a categorical perception experiment. The solid line, which shows the percent of sounds identified as /da/ as voice onset time, is varied from 0 to 80 msec. The dotted line shows the percent of sounds identified as /da/ after adaptation to /da/ for 2 minutes. The phonemic boundary's shift to the left indicates that /da/ is heard less often after adaptation. (From Eimas & Corbit, 1973.)

Both categorical perception and the invariant production of each phoneme despite changes in context led Liberman to suggest that our perception of speech is linked with the way we produce it. We are now ready to consider this idea in more detail.

The link between perception and production. What is this link between perception and production that we have been talking about? Liberman feels that "perception appears to be tied to articulation" (1967, p. 453) because, as we have seen above, each phoneme is best represented not by the acoustic signal (which varies with context) but by its pattern of articulation (which is essentially invariant with context).

The problem is: How do we tell how someone is producing a particular sound? According to Liberman, we accomplish this by using a **phonetic decoder**—a device specialized to recognize sounds that are characteristic of speech. This device receives and "decodes" the speech signal to indicate how it was produced by the speaker. To accomplish this feat, the decoder uses acoustic cues provided by the speech sounds. For example, one cue, which indicates closure of the auditory tract (important for the production of stop consonants such as /d/ and /t/), is a brief period of silence of the speech signal (Liberman & Studdert-Kennedy, 1978). There are, of course, many other cues present in the speech signal that we won't describe here. The important thing, according to the motor theory of speech perception, is that these acoustic cues stimulate a decoder specialized to deal with speech sounds and that the decoder's function is to determine how those sounds were produced by the speaker's vocal tract. Once we know how the speaker produced the sound, we can easily identify it by its unique pattern of articulation.

Box 14.1 Can Infants Perceive Speech?

Peter Eimas and co-workers (1971) have shown that very young infants may be able to perceive speech. The evidence for this early perception of speech comes from the results of categorical perception experiments similar to those run on adults. Eimas found that infants as young as one month old perform similarly to adults in these categorical perception experiments, in that they perceive the difference between two sounds with voice onset times (VOTs) that span a phonetic boundary and therefore sound different to adults (VOTs = +20 and +40 msec, which sound like /ba/ and /pa/, respectively), but they perceive little or no difference between two sounds with VOTs that are on the same side of the phonetic boundary and therefore sound the same to adults (VOTs = +60 and +80 msec, which both sound like /pa/).

How is it possible to tell whether or not a one-month-old infant can tell the difference between two sounds? Eimas made use of the fact that an infant will suck on a nipple in order to hear a series of brief speech sounds. If, however, the same speech sounds are repeated over and over, the infant eventually habituates to these sounds (see pp. 316–317, in Chapter 12) and the rate of sucking decreases. By presenting a new stimulus when the rate of sucking has decreased, we can determine whether the new stimulus sounds the same or different to the infant. If the new stimulus sounds different, dishabituation will occur and the rate of sucking will increase. If the new stimulus sounds the same, however, habituation will continue and the rate of sucking will either stay the same or decrease further.

Look at the results in the left graph on the next page. The number of sucking responses made when no sound was presented is indicated by the point at B. When sucking results in the presentation of a sound with a VOT of +20 msec (sounds like /ba/ to an adult), the number of sucking responses increases to a high level; then, after 3 minutes, the number of sucking responses begins to decrease. When the VOT is changed to +40 msec (sounds like /pa/ to an adult), the number of sucking responses increases, as indicated by the points to the right of the dashed line. This result means that the infant perceives a difference between sounds with VOTs of +20 and +40 msec. The center graph, however, shows that changing the VOT from +60 to +80 msec (both sound like /pa/ to an adult) has only a small effect on sucking, indicating that the infants perceive little, if any, difference between the two sounds. Finally, the results for a control group (the right graph) show that when the sound is not changed, the number of sucking responses decreases throughout the experiment.

These results show that when the VOT is shifted across the phonetic boundary (left graph), the infants perceive a change in the sound, and when the VOT is shifted on the same side of the phonetic boundary (center graph), the infants perceive little or no change in the sound. That infants as young as one month of age are capable of categorical perception is particularly impressive, considering that these infants have had virtually no experience in producing speech sounds and only limited experience in hearing them. We can, in fact, draw an analogy between Hubel and

The idea that one step in perceiving speech is to determine what is happening in the speaker's vocal tract may seem strange. However, proponents of the motor theory point out that since humans both perceive and produce speech, it makes sense that perception and production involve similar mechanisms. As Liberman puts it, "It seems unparsimonious to assume that the speaker-listener employs two entirely separate processes of equal status, one for encoding language and the other for decoding it. A simpler assumption is that there is only one process, with appropriate linkages between sensory and motor components" (1967, p. 452).

The motor theory of speech perception has greatly influenced research in speech perception for the almost 20 years since it was introduced. However, soon after it was proposed, it became clear that one of the main postulates of the theory—that the way each phoneme is produced is invariant with context—is not strictly true. The evidence leading to

Wiesel's kittens, whose adultlike receptive fields indicate that kittens have feature detectors for visual stimuli before they have had any visual experience (see pp. 330–331, in Chapter 12), and Eimas's infants, whose adultlike categorical perception indicates that they have mechanisms for detecting speech stimuli at a very early age.

A word of caution, however, is in order regarding the interpretation of Eimas's results. That infants may possess mechanisms for detecting speech sounds does not necessarily mean that infants recognize these sounds as speech. That capacity probably develops later—the result of learning gained as the infant listens to the speech of those around him (Aslin & Pisoni, 1980; Walley, Pisoni, & Aslin, 1981).

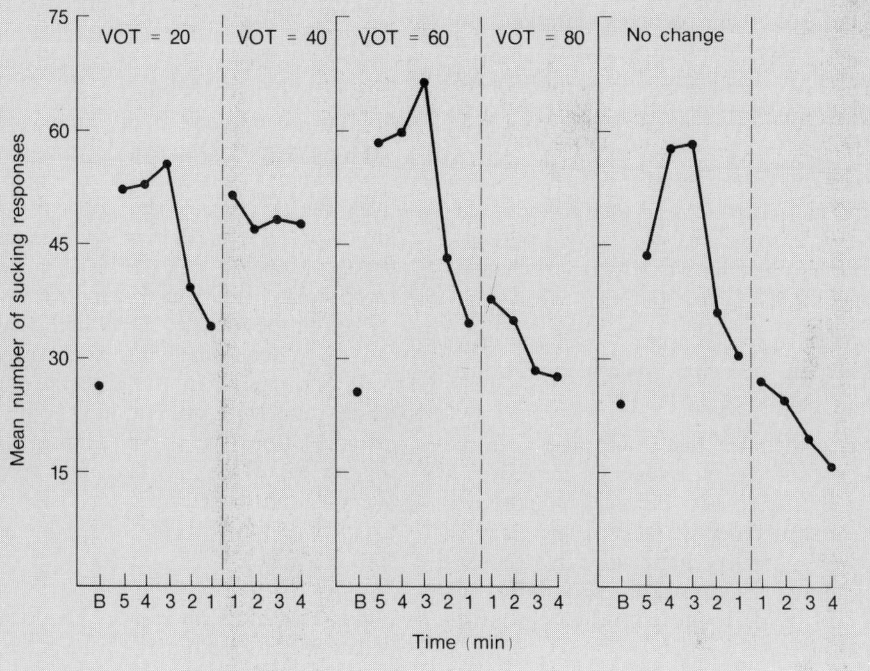

this conclusion came from experiments in which the *electromyogram (EMG),* an electrical response that indicates muscle activity, was recorded from various parts of the vocal tract during speech. These experiments showed that the muscle contractions accompanying production of a specific phoneme differ, depending on which phonemes come before or after that phoneme. Thus, while the pattern of articulation for a given phoneme does remain invariant with context, the muscular movements for a given phoneme are apparently not strictly invariant, as was thought when motor theory was first proposed (MacNeilage, 1970).

The main problem with motor theory for many researchers is that it raises as many questions as it answers. If we accept that acoustic cues trigger a phonetic decoder that tells us how a given sound was produced, we are still left with the question of how this hypothetical decoder works and how it pairs acoustic cues with specific modes of production. Therefore, many researchers feel that the motor theory's emphasis on speech production is unnecessary and that it makes more sense to look for information in the acoustic signal that indicates the presence of the different phonemes.

Information in the Acoustic Signal

Acoustic cues for perceiving phonemes. Despite variations in the acoustic signal due to context, is there enough information in the acoustic signal to enable us to identify a phoneme? This may seem like an innocent and reasonable enough question, but behind it lies one of the hottest controversies in speech research. This controversy centers on the following two conceptions about the way speech perception may work:

1. We perceive speech by means of a mechanism that is specialized to deal with sounds characteristic of speech. Motor theory's phonetic decoder is one example of such a mechanism (Repp, 1982).
2. We perceive speech as we would any other sound; no specialized speech processor is needed (Searle et al., 1979).

Many researchers feel that if information in the acoustic signal sufficiently enables us to identify a phoneme, a special decoder becomes unnecessary; it can then be argued that we perceive speech as we do any other sound, perhaps aided by neurons resembling feature detectors that respond not only to speech but to any sound with the appropriate characteristics.

Researchers have found that if they look at the speech signal in all its complexity (as opposed to simplified hand-drawn spectrograms, like the ones in Figure 14.4), they find much information that could signal the presence of specific phonemes without the need for a specialized speech decoder. There are many acoustic cues in the speech signal, including, among others, voice onset time, the duration of the formant transitions, the presence of silences in the signal, and the presence of large intensity changes in the signal. Even when context changes some of these cues, there may be enough overlapping cues to enable the listener to determine which phoneme is present. This way of thinking is similar to our approach to the problem of depth perception. We perceive an object's depth by taking many cues, both monocular and binocular, into account. A particular depth cue may not unambiguously indicate an object's depth in a particular situation, but, by combining all the available information, we can accurately perceive the object's depth. Perhaps a similar situation exists for the perception of speech. All the cues may not be present at all times, but those present may provide enough information to enable us to perceive speech.

In attempting to identify phonemes based on the acoustic signal, however, we needn't rely solely on the presence of numerous cues that may change in different contexts. S. E. Blumstein and K. N. Stevens (1979) have shown that short-term spectra—like the one in Figure 14.3, which depicts the information present in the first 26 msec of a phoneme's speech signal—can indicate with fairly good reliability the presence of the stop consonants /t/, /p/, /d/, /g/, /b/, and /k/, even when the context in which these consonants are found is changed. Therefore, these researchers argue that there is invariant information in the acoustic signal itself that the listener can use to determine which sounds are present.

If information in the acoustic signal indicates which sounds are present, how is this information extracted from the signal? Numerous researchers suggest that there may be neural detectors (much like the feature detectors for vision, discussed in Chapter 2) tuned to fire to specific aspects of the speech signal.

Feature detectors for speech. The idea that feature detectors for speech may exist has been supported by the results of **selective adaptation** experiments analogous to the visual grating adaptation experiment of Figure 2.34. In the visual experiment, adaptation to a grating of a particular orientation dims our perception of gratings with that orientation but has little effect on gratings with other orientations. We explain this selective dimming effect by assuming that adaptation to a particular orientation fatigues feature detectors sensitive to that orientation but does not affect feature detectors sensitive to other orientations.

Following this idea, Peter Eimas and John Corbit (1973) reasoned that an analogous effect might influence the results of a categorical perception experiment like the one in Figure 14.7. They reasoned that if adaptation to a particular feature fatigued the detector that responds to that feature, then listeners should be less likely to hear a syllable with that feature. For example, in the experiment of Figure 14.7, the /d/ of /da/ is voiced, and the /t/ of /ta/ is unvoiced. If we adapt a listener by repeating a voiced syllable, such as /da/ or /ba/, for 2 minutes, this selectively adapts a feature detector that responds to voicing; when we ask the listeners to again label the syllables, they are less likely to perceive /da/ than they were before the adaptation. That is, the curve of Figure 14.7 moves to the left, as indicated by the dotted line, so /da/ is heard less often and /ta/ is heard more often.

The results of Eimas and Corbit's selective adaptation experiment support the idea that feature detectors for speech exist, just as the results of visual selective adaptation experiments support the idea that feature detectors for vision exist. In both cases, presenting an adapting stimulus with a specific property (such as orientation for vision and voicing for speech) decreases the response of the feature detector that responds to that property.

***Are the feature detectors* linguistic *or* auditory?** Eimas and Corbit's selective adaptation experiment suggests that feature detectors help us identify the sounds of speech. Two ideas have been put forth regarding the nature of these feature detectors:

1. These detectors are *linguistic,* that is, tuned to respond specifically to the sounds of language.
2. These detectors are *acoustic,* that is, tuned to respond to specific sounds that needn't be related to the sounds of language.

These two ideas are related to the controversy, mentioned above, about how speech perception may work. Here again, one view suggests that speech is so special that it needs its own mechanisms, while the other view says that speech can be explained in terms of the same mechanisms that explain our perception of other sounds.

The results of the first selective adaptation experiments were interpreted as showing that selective adaptation involves linguistic detectors sensitive to sounds like phonemes. In the last 10 years, however, accumulated evidence has convinced many researchers that selective adaptation primarily involves auditory detectors sensitive to sounds in general (Pisoni & Tash, 1975; Sawusch, 1977; Eimas & Miller, 1978; Sawusch & Jusczyk, 1981).

One experiment that argues for the auditory nature of selective adaptation employs an effect called **audiovisual speech perception,** which was discovered in 1976 by Harry McGurk and John MacDonald. McGurk and MacDonald prepared the stimuli for their experiment by dubbing the sounds /ba-ba/ onto a videotape of a woman who was making the lip movements for the sounds /ga-ga/. However, when subjects viewed this videotape, they reported hearing /da-da/ (Figure 14.8). Thus, viewing lip movements that do not match the sound being produced changes the subject's perception of the sound (McGurk & MacDonald, 1976; MacDonald & McGurk, 1978; Summerfield, 1979).

Martin Roberts and Quentin Summerfield (1981) put this audiovisual effect to work in an ingenious categorical perception experiment. They first did an experiment in which /ba/ was perceived on the left side of the phonetic boundary and /da/ was perceived on the right side of the boundary. Adaptation of the subjects to the syllable /ba/ shifted the phonetic boundary to the left, so /ba/ was heard less often than before adaptation. This result was expected, because it essentially repeats the Eimas and Corbit experiment of Figure 14.7. In the Eimas and Corbit experiment, /da/ was perceived on the left, /ta/ was perceived on the right, and adaptation to /da/ pushed the phonetic boundary to the left.

Roberts and Summerfield then used the audiovisual effect by again adapting the subjects to the syllable /ba/ while they watched a videotape of a person making lip movements for the syllable /ga/. Thus, subjects were being adapted by the acoustic stimulus for the syllable /ba/, but, due to the audiovisual effect, they *perceived* the syllable /da/. The acoustic explanation for selective adaptation predicts that, since the acoustic signal for /ba/ is entering the subject's ears during adaptation, adaptation should push the phonetic boundary to the left, causing /ba/ to be heard less often. The linguistic explanation for selective adaptation predicts that, since the subjects perceive the speech sound /da/ during adaptation, adaptation should push the phonetic boundary to the right, causing /da/ to be heard

Figure 14.8 Audiovisual speech perception. The woman is making the lip movements for /ga-ga/, but the actual sound is /ba-ba/. The listener, however, reports hearing the sound /da-da/.

less often. The results of this experiment support the acoustic explanation. Even though the subjects hear /da/ during adaptation, the phonetic boundary is pushed to the left so that, after adaptation, /ba/ is heard less often. Thus, selective adaptation appears to be caused not by what the subject perceives but by the nature of the acoustic stimulus entering the subject's ears.

The above evidence suggests that perhaps speech is detected by means of feature detectors that respond to auditory sounds in general. Since the sounds of speech are complex, we would expect these feature detectors to respond to complex sounds, and a few such feature detectors have been found. For example, Whitfield and Evans (1965) found cells in the auditory cortex of the cat that do not respond to single pure tones but do respond to smooth changes in the frequency of the tone. Some cells respond only when the frequency of the tone is swept from low to high frequencies, and others respond when frequency is swept from high to low. It is interesting to note that these cells, which Whitfield and Evans called *frequency sweep detectors,* respond to stimuli resembling the upward and downward frequency sweeps of the formant transitions of speech (see Figure 14.4).

It should be obvious from the above discussion that researchers in the field of speech perception do not agree on how speech perception works. Some of the viewpoints held by various researchers are:

1. The speech stimulus must be processed by a phonetic decoder that is closely linked to the way speech is produced.
2. There is enough information in the acoustic signal to make a phonetic decoder unnecessary.
3. Speech perception is based on specialized feature detectors that respond only to linguistic stimuli.
4. Speech perception is based on feature detectors that respond to acoustic signals in general.
5. Speech perception is based on a combination of linguistic and acoustic feature detectors.
6. Speech perception can be explained without talking about feature detectors at all.

Clearly, whatever explanation of speech perception turns out to be correct, we cannot fully understand speech perception by considering only how we perceive such small segments of speech as phonemes. When we listen to someone talking, we don't just hear phonemes; we hear words, sentences, and thoughts. To complete our discussion of speech perception, therefore, we will turn from our consideration of isolated phonemes to look at some of the properties of conversational speech.

Conversational Speech

We can usually understand most people when they talk to us, even though (1) no clear boundaries exist between words, and (2) the sloppy pronunciation in conversational speech makes about half of the words unintelligible when taken out of context:

1. No clear boundaries exist between words. Though it may seem that there is a slight break between each word in a conversation, a sound spectrogram shows that it is often difficult to tell where one word ends and the next begins in conversational speech. A good example of this lack of boundaries between words is shown in the spectrogram of "I owe you a yo-yo" in Figure 14.9. From this spectrogram, it is not at all obvious where one word ends and the other begins, and even an experienced spectrogram reader would find it extremely difficult to locate the individual words.

It becomes obvious that there are no spaces between words when you consider how a foreign language sounds. To someone unfamiliar with a language, the sounds of that language seem to speed by in an unbroken string; however, to a speaker of that language, the words seem separated, just as the words of English seem separated to you. Since these separations are not contained in the acoustic message, our knowledge of the language must help us perceive these separations.

2. The sloppy pronunciation of most words in conversational speech makes about half of the words unintelligible when taken from their fluent context and presented alone. Irwin Pollack and J. M. Pickett (1964) experimentally demonstrated this difficulty in understanding words isolated from conversational speech. They recorded the conversations of subjects who sat in a room waiting for the experiment to begin. When the subjects were then presented with recordings of single words from their own conversations, they could identify only half the words, even though they were listening to their own voices!

You might think at first that Pollack and Pickett's subjects were particularly sloppy speakers. But try saying the following sentence at the speed you would use in talking to a friend: "This was a best buy." How did you say "best buy"? Did you pronounce the /t/ of "best," or did you say "bes buy"? What about, "She is a bad girl"? While saying this rapidly, notice whether your tongue hits the top of your mouth as you say the /d/ of "bad." Many people omit the /d/ and say "ba girl." Finally, what about, "Did you go to the store?" Did you say "did you" or "dijoo"?

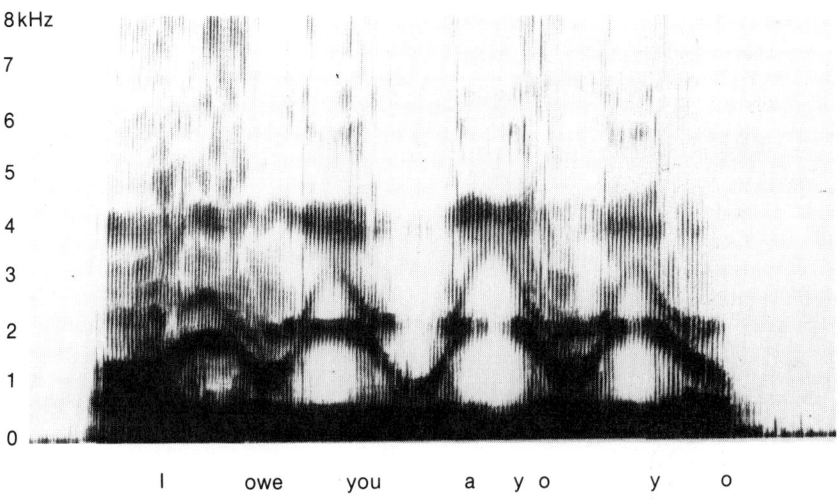

Figure 14.9 Spectrogram of "I owe you a yo-yo." (Spectrogram courtesy of Ron Cole.)

That people speak differently in conversational speech than when speaking slowly is also shown by the spectrograms of Figure 14.10(a) and (b). The spectrogram in Figure 14.10(a) is for the question, "What are you doing?", spoken slowly and distinctly, whereas the spectrogram in Figure 14.10(b) is for the same question taken from conversational speech. "What are you doing?" becomes "Whad'aya doin?" in conversational speech, and this difference is easily seen in the spectrogram. While the patterns for the first and last words ("What" and "doing") are similar in both spectrograms, the pauses between words are absent or much less obvious in the spectrogram of Figure 14.10(b), and the middle of this

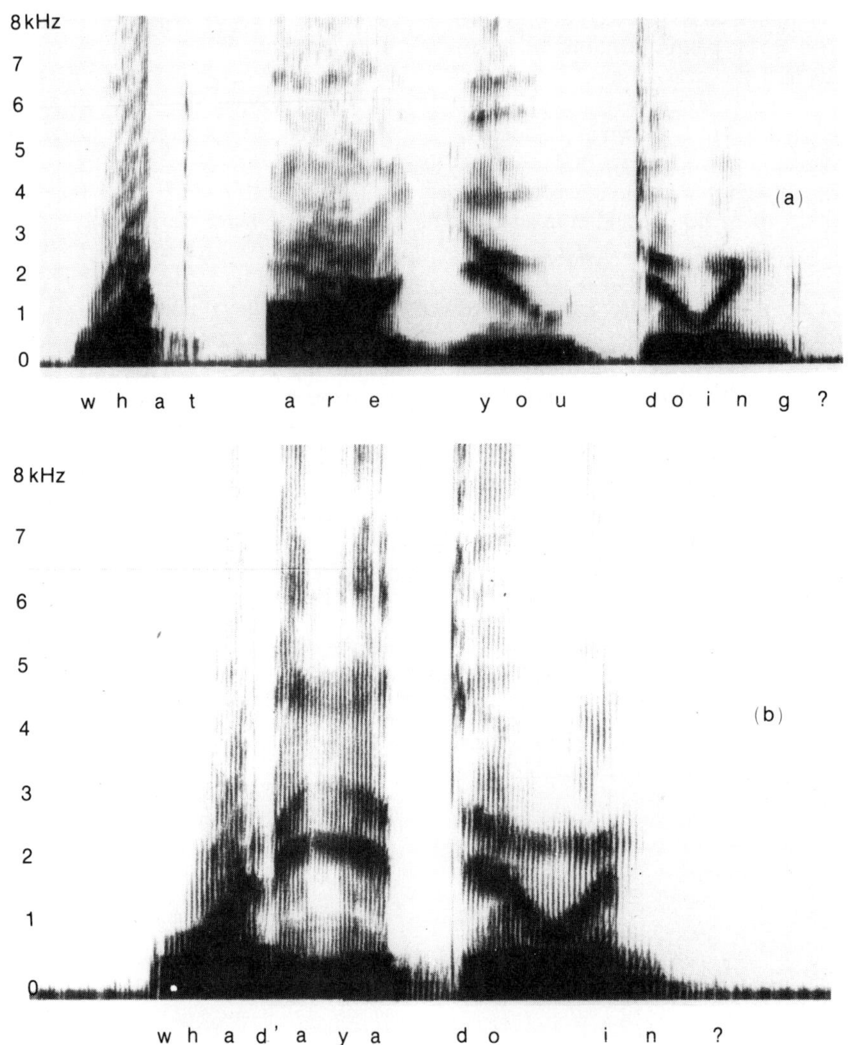

Figure 14.10 (a) Spectrogram of "What are you doing?", pronounced slowly and distinctly. (b) Spectrogram of "What are you doing?", as pronounced in conversational speech. Note that (b) has been enlarged so it is as wide as (a). However, (a) lasts about 2.1 seconds, while (b) lasts only about 0.9 seconds. (Spectrograms courtesy of Ron Cole.)

spectrogram is completely changed, with a number of speech sounds missing.

Though there are often no breaks between words in conversational speech, and though speech is sloppy, we somehow understand what people are saying! We do this by taking context into account. In the next sections, we will consider some experiments that show how the presence of context helps make conversational speech intelligible.

Putting Breaks Between Words

If there are no breaks between words in normal speech, what puts the breaks there? The answer to this question is *meaning*. Our knowledge of the language gives meaning to the sounds we hear, which helps us carry out the process of **segmentation**—putting breaks between words. With a few examples, we can illustrate how meaning results in segmentation. Read the following words: Anna Mary Candy Lights Since Imp Pulp Lay Things. Now that you've read the words, what do they mean? If you think that this is a list of unconnected words, beginning with the names of two girls, Anna and Mary, you are right; but if you read this series of words a little faster, ignoring the spaces between the words on the page, you may hear a connected sentence that does not begin with the names Anna and Mary. The resulting connected sentence—which is printed at the bottom of the next page (but don't peek unless you've tried reading the words again)—has become segmented in a way completely different from the way the words are printed on the page, and this segmentation is put there by your knowledge of the meaning of the sounds.

Pairs of words that flow together in speech also exemplify how segmentation results from meaning: "big girl" can be interpreted as "big Earl," and the interpretation you pick probably depends on the overall meaning of the sentence in which these words appear. This example is similar to the familiar "I scream, you scream, we all scream for ice cream" that many people learn as children. The different segmentations of "I scream" and "ice cream" are put there by the meaning of the sentence.

For a final example of how segmentation depends on meaning, read the following phrase fairly rapidly to someone else: "In mud eels are, in clay none are," and ask him or her to write the phrase. Here are some responses to this phrase, obtained in an experiment by Raj Reddy (1976): "In muddies, sar, in clay nanar"; "In may deals are, en clainanar"; "In model sar, in claynanar." In the absence of any context, Reddy's listeners clearly had difficulty figuring out what the phrase meant and, therefore, forced their own interpretation on the sounds they heard. Had the listeners known that the passage was taken from a book about where amphibians live, their knowledge about possible meanings of the words would facilitate segmentation and increase their probability of decoding the sentences correctly. In the next section, we will look at another example of how context influences perception.

The Phonemic Restoration Effect

Richard Warren (1970) did an experiment in which subjects listened to a tape recording of the passage: "The state governors met with their respective legislatures convening in the capital city," in which the first /s/ in "legislatures" was replaced by the sound of a cough. The subjects were told that there would be a cough somewhere in the sentence and that they should indicate where in the sentence the cough occurred. The result of this experiment was that no subject identified the correct position of the cough, and, even more interesting, none of the subjects noticed that the /s/ in "legislatures" was missing. This effect, which Warren calls the **phonemic restoration effect,** was even experienced by students and staff in the psychology department who knew that the /s/ was missing.

The phonemic restoration effect shows that the auditory system *fills in* the sound that, given the context of the rest of the word, should have occurred. In fact, this filling-in effect can even be influenced by the meaning of words *following* the missing phoneme. For example, the last word of the phrase "There was time to *ave . . ." (where the * indicates the presence of a cough or other sound) could be "shave," "save," "wave," or "rave," but subjects heard the word "wave" if the remainder of the sentence had to do with saying goodbye to a departing friend. Thus, auditory information in a sentence is apparently stored until the subsequent context identifies the obliterated phoneme, at which point the listener hears the phoneme!

Semantics, Syntax, and Speech Perception

Some experiments have shown that words are more intelligible when heard in the context of a grammatical sentence than when presented as items in a list of unconnected words. An experiment by George Miller and Stephen Isard (1963) investigated how **semantics** and **syntax** affect the perception of speech. Semantics specifies whether or not it is appropriate to use a word in a sentence based on the word's meaning, and syntax specifies which structures of a sentence are allowed. Let's illustrate what we mean by semantics and syntax with some examples. "The boy spoke a word" is a perfectly good sentence semantically and syntactically. If, however, we change the sentence to "The boy spoke a triangle," it makes no sense. The use of the word "triangle" is semantically incorrect, because the meaning of the word "triangle" does not fit into this sentence; therefore, we call this a *semantically anomalous* sentence. Note that a semantically anomalous sentence is still grammatically and syntactically correct; however, we can change the sentence further to make it syntactically incorrect, by changing the order of the words. Changing the sentence to "Spoke triangle the boy a" turns it into a grammatically and syntactically incorrect string of words, because the various parts of speech (nouns, verbs, etc.) are not in the correct order.

Miller and Isard constructed sentences that fell into three classes: (1) normal grammatical sentences, (2) anomalous sentences (semantically incorrect), and (3) ungrammatical strings of words (syntactically incorrect). Five examples of normal sentences they used are:

Gadgets simplify work around the house.
Accidents kill motorists on the highways.
Trains carry passengers across the country.
Bears steal honey from the hive.
Hunters shoot elephants between the eyes.

These normal grammatical sentences were then changed into the following five semantically anomalous sentences, by taking one word from each normal sentence:

Gadgets kill passengers from the eyes.
Accidents carry honey between the house.
Trains steal elephants around the highways.
Bears shoot work on the country.
Hunters simplify motorists across the hive.

Finally, five ungrammatical strings of words were produced by haphazardly rearranging the words as follows:

Around accidents country honey the shoot.
On trains have elephants the simplify.
Across bears eyes work the kill.
From hunters house motorists the carry.
Between gadgets highways passengers the steal.

Miller and Isard constructed 50 sentences of each type and recorded these 150 sentences in random order on a tape. Subjects then listened to the tape through earphones and were asked to repeat aloud what they heard as they were hearing it. This technique, which is called **shadowing,** results in a record of what the subjects heard. The subjects' responses were tape-recorded and later scored for the number of complete sentences or strings of words repeated exactly. The results of this scoring showed that 89 percent of the normal sentences, 79 percent of the anomalous sentences, and 56 percent of the ungrammatical strings were repeated exactly. This result indicates that subjects must be making use of semantic *and* syntactic information when perceiving speech, because when semantic information is lost, as was the case in the anomalous sentences, performance drops; and when syntactic information is lost, as was the case in the ungrammatical strings of words, performance drops even further. In fact, these differences among the three types of stimuli became even greater when the subjects heard the stimuli in the presence of a background noise. For example, at a moderately high level of background noise, 63 percent of the normal sentences, 22 percent of the anomalous sentences, and only 3 percent of the ungrammatical strings were perceived correctly. This is impressive evidence that listeners use both semantic and syntactic information in their perception of sentences.

From the results of the experiments discussed above, we can conclude that speech perception depends on *both* the acoustic information in phonemes and the contextual information provided by

Answer: An American delights in simple playthings.

Box 14.2 What Was That Word Again?

Have you ever noticed that strange things happen if you repeat the same word over and over again? Try repeating the word "house" over and over (househousehouse . . .). When you do this, the word eventually becomes meaningless, and it may also begin to sound different (like sowsowsow-sowsow . . .). The word's loss of meaning is called **verbal satiation** and the change in the word's sound is called the **verbal transformation effect.**

The verbal transformation effect occurs much more impressively if, instead of repeating the word yourself, you hear someone else repeat it. Richard Warren (1961, 1968) (who also demonstrated the phonemic restoration effect) had subjects listen to 3- to 5-minute tapes of repeating words and found that they heard many words in addition to the one presented. For example, the subjects in Warren's experiments heard the following words when listening to repetitions of the word "tress": stress, stressed, addrest, address, dress, best-drest, drest, dress-best, best-dress, Jewish, Jewess, Joyce, floris, florist, Esther, best, burst, a burst, purse, spur, stir, spurse, spur-stir.

Warren suggests that the verbal transformation effect reflects mechanisms of perceptual organization that are used to enhance the comprehension of normal speech. These types of perceptual organization would be needed, for example, in situations where normal speech might be sloppy and have a number of possible interpretations. In the case of normal speech, the context of the conversation usually helps us organize the sounds into the word appropriate to the conversation. In the verbal transformation effect, no context (other than the original word) is available, and this lack of context allows many different responses. (Warren did, in fact, find that the meaning of the original word did sometimes influence the transformed words.)

The ability of the auditory system to reorganize speech stimuli into different patterns was demonstrated in another way, 25 years before the verbal transformation effect was described. In 1936, B. F. Skinner (who is best known for his writings on learning theory) described a device called a **verbal summator.** This device presented short strings of meaningless syllables made up of vowel sounds such as "ah-uh-uh-oo-uh." The sounds were played softly and were preceded by instructions such as "I have here a phonograph record of a man talking. He is not speaking very clearly, but if you listen carefully you will be able to tell what he is saying. I will repeat each sample as many times as you like. When you hear what he is saying, tell me what it is." After the sounds were repeated a number of times, most subjects reported that they heard meaningful phrases, such as "Where are you going?"

In Skinner's verbal summator, the subject's responses to the sounds could not be influenced by meaning, since the sounds themselves had no meaning. Skinner found, however, that the subject's response was sometimes influenced by the context of the situation. For example, upon hearing loud talking in the hallway, one subject included the word "loudmouth" in his response, and a tired subject said that he heard the phrase "Please let me go home!" Skinner suggested that this type of test might be a "verbal ink blot," with a subject's responses being influenced by his or her personality. Although the verbal summator technique has not lived up to its promise as a substitute for the ink blot test, it does demonstrate the auditory system's amazing ability to organize meaningless material into meaningful perceptions (Grings, 1942).

words and sentences. We can appreciate the interdependence of the acoustic and contextual units of speech when we realize that, although we use the context to help us to understand the acoustic signal, the acoustic signal is the starting point for determining the context. If this sounds vaguely familiar, it's because this is a good example of the bottom-up and top-down processing we discussed in Chapter 7. We process from bottom-up by taking into account the information present in the acoustic signal, and we process from top-down by taking into account the meanings contained in words, sentences, and paragraphs. Look at it this way: there may be enough information in my sloppy handwriting so that a person could decipher it, using bottom-up processing, solely on the basis of the squiggles on the page; but my handwriting is much easier to decipher if, using top-down processing, the person takes the meanings of the words into account. Speech perception apparently works in a similar way. Though most of the information is contained in the acoustic signal, taking meaning into account makes understanding speech much easier.

Summary

1. A phoneme is the shortest segment of speech which, if changed, would change the meaning of a word.
2. The sound spectrogram, which is a plot of frequency versus time, provides a visual picture of the speech stimulus.
3. The short-term spectrum shows in detail which frequencies are produced during a fairly short period of time.
4. The hypothesis that each phoneme is signaled by its own acoustic cue is disproved by the effect of context—the pattern of frequencies associated with a particular phoneme is often influenced by other phonemes.
5. In speech the problem of invariance refers to the constancy of the listener's perception of a phoneme, even when context changes the phoneme's acoustic cues.
6. The motor theory of speech perception grew out of the idea that the problem of invariance cannot be explained by looking at the acoustic signal.
7. The production of consonants can be described by the consonant's voicing, its place of articulation, and its manner of articulation. Together, these three factors are called the pattern of articulation of the consonant. Each consonant has a unique pattern of articulation.
8. That our perception of a phoneme and the way we produce the phoneme remains constant, regardless of the context, led Alvin Liberman to propose the existence of a link between perception and production that can explain how we perceive speech.
9. In a categorical perception experiment, changing voice onset time (VOT) in small steps has no affect on our perception until the VOT crosses a phonetic boundary. Changing VOT across a phonetic boundary causes our perception to change suddenly from one phoneme to another.
10. Infants as young as one month old perform similarly to adults in categorical perception experiments. This result suggests that infants may possess mechanisms for detecting speech sounds.
11. The motor theory of speech perception states that perception is tied to articulation. It is hypothesized that a phonetic decoder receives the speech signal and decodes it to indicate how that signal was produced by the speaker.
12. Not all researchers accept the motor theory of speech perception. Many feel that the motor theory's emphasis on speech production is unnecessary and that we should look for information in the acoustic signal, that indicates the presence of different phonemes.
13. Many researchers feel that there is enough information in the acoustic signal to enable us to identify a phoneme without a phonetic decoder.
14. Some researchers feel that speech may be detected by neurons analogous to the feature detectors of vision. This idea has been supported by the results of selective adaptation experiments.
15. Some researchers feel that feature detectors for speech are linguistic, that is, tuned to respond specifically to the sounds of language. Others feel that these detectors are acoustic, that is, tuned to respond to specific sounds that needn't be related to the sounds of language.
16. The results of a selective adaptation experiment that made use of an effect called audiovisual speech perception argue for the auditory nature of speech detectors.

17. There is great disagreement among researchers as to how speech perception works.

18. To understand speech perception, we must take into account that conversational speech has no real breaks between words and is generally so sloppy that we can only recognize half the words when they are presented alone.

19. The process of segmentation—putting breaks between words—is aided by our knowledge of the meanings of the words.

20. The phonemic restoration effect shows that the context in which a phoneme appears can cause us to hear that phoneme, even if its sound is obscured by noise.

21. The verbal transformation effect may reflect mechanisms of perceptual organization that are used to enhance the comprehension of normal speech.

22. Sentences are easier to understand if they are semantically and syntactically correct. Making sentences semantically anomalous reduces a listener's ability to correctly identify the words in the sentence, and changing sentences into ungrammatical strings of words, by eliminating syntax, further decreases the listener's ability to correctly identify the words.

23. Speech perception depends on both acoustic and contextual information. We process from bottom-up by taking into account the information present in the acoustic signal, and we process from top-down by taking into account the meanings contained in words, sentences, and paragraphs.

Glossary

Acoustic cue A pattern of frequencies-over-time associated with a particular phoneme. (386)

Acoustic signal A sound's pattern of frequencies-over-time. (383)

Audiovisual speech perception A person views a speaker on a videotape in which the accompanying sound track does not match the speaker's lip movements. Audiovisual speech perception refers to changes in the person's perception of the sound track caused by viewing the speaker's lip movements. (393)

Categorical perception As voice onset time is changed over a large range, a listener perceives only two discriminable phonemes, one on one side of the phonetic boundary and another on the other side of the phonetic boundary. (388)

Formant A band of energy, characteristic of vowels, that shows up as a horizontal band on the sound spectrogram. (384)

Formant transition A rapid shift in frequency immediately preceding a formant. (386)

Invariance (in speech) Although acoustic cues for a phoneme change with different contexts, the sound of the phoneme does not change. (386)

Manner of articulation The mechanical means by which a consonant is produced. (387)

Motor theory of speech perception This theory postulates that we perceive speech by determining—by means of a device called a phonetic decoder—how a speech signal was produced by the speaker. Once we know how the signal was produced, we can identify that signal, since each sound is produced in a unique way. (386)

Pattern of articulation The combination of voicing, place of articulation, and manner of articulation characteristic of each phoneme. (387)

Phoneme The shortest segment of speech which, if changed, changes the meaning of a word. (383)

Phonemic restoration effect If a phoneme in a meaningful statement is obscured by noise, the auditory system "fills in" the phoneme so that a listener is not aware that the phoneme is missing. (397)

Phonetic boundary In a categorical perception experiment, the voice onset time at which perception abruptly changes from one phoneme to another. A listener cannot tell the difference between two phonemes on the same side of the phonetic boundary but can tell the difference between two phonemes on opposite sides of the boundary. (388)

Phonetic decoder A device proposed by the motor theory of speech perception that can determine and indicate how a particular speech signal was produced by a speaker. (389)

Place of articulation The place obstructed in the airstream during the production of a consonant. (387)

Segmentation The process of dividing a speech signal into individual words by creating perceptual breaks between each word. (387)

Selective adaptation In speech, selective adaptation refers to a procedure in which (1) a listener's phonetic boundary is determined, (2) the listener is selectively adapted by being repeatedly exposed to a particular syllable, and (3) the phonetic boundary is redetermined. The selective adaptation procedure, if effective, causes a change in the phonetic boundary. (392)

Semantics Specifies whether or not it is appropriate to use a word in a sentence, based on the word's meaning. (398)

Shadowing A procedure in which a listener is asked to repeat a message aloud as he or she hears it (see Chapter 7). (398)

Short-term spectrum A graph indicating the amount of energy present at each frequency in the acoustic signal over a short period of time. (384)

Sound spectrogram A display that shows the amount of energy present at different frequencies during the entire time course of a speech stimulus. (383)

Syntax Specifies which structures of a sentence are allowed. (398)

Verbal satiation The loss of a word's meaning that sometimes occurs if the word is repeated over and over. (399)

Verbal summator A device developed by B. F. Skinner that presents short strings of meaningless syllables. (399)

Verbal transformation effect The change in a word's sound that sometimes occurs if the word is repeated over and over. (399)

Voice onset time (VOT) The time delay between the beginning of a sound and the beginning of voicing. (388)

Voicing Refers to the state of the vocal cords during production of a phoneme. Phonemes that cause vibrations of the vocal cords are voiced, and phonemes that cause no vibrations are unvoiced. (387)

Chapter Fifteen

Smelling and Tasting

OLFACTION

No study of the senses would be complete without considering the sense of smell (or olfaction, as it is usually called in the scientific literature). Olfaction is essential for the survival of many animals and makes life much more interesting for humans. That many animals rely on their sense of smell for survival is reflected in the relative sizes of their olfactory organs. Dogs, for example, who spend a good portion of their waking hours sniffing, have olfactory mucosa much larger than a human's; and sheep, who rely on their noses to find food, have olfactory organs that take up a large portion of their skull.

Humans, on the other hand, could live without a sense of smell if they had to. But life would certainly be less interesting without good smells from the kitchen or the rain-freshened air after a spring shower, and it might be a little more dangerous if we couldn't smell food that has spoiled or gas leaking from a defective oven.

Many writers, commenting on our attitude toward smells, have pointed out that in our society we tend to avoid many smells. As William Cain (1978), a leading researcher on smell, says,

> There is a strong effort to manage man's olfactory environment. It is generally felt that, with few exceptions, both indoor and outdoor air should be odorless. Odors produced by warning agents, perfumes, and foods constitute permissible exceptions, but these may be welcome only at certain times, in certain places and for certain durations.
>
> It may be argued that we are too obsessed with, and hence strive to overmanage, some aspects of the olfactory environment. Do you take steps to ensure that your home does not have "house-itosis"? Do your clothes, hands, and armpits have just a hint of yummy lemon-fresh fragrance? Does your bathroom smell like the great outdoors?

And E. T. Hall, in his book *The Hidden Dimension* (1966), makes a similar point, with special reference to Americans:

> In the use of olfactory apparatus Americans are culturally underdeveloped. The extensive use of deodorants and the suppression of odor in public places results in a land of olfactory blandness and sameness that would be difficult to duplicate anywhere else in the world.

Why this obsession with smells? Perhaps people's feelings about smells have to do with the strong reactions that olfaction is capable of eliciting. To support the idea that no other sense elicits such a wide range of emotional reactions to simple stimuli, John Levine and Donald McBurney (1983) point out that it is implausible to imagine a color or a tone that could either empty a building of its occupants as rapidly as could the smell of smoke or command the high price of some perfumes.

Despite the powerful effects that smells can exert, the human olfactory system has a reputation for being deficient. Humans have, in fact, been called **microsmatic** (lacking a keen sense of smell), in contrast to many animals, who are called **macrosmatic** (having a keen sense of smell). Although many animals are more sensitive to smells than humans, calling humans microsmatic might somewhat overstate the case. In fact, recent research indicates that the human olfactory system is quite a bit more impressive than it was once thought to be. Let's consider some of the evidence uncovered by this research.

Some Myths About Human Olfaction

Myth #1: Human Olfactory Receptors Are Less Sensitive Than Animals'

The idea that human smell *receptors* are much less sensitive than those of other animals arose because some animals are much more sensitive than humans to odors. The most familiar example of this is the dog, which deserves its reputation for being able to detect very faint smells. Mairico Burton (1972) relates the story of a dog the Cairo police used to find a stolen donkey that had walked across rocky ground 4 days earlier. The dog put its nose to the donkey's trail and followed the scent right up to the door of the house where the donkey was being hidden. This ability to follow very faint smells has been experimentally confirmed in the laboratory: dogs can detect most substances in concentrations 100 times lower than concentrations humans can detect (Moulton, 1977).

But is this greater sensitivity of the dog evidence that the human's receptors are less sensitive than the dog's? Not necessarily. Remember Hecht, Shlaer, and Pirenne's (1942) experiment, in which they determined that it takes only a single quantum of light to excite a visual receptor? (See Box 2.1.) They determined this by precisely measuring how much light entered the eye at threshold and then calculating how much of this light actually reached the visual receptors. Doing a similar calculation for the olfactory system, H. deVries and M. Stuiver (1961) showed that it takes only one molecule of odorant to excite a human's olfactory receptor. Since nothing could be more sensitive than one molecule per receptor, the dog's greater sensitivity must be due to something else—that something else is the *number* of receptors: about one billion in the dog, compared to about 10 million for man (Moulton, 1977; Dodd & Squirrell, 1980).

Myth #2: Our Ability to Detect Differences in Smell Intensity Is Poor

The ability to detect differences in intensity is indicated by the difference threshold (see p. 12), and, in the past, olfaction has been reputed to have the largest difference threshold of all the senses, with typical values ranging from about 25 to 33 percent (Gamble, 1898; Stone & Bosley, 1965). That is, the concentration of an odorant must be increased by 25–33 percent before a person can detect an increase in odor intensity.

Recently, William Cain (1977) measured the difference threshold for a number of odorants by presenting two odorants of different concentrations on each trial and asking subjects to judge which was more intense. He presented the odorants by placing a small amount of each substance onto an absorbent cotton ball, in a glass vessel designed for olfactory testing. His results were better than those of most other studies, with an average difference threshold for three odorants of 19 percent, and a relatively low difference threshold of 7 percent for one of the odorants, n-butyl alcohol.

But Cain didn't stop there, because an average difference threshold of 19 percent still seemed high to him. He next analyzed the stimuli he had presented to his human subjects, using a **gas chromatograph,** a device that accurately measures the concentration of the vapor given off by each stimulus. Cain found what he had suspected: stimuli supposed to have the same concentration actually varied considerably, apparently due to variations in adsorption by the walls of the glass vessel and to differences in the airflow pattern through the cotton in different samples.

Based on his knowledge of signal detection theory (see Appendix A, p. 435), Cain hypothesized that this large variability in the stimulus might explain the large difference threshold. To understand how large variations in the stimulus can lead to a large difference threshold, look at Figure 15.2. Figure 15.2(a) shows probability distributions that indicate the perceptual effects caused by a low- and high-concentration stimulus with exactly the same concentration on each trial. These distributions indicate that the most likely perceptual effect for the low-concentration stimulus is 100, but effects ranging from 98 to 102 are also possible; similarly, the most likely perceptual effect for the high-concentration stimulus is 105, but effects ranging from 103 to 107 are also possible. That perceptual effects may vary, even when the stimulus is totally constant, is a common finding, as you may remember from our discussion of perceptual measurement (see p. 8). The important thing about the curves in Figure 15.2(a) is that they are fairly narrow and, therefore, do not overlap. This lack of overlap makes it easy to distinguish the two stimuli—any perceptual effect between 98 and 102 belongs to the low stimulus, and any perceptual effect between 103 and 107 belongs to the high stimulus.

Figure 15.2(b) shows what happens to the probability distributions when the concentrations of the low and high stimuli vary from trial to trial. These curves are wider than the ones in 15.2(a), because there are now two sources of variability: (1) the natural variability in the observer's judgments, which occurs even when stimuli are exactly the same on each trial (as in Figure 15.2a), and (2) the trial-to-trial variability in the concentrations of the stimuli. These wider curves create a problem for the observer: the curves overlap between 100 and 105; so, if the subject experiences a perceptual effect of, say, 103, he or she cannot really tell whether this effect was caused by the low or the high stimulus. Therefore, it will be more difficult to distinguish the two stimuli in Figure 15.2(b) than those in 15.2(a), even through the average difference in the concentrations of the stimuli is the same in both situations.

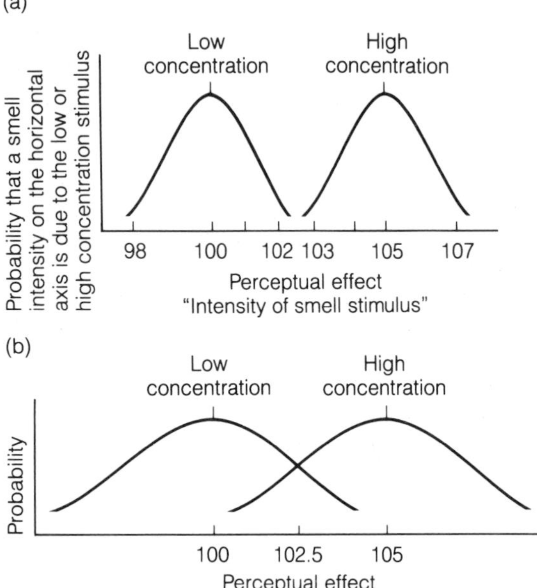

Figure 15.2 (a) The perceptual effects caused by two smell stimuli with exactly the same concentration on each trial. The low-concentration stimulus has a concentration of 100 on every trial, while the high-concentration stimulus has a concentration of 105 on every trial. Although concentration is constant for each stimulus, there is some variability in the observer's judgments, just as occurs in any psychophysical experiment. Since the two distributions do not overlap, however, the observer can still easily distinguish the two stimuli. (b) The perceptual effects for two smell stimuli with the same average concentrations as in (a); in this case however, there is some variability in the stimulus concentration from trial to trial. This stimulus variability broadens the curves and makes it more difficult to distinguish the two stimuli.

Based on his finding that olfactory stimuli presented on cotton balls are highly variable, Cain concluded that the large difference threshold for olfaction may result not from a deficiency in the nose's discriminating power but from the difficulty in precisely controlling the concentrations of the olfactory stimuli being presented. He tested this conclusion with an **olfactometer,** a device that presents olfactory stimuli with much greater precision than cotton balls can. When stimulus variability was decreased in this way Cain found an average difference threshold of 11 percent, with n-butyl alcohol having an impressively low threshold of only 5 percent. These figures, which rival difference thresholds for vision and hearing, show that our ability to detect differences in smell intensity is, in fact, not poor compared to the other senses.

Myth #3: Our Ability to Identify Odors Is Poor

The idea that our ability to identify odors is poor comes from experiments in which people are presented with a series of odorants and asked to tell the experimenter what they are. In a typical experiment, Trygg Engen and Carl Pfaffmann (1960) asked subjects to assign a label to each of 36 different stimuli, based on their smell. Each labeled odorant was then presented again, and the subjects were asked to remember the label he or she had previously assigned to that odorant. Even though the subjects were given a number of trials and were reminded of the correct labels for stimuli they did not identify correctly, they were able to correctly identify only 17 of the 36 stimuli.

Why did people fail to identify over half of the odorants in the Engen and Pfaffmann experiment? J. A. Desor and Gary K. Beauchamp (1974) thought that one reason might be that most of Engen and Pfaffmann's odorants were unfamiliar chemicals, such as hexane and nitrobenzene. Desor and Beauchamp, therefore, asked subjects to identify familiar materials such as coffee, bananas, and motor oil. When confronted with these familiar substances, subjects could still only identify about half of them correctly—the same result Engen and Pfaffmann obtained for unfamiliar chemicals. However, if Desor and Beauchamp identified the substances for their subjects when they first presented them and then reminded subjects of the correct identification if they failed to respond correctly on subsequent trials, their subjects could, after some practice, correctly identify 63 of 64 substances.

According to Cain (1979, 1980), Desor and Beauchamp's subjects identified odors so well because they were provided with the correct names, or labels, at the beginning of the experiment. In his own experiments, Cain showed that if subjects assign a correct label to a familiar object the first time they smell it (for example, labeling an orange "orange"), they usually identify it correctly the next time it is

Box 15.1 The Odorizing of America

Artificial odors have been with us for a long time, in the form of perfumes, colognes, and after-shave lotions calculated to appeal to the opposite sex, and room deodorizers designed to mask the smell of Uncle Fred's cigar. Recently, however, the use of artificial fragrances has reached an all-time high. Soaps used to contain about 1 percent fragrance, but fragrances now account for up to 10 percent of the content of soaps such as Irish Spring. Shampoos such as Agree and Herbal Essence have achieved great success largely because some people enjoy smelling things like wild strawberries or apricot nectar while they shower. Less obvious applications of artificial odors are the fragrances added to concrete to combat the "wet cement" smell in new buildings, those added to carpeting to reduce "new carpet" smell, and those which reduce the smell of resins in permanent-press fabrics.

With the increased presence of artificial fragrances in many products, perhaps the next step was inevitable: the Aroma Disc System, proposed by Charles of the Ritz. In an advertising brochure, the Aroma Disc System is billed as "the next frontier in home entertainment," and a story in the June 6, 1983, issue of *The New Yorker* describes the system as "to one's nose what a stereo is to one's ears, or a television set is to one's eyes." The Aroma Disc System allows you to choose what your immediate environment will smell like, simply by inserting a mylar disc into a disc player. A combination of pressure and heat releases fragrance oil from the disc, and within 2 minutes an average-sized room fills with whatever aroma you have chosen, be it Ocean Breeze ("The robust feeling of a walk along a beach in the early morning hours"), Country Moods ("The fun of an early autumn hayride"), Movie Time ("The nostalgic smell of buttered popcorn at the theatre"), or one of the 40 other fragrances available on either short-playing or long-playing discs.

The New Yorker's description of the aromas produced by the discs sounds intriguing indeed: "When Movie Time, for instance, was breathed directly, it produced less the sensation of being in a movie theater than the feeling of standing knee-deep in popcorn as melted butter was poured over our head. . . . When we put on A Dozen Roses, it seemed that the entire Brooklyn Botanic Garden had blossomed on our desk, in the fertile soil between typewriter and pencil cup."

While it remains to be seen whether a product like the Aroma Disc System will be commercially successful, there is no doubt that we have entered an era in which artificial odors will continue to play an increasing role in our day-to-day lives.

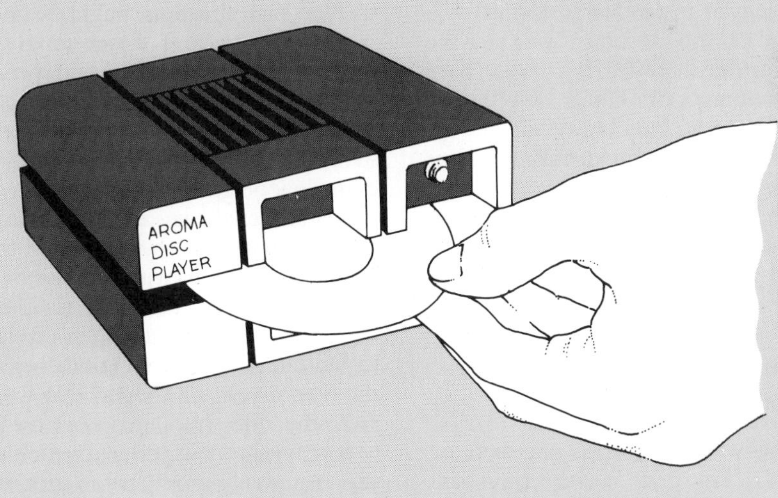

presented. However, if they assign an incorrect label to an object the first time they smell it (for example, labeling machine oil "cheese"), they usually misidentify it the next time it is presented. But if subjects are supplied with the correct labels right away, they easily identify the odors later. Thus, according to Cain, when we have trouble identifying odors, this trouble results not from a deficiency in our olfactory system but from an inability to retrieve the odor's name from our memory.

The amazing thing about the role memory plays in odor identification is that knowing the correct label for the odor actually seems to transform our perception into that odor. Cain (1980) gives the example of an object initially identified as "fishy-goaty-oily." When the experimenter tells the subject that the fishy-goaty-oily smell actually comes from leather, the smell is then transformed into that of leather. I recently had a similar experience. A friend of mine kindly gave me a bottle of Aquavit, a Danish drink with a very interesting smell, for Christmas. In the spirit of the holidays, I was sampling this drink with some friends, and as we drank it we tried to identify its smell. Many odors were proposed ("anise," "orange," "lemon"), but it wasn't until someone turned the bottle around and read the label on the back that the truth became known: "Aquavit ('Water of Life') is the Danish national drink—a delicious, crystal-clear spirit distilled from grain, with a slight taste of caraway." Upon hearing the word "caraway," the previous hypotheses of anise, orange, and lemon were instantly transformed into caraway. It seemed obvious as soon as we knew the answer. To demonstrate this effect to yourself, have a friend collect a number of familiar objects and, without looking, try your hand at identifying the odors. You will find that you can identify some but not others, and when your friend tells you the correct answer for the ones you missed, you will wonder how you could have failed to identify such a familiar smell. But don't blame your misses on your nose; blame your memory!

Myth #4: Animals Can Use Odors to Communicate, but Humans Can't

We will see below, when we discuss pheromones, that the first part of this myth is correct: animals are, in fact, very capable of communicating with odors, and smell plays an important role in their lives. As McKenzie (1923) has remarked about the dog: "He can recognize his master by sight, no doubt, yet, as we know, he is never perfectly satisfied until he has taken stock also of the scent, the more precisely to do so bringing his snout into actual contact with the person he is examining. It is as if his eyes might deceive him, but never his nose." Humans, however, are constrained from behaving like dogs. Except in the most intimate situations, it is considered poor form to smell other people at close range. However, what if we lived in a society that condoned this kind of behavior? Could we identify other people based on their smell? A recent experiment suggests that the answer to this question might be "yes."

Michael Russell (1976) had subjects wear undershirts for 24 hours, without showering or using deodorant or perfume. The undershirts were then sealed in a bag and given to the experimenter, who, in turn, presented each subject with three undershirts to smell: one was the subject's own shirt, one was a male's, and one was a female's. About three-quarters of the subjects succeeded in identifying their own undershirt, based on its odor, and also correctly identified which of the other shirts were worn by males or females (see also McBurney et al., 1977, for a similar experiment). This result certainly doesn't suggest that people can identify other people solely on smell, but it does suggest that our ability to use smell in such situations might be underrated.

The phenomenon of **menstrual synchrony** also suggests a role for smell in interpersonal relations. Martha McClintock (1971) noted that women who live or work together often report that their menstrual periods begin at about the same time. For example, one group of seven female lifeguards had widely scattered menstrual periods at the beginning of the summer, but by the end of the summer, all began their periods within 4 days of each other. To investigate this phenomenon, McClintock asked 135 females, aged 17–22, living in a college dormitory, to indicate when their periods began throughout the school year. She found that women who saw each other often (roommates or close friends) tended to have synchronous periods by the end of the school year. After ruling out factors such as awareness of the other person's period, McClintock concluded that "there is some interpersonal physiological process which affects the menstrual cycle."

What might this physiological process be? Michael Russell and co-workers (1980) did an experiment which suggests that smell might have something to do with this physiological process. He had a "donor" woman wear cotton pads in her armpits for 24 hours, three times a week. The sweat extracted from these pads was then rubbed onto the upper lip of a woman in the "experimental group." A control group of women received the same treatment, but without the sweat. The results for the experimental group showed that prior to the experiment, there was an average of 9.3 days between the onset of the donor's and subject's periods, but after 5 months, the average time between onset was reduced to 3.4 days. The control group showed no such synchrony. Since the donors and the subjects in the experimental group never saw each other, Russell concludes that odor must be the factor that causes menstrual synchrony.

The evidence above indicates that smell at least potentially plays some role in human communication. The evidence available to date, however, is only suggestive, and in our society the role of smell in human communication is surely small. To find strong evidence for odor as a method of communication, we must turn to animals.

Odor and Animal Communication: Pheromones

Smell provides the dominant means of communication in many animals, but it does much more than that. Many animals release chemicals called **pheromones,** which, when sensed by other animals of the same species, cause specific reactions (Karlson & Luscher, 1959). There are two major classes of pheromones, **primers** and **releasers.** Primers usually trigger a chain of long-lasting physiological (usually hormonal) effects in another animal. For example, Hilda Bruce (1959) found that if a female mouse which has just mated is exposed to the smell of a strange male mouse within 24 hours, the smell of the strange male mouse prevents the just-mated female mouse from becoming pregnant (the "Bruce effect").

Releasers, on the other hand, usually trigger an immediate behavioral reaction in another animal. Examples of a few of the behaviors caused by releasers are:

1. *Sex.* Chemicals that control sexual behavior are the most powerful of the pheromones, with extremely small quantities effective over long distances. For example, the pheromone bombykol, released by the female silkworm moth, can attract a male from over 3 km away; and though a single female contains only about .01 millionth gram of bombykol, this is enough chemical to potentially attract one billion males (Wilson, 1963)!

Many sexual pheromones have a dual function: they attract a mate, and they trigger the sequence of stereotyped behaviors necessary for mating. Sometimes this stereotyped mating response is triggered even if the pheromone is presented in the wrong context: male tortoises have been observed mounting such inappropriate objects as a head of lettuce over which a female had recently climbed (Shorey, 1977).

2. *Aggression.* Honeybee workers disturbed at the hive release an alarm pheromone (isopental acetate) from their sting chambers, which attracts other bees and causes them to attack objects in the vicinity of the hive. When the bees sting the enemy, additional pheromone is released to cause more bees to attack the potential intruder. This pheromone effect is probably responsible for the phenomenon, well known to beekeepers, that more than one bee will often sting the same spot (Shorey, 1977).

3. *Disposing of the dead.* Within a few days after an ant dies, the chemical decomposition products of the dead ant stimulate worker ants to carry the corpse to the refuse pile outside the nest. When living ants are experimentally daubed with the chemical decomposition products, they are carried to the refuse pile. After being dumped on the refuse pile, the ant promptly returns to the nest, only to be carried out again, and this process continues until the ant's "death smell" has worn off (Wilson, 1963).

All of the above are examples of how pheromones affect the behavior of nonmammals. There is also ample evidence that the sense of smell plays an important role in regulating the behavior of many mammals. For example, the scent marking practiced by many mammals has been linked to aggressive behavior. Animals mark either objects in the environment or other animals by rubbing the scent glands on their bodies against them, after which aggressive behavior often occurs (Ralls, 1971).

Pheromones also play an important role in regulating sexual behavior in many mammals. For example, a vaginal discharge of the female golden hamster causes males to mate within seconds of being exposed to the female. The male will also attempt to mate with another male that is smeared with this discharge, but this same male loses all interest in mating if its olfactory bulbs (see "Structure of the Olfactory System," below) are removed (Devor, 1977). A similar effect occurs in dogs. Female dogs in heat give off a special odor that attracts male dogs. If this odor is smeared onto a female that is not in heat, a male will attempt to mate with the female, even though the male showed no interest in mating minutes earlier, before application of the odor (Goodwin et al., 1979).

Before leaving the topic of pheromones, we should note that many investigators object to applying the term "pheromone"—which was originally developed to deal with fairly stereotyped, genetically programmed insect behaviors—to more complex mammalian behaviors, preferring instead to talk about "chemical signals" when referring to mammals (Beauchamp et al., 1976). In the early 1970s, evidence seemed to show that chemical signals control the sexual and reproductive behavior of monkeys (Michael & Kaverne, 1968; Michael et al., 1971). However, recent evidence (Goldfoot et al., 1978) indicates that olfaction may not, in fact, control reproductive behavior in monkeys, and a paper reviewing all the evidence on the role of pheromones in monkey sexual behavior concluded that: "It is probable that olfaction . . . influences behavior, but it seems unlikely that chemical communication plays any significant role in the control of higher primate reproductive and sexual behavior" (Rogel, 1978).

Whether or not olfaction plays a significant role in reproductive and sexual behavior in monkeys or humans, the above discussion should convince you not only of the importance of olfaction in animal behavior but also of the impressive capabilities of the human olfactory system. Let's now consider how this system works.

Structure of the Olfactory System

In Figure 15.3, stimuli from the rose enter the nose and find their way to the olfactory mucosa and the receptors in the mucosa (Figure 15.4). Molecules of odorant contact the cilia of the receptors and produce an electrical signal that travels along nerve fibers to the **olfactory bulb.** The olfactory bulb is analogous to the retina in that it is here that the initial processing of the signals generated in the receptors takes place; the olfactory bulb is where fibers from the receptors first synapse, and it also contains many additional synapses and complex connections, as does the retina.

From the olfactory bulb, fibers travel to a number of places in the brain, including the amygdala, the hippocampus, and the hypothalamus—all of which play roles in the regulation of feeding, drinking, and reproductive behavior—as well as the thalamus, where all the other senses also synapse. Unlike vision, hearing, or touch, which have well-defined cortical receiving areas, no such area has been located for smell. However, the *pyriform cortex,* an area on the underside of the brain, beneath the occipital cortex (see Figure 2.11), receives olfactory inputs; and an area in the frontal lobe has recently been found that also appears to be important in olfaction (Tanabe et al., 1975).

The Stimulus for Smell

Before we describe the processes of transduction and coding in the olfactory system, let's first consider the nature of the stimulus for smell. When you smell something, some molecules of the substance you smell have left the substance and traveled through the air into your nose. Because the invisible molecules we smell travel slowly through the air, it is difficult to tell exactly when these molecules hit the receptors and, consequently, it is difficult to determine how much time elapses between the time a molecule reaches the receptors and the time an electrical response is recorded from the olfactory system. It is also difficult to determine the exact concentration of the stimulus that reaches the receptors, since molecules of an odorant may deposit themselves on other surfaces inside the nose, before

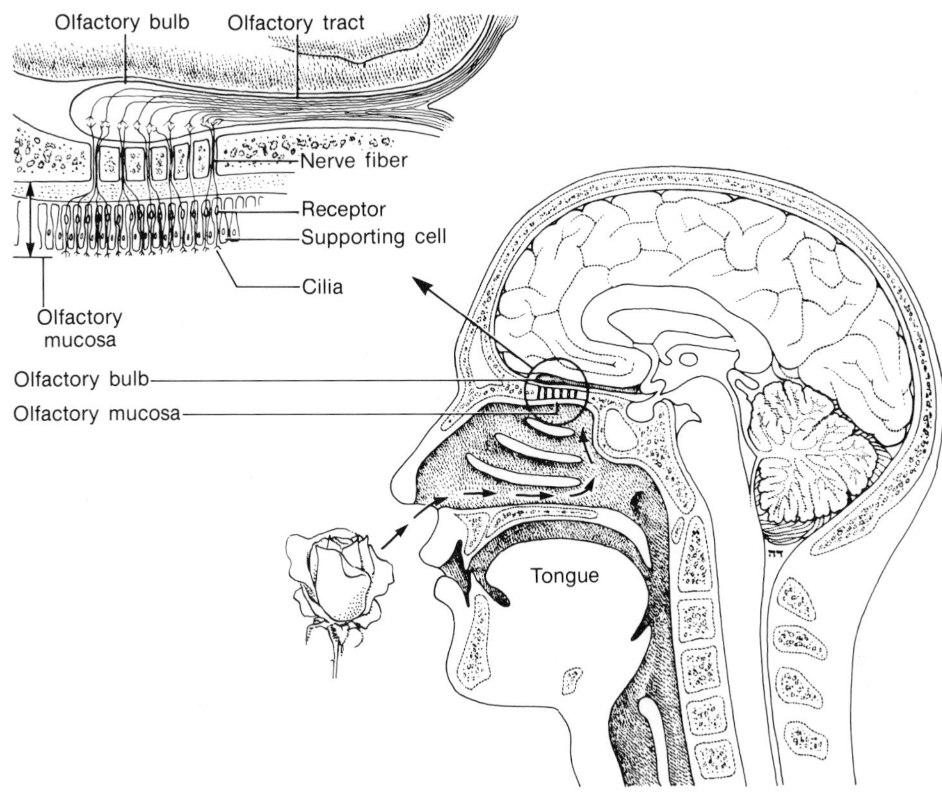

Figure 15.3 The olfactory system. (Adapted from Amoore et al., 1964.)

reaching the receptors. All this makes olfactory research quite complicated.

The above problems in delivering the stimulus, however, cause less trouble for smell research than the problem of determining which properties of the stimulus should be studied. To understand what we mean by this problem, consider vision and hearing. The first step in studying these senses was to identify the physical properties of the stimulus that, when changed, alter the perception of the stimulus. Thus, early researchers in vision found that changing the physical property of wavelength changes the hue of a light. For example, our perception can be changed from blue to red by simply increasing the wavelength of light from 400 to 650 nm. In fact, we can see all the hues of the spectrum as we increase the wavelength, and each hue is similar to the one that just precedes it. Similarly, early researchers in hearing found that changing the physical property of frequency changes the pitch of a sound. We can change our perception from a low pitch to a high pitch by simply increasing the frequency, and when we do this, each tone seems to follow from the preceding one.

The psychophysically determined linkages between wavelength and hue and between frequency and pitch identified wavelength and frequency as important physical properties to study in vision and hearing, pointing the way for physiological experiments relating wavelength and frequency to the activity of the nervous system. Thus, we obtained a good deal of our knowledge of vision and hearing by first identifying the quality to be studied, then determining the physical property of

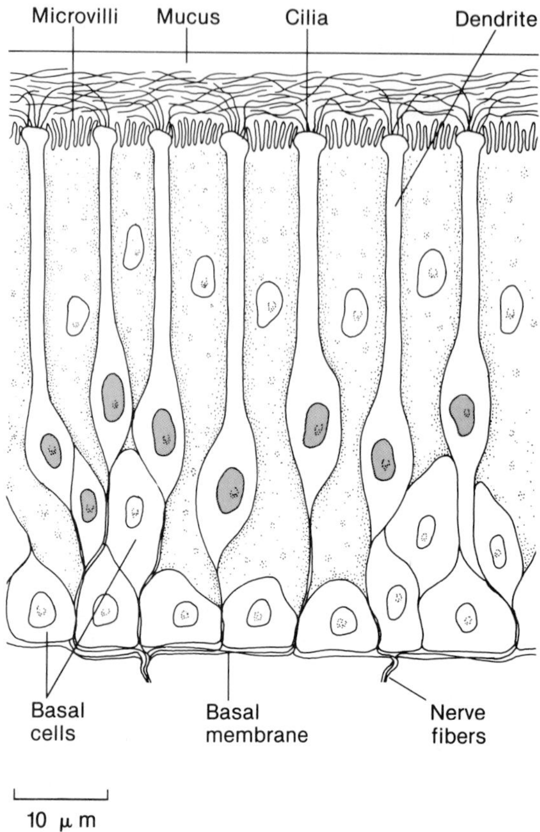

Figure 15.4 The olfactory receptors and mucosa. A smell stimulus reaches the mucus layer and stimulates the cilia attached to the olfactory receptors. Note that each receptor is separated from its neighbor by a thick supporting cell.

the stimulus linked to that quality, and, finally, determining how changing this physical property changes the activity of the nervous system.

One reason that our knowledge of smell is much more limited than our knowledge of vision or hearing is that we have not yet identified a physical property analogous to wavelength or frequency that would enable us to predict what the odor will be, given the physical property. The most important factors in determining odor seem to be the overall shape and size of the odorant molecule, as well as chemical and physical properties such as volatility and solubility. However, we are far from knowing exactly how each of these properties determines our response to odors. For example, the threshold for detecting β-ionone is 0.007 μgrams (1 μgram = 1 millionth of a gram) per liter of water, and the threshold for detecting ethanol is 100,000 μgrams per liter of water. Why is β-ionone 10 million times stronger than ethanol? We can't point to any chemical or physical property that will enable us to answer this question (MacLeod, 1980).

Perhaps the chemical structure of a molecule is the most logical property for determining odor quality. We might expect that molecules with similar structures would smell the same, and this is often true. However, as we will see below, in many cases, molecules with very similar structures smell different, and in other cases, such as the one shown in Figure 15.5, two molecules may have very different structures but smell similar.

Odor Quality

Odor Classification

One problem in dealing with odor quality is that there are thousands of different odors which we can't adequately describe, because we lack a specific language for odor quality. For example, if you asked people to smell the chemical β-ionone, they would probably say that it smells like violets. This description, it turns out, is fairly accurate, but if you compare β-ionone to real violets, they smell different. The perfume industry's solution is to use names such as "woody violet" and "sweet violet" to distinguish between different violet smells, but this hardly solves the problem we face in trying to determine how olfaction works.

A large number of attempts have been made to find a way to classify odors and so bring some order to this confusing situation. One of the best-known attempts is Henning's **odor prism,** shown in Figure 15.6. Henning's prism has six corners, at which the qualities putrid, ethereal, resinous, spicy, fragrant, and burned are located. Odors lying along an edge of the prism resemble the qualities at the four corners of the surface, in proportion to their nearness to each corner. For example, Figure 15.7 shows the face of the prism that has fragrant, ethereal, resinous, and spicy at its corners. From its location on the ethereal-resinous edge, we can see that lemon

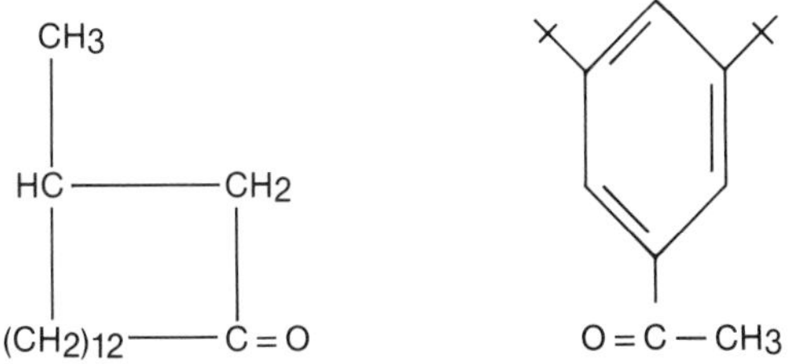

Figure 15.5 Two odorant molecules that have different structures but the same musky smell. (From MacLeod, 1980.)

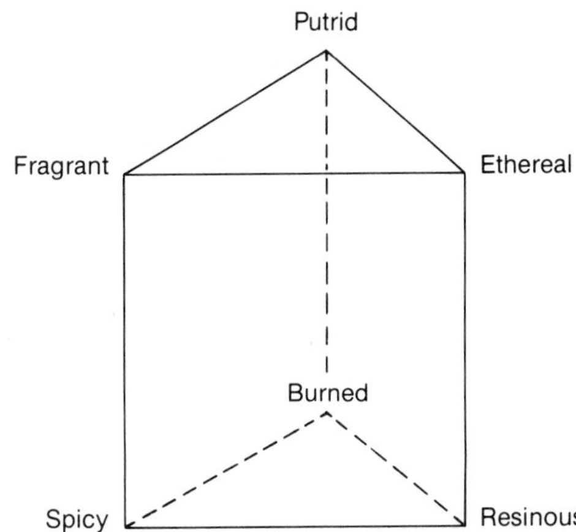

Figure 15.6 Henning's odor prism. (From Woodworth, 1938.)

oil has both ethereal and resinous properties but that it is more like ethereal, since it is closer to the ethereal corner.

Another classification scheme was proposed by John Amoore, who concluded that there are seven *primary odors* and seven *complex odors*. By first listing hundreds of different chemical compounds, along with a description of the odor of each compound, Amoore grouped odors with similar qualities and found that the following 14 groups accommodated most of the odors: camphoraceous, pungent, floral, ethereal, pepperminty, musky, putrid, almond, aromatic, aniseed, lemon, cedar, garlic, and rancid. Amoore reasoned that the categories containing the largest number of chemicals were primary odors, while the categories containing few chemicals were complex odors. Following this reasoning, he somewhat arbitrarily called odors in the seven largest categories (the first seven listed above) primary and the rest, complex. We can appreciate the arbitrariness of this decision by noting that there are 28 molecules in the putrid group and 23 in the almond group and that putrid is classified as a primary odor whereas almond isn't. The seven primary odors, along with an example of a substance with that odor, are listed in Table 15.1.

Unfortunately, none of the odor classification schemes so far proposed (including Henning's and Amoore's) is adequate. Many schemes propose too

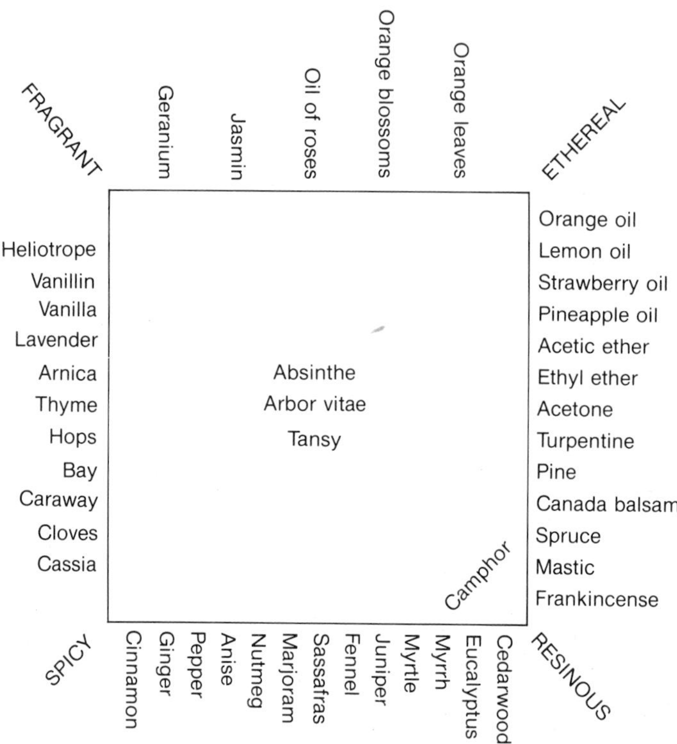

Figure 15.7 The face of Henning's smell prism that we see in Figure 15.6, showing the many smells that fall between the basic ones at the corners of the prism. (From Woodworth, 1938.)

few classifications, thereby making it impossible to find a class for some odors, and others propose categories so broad or ambiguous that some subjects might judge a particular odor to be in one category while others would judge the same odor to be in another category. This lack of a good system of odor classification has led John Levine and Donald McBurney (1983) to sum up the situation in this way: "Of the many systems of classifying odors that have been proposed over the centuries, none has ever done much for the field except decorate textbooks."

Table 15.1

Primary odor	*Substance*
Ethereal	Dry-cleaning fluid
Camphoraceous	Moth repellent
Musky	Angelina root oil
Floral	Roses
Minty	Mint candy
Pungent	Vinegar
Putrid	Bad egg

The Stereochemical Theory of Odor

Although Amoore's classification scheme is open to the above criticism of its arbitrariness, his scheme has drawn attention because of his observation that molecules in the first five categories above have similar shapes. Amoore built molecular models of many of the chemicals in each class and concluded that "models of molecules that smell alike also look alike." This observation formed the basis for his **stereochemical theory of odor,** which postulates both that there are different molecular shapes for different odor qualities and that there are "sites" on the olfactory receptors shaped to accept only molecules with the correct shape. Figure 15.8 shows some molecular models and models of the olfactory receptor sites into which these molecules are supposed to fit.

Despite the appeal of this idea, Amoore has been unable to find any evidence for his receptor sites and has therefore stated that "the site-fitting model for olfaction is evidently of rather limited value" (Amoore, 1970, p. 138). As was the case for odor classification schemes, Amoore's idea of receptor sites has decorated many textbooks.

What remains of Amoore's stereochemical theory, however, is still of interest to us, because he did demonstrate a relationship between the shape of a molecule and its odor. Amoore established the relationship between shape and odor by picking a standard chemical for each primary odor and then asking subjects to compare other odors in the same group to this standard. This procedure produced a psychophysical *similarity rating* for each odor in the group. To compare this similarity rating to the molecular shape, Amoore photographed models of each chemical and, using a computer, compared the silhouettes of each chemical to those of the standard chemical. The computer provided Amoore with a rating of similarity of shape to go along with his rating of similarity of odor, and when he plotted shape similarity versus odor similarity, he found that there was some relationship between them. That is, molecules that were more similar in shape to the standard were judged to be more similar in odor to the standard.

Thus, some correlation has been demonstrated between a physical property (molecular shape) and

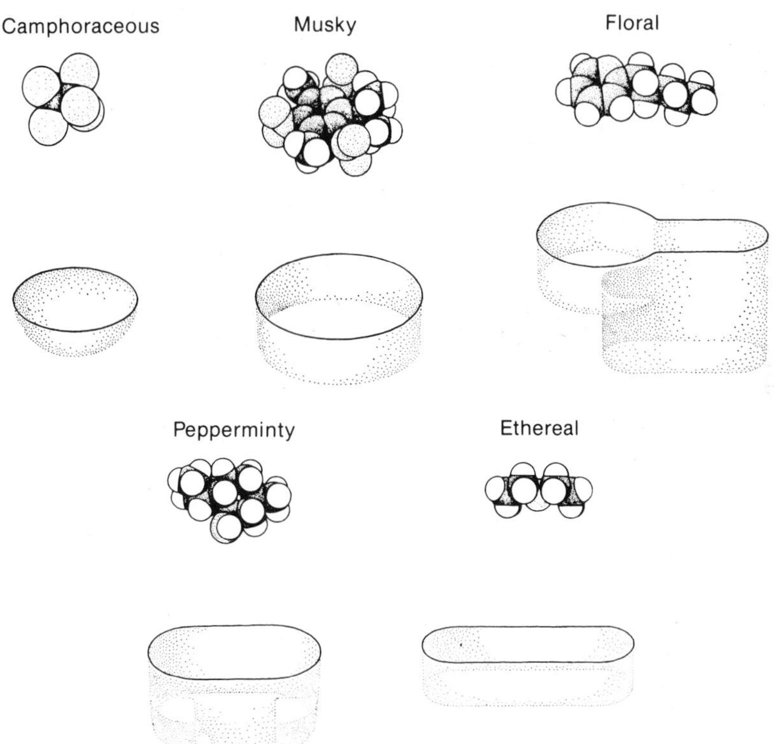

Figure 15.8 Molecular models and the receptor sites into which these molecules fit, according to Amoore's (1964, 1970) stereochemical theory of odor.

odor quality. Unfortunately, this is by no means a perfect relationship, because some molecules with identical similarity ratings for shape have very different similarity ratings for odor. This lack of a perfect relationship between molecular shape and odor quality reflects the fact that odor quality is also affected by properties such as chemical reactivity and the electrical charge of elements that make up a molecule. Thus, the two molecules shown in Figure 15.9, while almost identical in structure, differ greatly in odor, the one on the left having a strong musk odor and the one on the right having no odor (Beets, 1978). Many other physical properties, in addition to molecular shape, apparently interact to determine odor quality. So, while the search for the physical properties that correspond to odor quality has met with some success, we are far from being able to predict a substance's odor from its physical properties.

Transduction

While some researchers have been trying to develop schemes of odor quality, others have attempted to develop theories of olfactory transduction. Though a number of theories of olfactory transduction try to explain how odor molecules result in an electrical response, at this point these theories are speculative and supported by minimal evidence. Most theories of transduction propose that odorant molecules interact with the receptor membrane in some way, causing a change in the properties of the membrane so that sodium or potassium can flow across it. It is proposed that just as the sodium and potassium flow in nerve fibers (see pp. 33–35, in Chapter 2) results in a change in the electrical charge in the nerve fiber, so the sodium and potassium flow across the olfactory receptor membrane results in a change in the electrical charge in the olfactory receptor.

Unfortunately, the above statement of the mechanism is quite speculative, and the preliminary nature of our understanding of olfactory transduction becomes clear when we realize that although the cilia are believed to contain the sites stimulated by odorant molecules, there is little direct evidence at present to support this (Mozell, 1971; Dodd & Squirrell, 1980).

Though much of the theorizing about olfactory transduction is speculative, there are some experimental data available to help us answer the question of olfactory coding: Once an electrical signal is generated in the receptors, how does the brain determine the quality of the odor?

The Code for Odor Quality

Coding at the Level of the Receptors

Do receptors respond to one or to many odorants? We should first ask whether there are olfactory receptors that respond to only one odorant or perhaps to a group of similarly smelling odorants. The answer to this question appears to be "no"; most receptors respond to a number of different odors. Evidence that receptors fire to many odorants comes from Don Matthews' (1972) recordings from receptors in the tortoise olfactory mucosa. His results, illustrated in Figure 15.10, show how 19 receptors respond to 27 different odorants. Note that most of the receptors respond to more than one odorant, with the ones on the far right responding to more than 10 of the 27 odorants. Results similar to these, showing that individual receptors respond to a

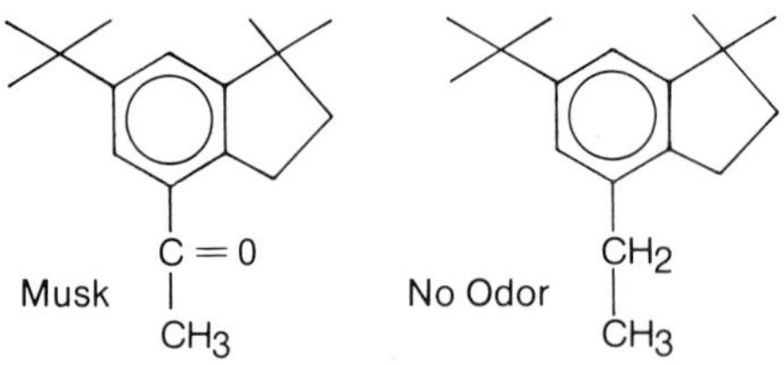

Musk $C=O$ / CH_3 — No Odor CH_2 / CH_3

Figure 15.9 Two molecules with similar structures but different odors.

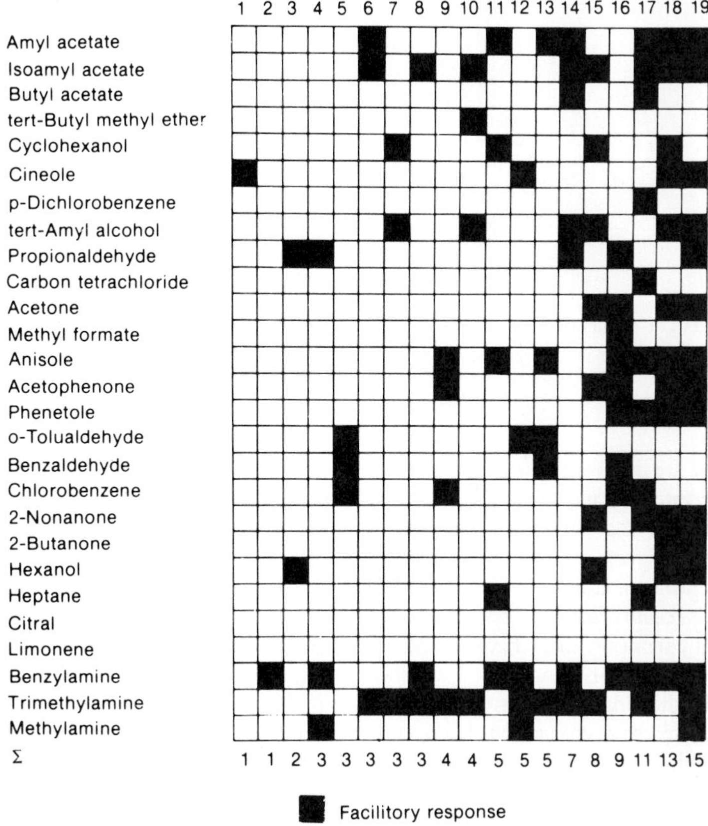

Figure 15.10 The responses of 19 different olfactory receptors of the tortoise to various stimuli. The darkened squares indicate that a stimulus elicits a response from a receptor. The receptors that respond to the fewest stimuli are on the left and those that respond to the greatest number of stimuli are on the right. (From Matthews, 1972.)

number of stimuli, have also been found in the frog (Blank, 1974; Holley et al., 1974) and the rabbit (Moulton, 1965).

Areas on the receptor surface respond to specific odorants. Though it is difficult to find single receptors that respond best to specific odorants, there is good evidence of areas on the mucosa that are sensitive to some odorants and not as sensitive to others. John Kauer and David Moulton (1974) showed that the front and back of the salamander's olfactory mucosa respond well to amyl acetate and the middle of the mucosa responds well to camphor. They showed this by designing a small nozzle that could present odorants to small areas of receptors on the mucosa. As they recorded from a neuron in the olfactory bulb, they moved the nozzle to different areas on the mucosa and found that although a particular olfactory bulb neuron responds to the stimulation of many different areas, it responds best to stimulation of one or two areas. Figure 15.11 shows the results of experiments on a number of neurons in the olfactory bulb for two stimuli, amyl acetate and camphor. Each oval indicates the area of mucosa that results in a maximal response to that chemical. Note that the distributions of these areas

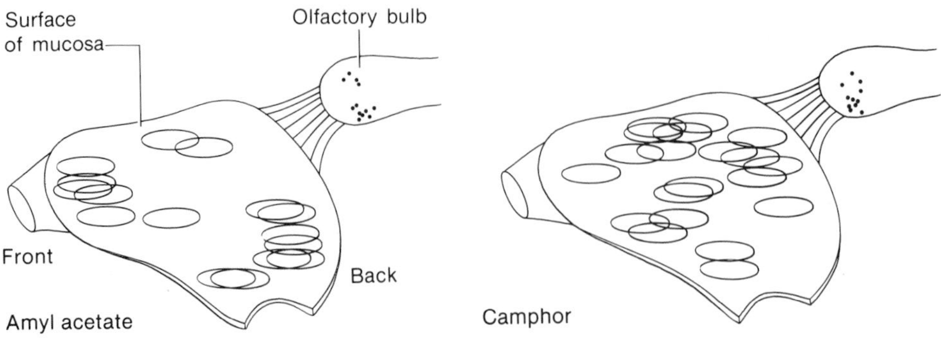

Figure 15.11 The results of Kauer and Moulton's (1974) determination of the area on the mucosa that responds best to amyl acetate (left) and camphor (right). Each oval represents the area of mucosa that elicits the largest response from a different neuron in the olfactory bulb.

of maximal response are different for the two chemicals. Large amyl acetate responses result from stimulation of receptors on the front or back of the mucosa, while large camphor responses result from stimulation of receptors nearer the middle of the mucosa. Thus, since receptors in different areas are sensitive to different chemicals, each chemical causes a different pattern of receptor firing.

Another way of achieving a different pattern of receptor firing for different chemicals has been suggested by Max Mozell. He has shown that different chemicals stimulate the olfactory receptors differently, not because of differences in receptor sensitivity, as demonstrated by Kauer and Moulton, but because of the way the chemicals distribute themselves on the olfactory mucosa.

Different chemicals distribute themselves differently on the receptor surface. In his **chromatographic theory** of smell, Max Mozell proposes that odorant molecules interact with the olfactory mucosa in a way similar to the way chemicals interact with a **gas chromatograph**, a device used to separate the different components of a chemical mixture. In gas chromatography, the mixture to be analyzed is transported by a carrier gas through a chromatographic column, which is filled with a material called the *sorbent*. As the mixture is carried through the column by the gas, some molecules travel through the column slowly, because they are attracted to the sorbent; other molecules, less strongly attracted to the sorbent, travel through the column more rapidly. Molecules that travel slowly are said to have long retention times in the column, while molecules that travel rapidly have short retention times. The different molecules of the mixture become separated as they flow through the column, with molecules having shorter retention times reaching the end of the column before molecules having longer retention times.

Mozell proposes that the olfactory mucosa behaves like the sorbent of the chromatograph and that, as odorant molecules flow over the mucosa, those with long retention times flow slowly and therefore stimulate receptors at the front of the mucosa more strongly, whereas molecules with short retention times flow more rapidly and therefore stimulate receptors more uniformly across the patch of mucosa. Thus, each molecule results in a different pattern of receptor stimulation, not because of differences in the sensitivity of the receptors but because of differences in the properties of the molecules themselves.

Mozell's theory was initially based on an experiment in which he simultaneously recorded from two branches of the olfactory nerve, the medial branch (MB), which signals activity of the receptors at the front of the mucosa, and the lateral branch (LB), which signals the activity of the receptors at the back of the mucosa (Mozell, 1964). He found that different molecules resulted in different ratios of LB/MB response, with some molecules causing a greater response in the LB ($LB/MB > 1.0$) and others causing a greater response in the MB ($LB/MB < 1.0$). This result alone does not prove that the odorant molecules are distributing themselves differently across the mucosa, because the same result could occur if the areas of mucosa sending signals through the LB and MB contained receptors sensitive to different molecules. However, in a series of experiments that span more than 10 years, Mozell produced the following additional evidence to support his theory.

1. That the time lapse between MB and LB responses is different for different chemicals supports the idea that different chemicals flow at different rates across the mucosa (Mozell, 1964).
2. If the direction of odorant flow is reversed so the flow is from back to front, the LB/MB ratios reverse. This is the result we would expect from chromatographic theory, because molecules with long retention times should stimulate the front of the mucosa most for the normal direction of flow and the back of the mucosa most for the reversed direction of flow (Mozell, 1966).
3. The retention times of odorant molecules on an actual gas chromatographic column, chosen to have a sorbent with properties like those of mucus, is correlated with the LB/MB ratios measured in the frog. That is, as the chromatographic theory predicts, molecules with small LB/MB ratios (which therefore stimulate the front of the mucosa more strongly) have long retention times, while molecules with large LB/MB ratios (which therefore stimulate the back more strongly) have short retention times (Mozell, 1970).
4. When the column of a gas chromatograph is replaced by the olfactory sac of a frog and odorants are injected into the chromatograph, the molecules migrate across the mucosa at different rates. This result shows that, even though the frog's mucosa is much shorter than the column of a normal chromatograph, it is long enough to separate different molecules, based on the different rates at which they flow across the mucosa (Mozell & Jagodowiez, 1973).
5. The concentrations of butanol molecules deposited on the mucosa have been directly measured by flowing radioactively labeled butanol molecules across the frog's mucosa and then freezing the mucosa to measure its level of radioactivity. These measurements show, as the theory predicts, different amounts of butanol on the front and back of the mucosa: the butanol concentration is high at the front of the mucosa and lower at the back. This result explains why butanol results in a large electrophysiological response from the MB, which serves the front of the mucosa, and little or no response from the LB, which serves the back of the mucosa (Hornung, Lansing, & Mozell, 1975; see also Hornung & Mozell, 1977).

This sequence of experiments is particularly interesting, because it shows how Mozell started with indirect evidence to support his theory and then steadily accumulated more evidence until he could directly support the theory. He began compiling indirect evidence by showing that there are different LB/MB ratios for different chemicals. This result suggested, but did not prove, that odorants may distribute themselves differently across the mucosa. Ten years later, by measuring butanol on the membrane and showing that the butanol distributes itself across the mucosa, Mozell provided direct evidence for his theory.

This strong evidence in favor of the idea that different odorant molecules distribute themselves differently on the olfactory receptors does not mean, however, that Kauer and Moulton's idea that there are areas on the mucosa sensitive to specific odorants is incorrect. The mechanisms proposed by Mozell and by Kauer and Moulton probably work together to result in a distinctive pattern of nerve firing for each odorant.

Coding in the Olfactory Bulb and Beyond

If distinctive patterns of nerve firing for different odorants are transmitted to the olfactory bulb, different odorants should cause different patterns of activity in the olfactory bulb. Recent experiments show that this appears to be the case.

K. B. Döving and A. T. Pinching's (1973, 1974) experiments are analogous to the stimulation deafness experiments we discussed on pages 359–360, in Chapter 13. In these experiments, animals were exposed to loud tones for long periods of time and then their cochleas were examined. Exposure to tones of different frequencies caused different areas of the cochlea to degenerate. Döving and Pinching asked what would happen to an animal's olfactory bulb if the animal were exposed to one odorant for a long period of time. To answer this question, they exposed each of a number of rats to a different odorant for 3 months and then examined the rats' olfactory bulbs. Their result was analogous to those of the stimulus deafness experiments: exposure to the odorants caused parts of the olfactory bulb to degenerate, and the pattern of degeneration was different for each odorant. Each odorant, however, did not have its own exclusive area on the olfactory bulb. Though each odorant exhibited a different overall pattern of degeneration, it also caused large areas to degenerate, thereby creating considerable overlap between the different patterns.

A more recent experiment, using a more elegant procedure, reached the same conclusion. William Stewart, John Kauer, and Gordon Shepherd (1979) used the 2-deoxyglucose (2-DG) technique, which, as we saw in Chapter 2, made it possible to visualize orientation columns in the visual cortex. We've come a long way since Chapter 2, so let's review the 2-DG technique. 2-deoxyglucose has three important properties. (1) Since its structure is similar to glucose, a primary source of energy for neurons, it is taken up by neurons as though it were glucose. The more active the neuron, the more 2-DG is taken up by the neuron. (2) When 2-DG is taken up by a neuron, it accumulates inside the neuron. (3) 2-DG can be labeled with a radioactive isotope, carbon 14. Therefore, by measuring the amount of radioactivity in various parts of the brain, we can determine which neurons were most active.

Stewart injected rats with radioactively labeled 2-DG and exposed them to either amyl acetate or camphor for 45 minutes, thereby activating neurons that would be stimulated by amyl acetate or camphor and causing them to take up 2-DG. After this 45-minute exposure, the rats were sacrificed, and their olfactory bulbs were examined to determine the pattern of radioactivity. The results, shown in Figure 15.12, indicate that different patterns of neurons are activated by amyl acetate and camphor.

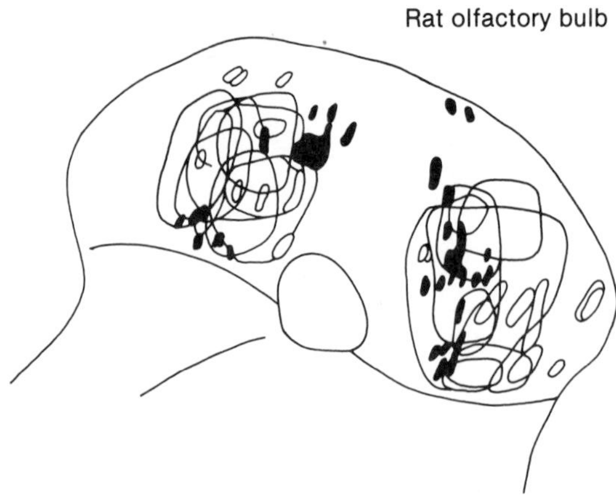

Figure 15.12 Areas of highest activity in the rat's olfactory bulb, caused by stimulation with camphor (dark areas) and with amyl acetate (open areas), as determined by the 2-DG technique. (From Stewart et al., 1979.)

Note, however, that although the patterns are different, each substance causes activity over a large area, and there is considerable overlap between the areas activated.

The results of both the receptor and olfactory bulb experiments, described above, point to a much more diffuse type of coding in the olfactory system than in the other sensory systems. For example, a touch to your hand activates mechanoreceptors in the parts of the hand touched, which causes activity in a fairly well defined area of cortex. In contrast, sniffing some amyl acetate activates a fairly diffuse pattern of receptors on your olfactory mucosa, which causes widespread activity in your olfactory bulb. This activity may be different than that generated by sniffing some other substance, but it is not precisely localized, as is the response to having your hand touched. Somehow, even though the coding in the olfactory system appears to be fairly diffuse, we are capable of distinguishing thousands of different odors.

Perhaps our ability to distinguish this large number of odors requires processing in centers higher than the olfactory bulb. We know little about the nature of this processing; however, some recent experiments by T. Tanabe and co-workers (1974, 1975) have uncovered an area of the brain, involved in olfaction, containing many neurons that respond to only a few odorant molecules. This area, which is called the **lateral postero-orbital frontal cortex (LPOF),** is located on the underside of the frontal lobe.

Tanabe showed by both behavioral and electrophysiological methods that the LPOF is important in olfaction. His behavioral test was simple. He impregnated two small pieces of bread with different odors and gave one of them a bitter taste. When each piece was given to a monkey, the monkey first smelled each piece and then ate it. But after determining which smell was associated with the bitter taste, the monkey was able to avoid the bitter piece of bread, solely on the basis of its smell, 81 percent of the time. Removal of the LPOF, however, reduced the ability from 81 percent to 26 percent. This large decrease in performance did not occur with the removal of other cortical olfactory areas.

Tanabe's electrophysiological results, shown in Figure 15.13, are of particular interest to us, because they show the degree to which eight different odorants caused neural responses in the olfactory bulb, amygdala, and LPOF. Each bar indicates the percentage of neurons responding to the number of odorants indicated on the horizontal axis. Note that few of the cells in the olfactory bulb and amygdala respond to only one odor, whereas half of the cells in the LPOF respond to only one odor. Neurons in the LPOF, then, are tuned to respond to much more specific odorants than are neurons in lower centers. From these results, it is tempting to draw an analogy between neurons in the LPOF and neurons, such as the hypercomplex cells of the visual system, that respond only to very specific visual stimuli. Such analogies, however, cannot be taken too seriously until we have more experimental evidence about information processing in the olfactory system.

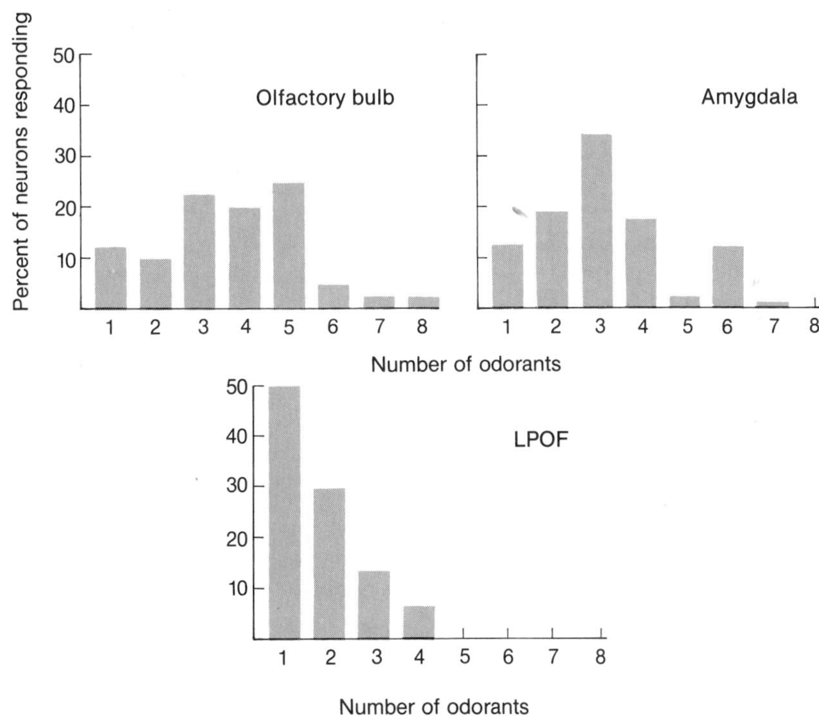

Figure 15.13 Histograms showing how neurons in the olfactory bulb, amygdala, and LPOF respond to eight different odorants. (From Tanabe et al., 1975.)

TASTE

Taste is usually thought of as a partner to smell, since they work together at mealtimes. As we put food into our mouths, the nose, conveniently located just above, adds flavor to our food. To demonstrate this to yourself, you have only to hold your nose while eating. When you do this, it becomes difficult to distinguish a piece of raw potato from an apple, and much of the flavor of meats, fruits, butter, and coffee is eliminated (Geldard, 1972).

But taste is a sense in its own right, with its own properties, many quite different than smell, and the pleasure we derive from eating owes a lot to the taste receptors on our tongue and in our mouth. Adding a little salt or sugar to food may affect its smell only slightly but can have a large effect on its taste. Interestingly enough, taste is perhaps the most public of all our senses, in that people often taste things together and often share their taste experiences as they eat: "This chicken would taste better with a little more salt," "I can't stand liver," "Your apple pie is fantastic, mom." When we share our taste experiences like this, we are emphasizing the *affective* aspect of taste; that is, we usually label tastes as pleasant or unpleasant, and these labels affect which foods we choose to eat and which foods we avoid.

Many factors influence how foods taste to us: how much we've already eaten, our past experiences with different foods, our genetic makeup, the food we've just finished eating, and our nutritional state, among others. As we have for the other senses in this book, we want to consider the physiological workings of the sense of taste, but first let's consider some of the factors that influence which foods we seek out and which we avoid.

Factors Influencing Food Intake

Internal State of the Organism

A restaurant near my house has fantastic banana cream pie. The first forkful is always great, and I find myself wishing they had given me a bigger piece. By the last forkful, however, the thrill is gone. I've had enough. This is a phenomenon that Cabanac (1971, 1979) calls **alliesthesia,** changed sensation. Our reaction to a taste stimulus may be positive when we first taste it, but this positive response may become negative after we've eaten for a while. To illustrate this effect, Cabanac describes an experiment in which he had people rate the pleasantness of a sugar solution. If they taste a sample and then spit it out, the sugar continues to get positive ratings over many samplings. If, however, people drink the sample each time they taste it, the originally pleasant sugar solution becomes unpleasant, and eventually the people refuse to drink any more. According to Cabanac, this experiment, and many others with similar results, illustrates that a given stimulus can be pleasant or unpleasant, depending upon signals from inside the body.

Genetics and Past Experience

It is generally assumed that many taste preferences are genetically determined. That is, people are born with a built-in preference for sweet foods, find bitter and sour foods unpleasant, and like salty foods at low concentrations but dislike them at high concentrations. There are good reasons for these built-in preferences. Sweetness usually indicates the presence of sugar, an important source of energy, whereas sourness or bitterness often indicates the presence of dangerous substances, such as poisons that result in sickness or death.

While people undoubtedly are born with built-in preferences for certain tastes, it is also true that not everyone likes the same foods. Could it be that different people taste things differently? In fact, there is evidence that people do taste things differently and that some of these differences could be due to genetic differences between people. One of the most well documented genetic effects in taste involves people's ability to taste the bitter substance **phenyltiocarbamide (PTC).** Linda Bartoshuk (1980) describes the discovery of this PTC effect:

> The different reactions to PTC were discovered accidentally in 1932 by Arthur L. Fox, a chemist working at the E. I. DuPont deNemours Company in Wilmington, Delaware. Fox had prepared some PTC, and when he poured the compound into a bottle, some of the dust escaped into the air. One of his colleagues complained about the bitter taste of the dust, but Fox, much closer to the material, noticed nothing. Albert

Box 15.2 Green Mashed Potatoes?

If, when you were younger, you discovered the magic of your mother's food coloring, you may have created, as I once did, such exotic foods as green mashed potatoes or blue applesauce. If you then tried to interest someone in eating your concoctions, you probably found that people are not enthusiastic about trying strangely colored foods.

The appearance of food plays an important role in people's attitudes about food, as evidenced by the large sums of money spent to produce appetizing-looking pictures of food to put on the cans, jars, and boxes that package the food. Another connection between vision and food is illustrated by the statement "That food looks good," which, translated, means "That food looks as if it would taste good." This statement is interesting, because it implies that we can decide if a particular food tastes good, based only on its appearance. Though most people would not go so far as to agree with this statement, most would agree that the appearance of their food does influence its desirability. However, only a few studies have been published on how color, one of the most important aspects of a food's appearance, influences a food's flavor.

Karl Duncker (1939) (whose work on induced movement was discussed in Chapter 11) found that subjects think that white chocolate candy tastes "milkier" and "less chocolatey" than brown chocolate candy. Experiments on how color affects the taste of liquids have shown that the color of a liquid can influence a subject's ability both to identify the flavor of the liquid and to detect small differences in taste between two liquids. For example, when 200 pharmacy students were asked to identify the taste of various colored syrups, most of them were unable to accurately identify the actual flavor when the syrups were colorless, and most had an even more difficult time when inappropriate colors were added to the syrups (Kanig, 1955).

The influence of color on taste has also been demonstrated in an experiment in which subjects were presented with two solutions of pear nectar, one containing 5.0 percent sucrose and the other containing 5.2 percent sucrose, and were asked to judge which was sweeter. When the solutions had no color, 65 percent of the subjects' responses were correct, but when the solutions had different colors (red, yellow, green, or blue), the accuracy of the responses dropped to 50 percent.

Similar results occurred when citric acid was added to one sample and subjects were asked to judge which of two samples was more sour. In this test, subjects were correct 81 percent of the time for uncolored samples and 65 percent of the time for colored samples. These results indicate that it is easier to judge small differences in flavor when both samples are colorless than when they are two different colors (Pangborn & Hansen, 1963). Apparently, our sense of flavor is influenced not only by our tongue and nose but also by our eyes!

F. Blakeslee, an eminent geneticist of the era, was quick to pursue this observation. At a meeting of the American Association for the Advancement of Science (AAAS) in 1934, Blakeslee prepared an exhibit that dispensed PTC crystals to 2,500 of the conferees. The results: 28 percent of them described it as tasteless, 66 percent as bitter, and 6 percent as having some other taste.

People who can taste PTC are described as *tasters,* and those who cannot are called ***nontasters*** (or **taste blind** to PTC). Molly L. Hall, Bartoshuk, and co-workers (1975) have found that most people who can taste PTC also perceive a bitter taste in caffeine at much lower concentrations than do nontasters, and Bartoshuk (1979) has reported a similar result for the artificial sweetener saccharin. That some people are much more sensitive to the bitter tastes of caffeine and saccharin than others is particularly interesting, since these two substances are found in many common foods. Caffeine makes coffee taste bitter to tasters but has little effect on nontasters, and saccharin, in the concentrations found in soft drinks, tastes two to three times more bitter to tasters than to nontasters. Maybe that's why I find many diet drinks very distasteful, whereas others have no problem drinking them.

Another taste that some people experience but others don't is called the **artichoke effect,** because some people taste water as sweet after eating artichokes. At the same AAAS meeting where Blakeslee studied people's sensitivity to the bitter taste of PTC, he also did an informal experiment on the artichoke effect. A dinner at the AAAS meeting included a salad consisting solely of artichokes and mayonnaise. After eating the artichokes, 60 percent of the diners found that the taste of water was altered, in most cases to sweet, whereas the rest of the diners experienced no effect (Bartoshuk, 1980). According to Bartoshuk, that some people experience this effect, while others do not, suggests that genetics may be behind this difference.

While some individual differences in taste may be due to genetics, others may be due to people's past experiences with different foods. Many Mexicans, for example, like chili peppers that would cause great distress to Americans. And I can vividly remember some of the meals an old roommate of mine from Nigeria used to cook; his liberal seasoning with red pepper seemed to enhance the taste for him, but it did little for me except greatly increase my consumption of water. Perhaps now that I've developed a taste for spicy Szechwan Chinese food, I would be more tolerant of my ex-roommate's red peppers.

Despite much anecdotal evidence that past experience with food can change people's food preferences, there is little experimental evidence that early experience with food results in permanent attachments to a particular food or flavor (Beauchamp & Maller, 1977). A recent experiment by Howard Moskowitz and co-workers (1975), however, does suggest that past experience may shape food preferences. Moskowitz first asked a group of Indian medical students to rate the pleasantness of various compounds and learned that they, like most other people, found sour compounds unpleasant. He then tested some Indians of the Karnataka province and learned that they found both citric acid and quinine to be pleasant tasting. This is quite different from the results with the Indian medical students, who had described the citric acid as having an unpleasant sour taste and quinine as having an unpleasant bitter taste. Moskowitz felt that past experience was the most likely explanation for the Karnataka Indians' strange preference for sour and bitter compounds. Their diet consisted of many sour foods, with the tamarind, a particularly sour fruit, making up a large portion of their diet. Being poor, they ate the tamarind out of necessity and, from constant exposure to this fruit, probably acquired a taste for sour foods. (It should be noted, however, that a genetic explanation for this phenomenon cannot be ruled out.)

Conditioned Taste Aversion

Food preferences can be affected not only by the long-term exposure to foods that results from daily eating patterns, as appears to be the case for the Karnataka Indians, but also by a single pairing of food with sickness. The first experiments to illustrate this effect were done by John Garcia and co-workers (Garcia, Ervin, & Koelling, 1966; Garcia, & Koelling, 1966) on rats. In a typical experiment, Garcia first determined that a rat will drink a sugar solution that tastes sweet to humans. The rats were then fed sugar water containing a poison that made them sick. After recovering from the resulting sickness, the rats would drink little or none of the sugar solution that, before being paired with sickness, they drank in large quantities. This avoidance of a taste after it is paired with sickness is called **conditioned taste aversion.**

Why do the rats avoid the sugar water after it is paired with sickness? One possibility is that pairing sugar water with sickness doesn't change the taste of the sugar water; instead, this pairing causes the rats to avoid the sugar taste, because they have learned that sickness follows it. On the other hand, the rats may avoid the sugar water because it takes on an unpleasant taste after they become sick. We cannot answer this question for the rat, since the rat can't tell us what it experiences; however, reports from humans support the idea that conditioned taste aversion actually changes the taste of the substance paired with sickness. A number of years ago, I experienced such an effect when I got sick about a half an hour after drinking one of my favorite drinks, cream soda. Even though I knew that the sickness had no actual connection to the cream soda (I had the 24-hour flu), the taste of the cream soda became associated with feeling sick, and for many years afterward cream soda tasted terrible to me. Other people have made similar observations (Garcia et al., 1974), and it has been shown that children made sick by chemotherapy treatments for cancer will avoid eating the ice cream they had eaten just before their chemotherapy injection (Bernstein, 1978).

Specific Hungers

We've already mentioned that people are born with a preference for certain tastes and that these genetically programmed taste preferences help people seek out food that is high in energy (indicated by their sweet taste) and avoid food that may be poisonous (indicated by their sour or bitter taste). In fact, taste appears to play a major role in regulating the intake of certain substances. For example, rats and people have a **specific hunger** for sodium, a necessary component of their diets. Rats deprived of sodium will increase their sodium intake to make up the deficit, and they use taste to recognize foods that contain sodium (Rozin, 1976).

A most dramatic demonstration that taste regulates this hunger for sodium is M. Nachman's (1963) experiment in which he created a need for salt in a rat by performing an adrenalectomy (removal of the adrenal gland), thereby causing the rat to eat large amounts of lithium chloride, even though this substance is toxic and makes the rat ill. The rat does this because lithium chloride tastes identical to sodium chloride, the substance the rat actually needs to correct the salt deficit created by the adrenalectomy.

Specific hunger for salt, analogous to that found in Nachman's adrenalectomized rats, has been reported in people who suffer from various diseases. In the 1930s, before the condition of specific salt hunger was widely recognized, a child whose adrenal cortex was diseased craved large amounts of salt. In an attempt to find out what caused this craving, the child was hospitalized, only to die after being placed on a standard hospital diet, which didn't satisfy the child's increased need for salt. Addison's disease also increases hunger for salt. A 34-year-old man with this disease was reported to routinely half fill a glass with salt before adding tomato juice and to cover his steak with a one-inch-thick layer of salt (Liphovsky, 1977).

The above examples illustrate some of the genetic, environmental, and biological factors that influence our sense of taste. Undoubtedly, our decision whether or not to ingest a particular food results from a complex interaction of genetically determined, experiential, and physiological influences (Rozin, 1976), and, because of its role in food selection, taste is of great importance in our day-to-day lives. We will now consider the physiological workings of the sense of taste, beginning at the most logical starting place—the tongue.

Structure of the Taste System

The surface of the tongue, shown in the chapter-opening illustration and in Figure 15.14, contains many ridges and valleys, due to the presence of structures called **papillae,** of which there are four kinds: (1) filiform papillae, shaped like cones, are found over the entire surface of the tongue, giving it its rough appearance; (2) fungiform papillae, shaped like mushrooms, are found at the tip and sides of the tongue; (3) foliate papillae are a series of folds along the sides of the middle of the tongue; and (4) circumvallate papillae, shaped like flat mounds surrounded by a trench, are found at the back of the tongue.

All these papillae except the filiform contain **taste buds,** with the human tongue containing a total of about 10,000 taste buds (Bartoshuk, 1971). Since

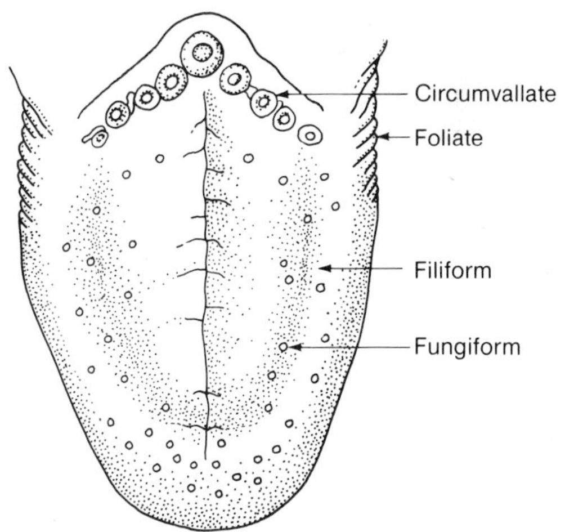

Figure 15.14 The tongue, showing the four different types of papillae.

the filiform papillae contain no taste buds, stimulation of the central part of the tongue, which contains only filiform papillae, causes no taste sensations. Figure 15.15 shows that each taste bud is made up of a number of receptor cells, each of which projects into a taste pore at the top of the bud. At this pore, the taste solution on the tongue contacts the taste cells, to generate the electrical signals that are transmitted along the fibers leaving the taste bud.

Fibers from the front of the tongue travel toward the brain in the **chorda tympani nerve**, and fibers from the back of the tongue travel toward the brain in the **glossopharyngeal nerve**. These nerves transmit signals to the solitary nucleus in the medulla, near the base of the brain (on top of the spinal cord), then to the thalamus and the parietal cortex. As is the case for olfaction, the cortical projections for taste are not precisely known; however, it appears that the central projections for taste are within or close to the tactile projection areas for the tongue in the somatosensory cortex (see Figure 2.11).

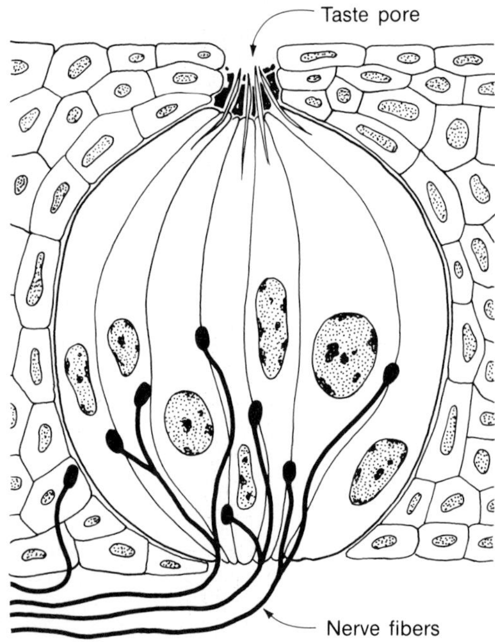

Figure 15.15 A taste bud of the foliate papillae. The taste bud consists of a number of cells, some of which are taste cells and some of which are supporting cells. (Adapted from Murray & Murray, 1970.)

Taste Quality

The Four Basic Tastes

There is somewhat more agreement about taste quality than about odor quality. Though many lists of taste qualities have been proposed over the centuries, almost all have included the four qualities of salty, sour, sweet, and bitter. For example, Aristotle's list of qualities, proposed over 2,000 years ago, included salty, sour, sweet, and bitter plus the tastes astringent, pungent, and harsh, while Zotterman's (1956) list includes salty, sour, sweet, and bitter, plus the taste of water.

One reason for this general agreement about salty, sour, sweet, and bitter is that these qualities are consistently reported by subjects; when tastes such as metallic or alkaline are reported, it is usually found that they result from a combination of smell and taste, rather than from stimulation of the taste buds alone.

Donald McBurney (1969) has applied the method of magnitude estimation (see p. 19, in Chapter 1) to the analysis of taste quality. He first rinses the subject's tongue with water and then flows the taste solution over the tongue for 5 seconds. Subjects are instructed to give magnitude estimates of the intensity of each of the four taste qualities for each solution. When this procedure is followed, some substances have a predominant taste, but many others result in combinations of the four tastes. For example, the compounds sodium chloride (salty), hydrochloric acid (sour), sucrose (sweet), and quinine (bitter) are the closest we can come to substances that each have only one of the four basic tastes, but the compound potassium chloride (KCl) has substantial salty and bitter components, as shown in Figure 15.16. Similarly, sodium nitrate ($NaNO_3$) results in a combined taste of salty, sour, and bitter.

Subjects, therefore, can describe their taste sensations based on these four qualities, and, even if given the option of using additional qualities of their own choice, they will usually stay with the four

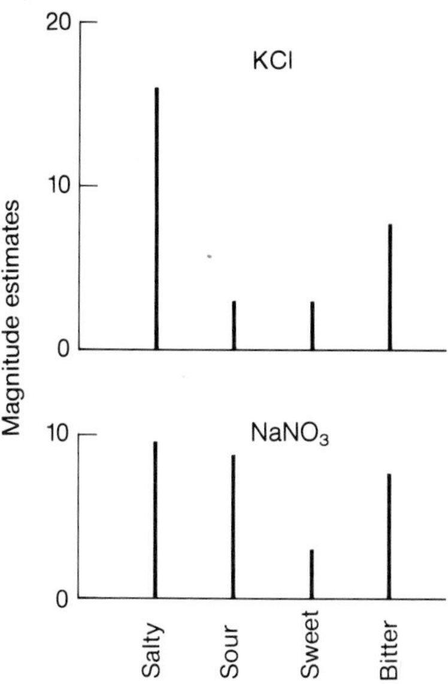

Figure 15.16 Contribution of each of the four basic tastes to the tastes of KCl and $NaNO_3$, is determined by the method of magnitude estimation. The height of the line indicates the size of the magnitude estimate for each basic taste. (From McBurney, 1969.)

basic tastes. Thus, salty, sour, sweet, and bitter appear to be adequate to describe the majority of our taste experiences.

The Taste of Water

Though it has been included in some people's lists of taste qualities, water has usually been considered to be tasteless. However, water can be given a taste by adapting the tongue to various other substances. For example, if water is flowed over the tongue after a salty solution, the water will taste sour or bitter. Adapting to sour or bitter causes a sweet **water taste,** and adapting to sweet causes a bitter water taste (McBurney & Shick, 1971). It is interesting both that adaptation can cause water to have its own taste and that the taste the water takes on is always one or more of the four basic taste qualities. That no new water tastes appear further supports the idea that there is something special about salty, sour, sweet, and bitter.

Physical Properties and Taste Quality

Even though the connections between the physical properties of molecules and taste quality are not clear-cut, there is increasing evidence that specific physical and chemical properties are characteristic of each basic taste. Table 15.2 lists each taste quality and the physical property associated with that quality (Beidler, 1978).

Despite good evidence that each quality depends on different physical properties, the exact physical properties involved for each quality are not precisely known, as is the case for smell. For one thing, the properties listed, especially for sweet and bitter, are very general, and even for sour and salty, for which we have more information, there are unsolved problems. For example, although sourness usually depends on the presence of a charged hydrogen atom (H+), some compounds with large amounts of H+ can be less sour than other compounds with much less H+. This lack of correlation between the amount of H+ and taste quality means that some other property is also involved in determining sourness. Salt poses another interesting problem, because it changes its quality as concentration changes. Thus, as the concentration of potassium chloride (KCl) is increased from low to high, this salt is perceived to be sweet, bitter, and, finally, salty.

We turn now from our discussion of physical properties and taste quality to taste coding.

Table 15.2

Quality	*Relevant physical property*
Sour	Organic and inorganic acids that release a hydrogen ion (H+) in solution. However, not all acids are predominantly sour.
Salty	Organic and inorganic salts. The cation (positively charged component of a molecule; Na+ in NaCl) is most important.
Sweet	Complex organic molecules, such as sugar.
Bitter	There is no good rule for bitter substances. Some are related to the structure of sweet molecules but have different molecular dimensions.

The Code for Taste Quality

Across-Fiber Patterns of Nerve Firing

If Figure 15.17 looks familiar, it's because you saw it in Chapter 2 as part of our discussion of sensory coding. Robert Erickson's demonstration that substances which taste alike to a rat have similar **across-fiber patterns** of nerve activity is excellent evidence for the idea that taste quality is determined by the firing pattern of a large number of fibers rather than by the responses of a few highly specific fibers. Other studies of individual cells in the taste buds of the rat and hamster, and of individual neurons in the taste relay stations in the medulla and thalamus of the rat, indicate that these cells respond to many different stimuli (Kimura & Beidler, 1961; Scott & Erickson, 1971).

More evidence in favor of across-fiber patterning comes from cross adaptation experiments. **Cross adaptation** is the reduction in the taste of one compound after adaptation to another compound. If the tongue is adapted to a compound with a predominant quality, such as sodium chloride (salt), this reduces the intensity of the taste resulting from stimulation by other compounds with the same quality. Thus, adapting the tongue to sodium chloride reduces the saltiness of other substances, while leaving other taste qualities unchanged.

The importance of cross adaptation is that the degree to which adaptation to one compound decreases the response to another tells us the degree to which these compounds share similar mechanisms. This point is best illustrated by looking at the results of an experiment done by David Smith and Marion Frank (1972). They electrophysiologically measured cross adaptation for a large number of salts in the chorda tympani nerve of the rat, by first determining the magnitude of the nerve's response to a test salt, then adapting the rat's tongue with an adapting salt, and, finally, remeasuring the nerve's response to the test salt.

Smith and Frank measured large amounts of cross adaptation between some compounds. For example, adapting with NaCl reduces the response to

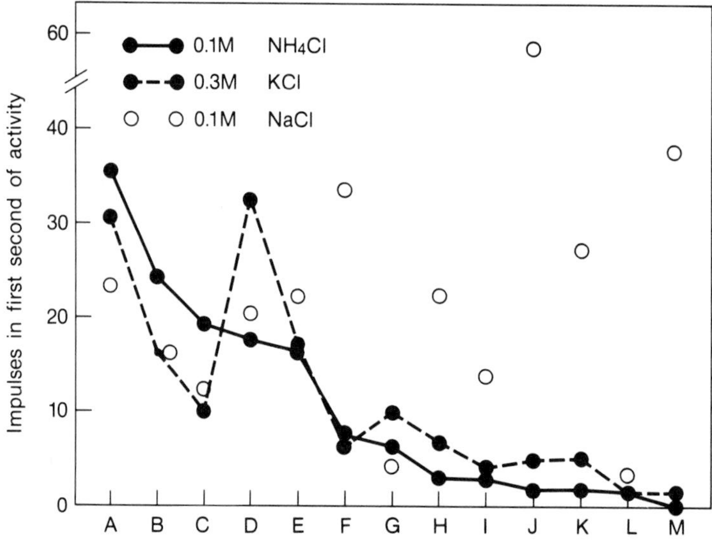

Figure 15.17 Across-fiber patterns of response to three salts in the rat. Each letter on the horizontal axis indicates a different single fiber. NaCl and KCl have similar across-fiber patterns and taste similar to each other. NaCl has a different across-fiber pattern and tastes different from Na_4Cl (see p. 59). (From Erickson, 1963.)

NaBr (sodium bromide) to zero. However, they found little cross adaptation between other compounds; adapting with NaCl had almost no effect on the response to KCl. To test the idea that greater cross adaptation between two compounds means that the compounds share similar mechanisms, Smith and Frank compared their measured amount of cross adaptation for each pair of salts to the across-fiber patterns of nerve firing for the same salts, as measured by Erickson (1963). This comparison indicated that the greater the cross adaptation between the two salts, the more similar their across-fiber patterns; thus, if two salts cross adapt well, they also cause many of the same nerve fibers to fire, and if they don't cross adapt well, they share few nerve fibers in common.

So far we have talked only about adapting the tongue to salt and then presenting another salt. What about adapting with a salty compound and then presenting a bitter compound? In general, adapting with a substance with a predominant quality, such as sodium chloride (salty), has little or no effect on the taste of a substance with a different predominant quality, such as quinine (bitter). The failure to cross adapt in these situations supports the idea that the four different taste qualities are caused by different mechanisms.

Labeled Lines

An alternative to the hypothesis that taste quality is coded by across-fiber patterning is the idea that different taste qualities are signaled by activity in specific nerve fibers. That is, the quality salty is signaled by activity in "salty fibers," sourness is signaled by activity in "sour fibers," and so on. This method of signaling taste quality is called **labeled lines,** because each nerve fiber is labeled as corresponding to a particular taste quality, in much the same way as different fibers in the skin correspond to specific qualities such as "warm," "cold," "touch," and "pain" (see pp. 88–90, in Chapter 4).

You might think at first that labeled lines would be an unlikely possibility for the sense of taste, because we saw above that a particular fiber rarely fires to only one quality, with most fibers responding to a number of the four basic tastes. However, recent evidence indicates that there are four different types of fibers, one for each basic taste quality. Each type of fiber responds best to one of the basic qualities and may also respond to one or more of the other qualities, but if we know to which quality a fiber best responds, we can usually predict the magnitude of its response to the other qualities. That is, each fiber has a fairly predictable response profile, as shown in Figure 15.18. This figure shows the response profiles of five "NaCl-best" fibers and five "HCl-best" fibers in the hamster. The NaCl-best fibers respond best to NaCl, respond less well to HCl, and respond only slightly or not at all to sucrose and quinine. The HCl-best fibers respond best to HCl, less well to NaCl, slightly to quinine, and slightly or not at all to sucrose. "Quinine-best" and "sucrose-best" fibers also have predictable response profiles.

The idea of labeled lines explains the fact, mentioned earlier, that many substances elicit a mixture of the four basic tastes. For example, a predominately salty substance might also have some sour and some bitter taste. According to the labeled line theory, the salty substance would cause vigorous firing in the "salt-best" fibers, which would result in a strong perception of saltiness. However, the salty substance would also cause smaller responses in the "sour-best" and "bitter-best" fibers, and the activity in these fibers would add slight sour and bitter tastes to the salty compound (Bartoshuk, 1978).

Additional evidence for the idea of labeled lines has come from recordings in higher animals such as the monkey, which appears to contain some fibers that respond only to specific stimuli, an example of which is shown in Figure 15.19 (Sato et al., 1975). This fiber responds poorly to sodium chloride, hydrochloric acid, and quinine but responds well to sucrose.

At present, it is premature to decide between across-fiber patterning and labeled lines for the sense of taste, because there is good evidence for both. The ultimate answer most likely will involve some combination of these two ideas. As we stated in Chapter 2: "The brain probably uses information from specifically tuned neurons *and* from the firing pattern of many neurons. . . ." While individual cells provide information about the nature of the stimulus, the overall firing pattern of many cells enables the brain to specify the stimulus more precisely.

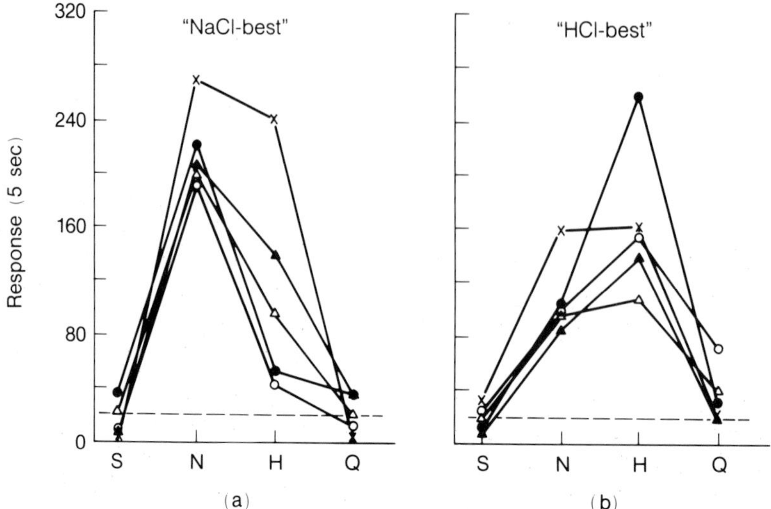

Figure 15.18 Response profiles of (a) five "NaCl-best" fibers and (b) five "HCl-best" fibers in the hamster. The letters on the horizontal axis stand for sucrose (S), sodium chloride (N), hydrogen chloride (H), and quinine (Q). The numbers on the vertical axis indicate the number of nerve impulses generated by each of these stimuli during the first 5 seconds of the response. (From Frank, 1973.)

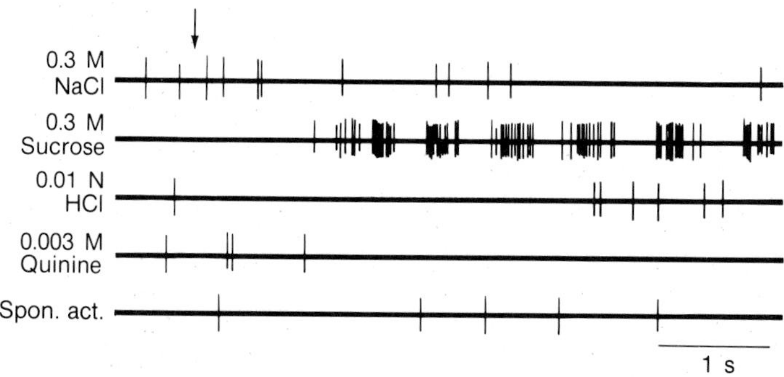

Figure 15.19 Response of a single fiber in the monkey's chorda tympani nerve to salt, sucrose, hydrochloric acid, and quinine. The bottom record indicates the rate of spontaneous activity. The arrow above the record for NaCl indicates the time of application of the stimuli. (From Sato et al., 1975.)

Summary

Olfaction

1. In our society we tend to avoid many smells, perhaps because the sense of smell is capable of eliciting strong reactions.
2. The idea that human smell receptors are much less sensitive than those of other animals is not true. It takes only one molecule of odorant to excite a human's olfactory receptor. Many animals have a keen sense of smell because they have a greater number of receptors than humans.
3. The large difference thresholds for olfactory

intensity, reported in some experiments, result from the difficulty in precisely controlling the concentrations of substances used as stimuli. When odorant concentrations are precisely controlled, the difference threshold for smell rivals the difference thresholds for vision and hearing.

4. When we have trouble identifying odors, this trouble results not from a deficiency in our olfactory system but from an inability to retrieve the odor's name from our memory.

5. Smell potentially plays some role in human communication.

6. Many animals release chemicals called pheromones, which, when sensed by other animals of the same species, trigger physiological or behavioral effects in these animals.

7. The receptors for smell are located in the olfactory mucosa. Contact of odorant molecules with the cilia of the receptors generates an electrical signal that travels to the olfactory bulb and then to higher olfactory centers.

8. Two of the problems in smell research are the lack of a good classification scheme for odor quality and our inexact knowledge of how the physical properties of odor molecules are linked to odor quality.

9. Two systems of classifying odors are Henning's odor prism and Amoore's stereochemical classification scheme. Neither system, however, has been generally accepted as being a fully adequate description of odor quality.

10. Amoore has demonstrated a relationship between the shape of a molecule and its odor. That two molecules almost identical in shape can differ greatly in odor, however, indicates that the relationship between molecular shape and odor quality is not perfect.

11. Most theories of olfactory transduction hypothesize that odorant molecules cause some change in the property of the receptor membrane, thus allowing sodium or potassium to flow across the membrane. At this point, however, these theories are speculative and backed by minimal evidence.

12. Most neurons in the olfactory system fire to a number of different odorants. This leaves open the possibility that the code for odor quality is determined by across-fiber patterning. However, behavioral work is needed before a strong case can be made for across-fiber patterning in the olfactory system.

13. Experiments in which small areas of the olfactory mucosa of the salamander were stimulated show that receptors in different areas of the mucosa are maximally sensitive to different chemicals.

14. Mozell's chromatographic theory states that odorant molecules interact with the olfactory mucosa in a way similar to the way chemicals interact with a gas chromatograph. Molecules with long retention times maximally stimulate the front of the mucosa, while molecules with short retention times maximally stimulate the back of the mucosa. This theory is supported by the results of a number of experiments.

15. Long-term exposure of animals to odorants causes degeneration of the olfactory bulb, with the pattern of degeneration being different for different odorants. Experiments in which rats are injected with radioactively labeled 2-deoxyglucose also indicate that different odorants result in different patterns of radioactivity in the olfactory bulb. In both the degeneration and the 2-DG experiments, there is a large area of overlap between the patterns for different odorants.

16. The results of both receptor and olfactory bulb experiments point to a much more diffuse type of coding in the olfactory system than in the other sensory systems.

17. A recently discovered olfactory center in the frontal lobe contains cells that each respond to fewer odorants than cells in other olfactory areas. This area, therefore, may represent a higher level of information processing, in which detectors for specific odors are present.

Taste

1. The internal state of the organism influences food intake. A given stimulus can be pleasant or unpleasant, depending upon signals from inside the body.
2. Many taste preferences are genetically determined. There is evidence that different people taste things differently and that some of these differences may be due to genetic differences between people.
3. Some differences in taste preferences may be due to people's past experiences with different foods.
4. Food preferences can be affected by a single pairing of food with sickness. This is called conditioned taste aversion.
5. A food's color can have a small effect on the food's taste.
6. Taste appears to play a major role in regulating the intake of substances essential for survival, such as salt.
7. The tongue contains four different kinds of papillae. Taste buds, each of which is made up of a number of taste cells, are found on all these papillae except the filiform. Fibers from the taste buds travel toward the brain in the chorda tympani nerve (for buds near the front of the tongue) or in the glossopharyngeal nerve (for buds near the back of the tongue).
8. Most taste researchers agree that there are four basic taste qualities: salty, sour, sweet, and bitter.
9. Water can be given a taste by first adapting the tongue to salty, sour, sweet, or bitter and then flowing water over the tongue.
10. Specific physical and chemical properties are characteristic of each basic taste, but the exact properties involved have not yet been precisely determined.
11. Psychophysical cross adaptation experiments indicate that if the tongue is adapted to a compound with a predominant quality, this reduces the intensity of the taste resulting from stimulation by other compounds having the same quality. However, adaptation with one quality has little effect on the intensity of a different quality.
12. Electrophysiological cross adaptation experiments indicate that the greater the cross adaptation between two salts, the more similar their across-fiber firing patterns. This finding supports the idea that the greater the amount of cross adaptation between two substances, the greater the similarity of the mechanisms responsible for their tastes.
13. Some evidence indicates that taste quality may be coded by an across-fiber pattern code. There is also evidence, however, consistent with the idea that taste quality is signaled by activity in specific nerve fibers. This method of signaling taste quality is called labeled lines, because each nerve fiber is labeled as corresponding to a particular taste quality.

Glossary

Across-fiber pattern In taste, the idea that different taste qualities are signaled by the firing pattern of a large number of nerve fibers. (428)

Alliesthesia "Changed sensation." Our reaction to a taste stimulus may be positive when we first experience it, but after repeated presentations our reactions may become negative. (422)

Artichoke effect Some people taste water as sweet after eating artichokes. (423)

Chorda tympani nerve A nerve that contains fibers that travel from the front of the tongue to the brain. (426)

Chromatographic theory of smell Max Mozell's idea that odorant molecules interact with the olfactory mucosa in a way similar to the way chemicals interact with a gas chromatograph. (418)

Conditioned taste aversion An aversion to the taste of a food due to pairing of the food's taste with sickness. (424)

Cross adaptation In taste, flowing one substance over the tongue affects a person's perception of another substance with the same quality. For example, adaptation with one salt might raise the threshold for detecting another salt. Adaptation across qualities, such as salt versus bitter, usually does not occur. (428)

Gas chromatograph A device that separates the components of a mixture of gases and accurately measures the vapor concentration of each one. (405)

Glossopharyngeal nerve A nerve that contains fibers that travel from the back of the tongue toward the brain. (426)

Labeled lines In taste, the idea that different taste qualities are signaled by activity in specific nerve fibers. (429)

Lateral postero-orbital frontal cortex (LPOF) An area on the underside of the frontal lobe of the cortex that may be involved in processing olfactory information. (421)

Macrosmatic Possessing a keen sense of smell. (404)

Menstrual synchrony Women who live together often have menstrual periods that begin at approximately the same time. (408)

Microsmatic Lacking a keen sense of smell. (404)

Odor prism Henning's system for classifying odors. (413)

Olfactometer A device that presents olfactory stimuli with great precision. (406)

Olfactory bulb The structure that receives signals directly from the olfactory receptors. (410)

Papillae Ridges and valleys on the tongue, some of which contain taste buds. There are four types of papillae: filiform, fungiform, foliate, and circumvallate. (425)

Phenyltiocarbamide (PTC) A bitter substance that some people *(tasters)* can taste and others *(nontasters)* can't. (422)

Pheromone A chemical released by an animal that causes specific physiological or behavioral reactions in another animal of the same species. (409)

Primer A pheromone that triggers a chain of long-lasting physiological (usually hormonal) effects in an animal. (409)

Releaser A pheromone that triggers an immediate reaction in another animal. (409)

Specific hunger A genetically programmed taste preference that helps an organism seek out food that meets specific nutritional needs. (425)

Stereochemical theory of odor Amoore's theory, which postulates that there are different molecular shapes for different odor qualities and that there are sites on the olfactory receptors shaped to accept only molecules with the correct shape. (414)

Taste blind With reference to the chemical PTC, those who cannot detect its bitter taste. (423)

Taste bud A structure that contains a number of taste receptors. (425)

Water taste Water can be given a taste by adapting the tongue to other substances. (427)

Appendix A

Signal Detection Theory

In this appendix, we will discuss the theoretical basis for the signal detection experiment described in Chapter 1. Our purpose will be to explain the theoretical bases underlying two ideas: (1) the percentage of hits and false alarms depends on the subject's criterion, and (2) a subject's sensitivity to a stimulus is indicated by the shape of the subject's ROC curve. We will begin by describing two of the key concepts of signal detection theory (SDT): signal and noise. (See Swets, 1964.)

Signal and Noise

To understand signal detection theory, we have to introduce the concepts of *signal* and *noise*. The signal is the stimulus presented to the subject. Thus, in the signal detection experiment of Chapter 1, the signal is the tone. The noise is all the other stimuli in the environment, and, since the signal is usually very faint, noise can sometimes be mistaken for the signal. Seeing what appears to be a flash of light in a completely dark room is an example of visual noise. Seeing a flash of light when there is none is what we have been calling a false alarm, which, according to signal detection theory, is caused by the noise. In the experiment in Chapter 1, hearing a tone on a trial in which no tone was presented is an example of auditory noise.

Let's now consider a typical signal detection experiment, in which a signal is presented on some trials and no signal is presented on the other trials. According to signal detection theory, rather than talk in terms of presenting a signal or no signal, we talk about presenting signal plus noise (S + N) or noise (N). That is, the noise is always present, and on some trials we add a signal. Either condition can result in the perceptual effect of hearing a tone, with a false alarm resulting if the subject indicates that she heard a tone on a noise trial and a hit resulting if the subject indicates that she heard a tone on a signal-plus-noise trial. Now that we have defined signal and noise, we need to introduce the idea of probability distributions for noise and signal plus noise.

Probability Distributions

Figure A.1 shows two probability distributions. The probability distribution on the left represents the probability that a given perceptual effect will be caused by noise (N), and the one on the right represents the probability that a given perceptual effect will be caused by signal plus noise (S + N). The key to understanding these distributions is to realize that "perceptual effect" is plotted on the horizontal axis. The perceptual effect is what the subject expe-

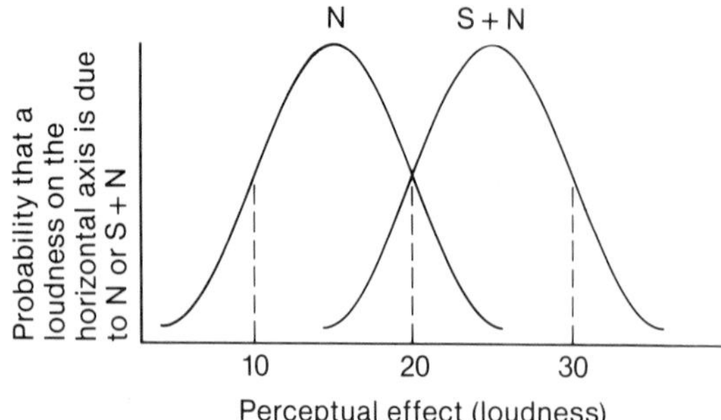

Figure A.1 Probability distributions for noise alone (N), on the left, and for signal plus noise (S + N), on the right. The probability that any given perceptual effect is caused by the noise (no signal is presented) or by the signal plus noise (signal is presented) can be determined by finding the value of the perceptual effect on the horizontal axis and extending a vertical line up from that value. The place where that line intersects the (N) and (S + N) distributions indicates the probability that the perceptual effect was caused by (N) or by (S + N).

riences on each trial; so, for an experiment in which the subject is asked to indicate whether or not a tone is present, the perceptual effect is the perceived loudness of the tone. Remember that in an SDT experiment the tone always has the same *intensity*. The *loudness* of the tone, however, can vary from trial to trial. The subject perceives different loudnesses on different trials, due either to trial-to-trial changes in attention or to the state of the subject's auditory system.

The probability distributions tell us what the chances are that a given loudness of tone is due to (N) or to (S + N). For example, let's assume that a subject hears a tone with a loudness of 10, on one of the trials of a signal detection experiment. By extending a vertical dashed line up from 10 on the "perceptual effect" axis in Figure A.1, we see that the probability that a loudness of 10 is due to (S + N) is extremely low, since the distribution for (S + N) is almost zero at a loudness of 10. There is, however, a fairly high probability that a loudness of 10 is due to (N), since the (N) distribution is fairly high at this point.

Let's now assume that, on another trial, the subject hears a tone with a loudness of 20. The probability distributions in Figure A.1 indicate that when the tone's loudness is 20, it is equally probable that this loudness is due to (N) or to (S + N). We can also see from Figure A.1 that a tone with a perceived loudness of 30 would have a high probability of being caused by (S + N) and only a small probability of being caused by (N).

Now that we understand the curves of Figure A.1, we can see the problem the subject confronts. On each trial, she has to decide whether no tone (N) was present or whether a tone (S + N) was present. However, the overlap in the probability distributions for (N) and (S + N) makes this judgment difficult. As we saw above, it is equally probable that a tone with a loudness of 20 is due to (N) or to (S + N). So, on a trial in which the subject hears a tone with a loudness of 20, how does she decide whether or not the signal was presented? According to signal detection theory, the decision the subject arrives at depends on the location of her *criterion*.

The Criterion

We can see how the criterion affects the subject's response by looking at Figure A.2. In this figure, we have labeled three different criteria: liberal (L), neutral (N), and conservative (C). Remember from our discussion in Chapter 1 that we can cause subjects to adopt these different criteria by means of

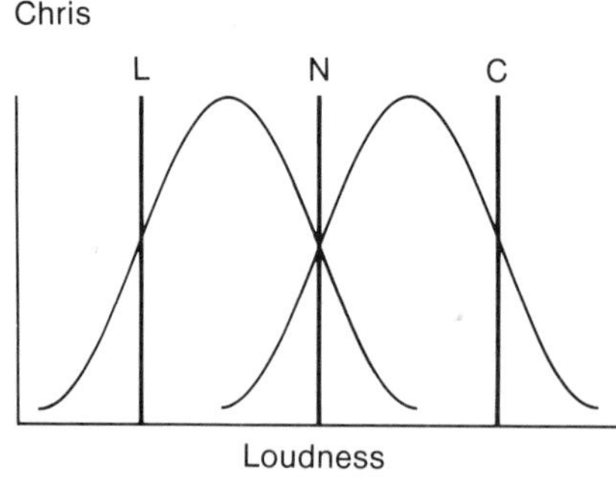

Figure A.2 The same probability distributions from Figure A.1, showing three criteria: liberal (L), neutral (N), and conservative (C). When a subject adopts a criterion, he or she uses the following decision rule: respond "yes" (I detect the stimulus) if the perceptual effect is greater than the criterion; respond "no" (I do not detect the stimulus) if the perceptual effect is less than the criterion (see text for details).

different payoffs. The key to understanding these criteria is to remember that once the subject adopts a criterion, he or she uses the following rule to decide how to respond on a given trial: if the perceptual effect is greater than (to the right of) the criterion, say "yes, the tone was present"; if the perceptual effect is less than (to the left of) the criterion, say "no, the tone was not present." Let's consider how different criteria influence the subject's hits and false alarms.

Liberal Criterion

To determine how criterion L will affect the subject's hits and false alarms, let's consider what happens when we present (N) and when we present (S + N). (1) Present (N): since most of the probability distribution for (N) falls to the right of the criterion, the chances are good that presenting (N) will result in a loudness to the right of the criterion. This means that the probability of saying "yes" when (N) is presented is high; therefore, the probability of a false alarm is high. (2) Present (S + N): since the entire probability distribution for (S + N) falls to the right of the criterion, the chances are excellent that presenting (S + N) will result in a loudness to the right of the criterion. Thus, the probability of saying "yes" when the signal is presented is high; therefore, the probability of a hit is high. Since criterion L results in high false alarms and high hits, adopting that criterion will result in point L on the ROC curve in Figure A.4.

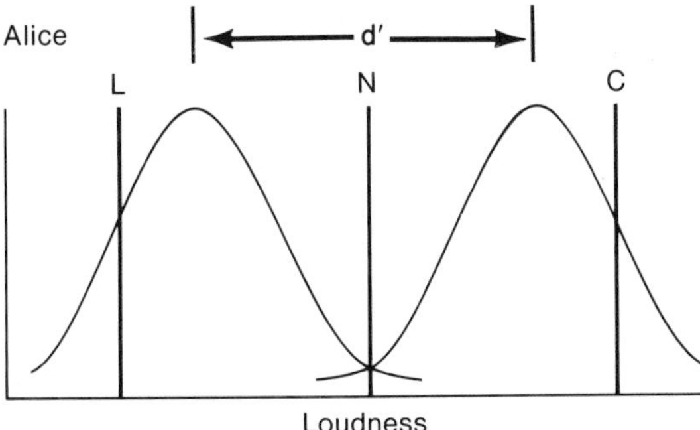

Figure A.3 Probability distributions for a subject who is extremely sensitive to the signal. The effect of increasing the subject's sensitivity is to move the (S + N) distribution to the right (see text for details).

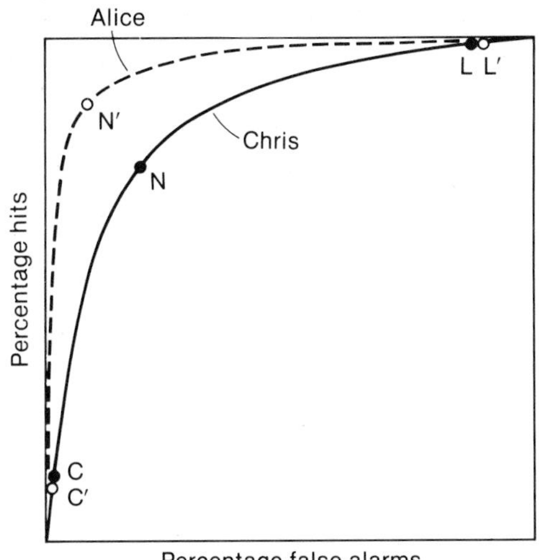

Figure A.4 ROC curves for Chris (solid) and Alice (dashed) (see text for details).

Neutral Criterion

(1) Present (N): the subject will answer "yes" only rarely when (N) is presented, since only a small portion of the (N) distribution falls to the right of the criterion. The false alarm rate, therefore, will be fairly low. (2) Present (S + N): the subject will answer "yes" frequently when (S + N) is presented, since most of the (S + N) distribution falls to the right of the criterion. The hit rate, therefore, will be fairly high (but not as high as for the L criterion). Criterion N results in point N on the ROC curve in Figure A.4.

Conservative Criterion

(1) Present (N): false alarms will be very low, since none of the (N) curve falls to the right of the criterion. (2) Present (S + N): hits will also be low, since only a small portion of the (S + N) curve falls to the right of the criterion. Criterion C results in point C on the ROC curve in Figure A.4.

You can see that when different criteria are applied to the probability distributions of signal detection theory, we generate the ROC curve in Figure A.4. But why are these probability distributions necessary? After all, in Chapter 1 we were able to explain how we got the ROC curve, simply on the basis of common sense. The reason the (N) and (S + N) distributions are important is that, according to signal detection theory, the subject's sensitivity to a stimulus is indicated by the distance (d′) between the peaks of the (N) and (S + N) distributions. With this fact in hand, we can show how the subject's sensitivity to a stimulus affects the shape of the ROC curve.

The Effect of Sensitivity on the ROC Curve

We can understand how the subject's sensitivity to a stimulus affects the shape of the ROC curve by considering what the probability distributions would look like for Alice, a subject with supersensitive hearing. Alice's hearing is so good that a tone which is barely audible to Chris sounds very loud to Alice. If presentation of (S + N) causes Alice to hear a loud tone, this means that Alice's (S + N) distribution should be far to the right, as shown in Figure A.3. In signal detection terms, we would say that Alice's high sensitivity is indicated by the large separation (d′) between the (N) and (S + N) probability distributions. To see how this greater separation between the probability distributions will affect Alice's ROC curve, let's see how she would respond when adopting liberal, neutral, and conservative criteria.

Liberal Criterion

(1) Present (N): high false alarms. (2) Present (S + N): high hits. The liberal criterion, therefore, results in point L′ on the ROC curve of Figure A.4.

Neutral Criterion

(1) Present (N): low false alarms. It is important to note that Alice's false alarms for the neutral criterion will be lower than Chris's false alarms for the neutral criterion, because only a small portion of Alice's (N) distribution falls to the right of the criterion. Compare Alice's situation to Figure A.2, in which some of Chris's (N) distribution is to the right of the neutral criterion. (2) Present (S + N): high hits. It is important to note that Alice's hits will be higher than Chris's, because all of Alice's (S + N) distribution falls to the right of the criterion. Compare Alice's situation to Figure A.2, in which not all of Chris's (S + N) distribution falls to the right of the neutral criterion. The neutral criterion, therefore, results in point N′ on the ROC curve in Figure A.4.

Conservative Criterion

(1) Present (N): low false alarms. (2) Present (S + N): low hits. The conservative criterion, therefore, results in point C′ on the ROC curve.

The difference between the two ROC curves in Figure A.4 is obvious. But before you conclude that the difference between these two ROC curves has anything to do with where we positioned Alice's L, N, and C criteria, see if you can get an ROC curve like Alice's from the two probability distributions of Figure A.2. You will find that no matter where you position the criteria, there is no way that you can get a point like point N′ (with very high hits and very low false alarms) from the curves of Figure A.2. In order to achieve very high hits and very low false alarms, the two probability distributions must be spaced far apart, as in Figure A.3.

Thus, increasing the distance (d′) between the (N) and (S + N) probability distributions changes the shape of the ROC curve. The greater the subject's sensitivity (d′), the more bowed is the ROC curve. In practice, d′ can be determined by comparing the experimentally determined ROC curve to standard ROC curves (see Gescheider, 1976); or, d′ can be calculated from the proportions of hits and false alarms that occur in an experiment, by using a mathematical procedure we will not discuss here. (Though we will not describe the mathematical procedure for calculating d′, we should note that this procedure makes it possible to determine a subject's sensitivity by determining only one data point on an ROC curve.)

Appendix B

What Is a Logarithm?

The logarithm of a number can be determined by looking in a log table, found in most math books, which lists numbers and their logarithms. The numbers in this table are determined from the following definition: *the logarithm of a number is the power to which 10 must be raised to equal that number.* For example, since 10 must be squared to equal 100 ($10^2 = 100$), the log of 100 is 2.0. Using this definition, we can construct the following tables:

Number (n)	$10^? = n$	*log n*
1	$10^0 = 1$	0
10	$10^1 = 10$	1
100	$10^2 = 100$	2
1,000	$10^3 = 1{,}000$	3

Number (n)	$10^? = n$	*log n*
2	$10^{0.3} = 2$	0.3
20	$10^{1.3} = 20$	1.3
200	$10^{2.3} = 200$	2.3
2,000	$10^{3.3} = 2{,}000$	3.3

These tables reveal an important property of logarithms: increasing the logarithm by 1.0 increases the number by a factor of 10. For example, if the log of the intensity of light A is 1.0 and the log of the intensity of light B is 2.0, then light B is 10 times more intense than light A. And if the log of the intensity of light C is 3.0, this light is 10 times more intense than light B and 100 times more intense than light A.

That one log unit represents a factor of 10 means that we can more easily deal with the large intensity ranges encountered by the senses. For example, if the intensity of a light that we can just barely detect in the dark equals 1.0, then the intensity of a 100-watt light bulb equals about 1,000,000,000,000 (Riggs, 1965a)! If, however, we convert these intensities to "log intensities," then the intensity at the threshold in the dark becomes 0 (log 1.0 = 0), and the intensity of our light bulb becomes 12. This conversion of the original intensity range of 1.0 to 1,000,000,000,000 into the log intensity range of 0 to 12 enables us to plot a graph in which we can represent the entire intensity range of seeing, without making the intensity axis of our graph unreasonably long.

Appendix C

Contrast Perception and Fourier Analysis

The idea that we perceive different spatial frequencies by means of a number of channels, each of which responds to a narrow range of frequencies, has found favor among many (though not all) sensory psychologists and physiologists. Some of the researchers who subscribe to the idea of frequency channels feel that the visual system may use these channels to help carry out something called a Fourier analysis of the stimulus. In order to understand Fourier analysis, we need to introduce Fourier's theorem.

Fourier's Theorem

Fourier's theorem was developed in the 1800s by French mathematician J. B. Fourier (pronounced Four-yay). Fourier's theorem states that any waveform (such as a square wave) can be broken down into a number of sine-wave components. It also follows from Fourier's theorem that any waveform can be synthesized by adding together its sine-wave components. Rather than introduce the complex mathematical formulas that Fourier developed, we will illustrate how Fourier's theorem works, by showing how a square wave can be constructed from a number of sine waves.

Our goal is to synthesize a square wave from a number of sine waves. This process, which is called *Fourier synthesis,* is carried out as shown in Figure C.1.

1. Start with a sine wave (a), with an amplitude 0.785 times that of the square wave we want to synthesize, and with a frequency equal to that of the square wave. This sine wave is called the *fundamental.*
2. Add to this sine wave another sine wave (b), with an amplitude equal to one-third the amplitude of the fundamental, and with a frequency three times the frequency of the fundamental. This sine wave is called the *third harmonic.*
3. When we add the fundamental (a) and third harmonic (b) together, positioning the two sine waves so that the trough of the fundamental is lined up with one of the peaks of the third harmonic, as indicated by the dashed line, we get curve (c). Notice that curve (c) is beginning to look like a square wave.
4. Add to curve (c) a sine wave (d), with an amplitude equal to one-fifth the amplitude of the fundamental, and with a frequency five

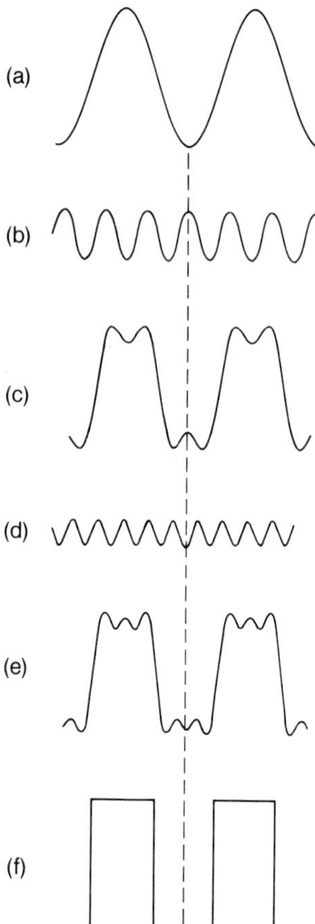

Figure C.1 Fourier synthesis of a square wave from a number of sine waves. Adding together the fundamental (a) and third harmonic (b) results in wave (c). Then adding the fifth harmonic (d) results in wave (e). The addition of each new harmonic brings the wave closer and closer to a square wave, until, after a few more harmonics are added, the square wave at (f) results. The dashed line is included to emphasize that these sine waves must be lined up correctly if a square wave is to result. For example, the peak of one of the waves of the third harmonic (b) must be lined up with the trough of the fundamental (a).

times the frequency of the fundamental. This sine wave is called the *fifth harmonic.*

5. When we add curves (c) and (d), we get curve (e), which looks closer to a square wave than curve (c).

To make our wave look even more like a square wave, we would add the seventh and ninth harmonics, and so on (you have probably noticed that to synthesize a square wave, we use only the odd harmonics). Every time we add a new harmonic, the result gets closer and closer to a square wave, until we eventually reach the square wave (f).

This demonstration illustrates Fourier's idea that a square wave is made up of a number of sine waves. But what does this have to do with contrast perception? To answer this question, let's consider an idea first proposed by Fergus Campbell (working with John Robson) in the 1960s.

Fergus Campbell Gives a Talk

One day in 1966, when I was a graduate student at Brown University, Fergus Campbell, a physiologist from the University of Cambridge, paid a visit to the psychology department and gave a very interesting talk. He presented the thesis that the visual system performs an analysis on the light entering the eye. Campbell suggested that the visual system responds to a square-wave grating by responding to the spatial frequencies of its component sine waves. At the time, the idea that the visual system could perform such a mathematical analysis of the stimulus seemed rather far-fetched, but Campbell presented some persuasive evidence to back up his idea. This evidence, plus work by other researchers, has made the idea that the visual system performs a Fourier analysis on the stimulus seem more probable now than it seemed in 1966.

One experiment he talked about was subsequently described in a paper by Campbell and John Robson (1968) entitled "Application of Fourier Analysis to the Visibility of Gratings." This experiment involved two gratings, a square-wave grating and a sine-wave grating, each with frequencies of 26 cycles per degree. If the visual system performs a Fourier analysis on these two gratings, then the sine-wave grating would remain unchanged (since, when a sine wave is Fourier analyzed, you end up with the same sine wave); but the square wave would be broken down into sine waves with frequencies of 26 cycles per degree (the fundamental), 78 cycles per degree (the third harmonic), and 130 cycles per degree (the fifth harmonic), as shown in Figure C.2. (There are more harmonics than this, but, as you will see, they turn out to be irrelevant.)

Now, let's look at the contrast sensitivity function (CSF) of Figure 10.20 and consider how the visual system responds to each of the sine waves that make up our sine- and square-wave gratings. Since both gratings are well above threshold, the visual system has no trouble detecting the 26 cycles/degree sine-wave grating and the 26 cycles/degree fundamental of the square-wave grating. However, as you can see from the CSF, the visual system is totally insensitive to the square wave's third and fifth harmonics (78 and 130 cycles/degree). Thus, as far as the visual system is concerned, it sees only the 26 cycles/degree sine wave, which is the square-wave grating's fundamental. Campbell and Robson predicted, therefore, that the square-wave grating should look like the sine-wave grating, and this, in fact, is what happened—the two were indistinguishable.

Our application of Fourier theory to visual gratings tells us that we should be able to tell the difference between the square-wave grating and the sine-wave grating only when some of the square wave's harmonics become visible. We can accomplish this by moving the two gratings closer to the observer. Since a grating's spatial frequency decreases as it is moved closer (see Figure 10.19), we can easily move the two gratings close enough to change their spatial frequencies from 26 cycles/degree to, say, 5 cycles/degree. When we do this, the fundamental of the square wave becomes 5 cycles per

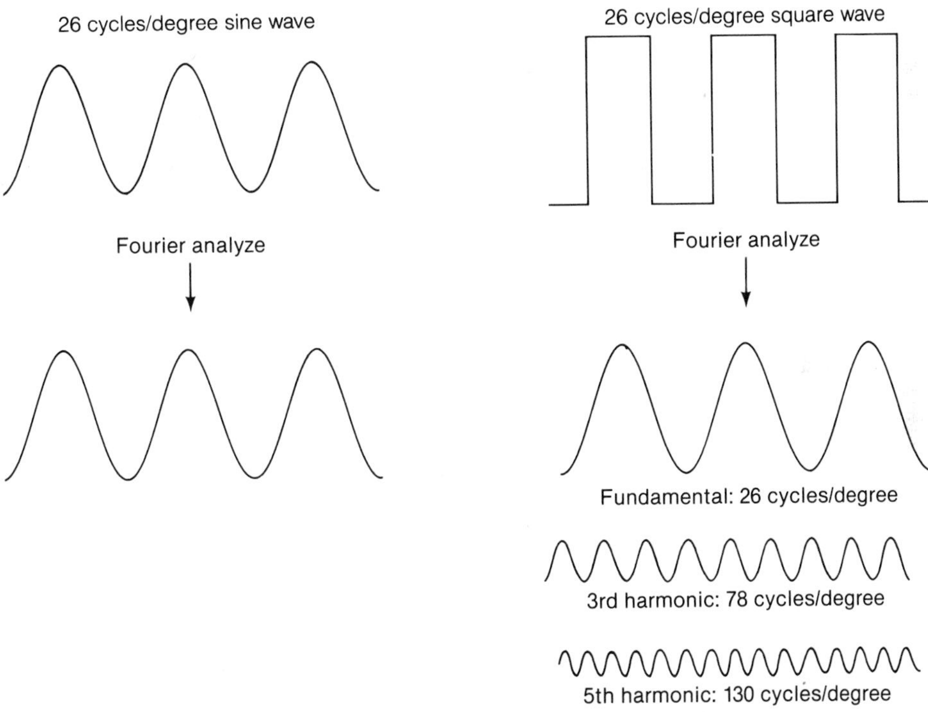

C.2 The sine-wave components of a 26-cycles-per-degree sine wave (left) and a 26-cycles-per-degree square wave (right), as determined by Fourier analysis. When we Fourier analyze the sine wave, we get the same sine wave. However, when we Fourier analyze the square wave, we get a number of sine waves; the fundamental (26 cycles/degree), the third harmonic (78 cycles/degree), and the fifth harmonic (130 cycles/degree) are shown here. If we were to add these three harmonics together, plus the seventh and ninth harmonics, we would end up with a function closely approximating the square wave.

degree, the third harmonic becomes 15 cycles per degree, and the fifth harmonic becomes 25 cycles per degree. Since the visual system will respond to frequencies of 15 and 25 cycles per degree, the square-wave grating now looks different than the sine-wave grating.

Since Campbell and Robson's experiments, other researchers (including Campbell and Robson) have provided further evidence which supports the idea that the visual system may perform a Fourier analysis on the stimulus. Therefore, some researchers have suggested that when an observer looks at a scene, the visual system uses Fourier analysis to break this scene down into its frequency components. According to this idea, just as we broke a square wave down into a number of sine waves of different frequencies, we also break a landscape down into sine waves of different frequencies, which are then signaled by the detectors, or channels, we described in Chapter 10. It is important to note here that, despite evidence that frequency-selective channels exist, it is by no means clear that the visual system actually uses these channels to perform a Fourier analysis on a whole scene; even if it does, we don't know whether, or how, the visual system uses this information to create perceptions. Thus, while we know that the spatial frequency of a stimulus definitely affects our perception, we are still uncertain as to the exact mechanism responsible for this effect.

Appendix D

Speech Production

In Chapter 14, we saw that the phonemes /d/ and /f/ could be described by their place of articulation, manner of articulation, and voicing. The place of articulation, manner of articulation, and voicing are indicated below for all the consonants.

Place of Articulation

For English speakers, there are seven major places of articulation (Clark & Clark, 1977). These places, and the consonants associated with them, are:

1. Bilabial: the two lips together *(p, b, m, w)*.
2. Labiodental: the bottom lip against the upper front teeth *(f, v)*.
3. Dental: the tongue against the upper front teeth (θ, ð).
4. Alveolar: the tip of the tongue against the alveolar ridge (see Figure 14.5) *(t, d, s, z, n, l)*.
5. Palatal: the tongue against the hard palate *(r, š, ž, č, ǰ, ỳ)*.
6. Velar: the tongue against the velum (*k, g*, ŋ).
7. Glottal: the glottis in the throat *(h)*.

Manner of Articulation

The six major categories corresponding to different means of articulation are:

1. Stop (or plosive): complete closure at the point of articulation. For example, /p/ is produced by completely closing both lips and then releasing a slight rush of air *(p, b, t, d, k, g)*.
2. Fricative: a constriction, but not complete closure, that sets up turbulence as air rushes through. Thus, to produce /f/, air is pushed between the upper teeth and lower lip *(f, v,* θ, ð, *š, ž, s, z, h)*.
3. Affricate: complete closure, followed by the rushing of air through a constriction. For example, /c/ as in church *(č, ǰ)*.
4. Nasal: the velum (see Figure 14.5) is lowered so that air passes through the nasal cavity. Try producing the sound /m/ while holding your nose shut. The pressure buildup you feel when you try this is caused by air being pushed into the nasal cavity *(m, n,* ŋ*)*.
5. Lateral: the tongue is shaped so that the main opening is on the sides *(l)*.
6. Semivowel: the tongue is shaped so that the main opening is in the middle *(w, r, y)*.

These different manners of articulation produce different sounds, and these differences can be seen in the sound spectrogram. For example, stops are characterized by a brief silent period, followed by a "pop" or "explosion" when the rush of air is released. This silent period and rush of air are clearly illustrated in Figure 14.2 by an open space, followed by a sharp line, in the spectrogram patterns of the stops /k/ and /t/ of "cat." Fricatives, on the other hand, result in a long-duration, high-frequency noise, due to the turbulence as air rushes through the teeth, as illustrated by the pattern for the /s/ of "shoo."

Voicing

Voiced consonants: *b, d, g, v, z, ž, ǰ, m, n, ð, ŋ, l, r, y, w.*

Unvoiced consonants: *p, t, k, f, θ, s, š, h, č.*

Pattern of Articulation

We noted in Chapter 14 that each phoneme has its own pattern of articulation, with a unique combination of voicing, place of articulation, and manner of articulation. The table below indicates the patterns of articulation for the phonemes /d/, /t/, /m/, /w/, /f/, and /v/. If we were to include the rest of the phonemes, we would see, in fact, that no two phonemes have the same pattern of articulation.

	d	*t*	*m*	*w*	*f*	*v*
Place						
Alveolar	x	x				
Bilabial			x	x		
Labiodental					x	x
Manner						
Stop	x	x				
Fricative					x	x
Nasal			x			
Semivowel				x		
Voicing						
Voiced	x		x	x		x
Unvoiced		x			x	

References

Abeles, M., and Goldstein, M. H. (1970) Functional architecture in cat primary auditory cortex: Columnar organization and organization according to depth. *Journal of Neurophysiology 33*, 172–187. (361)

Albers, J. (1975) *Interaction of color*. New Haven, CT: Yale University Press. (118)

Allen, T. W., Walker, K., Symonds, L., and Marcell, M. (1977) Intrasensory and intersensory perception of temporal sequences during infancy. *Developmental Psychology 13*, 225–229. (328)

Ammons, C. H., Worchel, P., and Dallenbach, K. M. (1953) Facial vision: The perception of obstacles out of doors by blindfolded and blindfolded-deafened subjects. *American Journal of Psychology 66*, 519–553. (366)

Amoore, J. E. (1970) *Molecular basis of odor*. Springfield, Ill.: Thomas. (415)

Amoore, J. E., Johnston, J. W., Jr., and Rubin, M. (1964) The stereochemical theory of odor. *Scientific American 210 (2)*, 42–49. (411, 415)

Anderson, D. E., Fisher, S. K., and Steinberg, R. H. (1978) Mammalian cones: Disc shedding, phagocytosis and renewal. *Investigative Ophthalmology and Visual Science 17*, 117–133. (74)

Anstis, S. M., and Gregory, R. L. (1964) The aftereffect of seen motion: The role of retinal stimulation and eye movements. *Quarterly Journal of Experimental Psychology 17*, 173–174. (306)

Arnheim, R. (1974) *Art and visual perception*, 2nd ed. Berkeley: University of California Press. (167)

Aslin, R. N. (1977) Development of binocular fixation in human infants. *Journal of Experimental Child Psychology 23*, 133–150. (322)

Aslin, R. N. (1981) Experiential influences and sensitive periods of perceptual development: A unified model. In *Development of perception, Vol. 2*, Aslin, R. N., Alberts, J., and Petersen, M. J. (Eds.), New York: Academic Press, pp. 45–93. (329, 343)

Aslin R. N., and Banks, M. S. (1978) Early visual experience in humans: Evidence for a critical period in the development of binocular vision. In *Psychology: From basic research to practice*, Sten-Schneider, H. Liebowitz, H. Pick, and H. Stevenson (Eds.). New York: Plenum. pp. 227–239. (341)

Aslin, R. N., and Pisoni, D. B. (1980) Some developmental processes in speech perception. In *Child phonology, Vol. 2: Perception*, G. Yeni-Konishian, J. F. Kavanagh, and C. A. Ferguson (Eds.). New York: Academic Press. (391)

Attneave, F. (1957) Physical determinants of the judged complexity of shapes. *Journal of Experimental Psychology 53*, 221–227. (178)

Attneave, F. (1971) Multistability in perception. *Scientific American 225(6)*, 62–71. (254)

Attneave, F., and Olson, R. K. (1971) Pitch as a medium: A new approach to psychophysical scaling. *American Journal of Psychology 84*, 147–166. (364)

Aubert, H. (1886) Die Bewegungsempfindung. *Archiv fuer die Gesamte Physiologic des Menschen und der Tiere 39*, 347–370. (289)

Awaya, S., Miyake, Y., Imayuni, Y., Shiose, Y., Kanda, T., and Komuro, K. (1973) Amblyopia in man, suggestive of stimulus deprivation amblyopia. *Japanese Journal of Ophthalmology 17*, 69–82. (339)

Bach-y-Rita, P. (1972) *Brain mechanisms in sensory substitution*. New York: Academic Press. (87)

Bach-y-Rita, P., Collins, C. C., Saunders, F., White, B., and Scadden, L. (1969) Vision substitution by tactile image projection. *Nature 221*, 963–964. (87)

Bach-y-Rita, P., Collins, C. C., Scadden, C., Holmlund, G. W., and Hart, B. K. (1970) Display techniques in a tactile vision substitution system. *Medical and Biological Illustration 20*, 6–12. (87)

Backus, J. (1977) *The acoustical foundations of music*, 2nd ed. New York: Norton. (375)

Baker, F. H., Grigg, P., and von Noorden, G. K. (1974) Effects of visual deprivation and strabismus on the response of neurons in the visual cortex of the monkey. *Brain Research 66*, 185–208. (331)

Banks, M. S. (1980) The development of visual accommodation during early infancy. *Child Development 51*, 646–666. (321)

Banks, M. S. (1982) The development of spatial and temporal contrast sensitivity. *Current Eye Research 2*, 191–198. (320)

Banks, M. S., Aslin, R. N., and Letson, R. D. (1975) Sensitive period for the development of human binocular vision. *Science 190*, 675–677. (341)

Banks, M. S., and Salapatek, P. (1978) Acuity and contrast sensitivity in 1-, 2-, and 3-month-old human infants. *Investigative Ophthalmology and Visual Science 17*, 361–365. (320)

Banks, M. S., and Salapatek, P. (1981) Infant pattern vision: A new approach based on the contrast sensitivity function. *Journal of Experimental Child Psychology 31*, 1–45. (319, 320)

Banks, W. P., and Prinzmetal, W. (1976) Configurational effects in visual information processing. *Perception and Psychophysics 19*, 361–367. (180)

Barlow, H. B., Blakemore, C., and Pettigrew, J. D. (1967) The neural mechanism of binocular depth discrimination. *Journal of Physiology 193*, 327–342. (215)

Barlow, H. B., and Hill, R. M. (1963) Evidence for a physiological explanation of the waterfall illusion and figural after-effects. *Nature 200*, 1345–1347. (307)

Bartlett, N. R. (1965) Thresholds as dependent on some energy relations and characteristics of the subject. In *Vision and visual perception*, C. Graham (Ed.). New York: Wiley. (79)

Bartoshuk, L. M. (1971) The chemical senses. I. Taste. In *Experimental psychology*, 3rd ed., J. W. Kling and L. A. Riggs (Eds.). New York: Holt, Rinehart and Winston. (425)

Bartoshuk, L. M. (1978) Gustatory system. In *Handbook of behavioral neurobiology, Vol. 1, Sensory integration,* R. B. Masterson (Ed.). New York: Plenum, 503–567. (429)

Bartoshuk, L. M. (1979) Bitter taste of saccharin: Related to the genetic ability to taste the bitter substance propylthiourial (PROP). *Science 205*, 934–935. (423)

Bartoshuk, L. M. (1980) Separate worlds of taste. *Psychology Today* (Sept.), 48–56. (422, 424)

Batteau, D. W. (1967) The role of the pinna in human localization. *Proceedings of the Royal Society of London, Series B 168*, 158–180. (373)

Beauchamp, G. K., Doty, R. L., Moulton, D. G. and Mugford, R. A. (1976) The pheromone concept in mammalian chemical communication: A critique. In *Mammalian olfaction, reproductive processes, and behavior*, R. L. Doty (Ed.). New York: Academic Press. (410)

Beauchamp, G. K., and Maller, O. (1977) The development of flavor preferences in humans: A review. In *Chemical senses and nutrition*, M. R. Kare and O. Maller (Eds.). New York: Academic Press, 291–311. (410, 424)

Beck, J. (1972) *Surface color perception*. Ithaca: Cornell University Press. (169)

Beck, P. W., Handwerker, H. O., and Zimmerman, M. (1974) Nervous outflow from the cat's foot during noxious radiant heat stimulation. *Brain Research 67*, 373–386. (88)

Beecher, H. K. (1972) The placebo effect as a nonspecific force surrounding disease and the treatment of disease. In *Pain: Basic principles, pharmacology, and therapy*, R. Janzen, W. D. Kerdel, A. Herz, C. Steichele, J. P. Payne, and R. A. P. Burt (Eds.). Stuttgart, West Germany: Georg Thiene. (91)

Beets, J. G. T. (1978) Odor and stimulant structure. In *Handbook of Perception, Vol. 6A*, E. C. Carterette and M. P. Friedman (Eds.). New York: Academic Press. pp. 245–255. (416)

Beidler, L. M. (1978) Biophysics and chemistry of taste. In *Handbook of Perception, Vol. 6A*, E. C. Carterette and M. P. Friedman (Eds.). New York: Academic Press. pp. 21–49. (427)

Békésy, G. von (1928) Zur Theorie des Horens: Die Schwingungsform der Basilarmembran. *Physikalische Zeitschrift 29*, 793–810. (357)

Békésy, G. von (1958) Funneling in the nervous system and its role in loudness and sensation intensity on the skin. *Journal of the Acoustical Society of America 30*, 399–412. (102)

Békésy, G. von (1959) Neural funneling along the skin and between the inner and outer hair cells of the cochlea. *Journal of Experimental Child Psychology 31*, 1236–1249. (102)

Békésy, G. von (1960) *Experiments in hearing*. New York: McGraw-Hill. (358, 359)

Békésy, G. von (1967) *Sensory inhibition*. Princeton: Princeton University Press. (102)

Berkley, M. A. (1981) Animal models of visual development: Behavioral evaluation of some physiological findings in cat visual development. In *The development of perception: Psychobiological perspectives*, R. N. Aslin, J. Alberts, and M. J. Petersen (Eds.). New York: Academic Press, 198–217. (331)

Bernstein, I. (1978) Learned taste aversions in children receiving chemotherapy. *Science 200*, 1302–1303. (425)

Bezold, W. von (1876) *The theory of color* (American edition). Boston: Prang and Company. (272)

Biederman, I. (1981) On the semantics of a glance at a scene. In *Perceptual organization*, M. Kubovy and J. Pomerantz (Eds.). Hillsdale, N.J.: Lawrence Erlbaum Associates. (191)

Blakemore, C. (1974) Developmental factors in the formation of feature extracting neurons. In *The neurosciences, 3rd study program*, F. G. Worden and F. O. Schmitt (Eds.). Cambridge, Mass.: MIT Press, 105–133. (339)

Blakemore, C. (1976) The conditions required for the maintenance of binocularity in the kitten's visual cortex. *Journal of Physiology 261*, 423–444. (339)

Blakemore, C. (1977) Genetic instructions and developmental plasticity in the kitten's visual cortex. *Philosophical Transactions of the Royal Society of London, Series B 278*, 425–431. (339)

Blakemore, C., and Campbell, F. W. (1968) Adaptation to spatial stimuli. *Journal of Physiology 200*, 11P–13P. (281)

Blakemore, C., and Cooper, G. F. (1970) Development of the brain depends on the visual environment. *Nature 228*, 477–478. (334, 339)

Blakemore, C., and Mitchell, E. D. (1973) Environmental modification of the visual cortex and the neural basis of learning and memory. *Nature 241*, 467–468. (336, 339)

Blakemore, C., and Sutton, P. (1969) Size adaptation: A new aftereffect. *Science 166*, 246–247. (277, 282)

Blakemore, C., and Tobin, E. A. (1972) Lateral inhibition between orientation detectors in the cat's visual cortex. *Experimental Brain Research 15*, 439–440. (292)

Blakemore, C., and Van Sluyters, R. C. (1975) Innate and environmental factors in the development of the kitten's visual cortex. *Journal of Physiology 248*, 663–716. (339)

Blank, D. L. (1974) Mechanism underlying the analysis of odorant quality at the level of the olfactory mucosa. II. Receptor selective sensitivity. *Annals of the New York Academy of Sciences 237*, 91–101. (417)

Blasdel, G. G., Mitchell, D. E., Muir, D. W., and Pettigrew, J. D. (1977) A combined physiological and behavioral study of the effect of early visual experience with contours of a single orientation. *Journal of Physiology 265*, 615–636. (336)

Blumstein, S. E., and Stevens, K. N. (1979) Acoustic invariance in speech production: Evidence from measurements of the spectral characteristics of stop consonants. *Journal of the Acoustical Society of America 66*, 1001–1017. (392)

Bonds, A. B. (1978) Development of orientation tuning in the visual cortex of kittens. In *Developmental neurobiology of vision*, R. D. Freeman (Ed.). New York: Plenum, 31–41. (331)

Borg, G., Diamant, H., Strom, C., and Zotterman, Y. (1967) The relation between neural and perceptual intensity: A comparative study of neural and psychophysical responses to taste stimuli. *Journal of Physiology 192*, 13–20. (56)

Boring, E. G. (1930) A new ambiguous figure. *American Journal of Psychology 42*, 444–445. (194)

Boring, E. G. (1943) The moon illusion. *American Journal of Physics 11*, 55–60. (243)

Boring, E. G. (1950) A history of experimental psychology, 2nd ed. New York: Appleton-Century-Crofts, 595. (166)

Boring, E. G., and Holway, A. H. (1940a) The moon illusion and the angle of regard. *American Journal of Psychology 53*, 109–116. (243)

Boring, E. G., and Holway, A. H. (1940b) The apparent size of the moon as a function of the angle of regard: Further experiments. *American Journal of Psychology 53*, 537–553. (243)

Bornstein, M. H. (1976) Infants are trichromats. *Journal of Experimental Child Psychology 21*, 425–445. (325)

Bornstein, M. H., Kessen, W. M., and Weiskopf, S. (1976) The categories of hue in infancy. *Science 191*, 201–202. (325)

Bowman, H. S., and Bedard, A. J. (1971) Observations of infrasound and subsonic disturbances related to severe weather. *Geophysical Journal of the Royal Astronomical Society 26*, 215–242. (370)

Boynton, R. M. (1972) Color vision. In *Experimental psychology*, 3rd ed., Vol. 1, *Sensation and perception*, J. W. Kling and L. A. Riggs (Eds.). New York: Holt, Rinehart and Winston, 315–368. (133)

Boynton, R. M. (1979) *Human color vision*. New York: Holt, Rinehart and Winston. (133)

Bregman, A. S., and Campbell, J. (1971) Primary auditory stream segregation and perception of order in rapid sequences of tones. *Journal of Experimental Psychology 89*, 244–249. (170)

Bregman, A. S., and Rudnicky, A. I. (1975) Auditory segregation: Stream or streams? *Journal of Experimental Psychology: Human Perception and Performance 1*, 263–267. (179)

Broadbent, D. E. (1958) *Perception and communication*. London: Pergamon. (199)

Brodatz, P. (1976) *Land, sea and sky: A photographic album for artists and designers*. New York: Dover. (223)

Brown, J. F. (1931a) The visual perception of velocity. *Psychologische Forschung 14,* 199–232. (289)

Brown, J. F. (1931b) The thresholds for visual velocity. *Psychologische Forschung 14*, 249–268. (289)

Brown, P. K., and Wald, G. (1964) Visual pigments in single rods and cones of the human retina. *Science 144*, 45–52. (76)

Bruce, H. (1959) An exteroceptive block to pregnancy in the mouse. *Nature 184*, 105. (409)

Brugge, J. F., and Merzenich, M. M. (1973) Responses of neurons in auditory cortex of the macaque monkey to monaural and binaural stimulation. *Journal of Neurophysiology 36*, 1138–1158. (375)

Bruner, J. S., and Minturn, A. L. (1955) Perceptual identification and perceptual organization. *Journal of General Psychology 53*, 21–28. (193)

Bryant, P. E., Jones, P., Claxton, U., and Perkins, G. M. (1972) Recognition of shapes across modalities by infants. *Nature 240*, 303–304. (328)

Bugelski, B. R., and Alampay, D. A. (1961) The role of frequency in developing perceptual sets. *Canadian Journal of Psychology 15*, 205–211. (193)

Buissert, P., and Imbert, M. (1976) Visual cortical cells: Their developmental properties in normal and dark reared kittens. *Journal of Physiology 255*, 511–525. (331)

Burgess, P. R., and Perl, E. R. (1973) Cutaneous mechanoreceptors and nociceptors. In *Handbook of sensory physiology*, Vol. 2, A. Iggo (Ed.). Berlin: Springer-Verlag, 29–78. (86, 88)

Burke, L. (1952) On the tunnel effect. *Quarterly Journal of Experimental Psychology 4*, 121–138. (309)

Burton, M. (1972) *The sixth sense of animals*. New York: Taplinger. (405)

Burzlaff, W. (1931) Methodologsche Beitrage zum Problem der Farbenhonstanz. *Zeitschrift fur Psychologie 119*, 177–235. (248)

Buswell, G. T. (1935) *How people look at pictures*. Chicago: Chicago University Press. (196)

Cabanac, M. (1971) Physiological role of pleasure. *Science 173*, 1103–1107. (422)

Cabanac, M. (1979) Sensory pleasure. *Quarterly Review of Biology 54*, 1–29. (422)

Cain, W. S. (1977) Differential sensitivity for smell: "Noise" at the nose. *Science 195*, 796–798. (405)

Cain, W. S. (1978) The odoriferous environment and the application of olfactory research. In *Handbook of perception*, Vol. 6A, E. C. Carterette and M. P. Friedman (Eds.). New York: Academic Press. 277–304. (404)

Cain, W. S. (1979) To know with the nose: Keys to odor identification. *Science 203*, 467–470. (406)

Cain, W. S. (1980) Sensory attributes of cigarette smoking. *Banbury Rpt. 3: A safe cigarette?* Cold Spring Harbor Laboratory, 239–249. (406, 408)

Campbell, F. W., and Robson, J. G. (1968) Application of Fourier analysis to the visibility of gratings. *Journal of Physiology 197*, 551–566. (281, 442)

Chapanis, A. (1947) The dark adaptation of the color anomalous. *Journal of General Physiology 30*, 423–437. (73)

Chapanis, A. (1965) Color names for color space. *American Scientist 53*, 327–346. (112)

Cherry, E. C. (1953) Some experiments on the recognition of speech, with one and with two ears. *Journal of the Acoustical Society of America 25*, 925–979. (198)

Clark, H., and Clark, E. (1977) *Psychology and language*. New York: Harcourt Brace Jovanovich. (387, 445)

Clark, W. C., and Clark, S. B. (1980) Pain responses in Nepalese porters. *Science 209*, 410–412. (17)

Clulow, F. W. (1972) *Color: Its principles and their applications*. New York: Morgan and Morgan. (117–119)

Cohen, W. (1957) Spatial and textual characteristics of the Ganzfeld. *American Journal of Psychology 70*, 403–410. (276)

Conel, J. L. (1939) *The postnatal development of the cerebral cortex*, Vol. 1. Cambridge: Harvard University Press. (318)

Conel, J. L. (1947) *The postnatal development of the cerebral cortex*, Vol. 3. Cambridge: Harvard University Press. (318)

Conel, J. L. (1951) *The postnatal development of the cerebral cortex*, Vol. 4. Cambridge: Harvard University Press. (318)

Cook, R. K. (1969) Atmospheric sound propagation. *Proceedings of the National Academy of Sciences 2*, 633–669. (370)

Costanzo, R. M., and Gardner, E. P. (1980) A quantitative analysis of responses of direction-sensitive neurons in somatosensory cortex of awake monkeys. *Journal of Neurophysiology 43*, 1319–1341. (103)

Crawford, M. L. J., and von Noorden, G. K. (1980) Optically induced concomitant strabismus in monkey. *Investigative Ophthalmology and Visual Science 19*, 1105–1109. (334)

Critchley, M. (1953) Tactile thought with special reference to the blind. *Brain 76*, 19–35. (106)

Culler, E. A., Coakley, J. D., Lowy, K., and Gross, N. (1943) A revised frequency-map of the guinea-pig cochlea. *American Journal of Psychology 56*, 475–500. (359)

Dallenbach, K. M. (1927) The temperature spots and end organs. *American Journal of Psychology 39*, 402–427. (88)

Delk, J. L., and Fillenbaum, S. (1965) Differences in perceived color as a function of characteristic color. *American Journal of Psychology 78*, 290–293. (120)

DeLoache, J. S., Strauss, M. S., and Maynard, J. (1979) Picture perception in infancy. *Infant Behavior and Development 2*, 77–89. (328)

Desor, J. A., and Beauchamp, G. K. (1974) The human capacity to transmit olfactory information. *Perception and Psychophysics 16*, 551–556. (406)

DeValois, R. L. (1960) Color vision mechanisms in monkey. *Journal of General Physiology 43*, 115–128. (129)

DeValois, R. L., and Jacobs, G. H. (1968) Primate color vision. *Science 162*, 533–540. (130, 133)

Devor, M. (1977) Central processing of odor signals: Lessons from adult and neonatal olfactory tract lesions. In *Chemical signals in vertebrates*, D. Muller-Schwarze and M. M. Mozell (Eds.). New York: Plenum, 529–545. (410)

deVries, H., and Stuiver, M. (1961) The absolute sensitivity of the human sense of smell. In *Sensory communication*, W. A. Rosenblith (Ed.). Cambridge, Mass.: MIT Press. (405)

Dews, P. B., and Wiesel, T. N. (1970) Consequences of monocular deprivation on visual behavior in kittens. *Journal of Physiology 206*, 437–455. (331)

Diamond, I. T., and Neff, W. D. (1957) Ablation of temporal cortex and discrimination of auditory patterns. *Journal of Neurophysiology 20*, 300–315. (365)

Dobelle, W. H. (1977) Current status of research on providing sight to the blind by electrical stimulation of the brain. *Journal of Visual Impairment and Blindness 71*, 290–297. (55)

Dobelle, W. H., Mladejovsky, M. J., Evans, J. R., Roberts, T. S., and Girvin, J. P. (1976) "Braille" reading by a blind volunteer by visual cortex stimulation. *Nature 259*, 111–112. (55)

Dobelle, W. H., Mladejovsky, M. J., and Girvin, J. P. (1974) Artificial vision for the blind: Electrical stimulation of visual cortex offers hope for a functional prosthesis. *Science 183*, 440–444. (55)

Dobson, V., and Teller, D. (1978) Visual acuity in human infants. Review and comparison of behavioral and electrophysiological studies. *Vision Research 18*, 1469–1483. (319)

Dodd, G. G., and Squirrell, D. J. (1980) Structure and mechanism in the mammalian olfactory system. *Symposium of the Zoology Society of London 45*, 35–56. (405, 416)

Döving, K. B., and Pinching, A. G. (1973) Selective degeneration of neurons in olfactory bulb following prolonged odor exposure. *Brain Research 52*, 115–129. (419)

Dowling, J. E., and Boycott, B. B. (1966) Organization of the primate retina. *Proceedings of the Royal Society of London, Series B 166*, 80–111. (41)

Duclaux, R., and Kenshalo, D. R. (1980) Response characteristics of cutaneous warm fibers in the monkey. *Journal of Neurophysiology 43*, 1–15. (88)

Duncker, D. K. (1929) Uber induzierte Bewegung (Ein Beitrag zur Theorie optisch wahrgenommener Bewegung). *Psychologische Forschung 12*, 180–259. (Summary in W. D. Ellis [1938] *A sourcebook of Gestalt psychology*. London: Kegan Paul, Trench, Trubner.) (301)

Duncker, D. K. (1939) The influence of past experience upon perceptual properties. *American Journal of Psychology 52*, 255–265. (423)

Durlach, N. I., and Colburn, H. S. (1978) Binaural phenomena. In *Handbook of perception*, Vol. 4, E. C. Carterette and M. P. Friedman (Eds.). New York: Academic Press, 365–466. (371)

Durrant, J., and Jovrinic, J. (1977) *Bases of hearing science*. Baltimore: Williams and Williams. (351, 352, 365)

Eimas, P. D., and Corbit, J. D. (1973) Selective adaptation of linguistic feature detectors. *Cognitive Psychology 4*, 99–109. (388, 392)

Eimas, P. D., and Miller, J. L. (1978) Effects of selective adaptation of speech and visual patterns: Evidence for feature detectors. In *Perception and experience*, H. L. Pick and R. D. Walk (Eds.). New York: Plenum, 307–345. (393)

Eimas, P. D., Siqueland, E. R., Jusczyk, P., and Vigorito, J. (1971) Speech perception in infants. *Science 171*, 303–306. (390)

Emmert, E. (1881) Grossenverhaltnisse der Nachbilder. *Klinische Monatsblaetter fuer Augenheilkunde 19*, 443–450. (238)

Engen, T. (1972) Psychophysics. In *Experimental psychology*, 3rd ed., J. W. Kling and L. A. Riggs (Eds.). New York: Holt, Rinehart and Winston, 1–46. (13)

Engen, T., and Pfaffmann, C. (1960) Absolute judgements of odor quality. *Journal of Experimental Psychology 59*, 214–219. (406)

Epstein, W. (1963) The influence of assumed size on apparent distance. *American Journal of Psychology 76*, 257–265. (208)

Erickson, R. R. (1963) Sensory neural patterns and gustation. In *Olfaction and taste*, Vol. 1, Y. Zotterman (Ed.). Oxford: Pergamon Press, 205–213. (58, 429)

Fagan, J. F. (1976) Infant's recognition of invariant features of faces. *Child development 47*, 627–638. (316, 327)

Fantz, R. L. (1961) The origin of form perception. *Scientific American 204*, 66–72. (319)

Fantz, R. L., Fagan, J. F., and Miranda, S. B. (1975) Early visual selectivity. In *Infant perception: From sensation to cognition*, L. B. Cohen and P. Salapatek (Eds.). New York: Academic Press, 249–345. (325, 326)

Fantz, R. L., Ordy, J. M., and Udelf, M. S. (1962) Maturation of pattern vision in infants during the first six months. *Journal of Comparative and Physiological Psychology 55*, 907–917. (316)

Fechner, G. T. (1860) *Elemente der Psychophysik*, Vol. 1. Leipzig: Breitkopf and Harterl. Translated by H. E. Adler, D. H. Howes, and E. G. Boring. New York: Holt, Rinehart and Winston. (7)

Feddersen, W. E., Sandel, T. T., Teas, D. C., and Jeffress, L. A. (1957) Localization of high frequency tones. *Journal of the Acoustical Society of America 5*, 82–108. (371)

Fiorentini, A., and Maffei, L. (1973) Contrast in night vision. *Vision Research 13*, 73–80. (320)

Fletcher, H., and Munson, W. A. (1933) Loudness: Its definition, measurement, and calculation. *Journal of the Acoustical Society of America 5*, 82–108. (369)

Fox, R., Aslin, R. N., Shea, S. L., and Dumais, S. T. (1980) Stereopsis in human infants. *Science 207*, 323–324. (322)

Frank, M. (1973) An analysis of hamster afferent taste nerve response functions. *Journal of General Physiology 61*, 588–618. (430)

Franzen, O., and Lindblom, U. (1976) Coding of velocity of skin indentation in man and monkey. A perceptual-neurophysiological correlation. In *Sensory functions of the skin in primates*, Y. Zotterman (Ed.). New York: Pergamon Press, 55–65. (56)

Freeman, R. D., and Pettigrew, J. D. (1973) Alterations of visual cortex from environmental asymmetries. *Nature 246*, 359–360. (341)

Freeman, R. D., and Thibos, L. N. (1973) Electrophysiological evidence that abnormal early visual experience can modify the human brain. *Science 180*, 876–878. (343)

Frey, M. von (1894) Beitrage zur Physiologie des Schmerzinns. *Berichte uber die Verhandlung der*

Koniglichen Sachsischen Gesellschaft der Wissenschaften zu Leipzig, Mathematisch-Physische Klasse 46, 185–196. (85)

Frey, M. von (1895) Beitrage zur Sinnesphysiologie der Haut. *Berichte uber die Verhandlung der Koniglichen Sachsischen Gesellschaft der Wissenschaften zu Leipzig, Mathematisch-Physische Klasse 47,* 166–184. (85)

Friedman, M. B. (1975) Visual control of head movements during avian locomotion. *Nature 225,* 67–69. (302)

Frishman, L. (1979) The velocity tuning of neurons in the lateral geniculate nucleus and retina of the cat. Doctoral Dissertation, Department of Psychology, University of Pittsburgh. (293)

Gamble, A. E. McC. (1898) The applicability of Weber's law to smell. *American Journal of Psychology 10,* 82–142. (405)

Garcia, J., Ervin, F. R., and Koelling, R. A. (1966) Learning with prolonged delay of reinforcement. *Psychonomic Science 5,* 121–122. (424)

Garcia, J., Hawkins, W. G., and Rusiniak, K. W. (1974) Behavioral regulation of the Milieu Interne in man and rat. *Science 185,* 824–831. (424)

Garcia, J., and Koelling, R. A. (1966) A relation of cue to consequence in avoidance learning. *Psychonomic Science 4,* 123–124. (424)

Gardner, E. (1975) *Fundamentals of neurology,* 6th ed., New York: Saunders. (86)

Gardner, M. B., and Gardner, R. S. (1973) Problem of localization in the median plane: Effect of pinnae cavity occlusion. *Journal of the Acoustical Society of America 53,* 400–408. (373)

Gelb, A. (1929) Die "Farbenkonstanz" der Sehding. *Handbook norm. path. Phys. 12,* 594–678. (251)

Geldard, F. A. (1972) *The human senses,* 2nd ed. New York: Wiley. (422)

Gescheider, G. A. (1976) *Psychophysics: method and theory.* Hillsdale, N.J.: Lawrence Erlbaum Associates. (7, 13, 438)

Gibson, E. H. (1969) *Principles of perceptual learning and development.* New York: Appleton-Century-Crofts. (188)

Gibson, E. H., and Walk, R. M. (1960) The "visual cliff." *Scientific American 202(4),* 64–71. (324)

Gibson, J. J. (1950) *The perception of the visual world.* Boston: Houghton Mifflin (220)

Gibson, J. J. (1962) Observations on active touch. *Psychological Review 69,* 477–491. (105)

Gibson, J. J. (1966) *The senses considered as perceptual systems.* Boston: Houghton Mifflin. (220, 227)

Gibson, J. J. (1968) What gives rise to the perception of motion? *Psychological Review 75,* 335–346. (293)

Gibson, J. J. (1979) *The ecological approach to visual perception.* Boston: Houghton Mifflin. (220)

Gilchrist, A. L. (1977) Perceived lightness depends on perceived spatial arrangement. *Science 195,* 185–187. (274)

Gilinsky, A. S. (1965) The effect of attitude upon the perception of size. *American Journal of Psychology 68,* 173–192. (240)

Ginsburg, A. (1983) Contrast perception in the human infant, unpublished manuscript. (321)

Goldfoot, D. A., Essock-Vitale, S. M., Asa, C. S., Thornton, J. E., and Leshner, A. J. (1978) Anosmia in male rhesus does not alter copulatory activity with cycling females. *Science 199,* 1095–1096. (410)

Goldstein, E. B. (1967) Early receptor potential of the isolated frog (*Rana pipiens*) retina. *Vision Research 7,* 837–845. (xvii)

Goldstein, E. B. (1975) The perception of multiple images. *AV Communication Review 23,* 34–68. (xvii)

Goldstein, E. B. (1978) Cone pigment regeneration in frogs and humans. In *Visual psychophysics and physiology,* J. Armington, J. Krauskopf, and B. Wooton (Eds.). New York: Academic Press, 73–84. (xvii)

Goldstein, E. B. (1979) Rotation of objects in pictures viewed at an angle: Evidence for different properties of two types of pictorial space. *Journal of Experimental Psychology: Human Perception and Performance 5,* 78–87. (xvii)

Goldstein, E. B. (1981) The ecology of Gibson's perception. *Leonardo 14,* 191–195. (226)

Goldstein, E. B., and Fink, S. I. (1981) Selective attention in vision: Recognition memory for superimposed line drawings. *Journal of Experimental Psychology: Human Perception and Performance 7,* 954–967. (198)

Gombrich, E. H. (1960) *Art and illusion.* Princeton: Princeton University Press. (210)

Goodwin, M., Gooding, K. M., and Regnier, F. (1979) Sex pheromones in the dog. *Science 203*, 559–561. (410)

Gossard, E. E., and Hooke, W. H. (1975) *Waves in the atmosphere*. Amsterdam: Elsevier. (370)

Graham, C. H. (1965) Perception of movement. In *Vision and visual perception*, C. Graham (Ed.). New York: Wiley, 575–588. (298)

Graham, C. H., Sperling, H. G., Hsia, Y., and Coulson, A. H. (1961) The determination of some visual functions of a unilaterally color-blind subject: methods and results. *Journal of Psychology 51*, 3–32. (134)

Granrud, C. E., Yonas, A., and Pettersen, L. (1982) A comparison of responsiveness to monocular depth information in 5- and 7-month-old infants. Unpublished manuscript. (324)

Green, D. M. (1976) *An introduction to hearing*. Hillsdale, N.J.: Lawrence Erlbaum Associates. (373)

Gregory, R. L. (1966) *Eye and brain*, 1st ed. New York: McGraw-Hill. (237, 245)

Gregory, R. L. (1973a) *Eye and brain*, 2nd ed. New York: McGraw-Hill. (246, 256)

Gregory, R. L. (1973b) The confounded eye. In *Illusion in nature and art,* R. L. Gregory and E. H. Gombrich (Eds.). New York: Scribner, 49–95. (256)

Gregory, R. L., and Wallace, J. G. (1963) Recovery from early blindness: A case study. *Experimental Psychology Society Monograph*, No. 2. (340)

Grether, W. F. (1939) Color vision and color blindness in monkeys. *Comparative Psychology Monograph 15*, 1–38. (133)

Griffin, D. R. (1969) The physiology and geophysics of bird navigation. *Quarterly Review of Biology 44*, 255–276. (370)

Grings, W. W. (1942) The verbal summator technique and abnormal mental states. *Journal of Abnormal and Social Psychology 37*, 529–545. (399)

Gross, C. G., Bender, D. B., and Rocha-Miranda, C. E. (1969) Visual receptive fields of neurons in inferotemporal cortex of the monkey. *Science 166*, 1303–1306. (187)

Gulick, W. L. (1971) *Hearing*. New York: Oxford University Press. (30, 351, 354)

Gyr, J. W. (1972) Is a theory of direct perception adequate? *Psychological Bulletin 77*, 246–261. (296)

Hall, E. T. (1966) *The hidden dimension*. Garden City, N.Y.: Doubleday. (404)

Hall, J. L. (1965) Binaural interaction in the accessory superior-olivary nucleus of the cat. *Journal of the Acoustical Society of America 37*, 814–823. (375)

Hall, M. J., Bartoshuk, L. M., Cain, W. S., and Stevens, J. C. (1975) PTC taste blindness and the taste of caffeine. *Nature 253*, 442–443. (423)

Hamilton, W. F., and Coleman, T. B. (1933) Trichromatic vision in the pigeon as illustrated by the spectral hue discrimination curve. *Journal of Comparative Psychology 15*, 183–191. (133)

Harman, G. (1974) Epistemology. In *Handbook of perception*, Vol. 1, E. C. Carterette and M. P. Friedman (Eds.). New York: Academic Press, 41–55. (7)

Harris, L., Atkinson, J., and Braddick, O. (1976) Visual contrast sensitivity of a 6-month-old infant measured by the evoked potential. *Nature 246*, 570–571. (319)

Hartline, H. K. (1938) The response of single optic nerve fibers of the vertebrate eye to illumination of the retina. *American Journal of Physiology 121*, 400–415. (46)

Hartline, H. K., Wagner, H. G., and Ratliff, F. (1956) Inhibition in the eye of limulus. *Journal of General Physiology 39*, 651–673. (41)

Hecht, S., Shlaer, S., and Pirenne, M. H. (1942) Energy, quanta, and vision. *Journal of General Physiology 25*, 819–840. (29, 404)

Heider, F., and Simmel, M. L. (1944) An experimental study of apparent behavior. *American Journal of Psychology 57*, 243–249. (309)

Held, R. (1965) Plasticity in sensory-motor systems. *Scientific American 213*, 84–94. (328)

Held, R., and Hein, A. (1963) Movement produced stimulation in the development of visually guided behavior. *Journal of Comparative and Physiological Psychology 56*, 872–876. (328)

Helmholtz, H. von (1852) On the theory of compound colours. *Philosophical Magazine 4*, 519–534. (122)

Helmholtz, H. von (1863) Die Lehre Von den Tonenpfindungen als physiologische Grundlege fur die Theorie der Musik. Translated by A. J.

Ellis (1954), *On the sensations of tone as a physiological basis for the theory of music*. New York: Dover. (355)

Helson, H. (1933) The fundamental propositions of Gestalt psychology. *Psychological Review 40*, 13–32. (177)

Helson, H., Judd, D. B., and Wilson, M. (1956) Color rendition with fluorescent sources of illumination. *Illuminating Engineering 51*, 329–346. (121)

Hensel, H. (1973) Cutaneous thermoreceptors. In *Handbook of sensory physiology*, Vol. 2, A. Iggo (Ed.). New York: Springer-Verlag, 79–110. (88)

Hering, E. (1878) *Zur Lehre vom Lichtsinne*. Vienna: Gerold. (125)

Hering, E. (1905) Grundzuge der Lehre vom Lichtsinn. In *Handbuch der gesammter Augenheilkunde*, Vol. 3, Chapter 13. Berlin (253)

Hering, E. (1964) *Outlines of a theory of the light sense*. Translated by L. M. Hurvich and D. Jameson. Cambridge: Harvard University Press. (125)

Hirsch, H. V. B. (1972) Visual perception in cats after environmental surgery. *Experimental Brain Research 15*, 405–423. (336)

Hirsch, H. V. B., and Spinelli, D. N. (1970) Visual experience modifies distribution of horizontally and vertically oriented receptive fields in cats. *Science 168*, 869–871. (334)

Hirsch, H. V. B., and Spinelli, D. N. (1971) Modification of the distribution of receptive field orientations in cats by selective visual exposure during development. *Experimental Brain Research 12*, 509–527. (334)

Hochberg, J. E. (1970) Attention, organization, and consciousness. In *Attention: Contemporary theory and analysis*, D. I. Mostofsky (Ed.). New York: Appleton-Century-Crofts, 99–124. (226)

Hochberg, J. E. (1971) Perception. In *Experimental psychology*, 3rd ed., J. W. Kling and L. A. Riggs (Eds.). New York: Holt, Rinehart and Winston, 396–550. (251)

Hochberg, J. E., Triebel, W., and Seaman, G. (1951) Color adaptation under conditions of homogeneous visual stimulation (Ganzfeld). *Journal of Experimental Psychology 41*, 153–159. (276)

Hodgkin, A. L., and Huxley, A. F. (1939) Action potentials recorded from inside a nerve fiber. *Nature 144*, 710–711. (36)

Hohmann, A., and Creutzfeldt, O. D. (1975) Squint and the development of binocularity in humans. *Nature 254*, 613–614. (341)

Holley, A., Duchamp, A., Revial, M. F., Juge, A., and Macleod, P. (1974) Qualitative and quantitative discrimination in the frog olfactory receptors: Analysis from electrophysiological data. *Annals of the New York Academy of Sciences 237*, 102–114. (417)

Holst, E. von (1954) Relations between the central nervous system and the peripheral organs. *British Journal of Animal Behaviour 2*, 89–94. (296)

Holway, A. H. and Boring, E. G. (1941) Determinants of apparent visual size with distance variant. *American Journal of Psychology 54*, 21–37. (234)

Hornung, D. E., Lansing, R. D., and Mozell, M. M. (1975) Distribution of butanol molecules along bullfrog olfactory mucosa. *Nature 254*, 617–618. (419)

Hornung, D. E., and Mozell, M. M. (1977) Factors influencing the differential sorption of odorant molecules across the olfactory mucosa. *Journal of General Physiology 69*, 343–361. (419)

Hubel, D. H., and Livingstone, M. (1982) Cytochrome oxidase blobs in monkey area 17: Response properties and afferent connections. *Society for Neuroscience Abstracts 8*, 706. (131)

Hubel, D. H., and Livingstone, M. (1983) Blobs and color vision. *Canadian Journal of Physiology and Pharmacology*. In press. (131)

Hubel, D. H., and Wiesel, T. N. (1959) Receptive fields of single neurons in the cat's striate cortex. *Journal of Physiology 148*, 574–591. (49, 51)

Hubel, D. H. and Wiesel, T. N. (1961) Integrative action in the cat's lateral geniculate body. *Journal of Physiology 155*, 385–398. (47)

Hubel, D. H., and Wiesel, T. N. (1962) Receptive fields, binocular interaction and functional architecture in the cat's visual cortex. *Journal of Physiology 160*, 106–154. (50)

Hubel, D. H., and Wiesel, T. N. (1963) Receptive fields of cells in striate cortex of very young, visually inexperienced kittens. *Journal of Neurophysiology 26*, 994–1002. (330, 331)

Hubel, D. H., and Wiesel, T. N. (1965a) Receptive fields and functional architecture in two nonstriate visual areas (18 & 19) of the cat. *Journal of Neurophysiology 28*, 229–289. (50, 51)

Hubel, D. H., and Wiesel, T. N. (1965b) Binocular interaction in striate cortex of kittens reared with artificial squint. *Journal of Neurophysiology 28*, 1041–1059. (334)

Hubel, D. H., and Wiesel, T. N. (1970a) The period of susceptibility to the physiological effects of unilateral eye closure in kittens. *Journal of Physiology 206*, 419–436. (333)

Hubel, D. H., and Wiesel, T. N. (1970b) Cells sensitive to binocular depth in area 18 of the macaque monkey cortex. *Nature 225*, 41–42. (215)

Hubel, D. H., Wiesel, T. N., and Stryker, M. P. (1978) Anatomical demonstration of orientation columns in macaque monkeys. *Journal of Comparative Neurology 177*, 361–379. (52)

Hurvich, L. (1981) *Color vision*. Sunderland, Mass: Sinauer Associates. (113)

Hurvich, L., and Jameson, D. (1957) An opponent-process theory of color vision. *Psychological Review 64*, 384–404. (126, 128)

Hyvärinin, J., and Poranen, A. (1978) Movement-sensitive and direction and orientation-selective cutaneous receptive fields in the hand area of the postcentral gyrus in monkeys. *Journal of Physiology 283*, 523–537. (101, 103)

Imbert, M. (1979) Maturation of visual cortex with and without visual experience. In *Developmental neurobiology of vision*, R. Freeman (Ed.). New York: Plenum, 43–50. (331)

Isenhour, J. P. (1975) The effects of context and order in film edition. *AV Communication Review 23*, 69–80. (310)

Ittleson, W. H. (1952) *The Ames demonstrations in perception*. Princeton, N.J.: Princeton University Press. (241)

Johnson, K. O., Darian-Smith, I., LaMotte, C., Johnson, B., and Oldfield, S. (1979) Coding of incremental changes in skin temperature by a population of warm fibers in the monkey: Correlation with intensity discrimination in man. *Journal of Neurophysiology 42*, 1332–1353. (60)

Judd, D. B., and Kelly, K. L. (1965) *The ISCC-NBS method of designating colors and a dictionary of color names*. U.S. National Bureau of Standards Circular 553, 2nd ed. (113)

Judd, D. B., MacAdam, D. L., and Wyszecki, G. (1964) Spectral distribution of typical daylight as a function of correlated color temperature. *Journal of the Optical Society of America 54*, 1031–1040. (116)

Julesz, B. (1971) *Foundations of cyclopean perception*. Chicago: University of Chicago Press. (221)

Kagan, J., Henker, B. A., Hen-Tov, A., Levine, J., and Lewis, M. (1966) Infant's differential reactions to familiar and distorted faces. *Child Development 37*, 519–532. (326)

Kaneko, A. (1970) Physiological and morphological identification of horizontal, bipolar and amacrine cells in goldfish retina. *Journal of Physiology 207*, 623–633. (36)

Kanig, J. L. (1955) Mental impact of colors in food studied. *Food Field Reporter 23*, 57. (423)

Kanizsa, G. (1955) Marzini quasi-percettivi in campi con stimolozione omogenea. *Rivista di Psicologia 49*, 7–30. (168)

Kanizsa, G. (1979) *Organization in vision*. New York: Praeger. (175)

Karlson, P., and Luscher, M. (1959) "Pheromones": A new term for a class of biologically active substances. *Nature 183*, 55–56. (409)

Kauer, J. S., and Moulton, D. G. (1974) Responses of olfactory bulb neurons to odor stimulation of small nasal areas in the salamander. *Journal of Physiology 243*, 717–737. (417)

Kaufman, L., and Rock, I. (1962a) The moon illusion I. *Science 136*, 953–961. (244)

Kaufman, L., and Rock, I. (1962b) The moon illusion. *Scientific American 207*, 120–132. (244)

Kellogg, W. N. (1962) Sonar system of the blind. *Science 137*, 399–404. (367)

Kenshalo, D. R. (1976) Correlations of temperature sensitivity in man and monkey, a first approximation. In *Sensory functions of the skin in primates, with special reference to man*, Y. Zotterman (Ed.). New York: Plenum, 305–330. (88, 90)

Kiang, N. Y. S. (1975) Stimulus representation in the discharge patterns of auditory neurons. In *The nervous system*, Vol. 3, E. L. Eagles (Ed.). New York: Raven, 81–96. (362, 384)

Kimura, K., and Beidler, L. (1961) Microelectrode study of taste receptors of rat and hamster. *Journal of Cell Physiology 58*, 131–140. (428)

Kinney, G. C., Marsetta, M., and Showman, D. J.

(1966) Studies in display symbol legibility, Part 12. *The legibility of alphanumeric symbols for digitalized television*. Bedford, Mass: Mitre Corporation. (190)

Knibestol, M., and Vallbo, A. B. (1976) Stimulus-response functions of primary afferents and psychophysical intensity estimation of mechanical skin stimulation in the human hand. In *Sensory functions of the skin in primates, with special reference to man*, Y. Zotterman (Ed.). New York: Plenum, 201–213. (56)

Knudsen, E. I., and Konishi, M. (1978a) Space and frequency are represented separately in auditory midbrain of the owl. *Journal of Neurophysiology 41*, 870–883. (375)

Knudsen, E. I., and Konishi, M. (1978b) Center-surround organization of auditory receptive fields in the owl. *Science 202*, 778–780. (375)

Koffka, K. (1935) *Principles of Gestalt psychology*. New York: Harcourt, Brace and World. (276)

Kolers, P. A. (1972) *Aspects of motion perception*. New York: Pergamon Press. (300)

Kosambi, D. D. (1967) Living prehistory in India. *Scientific American 216* (Feb.), 105. (91)

Kozlowski, L., and Cutting, J. (1977) Recognizing the sex of a walker from a dynamic point-light display. *Perception and Psychophysics 21*, 575–580. (190)

Krauskopf, J. (1963) Effect of retinal image stabilization in the appearance of heterochromatic targets. *Journal of the Optical Society of America 53*, 741–743. (273)

Kreithen, M. L., and Quine, D. B. (1979) Infrasound detection by the homing pigeon: A behavioral audiogram. *Journal of Comparative Physiology 129*, 1–4. (370)

Kris, J. von (1896) Uber die Funktion der Netzhautstabhen. *Zeitschrift fuer Psychologie 9*, 81. (68)

Kruger, L. M. (1970) David Katz: Der Aufbau Der Tastwelt (The world of touch): A synopsis. *Perception and Psychophysics 7*, 337–341. (105)

Kuffler, S. W. (1953) Discharge patterns and functional organization of mammalian retina. *Journal of Neurophysiology 16*, 37–68. (46)

Künnapas, T. (1957) Experiments on figural dominance. *Journal of Experimental Psychology 53*, 31–39. (175)

Kusajima, T. (1974) *Visual reading and braille reading: An experimental investigation of the physiology and psychology of visual and tactual reading*. New York: American Foundation for the Blind. (107)

LaBarbera, J. D., Izard, C. E., Vietze, P., and Parisi, S. A. (1976) Four- and six-month-old infants' visual responses to joy, anger, and neutral expressions. *Child Development 47*, 535–538. (321)

Lashley, K. S. (1916) The color vision of birds. I. The spectrum of the domestic fowl. *Journal of Animal Behavior 6*, 1–26. (133)

Leeper, R. W. (1935) A study of a neglected portion of the field of learning: The development of sensory organization. *Journal of Genetic Psychology 46*, 41–75. (193)

LeGrand, Y. (1957) *Light, color and vision*. London: Chapman and Hall, Ltd. (126, 132)

Lele, P. P., and Weddell, G. (1956) The relationship between neurohistology and corneal sensibility. *Brain 79*, 119–154. (86)

Lerman, S. (1966) *Basic ophthalmology*. New York: McGraw-Hill. (145)

Levine, J. (1955) Consensual pupillary reflex in birds. *Science 122*, 690. (78)

Levine, J. M., and McBurney, D. H. (1983) The role of olfaction in social perception and behavior. In *Physical appearance, stigma, and social behavior: The Ontario Symposium*, Vol. 3, C. P. Herman, M. P. Zanna, and E. T. Higgins (Eds.). Hillsdale, N.J.: Lawrence Erlbaum Associates. In press. (404, 414)

Lewis, E. R., Zeevi, Y. Y., and Werblin, F. S. (1969) Scanning electron microscopy of vertebrate visual receptors. *Brain Research 15*, 559–562. (68)

Liberman, A. M., Cooper, F. S., Shankweiler, D. P., and Studdert-Kennedy, M. (1967) Perception of the speech code. *Psychological Review 74*, 431–461. (386, 389, 390)

Lichten, W., and Lurie, S. (1950) A new technique for the study of perceived size. *American Journal of Psychology 63*, 280–282. (237)

Lindsay, P. H., and Norman, D. A. (1977) *Human information processing*, 2nd ed. New York: Academic Press. (184, 194)

Liphovsky, S. (1977) The role of the chemical senses in nutrition. In *The chemical senses and nutrition*, M. R. Kare and O. Muller (Eds.). New York: Academic Press, 413–428. (425)

Loftus, G. R., and Mackworth, N. H. (1978) Cognitive determinants of fixation location during picture viewing. *Journal of Experimental Psychology: Human Perception and Performance 4*, 565–572. (198)

Lowenstein, W. R. (1960) Biological transducers. *Scientific American 203*, 98–108. (28, 95)

Lowenstein, W. R., and Skalak, R. (1966) Mechanical transmission in a pacinian corpuscle: An analysis and a theory. *Journal of Physiology 182*, 346–378. (95)

Luria, A. R. (1966) *Higher cortical functions in man*. New York: Basic Books. (183)

MacDonald, J., and McGurk, H. (1978) Visual influences on speech perception processes. *Perception and Psychophysics 24*, 253–257. (393)

MacLeod, A. J. (1980) Chemistry of odours. In *Olfaction in mammals*, D. M. Stoddart (Ed.). New York: Academic Press. (Also in *Symposium of the Zoological Society of London 45*, 15–34.) (412)

Mackworth, N. H., and Morandi, A. J. (1967) The gaze selects informative details within pictures. *Perception and Psychophysics 2*, 547–552. (195)

MacNeilage, P. F. (1970) Motor control of serial ordering of speech. *Psychological Review 77*, 182–196. (391)

Mann, I. C. (1964) *The development of the human eye*. London: British Medical Association. (318)

Marks, W. B. (1965) Visual pigments of single goldfish cones. *Journal of Physiology 178*, 14–32. (133)

Marks, W. B., Dobelle, W. H., and MacNichol, E. F. (1964) Visual pigments of single primate cones. *Science 143*, 1181–1183. (76, 133)

Marr, D. (1982) *Vision*. San Francisco: Freeman. (226)

Masland, R. H. (1969) Visual motion perception: Experimental modification. *Science 165*, 819–820. (306)

Matthews, D. F. (1972) Response patterns of single neurons in the tortoise olfactory epithelium and olfactory bulb. *Journal of General Physiology 60*, 166–180. (416)

Maurer, D., and Salapatek, P. (1976) Developmental changes in the scanning of faces by young infants. *Child Development 47*, 523–527. (326)

Mayer, D. J. (1979) Endogenous analgesia systems: Neural and behavioral mechanisms. In *Advances in pain research and therapy*, Vol. 3, J. J. Bonica (Ed.). New York: Raven, 385–410. (91, 94)

McBurney, D. H. (1969) Effects of adaptation on human taste function. In *Olfaction and taste*, C. Pfaffmann (Ed.). New York: Rockefeller University Press, 407–419. (426)

McBurney, D. H., Levine, J. M., and Cavanaugh, P. H. (1977) Psychophysical and social ratings of human body odor. *Personality and Social Psychology Bulletin 3*, 135–138. (408)

McBurney, D. H., and Shick, T. R. (1971) Taste and water taste of twenty-six compounds for man. *Perception and Psychophysics 10*, 249–252. (427)

McClintock, M. K. (1971) Menstrual synchrony and suppression. *Nature 229*, 244–245. (409)

McGurk, H., and MacDonald, J. (1976) Hearing lips and seeing voices. *Nature 264*, 746–748. (393)

McKenzie, D. (1923) *Aromatics and the soul: A study of smells*. New York: Hoeber. (408)

Mello, N. K., and Peterson, N. J. (1964) Behavioral evidence for color discrimination in cats. *Journal of Neurophysiology 27*, 323–333. (133)

Melzak, R. (1973) *The puzzle of pain*. New York: Basic Books. (91, 94)

Melzak, R., and Dennis, S. G. (1978) Neurophysiological foundations of pain. In *The psychology of pain*, R. A. Sternbach (Ed.). New York: Raven, 1–266. (92)

Melzak, R., and Wall, P. D. (1962) On the nature of cutaneous sensory mechanisms. *Brain 85*, 331–356. (88)

Melzak, R., and Wall, P. D. (1965) Pain mechanisms: A new theory. *Science 150*, 971–979. (91, 93)

Metzger, W. (1930) Optische Untensuchengen am Ganzfeld. II. Zur Phanomenologic des homogenen Ganzfelds. *Psychologische Forschung 13*, 6–29. (276)

Meyer, D. R., and Anderson, R. A. (1965) Colour discrimination in cats. In *Color vision*, CIBA Foundation Symposium. London: Churchill, 324–344. (133)

Michael, C. R. (1969) Retinal processing of visual images. *Scientific American 220(5)*, 104–114. (133)

Michael, R. P., and Kaverne, E. B. (1968) Pheromones in the communication of sexual status in primates. *Nature 218*, 746–749. (410)

Michael, R. P., Kaverne, E. B., and Bonsall, R. W.

(1971) Pheromones: Isolation of male sex attractant from a female primate. *Science 172*, 964–966. (410)

Michotte, A. (1963) *The perception of causality*. New York: Basic Books. (307)

Miller, G. A., and Isard, S. (1963) Some perceptual consequences of linguistic rules. *Journal of Verbal Learning and Verbal Behavior 2*, 212–228. (398)

Miller, J. D. (1974) Effects of noise on people. *Journal of the Acoustical Society of America 56*, 729–764. (364)

Mitchell, D. E. (1981) Sensitive periods in visual development. In *Development of perception*, Vol. 2, R. N. Aslin, J. R. Alberts, and M. R. Petersen (Eds.). New York: Academic Press, 3–43. (331)

Mitchell, D. E., Reardon, J., and Muir, D. W. (1975) Interocular transfer of the motion aftereffect in normal and stereoblind observers. *Experimental Brain Research 22*, 163–173. (341)

Mitchell, D. E., and Ware, C. (1974) Interocular transfer of a visual aftereffect in normal and stereoblind humans. *Journal of Physiology 236*, 707–721. (341)

Mitchell, D. E., and Wilkinson, F. (1974) The effect of early astigmatism on the visual resolution of gratings. *Journal of Physiology 243*, 739–756. (342)

Moskowitz, H. R., Kumraich, V., Sharma, H., Jacobs, L., and Sharma, S. D. (1975) Cross-cultural difference in simple taste preference. *Science 190*, 1217–1218. (424)

Moulton, D. G. (1965) Differential sensitivity to odors. *Cold Spring Harbor Symposium on Quantitative Biology 30*, 201–206. (417)

Moulton, D. G. (1977) Minimum odorant concentrations detectable by the dog and their implications for olfactory receptor sensitivity. In *Chemical signals in vertebrates*, D. Miller-Schwarze and M. M. Mozell (Eds.). New York: Plenum, 455–464. (404)

Mountcastle, V. B., and Powell, T. P. (1959) Neural mechanisms subserving cutaneous sensibility, with special reference to the role of afferent inhibition in sensory perception and discrimination. *Bulletin of the Johns Hopkins Hospital 105*, 201–232. (101)

Movshon, J. A., and Van Sluyters, R. C. (1981) Visual neural development. *Annual Review of Psychology 32*, 477–522. (339)

Mozell, M. M. (1964) Olfactory discrimination: Electrophysiological spatiotemporal basis. *Science 143*, 1336–1337. (418)

Mozell, M. M. (1966) The spatiotemporal analysis of odorants at the level of the olfactory receptor sheet. *Journal of General Physiology 50*, 25–41. (419)

Mozell, M. M. (1970) Evidence for a chromatographic model of olfaction. *Journal of General Physiology 56*, 46–63. (419)

Mozell, M. M. (1971) The chemical senses. II. Olfaction. In *Experimental psychology*, 3rd ed., J. W. Kling and L. A. Riggs (Eds.). New York: Holt, Rinehart and Winston, 193–222. (416)

Mozell, M. M., and Jagodowiez, M. (1973) Chromatographic separation of odorants by the nose: Retention times measured across *in vivo* olfactory mucosa. *Science 181*, 1247–1249. (419)

Muir, D.W., and Mitchell, D. E. (1975) Behavioral deficits in cats following early selected visual exposure to contours of a single orientation. *Brain Research 85*, 459–477. (336)

Müller, J. (1842) *Elements of physiology*. Translated by W. Baly. London: Taylor and Walton. (57)

Murray, R. G., and Murray, A. (1970) The anatomy and ultrastructure of taste endings. In *Taste and smell in vertebrates*, G. E. W. Wolstenholme and J. Knight (Eds.). London: Churchill, 3–25. (31, 426)

Nachman, M. (1963) Taste preferences for sodium salts by adrenalectomized rats. *Journal of Comparative and Physiological Psychology 55*, 1124–1129. (425)

Nathan, P. W. (1976) The gate control theory of pain. *Brain 99*, 123–158. (94)

Navon, D. (1977) Forest before trees: The precedence of global features in perception. *Journal of Experimental Psychology: General 9*, 353–383. (191)

Neisser, U., and Becklen, R. (1974) Selective looking: Attending to visually specified events. *Cognitive Psychology 7*, 480–494. (198)

Nelson, R. J., Sur, M., Fellerman, D. J., and Kaas, J. H. (1980) Representations of the body surface in postcentral parietal cortex of macaca fasicularis. *Journal of Comparative Neurology 192*, 611–643. (101)

Newton, I. (1704) *Optiks*. London: Smith and Walford. (4, 114)

Nolan, C. Y., and Kederis, C. J. (1969) *Perceptual factors in braille word recognition.* New York: American Foundation for the Blind. (106, 107)

Norman, D. A. (1968) Toward a theory of memory and attention. *Psychological Review 75*, 522–536. (106, 199)

Norman, D. A. (1976) *Memory and attention*, 2nd ed. New York: Wiley. (194)

Nottebohm, F. (1970) Ontogeny of bird song. *Science 167*, 950–956. (337)

O'Brien, V. (1958) Contour perception, illusion, and reality. *Journal of the Optical Society of America 48*, 112–119. (269)

O'Day, W. T., and Young, R. W. (1978) Rhythmic daily shedding of outer segment membranes by visual cells in the goldfish. *Journal of Cell Biology 76*, 593–604. (75)

Olson, C. R., and Freeman, R. D. (1975) Progressive changes in kitten striate cortex during monocular vision. *Journal of Neurophysiology 38*, 26–32. (333)

Olson, C. R., and Pettigrew, J. D. (1974) Single units in visual cortex of kittens reared in stroboscopic illumination. *Brain Research 70*, 189–204. (338)

Olson, R. R., and Attneave, F. (1970) What variables produce similarity grouping? *American Journal of Psychology 83*, 1–21. (178)

Oyama, T. (1960) Figure-ground dominance as a function of sector angle, brightness, hue, and orientation. *Journal of Experimental Psychology 60*, 299–305. (175)

Palmer, S. E. (1975) The effects of contextual scenes on the identification of objects. *Memory and Cognition 3*, 519–526. (191)

Pangborn, R. M., and Hansen, B. (1963) The influence of color on discrimination of sweetness and sourness in pear-nectar. *American Journal of Psychology 76*, 315–317. (423)

Pearlman, A. L., and Daw, N. (1970) Opponent color cells in the cat lateral geniculate nucleus. *Science 167*, 84–86. (133)

Peebles, D. R., and Teller, D. Y. (1975) Color vision and brightness discrimination in two-month-old human infants. *Science 189*, 1102–1103. (325)

Penfield, W., and Rasmussen, T. (1950) *The cerebral cortex of man.* New York: Macmillan. (99)

Penrose, L. S., and Penrose, R. (1958) Impossible objects: A special type of illusion. *British Journal of Psychology 49*, 31–33. (226)

Pettigrew, J. D. (1974) The effect of visual experience on the development of stimulus specificity by kitten cortical neurons. *Journal of Physiology 237*, 49–74. (331)

Pettigrew, J. D., and Freeman, R. D. (1973) Visual experience without lines: Effects on developing cortical neurons. *Science 182*, 599–601. (338)

Pick, A. D. (1965) Improvement of visual and tactual form discrimination. *Journal of Experimental Psychology 69*, 331–339. (188)

Pick, A. D., Thomas, M. L., and Pick, H. L. (1966) The role of grapheme-phoneme correspondences in the perception of braille. *Journal of Verbal Learning and Verbal Behavior 5*, 298–300. (107)

Pinching, A. G., and Doving, K. B. (1974) Selective degeneration in rat olfactory bulb following exposure to different odors. *Brain Research 82*, 195–204. (419)

Pirchio, M., Spinelli, D., Fiorentini, A., and Maffei, L. (1978) Infant contrast sensitivity evaluated by evoked potentials. *Brain Research 141*, 179–184. (320)

Pisoni, D. B., and Tash, J. B. (1975) Auditory property detectors and processing place features in stop consonants. *Perception and Psychophysics 18*, 401–408. (393)

Poggio, G. F., and Mountcastle, V. B. (1960) A study of functional contributions of the lemniscal and spinothalamic systems to somatic sensibility: Central nervous mechanisms in pain. *Bulletin of the Johns Hopkins Hospital 106*, 266–316. (98)

Pollack, I., and Pickett, J. M. (1964a) The intelligibility of excerpts from conversational speech. *Language and Speech 6*, 165–171. (395)

Pollack, I., and Pickett, J. M. (1964b) Intelligibility of excerpts from fluent speech: Auditory versus structural context. *Journal of Verbal Learning and Verbal Behavior 3*, 79–84. (395)

Pomerantz, J. R. (1981) Perceptual organization in information processing. In *Perceptual organization*, M. Kubovy and J. Pomerantz (Eds.). Hillsdale, N.J.: Lawrence Erlbaum Associates. (178, 179)

Pomerantz, J. R., Sager, L. C., and Stoever, R. J.

(1977) Perception of wholes and their component parts: Some configurational superiority effects. *Journal of Experimental Psychology: Human Perception and Performance 3*, 422–435. (190)

Prinzmetal, W., and Banks, W. P. (1977) Good continuation affects visual detection. *Perception and Psychophysics 21*, 389–395. (181)

Pritchard, R. M. (1961) Stabilized images on the retina. *Scientific American 204(6)*, 72–78. (271)

Purkinje, J. E. (1825) *Neuerre Beitrage zur Kenntniss des Sehens in Subjectiver Hinsicht*. Berlin: Reimer. (73)

Ralls, K. (1971) Mammalian scent marking. *Science 171*, 443–449. (410)

Ratliff, F. (1965) *Mach bands: Quantitative studies on neural networks in the retina*. New York: Holden-Day. (42, 117)

Rechtschaffen, A., and Mednick, S. A. (1955) The autokinetic word technique. *Journal of Abnormal and Social Psychology 51*, 346. (304)

Reddy, D. R. (1976) Speech recognition by machine: A review. *Proceedings of the Institute of Electrical and Electronic Engineers 64*, 501–531. (397)

Regan, D., and Beverley, K. I. (1979) Visually guided locomotion: Psychophysical evidence for a neural mechanism sensitive to flow patterns. *Science 205*, 311–313. (226)

Regan, D., and Cynader, M. (1979) Neurons in area 18 of cat visual cortex selectively sensitive to changing size: Nonlinear interactions between responses to two edges. *Vision Research 19*, 699–711. (226)

Repp, B. H. (1982) Phonetic trading relations and context effects: New experimental evidence for a speech mode of perception. *Psychological Bulletin 92*, 81–110. (392)

Reynolds, D. V. (1969) Surgery in the rat during electrical analgesia induced by focal brain stimulation. *Science 164*, 444–445. (93)

Riesen, A. H. (1947) The development of visual perception in man and chimpanzee. *Science 106*, 107–108. (330)

Riggs, L. A. (1965a) Light as a stimulus for vision. In *Vision and visual perception*, C. Graham (Ed.). New York: Wiley. (209, 439)

Riggs, L. A. (1965b) Visual acuity. In *Vision and visual perception*, C. Graham (Ed.). New York: Wiley. (80)

Roberts, M., and Summerfield, Q. (1981) Audiovisual adaptation in speech perception. *Perception and Psychophysics 30*, 309–314. (393)

Robinson, D. L., and Wurtz, R. (1976) Use of an extra-retinal signal by monkey superior colliculus neurons to distinguish real from self-induced stimulus movement. *Journal of Neurophysiology 39*, 852–870. (298)

Robinson, J. O. (1972) *The psychology of visual illusion*. London: Hutchinson and Company. (246)

Rock, I. (1974) The perception of disoriented figures. *Scientific American 230(1)*, 78–85 (197)

Rock, I., and Kaufman, L. (1962) The moon illusion II. *Science 136*, 1023–1031. (244)

Rogel, M. (1978) A critical evaluation of the possibility of higher primate reproductive and sexual pheromones. *Psychological Bulletin 85*, 810–830. (410)

Root, W. (1974) Of wine and roses. *New York Times Magazine*. December 22, 1974, p. 14 *et seq*. (188)

Rose, J. E., Brugge, J. F., Anderson, D. J., and Hind, J. E. (1967) Phase locked response to low frequency tones in single auditory nerve fibers of the squirrel monkey. *Journal of Neurophysiology 30*, 769–793. (357)

Ross, H. E. (1974) *Behavior and perception in strange environments*. New York: Basic Books. (209)

Ross, H. E., and Ross, G. M. (1976) Did Ptolemy understand the moon illusion? *Perception 5*, 377–385. (242)

Rozin, P. (1976) The selection of foods by rats, humans, and other animals. In *Advances in the study of behavior*, J. S. Rosenblatt, R. A. Hinde, and C. Beer (Eds.). New York: Academic Press. (425)

Rubin, E. (1915) *Synoplevede Figurer*. Copenhagen: Gyldendalske. (173)

Rushton, W. A. H. (1961) Rhodopsin measurement and dark adaptation in a subject deficient in cone vision. *Journal of Physiology 156*, 193–205. (70, 71)

Rushton, W. A. H. (1964) Colour blindness and cone pigments. *American Journal of Optometry and Archives of the American Academy of Optometry 41*, 265–282. (134)

Russell, M. J. (1976) Human olfactory communication. *Nature 260*, 520–522. (408)

Russell, M. J., Switz, G. M., and Thompson, K. (1980) Olfactory influence on the human menstrual cycle. *Pharmacology, Biochemistry and Behavior 13*, 737–738. (409)

Rutherford, W. (1886) A new theory of hearing. *Journal of Anatomy and Physiology 21*, 166–168. (355)

Sakata, H., and Iwamura, Y. (1978) Cortical processing of tactile information in the first somatosensory and parietal association areas in the monkey. In *Active touch*, G. Gordon (Ed.). New York: Pergamon Press, 55–72. (104)

Sakata, H., Shibutani, H., and Kawano, K. (1977) Spatial selectivity of "visual" neurons in the posterior parietal association cortex of the monkey. Abstract, 27th International Congress of the Physiological Society. (See Sakata & Iwamura, 1978.) (302)

Salapatek, P. (1975) Pattern perception in early infancy. In *Infant perception: From sensation to cognition*, Vol. 1, L. B. Cohen and P. Salapatek (Eds.). New York: Academic Press, 133–248. (326)

Salapatek, P., and Banks, M. S. (1978) Infant sensory assessment: Vision. In *Communicative and cognitive abilities: Early behavioral assessment,* F. D. Minfie and L. L. Lloyd (Eds.). Baltimore: University Park Press, 61–106. (320)

Salapatek, P., Bechtold, A. G., and Bushness, E. W. (1976) Infant visual acuity as a function of viewing distance. *Child Development 47*, 860–863. (319)

Sato, M., Ogawa, H., and Yamashita, S. (1975) Response properties of macaque monkey chorda tympani fibers. *Journal of General Physiology 66*, 781–810. (429)

Sawusch, J. R. (1977) Peripheral and central processes in selective adaptation of place of articulation in stop consonants. *Journal of the Acoustical Society of America 62*, 738–750. (393)

Sawusch, J. R., and Jusczyk, P. (1981) Adaptation and contrast in the perception of voicing. *Journal of Experimental Psychology: Human Perception and Performance 7*, 408–421. (393)

Scharf, B. (1975) Audition. In *Experimental sensory psychology*, B. Scharf (Ed.). Glenview, Ill.: Scott, Foresman, 112–149. (373)

Schiffman, H. R. (1967) Size-estimation of familiar objects under informative and reduced conditions of viewing. *American Journal of Psychology 80*, 229–235. (210)

Schubert, E. D. (1980) *Hearing: Its function and dysfunction*. Wien: Springer-Verlag. (350, 352, 358)

Schultze, M. (1866) Aur Anatomie und Physiologie der Retina. *Arch. Mikroskop. Anat. 2*, 165–286. (67)

Schultze, M. (1872) Sehorgan I. Die Retina. In *Handb. d. Lehr von d. Geweben, Vol. 2*, S. Striker (Ed.). Leipzig: W. Engelmann. (Translated in S. Striker, *Manual of human and comparative histology*, Vol. 3, 1873.) (68)

Schwartz, A. S., Perez, A. J., and Azulaz, A. (1975) Further analysis of active and passive touch in pattern discrimination. *Bulletin of the Psychonomic Society 6*, 7–9. (105)

Schweitzer-Tong, D. (1976) Effect of adaptation on intensity-response relations in the dorsal lateral geniculate nucleus of the cat. Doctoral dissertation, Department of Psychology, University of Pittsburgh. (267)

Scott, T. R., and Erickson, R. P. (1971) Synaptic processing of taste-quality information in thalamus of the rat. *Journal of Neurophysiology 34*, 868–884. (428)

Searle, C. L., Jacobson, J. Z., and Rayment, S. G. (1979) Stop consonant discrimination based on human audition. *Journal of the Acoustical Society of America 65*. 799–809. (392)

Sechzer, J. A., and Brown, J. L. (1964) Color discrimination in the cat. *Science 144*, 427–429. (133)

Sekuler, R., Hutman, L. P., and Owsley, C. J. (1980) Human aging and spatial vision. *Science 209*, 1255–1256. (282)

Selfridge, O. G. (1959) Pandemonium: A paradigm of learning. In *The mechanization of thought processes*. London: Her Majesty's Stationery Office. (184)

Shea, S. L., Fox, R., Aslin, R., and Dumais, S. T. (1980) Assessment of stereopsis in human infants. *Investigative Ophthalmology and Visual Science 19*, 1400–1404. (322)

Sherif, M. (1935) A study of some social factors in perception. *Archives of Psychology 187,* 1–60. (304)

Sherk, H., and Stryker, M. P. (1976) Quantitative study of cortical orientation selectivity in visually inexperienced kittens. *Journal of Neurophysiology 39*, 63–70. (331)

Shorey, H. H. (1977) Pheromones. In *How animals communicate*, T. A. Sebeck (Ed.). Bloomington: Indiana University Press, 137–163. (409)

Sinclair, D. C. (1955) Cutaneous sensation and the doctrine of specific energy. *Brain 78*, 584–614. (86)

Skinner, B. F. (1936) The verbal summator and a method for the study of latent speech. *Journal of Psychology 2*, 71–107. (399)

Sloan, L. L., and Wollach, L. (1948) A case of unilateral deuteranopia. *Journal of the Optical Society of America 38*, 502–509. (134)

Smith, D., and Frank, M. (1972) Cross-adaptation between salts in the chord tympani nerve of the rat. *Physiology and Behavior 8*, 213–220. (428)

Smith, E. E., and Spoehr, K. T. (1974) The perception of printed English: A theoretical perspective. In *Human information processing: Tutorials in performance and cognition*, B. H. Kantowitz (Ed.). Hillsdale, N.J.: Lawrence Erlbaum Associates. (194)

Smith, K. R. (1947) The problem of stimulation deafness. II. Histological changes in the cochlea as a function of tonal frequency. *Journal of Experimental Psychology 37*, 304–317. (359)

Smith, K. R., and Wever, E. G. (1949) The problem of stimulation deafness. III. The functional and histological effects of high frequency stimulus. *Journal of Experimental Psychology 39*, 238–241. (360)

Smith, P. C., and Smith, O. W. (1961) Ball throwing responses to photographically portrayed targets. *Journal of Experimental Psychology 62*, 223–233. (219)

Sovijarvi, A. R. A., and Hyvärinin, J. (1974) Auditory cortical neurons in the cat sensitive to the direction of sound source movement. *Brain Research 73*, 455–471. (376)

Spoehr, K. T., and Lehmkuhle, S. W. (1982) *Visual information processing*. San Francisco: Freeman. (194)

Steinberg, R. H., Wood, I., and Hogan, M. A. (1977) Pigment epithelial ensheathment and phagocytosis of extrafoveal cones in human retina. *Transactions of the Royal Society of London, Series B 277*, 459–471. (74)

Stevens, J. K., Emerson, R. C., Gerstein, G. L., Kallos, T., Neufeld, G. R., Nichols, C. W., and Rosenquist, A. C. (1976) Paralysis of the awake human: Visual perceptions. *Vision Research 16*, 93–98. (296)

Stevens, S. S. (1957) On the psychophysical law. *Psychological Review 64*, 153–181. (19)

Stevens, S. S. (1961) To honor Fechner and repeal his law. *Science 133*, 80–86. (19)

Stevens, S. S. (1962) The surprising simplicity of sensory metrics. *American Psychologist 17*, 29–39. (19–22)

Stevens, S. S., and Volkman, J. (1940) The relation of pitch to frequency: A revised scale. *American Journal of Psychology 53*, 329–353. (355)

Stewart, W. B., Kauer, J. S., and Shepherd, G. M. (1979) Functional organization of rat olfactory bulb analyzed by the 2-deoxyglucose method. *Journal of Comparative Neurology 185*, 715–734. (420)

Stone, H., and Bosley, J. J. (1965) Olfactory discrimination and Weber's law. *Perceptual Motor Skills 20*, 657–665. (405)

Strauss, M. S., and Curtis, L. E. (1983) Infant perception of numerosity. *Child Development*. In press. (326)

Stryker, M. P., Sherk, H., Leventhal, A. G., and Hirsch, H. B. (1978) Physiological consequences for the cat's visual cortex of effectively restricting early visual experience with oriented contours. *Journal of Neurophysiology 41*, 896–909. (338)

Summerfield, Q. (1979) Use of visual information for phonetic perception. *Phonetica 36*, 314–331. (393)

Supa, M., Cotzin, M., and Dallenbach, K. M. (1944) "Facial vision": The perception of obstacles by the blind. *American Journal of Psychology 57*, 133–183. (366)

Svaetichin, G. (1956) Spectral response curves from single cones. *Acta Physiologica Scandinavica Supplementum 134*, 17–46. (129)

Swets, J. A. (1964) *Signal detection and recognition by human observers*. New York: Wiley. (435)

Talbot, W. H., Darian-Smith, I., Kornhuber, H. H., and Mountcastle, V. B. (1968) The sense of flutter-vibration: Comparison of the human capacity with response patterns of mechanoreceptive afferents from the monkey hand. *Journal of Neurophysiology 31*, 301–334. (96)

Tanabe, T., Iino, M., Oshima, Y., and Takagi, S. F. (1974) An olfactory area in the prefrontal lobe. *Brain Research 80*, 127–130. (420)

Tanabe, T., Iino, M., and Takagi, S. F. (1975) Discrimination of odors in olfactory bulb, pyriform-amygdaloid areas and orbito-frontal cortex of the monkey. *Journal of Neurophysiology 38*, 1284–1296. (410, 420)

Tansley, K. (1965) *Vision in vertebrates*. London: Chapman and Hall. (78, 133)

Tart, C. T. (1971) *On being stoned*. Palo Alto: Science and Behavior Books. (5)

Taylor, M. M., Lederman, S. J., and Gibson, R. H. (1973) Tactual perception of texture. In *Handbook of perception,* Vol. 3, E. C. Carterette and M. P. Friedman (Eds.). New York: Academic Press. (105)

Teller, D. Y., Morse, R., Borton, R., and Regal, D. (1974) Visual acuity for vertical and diagonal gratings in human infants. *Vision Research 14*, 1433–1439. (319)

Teller, D. Y., Peeples, D. R., and Sekel, M. (1978) Discrimination of chromatic from white light by two-month-old human infants. *Vision Research 18*, 41–48. (325)

Ternus, J. (1926) Experimentelle Untersuchungen uber Phanomenale Identitat. *Psychologische Forschung 7*, 81–136. (Summary in W. D. Ellis [1938] *A sourcebook of Gestalt psychology*. London: Kegan Paul, Trench, Trubner, 149–160.) (299)

Teuber, H-L. (1960) Perception. In *Handbook of physiology*, Section 1, Vol. 3, J. Field, H. W. Magoun, and V. E. Hall (Eds.). Washington, D.C.: American Physiological Society. (296)

Teuber, H-L, and Bender, M. B. (1949) Alterations in pattern vision following trauma of occipital lobes in man. *Journal of General Psychology 40*, 37–57. (5)

Thorpe, W. H. (1958) Further studies on the process of song learning in the chaffinch (*Fringilla coelebs gengleri*). *Nature 182*, 554–557. (337)

Thouless, R. H. (1931) Phenomenal regression to the real object I. *British Journal of Psychology 21*, 339–359. (247)

Tomita, T., Kaneko, A., Murakami, M., and Paulter, E. L. (1967) Spectral response curves of single cones in the carp. *Vision Research 7*, 519–531. (133)

Tonndorf, J. (1960) Shearing motion in scala media of cochlear models. *Journal of the Acoustical Society of America 32*, 238–244. (358)

Trevor-Roper, P. (1970) *The world through blunted sight*. Indianapolis: Bobbs-Merrill. (342)

Tretter, F., Cynader, M., and Singer, V. (1975) Modification of direction selectivity of neurons in the visual cortex of kittens. *Brain Research 84*, 143–149. (338)

Triesman, A. M. (1969) Strategies and models of selective attention. *Psychological Review 76*, 282–299. (199)

Tulving, E., and Gold, C. (1963) Stimulus information and contextual information as determinants of tachistoscopic recognition of words. *Journal of Experimental Psychology 66*, 319–327. (194)

Tulving, E., Mandler, G., and Baumal, R. (1964) Interaction of two sources of information in tachistoscopic word recognition. *Canadian Journal of Psychology 18*, 62–71. (194)

Vallbo, A. B., and Hagbarth, K. E. (1967) Impulses recorded with microelectrodes in human muscle nerves during stimulation of mechanoreceptors and voluntary contractions. *Electroencephalography and Clinical Neurophysiology 23*, 392. (56)

Vallbo, A. B., and Hagbarth, K. E. (1968) Activity from skin mechanoreceptors recorded percutaneously in awake human subjects. *Experimental Neurology 21*, 270–289. (56)

Vallbo, A. B., and Johansson, R. S. (1976) Skin mechanoreceptors in the human hand: Neural and psychophysical thresholds. In *Sensory functions of the skin in primates, with special reference to man*, Y. Zotterman (Ed.). New York: Plenum. (56)

Vallbo, A. B., and Johansson, R. S. (1978) The tactile sensory innervation of the glabrous skin of the human hand. In *Active touch*, G. Gordon (Ed.). New York: Oxford University Press, 29–54. (97, 99)

Valvo, A. (1968) Behavior patterns and visual rehabilitation after early and long-lasting blindness.

American Journal of Ophthalmology 65, 19–23. (340)

Van Sluyters, R. C., and Blakemore, C. (1973) Experimental creation of unusual properties in visual cortex of kittens. *Nature 246*, 506–508. (338)

Verheijen, F. J. (1961) A single afterimage method demonstrating the involuntary multi-directional eye movements during fixation. *Optica Acta 8*, 309–311. (273)

von Noorden, G. K., and Maumanee, A. E. (1968) Clinical observations on stimulus deprivation amblyopia (*amblyopia ex anopsia*). *American Journal of Ophthalmology 65*, 220–224. (339)

Wald, G. (1964) The receptors of human color vision. *Science 145*, 1007–1017. (72, 76)

Wald, G. (1968) The molecular basis of visual excitation. *Science 162*, 230–239. (70)

Wald, G., and Brown, P. K. (1958) Human rhodopsin. *Science 127*, 222–226. (72)

Wald, G., and Brown, P. K. (1965) Human color vision and color blindness. *Cold Spring Harbor Symposia on Quantitative Biology 30*, 345–359. (76, 123)

Walk, R. D. (1968) Monocular compared to binocular depth perception in human infants. *Science 162*, 473–475. (325)

Walk, R. D. (1978) Perceptual learning. In *Handbook of perception,* Vol. 9, E. C. Carterette and M. P. Friedman (Eds.). New York: Academic Press, 257–297. (188)

Walk, R. D., and Dodge, S. H. (1962) Visual depth perception of a 10-month-old human infant. *Science 137*, 529–530. (325)

Wallach, H. (1959) The perception of motion. *Scientific American 201(1)*, 56–60. (302)

Wallach, H. (1963) The perception of neutral colors. *Scientific American 208(1)*, 107–116. (251)

Wallach, H., Newman, E. B., and Rosenzweig, M. R. (1949) The precedence effect in sound localization. *American Journal of Psychology 62,* 315–336. (373)

Walley, A. C., Pisoni, D. B., and Aslin, R. N. (1981) The role of early experience in the development of speech perception. In *The development of perception: Psychobiological perspectives*, R. N. Aslin, J. Alberts, and M. J. Petersen (Eds.). New York: Academic Press, 219–235. (391)

Ward, W. D., and Glorig, A. (1961) A case of firecracker induced hearing loss. *Laryngoscope 71*, 1590–1596. (364)

Ware, C., and Mitchell, D. E. (1974) On interocular transfer of various visual aftereffects in normal and stereoblind observers. *Vision Research 14*, 731–735. (341)

Warren, R. M. (1961) Illusory changes of distinct speech upon repetition—the verbal transformation effect. *British Journal of Psychology 52*, 249–258. (399)

Warren, R. M. (1968) Verbal transformation effect and auditory perceptual mechanisms. *Psychological Bulletin 70*, 261–270. (399)

Warren, R. M. (1970) Perceptual restoration of missing speech sounds. *Science 167*, 392–393. (397)

Warren, R. M., Obuseck, C. J., and Acroff, J. M. (1972) Auditory induction of absent sounds. *Science 176*, 1149. (171)

Watkins, C. R., and Mayer, D. J. (1982) Organization of endogenous opiate and nonopiate pain control systems. *Science 216*, 1185–1192. (94)

Weber, E. H. (1834) *De pulsu, resorptione, auditu et tactu: Annotationes anatomical et physiological.* Leipzig: Koehler. (12)

Webster's new collegiate dictionary. (1956) Springfield, Mass.: Merriam. (112)

Weinstein, S. (1968) Intensive and extensive aspects of tactile sensitivity as a function of body part, sex, and laterality. In *The skin senses*, D. R. Kenshalo (Ed.). Springfield, Ill.: Thomas, 195–218. (97)

Weisenberg, M. (1977) Pain and pain control. *Psychological Bulletin 84*, 1008–1044. (91, 92)

Werner, G., and Mountcastle, V. B. (1965) Neural activity in mechanoreceptive cutaneous afferents: Stimulus-response relations, Weber functions, and information transmission. *Journal of Neurophysiology 28*, 359–397. (56)

Werner, J. S., and Wooten, B. R. (1979) Human infant color vision and color perception. *Infant Behavior and Development 2*, 241–274. (325)

Wertheimer, M. (1912) Experimentelle Stuidien uber das Sehen von Beuegung. *Zeitschrift fuer Psychologie 61*, 161–265. (166, 301)

Wever, E. G. (1949) *Theory of hearing*. New York: Wiley. (356, 361)

White, B. W., Saunders, F. A., Scadden, L., Bach-y-Rita, P., and Collins, C. (1970) Seeing with the skin. *Perception and Psychophysics 7*, 23–27. (87)

White, J. (1968) *The birth and rebirth of pictorial space*, 2nd ed. London: Faber and Faber. (210)

Whitfield, I. C., and Evans, E. F. (1965) Responses of auditory cortical neurons to stimuli of changing frequency. *Journal of Neurophysiology 28*, 655–672. (366, 394)

Whitsel, B. L., Roppolo, J. R., and Werner, G. (1972) Cortical information processing of stimulus motion on primate skin. *Journal of Neurophysiology 35*, 691–717. (103)

Wiesel, T. N., and Hubel, D. H. (1963) Single cell responses in striate cortex of kittens deprived of vision in one eye. *Journal of Neurophysiology 26*, 1003–1017. (332)

Wiesel, T. N., and Hubel, D. H. (1974) Ordered arrangements of orientation columns in monkeys lacking visual experience. *Journal of Comparative Neurology 158*, 307–318. (331)

Wilson, E. O. (1963) Pheromones. *Scientific American 208(5)*, 100–114. (409)

Wittreich, W. J. (1959) Visual perception and personality. *Scientific American 200(4)*, 56–60. (241)

Wolff, B. B., and Langley, S. (1968) *American Anthropologist 70*, 494. (17)

Woodworth, R. S. (1938) *Experimental psychology*. New York: Henry Holt and Company. (413)

Woolsey, C. N., Marshall, W. H., and Bard, P. (1942) Representation of cutaneous tactile sensibility in the cerebral cortex of the monkey as indicated by evoked potentials. *Bulletin of the Johns Hopkins Hospital 70*, 399–441. (99)

Wyszecki, G., and Stiles, W. S. (1967) *Color science: Concepts and methods, quantitative data and formulas*. New York: Wiley. (116)

Yager, D., and Thorpe, S. (1970) Investigation of goldfish color vision. In *Animal psychophysics*, W. S. Stebbens (Ed.). New York: Appleton-Century-Crofts, 259–275. (133)

Yarbus, D. L. (1967) *Eye movements and vision*. New York: Plenum. (195)

Yonas, A., Granrud, C. E., and Pettersen, L. (1983) Infant sensitivity to relative size information for distance. *Developmental psychology*, in press. (325)

Yonas, A., Pettersen, L., and Granrud, C. E. (1982) Infant's sensitivity to familiar size as information for distance. *Child Development 53*, 1285–1290. (317)

Young, R. A. (1967) The renewal of photoreceptor cell outer segments. *Journal of Cell Biology 33*, 61–72. (74)

Young, R. W., and Bok, D. (1969) Participation of the retinal pigment epithelium in the rod outer segment renewal process. *Journal of Cell Biology 42*, 392–403. (74)

Young, T. (1802) On the theory of light and colours. *Philosophical Transactions of the Royal Society of London 92*, 12–48. (122)

Young-Browne, G., Rosenfeld, H. M., and Horowitz, F. D. (1977) Infant discrimination of facial expression. *Child Development 48*, 555–562. (321)

Zimmerman, M. (1979) Peripheral and central nervous mechanisms of nociception, pain, and pain therapy: Facts and hypotheses. In *Advances in pain research and therapy,* Vol. 3, J. J. Bonica, J. D. Liebeskind, and D. G. Albe-Fessard (Eds.). New York: Raven, 3–32. (88, 91)

Zotterman, Y. (1939) Touch, pain, and tickling: An electrophysiological investigation of cutaneous sensory nerves. *Journal of Physiology 95*, 1–28. (90)

Zotterman, Y. (1956) Species differences in the water taste. *Acta Physiologica Scandinavica 37*, 60–70. (426)

Name Index

Artists and Photographers

Subject Index